educating the disadvantaged

educating the disadvantaged

SCHOOL YEAR 1968-1969

Edited by Allan C. Ornstein

AMS PRESS
NEW YORK

91669

PREFACE

Whether we have the knowledge, will, or financial means to solve the problems of educating the disadvantaged is a difficult question. The increasing number of investigators involved in analyzing such a problem and the prodigious amount of research and experimentation reflect our concern and urgent desire to <u>act</u>. In response to the growing concern, this yearbook represents a modest effort in compiling recent journal and magazine articles of significance.

The yearbook is not intended to be used as a text, but as a supplementary or library reference. It is designed for professors, school administrators, civil rights workers, and other interested investigators, who often lack sufficient time to keep up with existing and proliferating literature pertaining to the disadvantaged.

To analyze the problem of educating the disadvantaged is to probe the social and educational fabric of the country as a whole. As such, the readings represent an interdisciplinary approach. They draw upon the scholarship of investigators in various social sciences, including law and education.

In choosing material for the readings, I have focused both on the prominent investigators of the field and comparitively unknown authors who have written pertinent articles. At the outset of this project I had very little idea of how the yearbook would be organized, for I was unaware of what articles or underlining themes would evolve. Consequently, I requested permission for more articles than could be used, and for this I apologize.

The reader may feel that what emerges is an emphasis on race, or what Gunner Myrdal terms the "American Dilemma," as if I believe that educating the disadvantaged is synonymous with educating black youth. However, the yearbook merely reflects significant writings of the previous school year. It is important to add that many viable articles appeared the previous summer, some of which are included.

I wish to express my appreciation to the authors and publishers who allowed their articles to be reproduced. A special word of thanks is extended to the *Journal of Negro Education* for use of several articles. Next, I acknowledge my appreciation to Roy Young and Gabe Hornstein of AMS Press for encouraging this venture. Finally, thanks is extended to Dr. Virgil A. Clift of the Department of Secondary Education at New York University, for having taken a particular interest in my professional growth.

June, 1968
Allan C. Ornstein

PREFACE

Publisher's Note

Educating the Disadvantaged is intended as an annual anthology of the best articles published within the preceding year. All those desiring more information regarding this publication, e.g., time of publication, price, etc. are advised to address their inquiries to: Editor-in-Chief
AMS PRESS, INC.
56 E. 13 St.
N.Y.C. 10003

CONTENTS

PART I

SOCIO-PSYCHOLOGICAL FACTORS AFFECTING THE DISADVANTAGED

SELF PERCEPTIONS OF CULTURALLY DISADVANTAGED CHILDREN

Anthony T. Soares and Louise M. Soares

Anthony T. Soares and Louise M. Soares, "Self-Perceptions of Culturally Disadvantaged Children," *American Educational-Research Journal,* January 1969, Vol. 6

SELF PERCEPTIONS OF CULTURALLY DISADVANTAGED CHILDREN*

Anthony T. Soares and Louise M. Soares

According to Prescott Lecky (1945), the individual is continually countered with two kinds of problems—maintaining inner harmony and harmony with his environment. Inner harmony is closely attuned to man's single purpose of self-consistency. "Any value entering the system which is inconsistent with the individual's valuation of himself cannot be assimilated." On the other hand, if an individual is constantly devalued by others, he will come to think of himself in similar terms. This is true because he cannot hold onto a view of himself (in this case, a picture of a worthwhile person accepted by others) which is inconsistent with the attitudes surround nᵦ him. Eventually, he comes to realize that the others' view is tne "correct" one. Thereafter, he also views himself as unfavorable. Yet, this attitude has now become consistent, and he holds onto it tenaciously. This changed self-attitude is apt to be manifested through his self-images. Therefore, once you surround an individual with certain expectations, he begins to live up to those same expectations (such as, when the individual is constantly treated as though he were less worthy or less important than others). "As they believe he is, he comes to believe he is" (Jourard, 1958).

* This study was part of a larger project entitled, "The Bridgeport Vocational Rehabilitation and Cooperative Education Project," which is supported by VRA Grant #RD 1818G, Department of Health, Education, and Welfare, Washington, D. C.—Dr. Paul A. Lane, Project Director.

Culturally disadvantaged children, according to much of the research (Witty, 1967), seem to mirror the negative attitudes of others and reflect the discrimination in their own negative self-images. Handicapped by poverty and grossly unstimulating conditions, they are characterized by a denigration of one's potential as a person and as a learner, by a low aspirational level in academic areas, by a need for immediate self-gratification rather than for future goals, and by a spirit of resignation (Havighurst & Moorefield, 1967; Tannenbaum, 1967).

With the weight of logic and evidence on negative self-images, is there any reason to expect a higher level of self-esteem from the disadvantaged? First, through intermittent reinforcement by similar agents and factors in the environment which serve as identification models and instruments for imitative learning, individuals in disadvantaged areas can acquire self-acceptance. Self-perceptions induced in this fashion are highly resistant to extinction, and the accrued self-satisfaction is indicative of low motivation for change (Wheat, Slaughter, & Frank, 1967).

Kohn (1959) suggests that parents of lower classes are more concerned with the surface elements of behavior than middle class parents, who give more consideration to those aspects which underlie good behavior. It may be, then, that a self-satisfaction or acceptance of self may result, in part, from having lower standards, and this in turn promotes low motivation for change. Indeed, the evidence indicates that integrated schools tend to produce a less positive academic self-image than the non-integrated schools, which are less pressurizing and less competitive in comparison (Coleman, 1966; Levine, 1968).

Second, the segregation imposed upon disadvantaged children insulates them, at least for the early years, from acquiring the negative attitudes from those who are not disadvantaged. Younger ones have not yet had to encounter the social demands or search for the social possibilities which will determine their disadvantagement unless they have achieved the symbols of competence—educational achievement, economic efficiency, or adult marital role (Havighurst & Moorefield, 1967).

It could be that, when the disadvantaged child reaches the more heterogeneous high school, he may find it a different world, a foreign environment perhaps, from what he had experienced, and so he does not continue to derive satisfactions and some measure of success from the school. The gains of the elementary years may give way to the greater pressures of the secondary school years when the youngsters are emerging as individuals and searching for an identity (Erikson, 1950).

Third, through the efforts of good teaching and effective education, disadvantaged children can stem the tide of their handicaps and increase their understanding of cultural differences and worth (Katz, 1964). The schools can help to overcome the deprecatory self-image and hopelessness, where they exist, through rich experiences, abundant resources, motivating support, and unending opportunities. "The great difference between the successful and the unsuccessful depressed-area school is staff" (Passow & Elliott, 1967).

For these reasons, negative self concepts are not necessarily a foregone conclusion, but rather an impetus for research. The present study was formulated for the expressed purpose of determining the direction and intensity of self-perceptions of disadvantaged children, and comparing them with children who are not disadvantaged.

THE PROBLEM

This study was basically concerned with the self concepts of disadvantaged children in the middle and upper grades of elementary school—those important developing years preceding high school. The five grade levels involved (four through eight) are crucial in helping the child to develop a positive self concept in regard to his ability to achieve some measure of success in the classroom. These years also involve a growing search for self-identity and a widening need for interrelationships. The disadvantaged child has these two problems magnified for him because he is less apt to have successful models to identify with and he is more apt to give up trying to achieve, since he has possibly faced continual frustration aggravated by his handicap. Furthermore, the problems extend to an ever-increasing lack of communication, hampering his relationships with others.

Self-perceptions comprise an important area for educational study, for how a student looks at himself often has an effect upon how he looks at school and how he performs in the classroom

(Spiegler, 1967). These self-perceptions include the *self concept* (how the individual believes himself to be at the moment), the *ideal concept* (how he wishes he were or hopes to become), and the various *reflected selves* (how he believes others view him). The concern of the present study was to compare the self-perceptions of disadvantaged children with those of children who are not generally described as disadvantaged. The researchers measured the views each student stated about himself, how he says he would like to be, and how he thinks other people look at him— his classmates, his teacher, and his parents.

More specifically, the following questions were raised concerning these self-perceptions:

1. Do disadvantaged and advantaged children have positive or negative self-perceptions?

2. Are disadvantaged children significantly different from advantaged children in their self-perceptions?

3. Are there significant differences between the self-perception scores of disadvantaged and advantaged children when they are grouped according to grade?

4. Are there significant differences between the self-perception scores of disadvantaged and advantaged children when they are grouped according to sex?

5. Are there significant differences between the self-perception scores of disadvantaged and advantaged children when they are grouped according to any combination of sex and grade?

SUBJECTS

There were 514 subjects used in an urban school system—229 from a public elementary school in a disadvantaged area and 285 from a public elementary school in an advantaged area of the same city; 244 girls and 270 boys; grades four throught eight, with a minimum of 40 students from each grade. Both groups of children live in segregated areas of the community and attend neighborhood schools. The disadvantaged children typically live in low-rent tenements or subsidized housing. The ethnic composition is about two-thirds Negro and Puerto Rican, and one-third White. The family income is less than $4,000, and many families receive state aid or welfare funds. Some children receive free breakfast every morning at their school through a federally sponsored project, and the Headstart Program has been in operation.

In contrast, the children who are not disadvantaged are generally from a middle class neighborhood in the city. There is usually at least one adult working in a steady job or profession with an income of over $7,000. The members of the family tend to live in one-family homes which they themselves own. The ethnic make-up is about 90 percent White and 10 percent minority groups. These more advantaged youngsters are not unlike middle class children in the suburbs, but there are few suburban counterparts for the disadvantaged children living in the city.

PROCEDURE

To ascertain the self-perceptions of the subjects, a variant of the measuring device used by the authors in previous research (Soares & Soares, 1964, 1965, 1966) was utilized in this study. Twenty pairs of bi-polar traits expressed in sentence form—each pair separated by four spaces of distance, whereby the subject rated himself according to whether he was "very" or "more" like the positive than the negative trait, or vice versa—were presented to the subjects for five different measures of their self-perceptions. The traits were the same for all five measures, although the sentence structure was changed to correspond with the particular self-perception measured—i.e., self concept, ideal concept, reflected self in the eyes of classmates, reflected self in the eyes of the teacher, and reflected self in the eyes of the parent.

Example:

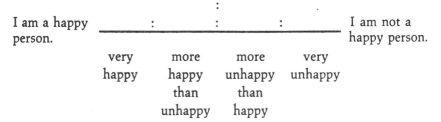

The example above is a typical item from the self-concept measure. For the ideal concept, the same item was changed to "I wish I were a happy person." For the reflected self-classmates (How he thinks his classmates view him), the item changed to "My friends think I am a happy person;" reflected self-teacher (How he thinks his teacher views him), "My teacher thinks I am a happy person;" and, for the reflected self-parent (How he thinks one of his parents views him), "My parent thinks I am a happy person."

A pilot project was first undertaken to determine whether the form devised would be appropriate, both in terms of language used and comprehension level. Single adjectives were used for this project but were later changed to the sentence form. The students in this pilot study contributed to the modification of the wording and directions of the instrument.

The five forms of the instrument were administered to the students at different times over a three-week period. The students did not know what they would do until the day they completed the form and were not told that they would be filling out other forms in the future. The fact that this was not a testing situation was stressed to the students.

Each of the five inventories was first given an index score. A check over the "very" on the positive end of the continuum received a score of $+2$; the "more" next to it, $+1$; "more" on the negative side, -1; "very" on the negative side, -2. These assigned positive and negative values were summed algebraically for each of the indices. The highest possible score was $+40$; the lowest, -40. The five scores were then statistically treated by an analysis of variance design.

TABLE 1

Analysis of Variance Results for Self Concept Scores

Source of Variation	d f	Sum of Squares	Mean Square	F Ratio
School	1	406.14	406.14	3.95*
Sex	1	35.58	35.58	n.s.
Grade	4	569.65	142.41	n.s.
School x Sex	1	410.11	410.11	3.99*
School x Grade	4	14,795.85	3,698.96	35.98**
Sex x Grade	4	573.35	143.34	n.s.
Sex x School x Grade	4	6,056.71	1,514.18	14.73**
Within	494	50,794.51	102.82	
Total	513	73,641.90		

$^*p < .05$
$^{**}p < .01$

RESULTS

Table 1 indicates significant differences on the self concept measure between the two schools and in the interactions of school with sex, school with grade, and school with sex and grade. An examination of Table 2 reveals that the children in the disadvantaged area school had the higher mean and the greater variability.

TABLE 2
Mean Self-Perception Scores and Standard Deviations for Disadvantaged and Advantaged Children

Self-Perception Measures	School A[a] N = 285		School B[b] N = 229		
	M	SD	M	SD	F ratios
Self Concept	20.12	9.60	22.84	10.85	3.95*
Ideal Concept	28.27	9.03	29.93	8.20	5.85*
Reflected Self —Classmates	20.92	11.28	22.73	12.78	2.84
Reflected Self —Teacher	20.00	12.24	22.96	13.25	7.01**
Reflected Self —Parent	19.70	11.51	22.25	12.18	8.39**

[a] School in advantaged area
[b] School in disadvantaged area
* $p < .05$
** $p < .01$

Table 3 shows significant differences on the ideal concept measure between the two schools and in the interaction of school with sex and grade. Referring back to Table 2 reveals again that the disadvantaged children had the higher mean but a smaller dispersion.

Table 4 has the analysis of the self-perception scores when the individual sees the self as reflected in his classmates' attitudes toward him. Only interactions were significant in this case—school with sex, school with grade, and school with sex and grade. It should be further pointed out that the school was the factor in each of these significant interactions. Table 2 again reveals the higher mean for the disadvantaged children as well as the higher standard deviation.

TABLE 3

Analysis of Variance Results for Ideal Concept Scores

Source of Variation	d f	Sum of Squares	Mean Square	F ratio
School	1	455.44	455.44	5.85*
Sex	1	100.35	100.35	n.s.
Grade	4	115.86	28.97	n.s.
School x Sex	1	14.29	14.29	n.s.
School x Grade	4	417.59	104.40	n.s.
Sex x Grade	4	590.65	147.66	n.s.
Sex x School x Grade	4	1,237.98	309.50	3.98*
Within	494	38,435.52	77.80	
Total	513	41,367.68		

* $p < .05$

TABLE 4

Analysis of Variance Results for Reflected
Self-Classmates Scores

Source of Variation	d f	Sum of Squares	Mean Square	F ratio
School	1	270.13	270.13	n.s.
Sex	1	33.04	33.04	n.s.
Grade	4	865.63	216.41	n.s.
School x Sex	1	681.85	681.85	4.83*
Sex x Grade	4	195.86	48.97	n.s.
School x Grade	4	3,442.20	860.55	6.09**
School x Sex x Grade	4	66,756.72	16,689.18	118.16**
Within	494	69,773.39	141.24	
Total	513	142,018.82		

* $p < .05$
** $p < .01$

Table 5 indicates the high significance of the school factor and the interactions of school with grade, and school with sex and grade, on the Reflected Self-Teacher scores. As before (see Table 2) the disadvantaged school children had the higher mean and standard deviation.

Table 6 shows that the highest and greatest number of significant F ratios occurred on the Reflected Self-Parent inventory,

TABLE 5

Analysis of Variance Results for Reflected
Self-Teacher Scores

Source of Variation	d f	Sum of Squares	Mean Square	F ratio
School	1	1,113.58	1,113.58	7.01**
Sex	1	50.03	50.03	n.s.
Grade	4	259.17	64.79	n.s.
Sex x School	1	174.25	174.25	n.s.
School x Grade	4	2,952.16	738.04	4.65**
Sex x Grade	4	1,303.60	325.90	n.s.
School x Sex x Grade	4	2,436.26	609.07	3.84**
Within	494	78,421.61	158.75	
Total	513	86,710.66		

** $p < .01$

TABLE 6

Analysis of Variance Results for Reflected
Self-Parent Scores

Source of Variation	d f	Sum of Squares	Mean Square	F ratio
School	1	1,068.16	1,068.16	8.39**
Sex	1	21.97	21.97	n.s.
Grade	4	4,592.33	1,148.08	9.01**
School x Sex	1	1,167.08	1,167.08	9.16**
School x Grade	4	966.12	241.53	n.s.
Sex x Grade	4	1,893.24	473.31	3.72**
School x Sex x Grade	4	1,876.27	469.07	3.68**
Within	494	62,915.77	127.36	
Total	513	74,500.94		

** $p < .01$

with no significance only on the sex-factor and the interaction of school with grade. Table 2 also reveals the higher mean and standard deviation for the school children in the disadvantaged area school.

Certain aspects of these six tables stand out when a comparison is made of the total picture. For all five self-perception scores, the disadvantaged children had consistently higher means than the advantaged children, with significance resulting on four of the five measures (excepting the Reflected Self-Classmates). In regard to the degree of variability, only on the Ideal Concept measure did the disadvantaged children indicate less dispersion than the advantaged children. For both schools, greater variation was shown on the three Reflected Self measures than the Self Concept or Ideal Concept.

On none of the five measures were sex differences indicated except in interaction with school or grade. Only one of the five self-perception scores revealed grade differences (Reflected Self-Parent), though there were more differences when grade was combined with sex or school.

The school and sex combination produced significance on three of the measures (Self Concept, Reflected Self-Parent, and Reflected Self-Classmates). The school and grade interaction was also significant for three sets of scores (Self Concept, Reflected Self-Classmates, and Reflected Self-Teacher), and in all cases the significance was at the .01 level. The .01 level of significance was also true for the interaction of sex and grade on the Reflected Self-Parent scores.

Because significant results occurred on all five measures for the interaction of the three factors—i.e., school, sex, and grade—and in only one case was this not at the .01 level of significance (Ideal Concept), it might be well to examine more closely the smallest units of the design. An inspection of Table 7 reveals a tendency toward lower mean scores for the boys as they progress from grade four to grade eight but toward somewhat higher mean scores for the girls as they progress through the grades.

The Duncan's method of analysis for comparison of means indicated significant differences between the boys in the two schools in the upper grades. Just the reverse was true for the girls. The significant differences between the two groups of girls occurred in the lower grades. For both sexes, the disadvantaged children generally indicated higher means than the advantaged children— with this being true for the boys in 20 of the 25 pairs of means, and 14 out of 25 for the girls. The standard deviations were also generally bigger for the disadvantaged boys and girls over the advantaged—indicating greater dispersion in 17 of the 25 pairs for the boys and 15 out of the 25 for the girls.

14

TABLE 7

Mean Self-Perception Scores and Standard Deviations for Disadvantaged and Advantaged Children

Grade and sex		SC M	SC SD	IC M	IC SD	RS–C M	RS–C SD	RS–T M	RS–T SD	RS–P M	RS–P SD
Boys:											
Four	n=42	23.14	9.84	29.43	7.99	21.73	12.51	20.79	11.76	22.86	10.26
	n=30	24.10	9.10	28.83	12.05	25.50	17.08	20.13	17.85	23.47	11.44
Five	n=33	20.21	9.68	29.03	6.31	24.41	8.11	22.00	12.43	21.58*	10.59
	n=29	22.93	12.95	30.45	10.82	27.66	13.88	24.76	16.20	26.76	11.66
Six	n=23	19.04	11.34	27.83	9.26	20.30	10.50	16.04*	11.59	19.74	9.89
	n=19	18.89	13.62	30.05	8.32	17.74	14.66	21.32	15.21	19.26	15.34
Seven	n=25	17.72**	8.56	26.84**	7.29	18.60**	10.36	16.72**	12.24	14.88**	11.39
	n=26	24.85	9.89	32.62	6.27	25.58	12.16	28.50	10.47	24.92	13.18
Eight	n=22	15.59**	9.76	27.55	5.80	13.14*	12.00	17.82	13.47	10.77**	13.54
	n=21	22.24	6.91	26.10	8.15	18.95	10.61	20.52	11.36	23.71	7.46
Girls:											
Four	n=33	20.82	7.57	28.15	7.23	19.39*	13.36	17.18*	16.16	18.00*	12.60
	n=21	22.62	10.24	28.71	8.78	24.86	12.14	24.71	10.86	27.57	6.87
Five	n=24	20.83	6.72	25.04*	14.68	21.08*	9.85	22.38	9.04	20.58	9.94
	n=18	18.11	13.17	30.78	8.41	17.06	11.79	18.67	12.99	17.06	12.94
Six	n=31	21.26	10.68	28.74	8.18	22.71	9.88	20.45*	11.33	22.23	10.16
	n=21	22.14	9.97	30.52	4.45	23.05	16.02	26.48	7.11	20.43	12.17
Seven	n=26	17.88	11.53	27.00	8.99	22.73	9.33	20.15	12.11	19.62	10.95
	n=24	19.54	11.52	29.92	8.03	19.25	11.76	20.54	11.66	16.08	12.41
Eight	n=26	21.58	8.29	31.69	4.90	22.65	7.60	25.42	8.57	22.81	8.49
	n=20	20.35	10.21	31.25	7.56	23.20	8.73	22.80	11.29	20.15	12.70

Self-Perception Measure

Note: The top line in each row of the grades is School A (advantaged group); the bottom line in each row is School B (disadvantaged group).
* p < .05; ** p < .01

DISCUSSION

Questions 1 and 2

It is most interesting to note that, not only did the disadvantaged group indicate positive self-perceptions, it also had higher self-perceptions than the advantaged group. These results are more readily understood when one notes that all the children involved attend neighborhood schools. In other words, disadvantaged children are exposed only to other disadvantaged people in school as well as at home and in their neighborhoods. As a corollary, the Coleman Report (1966) postulated that, when Negro pupils became part of an integrated school system, their self concepts diminished. Meanwhile, advantaged children associate only with other advantaged persons in school and at home. The ensuing associations and challenges for the disadvantaged have an effect upon the level of aspiration they hold for themselves and which others have of them. Since they are functioning according to expectations by teachers and parents, they are satisfied with themselves—hence, a positive self concept and reflected self.

On the other hand, the advantaged child may be more pressured than he should be by his parents and other adults. If he does not measure up to their expectations, the result may be lower self-esteem and lower (even though positive) self-perceptions.

Questions 3, 4, and 5

There were no significant differences between the sexes. However, there were some differences within both sexes between the disadvantaged and advantaged groups. In comparing boys with girls, advantaged girls tended to be higher than advantaged boys and disadvantaged boys were higher than disadvantaged girls. In other words, lower self-perceptions can be expected where the burdens are greater. The lower class woman must often engage in activities and manifest qualities which, in the middle class, are attributed to the male (Smilow, 1965). Furthermore, it is the son rather than the daughter in the lower-class home which is focused upon by the mother as the primary object of love and nurturance (Smilow, 1965). With middle-class males, greater pressures are exercised upon them during their early middle childhood years (the precise ages of the subjects in the present study); whereas for females in the middle class, the pressures do not begin to mount until during and after adolescence (Richards, 1966). Then too, in the elementary school, girls and boys are educated identically, and there is continual reinforcement of expectations of equality (Richards, 1966). It is not until entrance into the secondary school that the academic pursuits, to which the girls have become committed, give way to the role expectations by society for the marriageable female. These relationships are further brought out by the greater differences between the two groups of boys in the upper grades and between the two groups of girls in the lower grades.

In the final analysis, of course, both disadvantaged and advantaged children in elementary school indicate positive self-perceptions, which are neither overly high nor unduly low. Therefore, despite their cultural handicap, disadvantaged children do not necessarily suffer from lower self-esteem and a lower sense of personal worth. It may well be that the common denominator is effective and realistic teaching. The challenge, then, is to help the disadvantaged students maintain their positive self-images and yet function at a more realistic and higher level of aspiration, with neither dropping out of school nor yielding to the pressures of the high school.

Continuing research needs to be done for a comparative analysis with other sized cities, with city and suburban communities, with segregated and integrated school systems, and with elementary and secondary levels, in order to dimensionalize still further the scope of self-perceptions and self-images of disadvantaged children.

REFERENCES

COLEMAN, JAMES S., et al. *Equality of Educational Opportunity.* Washington, D. C.: Office of Education. U. S. Department of Health, Education, and Welfare, 1966. 743 pp.

ERIKSON, ERIK H. *Childhood and Society.* New York: W. W. Norton & Co., 1950. 445 pp.

HAVIGHURST, ROBERT J., & MOOREFIELD, THOMAS E. "The Disadvantaged in Industrial Cities." In P. S. Witty (Ed.), *The Educationally Retarded and Disadvantaged.* Sixty-sixth yearbook, Part I. Chicago, Ill.: National Society for the Study of Education, 1967. pp. 8-20.

JOURARD, SIDNEY M. *Personal Adjustment*. New York: The Macmillan Co., 1958. 462 pp.

KATZ, IRWIN. "Review of Evidence Relating to the Effects of Desegregation on the Intellectual Performance of Negroes." *American Psychologist* 19: 381-399; June 1964.

KOHN, MELVIN L. "Social Class and Parental Values." *American Journal of Sociology* 64: 337-351; June 1959.

LECKY, PRESCOTT. *Self-Consistency, A Theory of Personality*. New York: The Island Press, 1945. 287 pp.

LEVINE, DANIEL U. "The Integration-Compensatory Education Controversy." *The Education Forum* 32: 323-332; March 1968.

PASSOW, A. HARRY., & ELLIOT, DAVID L. "The Disadvantaged in Depressed Areas." In P. A. Witty (Ed.), *The Educationally Retarded and Disadvantaged*. Sixty-sixth yearbook, Part I. Chicago, Ill.: National Society for the Study of Education, 1967. pp. 20-39.

RAINWATER, LEE, COLEMAN, RICHARD P., & HANDEL, GERALD. "The Inner Life and the Outer World of the Working-man's Wife." In M. B. Sussman (Ed.), *Sourcebook in Marriage and the Family*. (Rev. ed.) Boston: Houghton Mifflin Co., 1963. pp. 180-186.

RICHARDS, CATHERINE V. "Discontinuities in Role Expectations of Girls." In W. W. Wattenberg (Ed.), *Social Deviancy Among Youth*. Sixty-fifth yearbook, Part I. Chicago., Ill.: National Society for the Study of Education, 1966. pp. 164-188.

SMILOW, ARLENE. "Family Structure, Sex Patterns, and Sex-Role Identification." (Mimeographed) Boston, Mass.: Training Center in Youth Development, Boston University, 1965. 42 pp.

SOARES, ANTHONY T., & SOARES, LOUISE M. "College Major as a Factor in Adjustment." *Journal of Physical Education* 62: 7-9; Sept.-Oct. 1964.

SOARES, ANTHONY T., & SOARES, LOUISE M. "A Study Involving 500 College Students: Adjustments During the Teacher-Training Period." *The Clearing House* 39: 415-418; March 1965.

SOARES, ANTHONY T., & SOARES, LOUISE M. "Self-Description and Adjustment Correlates of Occupational Choice," *Journal of Educational Research* 60: 27-31; September 1966.

SPIÉGLER, CHARLES G. "Provisions and Programs for Educationally Disadvantaged Youth in Secondary Schools." In P. A. Witty (Ed.), *The Educationally Retarded and Disadvantaged*. Sixty-sixth yearbook, Part I. Chicago, Ill.: National Society for the Study of Education, 1967. pp. 184-210.

TANNENBAUM, ABRAHAM J. "Social and Psychological Considerations in the Study of the Socially Disadvantaged." In P. A. Witty (Ed.), *The Educationally Retarded and Disadvantaged.* Sixty-sixth yearbook, Part I. Chicago, Ill.: National Society for the Study of Education, 1967. pp. 40-63.

WHEAT, WILLIAM D., SLAUGHTER, ROBERT, & FRANK, JEROME D. *Rehabilitation of Chronically Ill Psychiatric Patients.* Final report, Project No. 155, Johns Hopkins University, 1967. 23 pp.

WITTY, PAUL A. (Ed.) *The Educationally Retarded and Disadvantaged.* Sixty-sixth yearbook, Part I. Chicago, Ill.: National Society for the Study of Education, 1967. 384 pp.

(*Received March, 1968*)

(*Revised June, 1968*)

AUTHORS

SOARES, ANTHONY T. *Address:* Department of Psychology, University of Bridgeport, Bridgeport, Conn. 06602 *Title:* Associate Professor in Psychology *Age:* 44 *Degrees:* B.S., M.Ed., Boston College; Ed.D., Univ. of Illinois *Specialization:* Educational psychology, learning, adjustment and personality.

SOARES, LOUISE M. *Address:* Dept. of Research, University of Bridgeport, Bridgeport, Conn. 06602 *Title:* Asst. Professor in Education & Psychology *Age:* 35 *Degrees:* B.A., M.Ed., Boston University; Ed.D., University of Illinois *Specialization:* Educational psychology, educational research & statistics, adjustment and personality.

THE INFLUENCE OF ENVIRONMENT AND EDUCATION

Fred T. Wilhelms

Fred T. Wilhelms, "The Influence of Environment and Education," *National Association of Secondary School Principals,* April 1969, pp. 1-36.

THE INFLUENCE OF ENVIRONMENT AND EDUCATION

Fred T. Wilhelms

In the early 1930's, a psychologist working with an orphanage in Iowa administered tests to two baby girls 13 and 16 months old, both daughters of feeble-minded mothers. He found developmental levels of six and seven months, confirming what the staff already suspected, that both girls were so retarded that they should not be offered for adoption. Therefore, they were transferred to an institution for mentally retarded girls, where each was cared for in a ward of some 20 older girls. Naturally enough, each baby became the darling of her ward; she was made over, taken on shopping trips by the supervisors, and, in a sense, "adopted" by one girl who assumed a sort of mothering role while the other girls stood by as doting "aunts."

Some six months later, in a visit to the institution, the psychologist was attracted by two vigorous, alert toddlers, whom he scarcely recognized as the same two babies. He tested them immediately and then twice more in the next year and a half. Each time the results showed a steady progression toward normal development, and at the ages of 40 and 43 months both girls were "well within the normal range."

Out of this chance encounter, supported by some other experiences, came the idea for an organized study. Eventually a total of ten girls and three boys, all under three years of age, were moved from the orphanage to the institution for the retarded. They were tested before the transfer and periodically thereafter. Since babies considered unsuitable for adoption were transferred, the median IQ of the group was only 65—the range, from 35 to 89. The experiment ended for each child when it was felt that he had attained "maximum benefit" from his stay at the institution.

In the course of these events a "contrast" group of 11 children was formed. The cases were selected retrospectively, the criteria being that they had been given intelligence tests when they were under two years of age and that they were still living in the orphanage when they were four. Their original intellectual potential was apparently quite a bit above that of the other 13, for at an average age of 16.6 months their median IQ was 90 and only two fell below 80.

The study centered, then, on two groups of children. The "experimental" group consisted of children of very low apparent potential; for periods ranging up to about two years they lived as "house guests" in the relatively rich environment of the institution for the mentally retarded—"rich" in the sense that they had many opportunities to interact with adults as well as with other children, to play with a variety of toys, to find their way around in a complex of stimulating experiences. The "contrast" group consisted in the main of children with considerably better apparent potential; they continued to live in the dull, monotonous environment of the orphanage where they were well fed and cared for in a physical sense, but where they had very little chance to play, to interact with other children or adults, or to explore a variety of new experiences.

When the children in the two groups were compared after their different experiences the changes were striking. The median IQ of the experimental group had moved up from 65 to 94; the gains ranged from 7 to 58 points, with three cases above 45 and all but two above 15. (In a follow-up on the 11 who had been adopted into families, *their* mean IQ had become 101.) Meanwhile, during the experimental period, the median IQ of the contrast group had fallen from 90 to 60. In a subsequent period some of the cases moved into a more favorable environment and recovered some of their losses, but even then their median still stood at 66.

What is one to think of such findings, which have since been essentially duplicated several times in somewhat similar studies? At the time of their publication they aroused furious controversy, and great energy was put into showing that they did not prove what they seemed to prove. It was not difficult to cast legitimate doubt on the statistics, for the number of cases was small, many variables were uncontrolled, and the intelligence scores of very young children were too wobbly to support refined calculations.

Nevertheless there can be no doubt that *something very important happened in the lives of those two groups of children.* If such doubt was ever justified it must have been dispelled by the follow-up study published in 1966 by one of the original investigators.[1]

---

[1] Harold M. Skeels, *Adult Status of Children with Contrasting Early Life Experiences.* Monograph No. 105 of the Society for Research in Child Development, 5750 Ellis Avenue, Chicago 60637: The Society. 1966. While centering on the follow-up study, this report recapitulates the original study in sufficient detail for the general reader, and also cites the more specialized works needed by the scholar.

In that follow-up study Skeels located all the subjects who were still living (one had died) to see "how they were doing." He did not re-test their intelligence or apply any detailed analysis; he simply wanted to know, in a general way, how competently they were living their lives.

What he found, to put it simply, was that the experimental group were "doing all right" on the scale of the modest homes into which they had been adopted. All 13 were self-supporting or married and functioning successfully as housewives. Their incomes averaged above $4,000. They had typically completed 12 years in public schools. A high proportion of them were rearing families of normal, healthy children.

The status of the contrast group (which it should be remembered included initially the abler children) was a contrast indeed. Four of them were still institutionalized and unemployed. With one exception the others were employed in low-level jobs, as dishwashers, etc. (The one exception had for peculiar reasons had a very different experience—really a rich experience—at the orphanage, and he became a highly successful man.) Typical incomes of those who were employed ran around $1,200, and their social status was equally low.

The precise figures of IQ rises and slumps might well be open to question. But whatever happened when the IQ's of the experimental group rose on the average by 28.5 points while those of the contrast group dropped by 26.2 points was reflected in their general levels of life competence many years later.

Possible Explanations

Even though the scientific conclusions from this one pioneering venture are not too secure, we have dwelt on it because it provides a means of raising certain questions. Clearly what had happened to those two clusters of children in their early years was fundamental and lasting, but *what was it* that happened? Presumably one could interpret the results in any of a number of ways; for example, one could say:

1. That each child at birth had an innate quantity of intelligence; one set of circumstances permitted it to function better than another so that the surface measurement known as the IQ varied; but the initial endowment remained a constant whether one could measure it or not.

2. That each child at birth had a potential for intelligence within certain limits; some circumstances enabled him to rise closer to the upper limit of that potential than others might have; but the limits remained the same.
3. That each child at birth had a set of organic equipment—receptors, motor equipment, a central nervous system—which, as physical organs, might be better or worse; but that his intelligence at any point in his life would be that which had developed out of his organic interaction through experience with his environment.

At the speculative level the question goes all the way back to whether there actually *is* anything that can justifiably be called "a person's intelligence"—if that means an inherent, permanent quality—or whether a person's intelligence at any period is simply "what has developed." At the practical level the question often is phrased as one of *proportion:* granting that there is some innate genetic element and also that environment and experience have some effect, *how much* does each contribute? To the educator the essential question may be how much room there is to maneuver—to what extent one is dealing with a quality that is fixed or one that is open to change. In any case, how much of whatever room to maneuver there may have been at the time of the child's birth still remains when he enters school or, later on, when he enters the secondary school?

Another serious question also arises out of all this. If the *ability to learn* is itself a variable, subject to improvement by deliberate effort, to what extent will it pay to invest directly in such effort as against investing solely in the traditional instructional work of the school? It is this question of basic policy which is the ultimate concern of this volume.

Changing Assumptions

Within the scientific community profound changes are sweeping through the very conception of intelligence. Only a short while ago the dominant concept was that of a personal quality of each individual, a quality innate and fixed. It was there at birth and it would progress to its maturation *pari passu* with chronological age and physical growth. The quality might not be measured adequately by an intelligence test; but the quality was there if one could only find the means of measuring it. Meanwhile, if one kept his fingers crossed in recognition of a possible lack of reliability—or even of validity—in the tests, it was perfectly proper to speak of a given child's *being* a child of such-and-such an IQ. And once that was established it was also perfectly proper to treat him educationally as if he were.

And now? Well, now nothing is quite that certain. No one wishes to dismiss the idea of a genetic endowment, though there are questions as to just what it is that gets inherited. And certainly the estimates of how genetic qualities are distributed among the socio-economic classes bear little resemblance to those of the past, when it was simply taken for granted that the "better families" had the better genes. No one wishes to deny that at, say, the seventh-grade level some children are very bright and others are dull. If anything, our recognition of the enormous degree of such differences has grown more acute. Only, more and more the question arises: If those who are now dull had been reared in the same homes and environments as those that are now bright, would they be the dullards they are? And if those who are now bright had been put into a poor environment from birth on, would they now be bright?

This writer is in no position—and has no desire—to impose some artificial consensus on an area of such turbulence, where every year brings in new data, new insights, and new questions. But this much can be said: There is a fresh excitement among students of intelligence and it is an excitement that springs from *hope*. More and more the image is one of a dynamic set of resources. To be sure, those resources may be starved, the latent powers may atrophy, and a child may drift to a low level of cognitive effectiveness. But the important message is that the latent powers can be stimulated and reinforced to produce a high order of cognitive effectiveness.

To catch some notion of the change in basic position, let us look at the views of four outstanding theoreticians and practitioners:

> In the light of evidence now available . . . it might become feasible to raise the average level of intelligence as now measured by a substantial degree. In order to be explicit, it is conceivable that this "substantial degree" might be of the order of 30 points of IQ.
>
> J. McVicker Hunt. *Intelligence and Experience*, p. 267. New York: The Ronald Press. 1961.

27

My own feeling, derived from what happens in classrooms in which both curriculum and teaching concentrate on the development of cognitive powers, is that, at least in this one area of learning, we could probably attain in 12 years of schooling, a level of maturity which is about 4 years beyond that which we now achieve.

> *Hilda Taba.* In a speech to the National Science Teachers Association and the Council for the Elementary Science International, Denver. 1965.

Examination of the literature yields no explanation or justification for any child with an intact brain, and who is not severely disturbed, not to learn all the basic scholastic skills.

> Martin Deutsch. "Facilitation Development in the Pre-School Child: Social and Psychological Perspectives." *Merrill-Palmer Quarterly.* Vol. 10, No. 3:249-263. July, 1964.

Essentially the view of intelligence that I shall present says that intelligence, rather than being fixed by genetic factors at birth, emerges as it is nurtured.

> Millie Almy, "New Views on Intellectual Development in Early Childhood Education." *Intellectual Development: Another Look.* Washington, D.C. ASCD. 1964. 120 pages.

Thinking of the tremendous implications of such statements, one's first reaction may be one of sorrow as he visualizes the enormous waste of abilities that might have been developed. But then the idea begins to sink in: Perhaps we never again have to permit such waste of human potential; maybe we have it just at our fingertips to generate a common level of abilities such as the race has never seen before. To say even this much risks seeming to treat as established fact what is better seen as a dazzling possibility. Not that the hope is without foundation; but a decent respect for scientific caution demands that we speak in reasonably measured terms and give some accounting of the evidence that has caused the shift in thinking.

Some Types of Evidence

As we have already said, it is not our intention to attempt a comprehensive review of all the data.[2] We shall, in fact, only sketch a few of the major *kinds* of data, documenting even this much only to the extent that may be helpful to an interested general practitioner. Having taken into account a much broader array of evidence than will be reported here, the writer believes that what is reported is reasonably representative of the larger body and consonant with it. But he does not pretend to have covered everything in this extremely complex field, and the reader may be well advised to maintain a decent skepticism.

The cues come in from a variety of sources, among them the study of animals. From a wide array of types of animal research studies let us look at just two. One line of investigation has shown that differentials in environment and experience produce changes in the anatomy and physiology of the brain itself. For example, in a typical study half of a sample of comparable laboratory rats were reared in a dull cage setting; the other half were given a rich environment of things to do, objects to play with, opportunities to explore. When the individuals were later sacrificed and their brains were analyzed, two differences stood out: those with the richer environment were found to have developed a heavier cortex, and the supply of cholinesterase in their brains was greater. It has also been shown that these effects can be reversed if rats which have enjoyed a rich environment are later reduced to a dull setting.

One could elaborate greatly on this extremely significant theme. For our purposes it may suffice to say that, on the basis of a variety of studies using various types of animals, it seems clear that richness of environment and experience stimulates the nervous system itself to a fuller development; and that the "improvement" is primarily in the "higher" associative structures of the brain. Furthermore, it is reasonable to believe that such effects are more marked as one moves up the scale from animals with relatively simple brains to those with the more complex.

---

[2] Probably the best single summary of the evidence available up until 1961 is in J. McVicker Hunt's *Intelligence and Experience,* already cited. Of course, much has been learned since then, but for the serious generalist this book remains the best starting-point.

Another line of investigation has related differentials in environment and experience to subsequent problem-solving ability or, if you will, "intelligence." For example, in work with dogs a number of experiments have used the device of having some puppies reared in cages while others from the same litters were reared as pets. Presumably the latter enjoyed a much richer environment in terms of opportunities to explore and to learn. On later tests of problem-solving and of general canine intelligence, the pet-reared dogs excelled the cage-reared group so consistently that there was little overlap between the top of the one distribution and the bottom of the other. This held true even when the two groups, after their initial differential treatment, were kept together in a "dog pasture" for periods up to a year; the differences in intellectual development seem to have had a quality of permanence. This general type of experimentation has been carried on many times and with various species of animals with consistent results. It was even done with two groups' of laboratory rats which had been selectively bred through many generations to produce one group that was "maze bright" and another that was "maze dull." One-half of a sample of each group was reared in a stimulating way and the other half in a nonstimulating one. Some shades of difference remained in their maze-solving ability. But, substantially, the rats from the maze-dull group which were raised in an educative environment behaved like bright rats; and those from the maze-bright group which were raised in a depressed environment behaved like dull rats.

Of course, the findings from animal studies cannot be applied point by point to man, but among animals the evidence seems incontrovertible that the level of achievement which an individual reaches is significantly affected by a pattern of early stimulation with an abundance of opportunity to explore, to play, and to solve problems. And there are strong indications that this differential effect increases in size and permanence as one moves up the scale in complexity of the brains involved. It is tempting—and logical—to assume that the effects will be greatest of all in human beings.

Work with Human Infants

When we turn to human beings we find some most fascinating work being done with very young infants. Contrary to the general impression that for some time they are nothing much more than an insistent, demanding alimentary canal, it appears that they begin to notice very early even slight changes in their environment. When devices are installed to reveal their heart-beats it becomes clear that even in the first few months of life they are responding actively to what goes on about them.

It appears also that very soon they begin reaching out for stimulation. It is as if they *want* something to happen—something a little, but not too much, out of the ordinary. If his crib is rigged so that a baby can cause music to play by wiggling or cause a mobile to move by waving his feet, he will soon be exerting himself to make it happen. If, a little later, playthings are available, he will keep stretching his ability to get at them and manipulate them. If the view is open to what is going on in the room he watches alertly. The key thing is that he *becomes* an alert, vigorous organism, always reaching out, becoming bored with what is too much the same, brought into active response by whatever is just a little bit dissonant.

By stark contrast a baby without opportunity to "mix it up" with his environment comes to withdraw and moves toward flaccidity. All too many babies in hospitals and other institutions have spent their first months with nothing to do and not even anything to look at except a white ceiling. (To keep off drafts a white cloth may be put around the crib so that they cannot even see their neighbors.) They are "changed" occasionally, their bottle is brought on schedule and propped up for them—and that is all life holds for them. Their subsequent reaction looks very much as if they just *give up*—as if they had kept waiting for something to happen and finally despaired. The re-action is total. They lose their muscular tone and lie flaccid; they sink into apathy. They do not even learn to sit up or walk until months or years after the normal time.

No one can surely detail as yet the impacts which these differ-ential environments may be having on ultimate cognitive ability, but there are many clues to indicate that the more creative environments are producing important learnings even in those first few months. There are demonstrable gains in powers of discrimination and of problem solving, and it may well be that something fundamentally formative of ultimate intelligence is going on in this first cognitive push, possibly even something that could never be done so well at any later time.

Of course, in our momentary concentration on cognitive development we must not forget that other essential developments are also involved. There has always been argument whether the retreat from development of isolated babies is caused by lack of stimulation or lack of love; and if the pendulum just now is on the side of stimulation, that is not to deny the other. For infancy is also the time of development of basic trust and affection and a happy outlook on the world. Anyway, the best imaginable context of stimulation must be in the happy, loving play of parents and family. Good mothers, especially, have often a positive genius for solving what Hunt calls "the problem of the match"—to keep always some little dissonance, some little need to stretch, before the baby to lead him on in tiny steps. If early stimulation can be proved to have the mind-building power it appears to have, the problem will be to teach parents and older siblings how to use it in a context of affectionate play. The work of Gordon and his associates at the University of Florida, actually analyzing little bits of play for their cognitive values and teaching their use, may well be part of the wave of the future.

As the Child Grows

When language enters the scene there can be no question at all of the importance of what families do. Human intelligence is highly dependent on symbolization. At all but the lowest levels, the ability to think about anything may be almost synonomous with the ability to put words to it. And there is a wealth of evidence to show that the ways some families communicate with children is dramatically more effective in tooling up their mental processes than the ways other families do it.

In our culture this is a matter closely associated with social classes. There are many exceptions on both sides, of course, but upper- and middle-class families tend to help their children learn the names of a large array of things (in conjunction with active contact with those things where possible). They help children with words that put an edge on their perceptions ("hard-soft," "round-square," "blue-green"). They answer questions in ways that stimulate more questions. They thread into their conversations the beginnings of reasoning and logic ("If we do this, what will happen next?"). Above all, they provide models of clear, articulate thought expressed in language that will bear the load of precision.

Lower-class families, by contrast, tend to talk less freely. (Mother and father, both working hard, may be around less in the first place; and may be less disposed toward playful chatter, in any case.) Their own language may not, at best, be very precise. They do not bother so much with nice discriminations in their perceptions. Their speech is characterized less by sequential logic than by short, discrete bursts. They communicate more by gesture and other nonverbal means, less by explicit verbalizations. They tend to treat questions and other innocent gambits of active children in ways that establish closure and probably discourage further exploration. Add the fact that they do not get children into as much meaningful contact with varieties of things and experiences, and the result is a learning environment which provides less vocabulary, less discrimination, less logic, and less creative play with words. It is a system which may produce a reasonably good affective relational set of signs and expressions but not a language of precision for the logical expression of ideas. From the schoolman's point of view, it is a system that produces modes of communication out of key with those of the school.

It is a common observation that the language deficit of lower-lower class children is so great that it is intellectually crippling. No one has to argue very hard to make a case for efforts to repair it. But it is tempting to speculate on what may be at stake here. Is it merely that the child knows more or fewer words, can express better or worse the ideas he already has? Or does the ideation itself change? Does intelligence change? Is it possible that, as in the case of the rats whose environment was enriched, the nervous system itself is changed? And if so, is the change permanent?

Factors that Make a Difference

It may be a long time before we can answer such questions—if, indeed, we ever can. Nevertheless, it is already clear that in the very early months and years of a child's life the development of his cognitive processes is significantly affected by the quality of his environment and experiences. But what are the factors that make the difference? Assume that an infant enjoys a decent stability on the affective side of his life—that he is loved and nurtured in ways that make for basic trust, happiness, self-esteem, and freedom from undue anxiety; what, then, are the ingredients essential to cognitive growth?

Speaking very broadly, one major essential seems to be *stimulation*. The child's environment ought to be interesting; there need to be people to watch, to communicate with, to play with. There need to be things to feel and manipulate (and chew!). There must be variety and challenge, too—problems to solve that involve some "stretch"; for even a baby can quickly grow bored, fall into routine habituation, and get stuck at one level of development. To supply just the right kind of stimulation is not so easy, however, for there are nice problems of "match"—the best mix of comfortable familiarity and slightly strange novelty; the best mix of pleasant routine and challenging stretch. Too much novelty may only be frightening, too much challenge only frustrating. We can take comfort from the fact that good mothers —many of them relatively untutored—show an intuitive genius for finding the mix that keeps a baby happily and comfortably pushing ahead. Their little games of "peek-a-boo," and so on, far from being mere entertainment, contain the beginnings of important intellectual structures. We ought to be able to learn from such mothers and teach others to utilize play educationally.

One qualifier may well be entered here, though it is hard to define with any precision. Apparently there is need, within a rich and varied pattern of stimulation, for enough order and structure to avoid a degeneration into a mere buzzing, blooming confusion. If there is too great a babble of talk, for instance, a child simply learns to tune out. If the things in his life are too helter-skelter, he may not learn to concentrate on one, explore it systematically, and build an orderly concept on it.

A second major ingredient, probably increasing in importance as the infant grows older, appears to be full and well-articulated *verbalization*. This is more than the development of a large vocabulary—though that is important. What is involved is a system of symbolization. This includes abstractions as well as the names of concrete things; and it includes a coherent though simple logic (based on perceptions of relationships, of cause and effect, etc.). Of course, there are nice problems of timing in this. One does not want a frantic pushing toward adult models. But judicious help can move a child along comfortably toward expressive language that will carry the load of some precision.

A third ingredient may well take the form of a kind of *sensory* sharpening. Perhaps this is nothing but the first and second put together; that is, having a rich variety of experiences.

At any rate it is evident that even small children can be aided to hear words accurately, to discriminate more finely in all the sensory modalities (touch and smell as well as sight and hearing), and just to *notice* more of their environment and react to it more vividly.

Once more, to explain at the theoretical level what all this adds up to may defy us, even while we know it produces a more alert, vigorous youngster, more able to learn. Maybe it actually modifies the brain and elevates the intelligence. Maybe it only puts sharper tools at the service of the existing organism. But, however that may turn out, there really can be no question but that it is possible to generate changes in functioning cognitive effectiveness so large and significant that they are worth great investment.

Finally, it is worth noting that the "essential ingredients" just described virtually constitute a definition of the difference between the worse homes and the better ones. Obviously, great gains would be made if we could somehow bring the less nurtural families closer to the existing practices of the better ones. One cannot help wondering whether intuitive practices of the more nurtural parents could not be still further improved on the basis of research.

Institutional Programs Aimed at Cognitive Development

During the past decade most of the work aimed at deliberate cognitive development has been focussed on children a little older than the babies we have been discussing, typically on the immediate "pre-school" period, with three-, four-, and five-year-olds. A number of projects have sprung up combining research with action in varying degrees. Rather than attempt a comprehensive review, we shall look at just two of the major efforts.[3]

THE INSTITUTE FOR DEVELOPMENTAL STUDIES. The oldest and most comprehensive of the projects is the Institute for Developmental Studies, now affiliated with the New York University School of Education, which has been directed by Martin Deutsch ever since its establishment in 1958. A multi-disciplinary organization,

---

[3] A more extended overview of such efforts is provided in Maya Pines' *Revolution in Learning.* (New York: Harper & Row, 1966.) Written primarily for the intelligent layman and in a journalistic style, it is, nevertheless, based on careful study. It is eminently readable.

its work has consisted of a "mutually reinforcing cycle of basic and applied research, demonstration programs, and their evaluation." Its earliest work was chiefly a series of technical research studies; since 1962 it has also been engaged in an educational program beginning with four-year-olds and now extending through the third grade. This experimental/demonstration program, upon which we shall focus, has at every stage been structured with great care, evaluated in hard-boiled fashion, and constantly revised. Operating in conjunction with the New York City schools, it takes its clientele from the city's disadvantaged groups—though the Institute staff do not see deprivation as being confined to the slums or the lower class.[4]

In a recent brochure the Institute listed a number of assumptions which have guided its work. The first four of these were:

(1) that the child's potential intelligence is not fixed at birth, (2) that manipulation of the environment can produce significant changes in the child's willingness and ability to learn, (3) that the child's development depends on the quality of his interaction with the world around him, particularly in the early years of his life, (4) that especially vital to intellectual development is the child's mastery of language and other symbolic systems and the concepts they convey.

Anyone who desires a full description of the demonstration enrichment program should go to Powledge's *To Change A Child*. It is possible here to make only a few general comments. At the pre-school level anyone familiar with the conventional nursery school would probably feel reasonably at home. Although Deutsch and his associates have no intention whatever of merely reproducing such a nursery school with its emphasis on easygoing, stress-free play, socialization, and letting the child "unfold," their program does have elements in common with it. Thus, they do work hard at building up the child's self-concept,

---

[4] Because of its multiple approach, the Institute's publications have tended to appear in separate research reports published in a variety of ways. Much of this material, plus new interpretations, has now been consolidated in Martin Deutsch and Associates, *The Disadvantaged Child* (Basic Books, Inc., New York, 1967). This is an extremely valuable background work, by no means applicable to the teaching of the disadvantaged only. It does not include a direct description of the demonstration enrichment program. For that an excellent resource is Fred Powledge, *To Change A Child* (Quadrangle Books, Inc., 180 North Wacker Drive, Chicago, Illinois 60606, 1967). Written in a highly readable, rather formalistic style, after close study at the Institute, this includes one of the best factual descriptions of a program and its teaching methods to be found anywhere.

playing up his name, giving him great personal attention and discerning praise; they do provide a rich variety of things to manipulate and play with; there is a spirited atmosphere of fun, and a warmth of affection.

However, the resemblances are mostly superficial. For instance, the "things" in the room are very carefully organized—segregated, one might almost say—to offset the jumble and confusion characteristic of these children's lives. Great effort is made to help a child "work" with one thing for a considerable period; if, *in toto*, the goal is to provide a great deal of stimulation, it is also to provide one clean-cut stimulus at a time. The things are also *used* educationally to a maximum; there is almost constant emphasis on sensorimotor and perceptual sharpening (e.g., comparison of lengths and weights and textures, naming of colors and shapes).

In this connection, Deutsch believes that Montessori's inventions deserve much more attention than they have been given. The large form board developed at the Institute for teaching the letters is reminiscent of her approach. So is the emphasis on tactile stimulation and discrimination. However, he feels that she grossly underemphasized verbalization.

As a consequence, at the Institute, *everything* gets verbalized! The trained teachers seize every opportunity to talk with the children—about stories, about their food and clothing, about excursions, about the things they are playing with. The talk is anything but random. Much of it is carefully designed to sharpen perceptions; so they talk about colors and shapes, about which of two towers of blocks is higher, about which animal is soft and furry and which is rough and hairy. It is designed to build vocabulary; so there is constant stress on naming things accurately. It is designed to stimulate fullness of expression and syntactical completeness; so there is a steady—but not high-pressured —attempt to elicit syntactically complete and fully expressive responses. Some of the most important background research has been done by Cynthia Deutsch on auditory discrimination, and this sort of training enters the verbal work, too.

By the standards of some other programs, this is not an aggressive, hard-pushing campaign. But neither, by any stretch of the imagination, is it dedicated to waiting for a child to unfold. Every element of its curriculum is focussed on personal and cognitive development, and there is a steady pressure for forward movement. Its aspirations have been summarized by Deutsch (*The Disadvantaged Child,* pp. 384-5):

At this point it seems appropriate to review briefly what we consider essential for the intervention environment and curriculum. The environment would demand development and stimulate it along certain parameters. The environment would include sensorimotor stimulation, opportunities for making perceptual discriminations, interacting with a verbally adequate adult, receiving some individual attention, linking words and objects and meaningfully relating them in stories or to varying experiential contexts, being assisted in experiencing positive self-identifications; being encouraged toward task perseverance, and being helped to receive both tangible and verbal rewards for relatively competent performance. Such an environment includes stimulation which would be demanding of responses consistent with achieved developmental capabilities, and which would have sufficient and continual feedback from adults.

And what does evaluation reveal as to the results? This is not easy to report in anything like clean-cut form. Occasionally Deutsch and his associates release some test scores, which generally show some superiority among the children who have been in the enrichment program, in rough proportion to the time they have spent in it. Thus, the 1967 brochure quoted earlier had this to say about the first group of children to come through to the third grade—a group who had entered too early to have the benefits of the more refined program later developed for the preschool period:

However, preliminary findings from the first, pilot group indicate significantly greater gains than their controls in measured general intelligence, reading achievement, and language ability. For example, on the Illinois Test of Psycholinguistic Ability (ITPA), a standardized language test, Institute children performed significantly better than their controls. On an Institute-developed battery of assessment inventories, measuring verbal and nonverbal skills and mastery of same/different concepts, Institute children were superior not only to their comparison group but to a Head Start group of children. Again, significant differences were found in favor of Institute children on the Gates-MacGinitie Reading Test, a standardized measure that emphasizes sight recognition of words, and on an Institute-constructed test of phonic skills. Institute children also surpassed national norms on the Gates-MacGinitie Test.

But, in general, the Institute staff make no great point of this sort of thing, perhaps because they are more interested in the subtler forms of feedback needed to revise the program than in anything like terminal measures of gain. This writer, having read widely among Deutsch's writings and having had a little personal contact with him, finds it more informative to analyze the judgments he appears to have arrived at after about a decade of research and experience. At the risk of oversimplification or even misinterpretation, the writer has the following impressions.

Deutsch sees the fuller potentiation of cognitive abilities as a *big* job. He rejects the notion that "Any program is better than no program" as well as the optimistic hope that a brief, short-run program will "wake up" dormant powers which can then go on on their own. He does not believe that a deprived child's deficits can be offset by simply supplying whatever was missed earlier. In other words, he recognizes that what we face is an extremely intricate job of curriculum-making, the results of which must constantly be tested in longitudinal studies leading to further revisions. He believes that in the case of deprived children the period of enrichment must reach at least from age four through the first three grades. And he thinks the program must be expensive—on the order of $1,200 a year, with two persons handling a group of about 17 children. While he has chosen to work at the early childhood level and sees it as the best opportunity, he does not believe that the opportunity ends there and he advocates continued effort with older children. And while he has been working with disadvantaged children, he feels that much of what his program offers is both needed by and transferable to other children, given appropriate adaptation.

Given such *caveats,* he appears to be confident that the job can be done. Though far from content with present achievements, he feels that the current program is "working." He feels strongly that any child "with an intact brain" can be enabled to do school work successfully—though he is skeptical whether the schools will adapt sufficiently to let him. He quotes with apparent approval estimates that IQ's can be raised by some 20 points. In other words this man, who has perhaps been at the center of more careful research and development than anyone else, and who sees clearly the difficulties involved, is in the final analysis confidently optimistic. In a key paragraph as to the possibilities he writes, *"The failure of such children to learn is the failure of the schools. . . ."*

Work of Bereiter and Engelmann. Of all the pre-school projects one might choose by way of illustration, the one carried on by Carl Bereiter and Siegfried Engelmann, then of the University of Illinois, has probably been the most completely focussed on the essentials of purely cognitive development. It may also be the most controversial, because, driven by a sense of urgency to help disadvantaged four-year-olds catch up academically in one year, they stripped away almost all the social amenities of the conventional nursery school. The result is a concentrated program of direct instruction which no doubt shocks many educators accustomed to a more leisurely approach.

Bereiter and Engelmann are acutely aware of this reaction, and apparently share some of it themselves. One senses (though this is hard to judge) that they also would prefer an enrichment program of the type advocated by Deutsch if it could be started early enough and carried through long enough. But, apparently judging that this is not realistically possible, they insist on the necessity of sticking to the highest-priority tasks. They see the typical disadvantaged child as coming into school roughly a year behind his middle-class peers, not in basic endowment but in the sorts of learning that lead to success in handling subject matter. (". . . What disadvantaged children lack is learning, not the fundamental capacity to learn." p. 5[5]) Therefore, if the child enters pre-school at age four he has two years to do in one in order to enter school on an equal footing. And the only way it can be done is to cut away everything except the academic essentials.

Whether they are right or wrong, the very "cleanness" of their experimental work makes it an excellent laboratory case for our present inquiry. Their rationale is definite. They read the evidence from other studies to indicate that an average deficit of about 15 points of IQ is characteristic of southern Negro and Puerto Rican immigrant children, placing close to half of them below the borderline of mental deficiency. In stable urban lower-class populations the average deficit is only five points, but, statistically even, this means that one-and-a-half times the normal number fall into the below-80 range. (Incidentally, since Bereiter

[5] For a complete statement of rationale as well as explicit description of content and methodology, see Carl Bereiter and Siegfried Engelmann, *Teaching Disadvantaged Children in the Pre-School* (Prentice-Hall, Inc., Englewood Cliffs, N.J. 1966).

and Engelmann use IQ figures rather freely, it is well to note that they regard the IQ only as "a very general sort of indicator of how much a child has learned that is relevant to success in school, compared to other children of his own age." p. 4) In these terms, they calculate an IQ of 95 at age 5 as equivalent to three months of retardation; an IQ of 90 as equivalent to six months; and an IQ of 85 as equivalent to a retardation of nine months.

However—and this is the key to their curriculum planning—they believe that, compared to these overall retardations of three to nine months, disadvantaged children commonly come to school at least a year behind in *language development*. Similarly, another area in which they are typically at least a year behind is in *reasoning ability or logical development*. Taken together, these two outstanding deficits may be combined as lack of *ability to manipulate symbols*—the ability which is the major factor in school achievement. Therefore, this must be the focus of the attack.

To test their ideas Bereiter and Engelmann have developed a program running two hours a day for one school year. The basic format has consisted of three teachers working with a group of 15 four-year-olds. The children have been selected to represent gross deprivation and poor prognosis. The setting has been one main room, deliberately kept rather bare of playthings and other "distractions," with three small "classrooms" set off from the main room.

Of the two daily hours, one is taken up by the group as a whole with the routines of snack-time, of toileting, and a small amount of singing (used largely to reinforce instructional purposes) and some other activities. In the other hour the group is divided into five-somes for three 20-minute classes in *language, arithmetic,* and *reading.* Each teacher handles one of the subjects exclusively, the small groups rotating to her in turn.

Judged by the usual standards of four-year-old programs, these classes are pretty strenuous affairs. Hard work and vigorous response are required. There is a system of rewards and punishments (initially mostly the giving or withholding of cookies until the children learn to respond to praise, after which it becomes the going currency of reward). There is tremendous emphasis on verbalization; even the arithmetic and reading periods are heavily loaded in this direction, though a good deal of content is taught.

There is steady insistence on clear enunciation of words. (A great problem with these children is that they run expressions together into "giant words," do not individuate out the component words, and therefore cannot use them flexibly in other expressions.) There is equal insistence on full, complete sentences, with a great deal of repetitive drill.

But one senses that the real target is the children's *thinking*. Much of the talk is in the form of logic. ("A big truck is not a little truck.") Great emphasis goes to the "little words" so often slurred over. ("Pick up the·red block *and* the yellow block" as against "Pick up the red one *or* the yellow one.") There is skill-building in categorizing. ("If you use it to hurt somebody it's a weapon. A gun is a weapon. A cow is not a weapon.") The work in arithmetic is concerned largely with the logic of equations. All in all, the classes are a direct approach to purely cognitive development with the use of symbols (numerical symbols and written symbols, but especially verbalization) as the key.

However, any facile generalization that all this proceeds in neglect of the child's self-concept—or at its expense—is probably wrong. Apparently, after a short time, the children take to the strenuous challenge with zest and thoroughly enjoy it. Though Bereiter and Engelmann influence their teachers not to get into a mothering relationship or into much demonstrative affection, there is a steady flow of recognition and praise and success experience.

Technically speaking, the greatest disagreement between Bereiter and Engelmann and most cognitive-development theorists may lie in the area of sensorimotor stimulation and experience. Most workers in this field bank pretty heavily on the use of educational "things," excursions, etc., if they do not actually incorporate Montessorian techniques and equipment. At the very least, Bereiter and Engelmann see the crucial deficit so overwhelmingly in the abstracting-reasoning-verbalizing area as to demand concentration there. Beyond this, they seem to argue that the sensorimotor experience base of the lower-class child is not so bad anyway, even if it is different.

Test scores on one group of 15 children revealed the following results: After seven months the children had achieved approximately normal standing, except as to vocabulary, on the verbal subtests of the Illinois Test of Psycholinguistic Abilities, and they were about six months ahead in the free, descriptive use of language. After nine months 11 of the 15 were at or above beginning second-grade norms in arithmetic. With respect to the more general factors measured by the Stanford-Binet the average IQ had moved to slightly above 100. (This test was first applied after two months of schooling, when, by the investigators' assumption, the usual one-shot "irrelevant" gain of 6-8 points had already taken place. The average IQ was then 93.)

The investigators' size-up of these test results is that it would be a mistake to assume that these children had acquired the overall background of more privileged children; they had not. But since an intelligence rests in part on such general background, their IQ scores were actually pulled down by this factor; in terms of more purely *academic* abilities, they estimate that these five-year-old "graduates" were behaving like children with IQ's of 110-120. In this connection the authors report that early in the year visitors tended to view the children as "culturally deprived" but that later in the year visitors' comments and questions were such as would be raised about culturally privileged, academically talented children. It seems valid to estimate that, in the view of Bereiter and Engelmann, their program had done precisely what they wanted it to do. A narrowly focussed academic program had produced narrowly focussed cognitive gains, so that in a purely cognitive way the children were equipped to go on with successful schoolwork. So far as this writer knows, there has been no follow-up study to find out whether they actually did.

THE TABA CURRICULUM PROJECT. So far we have been looking mostly at work in the pre-school years aimed at a primary cognitive development. By contrast, the work of the late Hilda Taba at San Francisco State College was placed in the upper grades and dealt with the higher processes of thought.

Such mental activities as generalizing from concrete situations, drawing inferences from a body of factual data, and applying such generalizations and inferences in a predictive way to new situations have commonly been held to be virtually the exclusive property of the brighter students. In fact, the degree of ability to handle such thought processes has sometimes been considered almost synonymous with a definition of intelligence. The question with which Taba started was whether this sort of ability could be *taught*—whether, at this level as well as at the lower levels, intelligence could be created.

Observing the work of many teachers, Taba noticed (what many recent analytical studies of the teaching process are confirming) that in typical classrooms there is really very little effort to stimulate or assist the higher levels of thought. Nearly all of a typical teacher's questions (which, more than anything else, set the level of intellectual activity) are pitched to the low level of knowledge of information and skill. She noticed also that when, on occasion, such a teacher "took a flier" at a high abstraction or big generalization, the class generally could not hold the high ground and things quickly dropped down with a thud, often with a change of subject. Taba sometimes illustrated this with a sort of graph:

She began to wonder whether, in place of the flat profile interspersed with sudden, unsuccessful leaps upward, one could not build a gentler upward slope or stairway, so that once a child or class reached the higher ground it could be held. She hypothesized that in order to do this one would have to analyze the process of abstraction or generalization into the component skills which underlie it. Then, she hoped, each of those skills could be systematically taught. And then the skills could be put together in systematic practice in the more abstract processes of making inferences and predictions, etc.

With the aid of several grants, Hilda Taba was able to explore the possibility in a preliminary way, train some teachers in a particular methodology, and eventually develop curriculum materials in the social studies so that the cognitive approach would be built into both curriculum and method.

Basic to all this, of course, was an analysis of the components of thinking which had to be taught if the highest levels were to be reached. Taba organized these into three "cognitive tasks," each involving three steps. Probably the best way to explain her ideas is to quote directly from her own description.[6]

---

[6] What follows is taken from Hilda Taba, *Teaching Strategies and Cognitive Functioning in Elementary School Children, Cooperative Research Project No. 2404.* (San Francisco State College, 1966.) Since this report is available in limited supply, if at all, and other reports are still in process, it may be best to address an inquiry to the Taba Curriculum Development Project in Social Studies, San Francisco State College, 1600 Holloway Avenue, San Francisco, Calif. 94132.

"This study focuses on three cognitive tasks: 1. concept formation; 2. generalizing and inferring through interpretation of raw data; 3. the application of known principles and facts to explain and predict new phenomena. (Note that these tasks do not necessarily encompass all processes of thought. They exclude, for example, critical and evaluative thinking *per se*.) In each of these tasks a distinction was made between two sets of operations: the overt activities in which the individuals engage and the covert mental operations that are required in order to perform the overt activities. The covert operations determine the sequence of the overt activities because they represent the sequential skills that are necessary at each step.

"TASK 1: CONCEPT FORMATION. In order to organize aggregates of information, individuals must engage in three types of activities, each of which is the prerequisite for the next one. He must, first, *enumerate* or *list* the items of information. He must then group those items according to some basis of similarity. Finally, he needs to develop categories and labels for these groups and subsume the items in groups under appropriate labels.

"Certain covert processes underlie these steps in overt activities. In order to *enumerate,* an individual must differentiate one item from another, such as differentiating the materials of which houses are built from other things also associated with building houses, such as tools and processes. This differentiating involves analyzing the global wholes and breaking them into specific elements with specific properties.

"The second step, that of *grouping,* calls for abstracting certain common characteristics in an array of dissimilar objects or events. These common characteristics become the basis for grouping the objects or events together, e.g., grouping hospitals, doctors and medicine together as something to do with health care. Naturally, the same objects and events may be grouped in several different ways. For example, hospitals, x-rays, and surgical equipment can be grouped together as health facilities, types of services, or as indices of standards of living, depending on the purpose of the grouping. As was pointed out in Chapter 1, children form groups on several different bases. They may group by functional relations (grouping together father and mother because they live together), proximity (grouping together tables and chairs because they are near each other), grouping together items that are part of the same activity such as cement, cement mixer and patio because the first two are items needed in building the last.

"*Categorizing,* combined with *subsuming,* calls for an awareness of a hierarchical system of super- and sub-ordination in which items of lower order of generality are subsumed under items of a higher order of generality. Only as individuals are able to see that objects and events can be arranged in hierarchical systems of super- and sub-ordination, can one say that they have acquired a scientific class system of categorization and conceptual organization.

"In the following chart, dealing with Task 1, the first two columns show the sequence of relationships between the overt and covert processes.

Cognitive Task 1: Concept Formation

Overt Activity	Covert Mental Operation	Eliciting Questions
1. Enumeration and listing	Differentiation	What did you see? hear? note?
2. Grouping	Identifying common properties, abstracting	What belongs together? On what criterion?
3. Labeling, categorizing	Determining the hierarchical order of items. Super- and sub-ordination	What would you call these groups? What belongs under what?

"These steps are sequential because the differentiation involved in listings must be mastered before it is possible to identify common properties and group them. Similarly, the ability to identify common properties of objects and events and to form groups according to common properties is a prerequisite to determining the classes to which they belong and categorizing them.

"TASK 2: INFERRING AND GENERALIZING. Generalizing and inferring from data takes place when students are required to cope with raw data, such as when they must see and interpret a film or compare the tools and techniques for producing goods from differing technologies. Essentially, this cognitive task consists of evolving generalizations and principles from processing concrete data. Several sub-processes are involved. The first, and simplest, is that of identifying specific points in a mass of data, such as identifying from a film the tools used in agricultural processes or, after a period of research and reading, selecting the relevant points regarding education in Latin America. This process is somewhat analogous to the listing or enumeration preceding grouping in the first task.

"The second process is to explain specific items of information or events, e.g., explaining why ocean currents affect temperature or why Mexico employs the "each one teach one" system to wipe out illiteracy. This process involves relating the points in information to each other to detect causal relations and to establish relationships.

"The third operation is that of forming inferences that go beyond that which is directly given. For example, after comparing data on population composition in certain Latin American countries and relating these to data on standards of living there, a student infers that countries with predominantly white populations tend to have a higher standard of living.

"The chart below depicts the overt activities, the covert mental operations and the sequence of the eliciting questions for the process of generalization.

Cognitive Task 2: Inferring and Generalizing

Overt Activity	Covert Mental Operations	Eliciting Questions
1. Identifying points	Differentiating, distinguishing relevant information from irrelevant	What did you note? see? find?

| 2. Explaining identified items of information | Relating points to each other; establishing cause and effect relationships | Why did so-and-so happen? Why is so-and-so true? |
| 3. Making inferences or generalizations | Going beyond what is given; finding implications, extrapolating | What does this mean? What would you conclude? What generalizations can you make? |

"TASK 3: APPLICATION OF PRINCIPLES. The essence of this task is using information already possessed to explain something new, to predict consequences of events, or to hypothesize about causes and effects. For example, if one knows what a desert is, the way of life a desert permits and how water affects agricultural production, one can predict what might happen to the desert way of life if water became available. This process is the reverse of the one involved in interpretation. While interpreting and generalizing from raw data is an inductive process, applying known facts and generalizations is a deductive process.

"Three distinct steps are involved in this task also. The first step is that of predicting or hypothesizing. This involves the covert processes of analyzing the problem and of recalling and retrieving knowledge relevant to the problem. The second step consists of explaining or supporting the predictions or hypothesis by identifying the causal links that lead from the described condition or problem to the hypothesis or prediction. The third step is that of verifying the explanation, prediction or hypothesis by checking its probability and universality. This involves logical reasoning; for example, the use of logical inferences to determine the necessary and sufficient conditions for the probability of a given prediction.

"The processes involved in applying principles can be represented schematically as follows.

Cognitive Task 3: Application of Principles

Overt Activity	Covert Mental Operation	Eliciting Questions
1. Predicting consequences, explaining unfamiliar phenomena hypothesizing	Analyzing the nature and the dimensions of the problem or condition	What would happen if . . . ?
2. Explaining and supporting the predictions and hypotheses	Determining the causal links leading to a prediction or hypothesis	Why do you think this would happen?
3. Verifying the predictions and hypotheses	Using logical reasoning to determine the necessary conditions and the degree of universality of the prediction or hypothesis	What would it take for so-and-so to be true? Would it be true in all cases? At what times? Etc."

As has already been observed, Taba was eventually able (a) to train a group of 4th-, 5th-, and 6th-grade teachers to work systematically through the sequential steps, and (b) to provide a social studies curriculum with such organization of thinking "built in." In the schools of Contra Costa County, California, she was able to carry on an effectiveness study with control groups for comparison (though the nature of the work plus administrative difficulties made anything more than rough comparisons difficult).

Inevitably, evaluation was tricky, and this project seems to have had even more than the usual difficulty in devising measurements that would quantify the results. To this writer, frankly, the best evidence came from Hilda Taba herself, in correspondence and in conversation. She was an extremely objective and scientifically skeptical person, far more inclined to worry about the remaining "bugs" in her work than to see the favorable side. Yet in this case, having stayed very close to the teachers and read endless tapescripts of their classes, she seemed absolutely certain that she was onto something—that the process was working even though the teachers were still far from consistent mastery of her techniques and the curriculum materials were still in a formative stage. Perhaps the best way to catch her own assessment is to quote bits of her "Summary and Observations" at the end of her project report:

> The chief hypothesis of the study was that if the students were given a curriculum designed to develop their cognitive potential and theoretical insights, and if they were taught by strategies specifically addressed to helping them master crucial cognitive skills, then they would master the more sophisticated forms of symbolic thought earlier and more systematically than could be expected if this development had been left to the accidents of experience or if their school experience had been guided by less appropriate teaching strategies. The assumption was that conscious attention to the various intellectual processes would be the chief factor that would affect the students' facility to transform raw data into useable concepts, generalizations, hypotheses, and theories.
>
> It had been specifically postulated that teachers' actions were one of the most important influences in guiding the thought processes of students. These actions could, on the one hand, encourage divergent styles of thought and develop both discipline and autonomy in the use of cognitive skills, supporting students and giving them freedom to explore alternatives, or, on the other hand, these actions could limit the kind of cognitive operations in which students engage and the answers considered acceptable.

Generally speaking, the results of this study confirmed these hypotheses.

* * *

Evidence from the tests developed within the study showed that in ability to discriminate, to infer from data, and to apply known principles to new problems, the groups which had been trained in the skills of the three cognitive tasks were superior to untrained groups. However, these results were not consistent. It was not clear to what extent these inconsistencies were influenced by inadequacy of the tests, by imbalance in the composition of the sample groups, or by variations in teaching style over and above the variable of training.

* * *

The trained groups produced not only a greater number of thought units, but also thought units of greater length and complexity. They also tended to deal with more sophisticated content. They tended to operate more frequently on higher levels of thought, for example categorizing data on multiple bases or employing class categories instead of the functional ones in organizing the data. . . . The experimental groups also tended to produce more abstract and complex inferences. They tended to engage in consecutive and logically related sequences of thought, and they were both inclined to and capable of supporting their inferences. Through these chains of reasoning the trained groups gave evidence of actually producing generalizations in class, instead of appearing to recite or recall them as did the untrained students. Perhaps the most distinct difference was the trained students' inclination to constrain their hypothesizing to the data and to a realistic view of the problem. While long causal leaps often characterized their thinking, so did also their willingness and ability to reinstate these causal chains when pressed to do so. Also the students under trained teachers seemed to be more inclined to extend the hypothesizing across a longer chain of causal factors than were those under untrained teachers. The latter seemed to specialize more in immediate consequences and possibilities. . . .

* * *

The relationship between general ability as measured by intelligence tests and level of thinking is still baffling, probably because general ability and verbal fluency seemed to be related. By and large the more able students talked more and consequently also produced more high level thought units than did the less verbal or less expressive students. On the other hand, the low ability students also participated more than they did usually. Many teachers remarked on their surprise at seeing the "silent phalanges" become active participants. . . .

Further, the strategies fostered a greater incidence of both high and low level thought in the more able students. Since orderly thought requires the thinker to establish facts before generalizing, and factual support also is necessary to validate predictions and hypotheses, the above results seem reasonable enough. With the available time and techniques it was impossible to establish beyond doubt when low level thought was used for its own sake and when it was used as material from which to produce more abstract and complex forms of thought.

However, reading the tapescripts left a strong impression that the trained groups assembled descriptive information for the purpose of discovering general principles from comparing and contrasting the descriptive data, while the untrained groups more often were satisfied merely with assembling it. . . .

*　　*　　*

For example, the sharpest differences between the thinking of the trained and the untrained groups were found in the frequencies of "chained thought," the combination of both low and high level thought units into logical inferential sequence. . . .

Some Concluding—and Personal—Observations

Compared to the mass of available data, the foregoing look into the evidence on the educability of cognitive abilities is extremely sketchy. It has, in fact, amounted to little more than putting the flashlight on a bit here and another there. In her paper, which follows, Patricia Waller also highlights findings drawn from another type of sources. But her treatment also is necessarily sketchy. The writer can only plead that he believes what has been cited to be a reasonably representative sample of what might have been cited (though whole blocks of findings, such as those on the possibility of stimulating divergent thinking or creativity, have been left out; and the whole body of recent work on the effects of nutrition and the potentials of chemical aids to learning and memory has been excluded in favor of purely educational treatment).

Anyway, for whatever his opinion may be worth, this writer stands scientifically convinced that an enormous breakthrough possibility has been discovered. Over the long history of the schools no other problem has dogged the teachers of every generation as has the poor ability of most students to grasp what the teacher was trying to teach. Over the long history of the economy and the society nothing else has limited productivity and progress as has the limited ability of most adults to think with precision and handle the general idea. If such mental abilities can be raised, on the average, by even a little bit, the result must be one of the most striking advances in human history. And this writer believes that they can be raised by more than a little bit.

He is surest of all that the low cognitive abilities of the vast depressed masses can at least be brought to something like "normal." But he is hardly less sure that the cognitive abilities of those we now consider our able students can be raised even more signally. (Which is precisely what he believes has been beginning to happen to some of the better students in some of the better schools during the past decade; for instance, the sensational advances in science and mathematics are hardly to be explained as simply "knowing more math and science"; these students are patently operating on a new cognitive level.)

As to technique, obviously a great deal still remains to be learned. Even the basic research is only in its beginnings. And even if it were already complete we should still face a long period of policy change, curriculum adaptation, and—above all—teacher education.

Nevertheless, at this stage it does not appear that the *technical* problems (as against the human problems of involving and moving large numbers of adults) are particularly difficult. Thus one of the key elements, in good homes as well as in pre-school programs, is an enrichment of varied stimulation. At the nursery-school level this may take the form of sensorimotor stimulation with planned use of educational toys, excursions, and other rather concrete experiences. At the secondary level an analogue may well lie along the lines of the "higher horizons" programs, opening up the cultural community. Or it may be a *vocational* enrichment program, bringing into awareness a vastly widened scope of career possibilities. At any level schools can choose in many, many ways between dull, monotonous environments and a rich vividness of contact and experience. *The difficulties are not technical.*

Another key area of cognitive development is in language—or, more accurately—symbolization. The job is to build a symbolic system and communication habits that will hold the edge of precision so essential in our modern technology and complex society. This is no small task with children whose natural language is adequate only to crude affective-relational cues. But the evidence is that the problem does yield to direct, well planned attack, and there is no school subject, no school year in which that attack is not appropriate. This may well be the point at which we are closest to pure technical difficulties, but teachers could be prepared to handle them.

The sharpening of perception and of discrimination appears to be another major contributor. This is almost a commonplace at the early-childhood level, where great emphasis is placed on feeling rough and smooth surfaces, discriminating colors, lengths, shapes, and weights, hearing the final sounds in words, etc. It is easy to overlook, at a higher level, that when Taba went after big-generalization thinking she first trained teachers and students to "see" more of the basic data, draw discriminations, among them, and build categories. The great discoveries in science are largely the end results of ultra-fine perception of discrepancies, and a science program at any level should contain a high element of training in acute perception (reminiscent of that student of Louis Agassiz who was set to work for days on end to see what he could see in one fish skeleton). Certainly a program in music or art or literature is not less rich in potential to train the finer perceptions and discriminations. It is exactly such niceness that puts the fine edge on thought.

To take just one final example, there is the lead that Taba has given us. Sensory stimulation, exact nomenclature, discrimination training, and so on are all good and necessary. But ultimately there are those higher processes of thought, of abstraction, of disciplined induction and inference and transfer to new situations. These also are the product of education and experience, and if we can open them up to children otherwise earthbound to the concrete and particular, this may be the greatest gain of all. Here, in terms of the long traditions of hackneyed teaching as the imparting of knowledge, we may face our greatest difficulties. Any genuinely insightful secondary teacher of science or mathematics or social science or whatnot must see helping students forward in the disciplined logic of his field—in the use of his discipline as an "engine of inquiry"—as a primary task. So far, the transactional analyses of actual typical teaching reveal dismayingly that it almost forecloses the students' opportunities to travel the high roads of thought. But if we work at it and supply better instructional materials, teachers will learn.

Undoubtedly there are other major lines of effort. But it would not be the function of this report to produce a methodological recipe, even if that were possible at this stage. We have gone even this far in describing lines of input only to make two points: First, when we talk of raising cognitive abilities, we are not talking of any one panacea. "Intelligence," finally, is an end product of many components, each susceptible of refinement. And, second, the opportunities to do what we need to do are inherent in every subject at every level. As a matter of fact, what needs to be done for the building of cognitive competence is totally congruent with what needs to be done for the better teaching of every discipline.

There remain two questions to be dealt with: (1) Are there "critical periods"? (2) Do the gains "wash out"?

Are There "Critical Periods"?

Assuming that some combination of experiencing and verbalizing in a context of love and happiness can give a significant cognitive push, must this be done at some particular period or be forever lost? We know that in the animal kingdom there are "critical periods" for certain kinds of learning (which seem to lengthen as one goes up the phylogenetic scale). Are there similar critical periods for human learning?

One thing is clear: Learning is a cumulative matter. Piaget has shown, for instance, that certain "structures" must mature before others can be started. Obviously a child who gets a head start has a progressively expanding base for cognitive activity, and his head start may progressively lengthen as a result. Deficits are thus cumulative also, with the added disaster that the child who enters a typical school with too great a deficit begins a cycle of failure that can spiral downward in increasing depth.

But this is not the same thing as a "critical period," which means that if some developments do not take place at one age they cannot take place—or take place so completely—at a later period. The question of the existence of such periods remains largely unanswered. Bloom[7] is most often quoted for his carefully reasoned estimates that a child attains 40% of all the intelligence he will ever have by age 4, and another 40% by age 8, leaving only 20% to be effected through the rest of his life. But Bloom himself carefully alerts his readers to the fact that his whole treatise is "based on things as they now are, and this includes the particular tests to measure intelligence, the child-rearing practices of families in Western cultures, and educational practices in the schools. It is conceivable that changes in any or all of these could produce a very different picture."

---

[7] Benjamin S. Bloom. *Stability and Change in Human Characteristics.* John Wiley & Sons, Inc. 1964.

Bloom makes an impressive argument that any human variable is most subject to change during that period when it generally changes most in the natural course of events, particularly as it refers to such physical items as growth and height. Thus differences in nutrition will obviously affect a boy's height most if they come at the time when he normally grows most rapidly. But this may be more in the nature of a logical construct as applied to cognitive growth. It is an oddity that while many stress this emphasis on early action to catch the periodicity of growth for certain gains, few seem equally concerned to catch those gains that normally come later. Thus, many investigators, using Piaget's framework, seek to identify the most favoring environment at the *sensorimotor* stage and the stage of *concrete operations,* but the list thins when we come to the stage of formal operations, beginning around age 11 or 12. The opening up of the most truly genuine phase of human intelligence coincides almost exactly with the opening year of the middle school; yet not only secondary educators but also the predominant literature of the field tends to relegate cognitive training as a matter for the pre-school or at most the early grades. All in all, while there is much in this body of research to back the idea that there are *best* times for certain kinds of cognitive growth, there seems to be nothing in it to forbid continuing effort beyond early childhood to upgrade ability to learn.

Do the Gains "Wash Out"?

Much has been made of this argument, particularly in relation to Operation Head Start. Even if we can achieve a quick jump in IQ, the argument runs, it soon disappears when the child leaves the special program.

Of course, in any deep sense, the argument is irrelevant. If we can devise enrichment programs to stimulate the growth of cognitive abilities at one stage, there is no logic in basing our policies on the assumption that we must provide planned deprivation later! The only real question is whether the thing can be done at all; if it can, we can find ways of going further with it.

Nevertheless, in terms of public decision-making, the question is important and must be dealt with. This writer has come to feel no doubt that gains *will* lack significance if nothing is involved but a brief period of enrichment followed by a barren program.

He has a hunch that Bereiter and Engelmann are right in saying that almost any fresh encounter with a pre-school situation will generate enough responsiveness to the testing situation, if nothing more, to produce an IQ gain of some 6 or 8 points; but other youngsters who wait till later and hit the fresh situation in kindergarten or first grade will feel the same effect; hence, even if the gain is permanent, which may be doubtful, it is irrelevant to the providing of enriched programs. This writer shares Deutsch's feeling that no quick, little program is going to cause the dormant intellect to blossom forth for all time; that enrichment programs should start earlier than age 4 and go through at least grade 3. In fact, there seems to be no logical alternative to starting early and going forward *continuingly*, with changing emphases and techniques as the years move on.

That such a program will produce gains that hold is powerfully illustrated in Israel. Confronted by the truly massive deprivation among the children of "Oriental" Jews and many Arabs, that nation has led all the rest in a program lasting from nursery school through the secondary years. The result has apparently been, to quote one other group of reviewers of this literature, that "It seems that a whole generation of culturally deprived and psychosocially disadvantaged children . . . has been 'pulled up by its bootstraps'."[8]

A Question of Investment

If, thus far, we have been somewhere near the right track, then a big question emerges as to our investment of educational energy and money.

By long tradition, the schools pour virtually all their time, money, and energy into the direct teaching of subject matter. And if blockages occur on that line the all-but-universal response is simply to "push harder" on the subject matter.

Reading provides the outstanding example. A great many children are in trouble with it from the start. Hundreds of thousands of them continue to fall further and further behind until their deficit in this one area virtually guarantees failure across the board. Teachers spend endless hours trying to bring

---

[8] Walter L. Hodges, Boyd R. McCandless, and Howard H. Spicker in collaboration with Isabel S. Craig, *The Development and Evaluation of a Diagnostically Based Curriculum for Preschool Psycho-Socially Deprived Children*, U. S. Office of Education, 1967. p. 11.

them up. Schools mount massive programs of remedial instruction. Gains are made, of course, but usually rather small ones, and these at tremendous cost.

One cannot help wondering whether it would not be more effective—and perhaps even easier and cheaper—to work directly on the learner himself as a learner, rather than always work directly on the reading (or other subject matter). If he could be changed *as a learner*, much of the rest might fall into place. Even if we cannot yet guarantee what dividends a new approach to educational investment might yield, it is obvious that there is now so much investment in futility that common sense demands a new look.

Yet, of course, to pitch the question in terms of economy is to put it in its lowest possible form. The real question is what route leads away from cumulative deficit and toward the highest cumulative power. With all the uncertainties there may be here, one truth is certain: The cognitive potentials of children are far greater than what is generally actualized. The fundamental error we have made has been to look at the intellectual character a youngster has so far developed and say, "This is it"—to look at the IQ he seems to possess and say "This is what *he is*." The fundamental corrective we need is to learn to ask, "Regardless of what this child is right now, what has he the potential to *become*?—and how can we help him in that becoming?" In the cognitive realm we can ask that question meaningfully only as we come to see how little intelligence is pre-formed at birth, how much it is the outgrowth of educational experience.

NEGRO YOUTH
AND PSYCHOLOGICAL MOTIVATION

Alvin F. Poussaint and Carolyn O. Atkinson

Alvin F. Poussaint and Carolyn O. Atkinson, "Negro Youth and Psychological Motivation," *Journal of Negro Education,* Summer 1968, Vol. 37 pp. 241-251.

NEGRO YOUTH AND PSYCHOLOGICAL MOTIVATION

Alvin F. Poussaint and Carolyn O. Atkinson

INTRODUCTION

It is the concern of this paper to explore some of the factors which we consider most relevant to the issue of the motivation of Negro youth. Primary among these are (1) the individual's self-concept, (2) certain of his patterned needs, and (3) the rewards which society offers for performance in any of its institutional areas. These motivations are clearly of two types: those internal to the individual (the first two), and those external to the individual (the third). In assessing implications for action to bring about a closer coincidence between the psychological motivation of Negro youth and society's demands for performance, it would seem important to consider the operation of both internal and external motivations in order to determine more precisely the nature of their relationship to behavior and to suggest in which direction an optimal meshing of these factors might lie. Before addressing ourselves to the operation of these motivators in black youth, it is necessary to explore briefly the genesis and character of the internal motivators and the nature of the external reward structure. Finally, we will explore the implications of various patterns of motivations for optimizing the performance of black youth.

I. NATURE OF INTERNAL AND EXTERNAL MOTIVATORS

Self-Concept: Mead,[1] Cooley,[2] and others[3] have written that the self arises through the individual's interaction with and reaction to other members of society — his peers, his parents, his teachers and other institutional representatives. Through identification and as a requisite for effective communication, Mead maintains, the child learns to assume the role of others with whom he interacts and also their attitudes, and these attitudes, thus assumed, condition his response to others' and to his own behavior. Mead further suggests that the collection of attitudes of the others with whom the individual interacts is organized in the "generalized other," that community which gives the individual his unity of self. Thus, the individual's self is shaped and developed by anticipating and assuming the attitudes and definitions of others toward him, and it is controlled through the adoption of the attitudes, norms, and values of the generalized other (community) toward him. To the extent that

---

[1] George H. Mead, *Mind, Self, and Society* (Chicago: University of Chicago Press, 1934), Part III.
[2] Charles H. Cooley, *Human Nature and the Social Order* (Glencoe, Ill.: Free Press, 1956), *passim*.
[3] *Sociological Quarterly* (entire issue), Vol. 7, No. 3, Summer, 1966.

the individual is a member of this community, its attitudes are his, its values are his, and its norms are his, and his image of himself is structured in these terms. Each self, then, though having its unique characteristics of personality, is also an individual reflection of the social process.[4] Similarly, Cooley has said that the self might be considered a looking-glass, since one's self-idea has three principal components: "the imagination of our appearance to the other person; the imagination of his judgment of that appearance; and some sort of self-feeling, such as pride or mortification."[5]

What, then, can we say about the ways in which the self-concept of black youth in white American society develops? The generalized other whose attitudes the black child assumes and the looking-glass into which he gazes both reflect the same judgment: he is inferior because he is black. The youth learns these self-attitudes not only from racist representatives of white society, but also from his black family and peers who have been socialized to believe that they are substandard human beings. These beliefs are reinforced when performance in accordance with them is rewarded by the larger society: the incompetent, inadequate, imbecilic, and irresponsible Negro is the Negro who has frequently been rewarded and has survived in American society while the competent, adequate, achieving, aggressive Negro has been systematically suppressed. Similarly, when the Negro has peered into the looking-glass of white society, he has seen black skin and kinky hair and he has seen that in this society white skin and straight

hair are valued and that the more closely a black man approximates this appearance, the more esteemed he is both by whites and by many Negroes.

Thus, the self of the black youth, developed in the lowest stratum of a color caste system, is shaped, defined, and evaluated by a generalized other which is racist or warped by racists. The black person's self naturally becomes a negatively esteemed one which is nurtured through contact with such institutionalized symbols of caste inferiority as segregated (*de facto* or *de jure*) schools, neighborhoods, and jobs and more indirect negative indicators such as the reactions of his own family. Gradually becoming aware of the meaning of his black skin, the Negro child comes to see himself as an object of scorn and disparagement, unworthy of love and affection, and he learns to despise himself and to reject those like himself. From that time on, his personality and style of interaction with his environment become molded and shaped in a warped, self-hating, and self-denigrating way. The looking-glass self reflects a shattered image.

This conceptualization of the development of the self of black youth is, of course, a generalization which, while holding in the main, no doubt has numerous exceptions. It is our feeling, however, that it is the rule rather than the exception which should concern us in our discussion here.[6] The operation of self-

---

[4] Mead, *op. cit.*
[5] Cooley, *op. cit.*, p. 184.

[6] It is important to point out that the attitudes of the generalized other have become more ambivalent in the last few years. As we suggest elsewhere, (A.F. Poussaint, "The Dynamics of Racial Conflict," *Lowell Lecture Series*, sponsored by Tufts-New England Medical Center, April 16, 1968), the normative perception of Negroes as inferior and impotent has been challenged by the

concept as a motivator of performance will be explored in Section II below.

Patterned Needs: In the course of the socialization process, the individual acquires needs which motivate and generate emotions. Three such needs concern us here: the need for achievement, the need for self-assertion or aggression, and the need for approval.

Among the attitudes of the generalized other which the individual internalizes are the norms and values of the wider community, including, of course, the major tenets of the Protestant Ethic-American Creed: with hard work and effort the individual can achieve success and it is this achievement that defines the individual's worth. If the individual internalizes these values, he is motivated to act consistent with them. Thus, the need for achievement (whatever its concrete manifestation) develops in Americans, black youth included (see discussion of aspirations below). The motive to seek achievement in accordance with the value is reinforced by the fact that one's self-esteem is heightened or maintained through behaving in a manner approved by the community. There is evidence[7] that this value is internalized by lower class and middle class, black and white,

and that the motive to achievement is similarly present. However, these same data suggest that this motive may have various consequences for behavior. We shall explore this further in Section II. We assume, however, that the need for achievement is generally a part of the personality structure of black youth, although its strength may vary from case to case and its behavioral manifestations may take different forms.

The values expressed in the Protestant Ethic imply that assertion of self, aggression, is an expected and admired form of behavior. Through the socialization process, the individual internalizes those attitudes which reinforce his basic need to assert himself or express himself aggressively. Thus, random and possibly destructive aggression is channelled into a legitimate and rewarded motive to self-actualization and achievement.

What happens to the black child's need for aggression and self-assertion? What has been the nature of his socialization with respect to expressing aggression? Since slave days and, to some extent, through the present, the Negro most rewarded by whites has been the "Uncle Tom," the exemplar of the black man who was docile and nonassertive, who bowed and scraped for the white boss and denied his aggressive feelings for his oppressor. In order to retain the most menial of jobs and keep from starving, black people quickly learned such servile responses as "Yassuh, Massa": passivity was a necessary survival technique. To be an "uppity nigger" was considered by racists one of the gravest violations of racial etiquette. Vestiges of this attitude remain to the present day, certainly in the South but even

---

facts of the civil rights and black consciousness movements: Negroes are bringing about changes in their environments through their own knowledge, efforts, and through seeing black as a positive force. To the extent that this aspect of the generalized other has been meaningfully presented to black youth, his self-conception has become more positive.

[7] Joan Gordon, *The Poor of Harlem: Social Functioning in the Underclass*, Report to the Welfare Administration, Washington, D. C., July 31, 1965, pp. 115 and 161 and Irwin Katz, "Academic Motivation and Equal Educational Opportunity," *Harvard Educational Review*, XXXVIII (Winter, 1968), 57-65.

in the North: blacks who are "too out-spoken" about racial injustices often lose their jobs or are not promoted to higher positions because they are considered "un-reasonable" or "too sensitive." It is significant that the civil rights movement had to adopt passive-resistance and nonviolence in order to win acceptance by white America. Thus, the black child is socialized to the lesson taught by his parents, other blacks, and white society: don't be aggressive, don't be assertive. Such lessons do not, however, destroy the need for aggression and assertiveness, and thus, the question to be explored in Section II is the direction of motivation arising from this need.

With the development of the self and through the process of identification, the individual's need for approval develops and grows as does his need not to be disapproved. As we have stated earlier, behavior following the achievement motive and expressive of the need for self-assertion is approved by the society and, thus, in a cyclical fashion, the need for approval motivates such behavior. On the other hand, we have suggested that for blacks in American society, behavior which is neither achievement-oriented nor self-assertive is often approved by both blacks and whites (for different reasons), and, thus, the need for approval may motivate blacks to be nonachievement-oriented and nonassertive. However, the need for approval may also be met through other unrelated behavior types. Section II considers how the need for approval motivates black youth and the extent that satisfaction is attained.

External Motivators: The rewards which the institutions of this society offer to those whose behavior meets their approval or is "successful" consist of money, prestige, power, respect, acclamation, love, and increasing amounts of each of these for increasingly "successful" behavior. The individual is socialized to know that these will be his if he performs according to expectations. Hence, these rewards act as external motivators of behavior. Negroes have learned of the existence of these rewards. They have also learned, however, that behavior for which whites reap these rewards does not result in the same consequences for them. In the various institutional areas of society, Negroes are often rewarded differentially from whites for the same behavior — if they are rewarded at all. Thus, the reward structure can often not be trusted by Negroes to operate as promised, and its strength as a motivator of behavior may be diminished.

II. The Operation of Internal and External Motivations

We turn now to a consideration of how these motivations — self-concept, needs, and external rewards — operate to affect the personality and behavior of Negro youth. This discussion is not intended to be exhaustive or to present all of the data related to any particular motivation. (We have had to be selective in our choice of examples and have focused for the most part, although not exclusively, on those dealing with lower-class youth.) Rather, we hope to suggest that particular motivations can have diverse consequences for behavior.

Self-Concept: We have said that the sort of self-concept that has been nurtured and rewarded in black people is one of inferiority and unworthiness. There have been numerous attempts to measure self-concept and to associate it with various forms of behavior — particularly educational achievement. While the validity of the measures has varied widely,[8] most have confirmed the weakness and negativeness of the Negro's self-concept. One notable exception is the finding of the Coleman Report. By that measure negligible differences were found between the self-concepts of Negroes and of whites: they were at approximately the same levels when controlled for a range of variables.[9] This finding would seem to have implications for achievement. Coleman did not find such to be the case. Of three expressions of attitudes and motivations measured in children in this study, level of self-concept was the weakest predictor of achievement (as measured by Coleman) for black children, while it was the strongest predictor of achievement for white children.[10] Thus, this study says that although self-concept may be high, it is not related to achievement. Other studies disagree with this finding saying that self-concept is high but inversely related to achievement, or that it is low and directly related to achievement.

In the first case, assuming the tendency to have high standards for one's performance to be indicative of one's self-evaluation, Katz suggests that low achievement is related to high self-evaluation. He says,

Conceivably, their [low achieving Negro boys'] standards were so stringent

and rigid as to be utterly dysfunctional. They seem to have internalized a most effective mechanism for self-discouragement. In a sense, they had been socialized to self-impose failure.[11]

He presents evidence which indicates that the anticipation of failure or harsh judgment by adults (e.g., in a test situation) produces anxiety in the child, and that in Negro children, this level of anxiety is highest in low achievers who have a high standard of self-evaluation.[12] Therefore, the variable of level of anxiety and resulting motivation to self-impose failure would seem to intervene making high self-evaluation dysfunctional for achievement.

Deutsch's work has shown that Negro children had significantly more negative self-images than did white children.[13] He maintains that among the influences converging on the black urban child

is his sensing that the larger society views him as inferior and *expects* inferior performance from him as evidenced by the general denial to him of realistic vertical mobility possibilities. Under these conditions, it is understandable that the Negro child would tend strongly to question his own competencies and in so questioning would be acting largely as others expect him to act, an example of what Merton has called the "self-fulfilling prophecy" — the very expectation itself is a cause of its fulfillment.[14]

Similarly, Coombs and Davies, who found that higher conceptions of scholastic ability and expectations for grades were re-

---

[8] While we recognize the limitations of many measures of self-concept and that self-concept is often defined by how it is measured, an exploration of these considerations within the scope of this paper is clearly impossible. Therefore, for the purposes of our presentation here, we are taking the measures of self-concept at face-value.

[9] James S. Coleman and others, *Equality of Educational Opportunity*, (Washington, D. C.: U. S. Office of Education, Government Printing Office, 1966), p. 281.

[10] *Ibid.*, p. 320.

[11] Katz, *op. cit.*, p. 60.
[12] *Ibid.*, pp. 61-62.
[13] Martin Deutsch, "Minority Groups and Class Status as Related to Social and Personality Factors in Scholastic Achievement," in Martin Deutsch and Associates, *The Disadvantaged Child* (New York: Basic Books, Inc., 1967), p. 106.
[14] *Ibid.*, p. 107.

lated to high achievement,[15] offer the important proposition that

> In the context of the school world, a student who is defined as a "poor student" (by significant others and thereby by self) comes to conceive of himself as such and gears his behavior accordingly, that is, the social expectation is realized. However, if he is led to believe by means of the social "looking-glass" that he is capable and able to achieve well, he does. To maintain his status and self-esteem becomes the incentive for further effort which subsequently involves him more in the reward system of the school.[16]

Such studies as that of Davidson and Greenberg have confirmed these views finding that the lower the level of self-esteem, the lower the level of achievement. In a study of children from Central Harlem, these authors found that higher levels of self-appraisal and ego strength — feelings of self-competence — were associated with higher levels of achievement. For example, high achievers were more able to give their own ideas and to express basic needs,[17] suggesting that a stronger self-concept is associated with a greater willingness to risk self-expression, certainly a prerequisite for achievement.

The evidence on the operation of self-concept as a motivator of behavior is conflicting. What is clear is that no evidence has been adduced to show that low levels of self-concept are associated with optimal levels of achievement, and since the self-esteem of black youth is generally more negative than that of whites and may motivate them not to perform optimally, the black youth clearly competes at a disadvantage with white youth.

PATTERNED NEEDS

(1) Need for Achievement: We stated earlier that American youngsters including black youth are socialized to the achievement motive, but that Negroes also learn that non-achieving behavior on the part of blacks is rewarded by many who occupy positions of power. Thus, we asked how the need for achievement operated to motivate behavior.

We assume that aspirations are a manifestation of the achievement motive. Consequently, among the most important findings in this area are those of Coleman[18] and Katz[19] who note very high aspirations (often higher than those of middle-class whites) with regard to schooling and occupational choice in Negro youth, and those of Katz[20] and Gordon[21] which indicate that the aspirations and demands for academic achievement of the parents of these youths are often exceptionally high. All of these sources agree, however, that the achievement of these youth is far from commensurate with either their own aspirations or those of their parents.[22] Thus the problem does not seem to be, as some have suggested,[23]

---

15 Helen H. Davidson and Judith W. Greenberg, *Traits of School Achievers from a Deprived Background* (New York: City College of the City University of New York, May 1967), pp. 133, 134.

16 R. H. Coombs and V. Davies, "Self-Conception and the Relationship Between High School and College Scholastic Achievement." *Sociology and Social Research*, (July, 1966), 468-469.

17 Davidson and Greenberg, *op. cit.*, pp. 133-134.

---

18 Coleman, *op. cit.*, pp. 278-280.

19 Katz, *op. cit.*, p. 64.

20 *Ibid.*, pp. 63-65.

21 Gordon, *op. cit.*, p. 115.

22 Coleman, *op. cit.*, p. 281; Katz, *op. cit.*, p. 63; Gordon, *op. cit.*, pp. 155, 160-161.

23 David P. Ausubel and Pearl Ausubel, "Ego Development Among Segregated Negro Children," in A. Harry Passow, ed., *Edu-*

one of insufficiently high levels of aspiration, but, rather, one of the articulation of aspirations with behavior. Gordon[24] and Katz[25] suggest that this discrepancy persists because the educational and occupational values and goals have been internalized, but for one reason or another, the behavior patterns requisite for their articulation have not been similarly learned.

On the other side of the coin, there is such evidence as that of Davidson and Greenberg that greater achievement motivation is associated with high achievement.[26] We do not, however, know whether the relationship is a causal one, and if so, the direction of causation. There are, of course, numerous cases in which high aspirations are associated with high achievement. We feel, however, that it is equally if not more important to concern ourselves with the operation of the achievement motive in the form of aspirations which are *not* translated into behavior.

(2) Assertion of Self, Aggression: The black man's socialization has been *not to* assert himself or to express aggression. Nevertheless, these needs persist, and our concern was to explore how they are expressed and how they motivate behavior.

One asserts himself for self-expression, to achieve his goals, and to control his environment. Thus, an individual's sense of control over his environment is an indicator of the extent to which his need for self-assertion is realized. Coleman found that Negroes have a much lower sense of control over their environment than do whites.[27] He also found, however, that of three attitudes measured (another was self-concept which we discussed earlier), sense of control over environment showed the strongest relationship to achievement.[28] Further, sense of control over environment increased for Negroes as the proportion of whites with whom they went to school increased.[29] This syndrome of findings indicates that for Negroes who *objectively* are less able to control their environment than are whites, a realistic inability to assert themselves meaningfully is a greater inhibitor of ability to achieve than any other variable; but it also suggests that when Negroes are interacting in a school situation which approximates the world in which they must cope — i.e., one with whites — their sense of control and achievement increases. Our emphasis here is not that black students' being in the presence of white students increases their sense of control and level of achievement, but that their being in a proximate real world suggests to them that they can cope in any situation, not just one in which they are interacting with others who have been defined as inferior.

Coleman's findings are supported by those of Davidson and Greenberg: high achievers were more able to exercise control and to cope more effectively with feelings of hostility and anxiety generated by the environment than were low achievers.[30] However, the response to feeling little sense of control over the environment may be not to attempt to control it or to assert oneself. For instance, com-

---

cation in *Depressed Areas* (New York: Teachers College Press, 1963), p. 135.

24 Gordon, *op. cit.*, pp. 115, 161.

25 Katz, *op. cit.*, p. 63.

26 Davidson and Greenberg, *op. cit.*, p. 58.

27 Coleman, *op. cit.*, p. 289.

28 *Ibid.*, p. 319.

29 *Ibid.*, p. 323-324.

30 Davidson and Greenberg, *op. cit.*, p. 54.

petition which may bring success may also bring failure. Thus, the efforts which may bring success to a black man are often not made even when the opportunity exists, no doubt for two reasons: first, the anxiety that accompanies growth and change through self-assertion is avoided if a new failure is not risked, and, therefore, a try is not made; second, the steady state of failure represented by non-achievement rather than by an unsuccessful trial is what many Negroes have come to know and expect, and they feel less psychologically discomforted with the more familiar. Deutsch points out, for example, that Negro male children for whom aggressive behavior has always been more threatening (compared with Negro girls) have lower levels of achievement on a number of variables than do Negro girls.[31]

A corollary of the need for self-assertion is the need for aggression; and frustration of efforts to control the environment are likely to lead to anger, rage and other expressions of aggression.[32] Aggression can be dealt with by suppressing it, leading one to act on the basis of a substitute and opposing emotional attitude such as compliance or docility. It can be channelled through legitimate activities — dancing, sports — or by identifying with the oppressor and putting all of one's energy into striving to be like him. Aggression can be turned inward and expressed in psychosomatic illness, drug addiction, or attacking those who are like you (other blacks) and whom you hate

as much as you hate yourself. Or it can be directed toward those who generate the anger and rage — those whom the individual defines as thwarting his inclination to self-assertion and aggression. This form of aggression can be either destructive or constructive: dropping out of school or becoming delinquent are examples of the former case, while participation in black social action movements is an example of the latter instance. We believe that this latter form of aggressive behavior is increasing in extent, that the old passivity is fading and being replaced by a drive to undo powerlessness, helplessness, and dependency under American racism.

The evidence from the Coleman Report and our own clinical experience suggest that need for self-assertion and aggression are stronger motivators of behavior, especially achievement, than are personality predispositions related to self-concept. Perhaps, therefore, more attention should be given to examining this dimension of personality as a motivator of the black youth's behavior than to continuing inquiries into his self-image.

(3) Need for Approval: We have said that as one's self develops, so too does his need for approval and his need not to be disapproved. Clearly in the American system, this need is often tied to the achievement motive and the motivation to self-assertion. An indicator of this association is that high achievers have a more positive attitude toward authority figures and conform more to adult demands.[33] Thus their behavior is approved by others who are likely to be significant others. Katz, however, maintains that in lower-class Negro homes,

---

[31] Deutsch, *op. cit.*, p. 108.

[32] Alvin F. Poussaint, "A Negro Psychiatrist Explains the Negro Psyche," *New York Times Magazine*, August 20, 1967, pp. 58-80. The following is a summary of what was elaborated in the *Times Magazine* on manifestatons of aggression.

---

[33] Davidson and Greenberg, *op. cit.*, p. 61.

children do not learn realistic (middle-class) standards of self-appraisal and therefore do not develop (as do middle-class children) the capacity for gaining "satisfaction through self-approval of successful performance."[34] Rather, he suggests, achievement should be motivated and rewarded by approval from fellow students and teachers.[35]

The extent to which black children are responsive to approval for achievement in middle-class terms is, however, problematic. Some evidence suggests that lower-class black children are motivated to gain approval through physical characteristics and prowess rather than through intellectual achievement as are middle-class white and black children.[36] Further, needs for approval, not often met in black children through the established institutional channels may be met by others outside of these legitimate institutional areas. For instance, delinquent sub-cultures are supportive and encouraging of the behavior of their members and such members are not often sensitive to the informal sanctions imposed by nonmembers of this sub-society.[37] If an individual's needs are not met by others to whose sanctions he is expected to be responsive, he will be less likely to fear their sanctions for nonperformance and will seek to have his needs met by others to whose rewards of approval he will then be responsive.[38] Thus, for black

youth no less than others, how the need for approval motivates behavior depends in large part upon how it is satisfied.

External Motivators: Society's offer of such external rewards as money, prestige and power to black people is highly capricious. How then do these usually tempting prizes motivate their behavior?

That blacks orient some aspects of their behavior to society's reward system is evidenced by the fact that many studies have shown that lower-class Negroes, as opposed to middle-class people, have a utilitarian attitude toward education, viewing it primarily in terms of its market value.[39] However, whether the job will be commensurate with education can never be anticipated. This inability to trust society to confer rewards consistently no doubt makes it difficult for blacks to be socialized to behave in terms of anticipating future reward for present activity. Thus it is that Deutsch found that young Negro children are unwilling to persist in attempting to solve difficult problems. They respond to such situations with a "who cares?" attitude.[40] Similarly, another study showed that when a reward was offered for successful work on a test, the motivation of the deprived youngsters increased considerably.[41]

In a New York program, young men who had been working primarily as clerks and porters were motivated to join a tutorial program for admission to a construction trade union apprenticeship program when they were promised that successful completion of the program (pass-

---

[34] Katz, *op. cit.*, p. 57.
[35] *Ibid*.
[36] Edmund W. Gordon and Doxey A. Wilkerson, *Compensatory Education for the Disadvantaged* (New York: College Entrance Examination Board, 1966), p. 18.
[37] Claude Brown, *Manchild in the Promised Land* (New York: MacMillan Company, 1965), *passim*.
[38] Talcott Parsons, *The Social System* (Glencoe, Ill.: The Free Press, 1951), Ch. 7.

[39] Gordon and Wilkerson, *op. cit.*, p. 18.
[40] Deutsch, *op. cit.*, p. 102.
[41] Elizabeth Douvan, "Social Status and Success Striving," cited in Frank Riessman, *The Culturally Deprived Child* (New York: Harper and Row, 1962), p. 53.

ing the union's examination) would result in their being hired immediately at
a salary often double what they were
able to command previously.[42]

However, motivation to achieve certain
rewards may have different consequences
for behavior. As Merton explained, when
the goals of society are internalized without a corresponding internalization of normative means for achieving these goals,
what often results is the resort to illegitimate (deviant) means to achieve the
socially valued goal.[43] Thus such deviant
forms of behavior as numbers running,
dope pushing, and prostitution net the
rewards of society, but the institutional
channels for their achievement were abandoned. That Negro children early learn
that such behavior is rewarded is suggested
by Gordon's study in which young (9-13
years) Central Harlem boys were asked
if they knew people who were rich and if
so, how they thought they got to be that
way. Of those who did, a majority said
that they thought they had gotten rich
through illegitimate means or luck.[44]

Consequently, for many black youth,
external rewards are weak motivators of
behavior since they are discriminatorily
and inconsistently given. The more immediate and direct the reward is, the
stronger a motivator it is likely to be.
However, as with all members of a
society which stresses success and achievement but offers unequal access to these
goals, Negro youth may be motivated to
seek rewards through illegitimate means.

III. IMPLICATIONS

What are the implications of our consideration of the motivation of Negro
youth for bringing about a better mesh
between motivation and productive behavior?

First, with respect to self-concept, all
institutional segments of society must
begin to function in a non-racist manner.
To the extent that the self is shaped with
reference to a generalized other, to that
extent will the black child's image be
impaired as long as America remains racist.
In the meantime, the growth of black
consciousness and pride have had salutary
consequences for the black's self-image.
Further, our evidence suggested that the
operation of self-image as a motivator
for behavior was like a self-fulfilling
prophecy: Negroes were told and believed that they were inferior and would
fail and therefore they failed. Thus for
the black child to be motivated to achieve
in school, the school must negate everything that the society affirms: it must
tell the child that he can succeed — and
then he will succeed.[45]

Second, the relationship between self-
concept and achievement is not clear cut,
but some evidence suggests that it is a
weaker motivator of behavior than the
motive to self-assertion and aggression.
We would, therefore, suggest that structural changes in the institutional arrangements of society — in the direction of
blacks' having the opportunity to be more
self-assertive and aggressive — would be
important improvements. The plans to
decentralize New York City schools, to
develop black business, and to organize
and channel black political power are significant steps in this direction. Among
the data pertaining to sense of control

[42] Personal communication (C. A.)
[43] Robert K. Merton, *Social Theory and
Social Structure*, (Glencoe, Ill.: The Free
Press 1957), ch. 4.
[44] Gordon, *op. cit.*, p. 164.

[45] Kenneth B. Clark, *Dark Ghetto* (New
York: Harper and Row, 1965), pp. 139-148.

of the environment was the fact that this variable increased as the proportion of whites in the schools increased. We suggested in the body of this paper a partial interpretation of that association. We would add here that participation in all-or-predominantly-black structures may well not be self-destructive if the black individual chooses rather than is forced to participate in them. For if he chooses, he is asserting control over his environment.

Third, most of the data indicate that Negro youth and their parents have high educational and occupational aspirations, which are not manifested in achievement levels. We would, therefore, suggest that something is wrong with schools if so much young potential is being wasted simply because it cannot be developed within the framework of traditional ways.

The reward systems of American society are totally irrelevant to the lives and aspirations of most black youth. Approval is rewarded primarily for forms of behavior in which the black youth has managed to achieve little proficiency; thus he is likely to be less willing to make the effort. Is there not some way in which the educational aspirations of black youth could be associated in academic pursuits with their interests and proficiencies — and rewarded consistently -- so that, in time, intellectual endeavors would have the same relevance to their lives that they have to the lives of the high achievers?

All of these implications suggest major structural changes. The day has come for American society when full freedom for its black citizens and its own survival demand such changes.

EARLY EDUCATION:
A COGNITIVE – DEVELOPMENTAL VIEW

Lawrence Kohlberg

Lawrence Kohlberg, "Early Education: A Cognitive-Developmental View,"
Child Development, March 1968, pp. 1013-75.

EARLY EDUCATION:
A COGNITIVE–DEVELOPMENTAL VIEW

Lawrence Kohlberg

This paper reviews the implications of the cognitive-developmental theories of Baldwin, Dewey, Piaget, and Vygotsky for preschool education. The conception of cognitive stage basic to these theories is analyzed, and the connection of a stage conception to an interactional (as opposed to a maturationist or environmentalist-training) view of the origins of mental structure is analyzed. Empirical studies are reviewed supporting the validity of this conception of intellectual development. Preschool programs of academic and linguistic training or stimulation are examined from this point of view. The conception of the preschool period as a critical period for the environmental stimulation of general intelligence is examined, considering general intelligence in both psychometric and Piagetian terms. It is concluded that the theories reviewed do not so much imply an emphasis upon specific forms of preschool intellectual stimulation as they do imply a systematic formulation of the cognitive-developmental components of the play, constructive, aesthetic, and social activities which have traditionally been the heart of the preschool.

A glance over the field of early education in America at the time of Jean Piaget's seventieth birthday reveals a curious contrast. While Piaget's ideas are salient wherever research is done on early cognitive development, their salience in formulations of goals and processes in early education is much less widespread. Enthusiasts for early cognitive stimulation often make reference to Piaget's ideas but adapt them to a viewpoint different than that held by him. Bruner (1960, 1966), Bruner, Oliver, and Greenfield (1966), and Hunt (1961, 1964) interpret Piaget's ideas as consistent with

---

This paper was written while the author was at the University of Chicago. The research of the author and his colleagues on the factorial structures of Piagetian tasks and their relations to psychometric tasks and to cultural deprivation has been supported by an Office of Education grant to the Early Education Research Center of the University of Chicago.

the notion that intelligence is a set of acquired information-processing skills and that any intellectual content can be taught early if the teaching is adapted to the child's cognitive level. On the opposite pole, the "child-development" tradition of preschool education has appealed to Piaget's ideas as part of a body of maturational theory including Freud (in Kessen, 1965), Gesell (1954), Isaacs (1933), and Spearman (1930). In this context, Piaget's ideas have been viewed as consistent with the notion that preschool educators should just let cognitive abilities grow and that the educator should concentrate upon helping the child to adjust and develop emotionally.

This ambiguity is not surprising in light of the fact that "if one looks carefully through Piaget's writings, one seldom, if ever, finds an attempt to deal with concrete problems of pedagogy or childrearing" (Elkind in Piaget, 1967, p. xvi). More fundamentally, however, the ambiguity is due to Piaget's rejection of traditional dichotomies implicit in much controversy about early cognitive learning. In the first place, Piaget discards the dichotomy between maturation and environmentally determined learning. He insists that cognitive processes emerge through a process of development which is neither direct biological maturation nor direct learning in the usual sense, since it is a reorganization of psychological structures resulting from organism-environment interactions (Elkind, 1967b; Flavell, 1963; Hooper, 1968; Piaget, 1964; Wallace, 1965). In the second place, Piaget discards the dichotomy between the cognitive (usually considered as a set of intellectual skills) and the social emotional. According to Piaget, social development, play, and art all have large cognitive-structural components and contribute to, and are contributed to by, cognitive development in the narrower sense.

Piaget's rejection of the maturation-learning and the cognitive-emotional dichotomies is part of a general intellectual tradition out of which Piaget's work grows. This tradition has been variously labeled the "functional-genetic" (Baldwin, 1906–1915; Dewey, 1930), the "symbolic inter-actionist" (Mead, 1934), and the "cognitive-developmental" (Kohlberg, 1966a, 1968b). In addition to Piaget and the American genetics functionalists, Werner (1948) and Montessori are also in part representatives of this tradition (Elkind, 1967b; Kohlberg, 1968a).

As we elaborate in the following sections, there are three broad streams of educational thought which vary from generation to generation in their statement, but which are each continuous in starting from the same assumptions. The first stream of thought commences with Rousseau (in Kessen, 1965) and is contemporarily represented in the ideas of followers of Freud and Gesell. This maturationist stream of thought holds that what is most important in the development of the child is that which comes from within him and that the pedagogical environment should be one which creates a climate to allow inner "goods" (abilities and social virtues) to unfold and the inner "bad" to come under the control of the inner good, rather than to be fixated by adult cultural pressures. The extreme of this view is presented by Neill (1960). The second "cultural training" stream of thought assumes that what is important in the development of the child is his learning of the cognitive and moral knowledge and rules of the culture and that education's business is the teaching of such information and rules to the child through direct instruction. This stream of thought can be traced from John Locke to Thorndike and Skinner (cf. Kessen, 1965). The clearest and most thoughtful contemporary elaboration of this view in relation to preschool education is to be found in the writing of Bereiter and Engelman (1966).

The third stream of thought, the "cognitive-developmental" or "interactional" view is based on the premise that the cognitive and affective structures which education should nourish are natural emergents from the interaction between the child and the environment under conditions where such interaction is allowed or fostered. More specifically, the basic postulates of this approach are:

1. The terms "cognition," "thought," or "intelligence" basically refer to adaptive actions upon objects or internalizations of such actions. Mature or adequate cognition is defined by an equilibrium or reciprocity between action and object. Cognition is defined as function (as modes of action) rather than as content (as sets of words, "verbal responses," associations, memories, etc.) or as a faculty or ability (a power of producing words, memories, etc.). The encouragement of cognitive development, then, is the provision of opportunities for activities of an organized or equilibrated form.

2. Cognition proceeds through stages of structural reorganization. While cognitive functions are present from birth, cognitive structures are radically different from one stage to the next.

3. The implication of structural reorganization in development is that the source of cognitive structure and of cognitive development is to be found neither in the structure and maturation of the organism nor in the teaching structures of the environment but in the structure of the interaction between organism and environment.

4. The optimal conditions for such structural organization entail some optimal balance of discrepancy and match between the behavior structures of the child and the structure of his psychological environment.

5. From birth, there are inherent motives for cognitive activities, but these motives too undergo structural change in development.

6. Both the "cognitive" and the "affective" are functions, not psychic contents or structures. Cognitive and affective development are parallel aspects of the structural transformations undergone in development.

While all of the above ideas are common to all writers in the cognitive-developmental tradition, Piaget's work has been the first to apply these assumptions to children's behavior in logically precise and empirically specified form. The implication of Piaget's work for education, then, may best be understood as giving greater precision to the general functional-genetic approach to education, presented in its most comprehensive form by Dewey (1913, 1930, 1938, 1965).

In the present paper, we shall first summarize the Piagetian (or cognitive-developmental) position and some exemplary research as it bears upon two related topics central to preschool education: first, the general role of experience in cognitive development, and, second, the issue of whether preschool cognitive experience defines a special or "critical" period in intellectual development. In the course of this discussion, we shall attempt to consider its implications for the introduction of various types of cognitive "curricula" into the preschool. In a forthcoming book (Kohlberg & Lesser, in press) we use this viewpoint to analyze the contributions of play, art, and social interaction to the child's development.

Part of the purpose of this paper is to examine some of the implications of Piaget's rather difficult notions of cognitive development for the concrete concerns of the preschool educator, because it may be of some practical use for educational policy. In part, it also seems of use for the clarification of theory itself. Piagetian theory must take account of research on early education as well as "pure" research on cognitive development if it is to undergo the elaboration and refinement required of a viable theory. Accordingly, this paper attempts to both elaborate the position and to review some of the findings which make it plausible. Such a review of a broad range of findings somewhat tangentially related to Piaget's ideas is bound to be somewhat cursory and superficial, but it will at least suggest areas where current findings and Piagetian theory must confront one another.

I. THE COGNITIVE-DEVELOPMENTAL APPROACH AND THE CONCEPT OF STAGE

We have suggested that the basic characteristics of the cognitive-developmental approach may be best grasped by contrasting them with theories of innate patterning and maturation on the one hand and theories of environmental associationistic learning on the other. As opposed to either set of theories, cognitive-developmental theories are "interactional," that is, they assume that basic mental structure is the product of the patterning of the interaction between the organism and the environment rather than directly reflecting innate patterns or patterns of event-structures (stimulus contingencies) in the environment.

The distinction between theories stressing the innate and theories stressing the acquired has often been thought of as a contrast in quantitative emphasis on hereditary biological factors as opposed to environmental stimulation factors in causing individual differences. When the problem is posed in such a fashion, one can be led to nothing but a piously eclectic "interactionism" which asserts that all concrete behavior is quantitatively affected by both hereditary and environmental factors. The theoretical issues are quite different, however. They are issues as to type of theory, that is, between conceptions of basic mental structure and the location of the principles producing this structure within or without the organism.

The statement just made presupposes a distinction between behavior differences in general and mental structure. Structure refers to the general characteristics of shape, pattern, or organization of response rather than to the rate or intensity of response or its pairing with particular stimuli. According to cognitive-developmental theory, all mental structure has a cognitive component (and all cognition involves structure). Many cognitive theories do not employ structural concepts. As an example, Baldwin (1968) terms a number of theories (including his own) "cognitive" because (a) they postulate a coding or representational process intervening between stimulus and response, and (b) they postulate that the learning of representations or maps may occur without any overt response and without any definite reinforcement for this learning. In addition to these more general assumptions, cognitive-developmental theory assumes that "cognitions" are internally organized wholes or systems of internal relations, that is, structure. Cognitive structures are rules for processing information or for connecting experienced events. Cognition (as most clearly reflected in thinking) means putting things together, relating events, and in cognitive theories this relating is assumed to be an active connecting process, not a passive connecting of events through external association and repetition. The process of relating events depends upon general categories which represent the modes of relating common to any experienced events, for example, causality, substantiality, space, time, quantity, and logic (i.e., the identities, inclusions, or implications of classes and propositions).

The awareness that the child's behavior has a cognitive structure or organizational pattern of its own which needs description independently of the degree of its correspondence to the adult culture is as old as Rousseau, but this awareness has only recently pervaded the actual study of cognitive development. Two examples of the revolution resulting from defining the structure of the child's mind in its own terms may be cited. The first is that of Piaget, whose first psychological effort was to classify types of wrong answers on the Binet test. By moving beyond an analysis of intellectual development in terms of number of right answers to an analysis in terms of differences in structure, Piaget transformed the study of cognitive development. The second example comes from the study of children's language, which was for a generation based on counting nouns and verbs as defined by conventional adult grammar. In the last decade, psychologists have approached children's grammar with the methods of structural linguistics, as if the child's language were that of an exotic tribe. While the implications of the Piagetian revolution in cognition and the structuralist revolution in language are far from clear, they have made the conception of mental structure a reality accepted even by associationistic S-R psychologists of cognition (cf. Berlyne, 1965).

It is evident, then, that general questions as to the origins and development of mental structure are not the same as questions regarding the origins of individual differences in behavior. As an example, the fact that one 6-year-old child may pass all the 6-year items on the Binet test and another fail them all might be attributed purely to hereditary differences in general intelligence, while the patterns of behavior involved in the child's actual test performance (knowing the word "envelope") may be purely culturally learned behavior. Because many American psychologists have been peculiarly concerned with individual differences rather than developmental universals, and because they have failed to understand the distinction between behavior differences in general and behavior structure, they have frequently misinterpreted European theories of development. It is because of this confusion that some American writers have misinterpreted Piaget's stages as "maturational" and have thought that he claimed intelligence is unaffected by environment, while others have correctly interpreted Piaget's stages as being based on the assumption of organism-environment interactions, but take this assumption as indicating that individual differences in intellectual performance are less hereditary than was long believed. In fact, there is nothing in Piaget's theory which suggests that individual differences in speed of development through his stages is not largely due to the hereditary factors which seem to account for at least half of the variance in the usual IQ tests.

Maturational theories, then, are not theories based on quantitative assumptions about the role of heredity. In terms of quantitative role, maturational or nativistic theories, like those of Gesell (1954) or Lorenz (1965), recognize the importance of environmental stimulation in modifying genetically grounded behavior patterns. In a similar sense, associationistic learning theorists, like Hull (1943) or Pavlov (1928), recognize the quantitative role of hereditary traits of temperament and ability in causing individual differences in personality and in rate and type of learning. The difference between the two types of theories is not in the recognition of both innate and environmental causal factors in development but in the belief about which set of factors are the source of basic patterning.

The contrast between the quantitative and structural roles awarded to experience becomes clear with regard to the issue of critical periods. Most research on the effects of experience upon development has postulated "critical periods" in which the individual is especially sensitive to environmental influence in a given domain. Yet this notion of extreme quantitative sensitivity depends upon a maturational or nativistic theory. The existence of a fixed time period, during which a certain amount of stimulation is required to avoid irreversible developmental deficits, presupposes an innate process of growth with an inner time schedule and an inner pattern which can be arrested or distorted by deficits of stimulation.

In the nativistic view, stimulation may be needed to elicit, support, and maintain behavior patterns, but the stimulation does not create these patterns, which are given by templates in the genotype. In fact, learning or environmental influence itself is seen as basically patterned by genetically determined structures. Learning occurs in certain interstices or open places in genetic patterns, and the structuring of what is learned is given by these patterns (Lorenz, 1965). As an example, "imprinting" represents a type of learning, a determination of response by environmental stimulation. However, the "learning" involved represents a specific sensitivity or open spot in a genetically patterned social-sexual response, phylogenetically determined to produce a tie to others of the species. As another example, an insect or bird may learn a specific "map" of the geography of its home place, but this map is structured by an innate organization of space in general (Lorenz, 1965).

In dealing with developmental changes, nativistic theories such as Gesell's (1954) have stressed the notion of unfolding maturational stages. The patterning of these age-specific behavioral forms, their order and timing, is believed to be "wired into" the organism. The organism grows as a whole so that the effort to teach or force early maturation in one area will either be ineffective or will disrupt the child's total pattern and equilibrium of growth.

In contrast to nativistic theories, learning theories may allow for genetic factors in personality and in ease of learning of a complex response, but they assume that the basic structure of complex responses results from the structure of the child's environment. Both specific concepts and general cognitive structures, like the categories of space, time, and casuality, are believed to be reflections of structures existing outside the child, structurings given by the physical and social world.

Almost of necessity, the view that structure of the external world is the source of the child's cognitive structure has led to an account of the development of structure in associationistic terms. From John Locke to J. B. Watson and B. F. Skinner (Kessen, 1965), environmentalists have viewed the structure of behavior as the result of the association of discrete stimuli with one another, with responses of the child, and with experiences of pleasure and pain.

At its extreme, this conception of mental structure has the following implications for early education:

1. Mind or personality is a set of specific responses to specific stimuli in the environment. Cognitive development is the result of guided learning, of recurrent associations between specific discriminative stimuli in the environment, specific responses of the child, and specific reinforcements following these responses.

2. "Cognition" is a matter of discrimination and generalization learning. Conceptual development occurs through learning overt or covert verbal labeling responses to discriminated and generalized classes of stimuli. Training in discrimination of the stimulus attributes implied by cultural concepts and generalization of response to these attributes leads to concept learning.

3. The child is born with very little patterning of personality or of mind. Accordingly, it is possible to teach a child almost any behavior pattern, provided one teaches in terms of the laws of association learning and provided one starts at an early age before competing response patterns have been learned.

4. It is important to start education early because early learning, if appropriate, facilitate later learning, while if they are inappropriate they impede later learning.

It is important to recognize that all these educational postulates of environmentalist theories of learning are not inconsistent with the innate determination of IQ or other traits of ability or temperament. These postulates do, however, suggest that teaching can go on without much prior understanding of the structure of a given desired behavior pattern as it "naturally" develops and as it relates to prior organismic behavior structures. Teaching instead requires primarily a careful statement of a behavior pattern considered desirable (e.g., a skill such as reading or arithmetic) in terms of specific responses. This pattern is then to be taught in accordance with general laws of learning believed applicable to the learning of all organisms (old or young, human or nonhuman) and to the learning of all behavior patterns.

In general, such a program implies a plan for shaping the child's behavior by successive approximation from responses he is now making to the desired end responses. At every step, immediate feedback or reward is desirable and immediate repetition and elaboration of the correct response is used. A careful detailed programing of learning is required to make sure that (a) each response builds on the preceding, (b) incorrect responses are not made since once made they persist and interfere with correct responses, and (c) feedback and reward are immediate.

We have contrasted the maturationist assumption that basic mental structure results from an innate patterning with the learning theory assumption that basic mental structure is the result of the patterning or association of events in the outside world. In contrast, the cognitive-developmental assumption is that basic mental structure is the result of an interaction between certain organismic structuring tendencies and the structure of the outside world, rather than reflecting either one directly.

This interaction leads to cognitive stages, which represent the transformations of simply early cognitive structures as they are applied to (or

80

assimilate) the external world and as they are accommodated to or restructured by the external world in the course of being applied to it.

The core of the cognitive-development position, then, is the doctrine of cognitive stages. Cognitive stages have the following general characteristics (Piaget, 1960):

1. Stages imply distinct or qualitative differences in children's modes of thinking or of solving the same problem at different ages.

2. These different modes of thought form an invariant sequence, order, or succession in individual development. While cultural factors may speed up, slow down, or stop development, they do not change its sequence.

3. Each of these different and sequential modes of thought forms a "structured whole." A given stage-response on a task does not just represent a specific response determined by knowledge and familiarity with that task or tasks similar to it; rather it represents an underlying thought-organization. An example is the stage of "concrete operations," which determine responses to many tasks which are not manifestly similar to one another on the "ordinary" dimensions of stimulus generalization. According to Piaget, at the stage of concrete operations, the child has a general tendency to maintain that a physical object conserves its properties on various physical dimensions in spite of apparent perceptual changes. This tendency is structural; it is not a specific belief about a specific object. The implication is that both conservation and other aspects of logical operations should appear as a consistent cluster of responses in development.

4. Cognitive stages are hierarchical integrations. Stages form an order of increasingly differentiated and integrated *structures* to fulfil a common function. The general adaptational functions of cognitive structures are always the same (for Piaget the maintenance of an equilibrium between the organism defined as a balance of assimilation and accommodation). Accordingly, higher stages displace (or rather reintegrate) the structures found at lower stages. As an example, formal operational thought includes all the structural features of concrete operational thought but at a new level of organization. Concrete operational thought or even sensorimotor thought does not disappear when formal thought arises but continues to be used in concrete situations where it is adequate or when efforts at solution by formal thought have failed. However, there is a hierarchical preference within the individual, that is, a disposition to prefer a solution of a problem at the highest level available to him. It is this disposition which partially accounts for the consistency postulated as our third criterion.

The question of whether cognitive stages "exist" in the sense just defined is an empirically testable question. It has been held by Kaplan (1966) and others that stages are theoretical constructions and that their theoretical value holds independently of whether or not they define empirical sequences in ontogeny. Every theoretical set of structural stages are defined in such a way that a higher stage is more differentiated and integrated than a lower stage. In this logical sense, a set of structural stages form a valid hierarchy regardless of whether or not the stages define an ontogenetic sequence.

In spite of this fact, it is extremely important to test whether a set of theoretical stages does meet the empirical criteria just listed. If a logical hierarchy of levels did not define an empirical sequence, the hierarchy would tell us little about the process of development nor would it justify our notion that the sequence is interactional in nature. If empirical sequence was not found, one would argue that the "stages" simply constituted alternative types of organization of varying complexity, each of which might develop independently of the other. In such a case, the "stages" could represent alternative expressions of maturation or they could equally well represent alternative cultures to which the child is exposed. It would hardly be surprising to find that adult physical concepts are more complex, more differentiated and integrated in educated Western culture than in a jungle tribe. The fact that the Western and tribal patterns are at different levels of structural organization, however, in itself tells us little about ontogenesis in either culture and leaves open the possibility that ontogenesis in either culture is simply a process of learning cultural content.

In contrast, if structural stages do define general ontogenetic sequences, then an interactional type of theory of developmental process must be used to explain ontogeny. If the child goes through qualitatively different stages of thought, his basic modes of organizing experience cannot be the direct result of adult teaching or they would be copies of adult thought from the start. If the child's cognitive responses differed from the adult's only in revealing less information and less complication of structure, it would be possible to view them as incomplete learnings of the external structure of the world, whether that structure is defined in terms of the adult culture or in terms of the laws of the physical world. If the child's responses indicate a different structure or organization than the adult's, rather than a less complete one, and if this structure is similar in all children, it is extremely difficult to view the child's mental structure as a direct learning of the external structure. Furthermore, if the adult's mental structure depends upon sequential transformations of the child's mental structure, it too cannot directly reflect the current structure of the outer cultural or physical world.

If stages cannot be accounted for by direct learning of the structure of the outer world, neither can they be explained as the result of innate patterning. If children have their own logic, adult logic or mental structure cannot be derived from innate neurological patterning because such patterning should hold also in childhood. It is hardly plausible to view a whole succession of logics as an evolutionary and functional program of innate wiring.

It has just been claimed that it is implausible to view a succession of cognitive stages as innate. This claim is based on an epistemological assumption, the assumption that there is a reality to which psychology may and must refer, that is, that cognition or knowing must be studied in relation to an object known.

The invariant sequences found in motor development (Ames, 1937; Shirley, 1931, 1931–1933) may well be directly wired into the nervous system. The fact that the postural-motor development of chimpanzees and man proceed through the same sequence suggests such a maturational base (Riesen & Kinder, 1952). The existence of invariant sequence in cognition is quite a different matter, however, since cognitions are defined by reference to a world. One cannot speak of the development of a child's conception of an animal without assuming that the child has experience with animals. Things become somewhat more complicated when we are dealing with the development of categories, that is, the most general modes of relating objects such as causality, substance, space, time quantity, and logic. These categories differ from more specific concepts, for example, the concept of "animal," in that they are not defined by specific objects to which they refer but by modes of relating any object to any other object. Every experienced event is located in space and time, implies or causes other events, etc. Because these categories or structures are independent of specific experiences with specific objects, it has been plausible for philosophers like Kant to assume that they are innate molds into which specific experiences are fitted. If structures or categories like space and time were Kantian innate forms, it is difficult to understand how these structures could undergo transformation in development, however.

The interactional account assumes that structural change in these categories depends upon experience. The effects of experience, however, are not conceived of as learning in the ordinary sense, in which learning implies training by pairing of specific objects and specific responses, by instruction, by modeling, or by specific practices of responses. Indeed, the effects of training are determined by the child's cognitive categories rather than the reverse. If two events which follow one another in time are cognitively connected in the child's mind, it implies that he relates them by means of a category such as causality, for example, he perceives his operant behavior as causing the reinforcer to occur. A program of reinforcement, then, cannot directly change the child's causal structures since it is assimilated to it.

If cognitive development occurs in terms of stages, then, an understanding of the effect of experience upon it requires three types of conceptual analysis customarily omitted in discussions of learning.

In the first place, it requires an analysis of universal structural features of the environment. While depending on structural and functional invariants of the nervous system, cognitive stages also depend upon universal structures of experience for their shape. Stages of physical concepts depend upon a universal structure of experience in the physical world, a structure which underlies the diversity of physical arrangements in which men live and which underlies the diversity of formal physical theories held in various cultures at various periods.

In the second place, understanding cognitive stages depends upon a logical analysis of orderings inherent in given concepts. The invariance of sequence in the development of a concept or category is not dependent upon a prepatterned unfolding of neural patterns; it must depend upon a logical analysis of the concept itself. As an example, Piaget postulates a sequence of spaces or geometrics moving from the topological to the projective to the Euclidean. This sequence is plausible in terms of a logical analysis of the mathematical structures involved.

In the third place, an understanding of sequential stages depends upon analysis of the relation of the structure of a specific experience of the child to the behavior structure. Piaget (1964) has termed such an analysis an "equilibration" rather than a "learning" analysis. Such an analysis employs such notions as "optimal match," "cognitive conflict," "assimilation," and "accommodation." Whatever terms are used, such analyses focus upon discrepancies between the child's action system or expectancies and the experienced event, and hypothesize some moderate or optimal degree of discrepancy as constituting the most effective experience for structural change in the organism.

In summary, an interactional conception of stages differs from a maturational one in that it assumes that experience is necessary for the stages to take the shape they do as well as assuming that generally more or richer stimulation will lead to faster advances through the series involved. It proposes that an understanding of the role of experience requires (a) analyses of universal features of experienced objects (physical or social), (b) analysis of logical sequences of differentiation and integration in concepts of such objects, and (c) analysis of structural relations between experience-inputs and the relevant behavior organizations. While these three modes of analysis are foreign to the habits of associationistic learning theorists, they are not totally incompatible in principle with them. While associationistic concepts are clumsy to apply to universal objects of experience or to the logical structures of concepts and to the problem of match, it can be done, as Berlyne (1961, 1965) has demonstrated. As yet, however, such associationistic analyses have not led to the formulation of new hypotheses going beyond translations of cognitive-developmental concepts into a different language.

The preceding presentation of the cognitive-developmental approach has been rather abstract. Accordingly, it may be useful to present an empirical example of a cognitive stage-sequence and elaborate why it requires an interactional theory of process for its explanation. The dream concept, studied by Piaget (1928), Pinard and Laurendeau (1964), and this writer (1966b), presents a simple example. The dream is a good example of an object or experience with which the child is familiar from an early age but which is restructured in markedly different ways in later de-

TABLE 1
SEQUENCE IN DEVELOPMENT OF DREAM CONCEPT IN
AMERICAN AND ATAYAL CHILDREN[a]

	SCALE PATTERN TYPES						
STEP	0	1	2	3	4	5	6
1: Not real—recognizes that objects or actions in the dream are not real or are not really there in the room	−	+	+	+	+	+	+
2: Invisible—recognizes that other people cannot see his dream	−	−	+	+	+	+	+
3: Internal Origin—recognizes that the dream *comes from* inside him	−	−	−	+	+	+	+
4: Internal Location—recognizes that the dream *goes on* inside him	−	−	−	−	+	+	+
5: Immaterial—recognizes that the dream is not a material substance but is a thought	−	−	−	−	−	+	+
6: Self-caused—recognizes that dreams are not caused by God or other agencies but are caused by the self's thought processes	−	−	−	−	−	−	+
Median age of American children in given pattern or stage (range = 4 to 8)	4, 6	4, 10	5, 0	5, 4	6, 4	6, 5	7, 10
Median age of Atayal of given pattern (range = 7 to 18)	8	8	10	16	12	11	...

[a] No. of American children fitting scale types = 72; not fitting = 18. No. of Atayal children fitting scale types = 12; not fitting = 3.

velopment. One of the general categories of experience is that of substantiality or reality. Any experience must be defined as either subjective or objective. As the child's structuring of this category develops, his experience of the dream changes. According to Piaget, the young child thinks of the dream as a set of real events rather than as a mental imagining. This represents the young child's "realism," his failure to differentiate the subjective appearance from objective reality components of his experience.

Table 1 indicates the actual steps of development which are found in children's beliefs about dreams. The first step (achieved by about 4 yr., 10 mo. by American middle-class children) is the recognition that dreams are not real events, the next step (achieved soon thereafter) that dreams cannot be seen by others. By age 6, children are clearly aware that dreams take place inside them, and, by age 7, they are clearly aware that dreams are thoughts caused by themselves.

The concept of stages implies an invariant order or sequence of development. Cultural and environmental factors or innate capabilities may make one child or group of children reach a given step of development at a much earlier point of time than another child. All children, however, should still go through the same order of steps, regardless of environmental teaching or lack of teaching.

Table 1 shows a series of patterns of pluses or minuses called Guttman (1954) scale types, suggesting that the steps we have mentioned form an invariant order or sequence in development. If there is an invariant order in development, then children who have passed a more difficult step in the sequence, indicated by a plus, should also have passed all the easier steps in the sequence and gotten pluses on all the easier items. This means that all children should fit one of the patterns on Table 1. For instance, all children who pass or get a plus on Step 3, recognizing the dream's internal origin, should also pass Step 2 and Step 1. The fact that only 18 out of 90 children do not fit one of these patterns is evidence for the existence of invariant sequence in the development of the dream concept. (This is more precisely indicated by a coefficient of reproducibility of 0.96 and an index of consistency of 0.83, calculated following Green [1956].)

The importance of this issue of sequence becomes apparent when we ask, "How does the child move from a view of dreams as real to a view of dreams as subjective or mental?" The simplest answer to this question is that the older child has learned the cultural definition of words like "dream" and "real." The child is frequently told by parents that his dreams are not real, that he shouldn't be upset by them, that dreams are in his mind, etc. In the learning view, this verbal teaching eventually leads the child from ignorance to knowledge of the culture's definition of the dream. It is a little hard for this verbal learning view to account for invariant sequence in the development of the dream concept since it seems unlikely that children are taught Step 3 later than Step 2 or Step 1.

The issue of sequence becomes more critical when sequence can be examined in cultures with different adult cognitive beliefs than our own (Kohlberg, 1966b). The Atayal, a Malaysian aboriginal group in Formosa, believe in the reality of dreams. Most adult Atayal interviewed on the dream equated the soul, the dream, and ghosts. Dreams, like ghosts, are neither thoughts nor things; dreams are caused by ghosts, and during the dream the soul leaves the body and experiences things in far places.

Interviews of Atayal boys and young men of various ages indicated a very interesting pattern of age development. The youngest Atayal boys were much like the youngest American boys in their responses. Up until the age of 11, the Atayal boy seemed to develop toward a subjective conception of the dream through much of the same steps as American children, though more slowly. As the table shows, the Atayal boys' answers fell into the same sequential scale pattern as the American boys. This suggests that the Atayal children tend to develop naturally toward a subjective concept of the dream up to age 11, even though their elders do not believe dreams are subjective and hence are giving them no teaching to this effect. Both the youngest children's conceptions of the dream as real and the school age children's view of the dream as subjective are their own; they are products of the general state of the child's cognitive development rather than the learning of adult teachings (though the adolescent's later "regression" to concepts like those held by the younger children does represent such direct cultural learning).

The apparent invariant universal sequence in the development of the dream concept in the absence of adult cultural support cannot be interpreted as being the direct result of maturational unfolding, since maturation is supported by the fact that the culture can "reverse" it by specific training, a reversal presumably very difficult to teach for maturational postural-motor sequences. A maturational interpretation is also contradicted by the fact that the Atayal children go through the same sequence more slowly than do their Taiwanese and American age-mates, presumably because the Atayal exist in a somewhat cognitively impoverished general culture, that is, they have less *general* experience. In this regard the Atayal children are like culturally deprived American slum Negro children, who also appear to go through the dream sequence more slowly than middle-class Negroes, even when the two groups are matched on psychometric intelligence (Kohn, in preparation).

The culturally universal invariants of sequence found in the dream concept can be adequately understood through a logical analysis of the stages themselves. The steps represent progressive differentiations of the subjective and objective which logically could not have a different order. The first step involves a differentiation of the *unreality* of the psychiac event or dream image. The next step involves the differentiation of the *internality* of the psychic event from the externality of the physical event. A still later step is the differentiation of the *immateriality* of the psychic event from the materiality of other physical events. This sequence corresponds to the logical tree shown in Figure 1.

It is apparent that the differentiation of the immaterial from the material presupposes the inside-outside distinction, since all immaterial events are inside the body (but not vice versa). It is also apparent that internality (location of the dream experience inside the body) presupposes unreality (recognition that the dream is not a real object), since a real object could hardly be in the body. The observed sequence, then, is one which corresponds to an inner logic of the concept of reality itself (Baldwin, 1906–1915).

It is apparent that dreams are universal features of the child's experience. It is also apparent that a considerable degree of conflict between

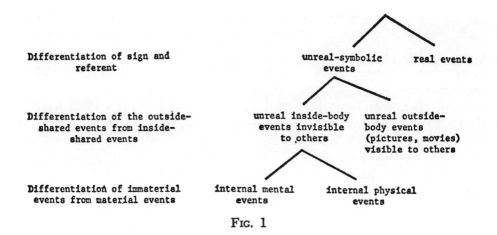

Differentiation of sign and referent	unreal-symbolic events	real events
Differentiation of the outside-shared events from inside-shared events	unreal inside-body events invisible to others	unreal outside-body events (pictures, movies) visible to others
Differentiation of immaterial events from material events	internal mental events	internal physical events

FIG. 1

the dream experience and the waking experience of reality is a universal feature of experience. This experienced conflict or disequilibrium is presumably the "motor" for movement through the sequence in the absence of adult teaching, though the discrepancies and matches in experience in this area have not been clearly specified.

The data on Atayal dream "regression" introduce a useful additional clarification of the nature of the cognitive-developmental approach. The approach is not a theory about the process by which *all* behavior change occurs, as "learning theories" are. It is rather a program of analysis. Some behavior changes are "structural" and "directed," as evidenced by proceeding through sequential stages, while other behavior changes are not. This is the first question for empirical investigation, since it determines any further theorizing about processes of development of the phenomena. Behavior changes which are universal, progressive, and irreversible require a different analysis than do reversible situation-specific learnings. While a cognitive-developmental approach may attempt to account for reversible situational learning, it may also be satisfied with associationistic accounts of situational learning. As an example, one might account for Atayal children's "regressive" learning of the adult culture's ideology as a reversible content-learning fitting associationistic notion of social training, modeling, and reinforcement; a learning that is superimposed upon the structural development of subjective-objective differentiation. It is only this latter type of change which requires the interactional equilibration theory of process described.

The Atayal example, however, also suggests that a third type of behavior change may require theoretical elaboration. While the Atayal example of culturally learned "regression" is extremely ambiguous, it is obvious that regression does sometimes occur, As is described elsewhere (Kohlberg, 1963; Linden, in preparation), Piaget cognitive tasks are passed at markedly lower levels by schizophrenic, brain-damaged, and senile subjects than by mental age controls. While longitudinal studies have not been carried out, we can assume that where brain damage or the onset of schizophrenia occurred in late childhood, actual regression (rather than failure of development) has occurred. It is obvious that processes accounting for such regressive change are distinct from those producing either progressive sequential change or those producing reversible specific learnings. We may decide to exclude such regressive processes from our analysis because they are outside the psychological system, a system based on the assumption of an intact nervous system, which does not need to account for the effects of a blow on the head or of senile organic deterioration upon behavior. Or we may decide that a developmental theory must include a systematic analysis or regression, along the lines outlined by Langer (1967).

The need to include an account of regression in a cognitive-developmental theory is suggested by some additional data from the Atayal study. The Atayal's learning of the adult dream ideology did not appear to be a smooth and painless superimposition of social content on an underlying cognitive structure. Rather it appeared to engender complications and conflict in the adolescent's cognitive responses. Atayal children acquired the conservation of mass of a ball of clay at the usual age (7 to 8). Nevertheless, at ages 11 to 15, the years of dream "regression," they partially "lost" conservation. The loss did not seem to be a genuine regression but an uncertainty about trusting their own judgment, that is, there was an increase in "don't know" responses. Apparently, adolescent confrontation with adult magical beliefs led them to be uncertain of their natural physical beliefs whether or not they were in direct conflict with the adult ideology. The findings on the Atayal, then, seem loosely compatible with experimental findings by Langer (1967), suggesting that some forms of cognitive conflict lead to progressive change while others lead to regressive change. The eventual goal of a cognitive-developmental theory, thus, may include a specification of the relatively rare types of discrepancies in experience which lead to backward movement as well as the types of discrepancies in experience leading to forward movement. All these analyses, however, presuppose a conception of development as relatively irreversible sequential change distinct from the ordinary conceptions of reversible situational learning employed by associationistic approaches.

II. RESISTANCE OF SEQUENTIAL COGNITIVE DEVELOPMENTS TO SPECIFIC TEACHING: EXPERIMENTS ON CONSERVATION

In the preceding section, we outlined an interactional theory of the role of experience which shares with maturationism a pessimism about the effect of specific teaching on cognitive-structural development. In a practical sense, the interactional view suggests that limited specific training experiences cannot replace the massive general types of experience accruing with age. Both views then agree in the factual importance of age-readiness but disagree in their interpretation of this fact. An example of evidence used for the maturational view is the finding of Gesell and Thompson (Gesell, 1954) that an untrained twin became as adept at tower building and stair climbing after a week of practice as was the trained twin who had been given practice in tower building and stair climbing over many weeks. As Hunt (1964) convincingly argues, while this finding shows the limited value of *specific training*, it does not show that the function in question does not depend upon *general experience*. The untrained twin was not just "maturing," he was walking and climbing on other objects than stairs; he was placing and manipulating other objects than block towers, etc. While the developmental and the maturational view may practically agree on the relative futility of early specific training of a function, the developmental view sees specific training as failing primarily because it cannot make up for the age-linked general experiential lacks of the young child rather than because it cannot make up for his neurological immaturity.

As an example, preschool children advanced in verbal knowledge and information are still almost as immature in level of development of the dream concept as are less verbally knowledgeable preschool children. Thus, Jack, a bright verbal child (Stanford-Binet MA = 6 yr., 10 mo.), age 5 years, 2 months, responds as follows to the dream task:. "Dreams come from God. God makes the dreams and puts them in balloons. The balloons float down from heaven and enter a dream bag under your stomach. In the dream bag there are some little men and a sergeant. They have a cannon that shoots the dream-balloons up into your head where they burst into pictures outside your head."

Jack here is much closer in developmental level to his chronological age-mates than to his mental age-mates. Yet his creative thinking and his possession of verbal concepts are high. Ongoing research by DeVries (in preparation) and others (Goodnow & Bethon, 1966) suggests that in general mildly retarded children are more advanced in Piaget concepts than younger average children of the same psychometric mental age and that average children are in turn more advanced than younger bright children of the same psychometric mental age. Our interpretation is not that Piaget stages represent age-fixed maturational unfoldings independent of psychometric ability but that cognitive-structural development depends upon massive general experience, a requirement which the "innately" bright child cannot short circuit. The psychometrically bright child is adept at organizing or "educing relations and correlates" in a cognitive field (Spearman, 1930), but the logical structure of the relations which are induced demands massive experience for its reorganization.

Much more comprehensive evidence to support the notion that specific training cannot substitute for age-linked general experience comes from the numerous experiments designed to teach conservation of mass, weight, or number to young children (Sigel & Hooper, 1968). These studies suggest that direct teaching of conservation through verbal instruction and reinforcement or through provision of observations of examples of conservation (e.g., weighing masses changed in shape on a balance) do not lead to the formation of a general or stable concept of conservation. Little change is induced by such methods.[1]

If specific experimental teaching seems to have only limited value for the attainment of conservation, general formal schooling appears to have no influence at all upon conservation. Conservation of number, mass, weight, and volume appears at the same age in schooled and unschooled subjects when other relevant variables are controlled. Probably the most definitive study on this question is that of Mermelstein (Mermelstein, 1964; Mermelstein & Shulman, 1967). Mermelstein compared the conservation responses on a number of tasks (including number) of 6- and 9-year-old Negro children of Prince Edward County who had been deprived of schooling with northern urban Negro children who had attended school. No significant differences were found between the two groups. An equally careful study by Goodnow showed no difference between unschooled Hong Kong children and comparable IQ schooled children in various types of conservation (Goodnow & Bethon, 1966). Price-Williams (1961) found that African Tiv children without schooling attained conservation on several tasks including number at about the same age Western children achieve conservation. Greenfield (1966) found some retardation on conservation in nonschooled Senegalese children, but this retardation disappeared when an appropriate form of the conservation task was used which eliminated set effects due to beliefs about magical attributes of white authorities. Kohlberg (1968a) hypothesized that Montessori schooling for young children might accelerate

---

[1] A general review is presented by Sigel and Hooper (1968). Some exceptions to our generalizations are reported in some studies, e.g., Sullivan's (1967) findings of partially generalized conservation induced through film instruction and Gelman's (1967) findings of partially generalized conservation induced through generalized discrimination learning set training. The only way in which the writer can integrate these findings with others is suggested by the older age (6 to 8) of Sullivan's experimental subjects. Using methods minimizing verbal complications, I find that the large majority of children this age possess conservation concepts. It seems likely that Sullivan's procedure led to the application of the conservation concept to new situations rather than to its formation. The same comment applies to the results of other studies in which conservation responses are increased by training the child to ignore irrelevant cues, to redefine the meaning of words like "bigger," etc. These studies are not studies indicating the possibility of early teaching of a conservation concept but rather indicating the possibility of its somewhat earlier elicitation by clarifying its situational relevance. Finally, rote-learning effects are probably responsible for some of the change reported.

conservation and transitivity because the Montessori training tasks are directed at sensorimotor experiences of quantitative measurement and comparison. While Montessori schooling over 9 months did significantly raise Stanford-Binet IQ, it failed to have any effects upon Piaget conservation tasks.

While the resistance of conservation to specific instruction is noteworthy, it is more significant to note that the conditions under which instruction does change conservation are those expected by cognitive-developmental theory. In the first place, the approach distinguishes between reversible situational learning and structural development. An associationistic theory of learning typically assumes that any learning is situation-specific (i.e., under the control of situational discriminative stimuli and reinforcers) and is reversible (i.e., can be extinguished). In the operant conditioning paradigm, the demonstration of reversibility (extinction and subsequent relearning) is part of the demonstration that the researcher has isolated the variables controlling behavior change. In contrast, both common sense and cognitive-developmental theory hold that cognitive development is generalized and irreversible. This constitutes the root meaning of the notion of cognitive structure. If the child has developed a concept of conservation, we expect that he will not lose it even in the face of contrary stimulation or social pressure. We also expect that he will invoke or apply the concept under conditions appropriate to the meaning of the concept rather than in terms of situational and sensory parameters extraneous to its meaning. It is obvious that insofar as structural change can be induced such change should take precedence over reversible situational learning as a focus of educational effort. There is no particular reason to expect that pre-school teaching of a reversible situation-specific type can have any lasting effect upon the child.

There is ample evidence that "naturally" developing conservation concepts have the structural properties mentioned. They typically cannot be reversed by trick demonstrations of nonconservation nor by social pressure from the experimenter (Kohlberg, 1963; Smedslund, 1961a). While some forms of conservation are more difficult than others, the order of difficulty tends to be regular (constituting a Guttman-scaled "horizontal decalage," e.g., conservation of mass, weight, and volume), and children showing conservation on a given task are likely to show it on others, that is, to generalize or transpose the concept in comparison to children of the same chronological or mental age who do not show conservation on that given task (Uzgiris, 1968).

In contrast, most of the effects of specific instruction in inducing conservation do not have the structural properties mentioned. Artificial acceleration of conservation seems to be limited in generalization. While generalizing across specific objects, training of number conservation does not seem to lead to acceleration of other forms of conservation (Gruen, 1968).

Apparent attainment of conservation so obtained seems to be partly or wholly reversible. Exposure to trick conditions suggesting nonconservation leads to loss of belief in conservation where conservation has been taught rather than developing naturally (Smedslund, 1961b).

We have stated that conservation responses are resistant to direct instruction and that often when they are not resistant (i.e., where conservation is induced) the response changes do not represent a genuine acquisition of conservation in the sense of an irreversible generalized belief in conservation. However, it also appears that some genuine acceleration of conservation may be induced if the instruction methods used follow from the conceptions of cognitive structure and of conflict and match implied by Piaget's theory. In the first place, successful induction of conservation is contingent upon the match in the sense that the child must already be near the level of attainment of conservation in terms of chronological and mental age. In the second place, some successful induction of conservation is achieved through stimulation of the development of the logical prerequisites of conservation defined by Piaget (e.g., the ability to make double classifications or to consider two dimensions simultaneously [Sigel, Roeper, & Hooper, 1968] or the stimulation of imaginative reversal [Wallach & Sprott, 1964]). In the third place, some successful induction of conservation results from creation of experiences in which nonconserving expectations lead to certain conditions of conflict (Langer, 1967; Smedslund, 1961a, 1961b).

In addition to the experimental findings mentioned, naturalistic studies support the notion that acquisition of conservation is contingent upon a background of general experience, as we have already discussed for the dream concept. Some degree of retardation in conservation appears in some semiliterate non-Western cultures, regardless of schooling (Greenfield, 1966; Hyde, 1959; Kohlberg, unpublished data on the Taiwan Atayal). Preliminary findings indicate that lower social class and "culturally disadvantaged" (Aid to Dependent Children) groups matched with middle-class subjects on Stanford-Binet mental age do more poorly on conservation tasks (Kohn, in preparation).

It seems unlikely that the "general experience" effects of social class and culture upon conservation are primarily or directly linguistic. The fact that conservation development is not directly contingent on language development is indicated by findings on the deaf (Furth, 1966). While these findings indicate some retardation of conservation among the deaf, this retardation is not marked, in spite of the fact that most of the deaf children studied have almost no facility with verbal language in any form. Much more marked deficits have been found in blind children of normal verbal IQ who do not appear to attain most forms of conservation reached by normal children at ages 5 to 7 until ages 9 to 11 (Nordan, 1967). The findings seems to be in line with Piaget's notions of the visual-motor roots of "concrete operations."

In summary, the conservation findings, like the dream-concept findings, clearly demonstrate that conservation is not a strict maturational product but is the product of interactional experience between organismic structure and environment. On the practical side, however, they do not give much support to the notion that development on basic Piaget-type cognitive functions can be markedly accelerated by deliberate intervention of a schooling variety, since such acceleration tends to be limited, specific, and contingent upon a narrow time gap between the intervention experience and the child's natural readiness. This readiness is determined by age, IQ, and the richness of the child's general background of stimulation.

III. PRESCHOOL CURRICULUM: SPECIFIC INTELLECTUAL INSTRUCTION

While differing in theory with the maturational view held by traditional "child development" preschool educators, the cognitive-developmental analysis just presented practically agrees with the maturationists that specific early training of cognitive functions is often useless. It should be noted that this conclusion holds for sequential age development in conceptual structures of a spontaneous sort, such as concepts of the dream or of conservation. Many preschool behavior changes associated with age are not of this type; some are primarily maturational (e.g., early motor development), while other behavior changes are more directly the result of instruction and reinforcement by socializing agents. We must now consider the relative contributions of specific instruction and of natural structural change to the preschool child's total cognitive development, in their implications for preschool programs.

Our viewpoint suggests that the speeding up of cognitive-structural change is extremely difficult to achieve but is likely to have long range general effects, since invariant sequence implies that advance in one step of development may lead to advance in the next step. In contrast, specific learnings are more easily achieved but are unlikely to have long range developmental effects. As an example, it is relatively easy to teach culturally disadvantaged preschool children to discriminate and name animals, but it is difficult to "teach" them conservation. Naming and discriminating unfamiliar animals may lead to some temporary rise in the Stanford-Binet in terms of vocabulary and picture-discrimination items. It is unlikely, however, in itself to lead to any future cognitive development which might lead to higher "general intelligence" some years later. By grade school, the children will have "spontaneously" picked up the labels and discriminations involved in any case. In contrast, "teaching" the children conservation might lead to an accelerated general development of arithmetical and classificatory operations.

We have contrasted structural change in natural concepts like conservation with specific information learning as objectives of preschool education. Many cognitive developments are neither one nor the other, however, but represent an organic mixture of structural and informational changes. These have been termed "scientific" as opposed to "spontaneous" concepts by Vygotsky (1962). The dream concept is a spontaneous concept, because while it requires some learning of cultural labels it is primarily organized around the child's direct experience of dreams and of related experiences involving differentiation of the mental-subjective from the physical-objective. In contrast, the concept of electricity depends upon verbal instruction for its organization and development. The child's experience of lightning, electric motors, etc. does not naturally lead to the organization of a structural concept of electricity. The development of such "scientific" concepts is obviously a major goal of elementary and high school education. It is not clear, however, that preschool children are capable of developing scientific concepts, that is cognitive organizations based on symbolic definitions of new concepts as opposed to being able to "fill in" verbal labels with their own natural conceptual organization. It seems likely that the "natural science" and "social studies" information given the preschool child is assimilated into the organization represented by the child's natural concepts. Concepts of life, death, birth, economic and occupational role, sex role, and many others appear to develop naturally through Piaget-type stages, regardless of preschool "scientific" informational input (Kohlberg, 1966a, 1968b). While teaching may contribute specific information at the preschool level, it is unlikely to lead to much in the way of "scientific" conceptualization. The acquisition of information about physical and social objects and events (preschool "natural and social science") does not itself produce the school-age capacity for classificatory and causal thought required for understanding natural and social events. Insofar as preschool "science" is the teaching of specific information without new cognitive organization, it seems somewhat similar to vocabulary teaching, an area of learning by children which does not require specific programed teaching by adults.

The most obvious example of mixed or "scientific" conceptual structure relevant to preschool are mathematical and arithmetic concepts. Piaget's theory stresses almost exclusively the natural components of number development "logical and arithmetical operations therefor constitute a single system that is psychologically natural, the second resulting from generalization and fusion of the first" (Piaget, 1952, p. viii). According to Piaget's theory, arithmetical operations (addition, multiplication, etc.) correspond to more general operations of thought which are internalizations of the child's actions upon concrete operations in the external world. In the field of arithmetic, operations presuppose (and lead to) conservation of number, that is, the invariance of number through all changes in spatial arrangement, etc. These operations, according to Piaget, are developing at around the same age (6 to 7) at which arithmetic is commonly taught, and the teaching of most phases of arithmetic depends upon the natural development of the cognitive structures of concrete operations and of conservation. The findings on the development and teaching of number conservation previously discussed as well as findings of natural sequence in arithmetical development (Dodwell, 1968; Kofsky, 1968; Wohlwill, 1968) related to sequence in the development of classification suggest that Piaget's view of the natural developmental base of arithmetic learning appears to be largely correct. Insofar as this view is correct, it suggests that the early teaching of arithmetic will lead only to rote learning of habits with no conceptual base.

An example of an opposed point of view is that of the "new math" curriculum, which, like Piaget, stresses understanding rather than the rote learning of habits, but which structures arithmetic teaching in logical sequences in an artificial symbolic language. Bereiter and Engelmann have adapted this approach to the preschool level, stating that "the extent to which arithmetic and everyday language share assumptions is the extent to which arithmetic can be taught as a foreign language" (1966, p. 123). While the cognitive-developmental approach agrees that linguistic-grammatical development reflects a process of developmental transformations of structure reminiscent of thought development, it stresses that the actual structural developments involved are quite different, as indicated by the fact that grammatical development is relatively complete in middle-class children at an age (4) at which they are not yet capable of concrete operational thought. Accordingly, the Piagetian is disposed to be skeptical of claims of teaching arithmetical understanding to children below the age (6 to 7) of concrete operations.

With specific regard to the Bereiter and Engelmann program, it is important to note that it has been successful in bringing preschool children to first-grade level according to the standards of arithmetic achievement tests (Bereiter, 1967). However, first-grade scores on arithmetic achievement tests can be readily achieved by rote knowledge of counting and very simply rote knowledge of addition and subtraction. Such scores can be achieved without the least genuine capacity to order quantitative relations. As an example, in our studies of conservation we ask children to pick the "more candy" for themselves, six pieces in a long row as opposed to seven pieces in a short row. Some preschool children count each row correctly but are unable to answer "Which is more, six or seven?" Others respond to the verbal question of "more" correctly, that is, they say seven is more than six, but when asked to pick the "more candy" for themselves pick the long row with six candies. Unsystematic observation by the writer indicated that some children in the Bereiter program made both the previous errors, although they had learned verbal series such as "six plus two equal eight," or "four plus zero equal four." It is difficult to know what such verbal learning indicates in the way of arithmetical thought in the absence of the underlying concrete operations which are presumably involved.

While the early teaching of arithmetic encounters the block of a lack of development of the concrete operational base required for mathematical understanding, it is not clear that it is useless for the child's later cognitive development in the sense in which specific vocabulary teaching of a random set of words may be said to be useless. It is abvious that some counting (and adding and subtracting) experiences are a prerequisite to arithmetical operations. It is also obvious that detailed skill in use of arithmetical operations requires the information and skill teaching customarily given in elementary school after the "natural" concrete operational base of arithmetic has already developed. It seems likely that the child may emerge from an early arithmetic program with a sense of interest and competence with numbers and with an ability to attend to arithmetic instruction, which allows him to retain his "headstart" throughout elementary school arithmetic programs. It should be noted, however, that such long-range effects of an early arithmetic program might be "artificial," in that they are based on a competitive advantage of the child who has had such a program. Such a finding could occur, and yet exposure of all children to preschool programs might lead to the same average performance at a later age as occurred without early instruction.

In any case, it is clear that mathematical learning is the learning of a set of concepts and skills with an extremely important natural base. This is reflected in the Piagetian elementary school math curriculum of Dienes (1963, 1965) and Lovell (1966) and partially in the Montessori math curriculum (Kohlberg, 1968a). The extent to which a mathematics curriculum which recognizes this natural base should orient to the preschool period is not at all clear.

So far we have discussed the issue of earlier teaching of portions of the elementary school curriculum involving logical, mathematical, and scientific concepts. Other portions of the elementary school curriculum, however, do not appear to be necessarily dependent upon the cognitive-structural changes typically occurring at ages 4 to 6. Learning the mechanics of reading and writing need not depend heavily upon the development of new levels of cognitive structure (categories of relation), although it may depend on the development of perceptual structure (Elkind, 1967a). Compared to the cognitive-structural transformations required for development of spoken language at age 2 or 3, the cognitive-structural requirements in tying together spoken and written signs seem modest. It is true that conventional methods of teaching reading ordinarily require considerable cognitive-structural capacity, just as they require considerable psychomotor maturity. It appears, however, that methods of teaching reading and writing can shortcut many requirements of both visuo-motor coordination and of cognitive-conceptual structurings and promote early learning on a simple discrimination-and-association basis. This is essentially what Moore (1968) has succeeded in doing with a number of preschool children. Moore's electric typewriter method bypasses both maturing motor skills (e.g., those involved in handwriting) and cognitive structurings by focusing on elementary active phonic sound-sight associations and the further association of these schemata into words.

Given the possibility of early teaching of reading and writing, is it desirable? Here it appears that the considerations suggested by Durkin (1965) are eminently sound. The major reason for such a program is that usually if a skill can be easily learned earlier it is more enjoyable for the child to learn it early. A good deal of learning to read and write in the elementary school is a tedious task for the 6- to 8-year-old, requiring drill, repetition, self-correction, and considerable insecurity in comparing the child's own performance with that of other children in the classroom. Because reading and writing (especially reading) are relatively low-level sensorimotor skills, there is nothing in the cognitive structure of the reading task which involves any high challenge to the older child. In contrast, the identification of letters and words (as well as repetitive pounding of Moore's typewriters) may be challenging fun for younger children. Many preschool children and kindergarten children have considerable desire for learning "big-kid" or adult skills such as reading, and find school a much more interesting place if there is opportunity for such learning. Thus, regardless of its effect on later abilities, the interest principle suggests that there is something to be gained by optional, relaxed, and well-thought-out programs of early reading.

It is important to recognize that the basic value to an approach like Moore's does not derive from the principle that earlier learning leads to greater general cognitive development but derives from the principle of optimal developmental match between the challenge of a task and the child's skills and interests.[2]

The second reason for an early reading program is, of course, to free the child's time in elementary school for cognitively more valuable activities than the mastery of the mechanics of reading and writing. This reason, of course, presupposes massive changes in the elementary schools. As long as the child goes to public shools in which the teaching of reading and writing are the primary content of the first three grades, early reading programs tend to leave the child doomed to boredom. Given such a change, however, the child would enter first or second grade not only with reading

---

[2] This same principle, suggesting that novel techniques may allow early learning of reading to be more enjoyable than later learning, also suggests that conventional methods of teaching reading might be better commenced at a later age than usual with the culturally disadvantaged. The contrast between the interest and the rate of learning of culturally disadvantaged adults in literacy programs and of disadvantaged children in school suggests thinking of such a possibility.

skills but with the cognitive capacity to make use of this skill, since the normal middle-class 6-year-old child is able to enjoy story or informational reading if he has the sensorimotor skills to do it.

While various forms of early stimulation and learning have value, then, they do not justify teaching things earlier than will come later with less effort, whether these be the standard school skills or whether they be intelligence or mental age type tasks as such. The cognitive-developmental approach agrees with maturationism in viewing the preschool period as one in which cognitive development is not sufficiently advanced for the traditional forms of intellectual instruction. The approach sees the preschool period as one in which the child has a qualitatively different mode of thought and orientation to the world than the older child, one in which he is prelogical, preintellectual or not oriented to external truth values. Cognitive-developmental theories and findings suggest that certain shifts in cognitive functioning occur around the ages of 5 or 6 which justify the traditional practice of starting formal intellectual training at about age 6. From this point of view, school starts at age 6, because it is at about that age that children attain the "concrete operations" which are necessary for so much of elementary school learning and thinking.[3] In a sense, these facts are especially limiting for early education for the disadvantaged. As discussed earlier, presumably because of generalized deficits in organized physical and social stimulation, disadvantaged children tend to be retarded in cognitive-structural development as much or more than they are in Binet-test "verbal" performance. For this and other reasons, it is even less possible to use traditional intellectual instruction techniques with disadvantaged preschool children than it is with middle-class preschool children. The notion that academic intellectual instruction can remedy the cognitive-structural retardation of culturally disadvantaged children, then, has little plausibility. Thus, the objectives of preschool programs for the disadvantaged must be phrased in other terms.

IV. PRESCHOOL CURRICULUM: LANGUAGE STIMULATION

The most common definition of preschool cognitive objectives has been in terms of language abilities or aptitudes. This interest in preschool lan-

---

[3] It should be noted that the view that age 5 to 7 is a watershed in cognitive development is one which is not contingent upon Piaget's particular description of this watershed in terms of "concrete operations." White (1965) has summarized a wide range of basic shifts occurring in the years 5 to 7 in areas of perception, discrimination, transposition and probability learning, and concept formation. All may be loosely characterized as shifts from associative to cognitive-conceptual modes of functioning. The attainment of Piaget's conservations, on its face a rather minor cognitive achievement, is found to correlate with a quite wide variety of attainments in the area of abstract-conceptual thought.

guage stimulation has arisen largely because of the obvious linguistic deficiencies of culturally disadvantaged children. Most persons focusing on preschool language stimulation have assumed that advances in language will cause advances in cognition. There is no direct experimental demonstration of this assumption, nor is there as yet any evidence that language-focused preschool programs are of any greater value than any other preschool programs in leading to improved cognitive functioning. The assumption, however, follows from so many different points of view that it seems extremely plausible.

One source of this hypothesis is S-R verbal mediation theory, which points to the role of implicit verbal labeling in processes of discrimination learning, concept attainment, and transposition learning (Berlyne, 1965; Reese, 1962; White, 1963). As Flavell and others have pointed out, the notion of verbal mediation must be broken down into (a) possession of the verbal sign, (b) spontaneous production of the verbal sign in a cognitive task, and (c) effective usage of the produced sign to mediate the task. A multiplicity of evidence suggests that mere knowledge of verbal labels does not in itself lead to effective verbal mediation in cognitive tasks. This evidence supports cognitive-developmental distinctions between knowledge of verbal labels (vocabulary) and their cognitive use in concept attainment or classification tasks. As an example, preschool children when asked to "put together the dolls that go together" characteristically do not separately group together all the boy dolls and all the girl dolls (categorical sorting) but rather put together a boy and a girl "because they play together" (relational sorting). By age 5 or 6 almost all normal children make such categorical sorts (Kohlberg, 1963; Stodolsky, 1965). The failure of preschool children to make use of categorical concepts is not directly due to ignorance of verbal labels, then, since the preschool children are able to group the male dolls together if explicitly told to do so. Instead it seems to be related to various Piaget concrete operations, as evidenced by the fact that categorical sorting forms a scale point in a sequence of Piaget operations (Kofsky, 1968; Kohlberg, 1963).

Flavell, Beach, and Chinsky (1966) have proposed that young children's cognitive deficits in many tasks are due to a generalized failure of children to spontaneously produce verbal signs in cognitive tasks, even though these signs are in their repetoire. Evidence for this hypothesis from studies by Flavell, Kohlberg, Luria, Vygotsky, and others is reviewed in Kohlberg, Yaeger, and Hjertholm (1968). The studies indicate that:

1. Older children engage in more private or self-directed speech on tasks than do younger children.

2. Bright young children engage in more private speech in tasks than do average young children.

3. Middle-class children use more private speech than do culturally disadvantaged children.

4. Children who use self-directed speech on some tasks do better than those who do not.

5. An experimental condition requesting self-directed speech leads to more self-directed speech and consequent improvement in performance.

6. Experimental prompting of self-directed speech does not, however, engender continued use of self-directed speech in situations where no prompting occurs. Spontaneous use of self-directed speech in memory tasks appears to be a relatively stable characteristic among children of a given age.

While these studies clearly indicate relations between private speech performance and cognitive functioning, the exact causal direction of this relation is not clear. The fact that older, brighter, and more culturally advantaged children engage in more private speech may indicate that cognitive advance is the cause rather than the effect of private speech production. While the studies of Flavell and his colleagues indicate improved performance after prompting of private speech, they also indicate improved performance if pointing (to the self) rather than talking (to the self) is experimentally prompted. These results are understandable because the task used was a serial memory rather than a cognitive-inferential task.

The findings, then, suggest that cognitive mediation requires something more than the possession and spontaneous production of verbal signs, though these latter may be necessary or facilitating conditions for the former. One line of thought has suggested that the structural-grammatical development of speech (rather than the possession and production of verbal labels) is largely responsible for the massive development of cognitive mediation in the preschool and early school years. This line of thought has been particularly influenced by Bernstein's (1961) characterization of social class differences in linguistic codes. In Bernstein's view, in addition to a "restricted code" shared by both classes, the middle class makes use of an "elaborated code" having distinctive stylistic and syntactical features as well as more cognitively abstract referential functions. The absence of exposure to this code in the lower class and the disadvantaged is believed to be influential in causing the poorer tested performance of the lower class in a number of intellectual tasks.[4]

---

[4] With regard to class differences in language, Schatzman and Strauss (1955) describe social class differences in language in terms similar to Bernstein's, but present a Piagetian view that failure to use an elaborated code in impersonal situations represents a certain "egocentricity" of perspective, i.e., a restriction of role-taking of the perspective of the listener and a failure to differentiate it from that of the self or other intimates. Following Mead (1934) they hold that the greater opportunities for participation and role-taking available to the middle class lead to a broader or more generalized perspective in communication. From

This conception has been particularly influential in the approaches to early education of the culturally disadvantaged, elaborated by Bereiter and Engelmann (1966), Deutsch (1965), and Hess and Shipman (1965). In particular, the Bereiter and Engelmann program focuses upon teaching the grammatical speech of the "elaborated code" as a "second language" to the culturally disadvantaged. (In this connection it may be pointed out that a goal of teaching standard English as a second language may best be achieved by exposing disadvantaged children to middle-class models in an integrated program [Kohlberg, 1967]).

While Bernstein's portrayal of parallels between cognitive and grammatical-stylistic aspects of language is intuitively convincing, the Piaget viewpoint suggests a number of qualifications as to the notion that the linguistic-grammatical aspects of the "elaborated code" are primary and determinative of the cognitive orientations involved. In Piaget's (1967, p. 98) view, "language is only a particular form of the symbolic function and as the individual symbol is simpler than the collective sign, it is permissible to conclude that thought precedes language and that language confines itself to transforming thought by helping it attain its forms of equilibrium by means of a more advanced schematization and a more mobile absraction. . . . The structures that characterize thought have their roots in action and in sensorimotor mechanisms deeper than linguistics. The more the structures of thought are refined, the more language is necessary for the achievement of this elaboration. Language is thus a necessary but not sufficient condition for the construction of logical operations. Language and thought are linked in a genetic circle where each necessarily leans on the other in interdependent formation. In the last analysis, both depend on intelligence itself, which antedates language and is independent of it."

Research support for Piaget's view comes from a recent study by Sinclair (1967). Sinclair found a marked association between success on conservation tasks and certain modes of language. Training increasing usage of these language modes, did not, however, lead to much greater success on the conservation tasks. With regard to the "concrete operations" which may be considered the primary structural achievement in the preschool beginning school period, we have noted that these develop without complex structural language in the deaf but seem markedly retarded in the blind. We also noted that the major features of grammatical language typically develop some years before "logical" concrete operational thought, so that development of linguistic structure is not sufficient for the develop-

---

this point of view the language form itself is less a directly transmitted subcultural entity than it is a reflection of a social perspective or cognitive orientation, and the educational problem is not to teach a syntactic code but to create opportunities for communication and role-taking at the level which will stimulate the development of a generalized perspective.

ment of cognitive structure. All these findings suggest that particular linguistic developments are not necessary conditions for cognitive-structural development.

The Piagetian view, then, holds that neither increased verbal labeling nor increased grammatical structuring are causally responsible for the basic cognitive developments of the later preschool years. It does hold that language may aid in "transforming thought by helping it attain its forms of equilibrium by a more advanced schematization and a more mobile abstraction." One way in which this may occur is suggested by Luria (1961) and Vygotsky (1962). Vygotsky believes that thought and speech have independent ontogenetic roots, that they "fuse" early in development and that the subsequent fate of thought is determined by the fact that thought in the older child (over 5 or 7) is a structure of interiorized speech. As we have noted, his suggestion that private speech is a way station between overt speech and interiorized inferential thought has received considerable support (Kohlberg, Yaeger, and Hjertholm, 1968). From this point of view, the shift from associative to conceptual modes in the years 4 to 7 can be seen as the result of the interiorization of language occurring in this period (Kohlberg, 1963). We cited earlier the fact that possession of verbal labels did not in itself lead the preschool child to use categorical class concepts. In Vygotsky's view, however, this conceptual failure of the preschool child may be due to his failure to use linguistic labels in an interiorized form. When the preschool child sorts objects, verbal labels seem to be "outside" the child as one of many perceptual attributes of the object, for example, the doll has a red necktie, it is big, and it is also called a boy. The label "boy" is not, however, an internal response subsuming all other external characteristics of the doll. For the older child, "boy" represents not one of many perceptual attributes of the doll but something over and above these individual attributes used to organize them. This may be because an internal verbal mediator organizes the concept, rather than acting as an external stimulus. In a similar spirit, Bruner et al. (1966) have suggested that the development of Piagetian conservation is related to the internalization of speech which frees the child from dominance by the immediate perceptual aspects of the situation. The Vygotsky analysis of internalization just discussed comes close to Piaget's view of concrete operations as the internalization of action. Whether "linguistic internalization" or "internalization of action" is stressed, however, it is clear that the stimulation of cognitive development involves something much more refined than the focus upon verbal labeling and grammar characterizing current preschool language-stimulation programs.

To summarize, cognitive-developmental theorists like Piaget and Vygotsky are in broad agreement as to the parallel and interdependent nature of the development of thought and speech. This parallelism of language and thought is most grossly reflected in the high correlations between measures of verbal development or knowledge and cognitive measures (like the Raven matrixes) which do not obviously depend upon verbal development. These correlations need not be interpreted as indicating that language development is the causal foundation of cognitive development, however. A more plausible interpretation is that the more basic cognitive abilities contributing to nonverbal tasks also contribute to language achievements (and, to some extent, vice versa).

The fact the preschoolers' cognitive ability and development is correlated with vocabulary scores does not mean that intervention to increase vocabulary will increase cognitive ability or development. A child's success in defining "envelope" correlates with general performance on the Stanford-Binet, but teaching him the word "envelope" will not increase his cognitive functioning. If this is true for a single word, it is true also for a dozen or a hundred. Theories such as Vygotsky's suggest sensitive points at which language development and cognitive development intersect. As these points come to be studied, we will probably find ways in which language stimulation can serve cognitive development. For the present, however, it must be stressed that language achievements should not be confused with general cognitive development. It is evident that the education of language achievement may have definite values apart from its effect upon general cognitive development, but it is unfortunate if educational thought is based upon a theoretical confusion between the two.

V. PRESCHOOL AS A CRITICAL PERIOD IN THE DEVELOPMENT OF PSYCHOMETRIC GENERAL INTELLIGENCE

We have suggested that age-linked structural change in the preschool period is necessary before the child is open to many forms of cognitive training. This does not imply a biological critical period, however. As we suggested earlier, the most extreme "critical period" notions of the importance of preschool cognitive stimulation rest as much upon a theory of maturational unfolding as do notions that early stimulation is unnecessary for later development because intelligence is innate.[5] This is because critical period concepts imply a biologically timed unfolding of a certain type of behavior, with a corresponding biologically based period of sensitivity to, or need for, normal supporting stimulation.

Although Hunt's (1961, 1964) use of Piaget in developing his own views sometimes suggests it, Piaget's theory does not imply critical periods

---

[5] While associationistic learning theorists often stress the importance of early learning, they provide little rationale for the notion that early learnings (or learning deficits) are critical or irreversible. While Hebb (1949, 1955) has distinguished between primary (irreversible and general) learning and secondary learning, this distinction has never been incorporated into a general learning theory nor operationalized in human research.

in intellectual development, insofar as the critical period concept implies (*a*) sensitivity to stimulation at a definite chronological time span, (*b*) greater sensitivity to stimulation at earlier than at later periods of development, or (*c*) irreversibility of the effects of early stimulus deprivation. The Piaget position holds that there are developmental phases of sensitivity, but these are tied to the child's behavioral level, not to chronological age. The position does hold that there are special sensitivities to stimulation at definite stages of development, and it implies that the effectiveness of stimulation is contingent upon its match with a given level of development. The child's perception of the world is determined by his stage of cognitive organization, and a stimulus is only a stimulus if it can match or be assimilated to already developed schemata. This was illustrated by the experimental work on training conservation cited earlier. "Teaching" of conservation was only found to be effective in children close in chronological mental age to the normal age of spontaneous attainment of conservation.

Not only does the position hold that stimulation is only effective under conditions of match but it holds experience at a given period of appropriate match is sufficient for development of a specific structure and does not require continual supplementation throughout life. Stages imply that cognitive structures are irreversible, that is, they are not subject to regression or extinction in the absence of the stimulation which originally facilitated their formation. (In this way Smedslund [1961a] was able to experimentally differéntiate the cognitive-structural development of conservation from its "conditioned" imitations.)

While the cognitive-developmental position implies the developmental phase specificity and irreversibility of effective stimulation, it does not imply that such stimulation must occur at a given point in time. Sensitivities to a stimuli are not determined by a chronological age or a maturational period but by the actual level of the child's cognitive structures, so that effectiveness of stimulation for conservation involves a match to mental, not chronological, maturity. (It might even be argued from the cognitive-developmental position that certain cognitive-enrichment programs should be timed later for culturally disadvantaged children because of cognitive retardation, rather than attempting to provide enrichment programs for these children at the age at which more advanced middle-class children are presumed to be receiving parallel stimulation.) The position does not imply that retarding stimulus deficits at an early time point are not reversible by compensating stimulation at a later time point. The stimulation necessary for normal development from one stage to the next should be effective in moving a retarded child to the next stage, even if the child has chronologically missed the time at which normal children received this stimulation.

Cognitive stages, then, do not imply chronologically determined and irreversible sensitive periods for stimulation. They also do not imply that earlier levels of development are generally more sensitive to critical stimulation than are later periods. Piaget's theory suggests that the child's sensitivity to environmental stimulation tends to increase rather than to decrease with development. Each level of cognitive development represents the capacity to be stimulated by, or to experience, something new. The child can only be stimulated by events or stimuli which he can partly assimilate, that is, fit into his already existing cognitive structures or schemata. The newborn baby is simply not sensitive to most of the events in the world around him. According to Piaget (cf. Hunt, 1961), the infant at first (Stage 1) responds only to those stimuli in the outside world which are directly related to his own activities, which fit innate reflexes. He next (Stage 2) responds to stimulus events which are associated with these reflexes, but only if he "perceives" them as caused by, or associated with, his own activity. Still later (Stage 4) he becomes interested in new events which he does not feel that he has directly caused, and, finally (Stage 5), he directly seeks to produce novel events. There is, then, a progression of stimulation to which the child becomes sensitive and which is required at succeeding levels of development. Even in a culturally deprived home, the kind of minimal simple stimulation that the infant requires is probably present, the kind of stimulation which will allow the exercise of sensorimotor schemata of one sort or another. As the child gets older and develops further he requires successively more complicated forms of stimulation, so that the effects of stimulus deprivation would be expected to become more critical as the child develops further and further.

Because the cognitive-developmental position distinguishes interactional cognitive stages from maturational physical-motor stages, it is reluctant to accept animal critical-period data as relevant to human intellectual development. Early deprivation of patterned light stimulation (Riesen, 1958), for instance, does seem to lead to practically irreversible defects in later visual perception among animals. This critical-period effect, however, is based largely on the specific requirements of a noncognitive neural growth going on at a specific time. Without light there is actual retinal degeneration. It is not clear whether early deprivation of patterned light stimulation has an irreversible effect. If it does, the irreversibility of this effect may be due to the existence of innately patterned mechanisms of pattern recognition, which depend upon some minimal input for their physiological maintenance.

The animal evidence for irreversible effects of deprivation upon definite cognitive structures is less clearcut. While stimulus deprivation appears to actually lead to lower brain weights, this does not appear to be a strict "critical-period" phenomena (Rosenzweig, 1966). Stimulus-deprived rats eventually gain in brain weight toward that of enriched-environment rats, suggesting only lower and slower brain-activity rates for the deprived, rather than early irreversible fixation or degeneration of a maturational structure. While the findings on critical periods in animals are themselves unclear, there are some basic further qualifications about generalizing from them to human intelligence. In human beings we find that there is a general intelligence factor. This consistency of an individual's performance from one cognitive task to another justifies us in calling any given performance "cognitive." No such general factor has ever been discovered in animal problem solving, learning, or perceptual functions. To the extent to which "maze-bright" rats are not bright at any other task, it is misleading to talk about intelligence or cognitive ability as being involved in maze-bright performance. Where early deprivation is found to have large and relatively stable effects upon later "problem solving," as in Thompson and Heron's (1954) study, it is not clear that the effects are due to cognitive-structural retardation or to social-emotional disturbance, distractibility, etc. Animal studies indicating the effects of early experience upon specific later sensory, motor, emotional, and conditioning patterns are uncertain in their import for cognitive development.

A second limitation to extrapolation from animal studies is that the sort of complete sensory social deprivation involved in animal experiments never occurs in human experience, even in the worst institutions. It can only occur in laboratory environment. Deprivation of all patterned light vision, of all tactual stimulation, of all thermal change, of all body contact with other organisms, etc., simply does not occur in natural settings. In general, the deprivation studies suggest that the minimal stimulation found in all natural settings is sufficient for normal maturation and that quantitative variations over this base line do not have the same significance as does complete deprivation. This provides another warrant for caution in extrapolation from animal experiments to natural variations in humans.

A third related limitation of extrapolation of animal critical-period notions to human intellectual development is the fact that the whole concept of cognition implies the capacity for equipotentiality or functional equivalence of a variety of stimuli. While a given type of sensory or motor input might be required for a certain sensory or motor function, cognitive structures can be based on a variety of different stimuli which are all functionally equivalent for cognitive development. This equipotentiality is suggested by the findings on conservation in the deaf and the blind. While complete absence of visual experience in the blind appears to sharply retard conservation development, this effect is not irreversible: the blind children eventually develop conservation. As judged by findings on general intelligence tests, the development of deaf, blind, and paralyzed children shows remarkably little irreversible deficit considering the severity of sensori-stimulus deprivation to which they are exposed. An account of the effects of cultural deprivation in terms of quasi-biological critical periods in sensory inputs is implausible when the much more obvious sensory deprivation of blind and deaf children does not have as marked effects as are attributed to the much more subtle forms of stimulus restriction found in culturally disadvantaged environments.

When we turn to the human field, then, the claim that early stimulus deprivation leads to irreversible cognitive deficit must be viewed with great caution. As increasingly careful work has been done in the effects of early deprivation in infants, the impressionistic conclusions of Spitz and Bowlby as to massive irreversible cognitive and developmental retardation due to maternal and stimulus deprivation in infancy have come increasingly under question (Robinson, 1968; Yarrow, 1964). A number of studies (Dennis & Najarian, 1957; Rheingold & Bayley, 1965) indicate that some observed retardation due to infant institutional deprivation, and some observed compensation by infant enrichment programs, wash out in later development.

The major factual considerations leading to the notion of a preschool critical period in cognition derive from neither animal nor institutionalization studies. The real basis for stressing preschool cognitive programs comes from the belated recognition by educators that differences in the child's educational achievement are primarily due to the characteristics of the child and of his home environment rather than to the child's elementary schooling as such. This point has been ably documented by Bloom (1964). According to Bloom, longitudinal studies indicate that about 50 per cent of the child's final intelligence and about 33 per cent of his performance on school achievement tests is predictable from measures of his intelligence before he enters school. While the fact that later achievement is quite predictable from intelligence test functioning at school entrance is unquestionable, the implication that the preschool era is a "critical period" for the environmental stimulation of intellectual development and that raising the IQ in this period is a practical and feasible goal for preschool programs is questionable.

The critical-period interpretation of test stabilization data starts from the finding that tests administered in the first year of life do not predict adult intelligence scores, that tests administered at school entrance sizably do predict these scores, and that there is only a small increase in predictability found if tests are administered later than school entrance. The critical-period interpretation of this large increase in predictability from age 1 to age 6 is due to the fact that environmental stimulation has "fixed" intellectual growth and functioning during this period. This interpretation, as elaborated by Bloom (1964), is based on two assumptions. The first is that the degree of predictability from a childhood test to an adult ability test is a function of the proportion of the pool of adult knowledge and skills tested which has developed at the childhood age. The second assumption is that the filling in of the ability pool between the two time points is largely a function of differential environment. Neither assumption seems tenable in light of other known findings concerning intelligence. The stability of intelligence tests after age 6 is not necessarily due to the completion of development at age 6 of half the elements composing adult ability but may be due to the continuing stable influence of both heredity and environment after this age. With regard to stabilization due to the environment, it should be recognized that the stimulation potential of home and neighborhood are more or less constant throughout childhood. The fact that low IQ of 6-year-olds from culturally deprived homes predicts to low IQ in adolescence does not necessarily indicate that the effect of environment on adult intelligence occurred primarily in the preschool years. The deprivation of the environment is fairly constant and continues to operate throughout the childhood years and accordingly contributes to the predictability of the preschool IQ to later intelligence.

With regard to stabilization due to heredity, there is also no reason to assume that this factor is completely manifest in early infancy or in the preschool years. With regard to the hereditary, no new evidence has accumulated in the last 25 years to modify earlier conclusions as to massive genetic components of general intellectual ability. It is not meaningful to specify definite quantitative estimates of hereditary and environmental contributions to intelligence, because such estimates depend upon the range of variation of heredity and of environments considered. If all the children considered grow up in middle-class surburban homes and schools, then most of the variation in their intelligence will be due to hereditary variability. If environments vary tremendously, so that some children are raised in orphanages without stimulation and some in a rich environment, then environment will account for much more of the variability in intelligence. In spite of these qualifications, it is safe to say that the twin studies suggest that at least 50 per cent of the reliable variation in general intelligence test scores (if reliably or repeatedly measured) at the school-age level among a "normally" reared, medically normal group of American children is contributed by hereditary factors. A very large portion of the predictability of later intelligence and achievement scores from scores on intelligence tests given at entrance to school, then, is the product of hereditary factors.

The major reason the hereditary contribution to stability of intelligence scores has been questioned recently is that infant tests do not predict to adult status, and it has been assumed that a hereditary factor should be manifested at birth. In fact, however, baby tests simply do not measure the same dispositions as do later intelligence tests, whether these dispositions be viewed as due to heredity or to environment. Baby tests were not constructed to measure cognition (i.e., education of relations and categories) but to record the age of appearance of sensory and motor responses.[6] Factor analytic studies indicate very little overlap between the content of baby tests and the content of intelligence tests, whereas they indicate something like a general cognitive factor in intelligence tests given after age 4.

Accordingly, the hereditary components of adult intelligence are not manifested in baby tests, which represent hereditary (and environmental) factors quite different than those influencing school-age or adult intelligence test functioning. Because of this, much of· the difference between the adult predictive power of infant tests and of school entrance tests is due to the fact that only the latter tap the hereditary contribution to adult intellectual status. This is demonstrated by the studies of Skodak, Skeels, and Honzik, reviewed by Jones (1954), which indicate a regular rise up until age 5 in the correlations between the IQ of children in foster homes and the education of their real mothers; this almost exactly parallels the rise in infant-mother correlations found for home-reared children. These correlations, then, cannot be attributed to stimulation by the real parents themselves. Rather, they indicate that the cognitive abilities of the adults (reflected in educational status or test performance) represent hereditary factors, which influence later cognitive performance of their children and are quite different from the hereditary factors influencing baby test performance.

The increase of predictability between infant tests and tests at school entrance is, then, largely the result of the fact that infant tests do not reflect the hereditary contribution to adult intelligence and is only in part the result of the filling in of intellectual skills by environment in these years. The weakness of the alternative "critical period" interpretation may be indicated by imagining findings in which baby tests at 1 month did not predict to adult intelligence, but baby tests at 7 months predicted 40 per cent of the variance of adult intelligence. The critical-period interpretive model would then require one to say: first, that 40 per cent of adult intellectual abilities were acquired in the first 6 months and, second, that their acquisition was primarily due to environment. In fact, the only plausible interpretation of the finding would be that the 1-month test was invalid as an intelligence test and that the 7-month test was a good indicator of the hereditary components of adult intellectual functioning.

We have claimed that neither cognitive-developmental theory nor empirical findings support the notion that the preschool period is a specially open period for stimulating general intelligence or general cognitive development. These conclusions are strengthened by the rather dis-

---

[6] This assumption is not clearly implausible, however, for the cognitive baby tests patterned after Piaget's baby observations, developed by Uzgiris and Hunt (1964) and by this writer (Kohlberg, 1961).

appointing findings concerning the actual effects of preschool cognitive stimulation upon performance on psychometric tests of general intelligence. Morrisett (1966) summarizes reviews of the literature (Fowler, 1968; Robinson, 1968) as well as unpublished work suggesting "that there is no compelling evidence for the long-term effectiveness of short-term educational intervention at the preschool level. Many preschool programs for disadvantaged children have shown that they make relatively large gains in intelligence test performance during the first year of the program; but this characteristic acceleration in intellectual growth is not always maintained during a second preschool year or when the children enter first grade." As one of many examples of such findings, we may cite a study of our own (Kohlberg, 1968a). An integrated Montessori program for Headstart children aged 3 and 4 led to a mean 14-point increase in Stanford-Binet IQ in the first 6 months. No significant further increase in IQ was found during the remaining 1½ years in which the children were in the program. The initial IQ increases could not be considered actual increases in general cognitive-structural development, since they were not paralleled by any significant increases in performance upon Piaget cognitive-structural tasks. The primary cause of the IQ increase was an improvement in attention and rapport with adults. Increases in rated attention in the classroom (as well as in the test situation) were marked during the first 6 months, and individual improvement in rated attention correlated .63 with improvement in Stanford-Binet IQ's during this period. In addition to attention, verbalization showed a sharp initial spurt related to improvement on IQ performance. In summary, then, it appears that the IQ changes were more a result of changes in cognitive motivation than a change in cognitive capacity. These changes in turn had a ceiling rather than moving continuously upward, and the motivational changes themselves did not lead to a later increase in cognitive capacity because of increased general learning.

VI. PIAGET CONCEPTS AND MEASURES OF PRESCHOOL INTELLECTUAL GROWTH

In the preceding section, we concluded that studies using psychometric tests indicate a heavy hereditary determination of intelligence and suggest that the effects of programs of preschool stimulation upon intelligence are rather minor and transient. We must now consider Hunt's (1961) suggestion that these conclusions may be specific to the concepts and methods employed by psychometric tests and might be revised by work with the newer concepts of methods of studying intelligence developed by Piaget.

It is not surprising to find that psychometric tests include a core of performance due to general cognitive ability of a partially hereditary nature, when this core constituted the rationale for their construction. The rationale of the general intelligence test of Binet, Spearman, and Wechsler (Spearman, 1930) is that of measuring a fixed biological capacity, as is implied in the division of performance into "g" (general ability) and "s" (specific experience) factors. Experience factors are largely consigned to "specificity" rather than to general intelligence. This rationale led to the construction of tests designed to wash out experience effects, partly by providing novel tasks and partly by providing a random and heterogeneous sample of tasks. Such tests lead to a sum score in which individual differences in experience with specific tasks might be expected to balance out. Stated differently, the Binet-Spearman approach has avoided defining basic cognitive achievements except in highly general terms ("education of relations and correlates") applicable to any task. Any item or achievement is a good intelligence test item if it elicits individual differences relating to other ability items. The more the item fails to correlate generally with all other items the worse or the more "specific experience loaded" the item is assumed to be.

There can be no question that this approach has yielded longitudinally stable and situationally general measures, which predict to all sorts of good outcomes in personality adjustment and in general problem solving as well as in scholastic achievement. However, the Spearman-Binet-Wechsler approach is not the only approach to yielding longitudinally stable and situationally general measures of cognitive development. In contrast to the psychometric approach to intelligence, the Piaget approach attempts to specify the basic concepts or operations characterizing each developmental era. It does not range over a wide variety of developmental items in order to wash out specific experience effects and leave a general rate of learning or development factor. Instead, it attempts to theoretically define some general cognitive operations and restricts items to those which may elicit such operations.

In a sense, then, Piaget's definition of intelligence or intellectual development is an a priori theoretical one, and it is irrelevant to him whether or not it leads to measures of situationally general and longitudinally stable individual differences. However, it is obvious that cognitive age-development as defined by Piaget's conceptions and cognitive age-development as defined by the Binet sampling approach must have some relation to one another. In fact the correlations between summed scores on Piaget tests and Binet scores are in the .70's for children of a given age (Kohlberg, 1966b; DeVries, in preparation). These findings seem to accord with Piaget's view that psychometric tests of intelligence get at the same thing as his tests, but in less pure and conceptually understandable form (1947, p. 154):

> It is indisputable that these tests of mental age have on the whole lived up to what was expected of them: a rapid and convenient estimation of an

individual's general level. But it is no less obvious that they simply measure a "yield," without reaching constructive operations themselves. As Pieron rightly pointed out, intelligence conceived in these terms is essentially a value-judgment applied to complex behavior. Inhelder was able to distinguish moronism from imbecility by the presence of concrete groupings and slight backwardness by an inability to reason formally. This is one of the first applications of a method which could be developed further for determining level of intelligence in general.

In this spirit, Pinard and Laurendeau (1964) have been developing a standardized method of assessing general intelligence or mental age with the Piaget procedures.

The writer's own view on this problem is somewhat different than that expressed by Piaget. My interpretation is that there is a hereditary general ability component of psychometric tests, a general "education of relations and correlates" or "rate of information-processing" factor, which contributes, along with other factors, to general cognitive-structural development as defined by Piaget. As I stressed earlier, the insistence of Piaget that *universal cognitive structures* are the result of interaction and are not pre-formed or maturational does not constitute a denial of the quantitative influence of heredity upon *individual differences in rate* of formation of these structures. It might be found that the rate at which experience was assimilated to create new cognitive structures was largely a function of genetic factors, and yet these structures would still be said to depend upon experiences as long as it was found that every child who developed the structures had had certain universal physical or social experiences.

While hereditary factors may enter into Piaget level, Piaget's theory also provides a definite rationale for the existence of item-general and longitudinally predictive differences in cognitive level based on differential amounts of general experience. The Piaget approach allows experiential effects to define general rather than specific differences in performance. General effects of experience are revealed in manner of handling a familiar object, specific effects in familiarity with the object itself. As an example, the dream experience is familiar to all children at every age, and the dream scale attempts to assess the qualitative mode of thought-response to the dream, not familiarity with it. It assumes that the structural level of the concept involves the general effects of experience and is not much affected by highly specific experience with the object in question. This focus is supported by the assessment of presence or absence of a level of thought or an intellectual operation, not assessment of speed and facility in its use. Piaget procedures treat the high school boy and Einstein as alike in possession of formal operations, though they differ greatly in their use. The generality of intellectual level in the Piaget view results from the fact that cognitive stages are structured wholes rather than from an innate rate factor. Intellectual performance is general because it rests on general operations which develop as total structures, not because it represents a general biological factor intersecting with specific experience or learnings (Smedslund, 1964).

In similar fashion, Piaget's theory may be used to account for the stability of intelligence without postulating an innate rate of growth factor. Longitudinal stability of cognitive level is implied by the existence of invariant sequences in cognitive development which has been found for many Piaget-type tasks (Sigel, 1964; Sigel & Hooper, 1968). Attainment of a given level of development implies successive attainment of all the preceding levels of development. Accordingly, relative cognitive maturity at a later age should be predictable from maturity at an earlier age without the assumption of an innate rate factor. If all children must go through an invariant sequence in cognitive development, children at a lower level at an earlier time point must go through more intervening stages and therefore will be relatively low at a later time point.

The writer and his colleagues (DeVries, in preparation; Kohlberg, 1963; Kohn, in preparation) have been engaged in research comparing psychometric and Piaget intellectual measures at ages 4 to 7 with regard to the following hypotheses derived from the framework just stated:

1. There should be a "general factor" among Piaget tests greater than that found among general psychometric items, but largely accounting for the general factor in the psychometric items.

2. Relative level on the Piaget tasks should be more longitudinally stable in the years 4 to 7 than would be expected from the stability of psychometric intelligence in this period.

3. Piaget items should depend more on general experience, and hence chronological age, than psychometric items. Accordingly, older average children should be more advanced on Piaget tasks than younger bright children matched for psychometric mental age.

4. Mere chronological aging should not, however, lead to greater development on Piaget items if the environment is very deprived. Culturally disadvantaged children, then, should show more retardation on nonverbal Piaget tasks than control children matched for psychometric mental age.

While much of the data from this research program has not yet been processed, some preliminary findings are available. While correlating with the Binet, Piaget tasks also hang together after Binet and other psychometric intellectual factors are removed. Presumably the intertask consistency of Piaget level represents a "general factor" independent of any innate rate factors entering into the Binet. The fact that chronological age correlates with the Piaget factor, with Binet mental age controlled, but that this correlation does not hold under conditions of cultural deprivation, gives additional support to the notion that the Piaget "factor" represents a general and longitudinally predictive residue of effects of experience upon cognitive development.

The logic and preliminary findings just mentioned suggest a number of reasons why Piaget measures might reflect general increments in cognitive development due to natural or educational experience better than do psychometric measures. In principle they resolve the paradox of the Binet, which almost forces us to view any educational increments as specific contents or as motivational sets not truly reflecting cognitive-structural development.[7] Insofar as Piaget measures of intelligence define general and sequential (longitudinally predictive) structural effects of general experience, they should be valuable in assessing the effects of various types of general cognitive-stimulation programs, whether or not these programs define accelerating Piagetian intellectual development as explicit objectives.

The possibility that Piagetian measures will detect some general and stable effects of preschool cognitive-stimulation programs more clearly than do psychometric measures does not, however, change the fundamental caution about preschool stimulation of general intelligence or cognitive development reflected in the previous section. The findings on acceleration of Piaget concrete operations indicate that such acceleration is neither easy nor does it typically generalize, either to other Piaget tasks or to Binet mental age tasks. With regard to the critical-period issue, it also does not appear that a wave of longitudinal, twin, and experimental studies using Piagetian measures would lead to radically different conclusions than those of the psychometric studies as to the role of heredity and of preschool experience upon long-range intellectual development. The fact that Piagetian and psychometric measures correlate as well as they do seems to preclude this possibility.

VII. CONCLUSIONS AS TO PRESCHOOL COGNITIVE OBJECTIVES

This paper has elaborated a view of preschool intellectual development as one of sequential structural change equipotentially responsive to a

---

[7] This was our interpretation of Binet increments in the Montessori program. We claimed they were due to attentional and verbalization factors rather than to general or cognitive-structural development, since the changes were not reflected in increments in Piaget performance. The study also suggested that this was not due to any failure of the Piaget tasks to assess general cognitive level. It was found that Piaget tests were more stable than the Binet tests, i.e., they yielded test-retest reliabilities between a 2- to 4-month period in the 90's. It was also found that when a child was initially high on the Piaget tests and low on the Binet tests, he would increase markedly on the Binet test at the later period. In other words, the Piaget tasks were more situation-free measures of cognitive capacity. Using nonverbal techniques (choice of lengths of gum, glasses of Coca Cola) to indicate possession of the conservation concept, the Piaget tasks elicited evidence of cognitive maturity masked by distractibility or shyness in the Binet situation. The Piaget tests, then, seemed to eliminate some "noncognitive" situational and verbal factors due to experience.

variety of specific types of experience but reflecting differences in the effects of general amount and continuity of organized experiences in the preschool age range. I have argued that specific types of preschool academic and linguistic training, even if immediately successful, are unlikely to have long-run general beneficial effects and that programs directed toward raising general psychometric intelligence are unlikely to have marked success. I have claimed that a Piagetian conception of methods of accelerating intellectual development (employing cognitive conflict, match, and sequential ordering of experience), a Piagetian focus upon basic intellectual operations, and a Piagetian procedure of assessment of general intellectual development might generate somewhat more general and long-range cognitive effects than would other approaches.

Basically, however, the Piaget approach does not generate great optimism as to the possibility of preschool acceleration of cognitive development (or of compensation for its retardation) nor does it lead to a rationale in which such acceleration (or compensation) is especially critical during the preschool years.

The cognitive-developmental approach suggests both modesty in the hopes of creators of preschool stimulation programs and modesty in the claims that one program of stimulation will differ markedly from another in its general impact upon the child. Cognitive-developmental theory, itself, is broadly compatible with a diversity of specific cognitive-stimulation programs, ranging from Moore to Montessori, insofar as all these programs define their cognitive goals developmentally and center on relatively active and self-selective forms of cognitive stimulation for the child (Kohlberg, 1968a). The compatibility of the cognitive-developmental view with a variety of programs is based first on its definition of cognitive advance in terms of natural lines of development rather than in terms of specifically taught "content." Second, this compatibility is based upon a concern with general forms of active experience, in terms of which a variety of specific types of stimulation are more or less functionally equivalent for cognitive development.

More generally, cognitive-developmental theory does less to suggest or support radical new preschool cognitive stimulation programs than it does to clarify the child-centered developmental approach to education expressed in its broadest form by John Dewey. The approach departs more from traditional child development concerns in providing a systematic analysis of the cognitive-structural and cognitive-interest implications of the play, aesthetic, constructive, and social activities which form the heart of the preschool than in suggesting narrowly "cognitive" activities in the preschool. Recent American Piagetian research on the preschool child has focused almost exclusively on children's quantitative and logical classificatory concepts, as indicated by Sigel and Hooper's (1968) anthology. It should be recalled, however, that Piaget and his followers have systematically studied the development of preschool children's play, their conversations with one another, their conceptions of life, of death, of reality, of sexual identity, of good and evil. The implications of these and other themes for the broader definition of preschool objectives are taken up elsewhere (Kohlberg & Lesser, in preparation).

REFERENCES

Ames, L. B. The sequential patterning of prone progression in the human infant. *Genetic Psychology Monograph*, 1937, **19**, 409–460.

Baldwin, A. Cognitive theory and socialization. In D. Goslin (Ed.), *Handbook of socialization*. New York: Rand McNally, 1968.

Baldwin, J. M. *Thoughts and things or genetic logic*. Vol. 3. New York: Macmillan, 1906–1915.

Bereiter, C. Progress report on teaching the disadvantaged. Urbana, Ill.: Institute for Research on Exceptional Children, 1967, mimeographed.

Bereiter, C., & Engelmann, S. *Teaching disadvantaged children in the preschool*. Englewood Cliffs, N.J.: Prentice-Hall, 1966.

Berlyne, D. *Conflict, arousal and curiosity*. New York: McGraw-Hill, 1961.

Berlyne, D. *Structure and direction in thinking*. New York: Wiley, 1965.

Bernstein, B. Social class and linguistic development: a theory of social learning. In A. Halsey, J. Floud, & C. Anderson (Eds.), *Education, economy, and society*. New York: Free Press, 1961.

Bloom, B. *Stability and change in human characteristics*. New York: Wiley, 1964.

Bruner, J. *The process of education*. Cambridge, Mass.: Harvard University Press, 1960.

Bruner, J. *Toward a theory of instruction*. Cambridge, Mass.: Harvard University Press, 1966.

Bruner, J., Olver, R., & Greenfield, P. *Studies in cognitive growth*. New York: Wiley, 1966.

Dennis, W., & Najarian. Infant development under environmental handicap. *Psychological Monographs*, 1957, **71**, (7, Whole No. 436).

Deutsch, M. The role of social class in language development and cognition. *American Journal of Orthopsychiatry*, 1965, **35**, 78–88.

DeVries, R. Performance of bright, average, and retarded children on Piagetian concrete operation tasks. Unpublished monograph, University of Chicago, Early Educational Research Center, in preparation.

Dewey, J. *Interest and effort in education*. Boston: Houghton Mifflin, 1913.

Dewey, J. Experience and conduct. In C. Murchison (Ed.), *Psychologies of 1930*. Worcester, Mass.: Clark University Press, 1930.

Dewey, J. *Experience and Education*. New York: Collier, 1963 (originally written in 1938).

Dewey, J. In R. Archambault (Ed.), *Dewey on education, a selection*. New York: Modern Library, 1965.

Dienes, Z. P. *An experimental study of mathematics*. London: Hutchinson, 1963.

Dienes, Z. P. *Modern mathematics for young children*. Harlow, England: Educational Supply Association, 1965.

Dodwell, C. Development of number concepts. In I. Sigel & F. Hooper (Eds.), *Logical thinking in children*. New York: Holt, Rinehart & Winston, 1968.

Durkin, D. Some issues in early reading. Unpublished paper, University of Illinois, Urbana, 1965.

Elkind, D. Reading, logic and perception. In J. Hellmuth (Ed.), *Educational therapy*. Vol. 2. Washington, D.C.: Special Child Publication, 1967. (a)

Elkind, D. Piaget and Montessori. *Harvard Educational Review*, 1967, 37, No. 4. (b)

Flavell, J. *The developmental psychology of Jean Piaget*. New York: Van Nostrand, 1963.

Flavell, J., Beach, D., & Chinsky, J. Spontaneous verbal rehearsal in a memory task as a function of age. *Child Development*, 1966, 37, 283–299.

Fowler, W. The early stimulation of cognitive development. In R. Hess & R. Bear (Eds.), *Preschool education: Theory, research and action*. Chicago: Aldine, 1968.

Furth, H. *Thinking without language; psychological implications of deafness*. New York: Free Press, 1966.

Gelman, R. Conservation, attention and discrimination. Unpublished doctoral dissertation, University of California, Los Angeles, 1967.

Gesell, A. The ontogenesis of infant behavior. In L. Carmichael (Ed.), *Manual of child psychology*. New York: Wiley, 1954.

Goodnow, J., & Bethon, G. Piaget's tasks: The effects of schooling and intelligence. *Child Development*, 1966, 37, 573–582.

Green, B. A method of scalogram analysis using summary statistics. *Psychometrika*, 1956, 21, 79–88.

Greenfield, P. On culture and conservation. In J. Bruner et al. *Studies in cognitive growth*. New York: Wiley, 1966.

Gruen, G. E. Experience affecting the development of number conservation in children. In I. Sigel & F. Hooper (Eds.), *Logical thinking in children: Research based on Piaget's theory*. New York: Holt, Rinehart & Winston, 1968.

Guttman, L. The basis for scalogram analysis. In S. A. Stouffer et al. *Measurement and prediction*. Princeton, N. J.: Princeton University Press, 1954.

Hebb, D. *Organization of behavior*. New York: Wiley, 1949.

Hebb, D. The mammal and his environment. *American Journal of Psychiatry*, 1955, 111, 1–9.

Hess, R., & Shipman, V. Early experience and the socialization of cognitive modes in children. *Child Development*, 1965, 36, 869–886.

Hooper, F. Piagetian research and education. In I. Sigel & F. Hooper (Eds.), *Logical thinking in children: research based on Piaget's Theory*. New York: Holt, Rinehart & Winston, 1968.

Hull, C. *Principles of behavior*. New York: Appleton-Century, 1943.

Hunt, J. McV. *Intelligence and experience*. New York: Ronald, 1961.

Hunt, J. McV. The psychological basis for using pre-school enrichment as antidote for cultural deprivation. *Merrill-Palmer Quarterly*, 1964, 10, 209–248.

Hyde, D. M. An investigation of Piaget's theories of the development of number. Unpublished doctoral dissertation, University of London, 1959.

Isaacs, S. *Social development in young children*. London: Routledge, 1933.

Jones, H. Environmental influences in the development of intelligence. In L. Carmichael (Ed.), *Manual of child psychology.* New York: Wiley, 1954.

Kaplan, B. The study of language in psychiatry. In S. Arieti (Ed.), *American handbook of psychiatry.* Vol. 3. New York: Basic Books, 1966.

Kessen, W. (Ed.) *The child.* New York: Wiley, 1965.

Kofsky, E. A scalogram study of classificatory development. In I. Sigel & F. Hooper (Eds.), *Logical thinking in children: research based on Piaget's theory.* New York: Holt, Rinehart & Winston, 1968.

Kohlberg, L. A schedule for assessing Piaget's stages of sensorimotor development in infancy. Unpublished schedule, Yale Univerity, 1961, mimeographed.

Kohlberg, L. Stages in children's conceptions of physical and social objects in the years 4 to 8—a study of developmental theory. Unpublished monograph, 1963, multigraphed (in preparation for publication).

Kohlberg, L. A cognitive developmental analysis of children's sex-role attitudes. In E. Maccoby (Ed.), *Development of sex differences.* Stanford, Calif.: Stanford University, 1966. (*a*)

Kohlberg, L. Cognitive stages and preschool education. *Human Development,* 1966, 9, 5–19. (*b*)

Kohlberg, L. Assessment of a Montessori program. Paper delivered at American Education Research Association, New York, February, 1967.

Kohlberg, L. The Montessori approach to cultural deprivation. A cognitive-development interpretation and some research findings. In R. Hess & R. Bear (Eds.), *Preschool education, theory, research and action.* Chicago: Aldine, 1968. (a)

Kohlberg, L. Stage and sequence: The developmental approach to socialization. In D. Goslin (Ed.) *Handbook of socialization.* New York: Rand McNally, 1968. (b)

Kohlberg, L., & Lesser, G. *What preschools can do: theories and programs.* Chicago: Scott, Foresman, in press.

Kohlberg, L., Yaeger, J., & Hjertholm, E. Private speech: four studies and a review of theory. *Child Development,* 1968, 39, 691–736.

Kohlberg, L., & Zigler, E. The impact of cognitive maturity upon the development of sex-role attitudes in the years four to eight. *Genetic Psychology Monograph,* 1967, 75, 89–165.

Kohn, N. The development of culturally disadvantaged and middle class Negro children on Piagetian tests of concrete operational thought. Doctoral dissertation, University of Chicago, in preparation.

Langer, J. The role of cognitive conflict in development. Paper delivered at meetings of Society for Research in Child Development, New York, March 21, 1967.

Linden, J. The performance of schizophrenic children upon a series of Piagetian tasks. Doctoral dissertation, University of Chicago, in preparation.

Lorenz, K. *Evolution and the modification of behavior.* Chicago: University of Chicago Press, 1965.

Lovell, K. Concepts in mathematics. In H. Klausneier & C. Harris (Eds.), *Analyses of concept learning.* New York: Academic, 1966.

Luria, A. R. *The role of speech in the regulation of normal and abnormal behavior.* New York: Liveright, 1961.

Mead, G. H. *Mind, self, and society.* Chicago: University of Chicago Press, 1934.

Mermelstein, E. The effect of lack of formal schooling on number development, a test of Piaget's theory and methodology. Unpublished doctoral dissertation, Michigan State University, 1964.

Mermelstein, E., & Shulman, L. S. Lack of formal schooling and the acquisition of conservation. *Child Development*, 1967, 38, 39–52.

Moore, O. K. Teaching young children to read. In R. Hess & R. Bear (Eds.), *Preschool education; theory, research, and action*. Chicago: Aldine, 1968.

Morrisett, L. Report of a conference on preschool education in *Items of the Social Science Research Council*, June, 1966.

Neill, A. S. *Summerhill*. New York: Hart, 1960.

Nordan, R. The development of conservation in the blind. Unpublished minor research paper, University of Chicago, 1967.

Pavlov, I. P. *Lectures on conditioned reflexes*. New York: Liveright, 1928.

Piaget, J. *The child's conception of the world*. New York: Harcourt Brace, 1928.

Piaget, J. *The psychology of intelligence*. London: Routledge, Kegen, 1947.

Piaget, J. *The child's conception of number*. London: Routledge, Kegan Paul, 1952.

Piaget, J. The general problem of the psychobiological development of the child. In J. M. Tanner & B. Inhelder (Eds.), *Discussions on Child Development*. Vol. 4. New York: International Universities Press, 1960.

Piaget, J. Cognitive development in children. In R. Ripple & V. Rockcastle (Eds.), *Piaget rediscovered, a report on cognitive studies and curriculum development*. Ithaca, N.Y.: Cornell University, School of Education, 1964.

Piaget, J. *Six psychological studies*. D. Elkind (Ed.). New York: Random House, 1967.

Pinard, A., & Laurendeau, M. *Causal thinking in children*. New York: International Universities Press, 1964.

Price-Williams, D. R. A study concerning concepts of conservation of quantity among primitive children. *Acta Psychologica*, 1961, 18, 297–305.

Reese, H. W. Verbal mediation as a function of age level. *Psychology Bulletin*, 1962, 59, 502–509.

Rheingold, H., & Bayley, N. The later effects of an experimental modification of mothering. In C. B. Stendler (Ed.), *Readings in child behavior and development*. New York: Harcourt, Brace & World, 1965.

Riesen, A. Plasticity of behavior; psychological aspects. In H. F. Harlow & C. N. Woolsey (Eds.), *Biological and biochemical bases of behavior*. Madison: University of Wisconsin Press, 1958.

Riesen, A., & Kinder, E. *The postural development of infant chimpanzees*. New Haven, Conn.: Yale University Press, 1952.

Robinson, H. The problem of timing in preschool education. In R. Hess & R. Bear (Eds.), *Preschool education: theory, research and action*. Chicago: Aldine, 1968.

Rosenzweig, M. Experimental complexity and cerebral change in behavior. Paper delivered at American Association for the Advancement of Science, Washington, D.C., December 30, 1966.

Schatzman, L., & Strauss, A. Social class and modes of communication. *American Journal of Sociology*, 1955, 60, 329–338.

Shirley, Mary M. The sequential method for the study of maturing behavior patterns. *Psychological Review*, 1931, 38, 501–528.

Shirley, Mary M. *The first two years, a study of twenty-five babies.* Minneapolis: University of Minnesota Press, 1931–1933. 2 vols.

Sigel, I. The attainment of concepts. In M. Hoffin & L. Hoffman (Eds.), *Review of child development research.* Vol. 1. New York: Russell Sage, 1964.

Sigel, I., & Hooper, F. (Eds.), *Logical thinking in children: research based on Piaget's theory.* New York: Holt, Rinehart & Winston, 1968.

Sigel, I. E., Roeper, A., & Hooper, F. H. A training of procedure acquisition of Piaget's conservation of quantity. In I. Sigel & F. Hooper (Eds.), *Logical thinking in children: research based on Piaget's theory.* New York: Holt, Rinehart & Winston, 1968.

Sinclair, H. *Acquisition du langage et development de la pensee.* Paris: Dunod, 1967.

Smedslund, J. The acquisition of conservation of substance and weight in children, III: Extinction of conservation of weight acquired normally by means of empirical control as a balance. *Scandinavian Journal of Psychology,* 1961, **2,** 85–87 (reprinted in Sigel & Hooper, 1968). (a)

Smedslund, J. The acquisition of conservation of substance and weight in children, V: Practice in conflict situations without external reinforcement. *Scandinavian Journal of Psychology,* 1961, **2,** 156–160, 203–210 (reprinted in Sigel & Hooper, 1968). (b)

Smedslund, J. Concrete reasoning: A study of intellectual development. *Monographs of the Society for Research in Child Development,* 1964, **29,** (2, Serial No. 93), 3–39.

Spearman, C. The psychology of "g." In C. Murchison (Ed.), *Psychologies of 1930.* Worcester, Mass.: Clark University Press, 1930.

Stodolsky, S. S. Maternal behavior and language and concept formation in Negro pre-school children: an inquiry into process. Unpublished doctoral dissertation, University of Chicago, 1965.

Sullivan, E. Acquisition of conservation of substance through film modeling techniques. In D. Brison & E. Sullivan (Eds.), *Recent research on the acquisition of substance* (Educational Research Series No. 2). Ontario: Ontario Institute for Studies of Education, 1967.

Thompson, W., & Heron, W. Environmental restriction and development in dogs. *Canadian Journal of Psychology,* 1954, **17,** No. 8.

Uzgiris, I. Situational generality of conservation. In I. Sigel & F. Hooper (Eds.), *Logical thinking in children: research based on Piaget's theory.* New York: Holt, Rinehart & Winston, 1968.

Uzgiris, I., & Hunt, J. McV. A scale of infant psychological development. Unpublished manuscript, University of Illinois, 1964.

Vygotsky, L. *Thought and language.* New York: Wiley, 1962.

Wallace, J. G. *Concept growth and the education of the child.* The Mears, Upton Park, Slough, Bucks: National Foundation for Education Research in England and Wales, 1965.

Wallach, L., & Sprott, R. Inducing number conservation in children. *Child Development,* 1964, **35,** 1057–1071.

Werner, H. *The comparative psychology of mental development.* Chicago: Wilcox & Follett, 1948.

White, S. Children's learning. In H. Stevenson (Ed.), *Child psychology: third yearbook of the National Society for the Study of Education.* Ch University of Chicago Press, 1963.

White, S. Evidence for a hierarchical arrangement of learning processes. In L sett & C. C. Spiker (Eds.), *Advances in child development and beh* Vol. 2. New York: Academic, 1965.

Wohlwill, J. A scalogram analysis of the number concept. In I. Sigel Hooper (Eds.), *Logical thinking in children: research based on P theory.* New York: Holt, Rinehart & Winston, 1968.

Yarrow, L. Separation from parents during early childhood. In M. L. H (Ed.), *Review of child development research.* Vol. 1. New York: Sage, 1964.

DEVELOPMENTAL SOCIOLINGUISTICS: INNER-CITY CHILDREN

Doris R. Entwisle

Doris R. Entwisle, "Developmental Sociolinguistics: Inner-City Children," *American Journal of Sociology,* July 1968, Vol. 74, pp. 37-49.

DEVELOPMENTAL SOCIOLINGUISTICS: INNER-CITY CHILDREN [1]

Doris R. Entwisle

ABSTRACT

In spite of the massive efforts aimed at early education of the culturally deprived, little solid information is available to guide these programs. It is assumed that cultural differences are important in language development and in cognitive development, but documentation of these assumptions is surprisingly sparse. Some data presented in this paper suggest, contrary to expectation, that inner-city children are more advanced on certain language measures than suburban children at the time of school entrance.

Linguistic data relate to many problems of sociological theory, such as the discreteness of social stratification and the integration of ethnic groups into the social system, and they are particularly informative vis-à-vis culture transmission and differences in socialization practices. Linguists studying language in its social context have worked mainly on dialect geography, however; and, so far, few data pertain to the interaction of language and social setting. As Hymes[2] points out, little is known about how personal and community beliefs and values impinge on the use of language, especially as this relates to language acquisition by children.

By age four the child has somehow learned most of the structural features of his native tongue, and by age eight he has learned a great deal about substitution properties of words. He knows that "little,"

for instance, will fill the same slot in a sentence as "big," even though he cannot define the word "adjective." The major development of language and verbal concepts occurs prior to age eight, so formal schooling may have little impact on it. The child's subculture may be the *only* substantial environmental influence because the young child's exposure to language is primarily auditory.

WORD ASSOCIATIONS AS DATA

Obtaining free associations to word stimuli is one way to study language development in young children because these associations are closely related to general linguistic competence and to verbal comprehension. This method has sharp limitations —the sample of language is minute—but associations can be secured from many different groups of children and analyzed by machine, permitting cross-cultural study of verbal concepts over a broad age span.[3]

[1] This work was supported by the National Institute of Child Health and Development, grant HD 00921-05, and was also aided by support from the Center for Study of Social Organization of Schools, Johns Hopkins University. The co-operation of staff and pupils in schools of Baltimore City is gratefully acknowledged. In particular, I am grateful to Dr. Orlando Furno, director of research, and to the following principals: Mr. Edwin Cohen, Mrs. Maria D. Hammond, Mr. Donald T. Leuschner, Mr. Wilfred M. Seaborne, Mr. Fuller C. Strawbridge, Mr. Henry N. West, and Miss Mildred A. Winter. The paper has benefited from comments by James Coleman, Robert Gordon, Edward McDill, and Arthur Stinchcombe.

[2] Dell Hymes, "Models of the Interaction of Language and Social Setting," *Journal of Social Issues,* XXIII (April, 1967), 8-28.

[3] Several atlases aid study of responses: For children in kindergarten, first, third, and fifth grades, see Doris R. Entwisle, *Word Associations of Young Children* (Baltimore: Johns Hopkins Press, 1966); for fourth-, fifth-, and sixth-grade children, see David S. Palermo and James J. Jenkins, *Word Association Norms* (Minneapolis: University of Minnesota Press, 1964). Atlases for other groups are listed in bibliographies of these books.

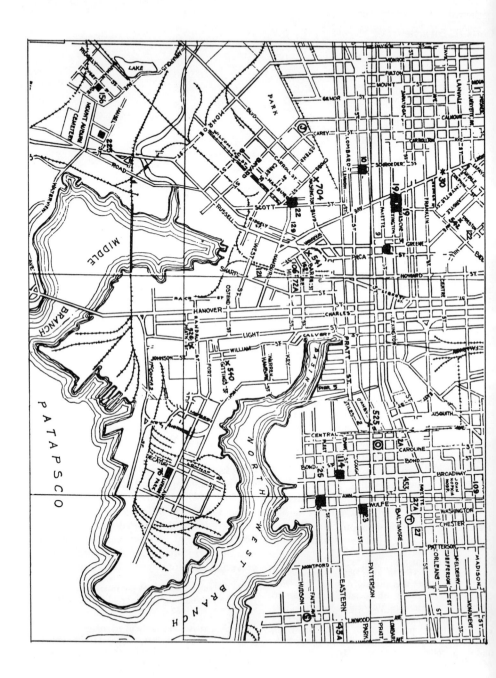

The validity of associations as indicators of linguistic development derives mainly from the correlation between grammatical sophistication and the appearance of paradigmatic associates and from the gradual emergence of responses typical of adults (therefore mature, by definition). We have gathered associations to common words ("table," "sell," "black," etc.), and so our data concern basic language skills. More refined and elaborate measures, such as sentence length, use of various grammatical

present study focuses on urban slum groups, both Negro and white, because we wished to see if extreme SES differences (slum vs. suburban) would have impact on language development when smaller SES differences (blue-collar vs. upper-middle class) had not.

METHOD

Data were gathered from children in Baltimore City, Maryland, who resided within census tracts (see Fig. 1) where

TABLE 1

DESIGN OF SUBJECTS IN SAMPLE

SUBJECTS	WHITE CHILDREN				NEGRO CHILDREN				GRAND TOTALS
	White Int.		Negro Int.		Negro Int.		White Int.		
	Med. I.Q.	Low I.Q.	Med. I.Q.	Low I.Q.	Med. I.Q.	Low I.Q.	Med. I.Q.	Low I.Q.	
Kindergarten:									
No. of children..	....	20	....	20	....	20	....	20	80
Average I.Q.*....	....	....	....	....	....	....	....	....	
First grade:									
No. of children..	20	20	17	20	20	20	9	20	146
Average I.Q.....	100.1	79.5	99.4	80.1	98.7	79.9	97.6	79.9	
Third grade:									
No. of children..	20	20	19	20	20	20	20	16	155
Average I.Q.....	99.7	80.8	100.3	80.5	99.9	80.6	99.6	81.1	
Fifth grade:									
No. of children..	20	20	20	20	20	20	20	20	160
Average I.Q.....	99.7	80.3	99.8	80.6	99.5	80.7	99.6	80.5	
Total.........	....	....	....	....	....	....	....	....	541

* No data available.

constructions, vocabulary size, and so on, might well demonstrate cleavage among groups that are equivalent on the word-association measures, or show differences of another kind from those we find. The reader should bear this in mind.

Prior to 1965 we sampled word associations for children representing various cultural and socioeconomic groups in Maryland and nearby regions of Pennsylvania.[4] There were strong differences between rural and suburban children but negligible differences between suburban blue-collar and suburban upper-middle-class groups. The

median family income is as low as $2,400. Elementary schools in the downtown area are very imbalanced racially, so to procure children whose living conditions were similar, schools with one racial group predominating were balanced by nearby schools with the other group predominant. For instance, school 19, all Negro, is balanced by

[4] Entwisle, *op. cit.* See also, Doris R. Entwisle, "Developmental Sociolinguistics: A Comparative Study in Four Subcultural Settings," *Sociometry,* XXIX (March, 1966), 67–84; and "Form Class and Children's Word Associations," *Journal of Verbal Learning and Verbal Behavior,* V (December, 1966), 558–65.

nearby school 10, mostly white, and the neighborhoods around the schools are similar. The design of the sample and the racial composition of the schools are shown in Tables 1 and 2. Negro and white children of average I.Q. (95–105) and low I.Q. (85 or less) were selected by using school records.[5] The entire design was replicated four times: white interviewers with white children, white interviewers with Negro children, Negro interviewers with white children, and Negro interviewers with Negro children. Racial groups are equivalent in terms of I.Q. and grade. Interviewers were all middle class with some college training. The interviewing procedure is reported completely elsewhere.[6]

The ninety-six stimulus words represent the several form classes (nouns, adjectives, verbs, pronouns, adverbs, and miscellaneous words). Nouns, adjectives, and verbs are stratified on frequency, so that there are eight high frequency (over 1,000), eight medium frequency (500–999), and eight low frequency (499 or less) of each according to the Thorndike-Lorge J-count. Other form classes do not permit a frequency division, so there are eight words of each kind.[7]

RESULTS

The results consist of lists of free associations. Data derived from these lists, such as frequency of primary responses, number of different responses, and percentages of paradigmatics, are the data analyzed. The "number of observations" in any analysis

[5] I.Q.'s for third- and fifth-grade children were mostly a Kuhlmann-Anderson score obtained in the second or fourth grade, respectively. First-grade children are given the Primary Mental Abilities (PMA) test on school entrance, and their I.Q.'s are based on four subtests, omitting the motor subtest.

[6] Entwisle, *Word Associations*.

[7] For a complete description of the stimulus list and its properties, as well as the method of determining form class of stimulus words and response words and frequency of stimulus words, see Entwisle, *Word Associations*.

consists of a response measure for a specific group of children (say, medium-I.Q., fifth-grade, Negro children interviewed by white interviewers) to a set of eight or more homogeneous stimulus words (say, adverbs or high-frequency nouns).

It has been widely observed that, with increasing age, form-class matching of stimulus and response increases, especially over the early school years, so the number of paradigmatics is the principal measure used.[8] (A paradigmatic response to "go" is

TABLE 2

RACIAL COMPOSITION OF SCHOOLS SAMPLED

School	Non-White	White	Total
1.............	207	3	210
6.............	1	460	461
10............	60	449	509
19 and A.......	1,447	0	1,447
22............	155	620	775
23............	0	394	394
114...........	447	18	465

"run.) Rates of paradigmatic responding for each subsample group are presented in Table 3.[9]

Age trends in paradigmatic responding obviously differ by form class. For in-

[8] Roger Brown and Jean Berko, "Word Association and the Acquisition of Grammar," *Child Development*, XXXI (March, 1960), 1–14; Susan Ervin, "Changes with Age in the Verbal Determinants of Word Association," *American Journal of Psychology*, LXXIV (September, 1961), 361–72; Entwisle, *Word Associations*. Also, for elementary school children, restricted and free associations are very highly related (Klaus F. Riegel, Ruth M. Riegel, Helen E. Smith, and Carole J. Quarterman, "An Analysis of Differences in Word Meaning and Semantic Structure between Four Education Levels" [unpublished manuscript, Department of Psychology, University of Michigan, November, 1964]), with close to 80 per cent overlap between free associations and associations given to instructions to produce superordinates, co-ordinates, contrasts, and so on. Thus free associations are highly related to comprehension of the word and ability to place words in appropriate contexts.

[9] In cases where subsamples were not equal to twenty, the response rate was adjusted proportionately.

TABLE 3

PERCENTAGES OF PARADIGMATIC RESPONSES, BALTIMORE CITY CHILDREN, 1965-66

FORM CLASS OF WORD	WHITE CHILDREN				NEGRO CHILDREN			
	White Int.		Negro Int.		Negro Int.		White Int.	
	Med. I.Q.	Low I.Q.	Med. I.Q.	Low I.Q.	Med. I.Q.	Low I.Q.	Med. I.Q.	Low I.Q.
First Grade								
High-freq. nouns.........	65.0	62.5	50.0	66.3	56.9	45.0	54.4	60.0
Med.-freq. nouns.........	62.5	58.8	56.3	68.7	61.9	44.4	66.9	58.7
Low-freq. nouns..........	60.6	58.8	50.6	61.9	54.4	48.7	48.7	53.1
Total nouns	62.7	60.0	52.3	65.6	57.7	46.0	56.7	57.3
High-freq. adj............	49.4	36.3	52.5	42.5	40.0	21.3	44.4	28.7
Med.-freq. adj............	44.4	35.0	46.9	36.3	40.0	26.3	37.5	26.9
Low-freq. adj............	43.7	26.9	38.7	26.9	34.4	17.5	37.5	25.0
Total adj..............	45.8	32.7	46.0	35.2	38.1	21.7	39.8	26.9
High-freq. verbs.........	34.4	28.7	31.3	26.9	20.6	28.1	25.0	29.4
Med.-freq. verbs.........	27.5	21.9	19.4	22.5	15.0	13.7	20.6	21.9
Low-freq. verbs..........	20.0	20.0	23.1	20.0	16.3	17.5	23.7	23.1
Total verbs............	27.3	23.5	24.6	23.1	17.3	19.8	23.1	24.8
Adverbs................	28.7	10.6	25.0	19.4	13.7	11.3	18.1	13.1
Pronouns...............	51.3	28.1	40.0	36.3	33.1	26.9	41.9	35.0
Third Grade								
High-freq. nouns.........	69.4	68.7	76.9	70.6	73.7	61.9	66.9	62.5
Med.-freq. nouns.........	75.0	70.6	76.3	68.1	76.9	64.4	75.0	65.0
Low-freq. nouns..........	75.6	75.6	90.0	68.7	67.5	66.3	75.0	61.9
Total nouns...........	73.3	71.7	81.0	69.2	72.7	64.2	72.3	63.1
High-freq. adj............	73.7	77.5	85.0	74.4	76.9	68.7	64.4	59.4
Med.-freq. adj............	64.4	61.3	71.9	63.1	70.0	63.7	62.5	46.9
Low-freq. adj............	53.1	53.7	66.3	55.0	55.0	48.1	53.1	43.1
Total adj..............	63.7	64.2	74.4	64.2	67.3	60.2	60.0	49.8
High-freq. verbs.........	55.6	50.6	55.0	42.5	57.5	39.4	50.0	48.1
Med.-freq. verbs.........	34.4	30.0	35.0	28.1	35.0	25.6	27.5	22.5
Low-freq. verbs..........	25.6	33.1	23.1	23.7	31.9	23.7	30.0	28.1
Total verbs............	38.5	37.9	37.7	31.5	41.5	29.6	35.8	32.9
Adverbs................	44.4	35.6	36.9	43.7	38.1	30.6	31.9	30.0
Pronouns...............	66.9	65.0	72.5	63.1	75.0	63.1	65.0	58.7

TABLE 3—*Continued*

FORM CLASS OF WORD	WHITE CHILDREN				NEGRO CHILDREN			
	White Int.		Negro Int.		Negro Int.		White Int.	
	Med. I.Q.	Low I.Q.	Med. I.Q.	Low I.Q.	Med. I.Q.	Low I.Q.	Med. I.Q.	Low I.Q.
	Fifth Grade							
High-freq. nouns	73.7	72.5	75.6	65.6	78.7	75.6	76.3	71.5
Med.-freq. nouns	80.6	75.0	75.6	76.9	80.6	75.0	85.0	81.3
Low-freq. nouns	89.4	84.4	93.7	84.4	88.1	83.1	85.3	83.7
Total nouns	81.3	77.3	81.7	75.6	82.5	77.9	82.3	78.7
High-freq. adj	93.7	85.0	90.6	88.1	85.6	87.5	91.9	91.3
Med.-freq. adj	79.4	76.9	86.3	71.9	75.0	75.0	79.4	76.9
Low-freq. adj	75.0	73.8	78.7	76.3	81.9	72.5	77.5	75.6
Total adj	82.7	78.5	85.2	78.7	80.8	78.3	82.9	81.3
High-freq. verbs	79.4	64.4	79.4	69.4	66.3	55.6	78.7	75.6
Med.-freq. verbs	49.4	36.9	43.7	38.7	41.9	36.9	52.5	43.1
Low-freq. verbs	53.1	44.4	43.7	51.9	45.0	45.6	64.4	46.3
Total verbs	60.6	48.5	55.6	53.3	51.0	46.0	65.2	55.0
Adverbs	61.9	50.6	57.5	53.1	62.5	44.4	58.1	54.4
Pronouns	77.5	71.9	80.6	72.5	66.9	75.0	73.1	85.6

stance, noun responses to nouns generally increase between kindergarten and fifth grade, but this increment is considerably less than that for adjectives or verbs. An analysis of variance of paradigmatic responses to nouns, adjectives, and verbs reveals a significant interaction ($p < .01$) among form class, grade, I.Q., race of child, and race of interviewer, so results are presented in terms of *individual* form-class analyses.[10]

Responses to adjectives.—The variance

[10] These findings are consistent with earlier work. See, for example, Entwisle, *Word Associations,* "Developmental Sociolinguistics," and "Form Class"; Also, Doris R. Entwisle and Daniel F. Forsyth, "Word Associations of Children: Effect of Method of Administration," *Psychological Reports,* XIII (July, 1963), 291–99; Doris R. Entwisle, Daniel F. Forsyth, and Rolf Muuss, "The Syntactic-Paradigmatic Shift in Children's Word Associations," *Journal of Verbal Learning and Verbal Behavior,* III (February, 1964), 19–29.

analysis for paradigmatic responses to adjectives shows a highly significant grade × I.Q. × race-of-interviewer × race-of-child interaction (see Table 4). At both first and third grades, Negro children are noticeably lower in seven out of eight comparisons. Differences between the races decrease with age, being 6–11 per cent at first grade and no more than 3 per cent by fifth grade.

Third-grade children are most affected by race of interviewers. When races of interviewers and children are mixed, Negro interviewers elicit more paradigmatics from white children than white interviewers elicit from Negro children, with one exception.

Suburban children from Baltimore with similar I.Q.'s were sampled in 1961–63 at two SES levels: (1) "high SES" suburban children whose fathers' average schooling amounted to 13.8 years and whose families had incomes of about $9,200; (2) "low SES" suburban children whose fathers had about 10.5 years of schooling and whose families had incomes of about $6,200. As mentioned earlier, the present study was undertaken partly to extend the variability on the socioeconomic dimension because it was thought that greater deprivation (family income at about $3,000) might yield language deficits, even though no differences had appeared between middle-class and working-class groups. Just the opposite seems to be true for first graders. Rates for first-grade slum children *exceed* rates

grade, so rates of development differ, but eventually all children attain the same level. At later grades, the early advantage of the slum children in terms of paradigmatic response rates to adjectives is lost.

Responses to verbs.—Previous work suggests that verbs continue to develop after fifth grade, but the major portion of development has occurred by then. (Adjective development is practically complete at third grade.)[11] Paradigmatic responses to verbs show somewhat different trends from those observed for adjectives (see Table 5). Although the impact of race differs by age,

TABLE 4

AVERAGE PERCENTAGES OF PARADIGMATIC RESPONSES TO ADJECTIVES;
GRADE × I.Q. × R.I. × R.C. INTERACTION*

| | WHITE CHILDREN | | | | NEGRO CHILDREN | | | |
| | White Int. | | Negro Int. | | Negro Int. | | White Int. | |
GRADE	Med. I.Q.	Low I.Q.	Med. I.Q.	Low I.Q.	Med. I.Q.	Low I.Q.	Med. I.Q.	Low I.Q.
1......	45.8	32.7	46.0	35.2	38.1	21.7	39.8	26.9
3......	63.7	64.2	74.4	64.2	67.3	60.2	60.0	49.8
5......	82.7	78.5	85.2	78.7	80.8	78.3	82.9	81.3

* R.I. = race of interviewer; R.C. = race of child.

for first-grade suburban children matched for I.Q. The medium-I.Q. slum children respond to adjectives much like the high-I.Q. (over 130) suburban children, and although the Negro slum children are less advanced than the white slum children, those of average I.Q. are responding at rates close to 10 per cent higher than either the high- or low-SES suburban white groups. The low-I.Q. white slum children are responding at rates close to those for the medium-I.Q. white suburban children, and the low-I.Q. Negro slum children are about the same as low-I.Q. white suburban children.

By third grade, however, medium-I.Q. slum children of both races *lag behind* suburban children. All children appear to attain the same asymptotic rate by fifth

racial differences do not vary from one I.Q. level to another. Frequency is apparently a more important variable as far as verbs are concerned.

For verbs, first-grade slum children are more advanced than first-grade suburban children at both I.Q. levels. Again, there is a reversal at third grade, and the relative advantage of the slum children disappears. At fifth grade, Negro slum children are about 5 per cent higher than white slum children *or* white suburban children of both I.Q. levels. Generally the same patterns with age and the same relative position of slum children with respect to suburban children are seen whether adjectives *or* verbs are analyzed.

[11] See Entwisle, *Word Associations.* Also see Palermo and Jenkins, *op. cit.*

Adverbs and pronouns.—Previous work shows that pronouns develop most rapidly between kindergarten and third grade. Adverbs, like verbs, continue to develop up to fifth grade and probably thereafter. A comparison of suburban and slum children on responses to adverbs and pronouns again documents the superiority of first-grade slum children and a falling behind at third grade. White slum children of medium I.Q. (100) closely resemble white suburban high-frequency adult responses with increasing age of the child. For instance, "chair," the primary adult response to "table," is more frequent at age ten than at age five. Frequency of primaries is a measure of maturity that is independent of other measures previously considered, and the relative advancement of first-grade slum children is again noted (see Table 6).

Responses that *increase* in frequency between first and third grades in the large

TABLE 5

AVERAGE PERCENTAGES OF PARADIGMATIC RESPONSES FOR
INTERACTIONS INVOLVING VERBS

	First Grade				Third Grade				Fifth Grade			
	White Int.		Negro Int.		White Int.		Negro Int.		White Int.		Negro Int.	
	Med. I.Q.	Low I.Q.	Med. I.Q.	Low I.Q.	Med. I.Q.	Low I.Q.	Med. I.Q.	Low I.Q.	Med. I.Q.	Low I.Q.	Med. I.Q.	Low I.Q.
High-freq........	29.7	29.1	25.9	27.5	52.8	49.4	56.3	40.9	47.8	70.0	72.8	62.5
Med.- freq......	24.1	21.9	17.2	18.1	30.9	26.3	35.0	26.9	50.9	40.0	42.8	37.8
Low-freq........	21.9	21.6	19.7	18.7	27.8	30.6	27.5	23.7	58.7	45.3	44.4	48.7
	White Int.		Negro Int.		White Int.		Negro Int.		White Int.		Negro Int.	
	White C.	Negro C.	Negro C.	White C.	White C.	Negro C.	Negro C.	White C.	White C.	Negro C.	Negro C.	White C.
Average........	25.4	23.9	18.5	23.9	38.2	34.4	35.5	34.6	65.3	60.1	48.5	54.5

children of high I.Q. (130) for both adverbs and pronouns. The relative positions of various I.Q. and racial slum groups are fairly consistent from grade to grade for both adverbs and pronouns. Suburban children are somewhat superior to slum children in paradigmatics to adverbs at fifth grade. With this exception, the findings altogether for pronouns and adverbs are reminiscent of findings for adjectives and verbs, respectively.

Development of high-frequency responses to nouns.—So far, only paradigmatic response rates have been considered. This section concerns primary responses (the single response with the highest frequency) to nouns, which show increments in suburban samples are arbitrarily defined as "mature," and the prevalence of "mature" responses in first-grade slum and suburban groups can be compared. For instance, the response "pepper" to "salt" increases in frequency from 44 per cent to 55 per cent in suburban children between first and third grades. First-grade slum children give this response 50 per cent of the time, and so in this primary response they are between first- and third-grade suburban children. All the responses listed in Table 6 increase in suburban children between first and third grades except "fly," "table," and "crayon," so all responses except these are mature. For the responses that decrease, "fly" and "table," the slum rates are lower than suburban rates, which is consistent with the notion that slum children are giving "more mature" responses. Slum children exceed suburban children at first grade on all other responses except for "color" and "bird." The suburban children are about ten points higher in average I.Q., a difference that would lead one to predict a higher rate for suburban children, rather than the reverse.

ban children for half of these noun responses.

Certain low-frequency words ("butterfly," "cocoon," etc.) must be heard infrequently by slum children, so one might guess that the lag displayed by slum children at third and fifth grades stems from reduced exposure to such words. The data do not support this. Suburban children of third and fifth grades are superior in terms

TABLE 6

Common Responses to Nouns (for High-Frequency and Medium-Frequency Stimuli)

Stimulus	Response	Suburban		Slum First Grade	
		First Grade	Third Grade	White	Negro
Bird	Fly	37.2	35.0	25.0	15.0
Chair	Table	20.8	18.9	15.0	15.0
Color	Red	12.1	18.9	10.0	20.0
	Crayon	8.6	0.0	10.0	0.0
Flower	Rose	6.4	12.9	20.0	15.0
Fly	Walk	0.0	17.2	20.0	0.0
Fruit	Apple	5.7	22.8	20.0	10.0
Hand	Arm	3.6	18.2	25.0	Finger 20.0*
Man	Woman	12.9	43.5	25.0	20.0
Music	Sing	11.4	12.9	10.0	Dance 20.0*
	Song	0.0	10.0	15.0	0.0
Ocean	Water	19.0	21.8	20.0	15.0
	Sea	10.0	40.0	15.0	0.0
River	Water	18.6	21.7	25.0	15.0
Salt	Pepper	44.3	56.4	50.0	40.0
Sheep	Lamb	15.7	22.5	35.0	30.0
Square	Circle	7.1	15.7	10.0	0.0
	Triangle	0.0	6.4	15.0	20.0
Table	Chair	36.1	51.4	60.0	30.0
Wing	Fly	22.5	39.0	25.0	15.0
	Bird	15.0	19.6	15.0	Chicken 10.0*

* High-frequency responses given by Negro children only, with high-frequency response of white children absent.

Negro slum children give some responses that are very different from white children —for instance, "chicken" to "bird," and "dance" to "music." Such differences may signify a different subcultural semantic structure and will be the topic of a future report. The Negro slum children do manifest many of the same mature responses as the white slum children ("triangle" in response to "square"), and the Negro slum children show rates *ahead* of white suburban children for half of these noun responses.

of high-frequency words as well as low-frequency words. Frequency does appear to be a more potent variable for slum children than suburban children, however, since ranges between high- and low-frequency stimuli for slum children are larger. Also, the interactions involving frequency noted with verbs suggest that young slum children may be exposed to the low-frequency stimuli on our list less often than suburban children. Frequency as currently measured (by counting occurrences of words in children's books) may not be appropriate for estimating frequencies of less common words of inner-city children. It turns out that slum children give the response "roach" six times as often as suburban children, for example.

DISCUSSION

The outcomes of this research we anticipated were: (1) again no difference between socioeconomic groups, or (2) a retardation in the slum groups because of their relatively greater cultural deprivation. Much evidence (paradigmatic responses to adjectives, verbs, pronouns, and adverbs, as well as primary responses to nouns, a measure independent of the others) suggests that first-grade white slum children are *more* advanced in linguistic development than suburban children of the same intelligence level.[12] To find slum children superior is both unanticipated and exciting because it raises important questions about cultural deprivation and also about the role of cultural factors in early linguistic development.

Previous work suggests that degree of urbanization may affect verbal development in young children. Briefly, it was found that rural Maryland children were behind suburban Maryland children; that Amish children residing in nearby areas of Pennsylvania were behind rural Maryland children; and that blue-collar and upper-middle-class suburban Maryland children, who dwelt in areas of similar urbanization, were about the same. Verbal interaction is probably less frequent for rural children

than for suburban children but equally likely for blue-collar and higher-status children. Customs of the Amish (little conversation between parents and children, lack of mass media, marked separation from neighbors, etc.) must discourage interaction even more than rural living per se, and this may account for the rural-Maryland Amish difference.

What characterizes inner-city living that could foster rapid early linguistic development? Homes are crowded, and television sets are practically universal. The slum child's verbal environment may be considerably enriched by television, and his almost unrestricted access to this medium may be the most important cause of the verbal acceleration we observe.[13] Also, there is little evidence to cite, but the pressures upon young slum children to become verbally proficient may be very powerful. Lower-class women are often employed, perhaps forcing the young slum child to acquire verbal skills because his needs must be met by persons other than his mother.

Psycholinguists, who have so far concentrated mainly on early childhood up to about age four, increasingly feel that language acquisition proceeds in line with some kind of internal monitoring.[14] To state the idea in an oversimplified way, the child is disposed to accept certain word orders and to ignore the numerous possibilities that do not occur. He seems genetically tuned to decode the sequences he hears. For simple verbal concepts, the verbal interaction required to support language acquisition activities may be more

---

[12] It seems likely that the "true" I.Q. of slum children testing at 100 may be higher than 100, yet test bias cannot account for the superiority of slum children because a test bias present at first grade could not evaporate by third grade. Third-grade children of average tested I.Q. should also be advanced on measures (verbs and adverbs) still displaying strong I.Q. differentials at age eight if the test-bias argument holds. This is not true; the slum children are behind on all measures by third grade, and then the medium-I.Q. slum children resemble the low-I.Q. suburban children.

[13] A more detailed discussion of television vis-à-vis subcultural differences in linguistic development is contained in Doris R. Entwisle, "Subcultural Differences in Children's Language Development," *International Journal of Psychology* (in press).

[14] See, for example, George A. Miller, "The Psycholinguists: On the New Scientists of Language," *Encounter*, XXIII (July, 1964), 29–37; Eric H. Lenneberg, *New Directions in the Study of Language* (Cambridge, Mass.: M.I.T. Press, 1966); David McNeill, "Developmental Psycholinguistics" (Cambridge, Mass.: Center for Cognitive Studies, Harvard University, 1966 [mimeographed]).

favorable for the very young slum child than for the suburban child.

In addition, the nature of interaction may favor the slum child. Hess and his associates[15] have observed verbal interaction occurring between Negro mothers and their preschool children from four social classes (college educated to welfare) as mothers attempt to teach their children simple conceptual tasks. Upper-status mothers use more speech, and more elaborate speech, than lower-class mothers, who use simple short sentences and gestures. Use of abstract words is directly related to social class level. The lower-class mothers are more apt to limit the range of choices open to the child and the time required to make a choice. Mothers differed little in affective elements of interaction, but greatly in the verbal and cognitive environments they presented to their children. Such class-specific modes of verbal interaction suggest how acquisition of early verbal skills could be aided at the expense of more sophisticated skills. The first-grade middle-class child could be temporarily at a disadvantage because exposure to more complicated models may not be optimum for acquisition of the very simplest concepts. Table 3 suggests this because the first-grade slum children, in spite of their general superiority, are *not* superior on low-frequency verbs.[16] At third grade, where they are generally inferior, the inferiority is much more noticeable for low-frequency verbs (20 per cent) than for high-frequency ones (7 per cent). In addition, at third grade, adverbs are noticeably depressed, especially for Negro children. Pronouns, by contrast, are not depressed at third grade,

[15] See Robert D. Hess and Virginia C. Shipman, "Early Experience and Socialization of Cognitive Modes in Children," *Child Development*, XXXVI (December, 1965), 869–86.

[16] This is consistent also with the observation that sheer exposure to speech at an early age is perhaps just as beneficial as expansions by the parent on incomplete utterances of the child (see Courtney B. Cazden, "Environmental Assistance to the Child's Acquisition of Grammar" [unpublished Ph.D. dissertation, Harvard University, 1965]).

and seemed to be the most highly developed of any form class at first grade. Pronouns are the most frequent class in spoken conversation, and their relative frequency must be higher for simple short interchanges than for complex utterances. Adverbs, on the other hand, express much more subtle meanings.

It is not clear what subcultural differences in verbal interaction could produce the Negro-white difference in paradigmatic rates. Dialect cleavage may operate when children are being interviewed (especially the youngest children). Middle-class Negro interviewers may differ more from lower-class Negro children than from lower-class white children because the speech of Negro college girls is more like that of the white community than the Negro slum. Dialect cleavage may also operate when the Negro preschooler attends to verbal models (mostly white speakers) presented via television.

Consistency with other data.—Our results are not so unexpected or so isolated as one might at first think. For instance, lower-class children of both races, when tested on comprehension of paragraphs of children's speech, do as well as middle-class children,[17] and lower-class and middle-class preschoolers[18] are equally good in applying morphological rules. Also, John,[19] using form-class matching in a word-association test as an index of maturity for first- and fifth-grade Negro children from lower-lower (slum), upper-lower, and middle-class families, finds no class differences at

[17] Martin Deutsch and Estelle Cherry-Peisach, "A Study of Language Patterns," *Instructor* (March, 1966). See also Estelle Cherry-Peisach, "Children's Comprehension of Teacher and Peer Speech," *Journal of Speech and Hearing Research* (in press).

[18] Thomas H. Shriner and Lynn Miner, "Morphological Structures in the Language of Disadvantaged and Advantaged Children," *Journal of Speech and Hearing Research* (in press).

[19] Vera P. John, "The Intellectual Development of Slum Children: Some Preliminary Findings," *American Journal of Orthopsychiatry*, XXXIII (October, 1963), 813–22.

first grade or fifth grade, although middle-class children have significantly larger vocabularies by fifth grade. I.Q. differences of from eight to eleven points favor middle-class over slum children in her study.

Linguistic differences associated with social class often fade away when I.Q. is held constant. In a study of speech quality in lower-class and middle-class children, variety of output in a timed speech sample showed a difference between lower-class and middle-class *only* when children also differed in I.Q.[20] Also, socioeconomic and class differences as reported on some parts of the Illinois test are very small and probably attributable to I.Q. bias, according to our re-analysis of some data for first-grade children obtained in Schenectady, New York.[21]

Actually there are few class differences in children's language behavior and general cognitive style that cannot be explained by the association between socioeconomic status and intellectual level. Although recent research points up the importance of environmental influences on the I.Q. a diffuse measure such as I.Q. does not lend itself either to fruitful hypothesis shaping or to fruitful practical recommendations. Little is done either to advance theory or to cope with current social problems by repeating I.Q. surveys of culturally deprived groups because two important questions are ignored: (1) whether there are differences in more specific areas of cognitive functioning, and (2) how such deficits (or advan-

tages) are related to specific features of the environment.

Our work shows that slum children are not retarded in a low-level kind of verbal functioning and, in fact, are probably advanced. To score at an average level on an I.Q. test while being advanced in one area (language) covered by the test might suggest that performance in other areas (number concepts, space perception) is below par. In checking this conjecture by comparing scores on the various subtests of the PMA, the verbal subtest was *not* consistently the highest, nor were there large differences in mental age between subtests. The implication is that smaller cognitive domains need to be investigated. Failure to identify specific areas and types of deficit may be one reason that programs for the culturally disadvantaged have so far had so little impact. The thrust of research needs to be toward considering social class a discrete set of experiences, and cognitive activities discrete processes. It has been repeatedly shown, for instance, that associative strength (measured by free-association response frequency) is an important determiner of recognition time or learning difficulty. If reading primers are constructed on the basis of middle-class response strengths that are inappropriate for lower-class semantic systems, then a further burden is given the lower-class child. This middle-class orientation is often pointed to, but little direct effort has been aimed at defining precisely what a lower-class orientation consists of. If, as our data mildly suggest, it is in the low-frequency verbal concepts and in the verb-adverb segments of language that slum children are most deficient, specific remedial efforts might be concentrated in these areas and directed toward older children in addition to the ones currently being attended to most in social action programs.

JOHNS HOPKINS UNIVERSITY

[20] Martin Deutsch, Alma Malirer, Bert Brown, and Estelle Cherry-Peisach, "Communication of Information in the Elementary School Classroom" (Cooperative Research Project No. 908 [Washington, D.C.: Office of Education, U.S. Department of Health, Education, and Welfare, 1964]).

[21] Vito M. Gioia, "A Comparison of Language Abilities in First-Grade Children from Differing Socioeconomic Groups" (unpublished Ph.D. dissertation, St. John's University, New York, 1965).

CURRICULUM STRATEGY BASED ON THE PERSONALITY CHARACTERISTICS OF DISADVANTAGED YOUTH

Virgil A. Clift

Virgil A. Clift, "Curriculum Stategy Based on the Personality Characteristics of Disadvantaged Youth," *Journal of Negro Education,* Spring 1969, pp. 94-104.

CURRICULUM STRATEGY BASED ON THE PERSONALITY CHARACTERISTICS OF DISADVANTAGED YOUTH

Virgil A. Clift

Listed below are characteristics one may expect to find among disadvantaged youth. Certainly no one individual would be expected to be characterized by all of these traits. It is true, however, that teachers who are working with typical classes where a large number of disadvantaged youth are enrolled will be able to identify many students who can be characterized by traits listed here.

In a very real sense, the traits listed represent disabilities, handicaps, or disadvantages which the individual has that make it very difficult, and almost always impossible, for him to function in school up to an acceptable level. Unless the teacher is able to ameliorate these ·problems, teaching does not produce desired results. All of the love the teacher may have for poor children, all of the respect she may be able to muster for minority children, all of the "hip" language she may use with children, and all of the other similar tricks and devices she may employ, are of no avail. Instead, the successful teacher of the disadvantaged must be a clinician who can help young people deal with traits or factors we know to be limiting the ability of these children to learn.

This being true, the daily teaching act, class period after class period, must focus on ameliorating traits or problems characteristic of the disadvantaged. Social studies, language arts, and all other areas of study must be organized and presented, in terms of content and method, so as to help students deal realistically with special characteristics peculiar to their personalities.

Characteristics presented here represent what the individual is like as a person. The next step is .to spell out objectives in each area or course the student pursues in school, grade by grade. These objectives must be specific, definitive and relate directly to helping the student solve or ameliorate personal problems.[1]

The traits or problems presented in this paper have been grouped under· three headings: (1) factors of personality, (2) factors of cognitive function, and (3) factors in relation to educational values.

It is often the case that subject matter in one field can be used more effectively than that from other fields to help students overcome certain of their specific problems. The task confronting the teacher is to select objectives which help students deal with their personal problems and at the same time help them to acquire essential knowledge. For example, the *Diary of Anne Frank, The Life of George Washington Carver,* or the *Life of Hans Christian Anderson* may do much more to help the youngster with a deeply ingrained negative self-image

---

[1] See: Benjamine S. Bloom, *et al., Taxonomy of Educational Objectives,* New York: David McKay Co., Inc. 1956; Robert F. Mager, *Preparing Educational Objectives.* Palo Alto: Fearon Publishers, 1962.

than some things currently being required. On the other hand, if we know the disadvantaged youngster tends to be more present-oriented and less aware of past-present sequences, we should try to modify our approach to teaching history and refrain from a total emphasis on chronological order which might remove the student 2,000 years from the present, when in reality, he may not be able to place events of five years ago in their proper relationship with those of five months ago. All of this is to emphasize that after objectives have been formulated, the next step is to select meaningful subject matter to achieve the objectives.

In the process just described there are three steps:

(1) Become acquainted with the traits or problems which characterize the disadvantaged child. Be able to recognize these in students.[2]

(2) State objectives for the course, subject area, and daily lessons which give greatest promise of relating directly to individual characteristics and to essential knowledge to be learned in a course or subject.

(3) Organize the subject, course, and daily lesson in a way that will make possible the achievement of the objectives.

For years educators have emphasized that we must "start where the students are." Characteristics of disadvantaged youth listed in this paper represent "where" these students are. It is the established consensus among teachers that all teaching must be related to objectives. Yet it is precisely in this area that all education is vulnerable because too often objectives are woefully inadequate, and sometimes meaningless.

Hopefully, one of the benefits which seems certain to come from our efforts to educate the disadvantaged will be more articulate statements of objectives. Another benefit will be a more systematic selection of subject matter to achieve educational objectives for individuals who bring to the learning situation different backgrounds of experience.

Educators often write about disadvantaged youth and their education as if there is something strange, mysterious and baffling about them. It will be helpful to remember that the disadvantaged are human beings, responding as any other human beings would respond, had they been exposed to the environment and forces the disadvantaged have. We come now to the traits which characterize disadvantaged youth.

EXPECTED CHARACTERISTICS OF CULTURALLY DISADVANTAGED YOUTH[3]

A. *Factors of Personality.*

1. He may exhibit negative feelings about his personal worth.

2. As a result of prolonged feelings of negative self-esteem, he may come to feel self-hatred and a rejection of his own ethnic, racial, national, or family group, but not his peer group.

3. Boys from certain disadvantaged groups (Negroes in particular) may suffer from role confusion and be completely

---

2 The major part of this paper is devoted to this step in the detailed enumeration of traits under the caption Expected Characteristics of Culturally Disadvantaged Youth.

3 Characteristics listed here were derived from related research, the behavioral sciences, and studies in connection with *Project APEX* at New York University.

unsure of their worth as a result of living in a matriarchal society.

4. He may suffer from the disorganizing impact of mobility, transiency, and similar factors which are caused by the fact that he is of minority status.

5. He may have absorbed some of the mental and emotional problems which are more commonly found in his family and peer-group than in the population as a whole.

6. He may feel frightened as a result of early emotional or physical abandonment by his parents.

7. Since the peer group exerts much greater influence on him at a much earlier age than in middle-class surroundings, he may reflect their values almost completely and have no sense of relating to an adult world.

8. He may have unrealistically high levels of *expressed* academic and vocational aspirations, which are an attempt to bolster his flagging self-esteem.

9. He will usually show, however, *low* levels of aspiration when concrete action is needed. This is very often a result of negative feelings toward himself and repeated attempts that have ended in failure.

10. His need for immediate financial independence because of early desatellization from his parents may make him emotionally unable to consider any form of education or training that will make him temporarily unable to be self-supporting. He may be emotionally unable to accept the idea of receiving money from his parents during the time that would be necessary for him to finish school.

11. He may exhibit an even greater fear of the unknown than is normal for children of his age group. He may respond to any new situation negatively.

12. He may show signs of an authoritarian personality which has been absorbed from his parents. This personality complex includes the need to dominate or be dominated, a tendency to view people as "in-groups" and "out-groups", relative resistance to change, or belief in a supernatural power which will eventually regulate the problems which the child faces. An authoritarian person is apt to be more ethocentric and prejudiced than others are.

13. Having grown up in an authoritarian home, in many cases, the child may seek an authoritarian leader in school. At the same time, he will evidence an underlying hostility toward authority of any kind, which will create ambivalent feelings and reactions.

14. He may show anxiety at having to work with two systems of values. The fact that in his culture certain actions or ways of living are accepted, but are rejected by the world of the school, may lead to confusion and hostility toward one or both of the systems of values.

15. He may respond primarily with anxiety to any threatening situation and may attempt to solve problems by repeated withdrawal.

16. He may indicate reactions of lethargy, apathy, and submission in any situation which he does not feel capable of mastering. These are usually suppressed feelings of aggression.

17. His massive anxiety and confusion may result in his being unable to maintain one kind of activity or reaction, and periods of submission (suppressed hostil-

ity) may alternate with periods of strong aggression and hostility.

18. He may show his feelings of resentment and hostility toward the rejecting majority group (the white middle class, in general).

19. If he feels unable to show his hostility, he may turn to reaction formation, where he will seemingly adopt the ideals and values of the majority culture, to the exclusion of other members of his own group.

20. His feelings of anxiety and sense of failure may lead him to withdraw from competition in the larger American scene, especially in relation to any activities that characterize the middle class.

21. He may show self-deprecatory reactions in any situation.

22. He may be prone to delinquent behavior because of family disorganization.

23. He may evidence feelings of shame about his family background which makes it more difficult for him to relate to others.

24. He may have deep-seated anxiety about achievement in any domain.

25. He may exhibit a complete lack of ego-involvement in school, and thus he may be a target for easy failure. This is due partly to the fact that the school, as he knows it, is completely incapable of meeting his emotional needs or helping him with his problems.

26. He may have built up a "fight for what is mine" psychology.

27. He may be rude and uncouth.

28. He sometimes shows little restraint and has few inhibitions.

29. He may be keenly sensitive to insult.

30. His major goals may seem to be "to grow up and get by."

31. He may be unconsciously bent toward self-destruction.

32. Companionship in the gang may be sought to make up for elements missing in family structure.

33. He may have a sense of values that is not only different from that of the middle class, but that may be beyond the comprehension of middle-class observers.

34. He may show no fear of personal injury, may have been encouraged to fight and not to be intimidated by police or others. In fact, he may have learned that this is the only thing that works with the slum landlord, the slum merchant, the dishonest bill collector, and the crooked cop.

35. He may have enjoyed so little attention and affection that he responds quite differently from the middle-class child when praised for success in school. He may have never experienced success and the gratifying feelings of success and security. He may be expected to respond differently from his middle-class counterpart for whom these have become a way of life.

36. He may be extremely bitter and justifiably so.

37. He may have a general feeling of being "hemmed-in" and as a result may crave excitement.

38. He frequently knows that he has been stereotyped as "dumb", "ignorant" or "worthless" and is hurt internally as a result.

39. He may be loud and boisterous

due in part to life style, or as a means of attracting attention, or because of lack of self restraint, or because he is excited due to anxiety, etc.

40. He may "giggle," exhibit loud laughter, and find humor in things that may not be the least bit funny to middle-class children who have enjoyed an entirely different background of experience.

41. He may have learned to make heavy use of survival skills needed for protection in the slum streets and in the gang. He may not know that the middle-class system expects a different kind of behavior.

42. The successful disadvantaged child may experience considerable trauma because he operates in terms of survival skills when in the slum environment, and in terms of accepting social skills of the middle class when in school. The successful disadvantaged child must operate in two very different worlds at the same time and thus develops two distinct personalities. As a result, he may on occasions be characterized as schizophrenic or may become disgusted or traumatized by all the hypocrisy and act out in various ways.

43. He may cope with authority figures by maintaining appropriate social distance, and by interacting with these figures on the basis of the formalized role rather than as persons.

44. He may feel himself the object of derision and disparagement and unworthy of succorance, affection, praise, etc., and may for that reason reject efforts of teachers and counselors to offer helpful encouragement or praise.

B. *Factors of Cognitive Function*

1. Even if high levels of perceptual sensitization and discrimination are present, these skills tend to be developed better in physical behavior than in visual, and better in visual behavior than in aural.

2. They tend to lack any high degree of dependence on verbal and written language for cognitive cues.

3. Many disadvantaged youth have not adopted receptive and expressive modes traditional to and necessary for success in school.

4. Their time-orientation varies from that expected for school. It is less consistent with reality.

5. They are characteristically *slower* than middle-class children in cognitive function.

6. They do not have good powers of concentration.

7. They are not generally persistent in problem-solving tasks.

8. They characteristically score low in recognition of perceptual similarities.

9. They tend to ignore difficult problems with a "so what" attitude.

10. They depend more on external than internal control of things.

11. They tend to have a more passive approach to problem-solving tasks.

12. Culturally deprived children have a restricted variety of stimuli to foster development of cognitive processes.

13. The particular stimuli they receive are less systematic, less sequenced. They are, therefore, less useful to growth and activation of cognitive potential.

14. They are limited by both the "formal" and "contentual" aspects of cognitive development. ("Formal" aspects are

those operations or behaviors by which stimuli are perceived. They have poorly developed auditory, visual, tactile aspects. "Contentual" aspects mean the actual content of knowledge and comprehension).

15. They lack in environmental information.

16. They have a poor general and environmental orientation.

17. Their concepts of comparability and relativity are not appropriately developed for their age level.

18. They lack ability to use adults as sources of information for satisfying curiosity.

19. They lack an ability to sustain attention.

20. They are farther away from their maturational ceiling as a result of experimental poverty. Therefore, they have poorer performance on I.Q. tests, and the tests tend to be poor indicators of their basic abilities.

21. They generally have not developed a concept of expectation of reward for accumulation of knowledge, task completion, or delaying gratification.

22. They have difficulty in seeing themselves in the past or in a different context.

23. Evidence indicates that they tend to be more present-oriented and less aware of past-present sequences.

24. They have difficulty working with time limitations.

25. They tend to have difficulty in handling items related to time judgments.

26. They are poor in judging figure-ground relationships.

27. Their spatial organization of the visual field may be impaired.

28. They may have memory disorders. Adults generally link past and present for children by calling to mind prior shared experiences. In lower-class homes they generally neglect to do this.

29. A combination of constriction in use of language and in shared activity with adults results in much less stimulation of early memory function.

30. The assignments that they receive at home tend to be motoric, short in time-span, and more likely to relate to very concrete objects. This is not attuned to school demands.

31. They usually experience a minimum of non-instructional conversation at home.

32. The lower-class home is not a verbally-oriented home. They, therefore, have little opportunity to hear concepts verbalized.

33. The ability to formulate questions is essential to data gathering in formulation of concepts of the world. Questions are not encouraged in their environment and are not responded to; therefore, this function does not mature.

34. They lack *training* in listening to a variety of verbal materials.

35. They lack an opportunity to observe high quality adult language use.

36. They learn inattention to sound, and "tune out" sounds; thus much of the talk they hear becomes "noise."

37. Lower-class children tend to differ from middle-class children in the definitions of common nouns. They give largely functional definitions. This is prominent at every age level.

38. One of the major differences between culturally deprived and non-culturally deprived children, is that the culturally deprived have a slower increase in use of formal (generic) responses and tend to use a high proportion of functional responses.

39. They are handicapped in anticipatory language skills, i.e., the correct anticipation of sequence of language and thought made possible by knowledge of context and syntactical regularities of a language.

40. They are most probably maturationally ready for more complex language functioning than they have achieved.

41. Speech sequences in lower-class homes tend to be temporarily very limited and poorly structured syntactically.

42. They may have a deficit in language development in subject continuity.

43. They have more expressive language ability than generally emerges in the classroom.

44. They are at a disadvantage when precise and somewhat abstract language is required for the solution of a problem.

45. It is possible that the absence of well-structured routine and activity in the home is reflected in difficulty in structuring language.

46. Their language development often lags behind their perceptual development.

47. The deprived child may not have the following types of information: his name, address, city, rudimentary concept of number relationships, differences between near and far, high and low, etc.

48. They have a tendency to concrete rather than symbolic approaches to problem solving.

49. They lack training in experimenting with identifying objects and having corrective feedback.

50. Their reading abilities are affected by poor auditory and visual discrimination.

51. Their general level of responsiveness is dulled.

52. They often have difficulty with the verb form "to be."

53. Often they have difficulty with subject and verb agreement.

54. They tend to use action verbs.

55. Usually they have difficulty in defining, comparing, judging, generalizing, etc.

56. They may have difficulty with auditory sequential memory.

57. A different perceptual disposition may be carried over into verbal expression, memory, concept formation, learning and problem solving.

58. There is a high level of undetected mental insufficiency among disadvantaged youth due to poor pre-natal care and environmental influences.

59. The thought process is more often inductive rather than deductive.

60. There is often little or no understanding of rewards that are not tangible or situations that are not "felt."

61. The home situation is ideal for disadvantaged youth to learn inattention. There is a minimum of constructive conversation and a maximum of non-instructional conversation directed toward the child, and most of it is in the background of confusion. Results: poor auditory discrimination, a skill very important to reading.

62. They have great difficulty in organizing response tempo to meet time limitations imposed by teachers. Middle-class teachers organize days by allowing certain amounts of time for each activity. The teacher may not realize that her view of time as life's governor may not be shared by all segments of society.

63. In disadvantaged homes, there is no setting of tasks for children, observing their performance, and rewarding of their completion in some way — nor is there disapproval if they do not perform properly or when they leave something unfinished. Much classroom organization is based on the assumption that children anticipate rewards for performance and will respond in these terms to tasks which are set for them.

64. The disadvantaged youth is not accustomed to using adults as a source for information, correction, reality testing as in problem solving, and for absorption of new knowledge. They have difficulty in relating to the teacher, therefore.

65. They are not prepared to question, or to demand clarification.

66. They do not come to school with verbal fluency which serves as a foundation for reading skills, and conceptual verbal activity. They have difficulty communicating with teachers.

67. They quickly lose interest in school if unsuccessful. This is due to weak ego development which they bring to school.

68. They have less deep-seated anxiety with respect to internalized needs for academic achievement and vocational prestige than middle-class children.

69. They may exhibit retarded academic growth as a result of actually having received poorer instruction and less instruction than other students. Slum schools have greater teacher turnover, more inexperienced teachers. This is also due to geographic mobility of low-income families.

70. They place greater stress on such values as money and tend to prefer agricultural, mechanical, domestic service, and clerical pursuits.

71. They make lower vocational interest scores in the literacy, esthetic, persuasive, scientific, and business areas than do middle-class adolescents.

72. They learn inattention in the preschool environment, and their level of responsiveness diminishes steadily. This is disasterous for structural learning situations in school.

C. *Factors in Relation to Educational Values*

1. There is no or very little interest in reading which is so valued by school. Reading is not valued or considered necessary in their environment.

2. They have not learned or been encouraged to concentrate, to persist in their studies, to have a long attention span. Teachers, therefore, often tend to term them stupid.

3. They have no feeling that economic position can be improved through effort and sacrifice.

4. They have no pressure to maintain a reputation for honesty, responsibility, and respectability.

5. They often do not focus on individual advancement, self-denial, and competent performance which leads to esteem for formal education, rationality, controlled and respectable behavior, hard

work, all of which are values of middle class parents, schools, and children.

6. They have no severe standards against aggression. Control of behavior is seen to have little relevance to social success or job maintenance.

7. They often recognize that they are not considered as "good" as middle class students who have been taught to control anger, inhibit direct aggression, etc., but they do not know why they are not considered as "good" as middle class students.

8. Cultural values which impinge upon them in school are meaningless.

9. Facts of a changing economy (decrease in menial or manual jobs) seem remote and external to them.

10. They display hostility to teachers and school administrators because they represent authority figures. They are often hostile toward any authority figures that they know have imposed constraints and administered punishments.

11. They lack an understanding of middle class teachers' mode of operation: kindness is misinterpreted as weakness; results in a disorientation as to how they should act.

12. They are used to unsupervised play, little parental influence, etc. Therefore, they are rebellious to the restrictiveness of school regulations.

13. They do not try to please teachers as a result of short term dependence on parents. They are not used to striving for parental approval.

14. They feel conflicts between personal interests, e.g., earning money, being with friends, wandering around, etc., and the goals and time demands of school.

15. They are often used to a mother who maintains considerable social and emotional distance from her children. They feel threatened when a teacher does not maintain this distance.

16. They are used to a mother who desires unquestioned domination over them with suppressive forms of control. Thus they often do not understand the coaxing atmosphere of school and school officials.

17. They have fear and suspicion of school. This stems from the general feeling of their segment of society: disengagement, nonintegration, mistrust with respect to major institutions of the large society.

18. They have little desire to work for far-distant goals of a college education, etc., when they know most of it is impossible. Result: lack of motivation.

19. They have even greater hostility toward school because their values and segment of society are threatened by school. They are aware of negative opinions the school has of them and their families. They know society looks down on "unmarried mothers," families on welfare, etc.

20. They are limited in terms of experience and gross knowledge as compared with middle class students due to a restricted environment. The result in school is failure after failure, increased sense of inferiority, and a more negative self-image. Their solution is to drop out.

21. Their status among their family and friends is not dependent on academic achievement, and academic achievement often has the opposite effect.

22. They come from an environment

that does not provide examples and models of social skills and work habits essential for success in school. The home does not teach initiative, creativity, and self-reliance — qualities which are rewarded at school.

23. Their cognitive style is not geared to academic work. Failure is practically guaranteed.

24. Misunderstanding and alienation are often inevitable because initiation into sex comes early for disadvantaged youth. School officials may consider them "immoral" for such things.

25. When a school population is composed entirely of a single ethnic group, or ethnically mixed, but culturally disadvantaged group, there are often not enough academically successful students to form a strong sub-group to withstand pressures of street gangs.

26. When the school population is mixed, a slum child is often barred from social membership in the group of academically successful students, and may find the risk of identifying with its values too great.

27. They are generally unfamiliar with tools confronted in school due to scarcity of objects of all types, but especially of books, toys, puzzles, pencils, and scribbling paper, in their homes.

28. They and their parents have no or little knowledge of the opportunities available in the middle and upper employment classifications. They have no way of learning incidentally or otherwise the basic skills, life style, and prerequisities for moving up the socio-economic ladder.

29. Parents and relatives most times feel it unbelievable that the child has potential or ability to raise above their own status in life; therefore, they tend to reinforce whatever apathy already exists.

30. They seldom if ever gain status and recognition from peers for academic attainment and success.

31. Higher education, technical education, etc., are thought to be prohibitive because of costs and ability to succeed.

32. They have little appreciation for beauty in art, music, drama, etc., and have generally become accustomed to a disorganized, cluttered personal environment.

33. They treasure items of immediate need and access to them.

34. They may have warped personalities and personality problems which stem from an inhospitable environment and make it impossible for them to function in a school environment.

35. The kinds of rewards the school gives have no meaning for them. They may feel just as well off without them.

36. They may conceive of their school and teachers as being of little worth or much less worth than other schools and other teachers (especially if they are segregated Negro schools or schools in depressed areas).

37. They often gain status among peers and in the community if they are disobedient and defy school regulations and school authority.

38. The life style, language and values of the educated person are so different from that of the disadvantaged child that he feels completely out of place with a person who is so different from him. It seems impossible and inconceivable that the teacher could have anything in common with him or really care for him.

39. They often have little pride in the American heritage and do not feel in any way related to it.

40. American heroes, traditions, institutions, etc., provide little inspiration. They see no way of emulating any of the great or even moderately successful men of the present or past.

41. They have usually had no help in evaluating their own potential ability and aptitude. They often have no realistic yardstick with which to measure their own personal resources.

42. They may show little respect for school property and even be destructive of it.

43. What appears to be faulty and poor judgment may be the result of woefully inadequate experience and a lack of information or facts on which to make valid judgments.

44. They may express fantasy on many levels.

45. They often tend to confuse kindness on the part of the teacher with weakness.

46. They may be prone to prejudices and "scapegoating."

47. Social-psychological obstacles may confront them due to the unreality of the text book world when it is put along side their own world.

48. School often interferes with present gratification in terms of peer status, earning power, and independence. It is often a place where they must return day after day to failure and to social situations where they are relegated to the lowest possible status.

49. They may revolt against school regulations and society by becoming delinquent which often helps them to become a member of the "in-group" and protects them against isolation in their real world.

50. Excessive success in school may be fraught with dangers from their peer group.

51. A tight social group is often developed among friends and provides security and solidarity. Their behavior, speech patterns, and values conflict with those of the school and thus the school is rejected.

52. The social systems operating in the school reject them and they have no techniques of becoming a part of any "in-group" that values academic achievement.

53. They see too much evidence and can point to too many examples that convince them that teachers and counselors dislike them, have no confidence in their ability to succeed, and do not respect their worth as individuals.

THE MEASUREMENT OF INTELLECTUAL CAPACITY AND PERFORMANCE

Winton H. Manning

Winton H. Manning, "The Measurement of Intellectual Capacity and Performance," *Journal of Negro Education,* Summer 1968, Vol. 37, pp. 258-267.

THE MEASUREMENT OF
INTELLECTUAL CAPACITY AND PERFORMANCE

Winton H. Manning

But the circle of our understanding
Is a very restricted area.
Except for a limited number
Of strictly practical purposes
We do not know what we are doing;
And even, when you think of it,
We do not know much about thinking.
What is happening outside the circle?

T.S. ELIOT

One of the ironies of the past decade has been the increasingly strident criticism of standardized tests by persons who see these measures as bulwarks of bias whose use denies equality of education and job opportunity to Negroes and other minority groups disproportionately represented in the poverty population. To be sure, some effects of these criticisms have been beneficial by stimulating among the research community an increased interest in bringing test methodology into a closer and potentially more productive relationship with educational and psychological theory.[1] The irony arises from the fact that objective tests of ability have historically been regarded in this country as useful social instruments in building a society based upon merit and accomplishment rather than on inherited privilege and social origins. Coupled with the disaffection expressed by spokesmen for the disadvantaged has been the decrying of tests by some persons whose concerns are mainly directed toward reforms within secondary and higher education. Some of these persons feel that tests do more harm than good in that they serve to reinforce an obsolete way of valuing human talent, and that insofar as they might be used as a tool of discrimination against, for example, creative people, they would also serve to perpetuate a system which is characterized as manipulative, coercive, intimidating, and authoritarian. Even more provocative is the view that tests represent a conceptualization of the structure of knowledge and how it is acquired by students that is at variance with their own perceptions and increasingly out of touch with the language and experience of young people.

It is not the purpose of this paper to explore the anatomy of the criticisms of testing; others already have dealt extensively with this topic.[2] However, no discussion of the problem of measuring intellectual performance and capacity as it relates to race and strivings for equality in American education can fail to recognize that today the spectre of these criticisms haunts any discussion of tests.

---

1 Anne Anastasi, "Psychology, Psychologists, and Psychological Testing," *American Psychologist*, XXII (April, 1967), 297-306.

2 Donald W. Fiske, "The Subject Reacts to Tests," *American Psychologist*, XXII (April, 1967), pp. 287-296; David Goslin, "Criticism of Standardized Tests and Testing, *Commission on Tests: Background Papers* (New York: College Entrance Examination Board, in press), pp. 33-65; Ann Pasanella, Winton H. Manning, and Nurham Findikvan "Bibliography of Test Criticism," *Commission on Tests: Background Papers* (New York: College Entrance Examination Board, in press, pp. 73-127.

My own perception of the problem has been influenced greatly over the past year by working on the staff of the Commission on Tests of the College Entrance Examination Board. The Commission on Tests is an independent body of distinguished teachers, researchers, writers and administrators that has been charged to conduct a three-year inquiry into present testing practices in education and to recommend changes in the nature of tests or their use which the Commission, in its own judgment, considers desirable or necessary to the enhancement of educational opportunity.

It is particularly appropriate for the College Board to sponsor such an inquiry because its efforts to enlarge access to higher education have historically found their chief expressions in the development of tests for college admissions. The nature of educational examinations — their definition, relevance, and equity — has important implications for a variety of sectors of our society. They serve as one of the critical determiners of the careers of young people, thereby touching the lives of many persons. They are highly visible examples of social science in action, and therefore must represent the best these sciences may offer to this problem. They are a principal means by which most schools and colleges appraise their students, and their influence on the life of these institutions, though subtle, is therefore pervasive. Further, in a nation and economy whose continued growth increasingly depends upon nurturing its human resources, tests are potent influences on the flow of talent through the educational system, and hence on the vitality of our national life.[3]

The Commission on Tests has not yet reached the halfway point in its inquiry and it would be premature for me to judge the tenor or character of its recommendations. What follows in this paper, therefore, should be understood to reflect the views of the author and only indirectly the deliberations of the Commission, although I freely acknowledge the stimulation and ideas I have received from its members.[4]

FUNCTIONS OF TESTS IN EDUCATION

Tests have become an integral part of the entire education process,[5] and any description of the functions they perform must necessarily be brief and partial. In general, the use of tests in education has ostensibly supported the objectives of both individual students and of institutions, although it is plainly evident that information systems derived from tests operate asymmetrically in respect to the needs and interests of these two parties. In brief, we may identify six functions of tests — three which are mainly in the interests of students, and three which are mainly in the interests of institutions. These are: (1) *Guidance functions* — the

---

[3] Kingsley Davis, "The Role of Class Mobility in Economic Development," *Population Review*, VI (July, 1962), 67-73; and Phillips Cutright, "Occupational Inheritance: A Cross-National Analysis," *American Journal of Sociology*, LXXIII (1968), 400-416.

[4] I would particularly like to express my gratitude to Professor David Tiedeman to whose counsel I am indebted.

[5] B. Alden Thresher has commented on the ubiquity of standardized tests within education by drawing a parallel between the testing movement and the development of the automobile; both began in minor ways in France at the turn of the century, both products were seized by Americans and thereafter produced and improved at an astonishing rate, both have become indispensible to the conduct of affairs in our society, and both have in recent years aroused grave doubts and frustrations as to their ultimate effects!

use of tests in information systems designed to foster a sense of planfulness, orderliness, and continuity within the careers of students. (2) *Elective functions* — the use of tests as alternative means for certification of competence for students whose preparation, background, or purposes are different from the majority of students — e.g. high school equivalency examinations and the College-Level Examination Program for unaffiliated adult students. (3) *Educative functions* — the use of tests as a part of the learning process so that a student may find an independent portrayal of his own attainments within the conceptual framework represented by the test itself. Fuller development of this function may be expected to coincide with more general use of computer aided instruction and testing. (4) *Selective and distributive functions* — the use of tests by institutions as a basis for systems of selection or classification designed to provide harmonizing of student characteristics and institutional resources and objectives. (5) *Prescriptive functions* — the use of tests by institutions as a basis for prescribing educational treatments designed to maximize attainment of desired educational outcomes, especially the effective remediation of educational deficits. (6) *Evaluative functions* — the use of tests by institutions to evaluate the effectiveness of their educational programs, and to provide a basis for comparison of educational outcomes with recognized standards or appropriate reference groups.

Major criticism of tests has tended to focus principally upon selective and evaluative functions of tests presumably because these are probably most salient from the standpoint of guaranteeing equality of opportunity. What is perhaps not generally recognized is that widespread application of measurement systems has also led to tests having acquired a *societal function*, in which the sample of behavior that constitutes the test (and hence scores deriving from it) comes to connote a view of man and the nature of human intellect that has important consequences as these influence social values regarding the worth of the individual and the dignity of various forms of work. This "aggrandizement" of the function of testing lies at the root of much of the antipathy expressed by the public, and in subtle ways has probably influenced educators and social scientists. The societal conception of the meaning of tests is related to a view that such measures tap innate, fixed, and predetermined human characteristics. Hunt[6] has reviewed this problem and offered constructive alternatives that are fortunately gaining increasingly wide acceptance.

From the perspective of the societal function of tests, a test score comes to be regarded by a student as a reward bestowed on him by the educational system. Pehaps even this fragmentary and biased perception of tests would not present an insuperable problem if he also believed and understood, as Kingsley Davis[7] has observed, that "there are two conditions that produce class mobility: inequality of rewards and equality of opportunity." But in the case of Negro youth impacted in the urban ghetto there is ample evidence of inequality of educational opportunity and immobility of social class. In the face of this, should anyone be surprised that hostility should be expressed toward tests as symbols of

---

6 J. McV. Hunt, *Intelligence and Experience* (New York: Ronald Press, 1961).

7 Kingsley Davis, *op. cit.*, p. 72.

inequality of the rewards bestowed by a rigid, repressive system?

By no means, however, has there been universal denunciation of tests by those concerned with breaking down the barriers to full and equal opportunity for participation in society. Speaking before the Commission on Tests, Kenneth Clark said:

> If I were doing any studies now . . . concerned with getting the American people to understand the enormity of the injustice inherent in differential educational quality of our biracial school systems, I would search for the most rigorous, objective, standardized test that was relevant to the question of educational achievement, and I would administer it to all of the children in public schools. [Then] I would present . . . the stark differential results and say to the American people: 'This is what you are doing by way of damming up human potential and human resources . . . You can either continue this and know . . . that you are spawning hundreds of thousands of human casualties, or you can make the necessary changes in the educational system to narrow this gap and, hopefully, obviate it.'[8]

When one places Kenneth Clark's statement next to the condemnations so frequently heard today, it starkly illustrates the paradoxical status of tests. Even more importantly, its implications throw out a challenge to the scientific community to provide rigorous, objective, standardized tests that will not only delineate the educational damage that Clark has pointed out, but also will provide a basis for educational diagnosis and treatment that will truly promote an unfolding of human potentialities in all children. It is my own feeling that present tests are demonstrably useful for a large number of practical purposes, including describing the effects of inequality of educational opportunity, but unless the theoretical basis on which tests are constructed is fundamentally changed they offer limited promise for indicating the ways that this damaged and wasted human potential can be recovered,. Unless tests are constructed to reveal the cognitive processes of the child, rather than simply the content and outcome of those processes, there is little hope that we can use them for educational prescription. To aim for testing systems that provide individual educational diagnosis and prescription is perhaps too grand or too remote an objective, but the possibility is real enough to warrant serious consideration.

The Interpretation of Test Score Differences

One of the benefits of extensive debate and reassessment of the status of tests has been the growth of sophistication in the use of such terms as "aptitude," "achievement," and "intelligence." It is not that these terms have become more finely differentiated in their meaning, but rather that distinctions formerly assumed to exist have fortunately become blurred so that terms such as "developed ability" are coming into more extensive use. This is not to say that it may not be useful to distinguish at times between aptitude and achievement, as does Kendrick[9] on the basis of relative susceptibility of im-

8 Kenneth Clark, Testimony before the Commission on Tests, meeting of June 6, 1967 in Washington, D. C.

9 S. A. Kendrick, "The Coming Segregation of Our Selective Colleges," *College Board Review*, No. 66, (Winter, 1967-68), 6-12.

provement as a result of direct tuition, or as does Shaycoft[10] upon the extent to which the measure is used to describe past accomplishment (achievement) or predict future performance (aptitude).

Data from a large number of studies comparing performance of Negro and white children on standardized tests of intelligence demonstrate differences which are very substantial.[11] Recently the widely discussed survey of equality of educational opportunity has documented still further the extent of the disparity in scores of Negro and white children on a variety of achievement and ability measures — verbal ability, non-verbal ability, reading comprehension, mathematics achievement, and general information in practical arts, natural science, social science and humanities.[12] In general, these studies suggest that by the twelfth grade averages for Negro students are about one standard deviation below averages of white students. This may be contrasted with the report by Nancy

Bayley[13] on the mental and motor test scores of infants, in which she found no differences between Negroes and whites at any period of development between birth and fifteen months in mental ability, and a slight superiority for Negro children in motor development throughout the first year. That mental test score differences do exist by the start of schooling and that the relative disadvantage of Negro children accumulates over time as a consequence of the differential school, family, cultural, and environmental milieu accompanying segregation, poverty and slums seems compelling in view of what we know about the effects of social and environmental factors on intellectual growth.[14]

An alternative hypothesis is, of course, that standardized tests of developed abilities and achievement are biased, or more reasonably, that present tests are so constituted that a very substantial portion of differences between Negro and white children is associated with factors specific to the white middle-class culture, thus falsely enhancing apparent differences between these two groups.

The subject of test bias is too complex to undertake extensive discussion in this review. For over forty years the question of bias in various kinds of tests has been

---

[10] Marion Shaycoft, *The High School Years: Growth in Cognitive Skills*, (Interim Report 3, Project TALENT, American Institute for Research, University of Pittsburgh, 1967), pp. 5-12.

[11] Audrey M. Shuey, *The Testing of Negro Intelligence*, Second Edition, (New York: Social Science Press, 1966) Wallace A. Kennedy, Vernon Van deRiet, and James White, "A Normative Sample of Intelligence and Achievement of Negro Elementary Children in the Southeastern United States," *Monographs of the Society for Research in Child Development*, XXVIII (1963), No. 6; Arthur R. Jensen, "Social Class, Race, and Genetics: Implications for Education," *American Educational Research Journal*, V (January, 1968), 1-42; and Susan S. Stodolsky and Gerald S. Lesser, "Learning Patterns in the Disadvantaged," *Harvard Educational Review*, XXXVII (Fall, 1967), 546-593.

[12] James S. Coleman *et al. Equality of Educational Opportunity*, (Washington, D. C.: U. S. Government Printing Office, 1966).

[13] Nancy Bayley, "Comparison of Mental and Motor Test Scores for Ages 1-15 Months by Sex, Birth Order, Race, Geographical Location, and Education of Parents," *Child Development*, XXXVI, (1965), 379-411.

[14] Cynthia Deutsch, "Learning in the Disadvantaged," in Herbert J. Klausmeier and Chester W. Harris, (eds.). *Analyses of Concept Learning* (New York: Academic Press, 1966, pp. 189-204; and David P. Ausubel and Pearl Ausubel, "Ego Development Among Segregated Negro Children," in A. Harry Passow (ed.), *Education in Deprived Areas* (New York: Teachers College, Columbia University, 1963), pp. 109-141.

under investigation beginning perhaps with the pioneer work of Klineberg.[15] It should be noted, however, that the fact of a difference between two groups does not in and of itself establish that bias exists; it merely suggests that the hypothesis should be examined.[16] So long as one is enmeshed in the problem of nature *versus* nurture, or insofar as tests come to acquire what I have called a "societal function" it seems inevitable that researchers should seek ways of removing cultural influences from tests. One may identify at least three approaches that have been followed in the attempt to remove culturally linked variance from a test. These are: (1) *Compensation* — a procedure in which items known to favor one group over another are balanced so that the means of the groups are equal. This has most frequently been applied to sex differences in tests of general ability, but suggestions for the inclusion of ghetto-based vocabulary items in tests of verbal ability would also fall in this category. This approach is quite limited in practice in that it has potential usefulness only if one is working toward global or omnibus tests. (2) *Elimination* — a procedure in which one successively eliminates items or types of items for which differences between groups occur, thus moving toward a culture-free test. The work of Eells and Davis[17] illustrates this approach. (3) *Substitution* — a procedure which aims at the identification of new intellectual factors, or new ways of measuring these, that offer promise as assessments of important psychological functions but without significant evidence of socio-economic bias. The work of Jensen[18] with miniature learning tasks, and of Rohwer[19] are examples of this approach.

Of these attacks on the problem the third procedure, that of substitution, seems relatively the most attractive and promising in view of the fact that attempts to develop culture-free or culture-fair tests have been extremely discouraging, if indeed they were not doomed conceptually from the start.

However, in a sense all of these procedures are irrelevant to the practical problem of devising tests that are useful in predicting the learning behavior of individuals within some already specified educational environment. To illustrate this matter one can cite the practical problem of tests designed to be predictive of criteria of achievement as presently defined within colleges and universities. The predictive validity of the Scholastic Aptitude Test (SAT) of the College Board has been examined in literally hundreds of studies across a wide range of institutions, students, and curriculums, with generally consistent results demonstrating that, like other carefully constructed tests of scholastic aptitude, it has substantial validity for the usual criterion of grades. Although the SAT has been

15 Otto Klineberg, "An Experimental Study of Speed and Other Factors in 'Racial Differences," *Archives of Psychology*, No. 93, 1928.

16 Irving Lorge, "Difference or Bias in Tests of Intelligence," in Anne Anastasi (ed.) *Testing Problems in Perspective* (Washington, D. C.: American Council on Education, 1966), pp. 465-471.

17 Kenneth W. Eells, *et al. Intelligence and Cultural Differences*, (Chicago: University of Chicago Press, 1951).

18 Arthur B. Jensen, "Intelligence, Learning, Ability, and Socioeconomic Status," Paper presented at symposium: *New Approaches to the Measurement of Intelligence*, Annual Convention of the American Educational Research Association, Chicago, Illinois, February 8, 1968.

19 William D. Rohwer, research reported by Arthur B. Jensen, *op. cit.* (11), p. 35.

subjected to some criticisms of bias, this has been primarily on the assumption that it must be so because differences are known to exist in mean scores between whites, Negroes, and other minority groups. Evidence that such differences exist for a variety of other tests, and that they are not simply or exclusively a function of social class alone, is given by Lesser, Fifer and Clark.[20]

The study by Clark and Plotkin[21] stimulated and reinforced discussion of bias in the SAT, but the design of this study has been shown to have such serious methodological shortcomings[22] that its conclusions are vitiated. More recent studies have shown that the SAT is as valid for predicting grades of Negro students within predominantly Negro colleges as it is for white students in predominantly white colleges.[23] Munday[24] has reported similar results using tests of the American College Testing Program. Within integrated colleges, Cleary[25] has also investi-

gated the question of predictive bias of the SAT. In her study she defined bias as a systematic under- or over-estimation of grades of Negro students when one uses for these students the same regression equation for predicting grades from test scores and high school rank as that used for all students in common. In the three colleges she studied, no evidence of predictive bias acting to the disadvantage of Negro students was found. Linn[26] has reanalyzed Cleary's data using only SAT scores as predictors and has obtained the same results. Still another approach to the question of bias is illustrated by examination of item bias in individual items of the PSAT by Cleary and Hilton.[27] In this study an item was defined as biased against a particular group if the discrepancy between performance on that item by members of the group differed by more than would be expected on the basis of the performance differences between groups on all of the other items in the test. The conclusion of this study was that "PSAT items cannot for all practical purposes be considered biased for either race or SES within race."[28]

The research studies cited do not, of course, finally settle the question of possible bias in scholastic aptitude tests; undoubtedly many more studies of this matter will be undertaken. The dilemma which these studies present, however, is

20 Gerald S. Lesser, Gordon Fifer, and Donald H. Clark, "Mental Abilities of Children from Different Social Class and Cultural Groups," *Monographs of the Society for Research in Child Development*, XXX (1965), No. 4.

21 Kenneth Clark and L. Plotkin, *The Negro Student at Integrated Colleges* (New York: National Scholarship Service and Fund for Negro Students, 1963).

22 Joel Campbell, *Testing of Culturally Different Groups* (Princeton, N. J.: Educational Testing Service, 1964).

23 Julian C. Stanley and Andrew C. Porter, "Correlation of Scholastic Aptitude Test Scores with College Grades for Negroes Versus Whites," *Journal of Educational Measurement*, IV (1967), pp. 199-218.

24 Leo Munday, "Predicting College Grades in Predominantly Negro Colleges," *Journal of Educational Measurement*, II (1965), 157-160.

25 T. Anne Cleary, *Test Bias: Validity of the Scholastic Aptitude Test for Negro and White Students at Integrated Colleges*, College Entrance Examination Board Research and Development Report No. 18

(Princeton, N. J.: Educational Testing Service, 1966).

26 Robert L. Linn, *Reanalysis of the Data of Miss Cleary's Predictive Bias Study*, (Princeton, N. J.: Educational Testing Service, 1967), (Mimeographed Memorandum).

27 T. Anne Cleary and Thomas L. Hilton, "An Investigation of Item Bias," *Educational and Psychological Measurement*, XXVIII (1968), pp. 61-75.

28 T. Anne Cleary and Thomas L. Hilton, *op. cit.*, p. 69.

illustrated by contrasting the statement of Kendrick[29] that "the reason the verbal test is not biased is that college programs are often biased. . . . tests predict the kinds of evaluations that the colleges will make of their students after instruction," and John Carroll's observation that "it seems obvious that meaningful verbal discourse is the primary tool of teaching. We expect students to learn most things by being told about them."[30]

Viewing tests as components of systems of guidance, selection, distribution and evaluation, it would seem important that we continue to regard these measurements as useful forecasts of future performance for Negro as well as white students. This does not mean that institutions should adopt an uncritical or routine use of test scores because this would, for example, ensure the realization of Kendrick's warning about the coming segregation of selective colleges.[31] But it does argue that test information should not be ignored as if it was simply not relevant in the instance of disadvantaged students.

Even more importantly, we must bear in mind that the functions of testing embrace other purposes than these just enumerated. In fact, it may be in the area of developing measurement instruments for *prescriptive* and *educative* functions that the genuine potentiality for educational improvement which proponents of testing have often promised will actually come to be realized. If tests of intellectual performance are to move beyond the strictly practical purposes of predicting educational success within conventional learning environments, it seems likely that the answer must be sought in the development of tests describing the processes underlying intellectual growth, that the search must center on the acquisition and use of language as the primary tool of learning, and that the educational model employed should be one of diagnosing inadequacies or dysfunctioning in linguistic behavior. Furthermore, there is reason to believe that tests developed along these lines would also be applicable to guidance, selective, distributive and evaluative functions. An effort to build prescriptive tests will require a profound redirection of testing in relation to psychological and sociological theory.

REDIRECTION OF TESTS

In recent years theories of the cognitive development of children have generally been divided over the role of language in intellectual functioning, with followers of Piaget regarding language processes as less fundamental whereas "American psychologists argue that mediation and language are at the heart of reasoning."[32] Without entering into this debate it seems probable that the effects of cultural deprivation on cognitive development are understandable in terms of the function of language as the means by which the individual incorporates and structures the environment into individual experience. Basil Bernstein[33] has proposed that forms

29 S. A. Kendrick, *op. cit.*, p. 11.

30 John Carroll, *On Learning From Being Told*, Research Memorandum 68-2, (Princeton, N.J.: Educational Testing Service), January, 1968.

31 S. A. Kendrick, *op. cit.*

32 Jerome Kagan, "A Developmental Approach to Conceptual Growth," in Herbert J. Klausmeier and Chester W. Harris (eds.), *Analyses of Concept Learning*, (New York: Academic Press, 1966), pp. 97-115.

33 Basil Bernstein, "Social Class and Linguistic Development: A Theory of Social Learning," in A. H. Halsey, Jean Floud, and C. A. Anderson (eds.), *Education, Economy,*

of spoken language in the process of their learning elicit, reinforce, and generalize distinct types of relationships with the environment and that certain linguistic forms involve a loss or acquisition of skills — both cognitive and social — which are strategic for educational and occupational success. That disadvantaged children acquire a somewhat different language system from middle-class children has been convincingly demonstrated by Deutsch[34] and others. Bernstein argues that the culture of poverty produces a distinctly different form of language (a *public* language) that by comparison with the *formal* language is simple, syntactically poor and inadequate for communication of ideas and relationships requiring precise formulation. The implications of this linguistic difference are serious, not only for the conceptualization of individual experience, but also for the affective relationships between teacher and child, who may become mutually alienated because of the breakdown in communication in herent in the use of different languages. Hess and Shipman[35] have described how, for culturally disadvantaged children, the central role of mother-child communications systems and family controls shapes the language of the child and consequently the cognitive styles of problem solving that he acquires. At the same time, we should remember that the "public" language, inadequate as it may be for the

intellectual tasks that society rewards, possesses an aesthetic quality of its own. Simple, powerful, direct, and rich in metaphor, it is also a language that emphasizes the individual as an end rather than a means.[36]

The saturation of educational tests with verbal aptitude is well known, and these tests are probably reasonably good, albeit indirect, indicators of the facility with which an individual can handle the formal language. Because the cognitive processes of labeling, hypothesis generation, evaluation and transformation depend upon linguistic behavior, problem solving even where the explicit content of the problem is non-verbal will inevitably employ the language of the individual. The common failure to recognize language as the foundation of reasoning probably explains why persons are baffled when disadvantaged children display about the same deficit on non-verbal intelligence tests as they do on verbal tests.

Another important consequence of redirecting the development of tests towards measurement of language processes would be the integration of the affective and motivational aspects of intellectual functioning with reasoning and other cognitive processes. The artificial separation of cognition from emotion, stemming from the days of nineteenth century school psychology, has been deplored but seldom seriously addressed within educational measurement. In this respect Bernstein[37] has observed that a "public" as contrasted with a "formal" language tends to minimize the experience of guilt, so that antisocial behavior and hostility are reinforced by the linguistic form itself. Such

and Society, (Glencoe, Illinos: Free Press, 1961), pp. 288-314.

[34] Martin Deutsch, "The Disadvantaged Child and the Learning Proeess," in A. H. Passow (ed.), *Education in Depressed Areas*, (New York:, Teachers College, Columbia University, 1963), pp. 163-180.

[35] Robert D. Hess and Virginia C. Shipman, "Early Experience and the Socialization of Cognitive Modes in Children," *Child Development*, XXXVI (1965), 869-886.

[36] Basil Bernstein, *op. cit.*
[37] *Ibid.*

a conceptualization offers the possibility of understanding underlying reasons for a finding of strong negative relationships between adult intelligence and behavior traits such as uncontrolled hostility and inability to delay gratification.[38]

The infusion of test theory with the mainstream of work in psycholinguistics and cognitive development seems to offer great promise, not only for disadvantaged youth but for all children. Indeed, a conceptualization of tests seems implicit in the eloquent and perceptive critique of compensatory education offered by Edmund Gordon;[39] without this redirection in tests many efforts at remediation will continue to end in frustration. In conclusion it seems certain that major improvements in psychological measurement will be needed if tests are to become of real use and significance in diagnosing sources of educational deficits, and in supporting directly prescriptive educational treatments.

SUMMARY

Present criticism of tests tends to obscure the real problems of measurement of intellectual development that lie beyond traditional concerns about cultural bias. Tests are held to be generally useful for a limited number of strictly practical purposes, but major improvements in measurement are needed if tests are to play a role in supporting educational programs of the future that parallels the usefulness tests have demonstrated in the past. The cultural role of language probably underlies the pervasiveness of verbal aptitude in present methods of assessing developed abilities, but a new direction for testing requires fundamental changes in the conception of measurement arising from new studies of language and cognitive development in children.

In summary the lines of T. S. Eliot,[40] given at the outset of the paper, seem to sum up the strengths, limitations, and needed directions for testing of intellectual capacity and performance. The circle of our psychometric understanding must be enlarged by what is happening outside that circle, especially in studies of psycholinguistics, thinking, and related processes.

----
[38] Nancy Bayley, "Behavioral Correlates of Mental Growth," *American Psychologist*, XXIII (1968), 1-17.

[39] Edmund W. Gordon and Doxey A. Wilkerson, *Compensatory Education for the Disadvantaged, Programs and Practices, Pre-School Through College*, (New York: College Entrance Examination Board, 1966), especially pages 156-189.

----
[40] T. S. Eliot, "The Family Reunion," in *The Complete Poems and Plays: 1909-1950*, (New York: Harcourt, Brace and Company, 1952), p. 291.

PART II

PERSPECTIVES FOR
TEACHING THE DISADVANTAGED

CHANGING THE GAME FROM "GET THE TEACHER" TO "LEARN"

Robert L. Hamblin, *et al.*

Robert L. Hamblin, *et al.,* "Changing the Game from 'Get the Teacher' to 'Learn,' " *Trans-action,* January 1969, pp. 20-31.

CHANGING THE GAME FROM "GET THE TEACHER" TO "LEARN"

Robert L. Hamblin, *et al.*

Almost any educator of experience will assure you that it is next to impossible—and often actually impossible —to teach normal classroom subjects to children who have extreme behavior problems, or who are "too young." Yet at four experimental classrooms of the Central Midwestern Regional Educational Laboratories (CEMREL), we have been bringing about striking changes in the behavior and learning progress of just such children.

In the 18 months of using new exchange systems and working with different types of problem children, we have seen these results:

■ Extraordinarily aggressive boys, who had not previously responded to therapy, have been tamed.

■ Two-year-olds have learned to read about as fast and as well as their 5-year-old classmates.

■ Four ghetto children, too shy, too withdrawn to talk, have become better than average talkers.

■ Several autistic children, who were either mute or could only parrot sounds, have developed functional speech, have lost their bizarre and disruptive behavior patterns, and their relationships with parents and other children have improved. All of these children are on the road to normality.

Our system is deceptively simple. Superficially, in fact, it may not even seem new—though, in detail, it has never been tried in precisely this form in the classroom before. In essence, we simply reinforce "good" behavior and nonpunitively discourage "bad" behavior. We structure a social exchange so that as the child progresses, we reinforce this behavior—give him something that he values, something that shows our approval. Therefore, he becomes strongly motivated to continue his progress. To terminate bizarre, disruptive or explosive patterns, we stop whatever has been reinforcing that undesirable behavior—actions or attention that teachers or parents have unwittingly been giving him in exchange, often in the belief that they were punishing and thus discouraging him. Study after study has shown that whenever a child persists in behaving badly, some adult has, perhaps inadvertently, been rewarding him for it.

"Socialization" is the term that sociologists use to describe the process of transforming babies—who can do little but cry, eat, and sleep—into adults who can communicate and function rather effectively in their society. Socialization varies from culture to culture, and, while it is going on all around us, we are seldom aware of it. But when normal socialization breaks down, "problems" occur —autism, nonverbal or hyperaggressive behavior, retardation, delinquency, crime, and so on.

The authors, after years of often interesting but by and large frustrating research, realized that the more common theories of child development (Freudian, neo-Freudian, the developmental theories of Gesell and Piaget, and a number of others) simply do not satisfactorily explain the socialization process in children. Consequently in desperation we began to move toward the learning theories and then toward the related exchange theories of social structure. Since then, working with problem children, our view has gradually been amplified and refined. Each experimental classroom has given us a different looking glass. In each we can see the child in different conditions, and can alter the conditions which hinder his socialization into a civilized, productive adult capable of happiness.

By the time they become students, most children love to play with one another, to do art work, to cut and paste, to play with Playdoh, to climb and swing on the playground, and so on. Most pre-schools also serve juice and cookie snacks, and some have television sets or movies. There is, consequently, no dearth of prizes for us to reward the children for good behavior. The problem is not in finding reinforcers, but in managing them.

The Basic System: Token Exchange

One of the simpler and most effective ways, we found, was to develop a token-exchange system. The tokens we use are plastic discs that children can earn. A child who completes his arithmetic or reading may earn a dozen tokens, given one by one as he proceeds through the lessons. And at the end of the lesson period comes the reward.

Often it is a movie. The price varies. For four tokens, a student can watch while sitting on the floor; for eight, he gets a chair; for 12, he can watch while sitting on the table. Perhaps the view is better from the table—anyway, the children almost always buy it if they have enough tokens. But if they dawdled so much that they earned fewer than four, they are "timed out" into the hall while the others see the movie. Throughout the morning, therefore, the children earn, then spend, then earn, then spend.

This token-exchange system is very powerful. It can

create beneficial changes in a child's behavior, his emotional reactions, and ultimately even his approach to life. But it is not easy to set up, nor simple to maintain.

At the beginning the tokens are meaningless to the children; so to make them meaningful, we pair them with M&M candies, or something similar. As the child engages in the desired behavior (or a reasonable facsimile), the teacher gives him a "Thank you," an M&M, and a token. At first the children are motivated by the M&Ms and have to be urged to hold on to the tokens; but then they find that the tokens can be used to buy admission to the movie, Playdoh, or other good things. The teacher tells them

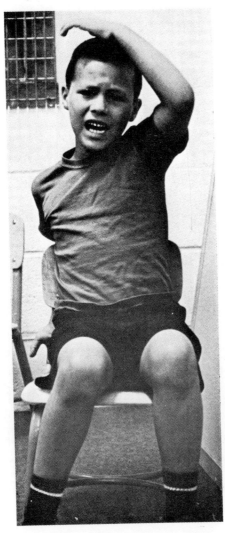

the price and asks them to count out the tokens. Increasingly, the teacher "forgets" the M&Ms. In two or three days the children get no candy, just the approval and the tokens. By then, they have learned.

There are problems in maintaining a token exchange. Children become disinterested in certain reinforcers if they are used too frequently, and therefore in the tokens that buy them. For instance, young children will work very hard to save up tokens to play with Playdoh once a week; if they are offered Playdoh every day, the charm quickly fades. Some activities—snacks, movies, walks outdoors— are powerful enough to be used every day.

As noted, the children we worked with had different behavior problems, reflecting various kinds of break- downs in the socialization process. Each experiment we conducted concentrated on a particular type of maladjust- ment or a particular group of maladjusted children to see how a properly structured exchange system might help them. Let us look at each experiment, to see how each problem was affected.

Aggression

Unfortunately, our world reinforces and rewards ag- gressive behavior. Some cultures and some families are open and brazen about it—they systematically and con- sciously teach their young that it is desirable, and even vir- tuous, to attack certain other individuals or groups. The child who can beat up the other kids on the playground is sometimes respected by his peers, and perhaps by his parents; the soldier achieves glory in combat. The status, the booty, or the bargaining advantages that come to the aggressor can become reinforcement to continue and esca- late his aggressions.

In more civilized cultures the young are taught not to use aggression, and we try to substitute less harmful patterns. But even so, aggression is sometimes reinforced unintentionally—and the consequences, predictably, are the same as if the teaching was deliberate.

In the long run civilized cultures are not kind to hyperaggressive children. A recent survey in England, for instance, found that the great majority of teachers felt that aggressive behavior by students disturbed more classrooms than anything else and caused the most anxiety among teachers. At least partly as a result, the dropout rates for the hyperaggressives was $2\frac{1}{2}$ times as great as for "normals," and disproportionate numbers of hyperaggressives turned up in mental clinics.

The traditional treatment for aggressive juveniles is punishment—often harsh punishment. This is not only of dubious moral value, but generally it does not work.

We took seriously—perhaps for the first time—the theory that aggression is a type of exchange behavior. Boys become aggressive because they get something for it; they continue to be aggressive because the rewards are continuing. To change an aggressive pattern in our experimental class at Washington University, therefore, we had to restructure appropriately the exchange system in which the boys were involved.

As subjects we (Ellis and Hamblin) found five extraordinarily aggressive 4-year-old boys, all referred to us by local psychiatrists and social workers who had been able to do very little with them. Next, we hired a trained teacher. We told her about the boys and the general nature of the experiment—then gave her her head. That is, she was allowed to use her previous training during the first period—and this would provide a baseline comparison with what followed after. We hoped she would act like the "typical teacher." We suspect that she did.

Let's Play "Get the Teacher"

The teacher was, variously, a strict disciplinarian, wise counselor, clever arbitrator, and sweet peacemaker. Each role failed miserably. After the eighth day, the average of the children was 150 sequences of aggression per day! Here is what a mere four minutes of those sequences were like:

Mike, John, and Dan are seated together playing with pieces of Playdoh. Barry, some distance from the others, is seated and also is playing with Playdoh. The children, except Barry, are talking about what they are making. Time is 9:10 A.M. Miss Sally, the teacher, turns toward the children and says, "It's time for a lesson. Put your Playdoh away." Mike says, "Not me." John says, "Not me." Dan says, "Not me." Miss Sally moves toward Mike. Mike throws some Playdoh in Miss Sally's face. Miss Sally jerks back, then moves forward rapidly and snatches Playdoh from Mike. Puts Playdoh in her pocket. Mike screams for Playdoh, says he wants to play with it. Mike moves toward Miss Sally and attempts to snatch the Playdoh from Miss Sally's pocket. Miss Sally pushes him away. Mike kicks Miss Sally on the leg. Kicks her again, and demands the return of his Playdoh. Kicks Miss Sally again. Picks up a small steel chair and throws it at Miss Sally. Miss Sally jumps out of the way. Mike picks up another chair and throws it more violently. Miss Sally cannot move in time. Chair strikes her foot. Miss Sally pushes Mike down on the floor. Mike starts up. Pulls over one chair. Now another, another. Stops a moment. Miss Sally is picking up chairs, Mike looks at Miss Sally. Miss Sally moves toward Mike. Mike runs away.

John wants his Playdoh. Miss Sally says "No." He joins Mike in pulling over chairs and attempts to grab Playdoh from Miss Sally's pocket. Miss Sally pushes him away roughly. John is screaming that he wants to play with his Playdoh. Moves toward phonograph. Pulls it off the table; lets it crash onto the floor. Mike has his coat on. Says he is going home. Miss Sally asks Dan to bolt the door. Dan gets to the door at the same time as Mike. Mike hits Dan in the face. Dan's nose is bleeding. Miss Sally walks over to Dan, turns to the others, and says that she is taking Dan to the washroom and that while she is away, they may play with the Playdoh. Returns Playdoh from pocket to Mike and John. Time: 9:14 A.M.

Wild? Very. These were barbarous little boys who enjoyed battle. Miss Sally did her best but they were just more clever than she, and they *always* won. Whether Miss Sally wanted to or not, they could always drag her into the fray, and just go at it harder and harder until she capitulated. She was finally driven to their level, trading a kick for a kick and a spit in the face for a spit in the face.

What Miss Sally did not realize is that she had inadvertently structured an exchange where she consistently reinforced aggression. First, as noted, whenever she fought with them, she *always lost*. Second, more subtly, she reinforced their aggressive pattern by giving it serious attention —by looking, talking, scolding, cajoling, becoming angry, even striking back. These boys were playing a teasing game called "Get the Teacher." The more she showed that she was bothered by their behavior, the better they liked it, and the further they went.

These interpretations may seem far-fetched, but they are borne out dramatically by what happened later. On the twelfth day we changed the conditions, beginning with B1 (see Figure 1). First, we set up the usual token exchange to reinforce cooperative behavior. This was to develop or strengthen behavior that would replace aggression. Any strong pattern of behavior serves some function for the individual, so the first step in getting rid of a strong, disruptive pattern is substituting another one that is more useful and causes fewer problems. Not only therapy, but simple humanity dictates this.

First, the teacher had to be instructed in how *not to reinforce* aggression. Contrary to all her experience, she was asked to turn her back on the aggressor, and at the same time to reinforce others' cooperation with tokens. Once we were able to coach her and give her immediate feedback over a wireless-communication system, she structured the exchanges almost perfectly. The data in Figures 1 and 2 show the crucial changes: a gradual increase in cooperation—from about 56 to about 115 sequences per day, and a corresponding decrease in aggression from 150 to about 60 sequences!

These results should have been satisfactory, but we were new at this kind of experimentation, and nervous. We wanted to reduce the frequency of aggression to a "normal" level, to about 15 sequences a day. So we restructured the

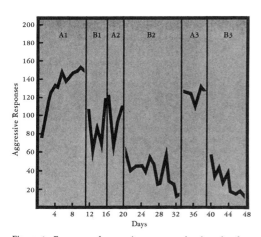

Figure 1. Frequency of aggressive sequences by days for five 4-year-old boys. In A1, A2 and A3 the teacher attempted to punish aggression but inadvertently reinforced it. In B1, B2 and B3 she turned her back or otherwise ignored aggression and thus did not reinforce it.

exchange system and thus launched A2.

In A2, we simply made sure that aggression would always be punished. The teacher was told to *charge* tokens for any aggression.

To our surprise, the frequency of cooperation remained stable, about 115 sequences per day; but aggression *increased* to about 110 sequences per day! Evidently the boys were still playing "Get the Teacher," and the fines were enough reinforcement to increase aggression.

So, instead of fining the children, the teacher was again told to ignore aggression by turning her back and giving attention and tokens only for cooperation. The frequency of aggression went down to a near "normal" level, about 16 sequences per day (B2), and cooperation increased to about 140 sequences.

Then, as originally planned, the conditions were again reversed. The boys were given enough tokens at the beginning of the morning to buy their usual supply of movies, toys, and snacks, and these were not used as reinforcers. The teacher was told to do the best she could. She was not instructed to return to her old pattern, but without the tokens and without our coaching she did— and with the same results. Note A3 in Figures 1 and 2. Aggression increased to about 120 sequences per day, and cooperation decreased to about 90. While this was an improvement over A1, before the boys had ever been exposed to the token exchange, it was not good. The mixture of aggression and cooperation was strange, even weird, to watch.

When the token exchange was restructured (B3) and the aggression no longer reinforced, the expected changes recurred—with a bang. Aggression decreased to seven sequences on the last day, and cooperation rose to about 181 sequences. In "normal" nursery schools, our observations have shown that five boys can be expected to have

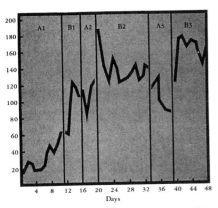

Figure 2. Frequency of cooperative sequences. In A1, A2 and A3 the teacher structured a weak approval exchange for cooperation and a disapproval exchange for noncooperation. In B1, A2, B2 and B3, she structured a token exchange for cooperation.

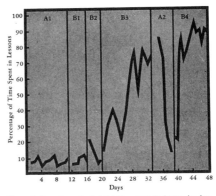

Figure 3. Percentage of scheduled time spent in lessons by days for five hyperaggressive boys. In A1 and A2, teacher structured approval exchange for attendance, disapproval for non-attendance. In B1 and B2, a token exchange for attendance was structured, but not effectively until B2 and B4.

15 aggression sequences and 60 cooperation sequences per day. Thus, from extremely aggressive and uncooperative, our boys had become less aggressive and far more cooperative than "normal" boys.

Here is an example of their new behavior patterns, taken from a rest period—precisely the time when the most aggressive acts had occurred in the past:

All of the children are sitting around the table drinking their milk; John, as usual, has finished first. Takes his plastic mug and returns it to the table. Miss Martha, the assistant teacher, gives him a token. John goes to cupboard, takes out his mat, spreads it out by the blackboard, and lies down. Miss Martha gives him a token. Meanwhile, Mike, Barry, and Jack have spread their mats on the carpet. Dan is lying on the carpet itself since he hasn't a mat. Each of them gets a token. Mike asks if he can sleep by the wall. Miss Sally says "Yes." John asks if he can put out the light. Miss Sally says to wait until Barry has his mat spread properly. Dan asks Mike if he can share his mat with him. Mike says "No." Dan then asks Jack. Jack says, "Yes," but before he can move over, Mike says "Yes." Dan joins Mike. Both Jack and Mike get tokens. Mike and Jack get up to put their tokens in their cans. Return to their mats.

Miss Sally asks John to put out the light. John does so. Miss Martha gives him a token. All quiet now. Four minutes later—all quiet. Quiet still, three minutes later. Time: 10:23 A.M. Rest period ends.

The hyperaggressive boys actually had, and were, double problems; they were not only extremely disruptive, but they were also washouts as students. Before the token system (A1), they paid attention to their teacher only about 8 percent of the lesson time (see Figure 3). The teacher's system of scolding the youngsters for inattention and taking their attention for granted with faint approval, if any, did not work at all. To the pupils, the "Get the Teacher" game was much more satisfying.

After the token exchange was started, in B1, B2, B3, and B4, it took a long, long time before there was any appreciable effect. The teacher was being trained from scratch, and our methods were, then, not very good. However, after we set up a wireless-communication system that allowed us to coach the teacher from behind a one-way mirror and to give her immediate feedback, the children's attention began to increase. Toward the end of B3, it leveled off at about 75 percent—from 8 percent! After the token exchange was taken out during A2, attention went down to level off at 23 percent; put back in at B4, it shot back up to a plateau of about 93 percent. Like a roller coaster: 8 percent without, to 75 with, to 23 without, to 93 with.

Normal Children

These results occurred with chronic, apparently hopeless hyperaggressive boys. Would token exchange also help "normal," relatively bright upper-middle-class children? Sixteen youngsters of that description—nine boys and seven girls, ranging from 2 years 9 months to 4 years

9 months—were put through an experimental series by Bushell, Hamblin, and Denis Stoddard in an experimental pre-school at Webster College. All had about a month's earlier experience with the token-exchange system. The results are shown in Figure 4.

Study in 15-Minute Periods

At first, the study hour was broken up into 15-minute periods, alternating between the work that received tokens, and the play or reward that the tokens could be used for. Probably because the children were already familiar with token exchange, no great increase in learning took place. On the 22nd day, we decided to try to increase the learning period, perhaps for the whole hour. In A2 (Figure 4), note that the time spent in studying went up rapidly and dramatically—almost doubling—from 27 to level off at 42 minutes.

During B, the token exchange was taken out completely. The teachers still gave encouragement and prepared interesting lessons as before. The rewards—the nature walks, snacks, movies, and so on—were retained. But, as in a usual classroom, they were given to the children free instead of being sold. The children continued at about the same rate as before for a few days. But after a week, attention dropped off slowly, then sharply. On the last day it was down to about 15 minutes—one-third the level of the end of the token period.

In A3, the token exchange was reinstituted. In only three days, attention snapped back from an average of 15 minutes to 45 minutes. However, by the end of A3, the students paid attention an average of 50 of the available 60 minutes.

A comparison of the record of these normals with the record of the hyperaggressive boys is interesting. The increase in attention brought by the token exchange,

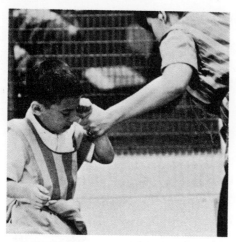

1. At first he thinks the whole procedure a joke.

2. She becomes more insistent.

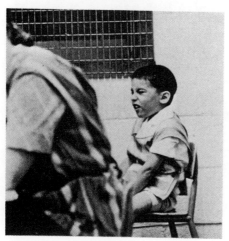

3. He discovers it is no joke.

A TOKEN
FROM THE TEACHER

Photographed by
DANIEL T. MAGDISON
of the CEMREL Staff

*The "token-exchange" system of learning
reinforcement calls, in essence, for the quick
and frequent reward and encouragement
of desirable behavior, and non-punitive
"timing-out"—usually by removing the child
—to discourage undesirable behavior.
By this means two-year-old children have
learned to read, violent ones to sit calmly
and study, and the autistic to speak and
to have hope.*

(Left) Teacher "timing out" a child by seating
him away from the others for a while.

(Right) Jimmy, an almost mute autistic child, is
rewarded with a corn chip for learning to say
"Nose."

ay 'Nose,' Jimmy.

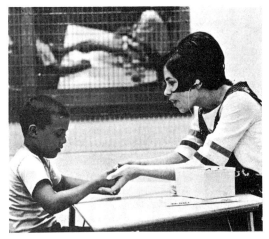

4. "Good boy, Jimmy!"

Nose,' Jimmy, *'nose!'* "

5. *"Good* boy!"

mmy says "nose.' "

6. Triumph and reward.

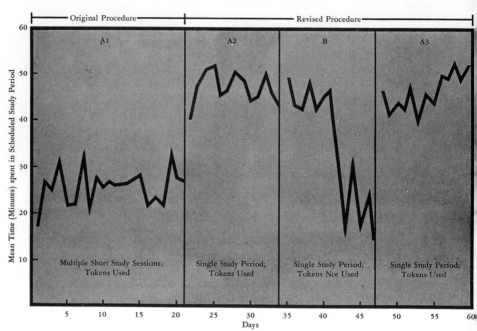

Figure 4. Sixteen upper-middleclass pre-schoolers. In A1, A2 and A3 the token exchange was used; in B, only approval.

from about 15 minutes to 50, is approximately threefold for the normal children; but for the hyperaggressive boys —who are disobedient and easily distracted—it is about eleven-fold, from 8 percent to 93 percent of the time. The increase was not only greater, but the absolute level achieved was higher. This indicates strongly, therefore, that the more problematic the child, the greater may be the effect of token exchange on his behavior.

The high rates of attention were not due to the fact that each teacher had fewer children to work with. Individualized lessons were not enough. Without the token exchange, even three teachers could not hold the interest of 16 children 2 to 4 years old—at least not in reading, writing, and arithmetic.

Praise and approval were not enough as rewards. The teachers, throughout the experiment, used praise and approval to encourage attention; they patted heads and said things like "Good," "You're doing fine," and "Keep it up"; yet, in B, when the token exchange was removed, this attention nevertheless ultimately declined by two-thirds.

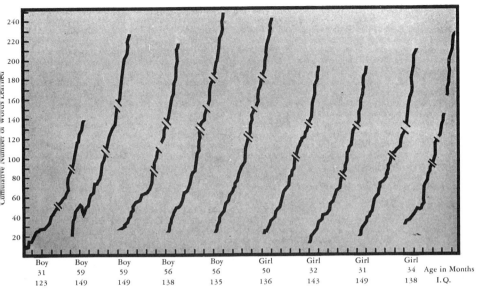

Figure 5. Number of sight-words learned through time by five 4- and 5-year-olds, and four 2- and 3-year-olds. Note that the younger children did about as well as the older ones—except for one boy whose I.Q. was somewhat lower than the others in the group. (Gaps indicate absences.)

Social approval is important, but not nearly so powerful as material reinforcers.

Finally, it is obvious that if the reinforcers (movies, snacks, toys, or whatever) do not seem directly connected to the work, they will not sustain a high level of study. To be effective with young children, rewards must occur in a structured exchange in which they are given promptly as recompense and thus are directly connected to the work performed.

The Very Young Child

According to accepted educational theory, a child must be about six and a half before he can comfortably learn to read. But is this really true, or is it merely a convenience for the traditional educational system? After all, by the time a normal child is two and a half he has learned a foreign language—the one spoken by his parents and family; and he has learned it without special instruction or coaching. He has even developed a feel for the rules

183

of grammar, which, by and large, he uses correctly. It is a rare college student who becomes fluent in a foreign language with only two and a half years of formal training—and our college students are supposed to be the brightest of our breed. Paul Goodman has suggested that if children learn to *speak* by the same methods that they learn to *read*, there might well be as many non-speakers now as illiterates.

What if the problem is really one of motivation? If we structured an exchange that rewarded them, in ways they could appreciate, for learning to read, couldn't they learn as readily as 5-year-olds?

We decided that for beginners, the number of words a child can read is the best test of reading ability. In an experiment designed by Hamblin, Carol Pfeiffer, Dennis Shea, and June Hamblin, and administered at our Washington University pre-school, the token-exchange system was used to reward children for the number of words each learned. The results are given in Figure 5. Note that the 2-year-olds did about as well as the 5-year-olds; their sight vocabularies were almost as large.

There was an interesting side effect: at the end of the school year, all but one of these children tested at the "genius" level. On Stanford-Binet individual tests, their I.Q. scores increased as much as 36 points. It was impossible to compute an average gain only because three of the children "topped out"—made something in excess of 149, the maximum score possible.

In general, the lower the measured I.Q. at the start, the greater the gain—apparently as a result of the educational experience.

The Non-Verbal Child

What happens when ghetto children are introduced into a token-exchange system? At our Mullanphy Street pre-school, 22 Afro-American children—age 3 to 5—attend regularly. All live in or near the notorious Pruitt-Igoe Housing Project, and most come from broken homes. When the school began, the teachers were unenthusiastic about a token exchange, so we let them proceed as they wished. The result was pandemonium. About half of the children chased one another around the room, engaged in violent arguments, and fought. The others withdrew; some would not even communicate.

After the third day, the teachers asked for help. As in the other experimental schools, we (Buchholdt and Hamblin) instructed them to ignore aggressive-disruptive behavior and to reward attention and cooperation with social approval and the plastic tokens, later to be exchanged for such things as milk, cookies, admission to the movies, and toys. The children quickly caught on, the disruptions diminished, and cooperation increased. Within three weeks of such consistent treatment, most of the children took part in the lessons, and disruptive behavior had become only an occasional problem. All of this, remember, without punishment.

Our attention was then focused upon the children with verbal problems. These children seldom started conversations with teachers or other students, but they would sometimes answer questions with a word or perhaps two. This pattern may be unusual in the middle classes, but is quite common among ghetto children. Our research has shown that children so afflicted are usually uneducable.

As we investigated, we became convinced that their problem was not that they were unable to talk as much as that they were too shy to talk to strangers—that is, to non-family. In their homes we overheard most of them talking brokenly, but in sentences. Consequently, we set up a token exchange for them designed specifically to develop a pattern of talking with outsiders, especially teachers and school children.

As it happened, we were able to complete the experiment with only four children (see Figure 6). During A1, the baseline period (before the tokens were used), the four children spoke only in about 8 percent of the 15-second sampling periods. In B1, the teachers gave social approval and tokens *only* for speaking; non-verbalisms, like pointing or headshaking, would not be recognized or reinforced. Note the increase in verbalization, leveling out at approximately 48 percent.

In A2 we reversed the conditions by using a teacher new to the school. The rate of talking dropped off immediately, then increased unevenly until it occurred in about 23 percent of the sample periods.

In B2 the new teacher reintroduced the token exchange for talking, and once more there was a dramatic rise: The speaking increased much more rapidly than the first time, ending up at about 60 percent. (This more rapid increase in known as the Contrast Effect. It occurs in part, perhaps, because the children value the token exchange more after it has been taken away.)

In the final test, we again took out the token exchange, and introduced yet another new teacher. This time the drop was small, to 47 percent.

We followed the children for three months after the end of the experiment. Their speech level remained at 48 percent, with little dropoff. This compares with the 40 percent talking rate for our other ghetto children, and the 42 percent rate for upper-middle-class children at the Washington University pre-school.

Frequency of speech, however, was not the only important finding. At the end of B1, the children spoke more often but still in a hesitant and broken way. By the end of B2, they spoke in sentences, used better syntax, and frequently started conversations.

Mothers, teachers, and neighbors all reported that the children were much more friendly and assertive. But some claimed that the children now talked too much! This could reflect individual bias; but there was little doubt that at least one child, Ben, had become an almost compulsive talker. He was given to saying hello to everyone he met and shaking their hands. So we terminated the experiment—what would have happened to Ben had we started *another* exchange?

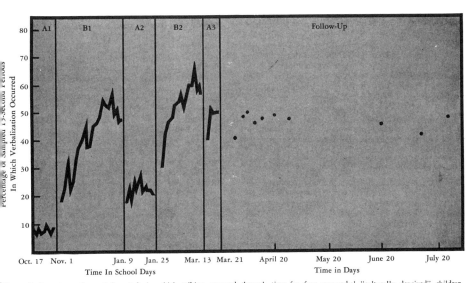

Figure 6. Percentage of sampled periods in which talking occurred through time for four non-verbal "culturally deprived" children, and through five experimental conditions. In each of the A conditions a new teacher was introduced, and she structured a token exchange for participation in lessons. In the B conditions, the teacher then structured a token exchange for talking. The follow-up was similar to the A conditions.

This experiment shows that token exchange can bring on permanent behavior change, but that the culture must reinforce the new behavior. Talking is important in our culture, and so is reading; therefore they are reinforced. But other subjects—such as mathematics beyond simple arithmetic—are not for most people. For behavior to change permanently it must be reinforced at least intermittently.

Autism

The problems of autistic children usually dwarf those of all other children. To the casual observer, autistic children never sustain eye contact with others but appear to be self-contained—sealed off in a world of their own. The most severe cases never learn how to talk, though they sometimes echo or parrot. They remain dependent upon Mother and become more and more demanding. They develop increasingly destructive and bizarre behavior problems. Finally, between 5 and 10 years old, autistic children ordinarily become unbearable to their families and at that point they are almost invariably institutionalized. Until recently, at least, this meant a rear ward to vegetate in until they died.

The breakthrough in therapy from autism came in 1964 when Dr. Ivar Lovaas and Dr. Montrose Wolfe and a graduate student, now Dr. Todd Risley, simultaneously developed therapy systems using well-established principles of operant conditioning. They were particularly successful with those children who randomly echoed or imitated words or sentences (this is called echolalia).

The therapy systems we have designed, developed, and tested, though similar in some ways to those developed by Lovaas, Wolfe and Risley, are quite different in others. First, we do not use punishment, or other negative stimuli.

We simply terminate exchanges that reinforce the autistic patterns, and set up exchanges that reinforce normal patterns. Second, our children are not institutionalized; they live at home, and are brought to the laboratory for twenty minutes to three hours of therapy per day. Third, as soon as possible—usually within months—we get the children into classrooms where a therapist works with four or five at a time. Fourth, we train the mother to be an assistant therapist—mostly in the home, but also in the laboratory. These changes were introduced for several reasons, but primarily in the hope of getting a better, more permanent cure for autism.

The Etiology of Autism

Is autism hereditary, as many believe? Our studies indicate that this is not the important question. Many mental faculties, including I.Q., have some physiological base. But the real issue is how much physiologically based potential is socially realized, for good or bad. As far as we can tell, the exchanges that intensify autism get structured inadvertently, often by accident; but once started, a vicious cycle develops that relentlessly drives the child further into autism.

When autism starts, the mother often reacts by babying the child, trying to anticipate his every need before he signals. Thus normal communication is not reinforced, and the child never learns to work his environment properly. But even if he doesn't know how to get what he wants through talking, he does learn, through association, that his oversolicitous and anxious mother will always respond if he acts up violently or bizarrely enough. And she must, if only to punish. He thus learns to play "Get mother's attention"; and this soon develops into "Get mother exasperated, but stop just short of the point where she punishes and really hurts." Here is an example (observed by Ferritor in the first of a series of experiments by the Laboratory's staff, not reported here):

Larry is allowed to pick out his favorite book. His mother then attempts to read it to him, but he keeps turning the pages so she can't. He gets up and walks away from the table. The mother then yells at him to come back. He *smiles* (a sign of pleasure usually but not always accompanies reinforcement). Mother continues to talk to the child to try to get him back for the story. Finally, he comes over to the table and takes the book away from her. She lets him and goes back to the bookcase for another book. He then sits down and she begins to read. He tries to get up, but his mother pulls him back. Again. Again. She holds him there. He gets away and starts walking around the room. Goes to the toy cabinet. Mother gets up to go over and take a toy away from him. He sits on the floor. The mother comes over and sits down by him. He gets up and goes over by the door and opens it and tries to run out. She tells him he has to stay. He *smiles*. She resumes reading. He gets up and starts walking around the table. She grabs him as he comes by. He *smiles*.

A clinical psychologist who had tested Larry did not diagnose him as autistic, but as an educable mental retardate with an I.Q. of perhaps 30. Yet he had gaze aversion and we suspected that Larry, like other autistics, was feigning inability as a way of getting what he wanted from his mother, and then from other adults. He began to respond to the attractive exchanges that we structured for him, and as we did, he began to tip his hand. For example, at one point when his mother was being trained to be an assistant therapist, the following incident occurred:

Mrs. C. told Larry that as soon as he strung some beads he could have gum from the gum machine that was across the room. For about 10 minutes he fumbled, he whined, all the time crying, saying "I can't." Finally, he threw the beads at his mother. Eventually, the mother had the good sense to leave the room, saying, "As soon as you 'string those beads, you can have your gum." With his mother out of the room, according to our observers he sat right down and, in less than 30 seconds, filled a string with beads with no apparent trouble.

Just two weeks later, after the mother had been through our 10-day training program, they again had a "story time."

The mother begins by immediately asking Larry questions about this book (the same book used a few weeks before). He responds to every question. She gives approval for every correct answer. Then she tries to get him to say, "That is a duck." He will not say it intel-

Robert L. Hamblin is a professor in sociology at Washington University and a Program Director for Instructional Systems for children with learning disabilities at CEMREL. This research is being continued with autistic, hyperactive and ghetto children at Washington University, and in the public schools. Dr. Hamblin, on sabbatical this year, is completing a book on this research, *Structured Exchange and the Socialization of Problem Children,* and another, *The Foundations of a New Social Psychology.*

David Buckholdt, and Daniel Ferritor are completing their dissertations at Washington University and are associate directors to Dr. Hamblin. David Buckholdt does experiments in the public schools with hyperaggressive and environmentally retarded children in the ghetto. Daniel Ferritor conducts experiments with autistic children. Desmond Ellis is an assistant professor of sociology at the University of North Carolina. Donald Bushnell is an assistant professor of sociology at the University of Kansas.

The work reported here was done by the Central Midwestern Regional Educational Laboratory, a private, nonprofit corporation supported in part as a Regional Educational Laboratory by funds from the U.S. Office of Education, Department of Health, Education and Welfare. The opinions expressed here do not necessarily reflect the position or policy of the Office of Education, and no official endorsement by the Office of Education should be inferred.

ligibly, but wants to turn the page. Mother says, "As soon as you say 'duck,' you may turn the page. Larry says "Duck" and turns the page. He *smiles*.

After seven minutes, Larry is still sitting down. They have finished one book and are beginning a second.

Most autistic children play the game "Look at me, I'm stupid," or "Look at me, I'm bizarre." These are simply attention-getting games that most adults repeatedly reinforce. Man is not a simple machine; he learns, and as he develops his abilities, he develops stronger and stronger habits. Thus, once these inadvertent exchanges get established, the child becomes more and more dependent, more and more disruptive, more and more bizarre, more and more alienated from the positive exchanges that are structured in his environment. What is sad is that the parents and the others in the child's life sense that something is terribly wrong, but the more they do, the worse the situation becomes.

It seems to those of us who have been involved in these experiments from the beginning that the exchange techniques and theories we have used have without question demonstrated their effectiveness in treating and educating problem children. Watching these children as they go peacefully and productively about their lessons toward the end of each experimental series is both an exhilarating and humbling experience. It is almost impossible to believe that so many had been written off as "uneducable" by professionals, that without this therapy and training— or something similar—most would have had dark and hopeless futures.

But it is not inevitable that so many hyperaggressive or environmentally retarded ghetto children become dropouts or delinquents; it is not inevitable that so many autistic children, saddest of all, must vegetate and die mutely in the back wards of mental hospitals.

FURTHER READING SUGGESTED BY THE AUTHORS:

The Analysis of Human Operant Behavior by Ellen P. Reese (Dubuque, Iowa: William C. Brown Company, 1966).

The Emotionally Disturbed Child in the Classroom by Frank Hewett (Boston: Allyn and Bacon, Inc., 1968).

Early Childhood Autism edited by J.K. Wing (London: Pergamon Press, Ltd., 1966).

Case Studies in Behavior Modification by Leonard P. Ullman and Leonard Krasner (New York: Holt, Rinehart and Winston, Inc., 1965).

HOW SHALL
THE DISADVANTAGED CHILD BE TAUGHT?

Marion Blank and Frances Solomon

Marion Blank and Frances Solomon, "How Shall the Disadvantaged Child Be Taught," *Child Development,* March 1969, pp. 47-61.

HOW SHALL
THE DISADVANTAGED CHILD BE TAUGHT?

Marion Blank and Frances Solomon

A 1-to-1 tutorial language program is illustrated in a series of dialogues between a teacher and a 4-year-old socially disadvantaged child. The teaching is analyzed both according to the deficiencies of the child's thinking and the techniques designed to foster the abstract thinking necessary to overcome these deficiencies. This program is contrasted to teaching done by a person trained in the traditional nursery school philosophy.

An eclectic approach to the teaching of language is usual in most preschool programs for disadvantaged children. Since their language deficiencies are extensive, it is hoped that the presentation of a massive array of possibly fruitful techniques is bound to lead to learning. In contrast, the present authors (Blank, 1968; Blank & Solomon, 1968) have presented the hypothesis that the deprived child's verbal weakness is so overwhelming that it blinds one to his more subtle but basic deficiency. This deficiency is the lack of a symbolic system for thinking. In order to develop this system, language is essential—but not all language is equally useful. In particular, we outlined a series of techniques in which the child was taught to use language so as to organize thoughts, to reflect upon situations, to comprehend the meaning of events, and to choose among alternatives. For example, one technique required the child to develop simple cause-and-effect models; for example, if the room is too bright when he comes in, he might be asked, "How can we make it darker in here?" These techniques are in direct contrast to methods focused mainly on enlarging vocabulary for description and communication.

We further postulated that this type of teaching could not be done in

This research was supported by U.S. Public Health Service grant K3-MH-10, 749. The authors wish to thank Miss E. Johnson and the staff of the Bronx River Day Care Center for their cooperation and participation in this research. Author Blank's address: Department of Psychiatry, Albert Einstein College of Medicine, 1300 Morris Park Avenue, Bronx, New York 10461.

the group situation. In observing children, even in small group settings, we have found that they often "tune out" when the teacher attempts to structure a lesson. Once that occurs, almost infinite teaching skill is required to re-engage the child's attention without losing the interest of the rest of the group. Therefore it was decided to conduct the teaching on the basis of short (15-minute), one-to-one sessions between the teacher and the child.

An exploratory program using these techniques was conducted with a group of 22 disadvantaged children ranging in age from 3 years 3 months to 4 years 7 months (Blank & Solomon, 1968). The children were divided into four groups, two tutored and two untutored, matched as closely as possible for age, sex, and Stanford-Binet IQ scores. In one tutored group, each of six children received individual teaching five times per week; in the second tutored group, six children received the same teaching three times per week. The tutoring involved taking the child for this short period from his classroom to a familiar room in the school. One untutored group of three children had daily individual sessions, but no attempt was made to tutor them. These children were exposed to the identical materials and were permitted to engage in any activity of their choice. This group was included to control for the possible role of individual attention alone in facilitating intellectual performance. Another untutored group of seven children remained in the regular nursery school program with no additional attention. After 3 months (approximately 12 and 7 hours of tutoring for the tutored groups, respectively) the mean IQ increases in groups tutored five and three times per week were 14.5 and 7.0 points, respectively; in the untutored groups the changes were 2.0 and 1.3 points.

In order to demonstrate these techniques in actual use, this paper presents two sessions with one of the 4-year-old children from the study. The sessions cover a 3-month period so as to illustrate the growth in her capacity to handle and structure cognitive material. A third session between this child and a nursery school teacher not trained in these techniques is also included here. We recorded a number of such sessions with teachers from established nursery schools. This was done to investigate the possibility that teachers might spontaneously adopt this approach to abstract thinking if permitted the opportunity of working on a one-to-one basis.

The commentary accompanying the dialogue is directed towards diagnosing both the deficiencies of the child's thinking and the success of the teacher's methods in overcoming these deficiencies. "Success," of course, is evaluated according to the rationale of our philosophy of teaching abstract thinking.

SESSION 1

Julie was a highly impulsive, voluble 4-year-old of Puerto Rican background. She was charming, but a will-o'-the-wisp. Many deficiencies obscured her latent brightness; chief among them was an attention span even shorter than that of her peers.

A teacher trained in the principles of the program is seen here conducting one of the first sessions with Julie. The dialogue reads slowly, but actually covered only 5 minutes of a 15-minute session.

After the child had been in the room for several minutes, the teacher introduced some drawing materials:

Dialogue	*Interpretation*
TEACHER: I'm going to draw a picture, and then you're going to make one just like it. I'll give you a paper. What color crayon would you like to use?	Teacher's statements are designed to: (1) Tune child in to intended activity; (2) Have her make a specific verbal choice which will determine her next action.
JULIE: Yellow. [Child chooses correctly, immediately starts drawing in usually impulsive manner.]	Had child's choice not been consistent with verbalization, teacher would have initiated interchange to correct child.
TEACHER: *Wait.* Don't draw anything yet.	Teacher attempts to delay impulsivity.
JULIE: [Halts and focuses.]	
TEACHER: [Draws a circle.] What did I draw?	Teacher was not concerned with label per se, but rather, with posing a question so as to keep the child's attention.
JULIE: A ball.	
TEACHER: Could you make that ball? Make one just like mine.	Using child's word, teacher utilizes imitation as a means of getting child to complete a simple task.
JULIE: [Succeeds.]	
TEACHER: Good, now, I'm going to make a line *across* the ball. Can you do that? [Teacher draws a line across the circle.]	Teacher is trying to integrate another concept into the work. Almost any elementary but relevant concept which would have increased the complexity of the situation would have been suitable (e.g., drawing another figure inside the circle).
JULIE: [Draws an incorrect line from top to bottom of a circle.]	Child has merely responded to the word "line." She has not heeded the total direction.
TEACHER: No, you drew it from the top to the bottom. We want it to go across. [Teacher indicates desired direction.]	
JULIE: [Draws line independently and correctly.] Now I went across.	Child's appropriate verbalization indicates understanding.

TEACHER: Very good. You know, we can also call a ball a circle. Do you know what I'm going to do with this circle? I'm going to get a green crayon and I'm going to fill in the *bottom half* of my circle. Would you like to get a green crayon and do the same thing? Fill it in so it looks like mine.

Since understanding is apparent, teacher introduces (1) the consensually validated label of circle, (2) again increases the complexity by the dual idea of *bottom* and *color*. To help child handle this increase in complexity, teacher perseveres with imitation ("do the same thing"). It would have been better here had the teacher not used the phrase "would you like . . . " since it lends itself to the child's using an automatic response of "no." Since choice was not at issue, a specific demand such as "please get" could have been put forth.

JULIE: I like this color. I like all colors. I like flowers, too. I got that kind of crayon. I like brown—it's dark. We could play in the dark and we be scared.

TEACHER: But we're working with the green.

This talk typifies the random associations of young children's thinking. Judgment is required to differentiate this from a creative use of spontaneous language.

Teacher evaluates child's monologue as rambling and refuses to be led by it. She attempts to refocus child so that the child can experience the opportunity of completing an assignment.

JULIE: [Continues drawing but keeps up rambling conversation.] I got my new clothes. I gotta lot of new clothes in my house.

TEACHER: Would you work a little faster on this bottom one?

Since rapid tempo for this child is pleasurable, teacher introduces it to aid the child in completing her work.

JULIE: [Completes task.]

TEACHER: Very good. Now, look what I'm going to do. I'm going to get a purple crayon. I'm going to make the top of my circle purple. Look how fast I do it. Can you do yours like this?

JULIE: Fast—right? [Completes task.]

Tempo retained as a means of handling child's short attention span.

Child responds well to incorporating tempo into task.

TEACHER: Show me the top of the circle.

JULIE: [Accomplishes task.]

TEACHER: Show me the bottom of your circle.

Teacher maintains concept of directionality.

Normally, opposites are not taught together. If child did not know "top," teacher would not go on to "bottom." Since the child knew, the teacher could attempt to introduce the opposite concept.

JULIE: [Does as she is asked.]

TEACHER: Very good, Julie. Turn your paper upside down. Now show me which is the top.

This action is designed as a first step in enabling the child to see that top is a relative concept.

JULIE: [Points to bottom.]

This response shows that the child's concept of top is tied to the specific place designated originally. This error is typical in the development of a concept from the specific to the general.

TEACHER: No, this is the top now. [Points to area.] The top is always the highest place. Everything has a top. When you turned your paper upside down, this became the top. Show me the top of your head.

Direct answers are usually avoided since the aim of the teaching is self-discovery. However, most factual information cannot be arrived at independently; therefore, the teacher gives this information. Teacher now begins to offer many examples of the concept.

JULIE: [Gestures correctly.]

TEACHER: Show me the top of the chair.

JULIE: [Satisfies this demand.]

Child is responding appropriately to concept posed by teacher. Thus, even though her response is nonverbal, it reflects thinking.

TEACHER: Show me the top of my boots.

Teacher specifically uses a low object to demonstrate that objects close to ground also have a "top."

JULIE: [Points correctly.]

TEACHER: Now, show me the top of the paper.

JULIE: [Points correctly.]

TEACHER: Show me the top of your drawing.

JULIE: [Gestures correctly.] The top is up here.

Child's correct response does not mean that she has a secure grasp of the concept, but she is developing a glimmering of the idea.

The teacher then reviewed the activities up to this point by having the child describe what they had done in that session (e.g., drawing, circle, across, top, bottom, same, color, etc.). Aid was given to help the child recall any significant omissions, and *she was made to ascertain whether her answers were correct*. If, for instance, she said she had used the color red, she was asked to find the drawing and determine if red was, in fact, the color used. If the child was unable to answer a question, the teacher might offer alternatives such as, "Did we draw a circle or a box?" Thus, assistance was given when needed, but the direct answer was rarely given. A basic precept of this study is that a self-discovered answer is most effective for the development of thinking.

This simple review of recent activities is a memory-strengthening task which is not to be confused with the aimless reporting elicited by questions such as, "What did you do yesterday?" Any answers given by the child to a question like the latter cannot be verified by the teacher. As a result, she has no means of demonstrating to the child whether his verbalizations correspond to reality. Therefore, all questions requiring memory in our program were restricted to verifiable events. These principles were continued throughout the teaching and are evident in the session that follows.

SESSION 2

The following dialogue with Julie is from a session held 3 months later. After entering the room, the teacher says:

TEACHER: Do you remember what we did when you were here yesterday?

The type of recall expected by now from child extends over greater time spans but is still verifiable. By contrast, in the early session, recall was restricted to tasks in the immediate session.

JULIE: Yes.

TEACHER: What did we do?

JULIE: I don't know.

Despite her affirmative answer to the previous question, the automatic negative response follows.

TEACHER: Let's see if I can help you. Is there anything on this table that we worked with the last time? [A limited variety of materials is present.]

Teacher presents visual aid to prod memory.

JULIE: [Points to blackboard.]

Child's gesture is correct.

TEACHER: That's just pointing. Tell me what we did.

Although a gesture would have been acceptable in an earlier session, teacher now demands a description, since child is capable of responding in language.

JULIE: We did—we did a square.

Without being given any hints, the child correctly describes the object she drew.

TEACHER: Right. What did we do with the square?

The teacher is making the child recount the next step in the past sequence.

JULIE: [Hesitates.]

TEACHER: Think about it for a minute.

Teacher makes a judgment that child can answer and delays offering help.

JULIE: We took it off. [Child refers to erasing.]

The pause has offered the child a chance to reflect. Her impulsive first answer has been replaced by accurate memory.

TEACHER: Good. Now, what did we use to take it off?

Teacher is continuing to focus on interrelated sequence of past events.

JULIE: I don't know.

TEACHER: [Brings blackboard forward.] All right—what would you do if you had a square on here and you wanted to get rid of it? How could you get it off?

Since child is encountering difficulty, teacher chooses a slightly easier level by offering a question which has several alternative answers (e.g., "What could you use to get it off?"). The child is thereby no longer limited to the past, where only one answer (the thing that actually happened) is correct.

JULIE: Maybe we could use paper.

Child is more successful with this relaxation in demand.

TEACHER: Why could we use paper? What would it do?

Teacher's question is to make child aware of the relationship between the object and the action for which it can be used.

JULIE: It could take it off. It could rub it off.

Child grasps this connection and expresses herself in clear language.

TEACHER: Fine. Now, remember what we did? We didn't use paper to take off the square. Do you remember what it was we *did* use?

JULIE: A sponge.

Child's answer is correct. The reduced complexity helped her recall the past sequence.

TEACHER: Very good. Would you get the sponge for me and wet it? Get a paper towel and wet that too. Wet them both.

This chain of commands is to help the child practice retaining several elements at one time.

JULIE: [Goes to sink in room and reaches, not for the requested items, but for the soap.]

This behavior illustrates the easy distractibility of a young child.

TEACHER: [Follows child over to sink.] Do we need the soap?

Teacher attempts to give aid by focusing on problem at hand.

JULIE: No. [Takes sponge and piece of paper toweling and starts to return to seat.]

Child has executed one segment of complex command in selecting the correct objects.

TEACHER: Do you remember what I asked you to do with the paper and sponge?

Teacher is offering assistance to help child remember last part of command. This emphasis on memory is intentional, since once a child has a grasp of how to relate past to present events, he has made a major gain in thinking.

JULIE: Uh huh. Wet them.

TEACHER: Fine. Then, do that.

JULIE: [Wets toweling and sponge.] They are full of water.

TEACHER: Do you need all that water?

Spontaneously verbalizes observation.

JULIE: [Shakes head to indicate "no."]

TEACHER: What could you do to get rid of the water that you don't need?

JULIE: [Squeezes water from both sponge and paper.]

Offers question to help child arrive at simple cause-and-effect relation.

TEACHER: What did you do?

Child's response is correct on action level.

JULIE: The water comes out.

TEACHER: That's fine Julie. You really didn't need all that water. [They return to the table.] Now, I'd like you to draw something for me on the blackboard.

Even when child acts appropriately, he may not understand the rationale for the action. Teacher's question was designed to elicit this awareness.

JULIE: What color?

TEACHER: What color would you like to use?

JULIE: Green [and selects green crayon.]

The specific color is not integral to completing the task. Therefore, here and whenever possible, teacher gives child the opportunity to exercise choice.

TEACHER: Green is fine. Draw some green lines for me.

As opposed to random grabbing, this action follows a specific direction.

JULIE: I'll make some big ones.

TEACHER: Okay. We can work with big ones. Oh! Those are very big lines. What will happen if you wipe the sponge on those lines?

Since child's wish is not in conflict with the goal of the lesson, the teacher incorporates it into the lesson. The question is designed to help the child predict future events.

JULIE: I don't know.

TEACHER: Think about it, Julie. If you put this sponge over your lines and wipe them, what will happen?

Even though teacher thought child could not predict the outcome, she posed this question to help child recognize that a significant event is about to occur.

JULIE: [Moves sponge over drawing.]

TEACHER: What's happening to the lines, Julie?

JULIE: [With surprise.] They're not there anymore!

By having been focused, child gets a flash of insight that an interesting process is occurring. By contrast, when given no direction, children frequently just accept common phenomena without understanding. For example, if teacher had merely said "erase it," child would have done so without any recognition of the processes involved.

TEACHER: [Holds sponge down to prevent child from lifting it.] If I lift up the sponge, what color is going to be on the sponge?

Another question to help child predict future events.

JULIE: White

Child automatically responds to word "color" by naming any color.

TEACHER: Why white?

Regardless of whether child's answer is correct or incorrect, teacher makes child justify response.

JULIE: Green.

TEACHER: Tell me why you said green? Why do you think it will be green?

This question is asked so that child begins to recognize that prediction is based on observation and must be justified.

JULIE: 'Cause I wipe it off.

The action she describes is one aspect of the cause-and-effect idea that teacher is trying to develop.

TEACHER: What did you wipe off?

This question is to bring in other aspects necessary for the completion of the cause-and-effect idea.

JULIE: The green color.

Achieves correct answer.

TEACHER: Let's see if you're right. [Lifts sponge.] Green! You're right. Very good.

Shows child that prediction was correct.

The discussion went on to consider issues such as the effects on the sponge of erasing different colors, what happens to the chalk after it is erased, how to get chalk out of a sponge, comparison of sponge and paper toweling as erasers, and so forth.

This lesson, which lasted 20 minutes, was conducted with interest and enthusiasm on the part of the child who 3 months before could not maintain a set for more than a few minutes.

The lesson that follows was given in the same week as Session 2. It was taught by one of the nursery school teachers who had been invited to visit the program. The teacher was told to teach a cognitively oriented lesson that she deemed appropriate for this age child.

SESSION 3

On this particular day, there were boxes of small plants in the room which the children were to plant outside. As she entered, Julie immediately looked at these flowers. The teacher noticed this and said:

TEACHER: Have you seen the flowers?

JULIE: I saw a beautiful flower outside.

Because the specific referent was not designated (i.e., the flowers in the room), child reacted only to the word "flower."

TEACHER: A beautiful flower? What color was it?

Teacher is led away from her initial referent and poses an unverifiable question.

JULIE: I don't know. It's a beautiful flower.

It is not possible to ascertain whether child's response is a superficial verbalization or an accurate description.

TEACHER: Did you put it in the ground?

Teacher appears to assume that child's comments reflect true interest. Thus, rather than initiating productive dialogue, teacher has limited herself to a very confined area.

JULIE: I picked it up.

This response is likely to be a simple rote association.

TEACHER: You picked it up? What kind was it?

Teacher here poses another unverifiable question.

JULIE: I don't know.

TEACHER: Was it little and yellow? Maybe it was a dandelion? Did you plant the flower? Was it a seed and now it's a flower?

Teacher's questions involve multiple concepts, including an understanding of plant metamorphosis. This example illustrates the paradox of many preschool language programs, in which it is common to ask extremely complex questions couched in deceptively simple terms. Because of the apparent simplicity, it is often not deemed necessary to give the aids necessary for grasping what are, in fact, complex ideas.

JULIE: [Nods.]

TEACHER: Why don't you draw a picture of the flower and then we can see what color it is.

Teacher assumes that child's poverty of language prohibits explanation and that if the verbal requirements are replaced through drawing, child's knowledge will be revealed. This may, in fact, be true. However, since child's drawing is not verifiable, teacher cannot determine its accuracy. Thus, dialogue with seeming conceptual content can often be aimless.

JULIE: I'd like to do any color flower.

TEACHER: I'd love to have a drawing of it.

In keeping with her permissive orientation, teacher drops her original request and follows child's superficial comment. If child were moving toward a productive idea of her own, this permissive acceptance would prove valuable.

JULIE: I'm gonna make a beautiful flower.

TEACHER: Good.

JULIE: What's this? [The child is referring to the design from the table which comes through on her drawing.]

Child is beginning to observe and question her surroundings.

TEACHER: That's the table cloth coming up; the pattern.

Teacher answers directly. The information requested by child is not simply factual but could be deduced by child herself through proper questioning.

An interchange about flowers then continued on the assumption that the child, in fact, had something definite she wanted to draw. The teacher did attempt to stimulate the child's recall of the specific flower but for this purpose again used unverifiable questions. After the child had drawn several flowers, the teacher said:

TEACHER: Do you know how many flowers you have there now?

Teacher here is attempting to lead child away from narrowness of flowers per se and integrate it with another concept, that is, number.

JULIE: Three. I'm 5 years old.

Child's association of one number with another has an understandable basis. However, her spontaneous use of the same words for a variety of phenomena (age, objects, etc.) suggests that she does not have a clear understanding of the concept of number. Although one would not expect greater understanding in a young child, one must be aware that confusion exists.

TEACHER: You're 5 years old? Maybe you could make flowers for how old you are. Do you know how many more you would need?

Teacher assumes that child can make an equation between numbers in terms of years and numbers of objects.

JULIE: Five.

Child does not answer question but, rather, repeats her response to earlier question.

TEACHER: Five *altogether*. And how many do you have here?

Teacher makes attempt to dissect the problem for simplification. However, the complexity involved requires an almost endless dissection, for example, "Five equals the number of years you are; each flower represents one year; the flowers do not equal the desired number of years; additional flowers must be drawn; you need to consider the number of flowers you have drawn relative to the desired number five, etc." This fantastic complexity is far beyond child's ability to comprehend, but is in effect what has been asked of her.

JULIE: I'll make one more. What kind of brown is this? It's a tree.

Child shows a primitive understanding that *more* is needed, but not specifically how much or why. Her leading back to color may be a combination of avoiding a difficult issue or another intrusion of an impulsive idea.

TEACHER: Oh, that's pretty, Julie. That's very, very, nice.

Topic of numbers has been discarded without any advance in child's knowledge.

JULIE: I bet it's time to wake up now.

Child is referring to the nap time of the rest of the nursery group.

TEACHER: What time do you get up?

Teacher has misinterpreted child's referent to mean the time she wakes up at home. This confusion is reasonable, and where teaching time is unlimited, it is of no special significance. In a language program with a highly restricted time element, however, it hampers the few opportunities available to teach a child how to interpret correctly other people's frames of reference.

JULIE: I get up five o'clock.

TEACHER: In the morning? [Incredulously.] Do you really wake up at five o'clock in the morning?

It is likely that child is perseverating the "five" from the earlier discussion.

JULIE: I do.

TEACHER: And what time do you come to school?

JULIE: I don't know what time—nighttime?

TEACHER: No.

JULIE: I think so; I got a clock. I'm tired.

This dialogue again illustrates the type of communication between a child and teacher which is often mistaken for a conceptual discussion (i.e., time, hours, daytime, nighttime, etc.) Child's lack of awareness of the absurdity of being in nursery school at night indicates that she is in a discussion beyond her depth. In her effort to respond, child is led to rely on prattle alone.

DISCUSSION

We believe that the first two dialogues illustrate the marked changes that occurred in this child after only 6 hours of tutoring. These 15-minute sessions took place three times a week over a 3-month period. Nine hours would have been the optimum during this time span, but absences reduced the total possible time allocated.

The changes in the behavior were corroborated by a rise of 12 points from 86 to 98 on the Stanford-Binet Intelligence Test. Similar changes which were statistically significant occurred for the total group of 12 children tutored as Julie had been. Although Julie's rise was only 12 points, one child's IQ rose 28 points. These changes occurred across a wide behavioral range including control of impulsivity, increase of attention span, and greater enjoyment in learning.

Verbal skills alone were not an indication of Julie's growth (and may well not be a good indicator for other children). For example, as her hyperactive state became more controlled, her initial *rate* of verbalization declined. In place of her scattered language outpouring, she began to harness the language skills she possessed and use them in a relevant and directed manner. No measures exist for discerning this growth in quality versus quantity of verbalization in the young child, although such measures are sorely needed.

It may be argued that any one-to-one situation may bring about this type of change. However, when the same nursery school teacher met with a control group of three children on an individual but nonteaching basis, there was no significant change. A relationship with an involved and warm adult has often been suggested as the missing link to learning. We submit that such a relationship is fruitless from a cognitive view, unless the time is structured and directed toward a language for cognition.

The session with the visiting teacher was included to offer clues as to why the one-to-one situation fails to develop thinking skills. We recognize that the dialogue is shown to a disadvantage in that the teacher was new to the situation and not well known to the child. However, it is repersentative of the type of session we recorded by a number of cooperating nursery school teachers. In addition, we feel that this sequence epitomizes the traditionally child-centered and permissive Gestalt of nursery school philosophy (see review by Weikart, 1967). In this type of program, which is designed to meet the needs of the middle-class child, language and intellectual development are placed *last* in a list of desired attributes to be developed. Even when cognitive skills are taught, the philosophy of "what does the child *want* to do" is the pervasive element.

This philosophy was clearly illustrated in the visiting lesson where the teacher severely limited the scope of the material by continuing to focus on casual comments of the child. Regardless of whether she mistook these remarks for real interest or whether she was guided by a consideration for a child's words, the teacher missed the opportunity to lead Julie toward developing the higher level concepts of which she was capable.

On the other hand, when the teacher did initiate material, she posed seemingly simple questions which, in reality, were of enormous complexity. Since the teacher did not have the techniques for analyzing where the child's difficulty lay, she assumed that the concepts involved were well beyond the child. The failure to recognize the complexity of her questions reinforces the philosophy that thinking cannot be accelerated but must merely wait until the child is "ready." The teacher thus abdicates her leadership in favor of the ephemeral concept of "readiness." Consequently, she sees her role as merely structuring the surroundings so as to set the stage for the spontaneous emergence of reasoning.

If this is the viewpoint of many nursery schools attended by middle-class children, the question arises as to how these children develop cognitive skills without special tutoring. It is generally assumed that they absorb them at home. However, if the middle-class teacher *avoids* fostering these skills, might not the middle-class parent similarly avoid this type of dialogue? Evidence indicates that, compared to the lower class, there is a much greater richness of verbal interchange between parent and child in the middle-class home (Freeburg & Payne, 1967). Thus, language is pervasive in these homes, and the child is exposed "naturally" to language skills throughout the day. The middle-class person is not accustomed to being limited to a special time (i.e., 15-minute periods) focused upon these skills, nor to the necessity for having such focusing. When a relevant situation arises, the middle-class parent will encourage discussion with his children. Such situations arise "normally" during the course of the day and are therefore taken for granted. However, such times rarely emerge during the course of the day of the lower-class child. These opportunities must be created for him. Consequently, the teaching situation may appear artificial and constricted, since the 15-minute period must be utilized with a maximum of efficiency in order to grasp every possible opportunity for cognitive growth.

REFERENCES

Blank, M. A methodology for fostering abstract thinking in deprived children. Paper presented at Ontario Institute for Studies in Education conference on "Problems in the Teaching of Young Children," Toronto, March, 1968.

Blank, M., & Solomon, F. A tutorial language program to develop abstract thinking in socially disadvantaged preschool children. *Child Development,* 1968, 39, 379–390.

Freeburg, N. E., & Payne, D. T. Parental influence on cognitive development in early childhood: a review. *Child Development,* 1967, 38, 65–87.

Weikart, D. P. Preschool programs: preliminary findings. Journal of Special Education, 1967, 1, 163–181.

[*Child Development,* 1969, 40, 47–61. © 1969 by the Society for Research in Child Development, Inc. All rights reserved.]

A TALK TO TEACHERS

Jonathan Kozol

Jonathan Kozol, "A Talk to Teachers," *The English Record,* October 1968, Vol. 19, pp. 2-14.

A TALK TO TEACHERS

Jonathan Kozol

We meet, I'm afraid, at a tragically appropriate moment. The nation is divided between a false facade of superficial mourning for a dead man [Martin Luther King] it seldom genuinely honored and a more authentic and gut-level terror that we are soon going to be obliged to pay a terrible price for the racism and brutality his murder symbolizes.

The over-riding fear, the constant question, is whether or not we are about to have a summer of unending urban riots. To my own mind the most saddening fact of all is that, in the long run, in terms of the ultimate issues, it is not going to much matter. More people may die and another thousand buildings may perhaps be burned or battered but the same problems will be with us even after the wreckage has been cleared away and, riots or not, destruction blatant and overt or destruction only gradual and ordinary, the same bitter problems of a divided society and of a nation torn by bigotry will still be with us in September.

I think that in America we love to believe in apocalyptic interventions. It would be comforting almost to think that a rebellion, no matter how devastating, no matter how expensive, would at least have the ultimate result of settling our problems. It is—unhappily—not so.

Broken glass and streams of blood will be good covers for news magazines in the middle of the summer—but they will not even begin to solve our problems. Probably they will not even destroy us.

They will *scare* us for a while and force our newspapers to write long editorials. And then we will go back to our ordinary American lives again and to our old, more quiet ways of dying.

It is for this reason, I believe, that now is as good a time as any to take an unforgiving second look at some of the ways in which we have defined the basic problems. I would like to focus on the schools. I would like to focus on the teachers. And I would like to get beyond some of the unproductive things that have been said already.

Jonathan Kozol won the National Book Award in 1968 for his "Death at an Early Age," subtitled "The Destruction of the Hearts and Minds of Negro Children in the Boston Public School," published by Houghton Mifflin Company. Mr. Kozol is now Educational Director of the Store-Front Learning Center in Boston's South End ghetto and continues to be one of the country's most articulate critics of racial prejudice in American schools. This paper was presented at the Annual Spring Conference of the New York State English Council in New York City, April 26, 1968.

The problem within the ghetto, stated in the very simplest possible terms, comes down to a very few plain and painful facts: Black kids, black parents and black leaders do not—by and large—either like or trust their schools or the kinds of white people who work in them. A great many black people, given even half a chance, would dearly love to burn the whole mess down and—unhappily, in a good many cases—would not be very much the losers if they succeeded.

I say this not facetiously but because I believe that many Negro people have been fortunate enough to recognize fairly early in their lives that the schools were not their friends, that the schools were not going to stand beside them in a struggle, that the teachers were not likely to stick out their necks on crucial issues.

I am going to try to be as frank as possible in attempting to anticipate the reactions to this statement among many of the people in this audience. Many of you, I can imagine, will protest at this kind of disloyal assertion on my part and will want to stand up and tell me that I am being insolent and speaking out of turn, needlessly defiant and unjustly disrespectful to my fellow-teachers: Don't I know—these people will want to ask—how many of the dedicated teachers of the inner city schools have given their lives to the education of young children?

To this, I am afraid, that there is only one real answer: It does not matter, in the long run, what I *think*—what matters in the long run is what the black communities BELIEVE. And what they *do* believe at the present time, throughout the nation, is that professional teaching hierarchies, principals, superintendents—are servants and acolytes of a hostile, unfriendly and ultimately unmerciful white structure which has trodden them down and kept their souls and lives in prison for over three hundred years and which still today oppresses their children, murders their leaders and disdains their own humanity.

If this is the case—if this is what the black communities believe—then the challenge for us is *not* to withdraw into a militant and stiff defensive posture in which we ward off criticism with our pious platitudes of "professional experience" and "long years of dedication" but to ask ourselves instead just exactly why it is that all our "professionalism" and all our inheritance of reiterated "dedication" seem to have had the ultimate effect of compelling most black people to despise us?

The deepest, most direct and most immediate personal experience that a black child in America is ever likely to have of white society is that which he will have within a public classroom—in the person of the school teacher. That experience, as we well know, is anything but happy. Bitterness and cynicism are the primary inheritance that most black children in America take from the classroom.

"Hate whitey!" cries the 14-year-old Negro student standing on the corner.

"Hate whitey!" repeats the 16-year-old drop-out as he sees a white policeman cruising through the ghetto.

But who is this whitey?? What white people do they *know?* What white man or white woman have they ever faced directly, known with intimacy, had a chance to assess and study and evaluate and learn how to trust or distrust—hate or admire?

Well, you know the answer as readily as I do: sometimes it's a slum-lord, a grocer, a money-lender, police officer or social worker—but in almost *all* cases it is a white school principal or a white school teacher. And it is from us, whether we know it or not, whether we like it or not, whether we can admit it or not, that black kids sooner or later get the message that white men and white women are people who—for one reason or another— they cannot take for real. Some teachers keep on repeating the same question, as though they haven't an idea in the world of a possible answer: Why don't they trust us? What on earth could we be doing wrong?

I don't think we really have to look far to find the answer. Teachers go out on strike for all sorts of good and palpable and powerful reasons: they strike for pay, they strike for better working conditions, they strike for extra benefits, occasionally they even strike for issues which have something to do, specifically, with the immediate demands of education: but *when,* the black community asks us, *did we ever strike to bring about racial integration? When*—they want to know—*did we ever strike to get racist Scott Foresman readers taken out of any grade-school classrooms? When*—they ask—*did the junior high school teachers of the ghetto ever strike to have the dishonest and openly bigoted and destructive Allyn and Bacon social studies textbooks taken out of their shelves and classrooms?*

You called us *culturally deprived*—the black parents tell us— you told us that we were the ones who lacked stability and values. All the while you, as the teacher, remained the keeper of the classroom and the guardian of its books and values. You were the ones who could examine those texts and prepare the lessons, ready the lesson-plans, state your approach, your purpose, your methods, and your evaluations. Yet all the while you failed for some reason to make the one most important and most obvious and necessary evaluation of them all: Are these books, are these values, are these areas of evasion and dishonesty consistent with democratic principles and with all that you (the teacher) are supposed to have known about the "professionalism" and "moral dignity" of education?

Allyn and Bacon, publishers: *Our America,*—a textbook for fourth grade children on our nation's history:

> 'Our slaves have good homes and plenty to eat.' . . . Most Southern people treated their slaves kindly. . . . 'When they are sick, we take good care of them.' No one can truly say, 'The North was right' or 'The Southern cause was the better.' For in Our America all of us have the right to our beliefs.

You were there—you were in the classroom—you were the one who had the education and the professional judgement and, supposedly, the moral character: *What did you do—what did you say?* (the Negro mother asks us) *If you ever protested, you must have done it in a whisper: we never heard you.* . . . *American Book Company, Publishers: Our Neighbors Near and Far:*

> The streets of this Oasis city of Biskra [in North Africa] are interesting. There are many different people upon them. Some who are white like ourselves have come here from Europe. Others are Negroes with black skins, from other parts of Africa. And many are bronze-faced Arabs who have come in from the desert to trade in the stores. . . .
>
> These people are fine looking. Their black eyes are bright and intelligent. Their features are much like our own, and although their skin is brown, they belong to the white race, as we do. It is the scorching desert sun that has tanned the skin of the Arabs to such a dark brown color.
>
> Yumbu and Minko are a black boy and a black girl who live in this jungle village. Their skins are of so dark a brown color that they look almost black. Their noses are large and flat. Their lips are thick. Their eyes are black and shining, and their hair is so curly that it seems like wool. They are Negroes and they belong to the black race.
>
> Two Swiss children live in a farmhouse on the edge of town. . . . These children are handsome. Their eyes are blue. Their hair is golden yellow. Their white skins are clear, and their cheeks are as red as ripe, red apples.

You were there—you were in the classroom—what did you say? What did you do? We were the uneducated—(the Negro mother, the Negro father tells us)—we were your maids and ironing-ladies, garbagemen and janitors. We were the ones who were illiterate, we were the ones who were culturally deprived. Daniel Moynihan has told the whole world what was wrong with *us*—but who has yet been able to explain to the world what in God's earth could have been wrong with *you?*

Allyn and Bacon, Publishers, Our World Today, another geography textbook, this one for junior high school:

> The people of South Africa have one of the most democratic governments now in existence in any country.
>
> Africa needs more capitalists. . . . White managers are needed . . . to show the Negroes how to work and to manage the plantations . . .

> The white men who have entered Africa are teaching the natives how to live.

You were there—you were the guardian of our children—what did you do?

And this (these things) the Negro child remembers—and the child who read that book five years ago, of course—is the full-grown black teenager of today, and he wants to know what you were doing or saying on these matters: He wants to know why you were silent, when you were the one who was the adult, the grown-up—the professional in that public classroom. You kept the cupboard. You prepared the meal. And what you fed the child—without remorse—was poison. Whether you taught math or physics, Russian, Chinese, English, French or cooking—you were there. You were an adult and you said nothing. There is no way in which you can escape responsibility.

The Negro mother and the Negro father speak to you, quietly: You went on strike (they say)—you went out on strike for your "professional rights and dignities" but you never once went out on strike for your rights *or* our rights as respectable human beings.

"Why is it they don't trust us?" ask the sweet and bewildered white school-ladies to each other.

Because we're frauds and it took the Negroes a long time to figure it out: but now they know it.

A couple of years back a highly respected board of inquiry sponsored by the Massachusetts State Board of Education issued a report documenting the fact of racial segregation in the Boston Schools. The report was signed by outstanding figures in all areas: the Catholic Archbishop, leaders of the Jewish and Protestant communities, the presidents of Boston University, M.I.T., Brandeis and Northeastern. . . .

In response to this report, a young Boston teacher, assigned to a third grade class within the ghetto, initiated a brief letter simply asserting in an unbelligerent manner that she, and other school teachers, were aware of the presence of racial segregation in their classroom, were aware of the deficiencies of their school buildings, and shared the sense of impatience and of discontent evinced both by the State Report and by the Black Community. She—like others—had heard the children singing when they were walking on the picket lines and she knew very well the words of one of the songs they sang:

"Which side are you on?" the song was asking, "Which side are you on?" It came out of the labor union struggles of the 1930's and was taken over by the white and Negro people in the Freedom Movement.

So here was this young white girl in the school system

trying, with a good heart, to give an answer and she appealed to her fellow-teachers in the system to do the same.

Ladies and gentlemen—there were at least 4,000 professional employees of the Boston Public Schools at that time. *Not 20 people would stand beside that one young teacher by affixing their signatures at the bottom of her letter.*

"Which side are you on?" the black parents were demanding.

And 3,980 professional employees of the Boston School System gave their answer. Then . . . in their faculty rooms, over their sandwiches and over their cups of coffee, the dedicated white ladies sat and stared at each other in sweet bewilderment —asking the time-honored question: "Why is it they don't trust us?"

Because they had done nothing to *deserve* being trusted: because they were not *trustworthy.*

The distance and the withdrawal on the part of a school faculty from its immediate community is, I think, well-known to many of us. Those among us who are acquainted with the classic faculty-room dialogue within a ghetto grade-school or a junior-high know well, I think, how older teachers coach the younger ones about the ways in which to deal and talk with Negro people: *Be careful,* is the message: *Don't be unguarded or informal. Don't let yourself be known to the black community in any way that might be vulnerable, that might reveal your feelings.*

The first advice that I received from my school supervisor was not to make use of the informal and casual word OKAY.

"I noticed you used the word OKAY three times this morning, Mr. Kozol"—said my superior. "OKAY is a slang word, Mr. Kozol. In the Boston schools we say ALL RIGHT, we do not say OKAY."

It seemed not worth the pain, not worth the trouble to reason with the man—to try to tell him that OKAY could be a very good and powerful word, that ALL RIGHT says nothing, that OKAY says everything, that President Kennedy used to say the word OKAY to his brothers, that good reporters say OKAY to their editors, football captains to their managers, pilots to the airport. I wanted to tell him that OKAY was a good word, an American word, an OKAY word—a word with life in it, and energy. But I didn't even argue with him. I just looked at him and nodded—and denied myself and said quietly, "All right."

There was the time, too, when I took a child over to visit in Cambridge. We visited the museums, went to call on an old classmate, had lunch with my girl friend, and went back to my own place to set up an electric train lay-out in the kitchen. The principal of my school heard of this visit in short order and later wrote of it in her report on me. She indicated in her report that unattractive conclusions might well be drawn of a man who takes a young child to visit in his home. Said the principal in her report, "I told Mr. Kozol of the possibilities. . . ."

I think, also, of the tragedy of a PTA meeting in my building at which I arrived a little late—late enough to stand a moment in the doorway and look out at the extraordinary scene in front of me. Parents on one side—teachers way over on the other. In the middle—a huge safe space of unoccupied and untouched chairs.

I looked and watched and wondered:

How did this happen?

Was it conceivably a random accident?

Was it just a fluke of timing?

Obviously—with all mercy, all reservation, all wish to be wise and kindly and compassionate and back-bending—one could not CONCEIVABLY write off the professional STUPIDITY, VULGARITY and sheer ROTTENNESS of the school principal and faculty in allowing this kind of situation to develop.

Was it not, I had to ask myself, part and parcel of the same stupidity that prevented white teachers from dropping in on Negro families, from driving kids home, from fooling around in a comfortable and easy-going way out in the schoolyard? Was it not the same tragedy, the same ignorance, the same brutality which allowed a school faculty to drive through the ghetto every morning with eyes looking neither to left nor to right, nor, in some cases, one felt, even down the middle? Teachers on one side—parents on the other. In the center, an area of graphic sterilization. No germs might travel, no blackness, no ugliness, no race-contagion, could journey the distance from the seated mothers of a black community and the prissy teachers, their legs and souls up-tight together in their safe and sexless little corner on the aisle.

I would like to be able to deserve to be called generous by my fellow-teachers and I recognize all too well that, in ringing such a note of outright indignation, I bring upon myself once again, as I have done before, the concerted rage of a profession of embattled people, teachers in panic, principals in frenzy, aroused to vengeance at the implications of their personal cowardice, deceitfulness and pathos.

Yet it is true. It is there before us every day. And the very rare exceptions only stand out to prove the rule.

Avoidance of intimacy—avoidance of blackness—avoidance of humanity. At times, the tragedy involved in such a stance withdrew into the background and all that remained was a kind of wild absurdity.

Absurdity seemed uppermost in a confrontation that developed once between our principal and one of the other Fourth Grade teachers. The teacher in question, a woman, happened to be Negro and happened to live in Roxbury and happened, as a matter of fact, to live in the precise neighborhood in which the school was situated. The principal had advised us to observe unusual caution in regard to any casual or day-to-day involvements with the black community. She did not, of course, use those words, but it was apparent to us all that this was her real meaning. So this teacher, the Negro woman I have just mentioned, went up and asked the principal what she expected of her.

"What if I'm in the supermarket," she asked, "and I meet the mother or father of one of my pupils there? What do you think I'm going to say?"

The principal was taken aback, obviously baffled by the situation. It did not accord properly with a reasonable understanding of such matters that a person ought to be living within the same community in which she also was a teacher. Our principal, however, was good at regaining her composure—she never lost it for long, nor lacked of authoritative resources for regaining it. And so in this case too she soon regained her self-possession, looked directly into the eyes of this young teacher, and said to her simply:

"Well then, in such a case all I can do is to advise you not to forget your professional dignity."

It is hard to know exactly how she meant this, or how indeed one is to lose dignity in the purchasing of groceries except by confirming to the mothers and fathers of a community that you, like them, possess an alimentary canal, need food, spend money, buy things cheaply. It is hard to know—but I don't even want to ask. What I would like to do instead is to ask what we can do for our part to change these things and to break down these walls of inhumanity.

I think, to start with, we have got to ask ourselves straightforwardly where most of these teachers and administrators *come* from—and in what ways they have been prepared for teaching. This, of course, is the real question and I am afraid—no matter what we say—the majority of us already know the answer.

They come from schools of education.

They come from teachers' colleges.

They do *not*, by and large, come from the liberal faculties of our major universities, but from those faculties which are geared to teacher-training.

I think it is time to place some of the blame where it belongs and to cease trying to placate those who are most likely to take offense at words of frankness.

Some schools of education (a few) are relatively competent and provide a rich and humane education. (For the sake of politeness, let us assume that the education faculty from which any of my listeners may have graduated was one of the exceptions.) By and large, this is simply not the case. Education schools, in their great numbers, are institutions which perpetuate precisely the kinds of uneasy and defensive behavior which I have been describing. At times they offer, I suppose, certain courses which may be truly helpful in a very few and highly selective areas of learning. Much of what they teach, however, is *not* necessary at all, has little relevance to the human or intellectual or moral demands to be placed upon a classroom teacher, and leaves her worse off than she was before she started.

In every other field we are willing to acknowledge the failure of a process of preparation when the products of that preparation prove unequal to the responsibilities for which they had thought that they had been prepared. *Only in education, it appears, do we attribute the blame for failure not to the training institution, not to the Education School nor even to the teacher—but to the consumer, the victim, the public, the Negro family and the Negro child.* Teachers, filled full with all the newest codification—with all the most recent and most sophisticated formulas of condescension concerning the supposedly under-motivated, lethargic and culturally disadvantaged Negro child—go out into the ghetto, memorize the words of their sociologists and suddenly find themselves bewildered and helpless, overwhelmed by the realities which are imposed upon them. Sometime—seeing the bewilderment with which so many education school graduates respond—I wonder if they would not have been better off in the beginning if they had had their courses, their training, their preparation right on the spot, right in the ghetto all along? What did they gain from all their courses in the philosophy of education, in methods and materials, in sociological examination of so-called "culturally deprived" but a wearisome and inappropriate and somehow dehumanizing sense of condescension—and an inflated and artificial image of their own individual importance as "professionals"?

Teachers tell us very frequently of the hostilities they encounter, the disappointments they face, the distrust their presence repeatedly engenders in their Negro pupils.

There was no such distrust of teachers in the Freedom Schools of Alabama and Mississippi.

There is no such distrust of teachers in the tutorial classes run by the various militant Negro community organizations in this country.

There is no such distrust in the classrooms of those experimental grade-schools begun and operated by the black communities.

Nor, I think we remember, has there ever been distrust of that sort within the Headstart Classes, Upward Bound Programs, or other independent educational projects of the War On Poverty.

Yet none of these programs that I have named are dominated by those whom we designate "professionals." It is, indeed, one is almost tempted to believe, the adamant *non*-professionalism—the amateur exuberance and uninhibited sense of personal commitment—which makes such programs possible and successful.

Why can we not bring some of the same energy and exuberance into the public classrooms? Is there no way to bring into these classrooms right away the kinds of people who will be able to earn the confidence of a black community because they will in fact share its aspirations? There are thousands of young, bright, brave and revolutionary pupils in the liberal colleges of this country and I know from my experience—from recent weeks and hours of long discussion among the parents and leaders of the black communities—that they are still needed and still *wanted* within the schools that serve the inner cities.

For all the recent militance, for all the rhetoric of separation, for all the talk about black schools with all-black children and black teachers, the authentic leaders of the black community will still tell us frankly that they cannot go it alone without white teachers. For a long while to come, the situation is going to remain the same—and the only question is whether we are going to give those children the worst or the best—the dreariest or the most exciting—the narrowest or the freest—that we have to offer.

The liberal and radical kids are there in our colleges right now. We send them to the Peace Corps, we give them to SNCC and S.D.S. or else we let them out on loan to Senator McCarthy but—poor economists that we are—we do not allow them to give their lives to the black children of the inner cities. Not, that is, unless they have previously agreed to have their brain picked dry and their outlook rendered sterile within the thankless surgery of one of our schools of education.

It is a reasonable question, I suppose, whether such kids would stick it out forever in a public classroom. Would they remain in teaching? Would they last for ten years? Would they last for forty? Would they be "dedicated" forever to their "professional" responsibility and obligation? In a curious sense, I almost hope that they would *not*—not, at any rate, in the manner in which those words have been interpreted up to now.

Rather an impulsive and energetic and unpredictable amateur than a drearily predictable, dedicated and dehydrated professional—and rather a person dedicated to life, and love, and danger, and activity, and action than to the wearisome and unchangeable sterility of chalk and stick and basic reader.

Recently in Newton a parent complained to a School official at an open meeting: "There is so much teacher-turnover within this system. Many of our teachers seem to leave so soon, after only three or four years in many cases, sometimes after seven."

Said the School official: "Of this we are not in the least ashamed. We would rather have teachers we can't keep than teachers we can't get rid of."

There, I believe, in few words, is a very good and adequate answer.

I see no shame in having high teacher-turnover—if what we are turning over is something fertile and exciting. Rather have a lively, attractive and exciting girl who will quit after five years because she has the healthy urge to marry—than a girl who will never quit, for that reason because she will never get an offer.

Many older people, I can well imagine, might consider the kind of proposal I have made impractical. They will tell me that young people, by and large, are selfish and ambitious to settle down, raise families, buy their ranch homes in the country, hire maids, have holidays abroad, earn lots of money. Young people, they say, may *talk* idealism but they will not act upon it. They will not make the sacrifice to stand up and serve as teachers.

When people tell me this—I always look at them for a moment—to think about their motives—and then I say that I do not know the kinds of young people they are speaking of. It was not the selfish and self-centered spoiled daughter of the selfish and the opulent rich man who ran the Freedom Schools in Mississippi and Alabama, who worked with the poor and the hungry for the Peace Corps in Argentina, Bolivia and Brazil. It was not the young man dreaming about a ranch-house and a million dollars who gave up his studies and his comfort and his security to go down South and risk his life, his respectability or his career, to walk a Negro citizen to the City Hall and give him the courage to go in and demand the right to register to vote.

Michael Schwerner was not thinking about cocktails, about sports cars or ranch-wagons when he lay down his life three years ago in Mississippi to help to make this nation free.

James Chaney was not calculating how he could make it to the top when he was buried at the bottom of the mud beneath a wall made out of stone in Mississippi, because he believed that black people still had the privilege to be free.

The young Unitarian minister, James Reeb, murdered three

years ago in Selma, Alabama was not worrying about nailing down a fancy parish, sending his kids to fancy schools and buying his wife a fancy way of living when he walked out upon the streets of that racist city and received a club over his head; and fell; and died.

There is a new nation within the old one in America. It is better than the old one; it is honest and it is not selfish and it is not afraid. The oldtime teachers, the oldtime autocrats, the oldtime political school administrators do not really want to believe that this can be the case. It is too threatening. It hurts them very badly. They are involved with guilt and with the memory of cowardice and with the fear of an unspeakable retribution. They knew about the racist books within their shelves and did not speak. They saw the Negro parents across the room and did not smile. They heard the moral challenge—the plea—coming out from within the black community and they did not answer. And now they are unwilling—they are unable—to believe that we can be more decent.

It is up to us to prove that they are wrong.

400,000 Negro kids are going to be attaining the age of eighteen this season. Of those 400,000, not 10% will have received an education equal to the white standards.

It will not be due to their mothers and their fathers.

It will not be due to a defective family-structure.

It will not be due to any inherent lack of intelligence or motivation.

It will be due to ineffective and irrelevant and dishonest EDUCATION.

There is no way to get around it. The facts are there and they are devastating.

We are going to have to look those facts straight in the face and take them seriously. The sweet white lady in the classroom who wears blinders, cannot make her way through to a rebellious generation of black children. The white bigot or false liberal who teaches his lesson, locks up his room, and hops into his car to return to his nice home within the safe suburbs, cannot and should not have a serious role within a ghetto classroom. There is only one kind of person who can make it work—and that is the person who, in his class and in his life, is ready to take a militant stand beside the black community. There is no other way to do it.

Often now, when I have finished with a lecture of this sort, young people come up to me, teachers just beginning or people who believe that they would like to teach, and they question me, and they ask me, it seems—almost as if it were an amazing and undecipherable riddle: "How is it, Mr. Kozol, that you were able to go in, as you did, to an angry and revolutionary Negro area and into a turbulent and unhappy and properly embittered classroom, a room in which kids had had substitutes half the winter, or emotionally unstable teachers, or teachers who despised them, or—more frequently—teachers who simply didn't really ever care—and did not right on the spot receive a knife in the side or, at the very least, an eraser or an elastic or a paperclip or a spitball in the eye?"

When this question is asked, I often am aware that the questioner expects a complicated answer—a subtle and elaborate and self-complimenting explanation of how I worked out and contrived some amazing and fascinating English lessons guaranteed to hook the most apathetic and lethargic students. It just is not so. There is a far more simple-minded answer. "Listen," I say; "I walked into a ghetto classroom, an inept amateur, knowing nothing. In my lapel there was a tiny little button that the children in that classroom recognized. It was white and black—an equal sign—you remember it, I hope—it was the symbol of the Civil Rights Movement in America. The children had *eyes* and they could *see*—and they had hearts and minds and they could feel and know. And they knew what that little button stood for. On Saturdays sometimes they saw me on a picket line in front of a dilapidated building whose absentee white landlord had been negligent. On Fridays sometimes, a little while before supper, they would see me and my girlfriend coming up the stairs of their own home to visit with their mother and their father and sometimes stay for dinner.

If it was revolutionary you may say, with a smile, it certainly was the most natural and easy and deeply satisfying kind of a revolution that a man or a woman could conspire.

Then—on Monday—I was in the classroom; and the kids would say "We saw you Saturday." Or another child would say, "He's got a pretty girlfriend." Or another one would say, "He's got a junky old beat-up raggedy car."

But the thing is—they were not angry any longer. And I wasn't a very excellent or fancy teacher—I can assure you—but I was someone they'd seen out in the real world and someone they were willing to take on as a real friend.

Well, there aren't many picket-lines any longer in America, and they don't sing Freedom Songs in this country any more, but the kids out in the ghettos are still turning to us in the same way and asking us the same question that they asked before.

"Which side are you on?" is what they're saying.

And, truly, there is no way to get around that question.

It hurts sometimes. It hurts terribly, I know. But each and every one of us has got to come up with his own answer.

227

ANXIETIES AND FORCES WHICH MITIGATE AGAINST GHETTO SCHOOL TEACHERS

Allan C. Ornstein

Allan C. Ornstein, "Anxieties and Forces Which Mitigate Against Ghetto School Teachers," *Journal of Secondary Education,* October 1968, pp. 243-254.

ANXIETIES AND FORCES WHICH MITIGATE AGAINST GHETTO SCHOOL TEACHERS

Allan C. Ornstein

We have the peculiar notion that we are doing good as long as we spend large sums of money. We believe that the problem of educating the disadvantaged can be solved by simply dispensing money to provide compensatory education, which we hope will guarantee "quality education" and "equality of opportunity" for the disadvantaged. In effect, we have adopted a "saturation approach" hoping that some programs will work. Yet, despite our huge outlay of money we are not making significant gains; more than ever, we face a vicious, stubborn cycle.

My purpose here is to come to grips with the problem, and suggest why we are failing. I am governed by a major assumption as to the reason for the problem and the stage that it has now reached. None of the compensatory programs has come up with a substitute for good teaching; no amount of money is adequate if teachers are doing an inadequate job. New schools, smaller classes, integrated textbooks, etc., are meaningless if teachers are indifferent. In short, it profits us little to spend billions of dollars on compensatory education and then place the students under ineffective teachers.

The idea that teachers are failing to reach and teach the disadvantaged is not new, but I suggest that we explore the reasons. The teachers are the victims of an intolerable system, and this causes them to become frustrated, angry, and finally, indifferent — so that almost everything we attempt now is a waste of time, money, and effort. Then, instead of being helpful, they are subjected to constant and unjust attacks by professors who are remote, not a part of or strongly attached to the actual school situation.

Teacher-training institutions do an appalling job of preparing teachers, even the distinguished, big-bellied colleges and universi-

ties fail miserably in their attempt. It is possible for a teacher to possess an advanced degree in education and instruction and still be ineffective in the classroom. Teachers who are assigned to "good" schools usually manage to get by, since their students have the ability and intrinsic motivation to behave well and learn on their own. However, whenever teachers are assigned to work with the disadvantaged, poor teacher training becomes obvious, because these students depend on good teaching. That a limited number of ghetto school teachers do succeed may be attributed to their unusual ability, which despite their poor training allows them to gain experience and effectively teach the disadvantaged. Here, however, we are confronted with a style — characteristics that seem to work well with disadvantaged youth, but were never developed by our teacher-training institutions.

The trouble with teacher training is twofold. First, only limited aspects of methodology can be supplied in advance of teaching, but virtually all the skills and knowledge basic to teaching are learned while teaching. Teachers develop competence and become aware of their role as teachers during the first two or three years of teaching, and not while they are in undergraduate school. Courses and textbooks require consolidation after teaching has begun, but as soon as prospective teachers graduate, their colleges abandon them. Thus, the most crucial period of training becomes the time when training is ended or there is a break in continuity. Second, courses consist merely of descriptions, recommendations, anecdotes, and success stories, all of which are

◆◆◆◆◆◆◆◆◆◆◆◆◆◆◆◆◆◆◆◆◆◆◆◆◆◆◆◆

ALLAN C. ORNSTEIN *is an Instructor in the School of Education at Fordham University, New York City.*

◆◆◆◆◆◆◆◆◆◆◆◆◆◆◆◆◆◆◆◆◆◆◆◆◆◆◆◆

nothing more than opinion, but often taken as gospel. Readings consist of glowing reports and advice, but fail to explain how or why the advice works. Even our best advice is a dead-end approach, a "gimmick" at best. What works for one teacher will not necessarily work for another, even with the same student. The best advice, in fact, can sometimes do the most harm. We fail to recognize that each teacher and student is unique, as well as their interactions.

☆　☆　☆

Eager but unprepared, the ghetto school teacher is usually doomed to failure. The disadvantaged are astute appraisers and knowing manipulators of their environment; they easily see through "gimmicks;" they often learn the educational cliches about themselves and answer or behave as they are expected to. They know what will upset the teachers, often better than the teachers know; they know just when to stop before it becomes unsafe or the teacher gets angry. They realize that threats are ineffectual and that the teacher's authority is limited; they usually assess the teacher as a person before they become interested in him as a teacher. A negative assessment — which is common, because of the different values and life styles of the teacher

and students — can provoke a dramatic incident, or it can be drawn out into a series of minor clashes. In either case, the students proceed to capitalize on the teacher's weaknesses, then ridicule and abuse him as a person, for example, derogating his personality and physical appearance. Once having demolished the teacher's self-respect and authority, they readily express indignation and contempt, and all their hostility and their resentment are directed at him.

The outcome is, the teacher soon tends to see his students as adversaries. The major task of teaching is replaced by discipline, and the teacher judges himself by his disciplinary prowess. Each day leaves him emotionally and physically exhausted. Anxiety overwhelms him, too, as he soon becomes aware that almost anything can happen. He is confronted by a bored and hostile class, thirty or thirty-five students he can no longer control. He sees no tangible results of hard work and feels no sense of accomplishment. For his own mental health, then, the teacher is forced to learn not to care. His apathy protects him; it is his defense; it is his way of coping with the meaninglessness and possible danger of his situation. Weekends and holidays become more important; he needs to rest, recuperate, and regain his strength and rational outlook. Sometimes he cannot wait, and becomes "ill" a day or two before the weekend. Sometimes he does not finish the term, or does not return for the next term.

The problem of "illness" and teacher turnover — the latter of which often leads to unfilled positions — results in excessive class coverages and loss of preparation periods, and detrimentally affects teaching morale and performance. The inability of ghetto schools to find willing *per diem* substitute teachers adds to the dilemma. The fact that teachers are required to cover additional classes — in most cases a strange one, which means the teacher is merely performing custodial work — creates for many uneasiness and emotional stress. This, in turn, further undermines teaching morale and performance, and causes more teachers to become "ill" and/or quit. More classes have to be covered; the students are not learning because they have many different teachers; the school's discipline problem worsens; and substitute teachers become even more difficult to recruit. Teaching morale and performance continue to deteriorate, resulting in still more absenteeism and departures, and the curtailment of the teaching-learning process. The cycle finally ends on the last day of the school year, but usually begins again in September.

Even when he is sincere, the teacher is often greeted with what to him is unwarranted cynicism. Constant questions and advice from social workers, police, and even other teachers have helped to create a feeling of suspicion on the part of the child. The child is surrounded by authorities who seem to castigate and further reject him for failing to appreciate what they have done for him. All authority becomes suspect. The child long since learned that the police are enemies. The teacher is now a new kind of "cop" who only keeps him in a different kind of jail, but a jail nevertheless. Some students are willing to learn the new rules, but many cannot, or will not.

Unfortunately, castigation and rejection are an almost intrinsic part of teaching. The development lesson is the type that most teachers use most of the time with most students. The teacher questions and the students answer, and when more than one student wishes to answer at the same time, it is the teacher who decides who will speak — or, from some children's point of view, who will be rejected. One is called on, and the others who were raising their hands cannot answer. The disadvantaged child is present-oriented and is unable to cope with this type of frustration and, since it occurs so often, it leads the child to reject the teacher and the learning process.

The most common method of evaluating students is with tests. The child's success or failure in school depends on his ability to take tests, and the accumulating learning deficit of the disadvantaged child just about guarantees failure as he is passed on from grade to grade. In effect, the test becomes just one more area of frustration and castigation, one more blow to an already weakened self-ego.

The child cannot escape being evaluated. Daily the teacher judges the child's work or lack of work, and communicates these judgments to the child, not with grades, but with facial expressions, or comments such as "who can help James?" The child realizes when he is confused and cannot cope with the learning situation, but rarely voices his plight, because the teacher seems to be castigating him for being stupid. It is little wonder that the child retreats from learning; the longer he remains in school the more evident is his retreat.

Delays are also common in all lessons. For example, in the lower grades the teacher may work with one group of students while another group works at something else. Some students are bound to finish before the teacher is ready for them, and often he asks them to find something else to do until he finishes, and may chastise them if they do not. Middle-class students obey the teacher, or at least will manage to appear busy, but the disadvantaged child has difficulty coping with delay and lacks self-control, and the ability to be "good" without a structured environment.

This kind of delay can also be observed in the secondary schools. The teacher gives the students an exercise to do; some students finish before others, and are unable to cope with the prospect of sitting and doing nothing. The teacher senses the problem and often asks, "How many need more time?" The teacher may be concerned with slower students, and give them more time, making no provisions for faster ones, or merely advising that they do "busy work" and frustrating them further. On the other hand, if the teacher discusses the exercise before everyone is finished, he is again castigating the slow-performing students and confirming their stupidity.

Then there are the minor delays — waiting to use the pencil sharpener, waiting to use the bathroom pass, waiting to line up for lunch or dismissal. It is precisely these delays that the disadvantaged child cannot cope with and which lead to disciplinary problems. Similarly, minor interruptions are common — students going to the teacher for advice, borrowing a pen or pencil, asking a question about obtaining a lunch pass, or permission to turn in today's homework tomorrow. Middle-class students can ignore these distractions or at least quickly resume their lesson; however, the disadvantaged have difficulty resuming work once they are distracted. These minor interruptions may result in a major delay, or in the teacher's losing control of the class.

☆　　☆　　☆

Isolation is usual for teachers in American schools. Formal observations and discussions of their teaching behavior are limited to one or two a year. Even the freshman teacher goes generally unobserved and unassisted, and the shock of initial year of teaching becomes his own private struggle. Inevitably, he makes many mistakes. Teachers who are assigned to "good" schools usually learn from their mistakes and piece together solutions to problems. However, those who are assigned to ghetto schools are usually unable to stand up alone under the cultural shock and process of getting adjusted to teaching the disadvantaged.

The teacher turns to his supervisors for help, but quickly learns that he must solve his own problems — or wait until he has been assaulted, threatened, or a knife has been flashed. His supervisors rarely can provide assistance on more than an emergency basis; even then, many teachers do not receive any assistance until weeks or months after the term has begun.

Often ghetto school supervisors are suffering from many of the same problems as the teacher, for example, lack of training and experience. Many are unwillingly appointed to the school; and like teachers, are "marking time" until they can transfer to a "better" school, or are prompted for not figuring in "the wrong headlines." The only difference is that they can shut their office doors, which some do, thereby divorcing themselves from the teacher's problems. They can divert their energies to writing impressive reports and devising programs that appear good on paper or look good to a visitor, but rarely if ever work. This is "playing the educator's game," giving their supervisors just what they want.

Of course, some supervisors are concerned and eager to provide assistance. Nonetheless, it is hard for them to avoid becoming inspectors and treating the teachers as subordinates. They start with the unfortunately true assumption that teachers are not teaching enough, and conclude that teachers must be coerced and controlled, checked and counter-checked. However, the unanticipated consequence of this teacher-supervisory relationship is the fostering of minimum acceptable teaching performance. These minimum standards tend to become common for most ghetto school teachers and thus become maximum standards as well. The teacher who deviates is often frowned upon and considered unrealistic. Minimum performance convinces the supervisors that their assumptions are correct; it puts added pressure on the supervisors to check more closely on the teachers and to further treat them as subordinates, which leads to increased tension and further decline of teaching morale. The teachers soon realize that they must battle both students and supervisors. Thus, the derogatory statements about ghetto school teachers become self-fulfilling prophecies.

As previously mentioned, every ghetto school has a few effective teachers, but they are never adequately rewarded or recognized by their profession. The teaching profession is probably the only one which does not reward superior performance, even superior performance under difficult circumstances. In effect, it rewards mediocrity. The absence of merit pay rewards the incapable and ineffective under the guise of professional equality. Furthermore, many incompetents are promoted to supervisory echelons. The very fact ·that the teacher remains in the classroom implies that he is a failure. The only compensation for effective teachers — as long as they are favored by their supervisors — is that they are usually given the "good" classes and fewer classes to teach, or are given the opportunity to leave the classroom entirely on a nonteaching assignment. Although this type of patronage system exists in almost all

schools, it is more pervasive in ghetto schools, primarily so that these teachers will not leave the school.

The result is that the new teachers, weak teachers, and those who are out of favor with their supervisors teach the most "difficult" classes, teach a maximum load, and are assigned to police the hallways and lunchroom. In most cases, it is precisely these teachers who cannot cope with the "difficult" classes and who need extra time to prepare themselves for their classes. Similarly, it is disheartening for a teacher who has to battle his students and supervisors to find out that some of his colleagues not only teach all the "good" classes, but are able to spend long periods in the teachers' lounge or cafeteria. Not only does this practice pit teacher against teacher, but it lessens professional integrity. Teachers in the nonpriviledged position often react by outright refusal to give assistance to the administration or to their colleagues, by spending less time on lesson preparation, or losing interest in teaching, etc. The situation fosters an attitude whereby teachers worry more about what they can get away with, than about what they can do. When teachers no longer care or are willing to help the growth of the school, morale deteriorates. Instead of supporting each other, they may purposely work against each other. The situation may become so bleak that the nonfavored group, that is, perhaps half the staff, may be "marking time."' In many large cities, the teachers' union attempted to remedy this situation by writing into their recent contracts a rotation system for nonteaching administrative positions. The result has been that many supervisors have rotated the nonteaching assignments within the same favored group of teachers.

☆   ☆   ☆

If the teacher is a provisional, his colleagues

sometimes advise him against returning for the next term before he gains permanent certification and is regularly appointed. If it is his misfortune to be already regularly appointed, he learns to "mark time" until he is allowed to transfer to a "better" school. If the teacher is regularly appointed, unless he is not trapped by approaching retirement, or by deferment from the army, he may be so depressed that he leaves the system or even the profession entirely.

Thus, many, if not most, permanent certified ghetto school teachers feel trapped by the school system. In order to reduce the turnover of teachers, many urban school systems require five or more years of service before a teacher can even be eligible for a transfer. What happens during the interim? The longer the teacher has to wait to be transferred from a school where he is "marking time," the more meaningless teaching becomes and the more cynical he becomes. Involvement, commitment, dedication, the joy of teaching, and the rest of the splendid educational clichés disappear from his thinking.

Who suffers more, the teacher or students, is questionable. Both are victims of the system and both victimize each other; both have dropped out in fact, if not in name, from the teaching-learning process. As for the teacher, his students seem disinterested and pay little tribute to his work; often they are hostile and alienated. Yet, a teacher's success and professional gratification depend on his teaching his students, knowing they are learning. Teaching is contagious but contagion can be good or bad. Both students and teachers are aware of their own feelings, and communicate these feelings to each other. If teachers don't care, then students learn not to care. The reverse is also true. When students are apathetic, teachers may become apathetic. Hostility and

alienation breed more hostility and alienation. If students come to school angry, teachers become angry. If students fail, in effect, teachers fail.

One hundred eighty days a year many ghetto school teachers face a living death — a feeling of helplessness and hopelessness — perhaps the bleakest existence any person can experience. Instead of teaching, they find that they must face a long-drawn-out humiliation, a state of loneliness and despair, in which the worst may be still to come and the only certainty is that there is no solution to their predicament in sight. The school year is a kind of jail sentence, and "torture" is not too strong a word to describe some of the things they have experienced in the classroom. Like prisoners who have given up hope, they adopt an air of indifference and willing incompetence; moreover, they act much more indifferent and incompetent than they normally are. Is this not a partial explanation of the indifference and incompetence that teachers often display in ghetto schools? Is this not one reason why ghetto school teachers adopt failure strategies? They are prisoners without hope!

☆ ☆ ☆

The school system — frequently characterized by deceit, incompetency, triviality and rigidity — and where the teacher is reduced to a file number and treated as an insignificant, powerless cog — reinforces the teacher's indifference for teaching. The system operates by siphoning teachers' energy and enthusiasm; it operates by first coercing teachers into and then preventing their escape from just about an impossible teaching situation and meaningless existence.

While the teachers are being assaulted, the system produces glowing reports. Pilot programs always seem to work, especially if evaluated by their directors. Instead of consulting the teachers, the system calls upon "experts" from local universities, governmental agencies, and foundations to reexamine and reorientate. The belief is, teachers are rank-and-file workers with no legitimate right to define policy — an outmoded theory based on business administration practices and adopted by education administrators for lack of a better system of ideas. Directions and decisions are passed on to teachers with no concern for them and no avenue of communication open to them, except by disrupting the system and striking. The entire system is organized to keep teachers at the bottom of the educational totem pole, or at best in a second-class position, with no ego-involvement in curriculum development, no participation in policy, and no means of sharing credit given to the schools. There are no teacher heroes, no public recognition of fine work or outstanding achievement. A teacher can gain recognition only by writing a book about his teaching experience — and then he had better leave the school. The system also creates an artificial division between teachers and supervisors; in fact, supervisors are organized to enforce the system and run roughshod over teachers because, supposedly, that is "the way things get done in the system." Teaching is the most important and difficult part of education; however, the salary difference and rewards between teachers and supervisors are wide, and recent teacher contracts indicate a widening trend. Although the activities of supervisors should be considered secondary and as assisting the major activity carried on by teachers, supervisors decide almost everything and take whatever praise may come — which increases the gap between them and teachers — but unfailingly impute poor achievement to the inadequacy of the teachers.

The system does more than uphold the ideals of hypocrisy; it fosters the myth that teaching is a profession. True, teachers compare — or at least contrast — their status and monetary rewards to the medical and legal professions. At best, they are semiprofessionals and their "Tie-City" ties and "brown-paper" mentality symbolize it; the difference is clear.

Teachers are entangled with large classes and cannot individualize their work. Professionals individualize their work with their clientele. Teachers defend the status quo and often reject innovations. Professionals continuously engage in research and seek new frontiers. While notable changes have been made in the last five years in the fields of science, medicine, etc., teaching methods have remained essentially unchanged for the last fifty years. Teachers are subject to the power hierarchy of their administrators. Professionals command major authority; their administration is in charge of secondary activities which facilitate the major activities performed by the professionals. Teachers are restricted by rigid bureaucratic rules of punctuality, attendance, dress, clerical assignments, etc. Professionals operate in a relatively free and informal setting. Teachers who remain teachers are considered failures, as previously mentioned. Success implies moving into administrative positions. Professionals are content in their work and consider administration undesirable. Teachers may be challenged by almost any parent or taxpayer; the community may dictate what they will teach and how, even in opposition to the teachers' "professional" judgment. Teachers have little or no political power. Professionals have strong lobbies. Teachers lack control even over standards of admittance to the field. Professionals determine their own criteria for meeting standards of admittance. If teachers were a professional group, there would be no need to assert their collective power through a union; the UFT would not challenge NEA leadership, or lack of leadership.

An important feeling for a teacher is at least to feel like a teacher, to compensate for his semi-professional status. Feeling like a teacher means the teacher and his students are in pursuit of learning together. It means that the students and teacher never give up hope, that the students become aware of their potential, that the teacher feels adequate. It implies a relationship between students and teacher, rapport, pleasure of knowing one another. Few ghetto school teachers have this feeling. Rather, they are disheartened and feel that they are wasting their lives in the classroom; they feel more like supply clerks, timekeepers, and policemen.

When teachers no longer feel like teachers, inevitably they must either quit their job or challenge and change the system, and improve their status by bettering their working conditions and salary. The UFT's strength is concentrated in the urban centers where it is fast becoming a luxury to feel like a teacher. The UFT does not seek to run the schools; it concentrates on the problems that arise as teachers attempt to teach, and most heavily on the problems stemming from teaching in ghetto schools. Under the guise of "quality education" and MES—pronounced mess—the UFT seeks "special services," smaller classes, lighter teaching loads, methods for dealing with the disciplinary problems, grievance machinery against supervisors, and finally, more money. Their thoughts are not with their students, as they claim, for most of them have already surrendered their faith and are too alienated. A dedicated teacher takes an inter-est in his students daily, not just when his contract expires. Sadly, ghetto school teachers cannot remain dedicated for long, but must learn the opposite if they are to survive the everyday classroom situation, with only rare exceptions. No system of mass, meaningless education can expect to recruit more than a sprinkling of exceptional teachers.

Having to fend against the students, supervisors, and system, the teachers often turn to the university for assistance, but even this fails. The professors formulate strategies for teaching the disadvantaged, but these are unrealistic and too general because the professors have little or no classroom experience with the disadvantaged, and are far too removed from the actual school situation — yet they are considered the "experts" in educating the disadvantaged. Instead of helping the teachers with their problems, the professors first patronize them, then criticize them for "negative attitudes," and finally, berate them for failing to understand and appreciate what has been done for them.

The professors commonly state that ghetto school teachers are uninterested in, if not antagonistic toward their students, and lack real comprehension of the problems of the disadvantaged. But if the teachers lack the understanding so necessary to work with disadvantaged students, surely the professors, who are middle class themselves and removed from the ghetto schools and communities, also lack exposure in this area; and, therefore, they are unable to provide real knowledge by which teachers may broaden their insights into the problems of the disadvantaged.

Teachers are also condemned for believing in the so-called "deprivation" theory — which is wittingly fostered by the professors. Recent research confirms the importance of family environment and early child deprivation. The accumulating learning deficit of the disadvantaged is a major cause for failure in school. When professors voice this theory, they are considered gallant and dedicated scholars, who deserve promotions. When the classroom teachers mention the child's background and environmental deprivation, they are immediately accused of having low expectations for these children, and emphasizing discipline. When the teachers use the professors' jargon — auditory, visual, cognitive, language deprivation — they are attacked by the professors for stereotyping and generalizing. When teachers accept I.Q. or reading scores as a valid measure of the child's present academic achievement and of what still needs to be accomplished, they are condemned for being prejudiced and confirming the child's low esteem and expectation of himself. Of course, it is never pointed out that the tests were originally developed — and they still are being developed — by professors.

The decision to abolish I.Q. tests in many school systems is supported by the professors, and illustrates their incongruity. The professors' "deprivation" theory is formulated and developed by measuring and comparing intelligence levels. Good, but must teachers abolish an instrument which has been developed and improved over generations and has proved its worth in measuring the potential of most students, in the hope that a more adequate test can be developed overnight? The scores made by the disadvantaged on I.Q. tests do not prove that the tests are unfair or the teachers prejudiced, but that the students lack present academic ability to succeed. Rather than abolish the test, why not improve their academic ability?

Not only are the professors' criticisms of ghetto school teachers unfair, but they are wholesale and generalized, based on preconceived opinions rather than on real teaching experience, and overlook the reasons for poor teaching and, therefore, have done grave injustice. The attacks subject the teachers to the same stereotyping that they blame teachers for using on their students. The harsh tone and constant criticism add to the problem of recruiting teachers, discourage the few competent and concerned teachers from remaining, and harden the already widespread feelings of indifference and futility, as well as reinforce poor teaching morale and performance.

Professors fail to recognize that these teachers were once idealistic and worked harder than others in other schools, but because of lack of adequate support and impossible bureaucratic conditions were forced to retreat from teaching. They fail to comprehend that ghetto school teachers would rather teach and feel like teachers and fulfill their commitments. Professors fail to appreciate that these teachers are overwhelmed by despair and need assistance, not criticism. They fail to realize that even they have abandoned and further alienated the teachers. More important, by criticizing their clientele, the professors are indirectly critizing themselves and their own inadequate job of teacher preparation. It is time for professors to stop attacking teachers. The fact that teachers are criticized and need to be reminded that they are failing indicates just how miserably the professors have failed with their own teaching.

Consequently, the remarks of the professors are beginning to have an apologetic ring. Some professors now admit they do not have the answers, while others claim they need the cooperation and even the assistance of the teachers; some talk about using ghetto school teachers as "clinical professors,'" while others advocate having teachers formulate their own strategies and inform the universities about what seems to work. Moreover, the professors claim they are coming "down from the hill," but how far down is speculative. Most of them are still standing safely on the sidelines and professing "mickey mouse" theories. Yet, the only place where learning and practice can be consolidated is in the public schools, not the universities.

Professors merely give lip service to what they say, and will continue to do so until they go into the classroom and teach the disadvantaged, test their theories, and experience what the teachers have experienced. Professors can read the literature in quiet offices and gain theoretical insights, but they need the actual experience and should have the opportunity to teach the disadvantaged at least for an "exchange year" — as a requirement for their rank promotions. Most of these professors would do well to accept the challenge they talk about, and apply for teaching licenses and positions and teach, before they vent their criticisms; there are many vacancies in ghetto schools and there is great need for dedicated and effective teachers. If the professors had the fortitude to work in ghetto schools, they might not paint such one-sided, dismal pictures of teachers. The truth is, however, most professors look down at and resent being called teachers, and are swift to indicate that they teach on the college or university level. Similarly, they would probably feel uncomfortable about going back into the classroom — even fear teaching disadvantaged youth — and would have to be coerced.

It would certainly be interesting — perhaps amusing — to see if the professors really know what they are talking about, if they are really "experts," or if they could do any better than the teachers they condemn. Not only do I dare them, but I question if some of them could be trusted alone in the classroom, especially if they are there long enough for the students to "size them up."

The teachers realize the professors' hypocrisy, resent it, and no longer trust or respect them. The result is a widening gap between the professors and teachers; moreover, as teachers become more educated and militant, the gap becomes more difficult to reconcile. Also, the gap widens over the discrepancy that teachers call reality. It is common practice among teachers to voice in their graduate courses, "That's all good theory, but it doesn't work." Of course, some professors advocate more realistic procedures for teaching the disadvantaged. They urge the use of audiovisual materials but rarely, if ever, demonstrate their use in their lectures. They remind teachers to teach concepts, but do not teach teachers how to teach concepts because, most likely, they do not know how themselves. They recommend that teachers change their lockstep method, but they use the same method in their own courses. They urge teachers to use role playing, but do not show how and when to use it.

Dull, repetitious, meaningless, and false, if these courses were not required for certification or promotion, most classrooms of education would be empty and the professors would be lecturing to the walls. Education courses do not help improve pedagogy, especially pedagogy with the disadvantaged.

Now the professors of education have safeguarded their jobs, and are assured that their courses will continue to be required, so the next step is for the professors to duplicate their lecture notes — which are sometimes yellowing — hand them out during the first session, send their clientele home, and have them return only for the final examination. There is no good reason to require anyone to leave his home in order to listen to humdrum hokum, useless clichés, and tiny bits of information.

The most amusing hokum is the glowing reports about successful programs for the disadvantaged and for teachers of the disadvantaged, as if the professors were reminding the teachers, "If you would change your attitudes, or if you knew what you were doing, you could succeed, too." Of course, if only half of these reports were true, there would no longer be a problem concerning the education of the disadvantaged, and the "experts" whom we pay for "expertise" would no longer be saying, "We do not have the answers."

The harsh fact is, reports can easily be filled with false data, procedures, strengths, and results. Very few directors of a program will jeopardize their chances for additional funds and admit their present program is a failure. Funds are readily available from governmental agencies and foundations for those who are in position to write up and submit a proposal for the education of the disadvantaged. That so many "experts" have suddenly become interested in this field indicates how profitable it has become. They are cashing in on an opportunity and getting the pie while the poor remain poor and the disadvantaged remain disadvantaged — and get the crumbs.

Apparently, little time or energy is spent on validating the various assumptions, or on anticipating the numerous variables that will affect a program. Guidelines and data are hurriedly put together to get the money while it is still available. The result is, the optimistic and portentous interpretations of these programs have ended chiefly in ambiguous and/or dismal outcomes. Nevertheless, because the private universities are increasingly dependent on this type of supported program, their folly is overlooked and, in fact, many universities have established offices and executives to work full time on program planning. Thus, professors are pressured to divert their energies from scholarship into developing such programs. The entire procedure illustrates one more hypocrisy which confronts the ghetto school teacher. Oh, yes, the programs are developed with the best interests of the teacher in mind. From beginning to end, from lofty objectives to fictitious conclusions, the programs are a tragic, but comical sortie.

Professors of education have been sitting idle — even though they know what they are doing is inadequate. They sit there, safeguarding their jobs, afraid that any major change will affect their security. The fact is, if they sit there long enough, and fail to reexamine, much less reorient what they are trying to accomplish in light of what they are veritably accomplishing, there will be no need to make decisions about how they can improve teacher training; it will be taken away from them — by the growing militant teacher unions, for example.

I submit that I have probably alienated my friends and former colleagues in school, whom I have in the past defended and praised, as well as my present partisans in college. However, I feel very strongly about what I have voiced.

As a writer and educator, it is safe to conclude on a positive or hopeful key. I refuse to conform to this "game," though many of my colleagues do it, some intentionally, some unintentionally. There are no sure or permanent solutions, no straight or sagacious roads to follow. The "sacred cows" of education, and the glowing reports and prophecies of success, can no longer mask the dim future. Most ghetto school teachers will continue to fail. Words will not prove me wrong, only time, and time is running out; for example, there is no guarantee that riots can always be confined to the summer.

Although it is considered inappropriate to criticize without offering solutions, this paper will risk that appearance, too. I am not trying to satisfy my readers or suggest what is currently fashionable — and unrealistic. We are fighting a losing battle. The depth and intensity of the problem of educating the disadvantaged are probably beyond our capacity to solve. The problem is not a matter of guns or butter, but spirit — spirit to teach, spirit to learn, a contagious, intangible element that is dying in the ghetto schools. The problem will worsen until the forces that are lined up against the teacher are abolished. But, such a change is unlikely because the educators upon whom we must rely are themselves a major cause of the problem. The harsh fact is, the control of educational policies and procedures rests with those who are working against the teachers.

REFERENCES

Corwin, Ronald G., *A Sociology of Education,* New York, Appleton-Century-Crofts, 1965.

Dunn, Joan, *Retreat From Learning,* New York, David McKay, 1955.

Etzioni, Amitai, *Modern Organizations,* Englewood Cliffs, New Jersey, Prentice-Hall, 1964.

Gordon, Edmund W.; Wilkerson, Doxey A., *Compensatory Education for the Disadvantaged,* New York, College Entrance Examination Board, 1966.

Holt, John, *How Children Fail,* New York, Pitman Publishing Corporation, 1964.

Hughson, Arthur, "The Case for Intelligence Testing," *Phi Delta Kappan,* November, 1964, pp. 106-108.

Jackson, Philip W., *Life in the Classroom,* New York, Holt, 1968.

Miller, Harry L. (ed.), "Recapitulation," *Education for the Disadvantaged,* New York, Free Press, 1967, p. 193.

Ornstein, Allan C., "What It Is Really Like For Most Slum-School Teachers," *Integrated Education,* October-November, 1967, pp. 48-52.

Ornstein, Allan C., "Why Ghetto-School Teachers Fail," *Phi Delta Pi Record,* April, 1968, pp. 99-101.

Ornstein, Allan C.; Milberg, Toby, "Problems Related to Teaching in Low Socio-Economic Areas," *Negro Educational Review,* July-October, 1967, pp. 70-82.

Wilkerson, Doxey A., "Research and Needed Emphasis in Research on the Education of Disadvantaged Children and Youth," *Journal of Negro Education,* Summer, 1964, pp. 346-357.

SUGGESTIONS FOR IMPROVING DISCIPLINE AND TEACHING THE DISADVANTAGED

Allan C. Ornstein

Alan C. Ornstein, "Suggestions for Improving Discipline and Teaching the Disadvantaged," *Journal of Secondary Education,* March 1969, Vol. 44 pp. 99-106.

SUGGESTIONS FOR IMPROVING DISCIPLINE AND TEACHING THE DISADVANTAGED

Allan C. Ornstein

The discussion of discipline has special reference to teaching the disadvantaged, since the problem is acute in most ghetto schools and is often considered the number-one problem for most teachers of the disadvantaged. Although discipline is not the major task, rather a necessary function of teaching, it often becomes the main concern in ghetto schools, and we usually judge the teacher's success in terms of the way he handles or disciplines a class. That a great many ghetto-school teachers "mark time" or request transfers indicates in part at least that they are unhappy with their disciplinary prowess and are unable to teach.

For our discussion the word discipline refers to the degree of order and control established in a group. It is a process in which the teacher's respect for his students and his understanding of and ability to manage their surface behavior and his own behavior go hand in hand.

It is not enough to provide teachers with psycho-sociological concepts and a list of positive qualities of the disadvantaged; it is essential, too, for the teacher to respect the child. Having middle-class values, most teachers measure progress on a middle-class scale. They encourage the child to succeed on their terms, therefore teaching the child that his values are wrong. To win their favor and receive the rewards of school that come with middle-class conformity, the child must give up his individuality and style of life. He must change his language, dress and manners; he must come to school clean, neat, and on time; he must not fight. This much sacrifice involves a loss of identity for the child. Thus, teachers are seen as condescending caretakers, who lack understanding or insight into his problems yet want to make him one of them. The clash between the expectations and life style of the disadvantaged and middle-class teachers is reflected in terms of "us" and "them," with the teachers siphoning off the "bright ones" from the group and preventing the rest of the group from expressing their values.

It does little good to belabor the teacher for his middle-class values. Teachers need only to be made aware of the differences in cultural values without viewing one as right or better. Instead of trying to reshape the disadvantaged child, teachers should accept his life style and improve him within the scheme of his own values. Indeed, teachers should maintain their system of values, but, at the same time, respect and enhance the child's own values in order to reach him. Children want respect and the opportunity to develop their own thinking in context within their life style.

Students behave according to what they perceive is their role. If they are expected to be stupid or hostile, they will behave accordingly and even learn the educational clichés of themselves. In this connection, the teacher

ALLAN C. ORNSTEIN *is an Instructor in the School of Education, Fordham University, New York City.*

should avoid generalizations and preconceived notions: "They're unteachable." "They're lazy." All they do is reflect the teacher's inability. The teacher must be convinced that the disadvantaged can learn because students who are not expected to learn will not learn, and will reinforce the original assumption.

Teachers should present a purposeful, related, but structured classroom atmosphere. The work the students do should be more a problem-solving basis, with students learning from each other, than a teacher-directed lesson. There should be opportunities for small groups to work together, planning panel discussions, and committee reports. This type of creative teaching is needed for all students, but it is needed more for the disadvantaged since teachers often are reluctant to experiment with them. Teachers must stop stereotyping the disadvantaged as problems and apathetic learners. Actually, the fostering of creative teaching should increase control in the classroom through added support and interest in the lesson.

Disadvantaged students should be encouraged to take the initiative and influence their own learning activities. Instead of the teacher dictating rules to students, the students should have the opportunity to govern their own behavior and learning. For example, the black-white struggle should be investigated in class, for it is a struggle which we hear or read about daily. Ignoring it, or teaching only safe subjects, implies a lack of respect and trust toward students. Students must be given the opportunity to voice their own opinions, being exposed to all sides before making decisions. They must be encouraged to bring civil rights and black power material to school to supplement the regular materials, especially when biased materials are used. Students need to understand what color and race mean by learning about black heroes and black culture. Recognizing that there are more colored people than white people in the world, they need to realize their potential power, not only in the world locally, as more blacks migrate to the cities. Not only should black students read Marian Anderson, George Washington Carver, and Martin Luther King, but, more so, Leroi Jones, Malcolm X, Stokeley Carmichael, and H. Rap Brown, even if discussion makes the white teacher feel uncomfortable or guilty. The basic principles of the Ku Klux Klan and the John Birch Society should be compared with those of SNCC, the Black Muslims, and the NAACP. The reason for the riots should be investigated, and hopefully how black students can take socially acceptable grass-roots action. Similarly, they need to organize demonstration marches, and sit-ins in order to handle real experiences. The fusion of reality with learning is the best way of getting the students excited, making school make sense, and making the task of discipline much easier.

Besides respecting the disadvantaged, the teacher should understand the manifestations of their behavior, and have a working knowledge of how they can help the students cope' with their problems. Ideally, the teacher functions within a guidance-oriented framework. He sets up "safety measures" for relieving classroom tensions and allows a measure of freedom from restraint, but at the same time establishes "limits" of acceptable behavior.

The teacher sees these children as they are, not as he wishes they were. He appraises their feelings and offers his friendship. Most disadvantaged children are extremely defensive and are accustomed to being rejected, sometimes even by their parents or guardian. They are not acquainted with having an adult, and for that matter an adult from the larger society, as a friend, but will enthusiastically welcome such a relationship once their initial apprehensions are proven groundless. Psychological safety and mutual trust then develop which are essential for maintaining good classroom management and mental health, as well as for helping the child with his problems. In turn, the child will look to the teacher for advice and will recognize him as a person of greater experience and understanding.

Too often a teacher creates a discipline problem or condemns a student before he tries to find the cause of his actions. This does not mean the teacher should condone the behavior in question, but he should use the child's actions as a point of departure for creating understanding. An aggressive student usually needs a friend, not a lecture, and his misconduct, whether verbal or physical, is usually the only way he can reveal that he needs help. Too often a teacher punishes a child for aggressiveness when what he needs is help. The teacher should distinguish between aggression that originates from immediate frustration and aggression that reflects hardened anger and contempt. The first kind can be handled by channeling the child's energies into more challenging and interesting activities. The second kind requires a firmer approach, with suitable rules and routine. For either situation, it is advisable that the teacher first try being a friend. The child's parents probably gave up on him, and so did other teachers. An effective approach is to try to understand the child and help him see his problems and the problems he is creating for his classmates.

The causes of aggression can be many; failure to understand the subject matter or see purpose in going to school, being asked to do something beyond one's capacity, conflicts in personality between the teacher and the child,

etc. By recognizing the child's major reason for noncooperation, the teacher and student can work together, not against each other. But no matter what the problem is, the teacher should be able to handle the exhibition of raw emotion when it arises, and help these children cope with and transfer their frustration and anger, both of which these children have a great deal of, into more constructive purposes.

Many disadvantaged children do not remember their contributions to events after a short time has elapsed. All disciplinary action, therefore, should be taken immediately after the incident, or as soon as possible. The children, likewise, get excited and become disorderly in groups. Since this behavior is infectious and can disrupt the entire class, the teacher should immediately stop the upset, provoked child or separate him from the group.

Disadvantaged children often do not take care of their possessions. They lose, destroy, misplace, and deface their school supplies and their personal belongings. To make matters worse, they often steal and hide things from each other, sometimes to obtain one of the many things they are denied, or just for sheer delight. Therefore, the teacher should remind students that they are responsible for their actions, and must look after their own belongings and whatever items the school lends them. Members of the group must be encouraged to work together, not against each other. Any theft or defacing of property must be accounted for — even if it means having to call a dean or supervisor — to stop a potentially intolerable condition, which can worsen if not checked.

Disadvantaged children are not accustomed to success within the larger society. As a consequence, when they do succeed, many cannot cope with it. Some do not know what to do; some become aggressive and some boisterous. Some will goad somebody less successful to copy them. Unless instantly curtailed, this will result in a verbal or physical confrontation. The teacher is required to be swift and capable of acting·as a judge. He does not ignore the students' clash of interests or their daring one another, which they call "wolfing". These children need the teacher's advice, and if he is fair they will appreciate it, even though they will not readily admit it.

Many behavioral problems, which teachers often experience with these students, can be avoided — if good judgement is used. There are no basic rules. It depends only on the teacher's using the right approach at the right time with the right child. Without stopping the lesson, a nod of the head, a snap of the finger, or a stern glance can be effective. Moving about the room and coming in close proximity to a student who is about to break the rules of the class may just be the thing that will alert the student and bring him back to the proper fold. Often the teacher can put his arm around the shoulder of a student and get his point across. But he should know who can be touched. He should never touch a stu-dent he does not know, or go close to someone who dislikes him or with whom he has little rapport, or who is tense and sensitive about being imposed upon.

When a child threatens another student,, the teacher should talk or "kid him down". The child wants a face-saving way out. If a child verbally harasses another student, the teacher does not get upset or make the situation an issue. Most of these children are continuously exposed to abusive language, and cannot help themselves when they are excited. An apology is sufficient. However, no matter what the problem is, it should not be aggravated by getting the child worked up to the point where he cannot help himself. Most violent outbursts, in fàct, occur when children try to preserve their dignity. The teacher should calm the student down and take direct action. He is certain the class is aware that the child was dealt with, because this type of behavior is contagious if allowed to go unchecked. Also, he makes the child realize that he is not rejecting him, but that he is rejecting his behavior and that he demands more respect.

The disadvantaged child learns at an early age to take no stock in promises. Promises are meaningless; they often have been in the past. A teacher who makes it a general rule not to make promises to these children will do better. Promises often involve adults, and adults represent authority. Adùlts whom he has known have lied to this child — why then should one with whom he has had no prior contact be obligated to tell him the truth? Promises have little influence over present acts — or for much time. They are considered signs of weakness. Also, any promise that is made must be carried out. The teacher who does not fulfill his promise breaks a contract, and these children will not forget; they conclude that he, too, cannot be trusted.

The teacher should be equally ready to refuse what is undesirable or unreasonable. A refusal is made with quiet firmness but without apology. It is factual, reasonable, and brief. Lengthy explanations have a defensive ring as if the teacher were unsure or preaching. The teacher appeals to the common sense of the child: "Now you know you're trying to take advantage." "I've been fair to you, but you're not being fair to me or the class.". "If you do this, you know you'll be in trouble." The proper approach is to suggest positive alternatives. "Now, wouldn't it be smarter if you do it this way?" "Your idea has merit, but let's see of there is another way to do it." If the child needs to be disciplined, the teacher should try to use the child's own values, and not impose a different middle-class set of values on him. A punitive climate is avoided, since it is damaging to class rapport. In the same vein, it is wrong to mistake good discipline for fear. Students stop caring, do not fight the teacher's efforts any more, but they despise him and have no interest in the subject.

Perhaps the best way to avoid trouble is by anticipating what is going to happen. This should become ingrained by the teacher being in the actual situation, doing something wrong, realizing what happened, and knowing the next time that he will anticipate and will not make the same mistake. For example, on the first day of school six children come to class unprepared — some accidentally and some intentionally. Of course, it is permissable for one child to borrow pencil and paper from a classmate, but when six children have to ask six others, and perhaps walk around the room to obtain them, control lessens. Anticipating this situation, the teacher has paper and sharpened pencils on hand.

Disadvantaged children will continuously test the teacher until they are convinced of his worth as a person. The teacher should be aware of what is happening, and be swift to use such incidents to his advantage, or together with the class joke about the situation and show his sharpness of wit. For example, the teacher walks into the room and finds an unflattering picture of himself drawn on the blackboard in front of the class. Instead of getting upset, the teacher says jokingly, "I see we have an artist among us." Without directly condemning the anonymity of the student he adds, "Would the artist like to sign his name?" Or the teacher can use the picture as a part of his lesson. The science teacher extends the arms of the picture and draws a test tube or bunsen burner, then proceeds with the actual demonstration. The social studies teachers commences his lesson, "The Closing of the Frontier," by drawing a cowboy hat, and so on.

When the teacher is exposed to ridicule or looks foolish, he admits it and laughs with the class; in fact, confirms that he looks foolish. False dignity, vanity, and excessive pride cause more disciplinary problems. Similarly, when the teacher makes a mistake, he admits it, but avoids lengthy explanations, since they have a defensive ring. When the teacher has to account for something he did, the explanation is clear and brief. An effective procedure is to make clear the position of the teacher, and/or to ask what the child would do if he were the teacher.

Socially maladjusted and emotionally disturbed children pose special challenges, and there are many to deal with in ghetto schools, especially because their home conditions are likely to have harmful effects on mental stability. These children may suffer from many psychological disturbances, and their school difficulty may be only one of its manifestations. Because they often cannot function in a regular classroom situation and because school seems a threat to them, their school problems snowball as they pass from grade to grade. Some are quiet and inhibited, passive and indifferent. They are too dispirited, lack self-confidence, and are afraid of the world around them. Some are easily provoked by minor frustrations. They lack self-control and cannot postpone gratification; their rage is immediately discharged. Some are demanding; their expectations are infantile and must immediately be satisfied. Some are alienated and extremely rebellious and unwilling to do work. This kind of child is probably the most difficult to deal with, since for them the teacher represents authority, which they resent.

Because of their inability to get along, socially maladjusted and emotionally disturbed children usually are hated by and feel isolated from the rest of the class. They are school failures and are afraid of more failure, no matter what its nature. What they need is a sympathetic and understanding teacher who will coax and help them understand themselves and adjust to their peer group. They need to be given work which they can successfully complete. They need to feel that they belong in the class and in school; for example, by working with their classmates on class projects and by participating in class and in extra-curricular activities. The fact is, they are usually interested in one field to the extent of potentially becoming experts; it is for the teacher to find their proper field of interest by closely scrutinizing their class work and by talking to them privately; their adjustment in life depends on this.

A teacher's self awareness reflects his ability to understand his own behavior and to perceive what is going on around him. All teachers should possess this self awareness, but the need is more recognized for the sterner task of teaching the disadvantaged. A teacher's self awareness means that he is more likely to be objective and accepting of himself and his students. By knowing himself, the teacher is more comfortable and feels less threatened by his students' behavior. In turn, he is less prone to react with hostility or criticism in a situation which calls for calmness or even humor.

The teacher's own behavior is a reflection of his personality; it is the sum quality of his physical and mental attributes. Not too many days of a school term elapse before the students size up their teacher and start to probe for sore spots. They will seize upon and react accordingly to any adult weaknesses, or for that matter strengths, the teacher displays, and most visible although probably not most significant are the physical attributes of the teacher. For example, a surprisingly large number of disadvantaged children exhibit a flair for and an appreciation of fashion. These children equate fashion and good taste in dress with knowledge or, in their own words, "being with it". Thus everything the teacher wears, and the way he wears it, is scrutinized by these children.

The "mental make-up" of the teacher is perhaps more significant, and in the end will dettermine the teacher's success or failure. It goes without saying that the person who is selected to teach disadvantaged youth must not be racially or socially prejudiced and must want to be there. No matter how knowledgeable or strong the teacher may be professionally, his attitude must be one of wanting to help the students he teaches, otherwise, he will be no teacher at all. The teacher must also be dedicated and committed to his role; otherwise, he will give up and become a cynic. The teacher must never lose confidence or express fear. Whatever teaching is instilled in the classroom must not be cancelled by the loss of his authority.

A teacher's behavior can be conscious or unconscious, obvious or subtle. The way a teacher talks, looks, or gestures communicates his feelings: anger, hostility, warmth, humor, etc. The fact that behavior is sometimes unconscious or subtle does not necessarily mean it's harmful. In fact, such patterns of behavior can sometimes make the difference between success or failure. Many times we hear that a teacher is effective in the classroom; yet, we are unable to explain the reasons, or if we do they are nebulous. Yet, the seemingly unnoticeable acts of behavior of both the teacher and the students are one explanation of a teacher's success or failure.

Some teachers resent or fear the disadvantaged because they are difficult to teach. Rather than feeling guilty, the teacher should realize that it is perfectly natural to have such sentiments, which arise when teachers, along with other people, feel threatened. Teachers who lose control in class or receive criticism tend to be more vulnerable and fearful of allowing their unconscious feelings and behavior to come to the surface. However, these teachers, more than others, need to confront themselves and gain understanding. They need a sense of security, so they will not take outbursts personally, not expect students to be always "good" or "proper". If teachers learned to evaluate themselves and their students in both separate and interacting perspectives, they would be able to evaluate their own effects in the classroom and their relationships with individual students.

In order to really know themselves, teachers must be willing to assess their own weaknesses and strengths. This is important in order to adopt realistic teaching styles appropriate to their own personalities. Disadvantaged students know what will upset teachers often better than their teachers know, readily learn the behavioral pattterns of their teachers, and sense what will make a teacher angry or lose control. Astute appraisers of their environment, the disadvantaged usually assess the teacher's worth as a person before they become at all interested in him as a teacher. A negative assessment can provoke aa dramatic incident, or it can be drawn out into a series of minor clashes. If the students demolish this teacher's authority, they will progress to criticism of his personality, commenting on his physical and mental attributes. Once, however, the teacher establishes himself, the attempts at assessment will be less frequent, and the tension resulting from the attempts will lessen.

One teacher may be strong enough to look at a disruptive student and make him stop whatever he is doing. Another teacher realizes his limitations, and gets results with a different approach — perhaps simply reminding the student that he is disturbing his classmates. But no matter what approach is used, the teacher must be himself, straight-forward. He cannot fake himself. The realities of life have made these children quite sophisticated in recognizing the phonies right away, and they deeply take offense to such deceit. Also, there is nothing more dangerous than trying to adopt a teaching style that does not fit one's personality. The teacher will never really be at ease, since what he is attempting to do does not come naturally.

Teachers must realize that they will have difficult students in their classes. If the situation becomes uncontrollable, and this is not uncommon with teachers of the disadvantaged, they will cause the teacher to feel a sense of despair and failure. It may take months, or even the entire year, before any of the students can get psychological help. Even then, there is no guarantee that the students will change or be "better" in class. In short, the teacher is forced to keep the students in the class, though the teacher and other students suffer. Merely informing the teacher that the class is difficult and it is understandable why he is unable to teach is not enough. Instructing the teacher that there are no pat answers, but to keep on trying anyway, is discouraging, too. Teachers need immediate help in dealing with their classroom problems. Textbooks and course work are too remote and cannot be realistically consolidated with the classroom situation.

Teachers need an educational clinic where they can telephone or register for help immediately, where they can express their anxieties or problems, and ask questions and gain insights into their feelings. No matter how naturally selfaware they seem, they can always use more help to understand themselves. For others, it may make the difference between gaining facility in coping with discipline problems or dropping out of the profession.

REFERENCES

1. Lichter, Solomon O. (ed.), *The Drop-Outs,* Glencoe, Illinois, Free Press, 1962.

2. Long, Nicholas J.; Newman, Ruth G., "The Teacher and His Mental Health," *The Teacher's Handling of Children in Conflict,* Bulletin of School Education, Indiana University, July, 1961, pp. 5-26.

3. Orstein, Allan C., "Guidance Practice for Teaching the Disadvantaged," *Selected Articles for Elementary School Principals,* Washington, D.C., National Education Association, 1968, pp. 26-29.

4. ...., "Reaching the Disadvantaged," *School and Society,* March 30, 1968, pp. 214-216.

5. ...., "Selecting Teachers for the Disadvantaged," *Negro Educational Review,* January, 1968, pp. 29-40.

6. Redl, Fritz, *Controls From Within,* Glencoe, Illinois, Free Press, 1952.

7. Trout, Lawana, "Involvement Through Slanted Languages," Peter G. Kontos and James J. Murphy (eds.), *Teaching Urban Youth: A Source Book for Urban Teachers,* New York, John Wiley, 1967, pp. 23-44.

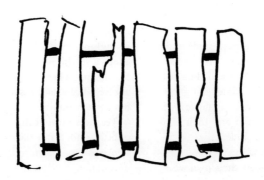

educating
the disadvantaged

educating the disadvantaged

SCHOOL YEAR 1968-1969

Edited by Allan C. Ornstein

AMS PRESS
NEW YORK

CONTENTS

PART I
RACE AND THE NATURE
OF THE URBAN SETTING

LIKE IT IS IN THE ALLEY

Robert Coles

Robert Coles, "Like It Is in the Alley," *Daedalus,* Fall 1968, Vol. 97, pp. 1315-1330.

LIKE IT IS IN THE ALLEY

Robert Coles

"In the alley it's mostly dark, even if the sun is out. But if you look around, you can find things. I know how to get into every building, except that it's like night once you're inside them, because they don't have lights. So, I stay here. You're better off. It's no good on the street. You can get hurt all the time, one way or the other. And in buildings, like I told you, it's bad in them, too. But here it's o.k. You can find your own corner, and if someone tries to move in you fight him off. We meet here all the time, and figure out what we'll do next. It might be a game, or over for some pool, or a coke or something. You need to have a place to start out from, and that's like it is in the alley; you can always know your buddy will be there, provided it's the right time. So you go there, and you're on your way, man."

Like all children of nine, Peter is always on his way—to a person, a place, a "thing" he wants to do. "There's this here thing we thought we'd try tomorrow," he'll say; and eventually I'll find out that he means there's to be a race. He and his friends will compete with another gang to see who can wash a car faster and better. The cars belong to four youths who make their money taking bets, and selling liquor that I don't believe was ever purchased, and pushing a few of those pills that "go classy with beer." I am not completely sure, but I think they also have something to do with other drugs; and again, I can't quite be sure what their connection is with a "residence" I've seen not too far from the alley Peter describes so possessively. The women come and go—from that residence and along the street Peter's alley leaves.

Peter lives in the heart of what we in contemporary America have chosen (ironically, so far as history goes) to call an "urban ghetto." The area was a slum before it became a ghetto, and there still are some very poor white people on its edges and increasing numbers of Puerto Ricans in several of its blocks. Peter was not born in the ghetto, nor was his family told to go there. They are Americans and have been here *"since way back before anyone can remember."* That is the way Peter's mother talks about Alabama, about the length of time she and her ancestors have lived there. She and Peter's father came north *"for freedom."* They did not seek out a ghetto, an old quarter of Boston where they were expected to live and where they would be confined, yet at least some of the time solidly at rest, with kin, and reasonably safe.

No, they sought freedom. Americans, they moved on when the going got *"real bad,"* and Americans, they expected something better someplace, some other place. They left Alabama on impulse. They found Peter's alley by accident. And they do not fear pogroms. They are Americans, and in Peter's words: *"There's likely to be another riot here soon. That's what I heard today. You hear it a lot, but one day you know it'll happen."*

Peter's mother fears riots too—among other things. The Jews of Eastern Europe huddled together in their ghettos, afraid of the barbarians, afraid of the *Goyim,* but always sure of one thing, their God-given destiny. Peter's mother has no such faith. She believes that *"something will work out one of these days."* She believes that *"you have to keep on going, and things can get better, but don't ask me how."* She believes that *"God wants us to have a bad spell here, and so maybe it'll get better the next time—you know in Heaven, and I hope that's where we'll be going."* Peter's mother, in other words, is a pragmatist, an optimist, and a Christian. Above all she is American: *"Yes, I hear them talk about Africa, but it don't mean anything to us. All I know is Alabama and now it's in Massachusetts that we are. It was a long trip coming up here, and sometimes I wish we were back there, and sometimes I'd just as soon be here, for all that's no good about it. But I'm not going to take any more trips, no sir. And like Peter said, this is the only country we've got. If you come from a country, you come from it, and we're from it, I'd say, and there isn't much we can do but try to live as best we can. I mean, live here."*

What is "life" like for her over there, where she lives, in the neighborhood she refers to as "here"? A question like that cannot be answered by the likes of me, and even her answer provides only the beginning of a reply: *"Well, we does o.k., I guess. Peter here, he has it better than I did, or his daddy. I can say that. I tell myself that a lot. He can turn on the faucet over there, and a lot of the* time, he just gets the water, right away. And when I tell him what it was like for us, to go fetch that water—we'd walk three miles, yes sir, and we'd be lucky it wasn't ten—well, Peter, it doesn't register on him. He thinks I'm trying to fool him, and the more serious I get, the more he laughs, so I've stopped.

"Of course it's not all so good, I have to admit. We're still where we were, so far as knowing where your next meal is coming from. When I go to bed at night I tell myself I've done good, to stay alive and keep the kids alive, and if they'll just wake up in the morning, and me too, well then, we can worry about that, all the rest, come tomorrow. So there you go. We do our best, and that's all you can do."

She may sound fatalistic, but she appears to be a nervous, hardworking, even hard-driven woman—thin, short, constantly on the move. I may not know what she "really" thinks and believes, because like the rest of us she has her contradictions and her mixed feelings. I think it is fair to say that there are some things that she can't say to me—or to herself. She is a Negro, and I am white. She is poor, and I am fairly well off. She is very near to illiterate, and I put in a lot of time worrying about how to say things. But she and I are both human beings, and we both have trouble—to use that word—"communicating," not only with each other, but with ourselves. Sometimes she doesn't tell me something she really wants me to know. She has forgotten, pure and simple. More is on her mind than information I might want. And sometimes I forget too: "Remember you asked the other day about Peter, if he was ever real sick. And I told you he was a weak child, and I feared for his life, and I've lost five children, three that was born and two that wasn't. Well, I forgot to tell you that he got real sick up here, just after we came. He was three, and I didn't know what to do. You see, I didn't have my mother to help out. She always knew what to do. She could hold a child and get him to stop crying, no matter how sick he was, and no matter how much he wanted food, and we didn't have it. But she was gone—and that's when we left to come up here, and I never would have left her, not for anything in the world. But suddenly she took a seizure of something and went in a half hour, I'd say. And Peter, he was so hot and sick, I thought he had the same thing his grandmother did and he was going to die. I thought maybe she's calling him. She always liked Peter. She helped him be born, she and my cousin, they did."

Actually, Peter's mother remembers quite a lot of things. She remembers the "old days" back South, sometimes with a shudder, but sometimes with the same nostalgia that the region is famous for generating in its white exiles. She also notices a lot of things. She notices, and from time to time will remark upon, the various changes in her life. She has moved from the country to the city. Her father was a sharecropper and her son wants to be a pilot (sometimes), a policeman (sometimes), a racing-car driver (sometimes), and a baseball player (most of the time). Her husband is not alive. He died one year after they all came to Boston. He woke up vomiting in the middle of the night—vomiting blood. He bled and bled and vomited and vomited and then he died. The doctor does not have to press very hard for "the facts." Whatever is known gets spoken vividly and (still) emotionally: "*I didn't know what to do. I was beside myself. I prayed and I prayed, and in between I held his head and wiped his forehead. It was the middle of the night. I woke up my oldest girl and I told her to go knocking on the doors. But no one would answer. They must have been scared, or have suspected something bad. I thought if only he'd be able to last into the morning, then we could get some help. I was caught between things. I couldn't leave him to go get a policeman. And my girl, she was afraid to go out. And besides, there was no one outside, and I thought we'd just stay at his side, and somehow he'd be o.k., because he was a strong man, you know. His muscles, they were big all his life. Even with the blood coming up, he looked too big and strong to die, I thought. But I knew he was sick. He was real bad sick. There wasn't anything else, no sir, to do. We didn't have no phone and even if there was a car, I never could have used it. Nor my daughter. And then he took a big breath and that was his last one.*"

When I first met Peter and his mother, I wanted to know how they lived, what they did with their time, what they liked to do or disliked doing, what they believed. In the back of my mind were large subjects like "the connection between a person's moods and the environment in which he lives." Once I was told I was studying "the psychology of the ghetto," and another time the subject of "urban poverty and mental health." It is hoped that at some point large issues like those submit themselves to lives; and when that is done, when particular but not unrepresentative or unusual human beings are called in witness, their concrete medical history becomes extremely revealing. I cannot think of a better way to begin knowing what life is like for Peter and his mother than to hear the following and hear it again and think about its implications: *"No sir, Peter has never been to a doctor, not unless you count the one at school, and she's a nurse I believe. He was his sickest back home before we came here, and you know there was no doctor for us in the county. In Alabama you have to pay a white doctor first, before he'll go near you. And we don't have but a few colored ones. (I've never seen a one.) There was this woman we'd go to, and she had gotten some nursing education in Mobile. (No, I don't know if she was a nurse or not, or a helper to the nurses, maybe.) Well, she would come to help us. With the convulsions, she'd show you how to hold the child, and make sure he doesn't hurt himself. They can bite their tongues real, real bad.*

"Here, I don't know what to do. There's the city hospital, but it's no good for us. I went there with my husband, no sooner than a month or so after we came up here. We waited and waited, and finally the day was almost over. We left the kids with a neighbor, and we barely knew her. I said it would take the morning, but I never thought we'd get home near suppertime. And they wanted us to come back and come back, because it was something they couldn't do all at once—though for most of the time we just sat there and did nothing. And my husband, he said his stomach was the worse for going there, and he'd take care of himself from now on, rather than go there.

"Maybe they could have saved him. But they're far away, and I didn't have money to get a cab, even if there was one around here, and I thought to myself it'll make him worse, to take him there.

"My kids, they get sick. The welfare worker, she sends a nurse here, and she tells me we should be on vitamins and the kids need all kinds of check-ups. Once she took my daughter and told her she had to have her teeth looked at, and the same with Peter. So, I went with my daughter, and they didn't see me that day, but said they could in a couple of weeks. And I had to pay the woman next door to mind the little ones, and there was the carfare, and we sat and sat, like before. So, I figured, it would take more than we've got to see that dentist. And when the nurse told us we'd have to come back a few times—that's how many, a few—I thought that no one ever looked at my teeth, and they're not good, I'll admit, but you can't have everything, that's what I say, and that's what my kids have to know, I guess."

What *does* she have? And what belongs to Peter? For one

thing, there is the apartment, three rooms for six people, a mother and five children. Peter is a middle child with two older girls on one side and a younger sister and still younger brother on the other side. The smallest child was born in Boston: *"It's the only time I ever spent time in a hospital. He's the only one to be born there. My neighbor got the police. I was in the hall, crying I guess. We almost didn't make it. They told me I had bad blood pressure, and I should have been on pills, and I should come back, but I didn't. It was the worst time I've ever had, because I was alone. My husband had to stay with the kids, and no one was there to visit me."*

Peter sleeps with his brother in one bedroom. The three girls sleep in the living room, which is a bedroom. And, of course, there is a small kitchen. There is not very much furniture about. The kitchen has a table with four chairs, only two of which are sturdy. The girls sleep in one big bed. Peter shares his bed with his brother. The mother sleeps on a couch. There is one more chair and a table in the living room. Jesus looks down from the living room wall, and an undertaker's calendar hangs on the kitchen wall. The apartment has no books, no records. There is a television set in the living room, and I have never seen it off.

Peter in many respects is his father's successor. His mother talks things over with him. She even defers to him at times. She will say something; he will disagree; she will nod and let him have the last word. He knows the city. She still feels a stranger to the city. *"If you want to know about anything around here, just ask Peter,"* she once said to me. That was three years ago, when Peter was six. Peter continues to do very poorly at school, but I find him a very good teacher. He notices a lot, makes a lot of sense when he talks, and has a shrewd eye for the ironic detail. He is very intelligent, for all the trouble he gives his teachers. He recently summed up a lot of American history for me: *"I wasn't made for that school, and that school wasn't made for me."* It is an old school, filled with memories. The name of the school evokes Boston's Puritan past. Pictures and statues adorn the corridors—reminders of the soldiers and statesmen and writers who made New England so influential in the nineteenth century. And naturally one finds slogans on the walls, about freedom and democracy and the rights of the people. Peter can be surly and cynical when he points all that out to the visitor. If he is asked what kind of school he would *like*, he laughs incredulously. *"Are you kidding?*

No school would be my first choice. They should leave us alone, and let us help out at home, and maybe let some of our own people teach us. The other day the teacher admitted she was no good. She said maybe a Negro should come in and give us the discipline, because she was scared. She said all she wanted from us was that we keep quiet and stop wearing her nerves down, and she'd be grateful, because she would retire soon. She said we were becoming too much for her, and she didn't understand why. But when one kid wanted to say something, tell her why, she told us to keep still, and write something. You know what? She whipped out a book and told us to copy a whole page from it, so we'd learn it. A stupid waste of time. I didn't even try; and she didn't care. She just wanted an excuse not to talk with us. They're all alike."

Actually, they're all *not* alike, and Peter knows it. He has met up with two fine teachers, and in mellow moments he can say so: *"They're trying hard, but me and my friends, I don't think we're cut out for school. To tell the truth, that's what I think. My mother says we should try, anyway, but it doesn't seem to help, trying. The teacher can't understand a lot of us, but he does all these new things, and you can see he's excited. Some kids are really with him, and I am, too. But I can't take all his stuff very serious. He's a nice man, and he says he wants to come and visit every one of our homes; but my mother says no, she wouldn't know what to do with him, when he came here. We'd just stand and have nothing to talk about. So she said tell him not to come; and I don't think he will, anyway. I think he's getting to know."*

What is that teacher getting to know? What *is* there to know about Peter and all the others like him in our American cities? Of course Peter and his friends who play in the alley need better schools, schools they can feel to be theirs, and better teachers, like the ones they *have* in fact met on occasion. But I do not feel that a reasonably good teacher in the finest school building in America would reach and affect Peter in quite the way, I suppose, people like me would expect and desire. At nine Peter is both young and quite old. At nine he is much wiser about many things than my sons will be at nine, and maybe nineteen. Peter has in fact taught me a lot about his neighborhood, about life on the streets, about survival: *"I get up when I get up, no special time. My mother has Alabama in her. She gets up with the sun, and she wants to go to bed when it gets dark. I try to tell her that up here things just get started in the night. But she gets mad. She wakes me up. If it*

*weren't for her shaking me, I might sleep until noon. Sometimes
we have a good breakfast, when the check comes. Later on,
though, before it comes, it might just be some coffee and a slice
of bread. She worries about food. She says we should eat what
she gives us, but sometimes I'd rather go hungry. I was sick a long
time ago, my stomach or something—maybe like my father, she
says. So I don't like all the potatoes she pushes on us and cereal, all
the time cereal. We're supposed to be lucky, because we get some
food every day. Down South they can't be sure. That's what she
says, and I guess she's right.*

"*Then I go to school. I eat what I can, and leave. I have two
changes of clothes, one for everyday and one for Sunday. I wait on
my friend Billy, and we're off by 8:15. He's from around here, and
he's a year older. He knows everything. He can tell you if a
woman is high on some stuff, or if she's been drinking, or she's off
her mind about something. He knows. His brother has a conver-
tible, a Buick. He pays off the police, but Billy won't say no more
than that.*

"*In school we waste time until it's over. I do what I have to.
I don't like the place. I feel like falling off all day, just putting
my head down and saying good-bye to everyone until three. We're
out then, and we sure wake up. I don't have to stop home first,
not now. I go with Billy. We'll be in the alley, or we'll go to see
them play pool. Then you know when it's time to go home. You
hear someone say six o'clock, and you go in. I eat and I watch
television. It must be around ten or eleven I'm in bed.*"

Peter sees rats all the time. He has been bitten by them. He
has a big stick by his bed to use against them. They also claim the
alley, even in the daytime. They are not large enough to be
compared with cats, as some observers have insisted; they are
simply large, confident, well-fed, unafraid rats. The garbage is
theirs; the land is theirs; the tenement is theirs; human flesh is
theirs. When I first started visiting Peter's family, I wondered
why they didn't do something to rid themselves of those rats, and
the cockroaches, and the mosquitoes, and the flies, and the mag-
gots, and the ants, and especially the garbage in the alley which
attracts so much of all that "lower life." Eventually I began to see
some of the reasons why. A large apartment building with many
families has exactly two barrels in its basement. The halls of the
building go unlighted. Many windows have no screens, and some
windows are broken and boarded up. The stairs are dangerous;

some of them have missing timber. ("*We just jump over them,*" says Peter cheerfully.) And the landowner is no one in particular. Rent is collected by an agent, in the name of a "realty trust." Somewhere in City Hall there is a bureaucrat who unquestionably might be persuaded to prod someone in the "trust"; and one day I went with three of the tenants, including Peter's mother, to try that "approach." We waited and waited at City Hall. (I drove us there, clear across town, naturally.) Finally we met up with a man, a not very encouraging or inspiring or generous or friendly man. He told us we would have to try yet another department and swear out a complaint; and that the "case" would have to be "studied," and that we would then be "notified of a decision." We went to the department down the hall, and waited some more, another hour and ten minutes. By then it was three o'clock, and the mothers wanted to go home. They weren't thinking of rats anymore, or poorly heated apartments, or garbage that had nowhere to go and often went uncollected for two weeks, not one. They were thinking of their children, who would be home from school and, in the case of two women, their husbands who would also soon be home. "*Maybe we should come back some other day,*" Peter's mother said. I noted she didn't say *tomorrow*, and I realized that I had read someplace that people like her aren't precisely "future-oriented."

Actually, both Peter and his mother have a very clear idea of what is ahead. For the mother it is "*more of the same.*" One evening she was tired but unusually talkative, perhaps because a daughter of hers was sick: "*I'm glad to be speaking about all these things tonight. My little girl has a bad fever. I've been trying to cool her off all day. Maybe if there was a place near here, that we could go to, maybe I would have gone. But like it is, I have to do the best I can and pray she'll be o.k.*"

I asked whether she thought her children would find things different, and that's when she said it would be "*more of the same*" for them. Then she added a long afterthought: "*Maybe it'll be a little better for them. A mother has to have hope for her children, I guess. But I'm not too sure, I'll admit. Up here you know there's a lot more jobs around than in Alabama. We don't get them, but you know they're someplace near, and they tell you that if you go train for them, then you'll be eligible. So maybe Peter might someday have some real good steady work, and that would be something, yes sir it would. I keep telling him he should pay more attention to school, and put more of himself into the lessons they give there. But he says no, it's no good; it's a waste of time; they don't care what happens there, only if the kids don't keep quiet and mind themselves. Well, Peter has got to learn to mind himself, and not be fresh. He speaks back to me, these days. There'll be a time he won't even speak to me at all, I suppose. I used to blame it all on the city up here, city living. Back home we were always together, and there wasn't no place you could go, unless to Birmingham, and you couldn't do much for yourself there, we all knew. Of course, my momma, she knew how to make us behave. But I was thinking the other night, it wasn't so good back there either. Colored people, they'd beat on one another, and we had lot of people that liquor was eating away at them; they'd use wine by the gallon. All they'd do was work on the land, and then go back and kill themselves with wine. And then there'd be the next day—until they'd one evening go to sleep and never wake up. And we'd get the Bossman and he'd see to it they got buried.*

"Up here I think it's better, but don't ask me to tell you why. There's the welfare, that's for sure. And we get our water and if there isn't good heat, at least there's some. Yes, it's cold up here, but we had cold down there, too, only then we didn't have any heat, and we'd just die, some of us would, every winter with one of those freezing spells.

"And I do believe things are changing. On the television they talk to you, the colored man and all the others who aren't doing so good. My boy Peter, he says they're putting you on. That's all he sees, people 'putting on' other people. But I think they all mean it, the white people. I never see them, except on television, when they say the white man wants good for the colored people. I think Peter could go and do better for himself later on, when he gets older, except for the fact that he just doesn't believe. He don't believe what they say, the teacher, or the man who says it's getting better for us—on television. I guess it's my fault. I never taught my children, any of them, to believe that kind of thing; because I never thought we'd ever have it any different, not in this life. So maybe I've failed Peter. I told him the other day, he should work hard, because of all the 'opportunity' they say is coming for us, and he said I was talking good, but where was my proof. So I went next door with him, to my neighbor's, and we asked her husband, and you know he sided with Peter. He said they were taking in a few here and a few there, and putting them in the

front windows of all the big companies, but that all you have to do is look around at our block and you'd see all the young men, and they just haven't got a thing to do. Nothing."

Her son also looks to the future. Sometimes he talks—in his own words—"big." He'll one day be a bombadier or "something like that." At other times he is less sure of things: "I don't know what I'll be. Maybe nothing. I see the men sitting around, hiding from the welfare lady. They fool her. Maybe I'll fool her, too. I don't know what you can do. The teacher the other day said that if just one of us turned out o.k. she'd congratulate herself and call herself lucky."

A while back a riot excited Peter and his mother, excited them and frightened them. The spectacle of the police being fought, of white-owned property being assaulted, stirred the boy a great deal: "I figured the whole world might get changed around. I figured people would treat us better from now on. Only I don't think they will." As for his mother, she was less hopeful, but even more apocalyptic: "I told Peter we were going to pay for this good. I told him they wouldn't let us get away with it, not later on." And in the midst of the trouble she was frightened as she had never before been: "I saw them running around on the streets, the men and women, and they were talking about burning things down, and how there'd be nothing left when they got through. I sat there with my children and I thought we might die the way things are going, die right here. I didn't know what to do: if I should leave, in case they burn down the building, or if I should stay, so that the police don't arrest us, or we get mixed up with the crowd of people. I've never seen so many people, going in so many different directions. They were running and shouting and they didn't know what to do. They were so excited. My neighbor, she said they'd burn us all up, and then the white man would have himself one less of a headache. The colored man is a worse enemy to himself than the white. I mean, it's hard to know which is the worst."

I find it as hard as she does to sort things out. When I think of her and the mothers like her I have worked with for years, when I think of Peter and his friends, I find myself caught between the contradictory observations I have made. Peter already seems a grim and unhappy child. He trusts no one white, not his white teacher, not the white policeman he sees, not the white welfare worker, not the white storekeeper, and not, I might add, me. There we are, the five of us from the 180,000,000 Americans who surround him and of course 20,000,000 others. Yet, Peter doesn't really trust his friends and neighbors, either. At nine he has learned to be careful, wary, guarded, doubtful, and calculating. His teacher may not know it, but Peter is a good sociologist, and a good political scientist, a good student of urban affairs. With devastating accuracy he can reveal how much of the "score" he knows; yes, and how fearful and sad and angry he is: *"This here city isn't for us. It's for the people downtown. We're here because, like my mother said, we had to come. If they could lock us up or sweep us away, they would. That's why I figure the only way you can stay ahead is get some kind of deal for yourself. If I had a choice I'd live someplace else, but I don't know where. It would be a place where they treated you right, and they didn't think you were some nuisance. But the only thing you can do is be careful of yourself; if not, you'll get killed somehow, like it happened to my father."*

His father died prematurely, and most probably, unnecessarily. Among the poor of our cities the grim medical statistics we all know about become terrible daily experiences. Among the black and white families I work with—in nearby but separate slums— disease and the pain that goes with it are taken for granted. When my children complain of an earache or demonstrate a skin rash I rush them to the doctor. When I have a headache, I take an aspirin; and if the headache is persistent, I can always get a medical check-up. Not so with Peter's mother and Peter; they have learned to live with sores and infections and poorly mended fractures and bad teeth and eyes that need but don't have the help of glasses. Yes, they can go to a city hospital and get free care; but again and again they don't. They come to the city without any previous experience as patients. They have never had the money to purchase a doctor's time. They have never had free medical care available. (I am speaking now of Appalachian whites as well as southern blacks.) It may comfort me to know that every American city provides some free medical services for its "indigent," but Peter's mother and thousands like her have quite a different view of things: *"I said to you the other time, I've tried there. It's like at City Hall, you wait and wait, and they pushes you and shove you and call your name, only to tell you to wait some more, and if you tell them you can't stay there all day, they'll say 'lady, go home, then.' You get sick just trying to get there. You have to give your children over to people or take them all with you; and the carfare is expensive. Why if we had a doctor around here, I could almost pay him with the carfare it takes to get there and back for all of us. And you know, they keep on having you come back and back, and they don't know what each other says. Each time they starts from scratch."*

It so happens that recently I took Peter to a children's hospital and arranged for a series of evaluations which led to the following: a pair of glasses; a prolonged bout of dental work; antibiotic treatment for skin lesions; a thorough cardiac work-up, with the subsequent diagnosis of rheumatic heart disease; a conference between Peter's mother and a nutritionist, because the boy has been on a high-starch, low-protein, and low-vitamin diet all his life. He suffers from one attack of sinus trouble after another, from a succession of sore throats and earaches, from cold upon cold, even in the summer. A running nose is unsurprising to him— and so is chest pain and shortness of breath, due to a heart ailment, we now know.

At the same time Peter is tough. I have to emphasize again *how* tough and, yes, how "politic, cautious and meticulous," not in Prufrock's way, but in another way and for other reasons. Peter has learned to be wary as well as angry; tentative as well as extravagant; at times controlled and only under certain circumstances defiant: *"Most of the time, I think you have to watch your step. That's what I think. That's the difference between up here and down in the South. That's what my mother says, and she's right. I don't remember it down there, but I know she must be right. Here, you measure the next guy first and then make your move when you think it's a good time to."*

He was talking about *"how you get along"* when you leave school and go *"mix with the guys"* and start *"getting your deal."* He was telling me what an outrageous and unsafe world he has inherited and how very carefully he has made his appraisal of the future. Were I afflicted with some of his physical complaints, I would be fretful, annoyed, petulant, angry—and moved to do something, see someone, get a remedy, a pill, a promise of help. He has made his "adjustment" to the body's pain, and he has also learned to contend with the alley and the neighborhood and us, the world beyond: *"The cops come by here all the time. They drive up and down the street. They want to make sure everything is o.k. to look at. They don't bother you, so long as you don't get in their way."*

So, it is live and let live—except that families like Peter's have a tough time living, and of late have been troubling those cops, among others. Our cities have become not only battlegrounds, but places where all sorts of American problems and historical ironies have converged. Ailing, poorly fed, and proud Appalachian families have reluctantly left the hollows of eastern Kentucky and West Virginia for Chicago and Dayton and Cincinnati and Cleveland and Detroit, and even, I have found, Boston. They stick close together in all-white neighborhoods—or enclaves or sections or slums or ghettos or whatever. They wish to go home but can't, unless they are willing to be idle and hungry all the time. They confuse social workers and public officials of all kinds because they both want and reject the city. Black families also have sought out cities and learned to feel frightened and disappointed.

I am a physician, and over the past ten years I have been asking myself how people like Peter and his mother survive in mind and body and spirit. And I have wanted to know what a twentieth-century American city "means" to them or "does" to them. People cannot be handed questionnaires and asked to answer such questions. They cannot be "interviewed" a few times and told to come across with a statement, a reply. But inside Peter and his brother and his sisters and his mother, and inside a number of Appalachian mothers and fathers and children I know, are feelings and thoughts and ideas—which, in my experience, come out casually or suddenly, by accident almost. After a year or two of talking, after experiences such as I have briefly described in a city hall, in a children's hospital, a lifetime of pent-up tensions and observation comes to blunt expression: *"Down in Alabama we had to be careful about ourselves with the white man, but we had plenty of things we could do by ourselves. There was our side of town, and you could walk and run all over, and we had a garden you know. Up here they have you in a cage. There's no place to go, and all I do is stay in the building all day long and the night, too. I don't use my legs no more, hardly at all. I never see those trees, and my oldest girl, she misses planting time. It was bad down there. We had to leave. But it's no good here, too, I'll tell you. Once I woke up and I thought all the buildings on the block were falling down on me. And I was trying to climb out, but I couldn't. And then the next thing I knew, we were all back South, and I was standing near some sunflowers—you know, the tall ones that can shade you if you sit down.*

"No, I don't dream much. I fall into a heavy sleep as soon as I touch the bed. The next thing I know I'm stirring myself to start in all over in the morning. It used to be the sun would wake me up, but now it's up in my head, I guess. I know I've got to get the house going and off to school."

Her wistful, conscientious, law-abiding, devoutly **Christian** spirit hasn't completely escaped the notice of Peter, for all his hard-headed, cynical protestations: "*If I had a chance, I'd like to get enough money to bring us all back to Alabama for a visit. Then I could prove it that it may be good down there, a little bit, even if it's no good, either. Like she says, we had to get out of there or we'd be dead by now. I hear say we all may get killed soon, it's so bad here; but I think we did right to get up here, and if we make them listen to us, the white man, maybe he will.*"

To which Peter's mother adds: "*We've carried a lot of trouble in us, from way back in the beginning. I have these pains, and so does everyone around here. But you can't just die until you're ready to. And I do believe something is happening. I do believe I see that.*"

To which Peter adds: "*Maybe it won't be that we'll win, but if we get killed, everyone will hear about it. Like the minister said, before we used to die real quiet, and no one stopped to pay notice.*"

Two years before Peter spoke those words he drew a picture for me, one of many he has done. When he was younger, and when I didn't know him so well as I think I do now, it was easier for us to have something tangible to do and then talk about. I used to visit the alley with him, as I still do, and one day I asked him to draw the alley. That was a good idea, he thought. (Not all of my suggestions were, however.) He started in, then stopped, and finally worked rather longer and harder than usual at the job. I busied myself with my own sketches, which from the start he insisted I do. Suddenly from across the table I heard him say he was through. Ordinarily he would slowly turn the drawing around for me to see; and I would get up and walk over to his side of the table, to see even better. But he didn't move his paper, and I didn't move myself. I saw what he had drawn, and he saw me looking. I was surprised and a bit stunned and more than a bit upset, and surely he saw my face and heard my utter silence. Often I would break the awkward moments when neither of us seemed to have anything to say, but this time it was his turn to do so: "*You know what it is?*" He knew that I liked us to talk about our work. I said no, I didn't—though in fact the vivid power of his black crayon had come right across to me. "*It's that hole we dug in the alley. I made it bigger here. If you fall into it, you can't get out. You die.*"

He had drawn circles within circles, all of them black, and then a center, also black. He had imposed an X on the center. Nearby, strewn across the circles, were fragments of the human body— two faces, an arm, five legs. And after I had taken the scene in, I could only think to myself that I had been shown "*like it is in the alley*"—by an intelligent boy who knew what he saw around him, could give it expression, and, I am convinced, would respond to a different city, a city that is alive and breathing, one that is not for many of its citizens a virtual morgue.

RACIALLY SEPARATE OR TOGETHER?

Thomas F. Pettigrew

Thomas F. Pettigrew, "Racially Separate or Together?," *Integrated Education,* January-February, 1969, pp. 36-56.

RACIALLY SEPARATE OR TOGETHER?[1]

Thomas F. Pettigrew

America has had an almost perpetual racial crisis for a generation. But the last third of the twentieth century has begun on a new note, a change of rhetoric and a confusion over goals. Widespread rioting is just one expression of this note. The nation hesitates; it seems to have lost its confidence that the problem can be solved; it seems unsure as to even the direction in which a solution lies. In too simple terms, yet in the style of the fashionable rhetoric, the question has become: Shall Americans of the future live racially separate or together?

This new mood is best understood when viewed within the eventful sweep of recent years. Ever since World War I, when war orders combined with the curtailment of immigration to encourage massive migration to industrial centers, Negro Americans have been undergoing rapid change as a people. The latest product of this dramatic transformation from southern peasant to northern urbanite is a second- and third-generation northern-born youth. Indeed, over half of Negro Americans alive today are below twenty-two years of age. The most significant fact about this "newest new Negro" is that he is relatively released from the principal social controls recognized by his parents and grand-

[1]This paper was the author's presidential address to the Society for the Psychological Study of Social Issues, delivered at the annual convention of the American Psychological Association in San Francisco, California on September 1, 1968. Its preparation was facilitated by Contract No. OEC 1-6-061774-1887 of the United States Office of Education.

parents, from the restraints of an extended kinship system, a conservative religion and an acceptance of the inevitability of white supremacy.

Consider the experience of the twenty-year-old Negro youth today. He was born in 1948; he was an impressionable six years old when the highest court in the land decreed against *de jure* public school segregation; he was only nine years old at the time of the Little Rock, Arkansas desegregation confrontation; he was twelve years old when the student-organized sit-ins began at segregated lunch counters throughout the South; and he was fifteen when the dramatic March-on-Washington took place and seventeen when the climactic Selma march occurred. He has literally witnessed during his short life the initial dismantling of the formal structure of white supremacy. Conventional wisdom holds that such an experience should lead to a highly satisfied generation of young Negro Americans. Newspaper headlines and social psychological theory tell us precisely the opposite is closer to the truth.

Relative Deprivation Theory . . .

The past three decades of Negro American history constitute an almost classic case for relative deprivation theory (Pettigrew, 1964, 1967). Mass unrest has reoccurred throughout history after long periods of improvement followed by abrupt periods of reversal (Davies, 1962). This pattern derives from four revolt-stirring conditions triggered by long-term improvements: (a) living conditions of the dominant group typically advance faster than those of the subordinate group; (b) the aspirations of the subordinate group climb far more rapidly than actual changes; (c) status inconsistencies among subordinate group members increase sharply; and (d) a broadening of comparative reference groups occurs for the subordinate group (Pettigrew, 1967).

Each of these four conditions typifies the Negro American situation today (Geschwender, 1964; Pettigrew, 1964, 1967). (a) Though the past few decades have witnessed the most rapid gains in Negro American history, these gains have generally not kept pace with those of white America during these same prosperous years. (b) Public opinion surveys document the swiftly rising aspirations of Negro Americans, especially since 1954. Moreover, (c) status inconsistency has been increasing among Negroes, particularly among the young whose educational level typically exceeds the low status employment offered them. Finally, (d) Negro Americans have greatly expanded their relevant reference groups in recent years; affluent referents in the richest country on earth are now routinely adopted as the appropriate standard with which to judge one's condition. The second component of unrest involving a sudden reversal has been supplied, too, by the Vietnam War. Little wonder, then, that America's racial crisis reached the combustible point in the late sixties.

The young Negro surveys the current scene and observes correctly that the benefits of recent racial advances have disproportionately accrued to the expanding middle class, leaving further behind the urban lower class. While the middle-class segment of Negro America has expanded from roughly five to twenty-five per cent of the group since 1940,[2] the vast majority of Negroes remain poor. Raised on the proposition that racial integration is the basic solution to racial injustice, the young Negro's doubts grow as opportunities open for the skilled while the daily lives of the unskilled go largely unaffected. Accustomed to a rapid pace of events, many Negro youth wonder if integration will ever be possible in an America where the depth of white resistance to racial change becomes painfully more evident: the equivocation of the 1964 Democratic Party Convention when faced with the challenge of the Mississippi Freedom Democratic Party; the Selma bridge brutality; the summary rejection by the 1966 Congress of antidiscrimination legislation for housing; the repressive reaction to riots from the Chicago Mayor's advocacy of police state methods to the New Jersey Governor's suspension of the Bill of Rights in Plainfield; and, finally, the wanton assassinations within ten weeks of two leading symbols of the integration movement. These events cumulated to create understandable doubts as to whether Dr. Martin Luther King's famous dream of equality could ever be achieved.

Shift in Militant Stance and Rhetoric . . .

It is tempting to project this process further, as many mass media accounts unhesitantly have done, and suggest that all of Negro America has undergone this vast disillusionment, that Negroes now overwhelmingly reject racial integration for separatist goals. As we shall note shortly, this is emphatically not the case. Nevertheless, the militant stance and rhetoric *have* shifted, and many whites find considerable encouragement in this new Negro mood. Indeed, strictly separatist solutions for the black ghettos of urban America have been most elaborately and enthusiastically advanced not by Negroes at all but by such white

---

[2] These figures derive from three gross estimates of "middle class" status: $6,000 or more annual family income, high school graduation or white-collar occupation. Thus, in 1961 roughly a fifth of Negro familes received in excess of $6,000 (a percentage that now must approach a fourth even in constant dollars), in 1960 22 per cent of Negroes over 24 years of age had completed high school, and in 1966 21 per cent of employed Negroes held white-collar occupations.

writers as newspaper columnist Joseph Alsop (1967a, 1967b) and W. H. Ferry (1968) of the Center for the Study of Democratic Institutions.[3] Nor should we confuse "black power" ideas as such with separatism, since there are numerous variants of this developing ideology, only a few of which portray a racially-separate United States as the desirable end-state. As a presumed intervening stage, black separatism is more concerned with group pride and "local control", more a retreat from whites than an attempt to dominate them. This contrasts with the traditional attempts at racial supremacy of white segregationists. Black separatism and white separatism present the danger that they might well congeal to perpetuate a racially-separate nation; but they are otherwise somewhat different phenomena as a cursory examination of their basic assumptions readily reveals.

Separatist Assumptions

White segregationists, North and South, base their position upon three bedrock assumptions. First, they maintain that separation benefits both races in that each feels awkward and uncomfortable in the midst of the other (Armstrong and Gregor, 1964). Whites and Negroes are happiest and most relaxed when in the company of "their own kind". We shall call this *"the comfortable assumption"*.

The second assumption of white segregationists is blatantly racist. The underlying reality of the nation's racial problem, they unashamedly maintain, is that Negroes are inherently inferior to Caucasians. The findings of both social and biological science place in serious jeopardy every argument put forward for *"the racial inferiority assumption"*, and an ever-decreasing minority of white Americans subscribe to it (Pettigrew, 1964). Yet it remains the essential substrata of white segregationist thinking; racial contact must be avoided, according to this reasoning, if white standards are not to be diluted. Thus, Negro attendance at a predominantly white school may benefit the Negro children, but it is deemed by segregationists as inevitably harmful to white children.[4]

---

[3]See, too, replies to Alsop by Schwartz *et al.* (1967, 1968). Alsop eagerly calls for giving up the effort to integrate schools racially in order to put all efforts into achieving separate but improved schools in the ghetto. Ferry goes further and advocates "black colonies" be formally established in American central cities, complete with treaties enacted with the federal government. Black militants, in sharp contrast, complain of being in a colonial status now but do not endorse it as a desired state of affairs.

[4]Analysis specifically directed on this point shows this contention not to be true for predominantly-white classrooms as contrasted with comparable all-white classrooms (U.S. Commission on Civil Rights, 1967; Vol. I, 160).

The third assumption flows from this presumption of white racial superiority. Since contact can never be mutually beneficial, it will inevitably lead to racial conflict. The White Citizens' Councils in the deep South, for example, stoutly insist that they are opposed to violence and favor racial separation as the primary means of maintaining racial harmony. As long as Negroes "know their place", as long as white supremacy remains unchallenged, "*the racial conflict assumption*" contends strife will be at a minimum.

Coming from the opposite direction, black separatists fundamentally base their position upon three parallel assumptions. They agree with "*the comfortable assumption*" that both whites and Negroes are more at ease when separated from each other. Some of this agreement stems from the harsh fact that Negroes have borne the heavier burden of desegregation and have entered previously all-white institutions where open hostility is sometimes explicitly practiced by segregationist whites in order to discourage the process. Yet some of this agreement stems, too, from more subtle situations. The demands by a few black student organizations on interracial campuses for all-black facilities have been predicated on "*the comfortable assumption*".

A second assumption focuses directly upon white racism. Supported by the chief conclusion of the National Advisory Commission on Civil Disorders (1968), black separatists label white racism as a central problem which so-called "white liberals" should confine their energies to eradicating. "*The white-liberals-must-eradicate-white-racism-assumption*" underlies two further contentions: namely, that "white liberals" should stay out of the ghetto save as their money and expertise are explicitly requested, and that it is no longer the job of black militants to confront and absorb the abuse of white racists.

The third assumption is the most basic of all, and is in tacit agreement with the segregationist notion that interracial contact as it now occurs makes only for conflict. Interaction between Negro and white Americans, it is held, can never be truly equal and mutually beneficial until Negroes gain personal and group autonomy, self-respect and power. "*The autonomy-before-contact assumption*" often underlies a two-step theory of how to achieve meaningful integration: the first step requires separation so that Negroes can regroup, unify and gain a positive self-image and identity; only when this is achieved can the second step of real integration take place. Ron Karenga, a black militant leader in Los Angeles, states the idea forcefully: "We're not for isolation, but interdependence. But we can't become interdependent unless we have something to offer. We can live with whites interdependently once we have black power" (Calame, 1968).

Each of these ideological assumptions deserves examination in light of social psychological theory and findings.

Social Psychological Considerations of Separatist Assumptions

The Comfortable Assumption

There can be no denying the reality of initial discomfort and ill-ease for many Negro and white Americans when they encounter each other in new situations. This reality is so vivid and generally recognized that both black and white separatists employ it as a key fact in their thinking, though they do not analyze its nature and origins.

The social science literature is replete with examples of the phenomenon. Kohn and Williams (1956), for instance, studied New York State facilities unaccustomed to Negro patronage. Negro researchers would enter a tavern, seek service and later record their experiences, while white researchers would observe the same situation and record their impressions for comparison. Typically the first reaction of waitresses and bartenders was embarrassment and discomfort; they turned to the owner or others in authority for guidance. When this was unavailable, the slightest behavioral cue from anyone in the situation was utilized as a gauge of what was expected of them. And if there were no such cues, confusion often continued until somehow the tense situation had been structured. Needless to add, the tension was at least as great for the potential Negro patron.

Other examples arise from small group and summer camp research. Irwin Katz (1964) has described the initial awkwardness in biracial task groups in the laboratory; white partners usually assumed an aggressive, imperious role, Negro partners a passive role. Similarly, Yarrow (1958) found initial tension and keen sensitivity among many Negro children in an interracial summer camp, much of which centered around fears of rejection by white campers. Not all Negroes and whites, of course, manifest this discomfort. Furthermore, such tension does not continue to pervade a truly integrated situation. Katz noted that once Negroes were cast in assertive roles behavior in his small groups became more equalitarian and this improvement generalized to new situations. Yarrow, too, observed a sharp decline in Negro anxiety and sensitivity which occurred after two weeks of successful integration at the summer camp. Similar increments in cross-racial acceptance and reductions in tension have been noted in new interracial situations in department stores (Harding and Hogrefe, 1952; Saenger and Gilbert, 1950), the merchant marine (Brothy,

1946), the armed forces (Stouffer *et al.*, 1949), public housing (Deutsch and Collins, 1951; Jahoda and West, 1951; Wilner *et al.*, 1955; and Works, 1961), and even among the Philadelphia police (Kephart, 1957).

Contact Effects Limited to the Situation

This is not to say that new interracial situations invariably lead to acceptance. As we shall note, the *conditions* of the interracial contact are crucial. Moreover, even under optimal conditions, the cross-racial acceptance generated by contact is typically limited to the particular situation. Thus, white steelworkers learn to work easily with Negroes as co-workers and vote for them as union officers; but this acceptance does not carry over to attitudes and action concerning interracial housing (Reitzes, 1953). A segregated society restricts the generalization effects of even truly integrated situations; and at times like the present when race assumes such overwhelming salience, the racial tension of the larger society may poison previously successful interracial settings.

Acquaintance and similarity theory helps to sort out the underlying process. Newcomb states the fundamental tenet as follows:

> Insofar as persons have similar attitudes toward things of importance to both or all of them, and discover that this is so, they have shared attitudes; under most conditions the experience of sharing such attitudes is rewarding, and thus provides a basis for mutual attraction (Newcomb *et al.*, 1965)

Rokeach has applied these notions to American race relations with some surprising results. He maintains that white American rejection of Negro Americans is motivated less by racism than by assumed belief and value differences. In other words, whites generally perceive Negroes as holding contrasting beliefs, and it is this perception and not race *per se* that leads to rejection. Indeed, a variety of subjects have supported Rokeach's ideas by typically accepting in a social situation a Negro with similar beliefs to their own over a white with different beliefs (Rokeach *et al.*, 1960; Rokeach and Mezei, 1966; Smith *et al.*, 1967; Stein, 1966; and Stein *et al.*, 1965).

Additional work specifies the phenomenon more precisely. Triandis and Davis (1965) have shown that the relative importance of belief and race factors in attraction is a joint function of the interpersonal realm in question and personality. Belief similarity is most critical in more formal matters of general personal evaluation and social acceptance, where racial norms are ambiguously defined. Race is most critical in intimate matters of marriage and neighborhood, where racial norms are explicitly defined. For interpersonal realms of intermediate intimacy, such as friendship, both belief and race considerations appear important. Moreover, there are wide individual differences in the application of belief similarity and race, especially in contact realms of intermediate intimacy.[5]

Isolation's Negative Effects

Seen in the light of this work, racial isolation has two negative effects both of which operate to make optimal interracial contact difficult to achieve and initially tense. First, isolation prevents each group from learning of the common beliefs and values they do in fact share. Consequently, Negroes and whites kept apart come to view each other as so different that belief dissimilarity typically combines with racial considerations to cause each race to reject contact with the other. Second, isolation leads in time to the evolution of genuine differences in beliefs and values, again making interracial contact in the future less likely.

A number of pointed findings of social psychological research support this extrapolation of interpersonal attraction theory. Stein *et al.* (1965) noted that relatively racially-isolated ninth-graders in California assumed an undescribed Negro teen-ager to be similar to a Negro teen-ager who is described as being quite different from themselves. Smith *et al.* (1967) found that belief similarity relative to racial similarity was more critical in desegregated settings, less critical in segregated settings. And the U.S. Commission on Civil Rights (1967), in its study of *Racial Isolation in the Public Schools*, found that both Negro and white adults who as children had attended interracial schools were more likely today to live in an interracial neighborhood and hold more positive racial attitudes than comparable adults who had known only segregated schools. Or put negatively, those Americans of both races who experienced only segregated education are more likely to reflect separatist behavior and attitudes as adults.

Racial separatism, then, is a cumulative process. It feeds upon itself and leads its victims to prefer continued separation. In an open-choice situation in Louisville, Kentucky, Negro children were far more likely to select predominantly white high

---

[5]This resolution of the earlier Triandis (1961) and Rokeach (1961) controversy takes on added weight when the data from studies favorable to the Rokeach position are examined carefully. That different interpersonal realms lead to varying belief-race weightings is borne out by Table 4 in Stein *et al.* (1965); that intensely prejudiced subjects, particularly in environments where racist norms even extend into less intimate realms, will act on race primarily is shown by one sample of whites in the deep South of Smith *et al.* (1967).

schools if they were currently attending predominantly white junior high schools.[6] From these data, the U.S. Commission on Civil Rights concluded: "The inference is strong that Negro high school students prefer biracial education only if they have experienced it before. If a Negro student has not received his formative education in biracial schools, the chances are he will not choose to enter one in his more mature school years" (U.S. Commission on Civil Rights, 1963).

Similarly, Negro adult products of segregated schools, the Civil Rights Commission (1967) finds, are more likely to believe that interracial schools "create hardships for Negro children" and less likely to send their children to desegregated schools than Negro products of biracial schools. Note that those who most fear discomfort in biracial settings are precisely those who have experienced such situations least. If desegregation actually resulted in perpetual and debilitating tension, as separatists blithely assume, it seems unlikely that children already in the situation would willingly opt for more, or that adults who have had considerable interracial contact as children would willingly submit themselves to biracial neighborhoods and their children to biracial schools.

A Social Cost Analysis is Needed

A social cost analysis is needed. The question becomes: What price comfort? Racially homogeneous settings are often more comfortable for members of both races, though this seems to be especially true at the start of the contact and does not seem to be so debilitating that those in the situation typically wish to return to segregated living. Those who remain in racial isolation, both Negro and white, find themselves increasingly less equipped to compete in an interracial world. Lobotomized patients are more comfortable, too, but they are impaired for life.

There is nothing inevitable, then, about the tension that characterizes many initial interracial encounters in the United States. Rather it is the direct result of the racial separation that has traditionally characterized our society. In short, separation is the cause, not the remedy, for interracial awkwardness.

---

[6]For twelve junior highs, the Spearman-Brown rank order correlation between the white junior high percentage and the percentage of Negroes choosing predominantly-white high schools is +.82 (corrected for ties)—significant at better than the one per cent level of confidence

The Assumptions of Racial Inferiority and
White-Liberals-Must-Eradicate-White-Racism

The second set of separatist assumptions raises related issues. Indeed, both of these assumptions also afford classical cases of self-fulfilling prophecies. Treat a people as inferior, force them to play subservient roles,[7] keep them essentially separate and the products will necessarily support the initial racist notions. Likewise, assume whites are unalterably racist, curtail Negro efforts to confront racism directly, separate from whites further, and the result will surely be continued, if not heightened, racism.

The core of racist attitudes, the assumption of innate racial inferiority, has been under sharp attack from social science for over three decades.[8] Partly because of this work, white American attitudes have undergone massive change over these years. For example, while only two out of five white Americans regarded Negroes as their intellectual equals in 1942, almost four out of five did by 1956—including a substantial majority of white Southerners (Hyman and Sheatsley, 1956; 1964). Yet a sizable minority of white Americans, perhaps still as large as a fifth, persist in harboring racist attitudes in their most vulgar and naive form. This is an important fact in a time of polarization such as the present, for this minority becomes the vocal right anchor in the nation's social judgment process.

Racist assumptions are not only nourished by separatism but in turn rationalize separatism. Equal-status contact is avoided because of the racist stigma branded upon Negro Americans by three centuries of slavery and segregation. Yet changes are evident in social distance attitudes, too. Between 1942 and 1963, the percentage of white Americans who favored racially desegregated schools rose from 30 to 63; and those with no objections to a Negro neighbor from 35 to 63 (Hyman and Sheatsley, 1964; Sheatsley, 1965). Nor has this trend abated during the recent five years of increasing polarization—a period which the mass media misinterpreted with the vague label of "backlash".[9] The most dramatic shifts have occurred in the South; the proportion of white Southern parents who stated that they would not object to having their children attend classes with "a few" Negro chil-

---

[7]For a role analysis interpretation of racial interactions in the United States, see Pettigrew (1964).

[8]One of the first significant efforts in this direction was the classic intelligence study by Klineberg (1935). For a summary of current scientific work relevant to racist claims in health, intelligence and crime, see Pettigrew (1964).

[9]The incorrect interpretation of present white animosities toward the Negro as a "backlash" is a classic case of the ecological fallacy; see Pettigrew (1966).

dren rose from only 38 per cent in 1963 to 62 per cent by 1965 (American Institute of Public Opinion, 1965). Consistently favorable shifts also characterized white opinion in the North. Here, a school with "a few" Negro children was declared objectionable by 87 per cent of white parents in 1963, by 91 per cent in 1965; a school where the student body was one-half Negro was acceptable to 56 per cent in 1963, to 65 per cent in 1965; and a school with a majority of Negro students found no objection among 31 per cent in 1963, among 37 per cent in 1965. Similar changes are evident in white attitudes in other realms and in more current surveys, though shifts in attitudes toward intimate contact have remained limited.

This slow but steady erosion of racist and separatist attitudes among white Americans has occurred during years of confrontation and change. To be sure, the process has been too slow to keep pace with the Negro's rising aspirations for full justice and complete eradication of racism. Yet this relentless trend parallelling the drive for integration should not be overlooked.

In a Period of Confrontation . . .

Thus, in a period of confrontation, dramatic events can stimulate surprisingly sharp shifts in a short period of time. Consider the attitudes of white Texans before and after the tragic assassination of Martin Luther King, Jr., the riots that followed his murder, and the issuance of the forthright Report of the

TABLE 1
PER CENT OF WHITE TEXANS WHO APPROVE*

Area of Desegregation	November 1967	February 1968	May 1968	May − $\dfrac{\text{Nov.} + \text{Feb.}}{2}$ Change
Same busses	65.6	66.6	75.6	+9.5
Same jobs	68.5	70.7	77.3	+7.7
Same restaurants	60.7	62.5	69.2	+7.6
Same hotels	55.2	55.4	62.5	+7.2
Same schools	57.1	60.4	64.3	+5.6
Teach your child	53.1	53.6	57.7	+4.4
Same churches	61.5	62.9	66.2	+4.0
Same social gatherings	42.1	42.4	45.3	+3.1
Live next door	34.2	36.2	36.8	+1.6
Same swimming pools	35.1	30.9	34.2	+1.2
Same house party	29.4	30.0	30.3	+0.6
College roommate of your child	21.4	21.5	21.4	−0.1

*These results are taken from R. T. Riley and T. F. Pettigrew, "Dramatic events and racial attitude change". Unpublished paper. Harvard University, August 1968. The data are from probability samples of white Texans drawn and interviewed by Belden Associates of Dallas, Texas specifically for the U.S. Office of Education Contract No. OEC 1-6-061-774-1887 to Harvard University.

National Advisory Commission on Civil Disorders (1968). Table 1 shows the data collected prior to the assassination in November 1967 and February 1968 and following the assassination in May 1968.

Observe the especially large change in the four realms of relatively formal contact—desegregation in busses, jobs, restaurants and hotels; the moderate change in realms of relatively informal contact—the desegregation of schools and churches; and the lack of significant change in realms of intimate contact— desegregation of social gatherings, housing, swimming pools, house parties and college dormitories. Despite the ceiling effect, approval increased greatest for those items already most approved. One is reminded of the Triandis and Davis (1965) breakdown of racial realms by degree of intimacy. The attitude change also varied among different types of white Texans; the young and the middle class shifted positively the most, again despite ceiling effects.[10] The tentative generalization growing out of these data is: In times of confrontation, dramatic events can achieve positive attitude changes among those whites and in those realms least subject to separatist norms.

Contact Studies . . .

The most solid social psychological evidence of racial attitude change comes from the contact studies. Repeated research in a variety of newly desegregated situations discovered that the attitudes of both whites and Negroes toward each other markedly improved. Thus, after the hiring of Negroes as department store clerks in New York City, one investigation noted growing acceptance of the practice among the white clerks (Harding and Hogrefe, 1952) and another noted rapid acceptance among white customers (Saenger and Gilbert, 1950). And a series of studies concentrating on public housing residents found similar results (Deutsch and Collins, 1951; Jahoda and West, 1951; Wilner *et al.*, 1955; and Works, 1961), as did studies on servicemen (Stouffer *et al.*, 1949; MacKenzie, 1948), the merchant marine (Brophy, 1946), government workers (MacKenzie, 1948), the police (Kephart, 1957), students (MacKenzie, 1948), and general small town populations (Williams, 1964). Some of these results can

---

[10]That the post-King murder data do not reflect merely temporary shifts is demonstrated by further data collected in Texas in August of 1968. Similar to these results was an overall shift of approximately five per cent toward favoring the racial desegregation of public schools noted among white Texans between two surveys taken immediately before and after the 1957 crisis in Little Rock. And, once again, the most positive shifts were noted among the young and the middle-class (Riley and Pettigrew; 1968).

be interpreted not as the result of contact, but as an indication that more tolerant white Americans seek contact with Negro Americans. A number of the investigations, however, restrict this self-selection factor, making the effects of the new contact itself the only explanation of the significant alterations in attitudes and behavior.

A major study by Deutsch and Collins (1951) illustrates this important literature. These investigators took ingenious advantage of a made-to-order natural experiment. In accordance with state law, two public housing projects in New York City were desegregated; in all cases, apartment assignments were made irrespective of race or personal preference. In two comparable projects in Newark, the two races were assigned to separate buildings. Striking differences were found between the attitudes toward Negroes of randomly selected white housewifes in the desegregated and segregated developments. The desegregated women held their Negro neighbors in higher esteem and were considerably more in favor of interracial housing (75 per cent to 25 per cent). When asked to name the chief faults of Negroes, they mentioned such personal problems as feelings of inferiority and oversensitivity; the segregated women listed such group stereotypes as troublemaking, rowdy and dangerous.

As discussed earlier, however, improvements in social distance attitudes are often limited to the immediate contact situation itself. Yet basic racist stereotypes are often affected, too. One white housewife in an interracial development put it bluntly: "Living with them my ideas have changed altogether. They're just people . . . they're not any different". Commented another: "I've really come to like it. I see they're just as human as we are" (Deutsch and Collins, 1951). And a Negro officer on an interracial ship off Korea summed it up candidly: "After a while you start thinking of whites as people".

On a National Scale

Recent surveys bear out these contact findings on a national scale. Hyman and Sheatsley (1964) found that the most extensive racial attitude changes among whites have occurred where extensive desegregation of public facilities had already taken place.[11]

---

[11]This is, of course, a two-way causal relationship. Not only does desegregation erode racist attitudes, but desegregation tends to come first to areas where white attitudes are least racist to begin with. The Hyman-Sheatsley (1964) finding cited, however, specifically highlights the former phenomenon: "In those parts of the South where some measure of school integration has taken place official action has *preceded* public sentiment, and public sentiment has then attempted to accommodate itself to the new situation".

And data from the Equal Educational Opportunity Survey—popularly known as "the Coleman Report"—indicate that white students who attend public schools with Negroes are the least likely to prefer all-white classrooms and all-white "close friends"; and this effect is strongest among those who began their interracial schooling in the early grades (Coleman *et al.*, 1966, 333). Recall, too, the similar findings of the U.S. Commission on Civil Rights (1967) for both Negro and white adults who had attended biracial schools as children.

Not all intergroup contact, of course, leads to increased acceptance; sometimes it only makes matters worse. Gordon Allport (1954), in his intensive review of this research concluded that four characteristics of the contact situation are of the utmost importance. Prejudice is lessened when the two groups: (a) possess equal status in the situation, (b) seek common goals, (c) are cooperatively dependent upon each other, and (d) interact with the positive support of authorities, laws or custom. Reviewing the same work, Kenneth Clark (1953) came to similar conclusions, and correctly predicted one year prior to the Supreme Court ruling against *de jure* public school segregation that the process would be successful only to the extent that authorities publicly backed and rigorously enforced the new policy.

The Allport statement of contact conditions is actually an application of the broader theory of interpersonal attraction. All four of his conditions maximize the likelihood of shared values and beliefs being evinced and mutually perceived. Rokeach's belief similarity factor is apparently, then, a key agent in the effects of optimal contact. Thus, following the Triandis and Davis (1965) findings, we would anticipate the attitude alterations achieved by intergroup contact, at least initially, to be greatest for formal realms and least for intimate realms—as with the changes wrought in white Texan attitudes by the dramatic events of early spring 1968.

Accordingly, from this social psychological perspective, the black separatist assumption that "white liberals" should eliminate white racism is an impossible and quixotic hope. One can readily appreciate the militants' desire to avoid further abuse from white racists; but their model for change is woefully inadequate. White liberals can attack racist attitudes publicly, conduct research on racist assertions, set the stage for confrontation. But with all the will in the world they cannot accomplish by themselves the needed Negro push, the dramatic events, the actual interracial contact which has gnawed away at racist beliefs for a generation. A century ago the fiery and perceptive Frederick Douglass (1962; 366–367) phrased the issue pointedly:

I have found in my experience that the way to break down an unreasonable custom is to contradict it in practice. To be sure in pursuing this course I have had to contend not merely with the white race but with the black. The one has condemned me for my presumption in daring to associate with it and the other for pushing myself where it takes it for granted I am not wanted.

The Assumptions of Racial Conflict and Autonomy-Before-Contact

History reveals that white separatists are correct when they contend that racial change creates conflict, that if only the traditions of white supremacy were to go unchallenged racial harmony might be restored. One of the quietest periods in American racial history, 1895–1915, for example, witnessed the construction of the massive system of institutional racism as it is known today—the nadir of Negro American history as Rayford Logan (1957) calls it. The price of those two decades of relative peace is still being paid by the nation. Even were it possible in the late twentieth century, then, to gain racial calm by inaction, America could not afford the enormous cost.

But if inaction is clearly impossible, the types of action called for are not so clear. Black separatists believe that efforts to further interracial contact should be abandoned or at least delayed until greater personal and group autonomy is achieved by Negroes. This is the other side of the same coin that leaves the struggle against attitudinal racism completely in the hands of "white liberals". And it runs a similar danger. Racism is reflected not only in attitudes but more importantly in institutionalized arrangements that operate to restrict Negro choice. Both forms of racism are fostered by segregation, and both have to be confronted directly by Negroes. Withdrawal into the ghetto, psychologically tempting as it may be for many, essentially gives up the fight to alter the racially-discriminatory operations of the nation's chief institutions.

The issues involved are highlighted in the schematic diagram shown in Figure 1. By varying contact-separation and an ideologically vague concept of "autonomy", four cells emerge that represent various possibilities under discussion. Cell "A" true integration, refers to institutionalized biracial situations where there is cross-racial friendship, racial interdependence, and a strong measure of personal autonomy (and group autonomy, too, if group is defined biracially). Such situations do exist in America today, but they are rare imbattled islands in a sea of conflict. Cell "B" represents the autonomous "black power" ghetto, relatively independent of the larger society and with a far more viable

FIGURE 1
SCHEMATIC DIAGRAM OF AUTONOMY AND CONTACT-SEPARATION*

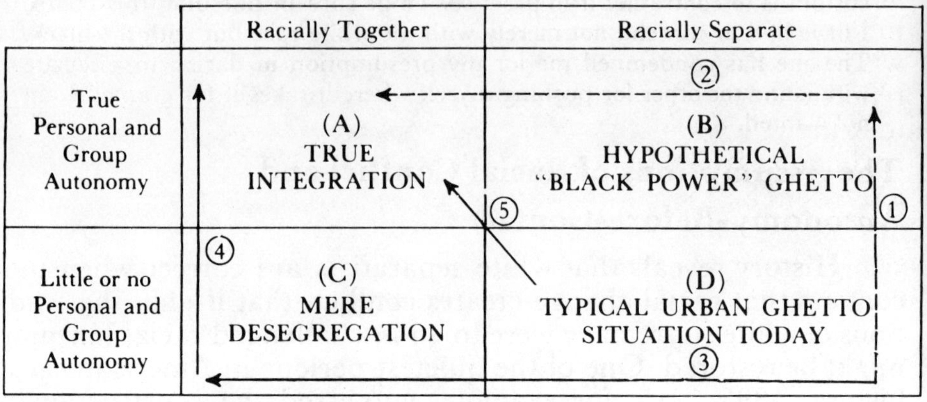

	Racially Together	Racially Separate
True Personal and Group Autonomy	(A) TRUE INTEGRATION	② (B) HYPOTHETICAL "BLACK POWER" GHETTO ①
Little or no Personal and Group Autonomy	④ (C) MERE DESEGREGATION	(D) TYPICAL URBAN GHETTO SITUATION TODAY ③

⑤ (on diagonal)

*The author is indebted to Professor Karl Deutsch, of Harvard University, for several stimulating discussions out of which came this diagram. Dotted lines denote hypothetical paths, solid lines actual paths.

existence than commonly the case now. This is an ideologically-derived hypothetical situation, for no such urban ghettos exist today. Cell "C" stands for merely desegregated situations. Often misnamed as "integrated", these institutionalized biracial settings include both races but little cross-racial acceptance and often patronizing legacies of white supremacy. Cell "D" represents today's typical Negro scene—the highly separate urban ghetto with little or no personal or group autonomy.

To Get from "D" to "A" . . .

Save for white separatists, observers of diverse persuasions agree that the achievement of true integration (cell "A") should be the ideal and ultimate goal. But there are, broadly speaking, three contrasting ways of getting there from the typical current situation (cell "D"). The black separatist assumes only one route is possible: from the depressed ghetto today to the hypothetical ghetto of tomorrow and then, perhaps, on to true integration (lines numbered 1 and 2 on Figure 1). The desegregationist assumes precisely the opposite route: from the present-day ghetto to mere desegregation and then, hopefully, on the true integration (lines numbered 3 and 4 in Figure 1). But there is a third, more direct route right across the diagonal from the current ghetto to true integration (line 5 in Figure 1). Experience to date combines with a number of social psychological considerations to favor the last of these possibilities.

The black separatist route has a surprising appeal for an untested theory; besides those whites who welcome any alternative to integration, it seems to appeal to cultural pluralists, white and black, to militant black leaders searching for a new direction to vent the ghetto's rage and despair, and to Negroes who just wish to withdraw as far away from whites as possible. Yet on reflection, the argument involves the perverse notion that the way to bring two groups together is to separate them further. One is reminded of the detrimental consequences of isolation in economics, through "closed markets", and in genetics, through "genetic drift". In social psychology, isolation between two contiguous groups generally leads to: (a) diverse value development, (b) reduced intergroup communication, (c) uncorrected perceptual distortions of each other, and (d) the growth of vested interests within both groups for continued separation. American race relations already suffer from each of these conditions; and the proposal for further separation even if a gilded ghetto were possible, aims to exacerbate them further.

No Access to the Tax Base . . .

Without pursuing the many economic and political difficulties inherent in the insulated ghetto conception, suffice it to mention the meager resources immediately available in the ghetto for the task. Recognizing this limitation, black separatists call for massive federal aid with no strings attached. But this requires a national consensus. Some separatists scoff at the direct path to integration (line 5 in Figure 1) as idealistic dreaming, then turn and casually assume the same racist society that resists integration will unhesitatingly pour a significant portion of its treasure exclusively into ghetto efforts. Put differently, "local control" without access to the necessary tax base is not control. This raises the political limitations to the black separatist route. The Irish-American model of entering the mainstream through the political system is often cited as appropriate to black separatism—but is it really? Faster than any other immigrant group save Jewish-Americans, the Irish have assimilated via the direct diagonal of Figure 1. Forced to remain in ghettos at first, the Irish did not settle for "local control" but strove to win city hall itself. Boston's legendary James Michael Curley won "Irish power" not by becoming mayor of the South Boston ghetto, but by becoming mayor of the entire city. There are serious problems with immigrant analogies for Negroes, since immigrants never suffered from slavery and legalized segregation. But to the extent an analogy is appropriate, Mayor Carl Stokes of Cleveland and Mayor Richard Hatcher of Gary are far closer to the Irish-American model than are black separatists.

Fate Control . . .

A critical part of black separatist thinking centers on the psychological concept of "fate control"—more familiar to psychologists as Rotter's (1966) internal control of reinforcement variable. "Until we control our own destinies, our own schools and areas", goes the argument, "blacks cannot possibly achieve the vital sense of fate control". And Coleman Report (Coleman *et al.*, 1966) data are cited to show that fate control is a critical correlate of Negro school achievement. But no mention is made of the additional fact that levels of fate control among Negro children were found by Coleman to be significantly higher in interracial than in all-Negro schools. Black separatists brush this important finding aside on the grounds that all-Negro schools today are not what they envision for the future. Yet the fact remains that interracial schools appear to be facilitating the growth of fate control among Negro students now, while the ideological contention that it can be developed as well or better in uniracial schools remains an untested and hypothetical assertion.

Despite the problems, black separatists feel their route (lines 1 and 2 in Figure 1) is the only way to true integration in part because they regard the indirect desegregation path (lines 3 and 4 in Figure 1) as an affront to their dignity. One need only know the blatantly hostile and subtly rejecting racial acts that typify some interracial situations to know to what this repudiation of non-autonomous desegregation refers (Cell "C" in Figure 1; Chessler, 1967). But it is conceptionally and practically useful to make a clear distinction between true integration (Cell "A" in Figure 1) and mere desegregation (Cell "C" in Figure 1). The U.S. Commission on Civil Rights (1967), in reanalyzing Coleman's data, found this distinction provided the tool for separating empirically between effective and ineffective biracial schools where whites form the majority. Negro student achievement, college aspirations, and sense of fate control proved to be highest in truly integrated schools when these schools are independently defined as biracial institutions characterized by no racial tension and widespread cross-racial friendship. Merely desegregated schools, defined as biracial institutions, typified by racial tension and little cross-racial friendship have scant benefits over segregated schools.

Allport Conditions for Optimal Contact

This civil rights commission finding reflects the Allport (1954) conditions for optimal contact. Truly integrated institutions afford the type of equal-status, common goal, interdependent and authority-sanctioned contact that maximizes cross-racial acceptance and Rokeach's belief similarity.[12] They apparently also maximize the positive and minimize the negative factors which Katz (1964, 1967) has carefully isolated as important for Negro performance in biracial task groups. And they also seem to increase the opportunity for beneficial cross-racial evaluations which may well be critical mediators of the effects of biracial schools (Pettigrew, 1967). Experimental research following up these leads is now called for to detail the precise social psychological processes operating in the truly integrated situation (Pettigrew, 1968).

The desegregation route (lines 3 and 4 in Figure 1) has been successfully navigated, though the black separatist contention that Negroes bear the principal burden for this effort is undoubtedly true. Those southern institutions that have attained integration, for example, have typically gone this indirect path. So it is not as hypothetical as the black separatist path, but it is hardly to be preferred over the direct integrationist route (line 5 in Figure 1).

The Self-Fulfilling Prophecy . . .

So why not the direct route? The standard answer is that it is impossible, that demographic trends and white resistance make it out of the question in our time. The self-fulfilling prophecy threatens once more. Secretary of Health, Education and Welfare, Wilbur Cohen, insists integration will not come in this generation —hardly a reassuring assertion from the chief of the federal department with primary responsibility for furthering the process.[13] The Secretary adopts the Alsop separatist argument and opts for programs exclusively within the ghetto, a position that makes extensive integration unlikely even a generation hence. One is reminded of the defenders of slavery who in the 1850's attacked

---

[12]Another white observer enthusiastic about black separatism even denies that the contact studies' conclusions are applicable to the classroom and other institutions which do not produce "continual and extensive equal-status contact under more or less enforced conditions of intimacy". Stember (1968) selectively cites the public housing and armed forces contact investigations to support his point; but he has to omit the many studies from less intimate realms which reached the same conclusions—such as those conducted in schools (Pettigrew, 1968), employment situations (Harding and Hogrefe, 1952; Kephart, 1957; and MacKenzie, 1948; and Williams, 1964), and even one involving brief clerk and customer contact (Saenger and Gilbert, 1950).

[13]Consistent with the thesis of this paper, a number of leading black separatists attacked the Cohen statement. For example, Bryant Rollins, separatist spokesman in Boston, called Cohen's statement "a cop-out" and described it as typical of "white bureaucratic racists who don't want to do anything" (Jordan, 1968).

the Abolitionists as unrealistic dreamers and insisted slavery was so deeply entrenched that efforts should be limited to making it into a benign institution.

If the nation acts on the speculations of Cohen, Alsop and Ferry, then, they will probably be proven correct in their pessimistic projections. For what better way to prevent racial change than to act on the presumption that it is impossible?

Urban Racial Demography . . .

The belief that integration is impossible is based on some harsh facts of urban racial demography. Between 1950 and 1960, the average annual increment of Negro population in the central cities of the United States was 320,000; from 1960 to 1966 the estimated annual growth climbed to 400,000. In the suburbs, however, the average annual growth of the Negro population has declined from 60,000 between 1950 and 1960 to an estimated 33,000 between 1960 and 1966. In other words, it would require about thirteen times the present trend in suburban Negro growth just to maintain the sprawling central city ghettos at their present size. In the nation's largest metropolitan areas, then, the trend is forcefully pushing in the direction of ever-increasing separatism.

But these bleak data are not the whole picture. In the first place, they refer especially to the very largest of the metropolitan areas—to New York City, Chicago, Los Angeles, Philadelphia, Detroit, Washington, D.C. and Baltimore. Most Negro Americans, however, do not live in these places, but reside in areas where racial integration is in fact possible in the short run were a good faith attempt to be made. The Harlems and Wattses, especially during this period of urban riots, have blinded some analysts into thinking of the entire Negro population as residing in such ghettos. Put differently, there are more Berkeleys and White Plainses—small enough for school integration to be effectively achieved—than there are New York Cities.

In the second place, the presumed impossibility of reversing the central city racial trends are based on anti-metropolitan assumptions. Without metropolitan cooperation, central cities—and many suburbs, too—will find their racial problems insoluble. So need we assume such cooperation impossible? Effective state and federal incentives are being proposed, and a few established, to further this cooperation. Moreover, some large Negro ghettos are already extending into the suburbs (e.g., Pittsburgh and soon in Chicago); the first tentative metropolitan schemes to aid racial integration are emerging (e.g., Boston, Hartford, and Rochester); and several major metropolitan areas have even consolidated (e.g., Miami-Dade County and Nashville-Davidson County).

Once the issue is looked at in metropolitan terms, its dimensions become more manageable. Negro Americans are found in America's metropolitan areas in almost the same ratio as white Americans; about two-thirds of each group resides in these 212 regions, so that on a metropolitan basis Negroes are not significantly more metropolitan than their one-ninth proportion in the nation as a whole.

Policy Implications

Much of the policy confusion seems to derive from the assumption that since *complete* integration in the biggest cities will not be possible in the near future, present efforts toward opening integration opportunities for both Negro and white Americans are premature. This thinking obscures two fundamental issues. First, the democratic objective is not total racial integration and the elimination of the ghetto; the idea is simply to provide an honest choice between separation and integration. This separation side of the choice is available today; it is integration that is closed to Negroes who would choose it. The long-term goal is not a complete obliteration of cultural pluralism, of distinctive Negro ghettos, but rather the transformation of these ghettos from today's racial prisons to tomorrow's ethnic areas of choice. Life within ghettos can never be fully satisfactory as long as there are Negroes who reside within them only because discrimination requires them to.

Second, the integrationist alternative will not become a reality as long as we disparage it, as long as we abandon it to future generations. Exclusive attention to within-ghetto enrichment programs is almost certain, to use Kenneth Clark's pointed word, to "embalm" the ghetto, to seal it in even further from the rest of the nation (making line 2 in Figure 1 less likely yet). This danger explains the recent interest of conservative whites in exclusive ghetto enrichment programs. The bribe is straightforward: "Stop rioting and stop demanding integration, and we'll minimally support separatist programs within the ghetto". Even black separatists are understandably ambivalent about such offers, as they come from sources long identified with opposition to all racial change. Should the bargain be struck, however, American race relations will be dealt still another serious blow.

What is Possible . . .

The outlines of the situation, then, are these: (a) widespread integration is possible everywhere in the United States save in the largest central cities; (b) it will not come unless present trends are reversed and considerable resources are provided for the process; (c) big central cities will continue to have significant Negro concentrations even with successful metropolitan dispersal; (d) large Negro ghettos are presently in need of intensive enrichment; and (e) some ghetto enrichment programs run the clear and present danger of embalming the ghetto further.

Given this situation and the social psychological considerations of this paper, the overall strategy needed must contain the following elements:

. . . (a) A major effort toward racial integration must be mounted in order to provide genuine choice to all Negro Americans in all realms of life. This effort should envisage by the late 1970's complete attainment of the goal in smaller communities and cities and a halting of separatist trends in major central cities with a movement toward metropolitan cooperation.

. . . (b) A simultaneous effort is required to enrich the vast central city ghettos of the nation, to change them structurally, and to make life in them more viable. In order to avoid embalming them, however, strict criteria must be applied to proposed enrichment programs to insure that they are productive for later dispersal and integration. Restructuring the economics of the ghetto, especially the development of urban cooperatives, is a classic example of productive enrichment. The building of enormous public housing developments within the ghetto presents a good illustration of counterproductive enrichment. Some programs, such as the decentralization of huge public school systems or the encouragement of Negro business ownership, can be either productive or counterproductive depending upon how they are focused. A Bundy Decentralization Plan of many homogeneous school districts for New York City is clearly counterproductive for later integration; a Regents Plan of a relatively small number of heterogeneous school districts for New York City could well be productive. Likewise, Negro entrepreneurs encouraged to open small shops and expected to prosper with an all-Negro clientele are not only counterproductive but are probably committing economic suicide. Negro businessmen encouraged to pool resources to establish somewhat larger operations and to appeal to white as well as Negro customers on major traffic arteries in and out of the ghetto could be productive.

A Mixed Integration-Enrichment Strategy

In short, a mixed integration-enrichment strategy is called for that contains safeguards that the enrichment will not impede integration. Recent survey results strongly suggest that such a mixed strategy would meet with widespread Negro approval. On the basis of their extensive 1968 survey of Negro residents in fifteen major cities, Campbell and Schuman (1968, 5) conclude:

> Separatism appeals to from five to eighteen per cent of the Negro sample, depending on the question, with the largest appeal involving black owner-ship of stores and black administration of schools in Negro neighborhoods, and the smallest appeal the rejection of whites as friends or in other informal contacts. Even on questions having the largest appeal, however, more than three-quarters of the Negro sample indicate a clear preference for integration. Moreover, the reasons given by respondents for their choices suggest that the desire for integration is not simply a practical wish for better material facilities, but represents a commitment to princi-ples of nondiscrimination and racial harmony.

Young men prove to be the most forthright separatists, but even here the separatist percentages for males sixteen to nineteen years of age ranged only from eleven to twenty-eight per cent. An interesting interaction between type of separatism and educa-tional level of the respondent appears in the Campbell and Schuman (1968, 19) data. Among the twenty-to-thirty-nine-year-olds, college graduates tended to be the more separatist in those realms where their training gives them a vested interest in competition-free positions—Negro-owned stores for Negro neigh-borhoods and Negro teachers in mostly-Negro schools; while the poorly educated were most likely to believe that whites should be discouraged from taking part in civil rights organizations and to agree that "Negroes should have nothing to do with whites if they can help it" and that "there should be a separate black nation here."

Negroes Want Both Integration and Black Identity

But if separatism draws little favorable response even in the most politicized ghettos, positive aspects of cultural pluralism attract wide interest. For example, forty-two per cent endorse the statement that "Negro school children should study an African language". And this interest seems rather general across age, sex and education categories. Campbell and Schuman (1968, 6) regard this as evidence of a broadly-supported attempt ". . . to emphasize black consciousness *without* rejection of whites . . . A substantial number of Negroes want *both* integration and black identity".[14] Or in the terms of this paper, they prefer cell "A" in Figure 1—"true integration".

The Campbell and Schuman data indicate little if any change from the pro-integration results of earlier Negro surveys (Brink and Harris, 1964; 1967). And they are consistent with the results of recent surveys in Detroit, Miami, New York City, and other cities (Meyer, 1967, 1968; and Center for Urban Education, 1968). Data from Bedford-Stuyvesant in Brooklyn are especially significant, for here separatist ideology and a full-scale enrichment program are in full view. Yet when asked if they would prefer to live on a block with people of the same race or of every race, eighty per cent of the Negro respondents chose an interracial block (Center for Urban Education, 1968). Interestingly, the largest Negro segment choosing integration—eighty-eight per cent—consisted of residents of public housing where a modest amount of interracial tenancy still prevails.

A final study from Watts links these surveys to the analysis of this paper. Ransford (1968) found that Negro willingness to use violence was closely and positively related to a sense of powerlessness, feelings of racial dissatisfaction and limited contact with whites. Respondents who indicated that they had no social contact with white people, "like going to the movies together or visiting each other's homes", were significantly more likely to feel powerless and express racial dissatisfaction as well as to report greater willingness to use violence. The personal, group and national costs of racial separatism are great.

A Final Word . . .

Racially separate or together? Our social psychological examination of separatist assumptions leads to one imperative: the attainment of a viable, democratic America, free from personal and institutional racism, requires extensive racial integration in all realms of life. To prescribe more separation because of discomfort, racism, conflict or autonomy needs is like getting drunk again to cure a hangover. The nation's binge of *apartheid* must not be exacerbated but alleviated.

---

[14]This is not a new position for Negro Americans, for their dominant response to Marcus Garvey's movement in the 1920's was essentially the same. Garvey stressed black beauty and pride in Africa and mounted a mass movement in the urban ghettos of the day, but his "back to Africa" separatist appeals were largely ignored.

REFERENCES

ALLPORT, G. W. *The nature of prejudice.* Cambridge, Mass.: Addison-Wesley, 1954.

ALSOP, J. No more nonsense about ghetto education! *The New Republic,* July 22, 1967, **157**, 18–23. (a)

ALSOP, J. Ghetto education. *The New Republic,* November 18, 1967, **157**, 18–23. (b)

American Institute of Public Opinion, press release, May 22, 1965.

ARMSTRONG, CLAIRETTE P. and GREGOR, A. J. Integrated schools and Negro character development: some considerations of the possible effects. *Psychiatry,* 1964, **27**, 69–72.

BRINK, W. and HARRIS, L. *The Negro revolution in America.* New York: Simon and Schuster, 1964.

BRINK, W. and HARRIS, L. *Black and white: a study of U.S. racial attitudes today.* New York: Simon and Schuster, 1967.

BROPHY, I. N. The luxury of anti-Negro prejudice. *Public Opinion Quarterly,* 1946, **9**, 456–466.

CALAME, B. E. A west coast militant talks tough but helps avert racial trouble. *The Wall Street Journal,* July 26, 1968, **172**, (1), 15.

CAMPBELL, A. and SCHUMAN, H. Racial attitudes in fifteen American cities. In The National Advisory Commission on Civil Disorders, *Supplemental studies.* Washington, D.C.: U.S. Government Printing Office, 1968.

Center for Urban Education. Survey of the residents of Bedford-Stuyvesant. Unpublished paper, 1968.

CHESSLER, M. *In their own words.* Atlanta, Ga.: Southern Regional Council, 1967.

CLARK, K. B. Desegregation: an appraisal of the evidence. *Journal of Social Issues,* 1953, **9**, 1–76.

COLEMAN, J. S., CAMPBELL, E. Q., HOBSON, C. J., McPARTLAND, J., MOOD, A. M., WEINFELD, F. D. and YORK, R. L. *Equality of educational opportunity.* Washington, D.C.: U.S. Government Printing Office, 1966.

DAVIES, J. C. Toward a theory of revolution. *American Sociological Review,* 1962, **27**, 5–19.

DEUTSCH, M. and COLLINS, MARY. *Interracial housing: a psychological evaluation of a social experiment.* Minneapolis: University of Minnesota Press, 1951.

DOUGLASS, F. *Life and times of Frederick Douglass: the complete autobiography.* New York: Collier Books, 1962 (original edition in 1892).

FERRY, W. H. Black colonies: a modest proposal. *The Center Magazine,* January 1968, **1**, 74–76.

GESCHWENDER, J. A. Social structure and the Negro revolt: an examination of some hypotheses. *Social Forces,* 1964, **43**, 248–256.

HARDING, J. and HOGREFE, R. Attitudes of white department store employees toward Negro co-workers. *Journal of Social Issues,* 1952, **8**, 18–28.

HYMAN, H. H. and SHEATSLEY, P. B. Attitudes toward desegregation. *Scientific American,* December 1956, **195**, 35–39.

HYMAN, H. H. and SHEATSLEY, P. B. Attitudes toward desegregation. *Scientific American,* July 1964, **211**, 16–23.

JAHODA, MARIE and WEST, PATRICIA. Race relations in public housing. *Journal of Social Issues,* 1951, **7**, 132–139.

JORDAN, R. A. Go-slow integration draws retorts. *The Boston Globe,* August 8, 1968, **194**, 2.

KATZ, I. Review of evidence relating to effects of desegregation on the performance of Negroes. *American Psychologist,* 1964, **19**, 381–399.

KATZ, I. The socialization of competence motivation in minority group children. In D. Levine (Ed.), *Nebraska symposium on motivation, 1967.* Lincoln: University of Nebraska Press, 1967.

KEPHART, W. M. *Racial factors and urban law enforcement*. Philadelphia: University of Pennsylvania Press, 1957.

KLINEBERG, O. *Negro intelligence and selective migration*. New York: Columbia University Press, 1935.

KOHN, M. L. and WILLIAMS, R. M., JR. Situational patterning in intergroup relations. *American Sociological Review*, 1956, **21**, 164–174.

LOGAN, R. W. *The Negro in the United States: a brief history*. Princeton, N.J.: Van Nostrand, 1957.

MACKENZIE, BARBARA. The importance of contact in determining attitudes toward Negroes. *Journal of Abnormal and Social Psychology*, 1948, **43**, 417–441.

MEYER, P. *A survey of attitudes of Detroit Negroes after the riot of 1967*. Detroit, Mich.: Detroit Urban League, in press.

MEYER, P. *Miami Negroes: a study in depth*. Miami, Florida: *The Miami Herald*, 1968.

National Advisory Commission on Civil Disorders. *Report*. Washington, D.C.: U.S. Printing Office, 1968.

NEWCOMB, T. M., TURNER, R. H. and CONVERSE, P. E. *Social psychology: the study of human interaction*. New York: Holt, Rinehart and Winston, 1965.

PETTIGREW, T. F. *A profile of the Negro American*. Princeton, N.J.: Van Nostrand, 1964.

PETTIGREW, T. F. Parallel and distinctive changes in anti-Semitic and anti-Negro attitudes. In C. H. Stember (Ed.), *Jews in the mind of America*. New York: Basic Books, 1966.

PETTIGREW, T. F. Social evaluation theory: convergences and applications. In D. Levine (Ed.), *Nebraska symposium on motivation, 1967*. Lincoln: University of Nebraska Press, 1967.

PETTIGREW, T. F. Race and equal educational opportunity. *Harvard Educational Review*, 1968, **38**, 66–76.

RANSFORD, H. E. Isolation, powerlessness, and violence: a study of attitudes and participation in the Watts riot. *American Journal of Sociology*, 1968, **73**, 581–591.

REITZES, D. C. The role of organizational structures: union versus neighborhood in a tension situation. *Journal of Social Issues*, 1953, **9**, 37–44.

RILEY, R. and PETTIGREW, T. F. Dramatic events and racial attitude change. Unpublished paper, Harvard University, 1968.

ROKEACH, M. Belief versus race as determinants of social distance: comment on Triandis' paper. *Journal of Abnormal and Social Psychology*, 1961, **62**, 187–188.

ROKEACH, M., SMITH, PATRICIA W. and EVANS, R. I. Two kinds of prejudice or one? In M. Rokeach (Ed.), *The open and closed mind*. New York: Basic Books, 1960.

ROKEACH, M. and MEZEI, L. Race and shared belief as factors in social choice. *Science*, 1966, **151**, 167–172.

ROTTER, J. B. Internal versus external control of reinforcement. *Psychological Monographs*, 1966, **80**, Whole no. 609.

SAENGER, G. and GILBERT, EMILY. Customer reactions to the integration of Negro sales personnel. *International Journal of Opinion and Attitude Research*, 1950, **4**, 57–76.

SCHWARTZ, R., PETTIGREW, T. and SMITH, M. Fake panaceas for ghetto education. *The New Republic*, September 23, 1967, **157**, 16–19.

SCHWARTZ, R., PETTIGREW, T. and SMITH, M. Is desegregation impractical? *The New Republic*, January 6, 1968, **157**, 27–29.

SHEATSLEY, P. B. White attitudes toward the Negro. In T. Parsons and K. B. Clark (Eds.), *The Negro American*. Boston: Houghton Mifflin, 1966.

SMITH, CAROLE R., WILLIAMS, L. and WILLIS, R. H. Race, sex and belief as determinants of friendship acceptance. *Journal of Personality and Social Psychology*, 1967, **5**, 127–137.

ɪEɪN, D. D. The influence of belief systems on interpersonal preference. *Psychological Monographs*, 1966, **80**, Whole no. 616.

ɪEɪN. D. D., HARDYCK, JANE A. and SMITH, M. B. Race *and* belief: an open and shut case. *Journal of Personality and Social Psychology*, 1965, **1**, 281–290.

ɪEMBER, C. H. Evaluating effects of the integrated classroom. *The Urban Review*, June 1968, **2**, (3–4), 30–31.

ɪOUFFER, S. A., SUCHMAN, E. A., DEVINNEY, L. C., STAR, SHIRLEY A. and WILLIAMS, R. M., JR. *Studies in social psychology in World War II*, Vol. I, *The American soldier: adjustment during army life.* Princeton, N.J.: Princeton University Press, 1949.

RIANDIS, H. C. A note on Rokeach's theory of prejudice. *Journal of Abnormal and Social Psychology*, 1961, **62**, 184–186.

RIANDIS, H. C. and DAVIS, E. E. Race and belief as determinants of behavioral intentions. *Journal of Personality and Social Psychology*, 1965, **2**, 715–725.

ɪnited States Commission on Civil Rights. *Civil rights USA: public schools, southern states, 1962.* Washington, D.C.: U.S. Government Printing Office, 1963.

ɪnited States Commission on Civil Rights. *Racial isolation in the public schools.* Vols. I and II. Washington, D.C.: U.S. Government Printing Office, 1967.

ɪILLIAMS, R. M., JR. *Strangers next door: ethnic relations in American communities.* Englewood Cliffs, N.J.: Prentice-Hall, 1964.

ɪILNER, D. M., WALKLEY, ROSABELLE and COOK, S. W. *Human relations in interracial housing: a study of the contact hypothesis.* Minneapolis: University of Minnesota Press, 1955.

ɪORKS, E. The prejudice-interaction hypothesis from the point of view of the Negro minority group. *American Journal of Sociology*, 1961, **67**, 47–52.

ɪARROW, MARIAN R. (Ed.) Interpersonal dynamics in a desegregation process. *Journal of Social Issues*, 1958, **14**, (1), 3–63.

THE NEW RACIALISM

Daniel P. Moynihan

Daniel P. Moynihan, "The New Racialism," *The Atlantic,* August 1968, pp. 35-40.

THE NEW RACIALISM

aniel P. Moynihan

T<small>HE</small> great enterprise on which the American nation was embarked when the Vietnam storm arose
was the final inclusion of the Negro American in
the larger American society. That the Negro was,
and still in considerable measure is, excluded none
will doubt. But it seems not less clear that this fact
of exclusion has been the lot of a very considerable
portion of the American people over the generations,
and the process of inclusion, of "national integration," in Samuel H. Beer's term, a process "in
which the community is being made more of a
community," has been going on almost from the
moment the fortunes of war and empire defined
this hopelessly heterogeneous people as made up
exclusively of General de Gaulle's "Anglo-Saxons."
In fact, at midcentury only 35 percent of the American people were descendants of migrants from Great
Britain and Northern Ireland. Most of the rest
have known greater or lesser degrees of exclusion —
and into the present. But none quite like that of the
Negro, and final, palpable equality for him became
the essential demand of our time, just as it became
the demand of the American presidency; only to
arouse among some elements of the society — in
greater or lesser degree in all elements — a pervasive fear and deep resistance. Laws in the hundreds
were passed, but changes were few. As the black
masses for whatever reasons became increasingly

violent, white resistance became more stubborn, even as it assumed more respectable forms: "Law and order."

This resistance has produced something of a stalemate, and in consequence a crisis. The essential symbol, and in ways the central fact, of black exclusion in white America is that the Negro is not permitted to move about freely and live where he will. Increasingly he is confined to the slums of the central cities, with consequences at once appalling to him and disastrous to the cities. The laws do not require this exclusion; in fact, they forbid it. Now also does the Supreme Court. But it prevails because of a process of private nullification by whites.

More and more one hears that this situation is likely to persist so long as to require that it be treated as a permanent condition. And largely as a result of this conclusion, a marked reversal appears to be taking place in what are generally seen as liberal circles on the subject of decentralized government and racial quotas. For a good half century now — longer than that, in truth — liberal opinion has held quite strong views on these issues and they are almost wholly negative. Nor have these views been in any sense marginal. Quite near to the core of the liberal agenda in the reform period that began at the turn of the century and continued almost to this moment we find two propositions.

The first is that local government is conservative or even reactionary. Such nostalgia as might have persisted about New England town meetings was seen as historically obsolete and ethnically inpplicable. Local government in New York, for xample, was known to be run by Irishmen, who vere bosses wielding vast but illegitimate power, •lacing unqualified men on public payrolls, conorting with criminals, and lowering the standards •f public life. In the South, local government was n the hands of racists, who systematically excluded Negroes from participation in public affairs, and nuch else as well. The West was far away. Hence he great thrust of liberal/intellectual political ffort, and central to liberal/intellectual political •pinion, was the effort to *raise* the level at which overnmental decisions were made above that of tate and local government, to that of the federal overnment. The great and confirming successes •f that effort were, of course, the Administrations •f Woodrow Wilson and Franklin D. Roosevelt. "States' rights" became a symbol of reaction. Distinguished public servants such as Paul Appleby leveloped the doctrine that those who insisted hat this or that governmental activity was best arried out at the local level were in fact opposed o such activity, and confident that in actuality he local government would do nothing. E. E. Schattschneider explained the whole thrust of liberal politics in terms of the effort to raise the evel at which the decisions were made. These riews had consequence. Three years ago, for exmple, when the Johnson Administration was about to come forth with a proposal for revenue-haring with state governments — the well-known Heller-Pechman plan — the proposal was vetoed by the labor movement on grounds that giving more esources to local powers could only strengthen the forces of conservatism and reaction.

The second general theme has to do with the whole issue of ethnic, racial (if one wishes to make a distinction between those two), and religious heterogeneity. These were matters which liberal opinion firmly held ought not to be subjects of public moment or acknowledgment. Rather as politics and women are proscribed as matters of conversation in a naval officers' mess, it was accepted that such categories existed, and given the doctrine of freedom of conscience, it was also accepted that religious diversity would persist, but in general, opinion looked forward to a time when such distinctions would make as little difference as possible. Opinion certainly aspired to the complete disappearance of ethnic characteristics, which were felt to have little, if any, validity. Increasingly, the identification of persons by race or religion, especially in application forms of various sorts, was seen as a manifestation of racism, of unavoidably malign intent.

It is hard to judge which is the more extraordinary: that Americans could have thought they could eliminate such identities, or that so little comment was made about the effort. (Resistance, then as now, was largely silent and ashamed.) Andrew Greeley has recently speculated that the historians of, say, the twenty-third or twenty-fourth century looking back to this time will find that, apart from the great population increase in the world, and its Westernization and industrialization, quite the most extraordinary event was the fusing of cultures in the American republic.

> The historians of the future will find it hard to believe
> that it could have happened that English, Scotch, and
> Welsh, Irish, Germans, Italians, and Poles, Africans,
> Indians, both Eastern and Western, Frenchmen, Span-
> iards, Finns, Swedes, Lebanese, Danes, Armenians,
> Croatians, Slovenians, Greeks, and Luxembourgers,
> Chinese, Japanese, Philippinos, and Puerto Ricans
> would come together to form a nation that not only
> would survive but, all things considered, survive reason-
> ably well. I further suggest that the historians of the
> future will be astonished that American sociologists,
> the product of this gathering in of the nations, could
> stand in the midst of such an astonishing social phenom-
> enon and take it so for granted that they would not
> bother to study it.

I agree, largely as I feel that future historians, relieved of our nineteenth-century preoccupation
with the appearance of industrialization and the
issue of who would control the artifacts thereof,
a preoccupation, in other words, with issues such
as capitalism, socialism, and Communism, will
also see that the turbulence of these times here
and abroad has had far more to do with ethnic,
racial, and religious affiliation than with these
other issues. Nonetheless, beginning with the New
Deal, federal legislation began prohibiting discrimination based on race and religion, and this
movement increasingly took the form of forbidding
acknowledgment even of the existence of such
categories. In New York, for example, a prospective employer simply may not ask to know the
religious or ethnic affiliation of an employee. A
dean of admissions may not ask for a photograph

of an applicant. The culmination of this movement, and given its insistence on absolute equality in competition, the high-water mark of social Darwinism in the United States was, of course, the Civil Rights Act of 1964.

Now, of a sudden, all this has changed. The demand for decentralization of government and local participation in decision-making about even the most global issues has become almost a leading issue with liberal thinkers and politicians. Distrust of Washington, once the sure giveaway of a conservative or reactionary mind, has become a characteristic stance of forward-looking young men. And now ethnic quotas have reappeared, although primarily in terms of racial quotas. That which was specifically forbidden by the Civil Rights Act is now explicitly (albeit covertly) required by the federal government. Employers are given quotas of the black employees they will hire, records of minority-group employment are diligently maintained, and censuses repeatedly taken. In universities in particular the cry has arisen for racial quotas, roughly representative of population proportions, in both university faculties and student bodies, and the proposal is most ardently supported by those who would have themselves considered most advanced in their social thinking. It would seem altogether to be expected that this process will continue, and come to be applied to all the most visible institutions of the land, starting, of course, with those most sympathetic to social change, and therefore most vulnerable to such pressure, and gradually, grown more legitimate, extended to the more resistant centers.

WHAT on earth happened? Taking these developments in the order that I listed them, one can perceive at least two sources of the thrust toward decentralization, both related to the racial stalemate and both of which can properly be described as the result of a learning process, and on that ground welcomed. The first is the discovery by liberal middle-class America that many of the institutions of urban working-class politics served important and legitimate purposes, and that the destruction of these institutions created a vacuum in which by and large Negroes now have to live. Having destroyed the power of the local bosses, we learn that the people feel powerless. Having put an end to patronage and established merit systems in civil service, we find that the poor and unqualified are without jobs. Having banished felons from public employment, we find that enormous numbers of men who need jobs have criminal records. Having cleaned up law enforcement, we find that crime is run by the Mafia (or whatever is the current term for slandering Italians), instead of the police, as was the case in the idyllic days of Lincoln Steffens' youth. Hence liberals now are urged to return to local organization with an enthusiasm ever so slightly tinged with the elitism of the middle-class liberal/radical who now as always is confident that he is capable of running anything better than anyone else, even a slum neighborhood. Middle-class radicals continue to insist the Negroes in Harlem are powerless, not least, one fears, because the one type who is *never* elected is the middle-class radical. (But to my knowledge there is hardly a single significant elected or appointed political, judicial, or administrative office in Harlem that is not held by a Negro.) Hence an ever increasing enthusiasm of liberal foundations and reform mayors for creating new "indigenous" community organizations and giving to them a measure of real or pretend power. Whether in fact outsiders can create an "indigenous" organization is problematic. (Would it not be good sport for the Landmarks Commission to assign to Mayor Lindsay's Little City Halls their traditional Tammany designations of Tuscorora Club, Iroquois Club, Onondaga Club?) But the effort is sincere, if withal tinged with a certain elitist impulse to manage the lives of the less fortunate.

On a different level, a movement toward decentralization has arisen largely from the emergence of what James O. Wilson has called the bureaucracy problem, the fact that "there are inherent limits to what can be accomplished by large, hierarchical organizations." Although Max Weber explained to us why large bureaucracies, once established, would work for themselves rather than the putative objects of their concern, it was not until the bureaucracies were established, and someone tried to do something with them, that any great number of persons came to see the point. Interestingly enough, this seems to have happened in the Soviet Union at about the same time as in the United States. For certain it is an endemic mood among men who went to Washington with John F. Kennedy. The problem involves not just the dynamics of large organizations, but also the ambitiousness of our society. As Wilson continues: "The supply of able, experienced executives is not increasing nearly as fast as the number of problems being addressed."

This is all to the good. It responds to reality; it reflects an openness to experience. Irving Kristol has remarked, echoing Sir William Harcourt at the turn of the century on the subject of socialism, "We are all decentralists now." The acknowledgment that race and ethnicity are persisting and consequential facts about individuals that ought in certain circumstances to be taken into consideration is long overdue. (Several years ago, to my ultimate grief, I tried to get the welfare establishment in Washington to abandon its "color-blind" policy which refused to record anything about the race of welfare recipients. Last year Southern committee chairmen brought about the enactment of vicious anti-Negro welfare legislation, which no one could effectively oppose because no one is supposed to "know" about such things.) But before lurching from one set of overstatements to another, is it not possible to hope that a measure of thought will intervene, and that the truth will be found, alas, somewhere in the middle?

The issues are intertwined, and tend to work against one another. Thus the fundamental source of equal rights for Negro Americans, for all Americans, is the Constitution. Where the federal writ runs, all men are given equal treatment. But this process is not directed by some invisible hand; it is the result of political decisions made year to year in Washington. "Local control" means a very different thing in Mississippi than it does in New York, and let us for God's sake summon the wit to see this before we enshrine the political principles of George C. Wallace in the temple of liberal rationalism. Paul Appleby knew· what he was talking about. An aggressive federal insistence on equal treatment for all races is indispensable to the successful inclusion of the Negro American into the large society.

Further, to argue that all things cannot be run from Washington is not to assert that neither can they be run from city hall. Unfortunately, a good deal of decentralization talk is fundamentally anti-government in spirit, and this can be a calamity in areas such as race relations. Giving a mayor enough untied federal funds to enable him to govern his city could release immensely creative energies. Forcing him to break up his administration into endlessly fractionating units will bring on anarchism at best and chaos at worst. Given the heterogeneous political community of most large cities, this potential for ethnic and racial chaos, Kristol remarks, is especially great.

School decentralization in New York seems to be encouraging just this. The problem is that now, as ever in the past, the lower classes of the city are ethnically quite distinct from what might be termed the bureaucratic classes, and neighborhoods tend to conform to those distinctions. The result is that conflict induced between the two groups gets ugly fast. Thus the New York *Times* reported that the militant picketing of I.S. 201 in east Harlem in 1967 was "flagrantly anti-Semitic." Similar tendencies have appeared in the Ocean Hill-Brownsville area where decentralization is being experimented with. A leaflet recently distributed there reads:

If African-American History and Culture is to be taught to our Black Children it Must Be Done By African-Americans Who Identify With And Who Understand The Problem. It Is Impossible For The Middle East Murderers of Colored People to Possibly Bring To This Important Task The Insight, The Concern, The Exposing Of the Truth That is a *Must* If The Years of Brainwashing And Self-Hatred That Has Been Taught To Our Black Children By Those Bloodsucking Exploiters and Murderers Is To Be Overcome.

A pretty sentiment, to which, not surprisingly, there are Jews capable of responding in kind. Charles E. Silberman, the distinguished author of *Crisis in Black and White,* recently demanded of an American Jewish Committee meeting that it

> face up to the raw, rank, anti-Negro prejudice that is within our own midst. We talk — endlessly — about Negro Anti-Semitism; we rarely talk about — let alone try to deal with — the Jewish Anti-Negroism that is in our midst and that is growing very rapidly.

All too familiar. And as Archbishop John F. Dearden of Detroit, president of the National Conference of Catholic Bishops, observed last year, in other cities of the nation the Negro-white confrontation is becoming a Negro-Catholic (Protestant-Catholic) encounter. *Plus ça change. . .*

THE danger is that we shall see the emergence of a new racialism. Not racism, a term — dreadfully misused by the Kerner Commission — that has as its indispensable central intent "the assumption that psychocultural traits and capacities are determined by biological race and that races differ decisively from one another" (Webster's *Third New International Dictionary*). There is a streak of the racist virus in the American bloodstream, and has been since the first "white" encounter with the "red" Indians. But it is now a distinctly minority position, and mainly that of old or marginal persons, with an occasional politician seeking to make use of what is left. Yet there is a strong, and persisting, phenomenon of racialism, defined as "racial prejudice or discrimination: race hatred." This is in no sense confined to "whites," much less "Wasps." (I use quotation marks. The geneticist Joshua Lederberg notes that it is scientifically absurd to call anyone in this country "black," and probably not accurate to speak of "whites" either.) Writing in a 1935 issue of *Race*, E. Franklin Frazier, for example, referred to W. E. B. DuBois's then current proposal that the Negro build a cooperative industrial system in America as "racialism." There is nothing mystical about racialism; it is simply a matter of one group not liking another group of evidently antagonistic interests. It is a profoundly different position from that of racism, with its logic of genocide and subordination. And it does no service whatever to this polity to identify as racist attitudes that are merely racialist and which will usually, on examination, be found to have essentially a social class basis. But our potential for this type of dissension is large and very likely growing. In the hands of ideologues (who often as not enjoy the chaos) or charlatans (who stand to benefit) or plain simpletons, many forms of decentralization in the modern city will give rise to racialism. Responsible persons should examine that prospect beforehand.

The question of quotas raises the same issue. As I am almost certain to be misunderstood — that appears to be an occupational hazard in this field (and I would seriously suggest that the training of any social scientist in years to come should include something equivalent to the processes by which psychiatrists are taught to anticipate and accept hostility) — let me offer a word or two by way of credentials. I believe it fair to say that I have been one of a smallish band of sociologists and political scientists who have insisted that race, ethnicity, and religion were and are relevant and functional categories in American life. I accept fully, as does Greeley, the Weberian analysis of E. K. Francis that the ethnic collectivity represents an attempt on the part of men to keep alive during their pilgrimage from *Gemeinschaft* to *Gesellschaft*, or as Greeley puts it, "from peasant commune to industrial metropolis," some of the diffuse, ascriptive, particularistic modes of behavior that were common to their past. I have argued in favor of the balanced political ticket; I have even been a member of one. I see the emergence of "black pride" as wholly a good thing. And so on. But at the same time, I would hope as we rush toward an ethnically, racially, and religiously conscious society that we try to keep our thinking just a bit ahead of events.

My concerns are twofold and come to this. First, I am worried that having so far been unable to assemble the political majority that would enable the nation to provide a free and equal place for the Negro in the larger society by what are essentially market strategies (full employment, income supplementation, housing construction, and suchlike), we will be driven to institutional strategies involving government-dictated outcomes directed against those institutions most vulnerable to government pressure. I don't like this mostly because I don't like that kind of government pressure. But I oppose it also because I fear the kind of rigidities that it can build into a society that obviously is most effective when it is most flexible.

Remember, the Negro middle class is on the move. A recent study at Columbia found that the proportion of Negroes with professional or technical occupations in New York City is distinctly higher than that of Irish or Italians.

If there is an ethnic balance "against" Negroes in many municipal bureaucracies today, there is likely to be one "for" them in the not distant future. These are for the most part truly integrated groups, which, much as do the Armed Forces, provide major opportunities for Negro advancement on purely equal terms involving neither discrimination nor preference. (When the Jewish principal at I.S. 201 resigned, his Negro deputy refused the job on grounds that she would not be appointed *as a Negro*. She had no need to be. Inspired or lethargic, brilliant or bright, she was on her way to a principalship on her own. That is what bureaucracy is like.)

My second concern is, to my mind, the greater. Once this process gets legitimated there is no stopping it, and without intending anything of the sort, I fear it will be contributing significantly to the already well-developed tendency to politicize (and racialize) more and more aspects of modern life. Thirty years ago Orwell wrote, "In our age there is no such thing as 'keeping out of politics.' All issues are political issues. . . ." I resist that. Not all issues. Not yet. Note that he added "and politics itself is a mass of lies, evasions, folly, hatred, and schizophrenia." Not all American politics. Not yet. But enough is, and we must therefore struggle against the effort of government, in some large general interest, to dictate more and more of the small details. It is necessary to be more alert to Robert A. Nisbet's observation that democracy is, fundamentally, "a theory and structure of *political power*," but that liberalism is "historically a theory of *immunity* from power."

This, to my mind, is something more than a generalized concern. For centuries it has been obvious that property is not always evenly distributed, and it has been more or less legitimate to talk about it. In America, however, in the modern world generally, there have grown up new forms of property and influence, not so readily perceived, and the people who possess them have been wisely content to leave it at that. Success, as Norman Podhoretz wrote, and as he learned, is a dirty little secret in America, which those who are successful very much dislike to see discussed in public. A quality which makes for social stability at this time is that different groups in the population value different kinds of success, and tend to be best at those they most value. But government knows little of such variegations, and I very much fear that if we begin to become formal about quotas *for* this or that group, we will very quickly come to realize that these are instantly translated into quotas *against*. This is painfully true in the field of education and culture, which to a very considerable degree at this particular moment in our history is exceptionally influenced by American Jews. It was in a certain sense in an effort to resist the processes that brought about this partial hegemony that the "older American" institutions imposed quotas in the first place, and it was to abet the process that the quotas were abolished. Those were in fact quotas on success, imposed against a disproportionately successful group.

Let me be blunt. If ethnic quotas are to be imposed on American universities and similarly quasipublic institutions, it is Jews who will be almost driven out. They are not 3 percent of the population. This would be a misfortune to them, but a disaster to the nation. And I very much fear that there is a whiff of anti-Semitism in many of these demands. I was interested that when demands for quotas were made at Harvard, the *Crimson* endorsed with some enthusiasm the idea of ethnic representation, if not exactly quotas, on the faculty, but the editors were not at all impressed with the advantages of extending the principle to the student body. I do not know what was on their mind, but I do know that if ethnic quotas ever should come to Harvard (surely they won't!), something like seven out of eight Jewish undergraduates would have to leave, and I would imagine it to be a higher proportion in the graduate schools. This, I repeat, would be a misfortune for them, but a disaster for a place like Harvard. And much the same exodus would be required of Japanese and Chinese Americans, especially in the graduate schools.

One assumes that America has known enough of anti-Semitism and anti-Oriental feeling to be wary of opening that box again. Especially now. Given the prominence of Jews in current American radical movements — the *Times* describes the student activists at Columbia as "typically very bright and predominantly Jewish" — and the hostage of Israel, Jews are at this moment perhaps especially exposed to conservative or reactionary pressures which could easily make an issue of "overrepresentation." Recalling what we did to Japanese Americans in World War II, we surely should be careful about exposing Chinese Americans today to reactionary pressures simply on the basis that mainland China is our enemy.

It comes down to a matter of prudence: of recognizing our potential for racialism, and guarding against it, while responding to real and legitimate racial needs. Thus Negroes need preferential treatment in some areas, and deserve it. The good sense of the country in the past has been to do this kind of thing by informal arrangements — the balanced ticket. At the present time Israel, for example, seems to be having success with similar arrangements for its Eastern Jewish immigrants. Can we not do as much?

I hope I would not be interpreted as resisting a more open acknowledgment of these factors. To the contrary, I feel they should be more in our minds, but at a private and informal level of concern. I am acutely aware, for example, of the debilitating imbalance in the ethnic origins of American social scientists. I say debilitating because it is the nature of heterogeneous societies such as ours that analysis that could in any way be taken as criticism is routinely rejected when the analyst is of a distinctly different group. That is the plain truth of it. And it is a truth much in evidence with respect to Negro studies at this time. Thirty years ago in this country anyone seeking to learn more *about* Negroes would have had to read books written *by* Negroes: Frazier, Drake, Cayton, Johnson, and others. Somehow that tradition, nobly begun by DuBois, faltered. There was not, for example, a single Negro social scientist on the research staff of the President's Advisory Commission on Civil Disorders. Now, with only a few exceptions, social science studies of Negroes are carried out by whites, and we are not to wonder that more and more the cry goes out from the slums that they are tired of that white magic and will listen no more. But Negroes are only one case, and not a particularly special one. American social science desperately needs to expand its ethnic, racial, and religious base, just as it has got to expand its interests in those areas.

Let me conclude with the words with which Nathan Glazer and I closed our own study of the city:

Religion and race define the next phase in the evolution of the American peoples. But the American nationality is still forming: its processes are mysterious, and the final form, if there is ever to be a final form, is as yet unknown.

CHARLIE DOESN'T EVEN KNOW HIS DAILY RACISM IS A SICK JOKE

Bob Teague

Bob Teague, "Charlie Doesn't Even Know His Daily Racism Is a Sick Joke," *The New York Times Magazine,* September 15, 1968, pp. 36-37, 142, ff.

CHARLIE DOESN'T EVEN KNOW HIS DAILY RACISM IS A SICK JOKE

Bob Teague

IF you look at the racial problem from a black man's point of view, you can see the jokes as well as the injustices. Which is to say that you can then understand this: The underlying syndrome that must be attacked is much more subtle than a white policeman's nightstick. It's more like a topsy-turvy vaudeville routine in which all the funny lines come from the straight men.

A favorite comic theme among the "concerned and enlightened" elements of white society is "Let's Stamp Out Racial Hatred." Hoo boy! Hatred has very little to do with the central problem, Charlie. What is done to and withheld from black folk day by day in this country is based on neither hate nor horror. On the contrary. It is coldly impersonal. Like the brains of precocious computers.

Simply put, it seems to me that white folk are convinced, deep in their bones, that the way they run this melting pot —with black folk unmelted at the bottom—is nothing more than the natural order of things.

What happens quite naturally, for example, is that a black *bon vivant* who shows up in a clean shirt at a posh restaurant is approached by white customers who beg him to get them a good table, please. There is nothing malicious about it. They simply think of black men in clean shirts as waiters.

Similarly, a black man caught on foot near a public parking lot is likely to be buttonholed by a pale proud patrician who wants his limousine fetched in a hurry.

And even the most militant white egalitarians are prone to compliment one another by saying, "That's real white of you, Edgar." Obviously, the notion that anything white is inherently superior to its black counterpart is built into the white American idiom, and thus into the white American mind.

Do you think it's accidental that the bad guys in Western movies are the ones in black sombreros?

THIS is not to suggest that white folk don't feel a respectable amount of guilt now and then, here and there. What the hell. They're human, too. In fact, I personally witnessed a veritable orgy of private and public breast-beating among whites early this year—that is, after they had recovered from the initial shock of learning from the President's Commission on Civil Disorders that "the main cause of black violence in the ghettos last summer was white racism."

Although I had reached a similar conclusion by the time I was 10 years black, I nevertheless judged the President's commission to be somewhat crude. You shouldn't spring a thing like that on 180 million unsuspecting suspects without warning. They didn't even have time to consult their lawyers.

Fortunately for the white masses, however—before their breasts had been pounded into lily-white pulp—a nationally famous Washington ventriloquist intervened. Through a captive puppet, he delivered a one-line joke that helped to bring white America back to normal. "It would be a mistake," the straight man said, "to condemn a whole society."

The implication was clear: Perhaps only a small minority of misguided whites were the culprits.

The collective sigh of relief was still in the air when a black civic leader, a former city councilman, died in East St. Louis. Naturally, since the natural order had been restored, the Valhalla Cemetery refused the corpse—on the ground that "everybody else buried in Valhalla is white." Who said the people who run cemeteries have no sense of humor?

A popular variation of the Valhalla skit was played this summer in the Republican political arena. Bold headlines stirred up a fuss around the two leading contenders for the G.O.P. Presidential nomination because each belonged to a private club, in different states, that bars black folk from membership—as if nearly all white folk don't belong to a Society of, a Committee to, a Council for or a Convention on that maintains the same standards of purity.

I am exposed to the same basic joke almost every time I walk into an all-white apartment building to keep an appointment with a friend. I see panic in the eyes of the pale residents coming out as I go in —trying to recall whether they locked their doors. And the doorman himself seems to be trying to remember the standard procedure for What to Do Until the Cops Come.

Although it has taken me many years to reach this point of view—perhaps because I managed a get-away of sorts from the ghetto—I understand now that neither the Valhalla Cemetery nor the doorman and the rest of white America are motivated by hate. To their way of thinking, the business of keeping black folk at a comfortable distance is not a matter of racism, not a choice between right and wrong. It's like fearing the bomb, saluting the flag and sending a card on Mother's Day. It's an automatic reflex action. In other words, no emotion of any kind is necessarily involved.

CONSIDER, for example, those magazine and newspaper advertisements for "flesh-colored" bandages. The color they mean blandly ignores the color of most flesh on this planet. Mine in particular. But the top bananas who dreamed up that bit would be sorely aggrieved if someone called them racists. Some of those chaps are probably card-carrying fellow-travelers in the N.A.A.C.P., and their wives probably sent food to the poor people's shanty-town in Washington. Their "flesh-colored" bandages are merely a profitable manifestation of a common assumption among white folk: White skin is what human flesh is *supposed* to look like. Anything else— black skin certainly—is irrelevant. Sort of a whimsical goof by Mother Nature.

How else can a black man explain those ubiquitous cosmetic ads showing a pale proud beauty using the facial lotion that promises to give her "the natural look"? The joke here is that this same beauty, and those who swear by "flesh-colored" bandages spend as much time in the sun as possible to darken their natural looks. They even buy chemical tans in bottles. And did you ever hear a commercial Goldilocks say, "Goodness gracious, my tan is much too dark"?

A spin-off joke from that particular farce is the honest pretense among whites that only their backward brothers— way down yonder in Mississippi —are hypersensitive to color. The white liberal party line says in effect that truly civilized whites regard black skin as a rather flamboyant costume for humankind, but nonetheless legitimate.

This is self-deception, of course. My experience has been that most white folk are so caught up in the seductive *mystique* of White Power that their brains are rarely brushed by the notion that the "natural order" in this country is in any way forced and unnatural.

Only last week one of my white friends—to be known here as Charlie—called my attention to one of those "flesh-colored" ads. Although Charlie is well past 35 and literate and had read similar ads over the years, he was seeing it clearly for the first time.

"Man, look at this," he said, wearing an embarrassed grin. "They even insult you in the ads, don't they?"

Charlie's insight is not yet complete, however. If it ever is, he'll say "we" instead of "they."

How could good old Charlie have missed the point of that joke for so many years and thus become an accessory to the largely unconscious white conspiracy? It was easy. Just as it is for white gossip columnists to report regularly that the sexy movie queen who appears to be nude on the screen is actually hiding the goodies in a "flesh-colored" bra. They wouldn't dream of explaining such illusions in terms of "a bra that virtually matched her skin." Those gossip columnists, by God, know "flesh color" when they see it.

ALL of which is to say that white folk are immersed in such a totally racist climate that—

like fish born in the ocean—they have no reason to suspect for a moment that they might be all wet. Wherever they look in this society, there are white institutions, habits, signs, symbols, myths and realities that reinforce their notion that black folk rank somewhere between King Kong and Frankenstein's monster on the scale of lower forms of life.

I recently read a best-selling novel which was not about the race problem. Yet the hero and his adversaries made the point again and again in passing that the busty blond heroine was clearly depraved and lost beyond recall since, between sexual acrobatics with the good guys, she allowed a "boogey" into her boudoir. That novel has sold more than 900,000 copies in the hard-cover editions, and more than two million more in paperback. I am not saying that its success is based in any way on its casual racial insults. The point is, it's a typical visual aid in the process of white indoctrination.

Television is even more effective in that respect. Here again, of course, white folk control both the medium and the message.

If a superintelligent visitor from another planet were to deduce, strictly from television, the nature of the 22 million black pariahs who exist

in the crevices of this society, he undoubtedly would get an impression that was 99 44/100 per cent pure nonsense. From the electronic evidence of omission, projected around the clock, the visitor might gather that black women are rather dull and sexless creatures. Apparently nothing known to science or Madison Avenue can help black girls to develop "the skin you love to touch." With scarcely a blond hair to call their own, they obviously are not the kind of broads who "have more fun." And without one toothbrush among them, they have no interest in the leading toothpaste that "gives your mouth sex appeal."

Black men are equally irrelevant among the fauna of the natural TV order. It is tacitly suggested, for instance, that they are socially backward — black Square Johns, so to speak. Otherwise they would be seen driving "the low-priced luxury car" to seduce more swinging chicks.

It's true that black satellites are sometimes seen in TV dramatic series, but usually as cardboard characters with virtually no lives of their own. They are perpetually in orbit around the full-blooded white supermen who perform brain surgery, fall in love, bounce children on their knees and worry about middle-aged spread.

MY impression is that many white folk would like to portray black people in a more sophisticated manner. But, alas, they cannot forget all those Tarzan movies of their youth. These made it official that black folk are natural-born spear carriers, dangerous savages and beasts of the white man's burdens.

Then, too, there are all those cannibal cartoons in the slick magazines put out by and for white folks. Who wouldn't be somewhat repelled by a black gourmet whose favorite entree is fricassee of Charlie?

Such examples of how black folk are systematically misrepresented or shut out from the stuff that the American Dream is made of are virtually endless. The smiling faces on greeting cards are never black faces. Department-store manikins don't resemble anyone you are likely to meet in the ghetto. And all plastic angels who symbolize the Christmas spirit are pink.

The net effect of these deceptions is that each tailor-made reality buttresses the other in the minds of whites. This explains in large measure why so many white folk are genuinely baffled by the grumbling and violence in the ghettos. Which is the basis for the popular white joke that ends with the punch line: "What do you people want?"

When black folk bother to spell out the answer to that riddle—with expectations that can only be described as naive —the consistent white responses add up to rather predictable pranks: another study of black frustration; another conference on brotherhood; another million-dollar crash program to tear down an old ghetto and replace it with a new ghetto.

As one of the best buffoons in the Federal Government observed after the riots last summer: "The very existence of the ghetto is un-American." But that line was much too oblique for most of white America to comprehend.

I AM not suggesting that white folk don't even try. On the contrary. They conscientiously integrate a school here and there—even if it means doing something silly, like busing half the youngsters from A to Z and the other half vice versa. At the same time, however, they automatically prevent black families from buying or renting homes near the school in question. And they bar black folk from the jobs that pay the kind of money that would enable them to afford such a pristine neighborhood.

But getting back to how hard white people try, I witnessed one of their truly valiant efforts against insuperable odds this year. The occasion was the hint dropped by the President's Commission on Civil Disorders that the "ghetto is created by whites, maintained by white institutions and condoned by white society."

Most white folk were truly sorry about that. They rushed

HARD SELL—"When a black customer shows up many white merchants make a special effort to unload whatever raunchy merchandise is in stock."

from their enclaves of affluence to the nearest ghetto to make amends. However, once in the wilds of Harlem and its scattered subdivisions, they simply could not resist telling corny jokes. Like the one Hitler told as he toured a concentration camp: "Jews stink."

What the Führer was smelling, of course, was Nazism. And in America the heady aroma of racism is equally confusing to the thin straight noses of the master race. Otherwise it would not be possible for those deadpan middle-class comedians to come up with such boffos as: "Why can't the black man pull himself up by his bootstraps like the other minorities have done?" While guarding the boots with bulldog tenacity day and night.

Admittedly, that is a rather large generalization. I have no doubt that some white skeptics will challenge me to prove it. My answer is this: Regard me as sort of a black J. Edgar Hoover. You didn't ask him to prove his public generalization that "Martin Luther King is one of the most notorious liars in the country."

Furthermore, I am prepared to generalize again. From my experience with white storekeepers over the years, I judge that many white merchants make a special hard-sell effort when a black customer shows. up — to unload whatever raunchy merchandise they have in stock.

Example: One of my soul sisters overheard a white housewife chewing out a white butcher for putting rotten meat on display. "Can't you see it's not fit to eat?" she demanded.

"Lady, this is not for you," the butcher said matter-of-factly. "It's for them. Believe me, they don't know any better. They're like pigs."

ALTHOUGH black folk are reluctant to admit it in this age of militant reassessment of their posi-

tion, they do feel a certain amount of pity for white folk now and then. Like Sam Bowers, who resigned this year as Grand Dragon of the United Ku Klux Klans in Georgia. Sam said he wanted "to work for a united America where black men and white men can stand shoulder to shoulder."

When I broadcast that item last spring, I couldn't help thinking: What grievous tortures poor old Sam must have suffered upon discovering the joke of white supremacy.

Another public confession was made recently at the opposite end of the spectrum by a self-declared white liberal—a Northern youth who had risked his life as a field worker in the civil-rights movement in Mississippi. Out of curiosity, he said, he took a trip on the LSD express. And the jig was up. Under the influence of the so-called mind-expanding drug, he realized for the first time that, in the Deep South of his soul, he honestly believed that black people were not now, never had been and never could be as deserving as whites. The immediate result of his insight was a nervous breakdown.

That young man was neither the first nor the last of his breed. The mass media these days are overpopulated with white liberals who portray themselves as "champions of the inarticulate masses." The sick joke here is that the masses—especially the black masses—are not at all inarticulate. They tell it like it is and like it ought to be—with precision, persistence and profanity.

But white society can't grasp the meaning of all that yammering—being too busy washing brains, their victims' and their own. They therefore have no real difficulty in maintaining their cool and the status quo in the face of massive protest and violence.

Being highly inventive jesters, white folk entertain themselves with a monologue that says, in effect, black folk are too stupid to realize that something phony is going on here. It goes like this: "It's the Communist agitators and Communist dupes who are behind all this violence."

One-liners like that are probably what killed vaudeville.

If black folk don't laugh out loud at such routines, it is because their funny bones are dulled from the same old stale material. Real comedy depends on surprises. So why should a black man chuckle over the annual Congressional Follies built around civil-rights legislation, for example? He knows in advance that the new Civil Rights Act is going to wind up like the so-called Open Housing Act of 1866 — unenforced and soon forgotten.

Enforcement, he is told, would "infringe on the rights" of the white minority. That's a good one, too. But it is as familiar as, "Why does a fireman wear red suspenders?"

As for the sight gags in white society's repertoire, these too have worn thin from overexposure. How many times can an individual black man be amused by the blind-cab-driver routine? After the 37th time, it no longer strikes him as suitable material for a laff-in.

DID I say "individual black man"? Actually, there is scarcely any such animal as far as white eyes can see. They recognize "the first Negro who" and "the only Negro to," but not as individuals — instead, as freaks or symbols. Which is to say that white folks have a habit of arbitrarily assigning a rather standard personality to a black man. His real self is like an iceberg, deeply submerged in a sea of white assumptions.

One of my soul brothers was recently promoted to an executive position with a giant corporation in New York City. He had earned it by bringing in more sales orders over the last five years than anyone else in his department. You can imagine how chagrined he was when several of his white colleagues dismissed his personal achievement with humorless jokes like this: "It pays to be black these days. Man, you've got it made."

Such an attitude is not founded primarily on jealousy, as it might appear on the surface. White folks are simply incapable of seeing a black man as anything beyond his blackness.

At least twice a year, for instance, I am approached for an interview by one national magazine or another. My experience as a newspaper reporter and television news broadcaster has provided me with a wealth of interesting material from face-to-face encounters with four Presidents, a half-dozen princesses, scores of prizefighters, hundreds of politicians, assorted pimps, paragons and pin-up queens. But not one white interviewer ever shows the slightest interest in anything except my blackness.

"What is the role of the black newsman?" they want to know.

"The role of a black man," I tell them off the record, "is or ought to be the same as it is for everybody else in his profession; in this case, to gather the facts and report them with as much integrity, clarity and objectivity as he can muster." End of interview.

I am also rather weary of getting letters from white television fans that read like this one:

"When you first began broadcasting the news on television, I watched you every night, but I realize now, years later, that I was so conscious of the fact that you were black that I didn't hear a word you said about

PANIC—"When I walk into an all-white apartment building to keep an appointment with a friend, the doorman seems to be trying to remember the standard procedure for What to Do Until the Cops Come."

the news. Now, I am happy to say, I still watch you every night, but only because you are a damn good newscaster...."

What I'm getting at here is that white folks are generally flabbergasted by a black man who can fly a plane, mix a martini, speak unbroken English or shoot a round of golf. Such a black man is something like the celebrated dog that could walk on its hind legs unassisted.

ABOUT the only realm of this society which seems to be perhaps one-third of the way toward the verge of catching the spirit of this thing called the free democratic society is professional sports. Even here a string of qualifying exceptions must be taken into account. To mention just a few:

Boxing is obsessed by the search for a "white hope"; football is convinced that a black quarterback could not lead his team to the goal line; and baseball, like all the others, shuts out black men from the managerial and decision-making level. And besides all that, there is a great deal of friction and apartheid on the so-called integrated teams.

But baseball still deserves a better grade than white Americans generally. In the first place, black players are no longer required to be supermen like Jackie Robinson. If you watch baseball these days, you see black men fumbling routine grounders, dropping flies, striking out with the bases loaded and winding up the season with microscopic batting averages. Just like whites. And no one

LEFT OUT—*"From the evidence of omission" in TV ads, one "might gather that black women are dull and sexless creatures."*

suggests that such derelictions are peculiar to one race or another.

Furthermore, if a white interviewer shows up in the locker room, he is full of questions about the spitball or the squeeze play that didn't quite work in the ninth. After all, why should a third baseman, even a black one, be limited to discussing racial jokes?

SO how long is it going to take the rest of this country to evolve even as little as baseball? In my judg-

ment, another 100 years at the very least, if this society manages to survive that long.

Why so much time? Well, it seems to me that while one side of those split personalities called white Americans is striving with all its might to open their minds and their society, the other side is being pulled in the opposite direction by what white Americans accept and automatically maintain as the natural order. As you can see for yourself, it is something of an unequal race. ■

THE NEGRO'S STAKE IN AMERICA'S FUTURE

Nathan Glazer

Nathan Glazer, "The Negro's Stake in America's Future," *The New York Times Magazine,* September 22, 1968, pp. 30-31, 90, ff.

THE NEGRO'S STAKE IN AMERICA'S FUTURE

Nathan Glazer

SOMETHING very strange is happening in the American racial crisis. On the one hand, the concrete situation of Negro Americans is rapidly improving. This is not only true when we look at economics—for we all know this is an inadequate measure of group progress, and that a people that feels oppressed will not be satisfied with the argument, "you never had it so good." But it is also true that things are improving when we look at political participation and power, and even when we look at the critical area of police behavior. Despite recent instances of police violence against black militants, there is no question that the police in city after city are becoming more careful in how they address Negro Americans and in the use of force and firearms. The history of police response to the riots alone demonstrates that.

On the other hand, as the Negro's situation improves, his political attitudes are becoming more extreme. The riots are called rebellions, and hardly any Negro leader bothers to deplore them these days. Militant groups become larger and their language and demands more shocking, even to a demand for political separation. This is sobering, for we know what may happen when a country begins to break up; look at Nigeria.

Social policy faces a dilemma; most of us—black and white, liberals and conservatives —believe that political and social attitudes reflect concrete conditions (when things get better people become more satisfied and less violent) and that we can change attitudes by changing conditions. When political attitudes become more extreme as conditions are improving, we resort to two explanations: the well-known revolution of rising expectations and the theory of Alexis de Tocqueville that the improvement of conditions increases the desire for change because people begin to feel stronger and more potent.

Both of these theories undoubtedly have some validity, but one's attitude toward them

85

must depend upon one's attitude toward society. One who looks upon American society as the French looked upon their Old Regime—as conservative, sclerotic, repressive, irrational and selfish—will look favorably upon the rise of extreme opinion and the crash of the American Old Regime. But one who sees American society as fundamentally democratic and responsive to people's wishes will be deeply concerned about its fate. That expectations rise is good; that they rise so fast that no policy of any type carried out by anybody can satisfy them is bad. That people feel powerful and free to express their resentments is good; that their resentment may overthrow a system capable of satisfying their needs and hopes is bad. There must be a point at which improvement will moderate extremism despite the revolution of rising expectations and the Tocquevillian hypothesis. But if such a point exists, we are getting further away from it rather than closer to it.

There is, of course, another possible explanation for what is happening: that the Negro is no longer interested in advancing within the American social system. The theory here is that Negroes have begun to see themselves as a subject people, and —like all such people—will be satisfied only by independent political existence. This is the direction that militant Negro demands have now begun to take, and if Negroes follow them this nation will have to use all its political ingenuity and creativity to avoid being torn apart. It is this rise of Negro separatism, and how we might respond to it, that I wish to explore here.

FIRST, let us show briefly that things *are* getting better. Many liberal shapers of opinion insist that the situation of the Negro has not changed or has grown worse. Sadly, social scientists, who should know better, are often among the worst offenders. Elliot Liebow, the writer of "Tally's Corner," a fine study of unemployed Negro men, states casually, for example, that "the number of the poor and their problems have grown steadily since World War II." Some who insist that the Negro's economic situation is getting worse point to the rising *absolute* gap between Negro and white incomes and ignore the fact that the *percentage* gap is diminishing. According to their logic, if at some fortunate time median white incomes are $10,000 and median nonwhite incomes are $8,000, one might conclude that Negroes are worse off than they were when whites made $5,000 and they made $3,250.

In October, 1967, the Bureau of Labor Statistics and the Bureau of the Census published a compendium of statistics on the social and economic conditions of the Negro. Here are some of the major findings.

Income: In 1966, 23 per cent of the nonwhite families had incomes of more than $7,000, and 53 per cent of white families made that much or more. Ten years earlier, using dollars of the same value, the figures were only 9 per cent for nonwhite families and 31 per cent for white families. Outside the South, Negroes did better: 38 per cent of nonwhite families had incomes above $7,000, against 59 per cent of white families.

Occupation: Between 1960 and 1966, the number of nonwhites in the better-paying and more secure job categories rose faster than the number of whites. There was a 50 per cent increase for nonwhites in professional, technical and managerial work, and a 13 per cent increase for whites; in clerical jobs the increases were 48 per cent for nonwhites and 19 per cent for whites; in sales, the changes were 32 per cent and 7 per cent, and among foremen and craftsmen they were 45 per cent and 10 per cent. During the same period, the proportion of nonwhites employed as laborers and in private households dropped.

Education: In 1960 there was a gap of 1.9 years between nonwhite and white males over 25 in median years of schooling; by 1966, there was a gap of only 0.5 years. In 1960, 36 per cent of nonwhite males and 63 per cent of white males over 25 had completed high school; by 1966, the figures were 53 per cent for nonwhite males and 73 per cent for white males. In 1960, 3.9 per cent of Negro males and 15.7 per cent of white males had completed college; in 1966, college graduates included 7.4 per cent of Negro males and 17.9 per cent of white males. This represents a 90 per cent increase in nonwhite college graduates and an increase of only 14 per cent among whites.

Housing: Between 1960 and 1966, there was a 25 per cent drop in the number of substandard housing units occupied by nonwhites (from 2.26 million to 1.69 million) and a 44 per cent increase in the number of standard units (from 2.88 million to 4.13 million).

Political participation: Negro voter registration in the South increased from 2.16 million in March, 1964, to 3.07 million in May, 1968, while Negro population remained stable. And the National Advisory Commission on Civil Disorders reported after a survey of 20 cities that they averaged 16 per cent in Negro population while Negroes accounted for 10 per cent of the elected political representatives. This figure must be interpreted in light of the fact that Negroes of voting age are generally a smaller fraction in the total Negro population than whites of voting age are in the white population; Negroes in cities have a higher proportion of young families and children, whites a higher proportion of the aged.

The police: Even on this sorest point of black-white relations, the Kerner Commission reports progress in one significant respect: there are now substantial numbers of Negroes on many city police forces. In Washington, 21 per cent of the force is Negro; in Philadelphia, 20 per cent; in Chicago, 17; St. Louis, 11; Hartford, 11; Newark, 10, and Atlanta, 10.

These are simply over-all measures. When one considers the number of programs devoted to getting Negroes into colleges, graduate schools and corporations, to raising their grades in the civil service and to moderating police attitudes, one must conclude that the situation of the Negro is improving.

OF course all these figures can be argued with. For instance, we have recently become aware that 14 per cent of Negro males and only 2 per cent of white males were not counted in the 1960 census, and if they were counted they would probably lower the average figures for Negro earnings, education, employment, housing. On the other hand, we probably have not been counting similar proportions of white and Negro males in earlier censuses, so any improvement indicated by change from one census or sample census survey to another is real.

It can also be argued that the quality of jobs held by Negroes, even if they are in white-collar and skilled-labor categories, is lower than that of the whites' jobs, and this is true. But the quality of jobs held by Negroes certainly has not decreased on the average. Fewer Negro professionals today are preachers, more are engineers.

Some people argue that the improvement in economic, educational and housing conditions is largely a result of the Negro's migration from the South to the North and West and from small towns and rural areas to big cities; if we were to study Negroes in the North and West alone, we would not find such marked changes over the last few years. But the statistics show improvement in every section.

Another argument is that these over-all measures of improvement apply only to the Negro middle class and stable working class, that the lower working class has shown no progress. But an unpublished analysis by Albert Wohlstetter of the University of Chicago indicates that the Negro lower-income group has recently made greater progress relative to the white lower - income group than have upper-income Negroes relative to the corresponding white group. It is true, however, that such other measures of social condition as the proportion of broken homes and illegitimacy continue to show worsening conditions among low - income Negroes.

Finally, one may argue that much of the advance to which I have pointed has taken place since the Vietnam War expanded in 1965, just as the previous economic advance of the Negro took place during the Korean War and ended with it. Though there was a relative decline or stagnation between the wars, the advances were not fully wiped out; it was rather that the rate of advance was not maintained. By now the build-up of Negro political power and national programs is so great, and the scale of recent achievements is so massive, that I cannot believe they will not continue after the war—

provided there is not a radical change in the political situation.

MORE striking, however, than the advance itself is that on the basis of our present statistics we cannot single out the Negro as a group which suffers unique deprivation as compared to other ethnic and racial groups which suffer from the effects of poor education, depressed rural background and recent migration to urban areas. Social scientists disagree on how to view Negroes in the context of the ethnic and racial history of the United States. One tendency is to emphasize the many unique things: the manner of their arrival (by force and in chains); the condition in which they lived for 200 years (slavery); the condition in which they have lived for the last 100 years (legal inferiority in much of the country), and the special role of the Negro in helping shape American culture and imagination.

But one can also view Negroes in the American context as part of a series of ethnic and racial groups that have moved into society and become a part of it. There is a new illusion which asserts that all white ethnic groups moving into American society have quickly achieved respectable levels of income, good living conditions and political power; that all racially distinct groups have been held back, and that the Negro, because of the unique character of slavery, is furthest back. The truth is nothing like this. Some white ethnic groups—the Jews, for instance—have shown a rapid economic rise; others have been much slower to achieve in this area. One of the economically backward white ethnic groups, the Irish, has been politically gifted, and its members are among elected officials at all levels in almost every part of the country. Other ethnic groups, such as Italians and Poles, have done poorly both economically and politically. Some racially distinct groups — the Japanese, for example—have done remarkably well in education and occupation; most others have done badly.

The Negro's situation is more complex than the gross simplification of having started at the bottom and having stayed there. By some measures, Puerto Ricans do worse in New York and Mexican Americans do worse in the Southwest. One can argue that the Negro is worse off than other groups in this country, but the difference is not great enough to explain by itself the special quality of despair and hysteria that dominates much Negro political discourse. Of course we must realize that our national obligation to improve the Negro's position is much greater than our obligation to those who came here voluntarily. The Negro is aware of this, and the inferiority of his position is thus more grating than it would be to other groups.

REGARDLESS of how we view their social position, a growing number of the 22 million United States Negroes believe that Americans are racists and that the only solution is some form of separate political existence. One indication of how far this trend has gone is in the use of words —"genocide," for example. In February, Stokely Carmichael, speaking to a Negro audience in Oakland, Calif., felt the need to justify his use of "genocide" in describing the dangers facing Negroes: ". . . we are not talking about politics tonight, we're not talking about economics tonight, we're talking about the survival of a race of people. . . . Many of us feel—many of our generation feel—that they are getting ready to commit genocide against us. Now many people say that's a horrible thing to say about anybody. But if it's a horrible thing to say, then we should do as Brother Malcolm said — we should examine history."

We have moved far since

February. An official of the Southern Christian Leadership Conference warns that genocide is a danger. James Baldwin, in The New York Times Book Review, asserts: "White America appears to be seriously considering the possibilities of mass extermination." By now even moderate leaders use the term "genocide," perhaps feeling they have to show they are not Toms. And by now, of course, white men who want to demonstrate their sympathy for Negroes also use the term—thus, Eliot Fremont - Smith, reviewing John Hersey's "The Algiers Motel Incident" in The New York Times, says that the book "shows America to be deeply—and unknowingly to most of its citizens — genocidal."

The public-opinion polls report rapid changes of attitude among Negroes. A Harris poll conducted *before* Martin Luther King's assassination concluded that the number of Negroes alienated rose from 34 per cent in 1966 to 56 per cent in 1968. The proportion of respondents who agreed with the statement "Few people really understand how it is to live like I live" rose from 32 per cent to 66 per cent; those who agreed that "People running the country don't really care what happens to people like ourselves"

rose from 32 per cent to 52 per cent. Yet in the same poll, 73 per cent of the respondents agreed that there had been more racial progress in recent years than previously.

More impressive than attitudes and the use of words, however, is action—the rioting, the expectation of guerrilla warfare, the rise of such groups as the Black Panthers, who call for armed resistance to the police, the freeing of black prisoners and — ultimately — a separate national political existence.

THERE are three points of view on what to do about rising extremism in the face of social improvement. One group contends that we must strengthen the police, create riot-control forces and put down extremism. A second holds that we must increase the rate of social improvement in the hope of creating a harmonious nation. The third position is that social improvement is no longer the issue, that separate political power for Negroes is the only thing that will satisfy them.

The majority of white Americans, I think, reject the first point of view, though most of them believe that the maintenance of civil order must be part of the national response to the crisis. The second position is the one for which the Kerner Commission has written a brief and to which, undoubtedly, most liberals subscribe. It is almost the only position open to one who believes, as I do, that our society is on the whole a success and that it can handle the complex and frightening problems of an advanced technology better than such alternatives as the varied assortment of Communist authoritarian states or the unexplicated utopia that is the vague hope of the New Left. The liberal position does, however, have at least one basic difficulty.

It is that we have already carried out social programs on an ever-expanding scale without any movement toward the reward of a united and peaceful nation that is the Kerner Commission's hope. Take the commission's own figures: "Federal expenditures for manpower development and training have increased from less than $60-million in 1963 to $1.6-billion in 1968. The President has proposed a further increase, to $2.1-billion, in 1969. . . . Federal expenditures for education, training and related services have increased from $4.7-billion in fiscal 1964 to $12.3-billion in fiscal 1969. . . . Direct Federal expenditures for housing and community development have increased

from $600-million in fiscal 1964 to nearly $3-billion in fiscal 1969." There have been similar increases in health and welfare expenditures.

I am left with the uneasy feeling that if these increases have taken place at the same time as the spread of urban riots and political extremism, it is questionable whether a further expansion will stem them. I am for expanding and improving the programs because they are our major means for achieving equality in education, housing and the like, but I do not think we can count on them to moderate attitudes; political attitudes have a life of their own and are not simply reflections of economic and social conditions. The demand for separatism will not easily be moderated by social programs. We must face up to it on its own terms.

White America must recognize that separatism means a host of things, many of them —positive identification with the group, greater political representation and economic power for the black man, the teaching of black history and arts in the schools—valuable and healthy for Negroes and American society. The major problem is the demand for territorial autonomy—a group of states set aside as a black nation or black enclaves in the cities with certain rights and powers. Certainly most white Americans will resist these demands for territorial autonomy and extraterritoriality.* One war has been fought to keep the nation united, and the sense of what all Americans gain from a united nation and what they might lose from a divided one is strong enough to insure that these demands will continue to be resisted. Nor is it clear that any substantial number of Negroes want autonomy. The leaders who demand it are powerfully supported, I think, not by the realities of the Negro condition and the hope they offer of improving it; but by powerful ideologies, in particular by the belief that American Negroes are a colonial people who must be freed from their colonial status even if they enjoy all the rights of every other American.

IF the demand for territorial independence captures the minds of Negroes, it will be because Americans—black and white—have failed to understand the relationship between their society and the groups that make it up. Many people see society as far more monolithic and homogeneous than it has ever been. I am afraid that whites will fight to retain something that has never existed and blacks will fight because they do not realize the enormous scope the society grants for group diversity and self-fulfillment.

Almost every group that has settled in this country has been nationalistic and separatist, and the laws have permitted for most of them a degree of separatism not yet reached by Negroes. Many groups have supported—sometimes with armed volunteers — nationalist leaders intent upon freeing or revolutionizing their homelands, even when this was a matter of great embarrassment to the United States. Most groups have maintained schools in their own languages and have tried to foster their religious and ethnic customs and beliefs among their children. The major outer limits set on the development of racial and ethnic groups in this country have been an insistence on political loyalty to the United States and a denial of territorial autonomy.

All Americans are aware of the prejudice almost all immigrant and racial groups have faced, but we tend to be less

---

*Greater local community control—over schools, police, urban renewal—is a definite possibility and even likelihood. It is territorial autonomy for black areas as such which raises the major issue.

aware of the adjustments our society has eventually made to accommodate them. We have, for instance, developed a political system in which groups of any substantial number are represented among appointed or elected officials; the system has worked well without any laws specifying how much or what kind of recognition should be given. The general freedom this country grants to business enterprises has aided the economic integration of minority groups. (Unfortunately, the ability to create independent economic bases is now considerably limited by — among other things — state and local licensing requirements, union regulations and Federal tax and accounting procedures. This, of course, makes it more difficult for the less sophisticated and literate to become successful in business.) We have granted full freedom to religious organization, and under its protection a wide range of educational, cultural, political and social activities is carried on.

Compared with most countries that have tried to create themselves out of a mixed population, there has been a certain genius in the American style of handling this problem. The principle has been that there is no formal recognition of an ethnic or racial group, but there is every informal recognition of the right to self-development and integration at the group's own rate and to independence in social, religious and political matters. The principle has often been ignored; we have enacted laws that discriminate against some groups — most notably, Negroes, but also American Indians and Orientals—and we have often restricted the development of certain groups through "Americanization" movements. But most breaks with these principles — from slavery to immigration quotas by race— have in the end been recognized as un-American and overturned by the courts and legislatures and, in the most important case; war.

To say that Negroes have been a part of this pattern may seem to be no more than a refusal to face the evil in American society. Prof. Robert Blauner of the University of California at Berkeley has argued forcefully that there are "colonized" peoples in the United States who do not fit the ethnic pattern I have described; among them, he says, are Negroes, American Indians and, to some extent, Mexican Americans. According to this argument, the self-regulated rate of integration prevailed only for European immigrants and, to a much more modest degree, prevails now for the Chinese and Japanese. Blauner contends that there has been a different pattern for peoples we have conquered or brought here as slaves: this is a pattern of internal colonization, whereby these groups have been made inferior to the "settlers" politically, economically, socially and culturally; for them the only meaningful course is the colonial one: rebellion, resistance and, conceivably, forceful overthrow of the "settler." If Professor Blauner is right, we settlers must figure out how to grant to the colonized the independence that will make them whole or how to resist their effort to take it and perhaps destroy the society in doing so.

For one basic reason, I think the Blauner argument is wrong. Whatever relevance the colonization theory may have had in the past—when Negroes lived as agricultural workers in the South, Mexican Americans in villages in the Southwest and Indians on their reservations —— it is scarcely relevant today, when three-quarters of American Negroes have moved to cities to become not only workers and servants but skilled workers, foremen, civil servants, professionals and white-collar workers of all types; when at a slower rate the same thing is happening to Mexican Americans, and when even Indians can free themselves from any politically inferior status by giving up the reservation and moving to the city, as more and more are doing. These moves are voluntary—or if involuntary to some extent, no more so than the migration of many other groups escaping political persecution and economic misery. They lead to the creation of a voluntary community of self-help institutions. They lead to a largely self-regulated rate at which group cultural patterns are given up and new ones adopted. It is all quite comparable to what happened to the European immigrant.

The existence of preju e and discrimination does not make the colonial analogy fit. They occur wherever different groups interact socially. Are the Algerian workers in the slum settlements around Paris and the Spanish and Turkish immigrant workers in Europe "colonized"? Or are they simply immigrants facing the discrimination that is so often the lot of immigrants? Nor are prejudice and discrimination insuperable obstacles to political and economic advancement. The important questions rather, are the *level* of discrimination, how it is reflected in *harmful policies*, what *state assistance* it gets and to what extent the *state acts against it*. Tested this way, the colonial analogy becomes meaningless. There has been a steady decline in all forms of expressed prejudice against Negroes; it is indicated by opinion polls and by everyday behavior. There is ever-stronger state action against prejudice and discrimination, even in parts of the South.

THE colonial pattern makes sense if there is a *legal* inferiority of the colonized, or if, even in the case of *formal* equality, in fact only tiny proportions of the colonized can reach high statuses. But this is not true of the Negro Americans — nor will it be true shortly of the Mexican Americans and, if they so choose, of American Indians. The fact is that instead of keeping these groups out of privileged statuses, most public policy and the policy of most large private institutions is to bring them in larger and larger numbers into privileged statuses —what else is the meaning of the work of the Federal Civil Service in upgrading minority employees, of the colleges in recruiting minority students in greater numbers than could normally qualify, of the various corporation programs for increasing numbers of minority-group executives and franchise holders? The scale of most of this effort is still much too small, but its aim is to speed up the incorporation of the minority groups into the mixed American society rather than to slow it down.

THE question of whether American Negroes are "colonized" is ultimately to be answered only by the Negroes. If they see themselves as being prevented by the American pattern from achieving the independence they want, they will do everything in their power to break the pattern. Then all Americans may have to choose between the suffering of another war of national unity and the dangers of separatism.

Three factors still argue against the eventual victory of the colonial theory. The first is the large number of Negroes who *are* integrated— civil servants, white-collar workers, union members, party members and elected officials. Second, there is the possibility that moderate social change may still pacify the militants. While they demand independence, they might be satisfied with more and better jobs, more political power, better schools and housing and as much institutional identity and control as the American society can allow. Finally, there is the enormous practical difficulty of satisfying the demand of a scattered people for territorial separation or of finding acceptable alternatives.

Among the factors working toward the success of the colonial analogy among Negroes is the importance to them of their experience in the South, where they were indeed colonized and where there remains in large sections the most unrelenting resistance to black equality. The colonial imagery of the South has been transported to the cities of East and West, which are largely free of colonialism. There it struggles against the immigrant analogy, and on the whole it is losing.

The second factor working for the colonial analogy is our failure to adopt rapidly enough new approaches to achieving effective equality for the Negro. Negro businesses must be created, subsidized, sustained and advised; job programs must become more meaningful; colleges must learn how to incorporate large numbers of minority students, and urban schools must undergo a transformation (though which one it is hard to say). All this is so demanding we may not succeed. Mayor Lindsay of New York, perhaps the dominant liberal member of the Kerner Commission, told businessmen what they must do to make the hard-core unemployed effective:

"You've got to literally adopt this kind of employe, be responsible for his total condition 24 hours a day, 7 days a week. . . . Adopt their families, a piece of the block where they live, a chunk of the city and its future. Know where they live, their economic condition, how their children are, whether there's a police problem, what the neighborhood pressures are. . . .

"The businessman who does hire the hard-core unemployed is going to be confronted with absenteeism, poor working habits, deficiencies in reading and writing, negative attitudes. . . ."

If this is what businessmen —and perhaps teachers—must do to employ and educate a substantial part of our minority population, we may not have the compassion, commitment and capacity to succeed.

THE third reason that the colonial analogy may win out is the inability of both blacks and whites to understand the American pattern of group incorporation. On the white side, there is a fear of Negro separatism and Negro power that is based on a failure to understand that every group has gone through—and some have maintained — a substantial degree of separatism; all have demanded, and many won, political representation in appointive and elected office and control over pieces of the political action.

As long as we do not

succumb to the temptation to become a society of fixed quotas and compartments, we can go some distance in meeting separatist demands. If suburban towns can have their own school systems and police forces, then I can see no reason why parts of a larger city cannot have them. In any case, when the authority of teachers and policemen has been destroyed —and it has in large measure been destroyed in ghetto areas —there is no alternative to some pragmatic adjustment to the creation of new social forms.

Among the blacks, too — and here they are joined by many whites — there is a failure to understand the relationship of the group to society, to understand that, even while prejudice and discrimination exist, those discriminated against can achieve their goals and a respected place in society. There is a failure to understand that different groups vary in their cultural characteristics and in the area and character of their achievements and that an owlish insistence on equality in every area and every characteristic denies the significance of special characteristics and achievements. There may come a time when the special gifts of the American Negro will mean a massive representation in politics or the arts, even if today they mean only an overrepresentation in such fields as professional sports. The special character of American group life—its acceptance of individual merit and its flexible arrangements for group character and pride — should not be destroyed by a demand for fixed quotas and their incorporation into legal and semilegal arrangements.

ABOVE all, I think, black militants and their too-complaisant white allies fail to understand that there *is* an American society with tremendous power to incorporate new groups—to their advantage and its own — and that this is not a *white* society. There is nothing so sad as to hear the Government, the universities and the corporations denounced as white racist institutions. A hundred years ago the same reasoning would have branded them English institutions, but the Germans and Irish became a part of them; 50 years ago they might have been called Christian institutions, but Jews became a part of them. They are not essentially white institutions today any more than they were essentially Christian 50 years ago or English a century ago. They will become white institutions only if Negro Americans insist on full political separation and decide for themselves that the American pattern of group life cannot include them. ■

ALTERNATIVE FUTURES FOR THE AMERICAN GHETTO

Anthony Downs

Anthony Downs, "Alternative Futures for the American Ghetto," *Daedalus,* Fall 1968, Vol. 97, pp. 1331-1378.

ALTERNATIVE FUTURES FOR THE AMERICAN GHETTO

Anthony Downs

IN THE past few years, the so-called "ghetto" areas of large American cities have emerged as one of the major focal points of national and local concern. Yet there have been very few attempts to develop a comprehensive, long-run strategy for dealing with the complex forces that have created our explosive ghetto problems.

Historically, the word "ghetto" meant an area in which a certain identifiable group was compelled to live. The word retains this meaning of geographic constraint, but now refers to two different kinds of constraining forces. In its *racial* sense, a ghetto is an area to which members of an ethnic minority, particularly Negroes, are residentially restricted by social, economic, and physical pressures from the rest of society. In this meaning, a ghetto can contain wealthy and middle-income residents as well as poor ones. In its *economic* sense, a ghetto is an area in which poor people are compelled to live because they cannot afford better accommodations. In this meaning, a ghetto contains mainly poor people, regardless of race or color.

Considerable confusion arises from failure to distinguish clearly between these different meanings of the word "ghetto." In the remainder of this analysis, I will use the word in its racial sense unless otherwise noted.[1]

The Population of Ghettos

In March 1966, there were 12.5 million nonwhites living in all U.S. central cities, of whom 12.1 million were Negroes. Since the Negroes were highly segregated residentially, this number serves as a good estimate of the 1966 ghetto population in the racial sense. Approximately 39 per cent of these racial ghetto residents had incomes below the "poverty level" (the equivalent of $3,300 per year for a four-person household), based upon data for 1964 (the latest available).[2]

On the other hand, in 1964 the total number of persons with incomes below the "poverty level" in all U.S. central cities was about 10.1 million. Approximately 56 per cent of these persons were white and 44 per cent were nonwhite.[3] Since there were about 11.3 million nonwhites altogether in central cities in 1964, the ghetto in its purely economic sense contained about 11 per cent fewer people than in its racial sense. Moreover, about 4.4 million persons were doubly ghetto residents in 1964—they were central-city citizens who were both poor and nonwhite.[4]

No matter which ghetto definition is used, it is clear that the population of ghettos is a small fraction of total U.S. population—less than 7 per cent. Moreover, future growth in the ghetto population will be dwarfed by future growth in the suburbs of metropolitan areas, which are predominantly white. From 1960 through 1980, those suburbs will gain about 40.9 million persons.[5] Thus the *growth* of suburban population in this period will be almost twice as large as the *total size* of all U.S. ghettos by 1980.

Any policies designed to cope with the ghetto must recognize that the concentrations of Negro population in our central cities are growing rapidly. In 1950, there were 6.5 million Negroes in central cities. In 1960, there were 9.7 million. This represents an increase of 49.2 per cent, or an average of 320,000 persons per year. In the same decade, the white population of central cities went from 45.5 million to 47.7 million, an increase of 2.2 million, or 4.8 per cent. However, in the largest central cities, the white population actually declined while the Negro population rose sharply.[6]

Since 1960, the growth of nonwhite population in central cities has continued unabated. White population growth in all those cities taken together has, however, ceased entirely. In 1966 the total Negro population of all central cities was about 12.1 million. This is a gain of 2.4 million since 1960, or about 400,000 persons per year. Thus the *absolute* rate of growth of ghettos per year has gone up to its highest level in history. In contrast, the white population of central cities in 1965 was 46.4 million, or 1.3 million *less* than in 1960. So for all 224 central cities considered as a whole, all population growth now consists of gains in Negro population.[7]

Moreover, nearly all Negro population growth is now occurring in ghettos, rather than in suburbs or rural areas. From 1960 to 1966,

89 per cent of all nonwhite population growth was in central cities, and 11 per cent was in suburbs. Nonmetropolitan areas (including the rural South) actually *lost* nonwhite population. This indicates that heavy out-migration from rural areas to cities is still going on.[8]

Future Ghetto Growth If Present Policies Continue

All evidence points to the conclusion that future nonwhite population growth will continue to be concentrated in central cities unless major changes in public policies are made. Not one single significant program of any federal, state, or local government is aimed at altering this tendency or is likely to have the unintended effect of doing so.[9] Moreover, although nonwhite fertility rates have declined since 1957 along with white fertility rates, ghetto growth is likely to remain rapid because of continued in-migration, as well as natural increase.

Recent estimates made by the National Advisory Commission on Civil Disorders indicate that the central-city Negro population for the whole U.S. will be about 13.6 million in 1970 and could rise to as high as 20.3 million by 1985. These estimates assume continued nonwhite in-migration at about the same rate as prevailed from 1960 to 1966. But even if net in-migration is reduced to zero, the 1985 central-city Negro population would be about 17.3 million.[10]

Within individual cities, rapid expansion of segregated ghetto areas will undoubtedly continue. Our 1967 field surveys in Chicago show that about 2.9 city blocks *per week* are shifting from predominantly white to nonwhite occupancy, mainly on the edge of already nonwhite areas. This is somewhat lower than the 3.5 blocks-per-week average from 1960 to 1966, but above the average of 2.6 from 1950 to 1960.[11] If such "peripheral spread" of central-city ghettos continues at nearly the same rate—and there is no present reason to believe it will not—then a number of major central cities will become over 50 per cent Negro in total population by 1985. These cities include Chicago, Philadelphia, St. Louis, Detroit, Cleveland, Oakland, Baltimore, New Orleans, Richmond, and Jacksonville. Washington, D.C., Newark, and Gary are already over 50 per cent Negro. The proportion of nonwhites in the public school systems in most of these cities now exceeds 50 per cent. It will probably be approaching 90 per cent by 1983—unless major changes in school programs and districting are adopted before then.[12]

This future growth has critical implications for a great many policy objectives connected with ghettos. For example, it has been suggested that school district boundaries within central cities should be manipulated so as to counteract *de facto* segregation by creating districts in which many Negroes and many whites will jointly reside. This solution is practical over the long run only when there is reasonable stability in the total size of these two groups. But when one group is rapidly expanding in a city where there is no vacant land to build additional housing, then the other group must contract. The only alternative is sharp rises in density which are not occurring. Therefore, as the Negro population expands in such cities, the white population inevitably falls. So possibilities for ending *de facto* segregation in this manner inexorably shrink as time passes. For this and other reasons, no policy toward ghettos can afford to ignore this rapid expansion of the Negro population.

The Complexity of the Ghetto Population and Ghetto Problems

To be accurate, every analysis of ghettos and their problems must avoid two tempting oversimplifications. The first is conceiving of the ghetto population as a single homogeneous group, all of whose members have similar characteristics, attitudes, and desires. Thus, because many ghetto residents are unemployed or "underemployed" in low-paying, transient jobs, it is easy—but false—to think of all ghetto households as plagued by unemployment. Similarly, because some ghetto residents have carried out riots and looting, whites frequently talk as though *all* ghetto dwellers hate whites, are prone to violence, or are likely to behave irresponsibly. Yet all careful studies of recent riots show that only a small minority of ghetto residents participated in any way, a majority disapprove of such activity, and most would like to have more contact with whites and more integration.[13]

In reality, each racial ghetto contains a tremendous variety of persons who exhibit widely differing attitudes toward almost every question. Many are very poor, but just as many are not. Many have radical views—especially young people; many others are quite conservative—especially the older people. Many are "on welfare," but many more are steadily employed.

This diversity means that public policy concerning any given ghetto problem cannot be successful if it is aimed at or based upon the attitudes and desires of only one group of persons affected by that problem. For example, take unemployment. Programs providing job training for young people could, if expanded enough, affect a large proportion of ghetto dwellers. But the inability of many adult ghetto men to obtain and keep steady, well-paying jobs is also a critical ghetto problem.[14] Also, many women with children cannot work because no adequate day-care facilities are available. Thus, public policy concerning every ghetto problem must have many complex facets in order to work well.

A second widely prevalent oversimplification of ghetto problems is concentration of remedial action upon a single substandard condition. For instance, improving the deplorable housing conditions in many slums would not in itself eliminate most of the de-humanizing forces which operate there. In fact, no single category of programs can possibly be adequate to cope with the tangled problems that exist in ghettos. Any effective ghetto-improvement strategy must concern itself with at least jobs and employment, education, housing, health, personal safety, crime prevention, and income maintenance for dependent persons. A number of other programs could be added, but I believe these are the most critical.[15]

The Location of New Jobs

Most new employment opportunities are being created in the suburban portions of our metropolitan areas, not anywhere near central-city ghettos.[16] Furthermore, this trend is likely to continue indefinitely into the future. It is true that downtown office-space concentrations in a few large cities have created additional jobs near ghettos. But the out-flow of manufacturing and retailing jobs has normally offset this addition significantly—and in many cases has caused a net loss of jobs in central cities.

If we are going to provide jobs for the rapidly expanding ghetto population, particularly jobs that do not call for high levels of skills, we must somehow bring these potential workers closer to the locations of new employment opportunities. This can be done in three ways: by moving job locations so new jobs are created in the ghetto, by moving ghetto residents so they live nearer the new jobs, or by creating better transportation between the ghetto and the locations of new jobs. The first alternative—creating new jobs in the ghetto—will not occur in the future under normal free-market conditions, in my opinion.

That nearly all *new* job opportunities will be located in suburbs does not mean that central cities cannot provide *any* employment to their Negro residents. There are still millions of jobs located in central cities. Just the turnover in workers regarding those jobs will open up a great many potential positions for Negro central-city residents in the future—if employers and other workers cease racial discrimination in their hiring and promotion practices. Nevertheless, as the total number of Negro central-city job-seekers steadily rises, the need to link them with emerging sources of new employment in the suburbs will become more and more urgent as a means of reducing unemployment in Negro neighborhoods.

Recently, a number of proposals have been advanced to create public subsidies or guaranteed profits encouraging free enterprise to locate new jobs in ghettos.[17] It is possible that they might work to some extent if the promised profits are high enough to offset the risks and disadvantages involved. Any ghetto improvement strategy must, however, face the problem of linking up persons who need employment with those firms which can provide it or those public agencies assigned to create it.

The Future "Cost Squeeze" on Local Governments

Traditionally, individual productivity has risen faster in the manufacturing, mining, construction, and agricultural sectors of our economy than in sectors where personal services are dominant —such as finance, insurance, and real estate; retailing; services; and government. The ability to employ larger amounts of capital per worker, coupled with technological change, has caused much larger increases in hourly output-per-worker in the former sectors than in the latter.

All sectors compete with one another for talent and personnel, and all use many of the same products as basic inputs. This means that wages and salaries in the service-dominated sectors must generally keep up with those in the capital-dominated sectors. This tends to place a "squeeze" on the cost of those activities for which individual productivity is hard to increase.

A recent analysis of the performing arts by economists William

Baumol and William Bowen highlighted this type of "cost squeeze" as the major reason why it is so difficult to sustain theaters, opera, symphonies, and ballet companies on a self-supporting basis.[18] A pianist cannot perform Chopin's Minute Waltz in 30 seconds, or spend half as much time learning how to play it, to improve efficiency. Yet his salary and the salaries of all the electricians, accompanists, administrators, and others needed for the performing arts are constantly raised to keep their living standards comparable with those of people in the sectors where wage gains can be offset by productivity increases.

Baumol has argued that a similar "cost squeeze" is one of the reasons why state and local expenditures have risen so fast in the postwar period. They increased 257 per cent from 1950 to 1966, as compared to 159 per cent for Gross National Product and 206 per cent for federal expenditures.[19] Moreover, Baumol believes that this pressure to increase service-oriented wages and salaries faster than real output-per-man-hour in the service-oriented sectors will generate an even bigger "explosion" of local and state government costs in the future. For one thing, a higher fraction of society is now and will be employed in public activities than ever before. So there is a steady increase in the proportion of persons whose compensation tends to rise faster than their real output. This reflects both rapid automation in non-service-oriented sectors and an increasing shift of consumer demand toward such services as education, entertainment, and government activities of all types.

The resulting upward pressure on local and state government costs—and tax needs—will undoubtedly be offset to some extent by two forces. The first is greater automation of services themselves through use of computers, closed-circuit TV, duplicating machines, and other devices. The second is the partial substitution of semiskilled and low-skilled assistants for highly-skilled professionals. For example, teachers' aids could relieve professional teachers of immense amounts of administration and paperwork, thereby freeing the latter for more effective use of their time.

Nevertheless, the huge future growth of suburban population will almost certainly force a continuance of the trend toward rising local and state taxes that has now gone on for twenty years. Similar upward pressure on revenue needs will be felt even more strongly by central-city governments. Center cities will contain ever higher proportions of low-income residents who need more services per capita than wealthier suburbanites.

This future "cost squeeze" is important to our analysis because of its impact upon the willingness of suburban taxpayers to help finance any large-scale programs aimed at improving ghetto conditions. Such programs would almost certainly require significant income redistribution from the relatively wealthy suburban population to the relatively poor central-city population. Yet suburbanites will be experiencing steadily rising local and state tax burdens to pay for the services they need themselves.

The "Law of Dominance"

The achievement of stable racial integration of both whites and nonwhites in housing or public schools is a rare phenomenon in large American cities. Contrary to the views of many, this is *not* because whites are unwilling to share schools or residential neighborhoods with nonwhites. A vast majority of whites of all income groups would be willing to send their children to integrated schools or live in integrated neighborhoods, *as long as they were sure that the white group concerned would remain in the majority* in those facilities or areas.

The residential and educational objectives of these whites are not dependent upon their maintaining any kind of "ethnic purity" in their neighborhoods or schools. Rather, those objectives depend upon their maintaining a certain degree of "cultural dominance" therein.[20] These whites—like most other middle-class citizens of any race—want to be sure that the social, cultural, and economic milieu and values of their own group dominate their own residential environment and the educational environment of their children. This desire in turn springs from the typical middle-class belief of all racial groups that everyday life should be primarily a *value-reinforcing* experience for both adults and children, rather than primarily a *value-altering* one. The best way to insure that this will happen is to isolate somewhat oneself and one's children in an everyday environment dominated by—but not necessarily exclusively comprised of—other families and children whose social, economic, cultural, and even religious views and attitudes are approximately the same as one's own.

There is no intrinsic reason why race or color should be perceived as a factor relevant to attaining such relative homogeneity. Clearly, race and color have no necessary linkage with the kinds of social, cultural, economic, or religious characteristics and values that can have a true functional impact upon adults and children. Yet I believe a majority of middle-class white Americans still perceive race and color as relevant factors in their assessment of the kind of homogeneity they seek to attain. Moreover, this false perception is reinforced by their lack of everyday experience and contact with Negroes who are, in fact, like them in all important respects. Therefore, in deciding whether a given neighborhood or a given school exhibits the kind of environment in which "their own" traits are and will remain dominant, they consider Negroes as members of "another" group.

It is true that some people want themselves and their children to be immersed in a wide variety of viewpoints, values, and types of people, rather than a relatively homogeneous group.[21] This desire is particularly strong among the intellectuals who dominate the urban planning profession. They are also the strongest supporters of big-city life and the most vitriolic critics of suburbia. Yet I believe their viewpoint—though dominant in recent public discussions of urban problems—is actually shared by only a tiny minority of Americans of any racial group. Almost everyone favors at least some exposure to a wide variety of viewpoints. But experience in our own society and most others shows that the overwhelming majority of middle-class families choose residential locations and schools precisely in order to provide the kind of value-reinforcing experience described above. This is why most Jews live in predominantly Jewish neighborhoods, even in suburbs; why Catholic parents continue to support separate school systems; and partly why so few middle-class Negro families have been willing to risk moving to all-white suburbs even where there is almost no threat of any harassment.

However demeaning this phenomenon may be to Negroes, it must be recognized if we are to understand why residential segregation has persisted so strongly in the United States, and what conditions are necessary to create viable racial integration. The expansion of nonwhite residential areas has led to "massive transition" from white to nonwhite occupancy mainly because there has been no mechanism that could assure the whites in any given area that they would remain in the majority after nonwhites once began entering. Normal population turnover causes about 20 per cent of the residents of the average U.S. neighborhood to move out every year because of income changes, job transfers, shifts in life-cycle position, or deaths. In order for a neighborhood to retain any given character, the persons who move in to occupy the resulting vacancies must be similar to those who have departed.

But once Negroes begin entering an all-white neighborhood near the ghetto, most other white families become convinced that the area will eventually become all Negro, mainly because this has happened so often before. Hence it is difficult to persuade whites not now living there to move in and occupy vacancies. They are only willing to move into neighborhoods where whites are now the dominant majority and seem likely to remain so. Hence the whites who would otherwise have moved in from elsewhere stop doing so.[22] This means that almost all vacancies are eventually occupied by nonwhites, and the neighborhood inexorably shifts toward a heavy nonwhite majority. Once this happens, the remaining whites also seek to leave, since they do not wish to remain in an area where they have lost their culturally dominant position.

As a result, whites who would be quite satisfied—even delighted—to live in an integrated neighborhood *as members of the majority* are never given the opportunity to do so. Instead, for reasons beyond the control of each individual, they are forced to choose between complete segregation or living in an area heavily dominated by members of what they consider "another group." Given their values, they choose the former.

Many—especially Negroes—may deplore the racially prejudiced desire of most white middle-class citizens to live in neighborhoods and use schools where other white middle-class households are dominant. Nevertheless, this desire seems to be firmly entrenched among most whites at present. Hence public policy cannot ignore this desire if it hopes to be effective. Moreover, this attitude does not preclude the development of racial integration, as long as whites are in the majority and believe they will remain so. The problem is convincing them that their majority status will persist in mixed areas in the face of past experience to the contrary. Even more difficult, the people who must be persuaded are not those now living in a mixed area, but those who must keep moving in from elsewhere to maintain racial balance as vacancies occur through normal population turnover.

Clearly, the dynamic processes related to this "Law of Dominance" are critical to any strategy concerning the future of American ghettos. They are especially relevant to strategies which seek to achieve stable residential or educational integration of whites and nonwhites, instead of the "massive transition" and "massive segregation" which have dominated the spatial patterns of nonwhite population growth in the past twenty years. Such stable integration will occur in most areas only if there is some way to guarantee the white majority that it will remain the "dominant" majority. This implies some form of "quotas" concerning the proportion of nonwhites in the facility or area concerned—even legally supported "quotas."

Unless some such "balancing devices" are *explicitly* used and reinforced by public policies and laws to establish their credibility, whites will continue to withdraw from—or, more crucially, fail to keep entering—any facility or area into which significant numbers of nonwhites are entering. This means a continuation of *de facto* segregation and a reinforcement of the white belief that any nonwhite entry inevitably leads to "massive transition." Even more importantly, it means continued failure to eliminate white perception of race as a critical factor by encouraging whites and nonwhites to live together in conditions of stability. Thus, in my opinion, the only way to destroy the racial prejudice at the root of the "Law of Cultural Dominance" is to shape current public policy in recognition of that "Law" so as to encourage widespread experience that will undermine it.[23]

The Concept of Social Strategy

Americans typically do not attempt to solve social problems by means of behavior patterns that could reasonably be considered "strategies." The concept of strategy implies development of a single comprehensive, long-range plan to cope with some significant social problem. But U.S. decision-making concerning domestic issues is too fragmented and diffused to permit the formulation of any such long-range plan regarding a given problem. Instead, we approach most social problems through a process which has been aptly labeled "disjointed incrementalism."[24] Each decision-maker or actor makes whatever choices seem to him to be most appropriate at that moment, in light of his own interests and his own view of the public welfare. For two reasons, he pays little attention to most of the consequences of his action upon others—especially the long-run consequences. First, no one has the detailed knowledge and foresight necessary to comprehend all those consequences. Second, no one has the time nor the energy to negotiate in advance with all others likely to be affected by his actions. So instead he acts "blindly" and waits for those who are hurt to complain or those who are benefited to applaud.

A process of mutual adjustment ensues. Those who are unduly harmed by each decision supposedly recoup their losses by exercising whatever economic, moral, or political powers are available to them. Those who benefit use their powers to encourage more of the same. Presiding over this melee is a set of mainly "reactive" governments and other public agencies. They keep altering the "rules of the game" and their own programs and behavior so as to correct any grievous imbalances that appear.

There is no guarantee that the checks and balances built into this uncoordinated process will effectively counteract every destructive condition or trend that emerges from it. It is certainly possible that each individual will be motivated by the incentives facing him to take actions that, when combined with those taken by others acting in a similar individualistic fashion, will lead to collective disaster.

So far in history, the system has been remarkably effective at avoiding such outcomes. Part of this success undoubtedly results from society's ability to generate in most of its citizens a single set of basic values and even broad policy objectives that exert a cohesive influence on their supposedly individualistic decisions. But another important ingredient in the system's success is the ability of enough significant actors in it to perceive threatening trends in time to formulate and carry out ameliorating policies.

This means they must accurately forecast any potentially dire outcome of current trends. They must also visualize alternative outcomes that would be preferable and are within the capabilities of society. Finally, they must devise policies and programs that will shift individual incentives so one of those alternatives will occur. In some cases, the ongoing trends that threaten society are strongly entrenched in its institutional structure. If so, alternatives that avoid the pending threats may not be attainable without fundamental changes in institutions. Those changes in turn may be possible only if a preponderance of powerful people in society share at least a broad concept of the need for change and the kinds of objectives motivating it. This concept closely resembles a social strategy. It visualizes a certain desired outcome, implies a wide range of policies by various actors necessary to attain that outcome, and serves as a "hidden coordinator" of seemingly individualistic behavior.

The above reasoning implies two conclusions crucial to this analysis. First, strategic thinking about social problems can play a vital role in stimulating social change even where decision-making is dominated by disjointed incrementalism. Second, the alternative outcomes conceived in such thinking can usefully include some which could not be achieved without major changes in existing institutions or values. For example, some of the strategies discussed herein require a highly coordinated set of policy decisions. Such coordination is unlikely to occur in the presently fragmentalized governmental structures of our metropolitan areas unless major changes in the incentives facing these governments are created.

I will therefore formulate several alternative strategies for coping with the problems posed by future ghetto growth, even though carrying out some of them would require a far more consciously coordinated development of social change than has been typical of America in the past.

Formulation of Major Alternative Strategies

Because of the immense complexity of our society, an infinite number of alternative future strategies regarding ghettos could conceivably be designed. But for purposes of practical consideration, this number must be narrowed drastically to a few that highlight the major choices facing us. Selecting these few is inescapably arbitrary—there is no "scientific" way to do it. I believe, however, that the narrowing of alternative ghetto futures can best be accomplished by focusing upon the major choices relating to the following three questions:

> To what extent should future nonwhite population growth be concentrated within the central cities, as it has been in the past twenty years?

> To what extent should our white and nonwhite populations be residentially segregated from each other in the future?

> To what extent should society redistribute income to relatively depressed urban areas or population groups in society in a process of "enrichment"?

Each of these questions can be answered with any one of a whole spectrum of responses from one extreme to the other. But for purposes of analysis, I believe we can usefully narrow these answers down to just two points on the spectrum for each question. This allows us to reduce the alternatives to the following:

Degree-of-Concentration Alternatives
1. Continue to concentrate nonwhite population growth in central cities or perhaps in a few older suburbs next to central cities. *(Concentration)*
2. Disperse nonwhite population growth widely throughout all parts of metropolitan areas. *(Dispersal)*

Degree-of-Segregation Alternatives
1. Continue to cluster whites and nonwhites in residentially segregated neighborhoods, regardless of where they are within the metropolitan area. *(Segregation)*
2. Scatter the nonwhite population, or at least a significant fraction of it, "randomly" among white residential areas to achieve at least partial residential integration. *(Integration)*

Degree-of-Enrichment Alternatives
1. Continue to provide relatively low-level welfare, educational, housing, job training, and other support to the most deprived groups in the population—both those who are incapable of working, such as the vast majority of public-aid recipients, and those who might possibly work, but are unemployed because of lack of skills, discrimination, lack of desire, or any other reason. *(Non-enrichment)*
2. Greatly raise the level of support to welfare, educational, housing, job-training, and other programs for the most deprived groups, largely through federally aided programs. *(Enrichment)*

Even narrowing the alternatives in this fashion leaves a logical possibility of eight different combinations. A number of these can, however, be ruled out as internally inconsistent in practice. For example, I believe it is extremely unlikely that any strategy of dispersing the nonwhite population throughout metropolitan areas could be accomplished without provision of substantially greater incentives to both nonwhites (to get them to move) and whites (to increase their willingness to accept large numbers of nonwhite in-migrants without strong resistance). Thus no combination of both dispersal and non-enrichment need be considered.

Similarly, in the very long run, concentration of future non-white population growth within central cities is probably inconsistent with integration. Many of those cities will become so preponderantly nonwhite that integration within their borders will be impossible. Admittedly, it may take two or more decades for this to occur in some central cities, and it might never occur in others. Nevertheless, some types of integration (such as in the public schools) will become impossible long before that if a concentration policy is followed. For these reasons, I will consider only one special combination containing both concentration and integration. This consists of continued concentration, but a build-up of a gradually expanding inner-city core of fully integrated housing and public facilities created through massive urban renewal. For reasons explained below, this strategy would require a significant enrichment program too.

This whole process of elimination leaves five basic alternative strategies relevant to future development of ghettos. For convenience, each has been assigned a short name to be used throughout the remainder of this article. These strategies can be summarized as follows:

1. *Present Policies:* concentration, segregation, non-enrichment.

2. *Enrichment Only:* concentration, segregation, enrichment.

3. *Integrated Core:* concentration, integration (in the center only), enrichment.

4. *Segregated Dispersal:* dispersal, segregation, enrichment.

5. *Integrated Dispersal:* dispersal, integration, enrichment.

Before these strategies are examined in detail, two things about them should be emphasized.

First, they apply to individual metropolitan areas. Therefore, it would be at least theoretically possible to adopt different strategies toward the ghetto in different metropolitan areas. There are, in fact, some convincing reasons why this would be an excellent idea.

Second, these strategies are formed from relatively extreme points on the relevant ranges of possibilities. Hence they could actually be adopted in various mixtures, rather than in the "pure" forms set forth above. This further strengthens the case for using a variety of approaches across the country. For purposes of analysis, however, it is fruitful to examine each of these strategies initially as though it were to be the sole instrument for coping with ghetto problems in all metropolitan areas.

The Present-Policies Strategy

In order to carry out this strategy, we need merely do nothing more than we do now. Even existing federal programs aimed at aiding cities—such as the Model Cities Program—will continue or accelerate concentration, segregation, and non-enrichment, unless those programs are colossally expanded.

I do not wish to imply that present federal and local efforts in the anti-poverty program, the public housing program, the urban renewal program, health programs, educational programs, and many others are not of significant benefit to residents of ghettos. They are. Nevertheless, as both recent investigations and recent violence have emphasized, existing programs have succeeded neither in stemming the various adverse trends operating in ghetto areas nor in substantially eliminating the deplorable conditions there. Therefore, the strategy of continuing our present policies and our present level of effort is essentially not going to alter current conditions in ghettos.

This may make it seem silly to label continuation of present policies as a specific anti-ghetto strategy. Yet failure to adopt effective policies is still a strategy. It may not be a successful one, but it nevertheless is an expression of society's current commitment and attitude toward the ghetto.

Thus, if we maintain our current programs and policies, segregated areas of residence in our central cities will continue to expand rapidly and to suffer from all the difficult problems inherent in both racial and economic ghettos.

The Enrichment-Only Strategy

The second fundamental ghetto future strategy I call "enrichment only." This approach is aimed at dramatically improving the quality of life within the confines of present ghetto areas and those nearby areas into which ghettos will expand in the future if concentration continues. I presume that any such policy would apply to the poverty meaning of ghetto more than the racial one—that is, any enrichment strategy would aim at upgrading the lowest-income and most disadvantaged citizens of our central cities, regardless of race. Nevertheless; a sizable proportion of such persons are nonwhites. Moreover, programs aimed at reducing racial discrimination in employment and in the quality of public services would form an important part of any strategy aimed at upgrading the most deprived groups. So the enrichment-only strategy would still concentrate upon the same areas as if it were to follow a racial policy.

The basic idea underlying the enrichment-only strategy (and part of every other strategy involving enrichment) is to develop federally financed programs that would greatly improve the education, housing, incomes, employment and job-training, and social services received by ghetto residents. This would involve vastly expanding the scale of present programs, changing the nature of many of them because they are now ineffective or would be if operated at a much larger scale, and creating incentives for a much greater participation of private capital in ghetto activities. Such incentives could include tax credits for investments made in designated ghetto areas, wage subsidies (connected with on-the-job training but lasting longer than such training so as to induce employers to hire unskilled ghetto residents), rent or ownership supplements for poor families, enabling them to rent or buy housing created by private capital, and others.[25]

It is important to realize that the enrichment-only strategy would end neither racial segregation nor the concentration of non-whites in central cities (and some older adjoining suburbs). It would help many Negroes attain middle-class status and thus make it easier for them to leave the ghetto if they wanted to. Undoubtedly many would. But, by making life in central-city ghettos more attractive without creating any strong pressures for integration or dispersal of the nonwhite population, such a policy would increase the in-migration of nonwhites into central cities. This would speed up the expansion of racially segregated areas in central cities, thereby accelerating the process of "massive transition" of whole neighborhoods from white to nonwhite occupancy.

The Integrated-Core Strategy

This strategy is similar to the enrichment-only strategy because both would attempt to upgrade the quality of life in central-city ghettos through massive federally assisted programs. The integrated-core strategy would also seek, however, to eliminate racial segregation in an ever expanding core of the city by creating a socially, economically, and racially integrated community there. This integrated core would be built up through large-scale urban renewal programs, with the land re-uses including scattered-site public housing, middle-income housing suitable for families with children, and high-quality public services—especially schools.

All of these re-uses would be based upon "managed integration" —that is, deliberate achievement of a racial balance containing a majority of whites but a significant minority of Negroes. Thus, the integrated-core strategy could be carried out only if deliberate racial discrimination aimed at avoiding *de facto* segregation becomes recognized by the Supreme Court as a legitimate tactic for public agencies. In fact, such recognition will probably be a necessity for any strategy involving a significant degree of integration in public schools, public housing, or even private residential areas. This conclusion was re ntly recognized by the Chicago Board of Education, its staff, and its consultants, who all recommended the use of quotas in schools located in racially changing neighborhoods to promote stable integration.[26]

The integrated-core strategy essentially represents a compromise between an ideal condition and two harsh realities. The ideal condition is development of a fully integrated society in which whites and Negroes live together harmoniously and the race of each individual is not recognized by anyone as a significant factor in any public or private decisions.

The first harsh reality is that the present desire of most whites to dominate their own environment means that integration can only be achieved through deliberate management and through the willingness of some Negroes to share schools and residences as a minority. The second harsh reality is the assumption that it will be impossible to disperse the massive Negro ghettos of major central cities fast enough to prevent many of those cities from eventually becoming predominantly, or even almost exclusively, Negro in population. The development of predominantly Negro central cities, with high proportions of low-income residents, ringed by predominantly white suburbs with much wealthier residents, might lead to a shattering polarization that would split society along both racial and spatial lines.

This strategy seeks to avoid any such polarization by building an integrated core of white and nonwhites in central cities, including many leaders of both races in politics, business, and civic affairs. Negro leadership will properly assume the dominant position in central-city politics in many major cities after Negroes have become a majority of the municipal electorates there. By that time, integration of leadership within those cities will, it is to be hoped, have become a sufficient reality so that leaders of both races can work together in utilizing the central city's great economic assets, rather than fighting one another for control over them.

Thus, the integrated-core strategy postulates that a significant movement toward racial integration is essential to keep American society from "exploding" as a result of a combined racial-spatial confrontation of central cities vs. suburbs in many large metropolitan areas. It also postulates that development of integration in the suburbs through massive dispersal cannot occur fast enough to avoid such a confrontation. Therefore, integration must be developed on an "inside-out" basis, starting in the core of the central city, rather than in the suburbs.

The Concept of Dispersal

The two dispersal strategies concerning the future of ghettos are both based upon a single key assumption: that the problems of ghettos cannot be solved so long as millions of Negroes, particularly those with low incomes and other significant disadvantages, are required or persuaded to live together in segregated ghetto areas within our central cities. These strategies contend that large numbers of Negroes should be given strong incentives to move voluntarily from central cities into suburban areas, including those in which no Negroes presently reside.

To illustrate what "large numbers" really means, let us postulate one version of dispersal which I call the "constant-size ghetto strategy." This strictly hypothetical strategy aims at stopping the growth of existing central-city ghettos by dispersing enough Negroes from central cities to the suburbs (or to peripheral central-city areas) to offset potential future increases in that growth. Taking the period from 1970 through 1975, estimates made by the National Advisory Commission on Civil Disorders show that the nonwhite population of all U.S. central cities taken as a whole would, in the absence of any dispersal strategy, expand from about 13.6 million to about 15.5 million.[27] Thus, if dispersal of nonwhites were to take place at a scale large enough to keep central-city racial ghettos at their 1970 level during the five subsequent years, there would have to be an out-movement of 1.9 million Negroes into the suburbs. This amounts to 380,000 per year.

From 1950 to 1960, the suburban Negro population of all U.S. metropolitan areas grew a total of only 60,000 per year. In that decade, the white population of suburban portions of our metropolitan areas (the so-called "urban fringe") increased by about 1,720,000 persons per year. Thus, 96.6 per cent of all suburban population growth consisted of whites. From 1960 to 1966, the Negro population growth in all suburban areas declined sharply to a rate of 33,300 per year. In fact, there was actually in-migration of Negroes from suburbs to central cities. But the white population in all suburbs went up an average of 1,750,000 per year. Thus the proportion of suburban growth made up of whites climbed to 98.1 per cent—an even higher fraction than in the decade from 1950 to 1960.[28] Undoubtedly, some of this white population increase was caused by an exodus of whites from central cities in response to the growth therein. If future Negro population growth in central cities were stopped by a large-scale dispersion policy, then white population growth in the suburbs would be definitely smaller than it was from 1950 through 1966. The size of the resulting decline would depend upon the fraction of white exodus from central cities that occurs in response to Negro growth, as opposed to such other factors as rising incomes, the aging central-city housing stock, and shifts in life-cycle position. If whites leave central cities in a one-to-one ratio with the expansion of Negro population therein, then a cessation of Negro ghetto growth would result in a large drop in white suburban growth. In that case, future suburban population increases would consist of about 23 per cent Negroes (based on very rough calculations). This contrasts with proportions of less than 5 per cent from 1950 through 1960 and less than 3 per cent from 1960 through 1966.

Clearly, such dispersal would represent a radical change in existing trends. Not only would it stop the expansion of Negro ghettos in central cities, but it would also inject a significant Negro population into many presently all-white suburban areas. It is true that policies of dispersal would not necessarily have to be at this large a scale. Dispersal aimed not at stopping ghetto growth, but merely at slowing it down somewhat could be carried out at a much lower scale. Yet even such policies would represent a marked departure from past U.S. practice.

Such a sharp break with the past would be necessary for any significant dispersal of Negroes. Merely providing the *opportunity* for Negroes to move out of ghettos would, at least in the short run, not result in many moving. Even adoption of a vigorously enforced nationwide open-occupancy law applying to *all* residences would not greatly speed up the present snail's-pace rate of dispersion. Experience in those states that have open-occupancy ordinances decisively proves this conclusion.

Hence, positive incentives for dispersion would have to be created in order to speed up the rate at which Negroes voluntarily move from central cities and settle in suburban areas. (Certainly no policy involving *involuntary* movement of either whites or Negroes should ever be considered.) Such incentives could include rent supplements, ownership supplements, special school-support bonus payments linked to the education of children moving out from ghettos, and other devices which essentially attach a subsidy to a person. Then, when the person moves, he and the community into which he goes get credit for that subsidy. This creates incentives both for him to move and for the community to accept him gladly. Both of the strategies involving dispersal would thus represent radical changes in existing practices.

Segregated vs. Integrated Dispersal

One of the fundamental purposes of any dispersal strategy is providing Negro Americans with real freedom of choice concerning housing and school accommodations. The experience of other ethnic groups indicates that Negroes would exercise that choice in suburban areas in a combination of two ways. Some individual Negro households would become scattered "randomly" in largely white residential areas. But other Negro households—probably a larger number—would voluntarily cluster together. This would create primarily Negro neighborhoods, or even primarily Negro suburban communities. Such a combination of both *scattering* and *clustering* would occur even if Negro households had absolutely no fears of hostility or antagonism from white neighbors. It is unrealistic to suppose, however, that *all* prejudice against Negro neighbors can be eliminated from presently all-white suburbs in the immediate future. As a result, even if a dispersal strategy is carried out, there will still be some external pressure against Negro newcomers. This will encourage an even higher proportion of in-coming Negro households to cluster together than would do so in the absence of all fears and antagonism. Moreover, public policies to accomplish dispersion might include deliberate creation of some moderate-sized clusters of Negro families, as in scattered-site public housing developments.

Once all-Negro clusters appear in previously all-white suburbs, there is a high probability that they will turn into "ghetto-lets" or "mini-ghettos." The same forces that produced ghettos in central cities are likely to repeat themselves in suburbs, though in a much less pathological form. Those pressures are a rapidly expanding Negro population, the "Law of Cultural Dominance" among whites, and at least some restriction of Negro choice in areas far removed from existing all-Negro neighborhoods. Therefore, once a Negro cluster becomes large enough so that Negro children dominate a local elementary school, the typical phenomenon of white withdrawal from the local residential real-estate market is likely to occur. This has already taken place regarding Jews and gentiles in many suburban areas. Thus, any dispersal strategy that does not explicitly aim at preventing segregation, too, will probably create new segregated neighborhoods in the suburbs.

This new form of *de facto* segregation will, however, have far less damaging effects upon Negroes than existing segregation concentrated in central cities. In the first place, if Negro clusters are deliberately created in almost all parts of the metropolitan area at once, whites will be unable to flee to "completely safe" suburbs without accepting impractically long commuting journeys. This will strongly reduce the white propensity to abandon an area after Negroes begin entering it. Moreover, the presence of some Negroes in all parts of suburbia will also make it far easier for individual Negro families to move into all-white neighborhoods on a scattered basis. Thus any dispersal policy that really disperses Negroes in the suburbs will immediately create an enormous improvement in the real freedom of residential choice enjoyed by individual Negro families. This will be true even if most of those families actually choose to remain in Negro clusters.

Second, any dispersal strategy would presumably be accompanied by strongly enforced open-occupancy laws applying to all housing. At present, these laws do not lead to scattering, but they would in the climate of a dispersal strategy. Then Negro willingness to move into all-white areas would rise sharply, and white antagonism toward such move-ins would drop.

Third, *de facto* residential segregation need not lead to segregated suburban schools. In relatively small communities, such as most suburbs, it is easy to bus students to achieve stable racial balance. Thus, the formation of clustered Negro housing would not have to cause the quality-of-education problems that now exist in central-city ghettos. True, if a given suburb became predominantly Negro, its schools might become quite segregated. In that case, school systems in adjoining suburbs might have to merge or at least work out student exchange procedures with the segregated community in order to counteract segregation. This may be difficult to accomplish (though in the climate of a dispersal strategy, it would be at least thinkable). Hence it is possible that some segregated school systems might appear in suburban areas. But Negro families would still have far more opportunities than they do now to move to areas with integrated schools.

A dispersal strategy that did not succeed in initially placing Negro households in almost all parts of the metropolitan area would be more likely to generate "ghetto-lets." Hence, if dispersal tactics call for initially concentrating on dispersion only to a few suburbs, it is quite possible that segregated dispersal would result. This implies that integrated dispersal could be attained in only two ways. Either the initial dispersal strategy must place Negroes in almost all suburban communities, or specific integration-furthering mechanisms—such as school and residential quotas—must be adopted.

The speculative nature of the above discussion illustrates that society needs to do much more thinking about what dispersal really means, how it might be achieved, what alternative forms it might take, and what its consequences would be.

In an article of this length, it is impossible to present an adequate analysis of each of the strategies described above. Certain factors will, however, have a crucial influence on which strategy actually prevails. These factors should be at least briefly mentioned here.

The Possibility of a Spatial-Racial "Confrontation"

Society's existing policies toward the ghetto are, by definition, those called for by the present-policies strategy. Yet there are strong reasons to believe that maintenance of these policies in ghettos is not possible. The striking increase in violence in big-city ghettos is probably related to a combination of higher aspirations, reduced sanctions against the use of violence, and continued deplorable slum conditions. If so, persistence of the present-policies strategy may continue to spawn incidents, riots, and perhaps guerrilla warfare. Then existing local police forces might have to be supplemented with para-military forces on continuous alert. Thus, the present-policies strategy might lead to further polarization of whites and Negroes and even to the creation of semi-martial law in big cities.

Moreover, when Negroes become the dominant political force in many large central cities, they may understandably demand radical changes in present policies. At the same time, major private capital investment in those cities might virtually cease if white-dominated firms and industries decided the risks of involvement there were too great. In light of recent disorders, this seems very likely. Such withdrawal of private capital has already occurred in almost every single ghetto area in the U.S. Even if private investment continues, big cities containing high proportions of low-income Negroes would need substantial income transfers from the federal government to meet the demands of their electorates for improved services and living conditions.

But by that time, Congress will be more heavily influenced by representatives of the suburban electorate. The suburbs will comprise 41 per cent of our total population by 1985, as opposed to 33 per cent in 1960. Central cities will decline from 31 per cent to 27 per cent.[29] Under a present-policies strategy, this influential suburban electorate will be over 95 per cent white, whereas the central-city population in all metropolitan areas together will be slightly over 60 per cent white. The suburban electorate will be much wealthier than the central-city population, which will consist mainly of Negroes and older whites. Yet even the suburbs will be feeling the squeeze of higher local government costs generated by rising service salaries. Hence the federal government may refuse to approve the massive income transfers from suburbs to central cities that the mayors of the latter will desperately need in order to placate their relatively deprived electorates. After all, many big-city mayors are already beseeching the federal government for massive aid—including Republicans like John Lindsay—and their electorates are not yet dominated by low-income Negroes.

Thus the present-policies strategy, if pursued for any long period of time, might lead to a simultaneous political and economic "confrontation" in many metropolitan areas. Such a "confrontation" would involve mainly Negro, mainly poor, and fiscally bankrupt larger central cities on the one hand, and mainly white, much wealthier, but highly taxed suburbs on the other hand. Some older suburbs will also have become Negro by that time, but the vast majority of suburbs will still be "lily white." A few metropolitan areas may seek to avoid the political aspects of such a confrontation by shifting to some form of metropolitan government designed to prevent Negroes from gaining political control of central cities. Yet such a move will hardly eliminate the basic segregation and relative poverty generating hostility in the urban Negro population. In fact, it might increase that population's sense of frustration and alienation.

In my opinion, there is a serious question whether American society in its present form could survive such a confrontation. If the Negro population felt itself wrongly "penned in" and discriminated against, as seems likely, many of its members might be driven to supporting the kind of irrational rebellion now being preached by a tiny minority. Considering the level of violence we have encountered already, it is hard to believe that the conditions that might emanate from a prolonged present-policies strategy would not generate much more. Yet the Negro community cannot hope to defeat the white community in a pitched battle. It is outnumbered 9 to 1 in population and vastly more than that in resources. Thus any massive resort to violence by Negroes would probably bring even more massive retaliation by whites. This could lead to a kind of urban *apartheid*, with martial law in cities, enforced residence of Negroes in segregated areas, and a drastic reduction in personal freedom for both groups, especially Negroes.

Such an outcome would obviously violate all American traditions of individual liberty and Constitutional law. It would destroy "the American dream" of freedom and equal opportunity for all. Therefore, to many observers this result is unthinkable. They believe that we would somehow "change things" before they occurred. This must mean that either the present-policies strategy would not lead to the kind of confrontation I have described, or we would abandon that strategy before the confrontation occurred.

Can the Present-Policies Strategy Avoid "Confrontation"?

What outcomes from a present-policies strategy might prevent this kind of confrontation? For one thing, if incomes in the Negro community rise rapidly without any additional programs, the Negro population of central cities may enter the middle class at a fast rate. If so, the Negro electorate that comes to dominate many major central cities politically by 1985 under the present-policies strategy may consist largely of stable, well-to-do citizens capable of supporting an effective local government.

To test this possibility, we have done some projections of incomes in the nonwhite population on a rough basis through 1983, assuming a present-policies strategy. These indicate that about two thirds of the nonwhite population at that time will have incomes *above* the existing poverty level—about the same fraction as at present. Since nonwhites will then form a much larger share of total central-city population, however, the percentage of *total* central-city population below the present poverty level might actually *rise* slightly. It is possible that nonwhite incomes might increase faster than in this forecast. Yet it is almost certain that the substitution of a relatively poor nonwhite group for a middle-income white group in central cities under a status-quo strategy will counterbalance likely increases in the incomes of nonwhites.

As a result, the electorate that will exist in major cities when Negroes become a majority will probably be just as poor as it is now (in real income terms). In contrast, the population in surrounding suburbs will be much wealthier than it is now. Thus, even if nonwhite incomes rise rapidly, there is still likely to be a significant "gap" between central-city and suburban income levels at that time—probably larger than at present.

Yet even under *present* conditions, many large central cities are critically short of revenue. Furthermore, in a generally wealthier society, it is highly probable that most central-city electorates will demand higher-than-existing levels of public service. Finally, the general cost of all government services will have risen sharply because of the productivity trends explained earlier. Hence, future central-city governments will have much higher costs, but not much greater resources than they do now. So rising incomes among nonwhites will not remove the fiscal pressure on central-city governments that is a key ingredient in the "confrontation" described above.

Moreover, the population group most responsible for violence and disturbances in central cities appears to consist of young Negro men between fifteen and twenty-four years of age. A high proportion of these people are unemployed because they lack skills (many are high school dropouts) and elementary training and motivation. This group will undoubtedly grow larger through natural increase and in-migration. Its problems are not likely to be solved under a status-quo strategy. Hence, even if the vast majority of nonwhites in central cities have increasing reason to abhor violence and riots, the *absolute size* of this more alienated group in 1975 will be 40 per cent larger than in 1966, and even larger by 1985.[30] This implies that at least part of this group might start actions forcing the kind of "confrontation" I have described.

Most of the other possible developments under a non-enrichment strategy that would avoid any major "confrontation" involve abandoning concentration of Negroes in central cities. Thus, some observers argue that members of the Negro middle class will increasingly move out to suburban communities as their incomes rise with no further encouragement from public programs. In this way, Negroes would be following the precedent of other ethnic groups. Up to now, there is no evidence that this has started to occur, even though a large Negro middle class already exists. But if such a pattern did evolve, it would amount to dispersal rather than the concentration implicit in the present-policies strategy.

Can Present Policies Be Sustained?

In any event, there appears to be significant probability—which I subjectively judge to be at least 25 per cent and perhaps as high as 75 per cent—that the present-policies strategy will prove unsustainable. If adopted, it would probably generate major repercussions that would force it to be abandoned. Society would be compelled either to suspend traditional individual rights and adopt martial law in cities or to institute major programs to improve ghetto conditions or to move toward wider dispersal of the Negro population, or some combination of these. Admittedly, there is no certainty that the present-policies strategy will lead to these outcomes. Nevertheless, I believe the probability that it will is high enough to make this strategy essentially self-defeating. Modern life is too dynamic for the status quo to be preserved for long.

Yet the present-policies strategy is the one society has so far chosen. Almost all current public policies tend to further concentration, segregation, and non-enrichment, as mentioned earlier. The few supposedly anti-concentration devices adopted, such as open-occupancy laws, have proved almost totally ineffective. All we have to do to confirm our choice of this strategy is to continue existing policies. In fact, avoiding this strategy will be difficult, because doing so will require major changes in present attitudes as well as in existing resource allocations.

The "Black Power" Case for the Enrichment-Only Strategy

The enrichment-only strategy is consistent with a current ideology that has come to be called the "Black Power" viewpoint. This viewpoint has been criticized by many, and some of its proponents have misused it to incite violence. Yet it is certainly an intellectually respectable and defensible position containing some persuasive elements.

The "Black Power" argument states that the Negro American population needs to overcome its feelings of powerlessness and lack of self-respect before it can assume its proper role in society. It can do so only by exerting power over the decisions that directly affect its own members. According to this view, a fully integrated society is not really possible until the Negro minority has developed its own internal strength. Therefore, the ideal society in which race itself is not an important factor can only come much later. It could exist only after Negroes had gained power and self-respect by remaining in concentrated areas over which they could assume political and economic control and direction. Hence this view contends that a future in which central cities become primarily Negro and suburbs almost entirely white would be an advantage rather than a disadvantage.

The "Black Power" view has several notable strong points. First, such assumption of local power would be fully consistent with the behavior of previous nationality groups, such as the Irish in New York and Boston. They, too, came up from the bottom of the social and economic ladder, where they had been insulted and discriminated against. And they did it by gaining political and economic control over the areas in which they lived.

Second, it is unquestionably true that one of the two most important factors providing Negroes with all their recent gains in legal rights and actual welfare has been their own forceful presentation of grievances and demands. (The other factor has been high-level prosperity in the economy in general.) Negro-originated marches, demonstrations, protests, and even riots have had immensely more impact in improving their actual power, income, and opportunities than all the "purely voluntary" actions of whites combined—including those of white liberals.

Third, time is on the side of the "Black Power" argument if current population growth and location trends continue. As pointed out earlier, Negroes are likely to become a majority of the electorate in many large American cities within the next fifteen years, unless radically new policies are adopted. By giving Negroes political control over these cities, this trend would provide them with a powerful bargaining position in dealing with the rest of society—a tool they now sorely lack.

Fourth, the "Black Power" viewpoint provides many key ideological supports for Negro self-development. It stresses the need for Negroes to become proud of their color and their history, more conscious of their own strengths. It also focuses their attention on the need for organizing themselves economically and politically. Hence it could provide a focal point for arousing and channeling the largely untapped self-development energies of the Negro American population. One of the greatest difficulties in improving ghettos is discovering effective ways in which the lowest-income and most deprived residents can develop their own capabilities by participating more fully in the decisions and activities that affect them. Such "learning by doing" is, in my opinion, a vital part of the process of bringing deprived people into the main stream of American society. Insofar as "Black Power" proponents could develop such mechanisms, they would immensely benefit American society.

There are, however, also significant flaws in the "Black Power" argument. First, Negroes do not in fact have much power in the U.S. Nor is it clear just how they can obtain power solely through their own efforts, particularly in the near future. "Black Power" advocates constantly talk about "taking what is rightfully theirs" because they are dissatisfied with what "whitey" is willing to turn over to them voluntarily. They also reject the condescension inherent in whites' "giving" Negroes anything, including more power. But what bargaining power can Negroes use to compel whites to yield greater control over the economic and political decisions that affect them?

There are two possible answers. First, they could organize themselves so cohesively that they would become a potent political and economic force through highly disciplined but fully legal action. Examples would be block voting and economic boycotts. So far, nearly all efforts at such internal organization have foundered on the solid rocks of apathy, lack of funds, internal dissension, and disbelief that anything could be accomplished.

Second, Negroes could launch direct action—such as demonstrations and marches—that would morally, economically, or physically threaten the white community. This approach has so far proved to be the most successful. But many Negroes believe it has not improved their situation as fast as is necessary. Hence, there is a tendency to shift the form of threat employed to more and more violent action in order to get faster and more profound results. This tendency need only influence a small minority of Negroes in order to cause a significant escalation of violence. Yet such an escalation might result in massive retaliation by the white community that would worsen the Negroes' position. What is needed is enough of a threat to cause the white community to start changing its own attitudes and allocation of resources in ways far more favorable to Negroes, but not so much of a threat as to cause withdrawal of all white cooperation and sympathy.

This conclusion points up the second flaw in the "Black Power" case: Ultimately, U.S. Negroes cannot solve their own problems in isolation, because they are fully enmeshed in a society dominated by whites. The solution to Negro problems lies as much in the white community as in the Negro community. This is especially true because whites control the economic resources needed to provide Negroes with meaningful equality of opportunity. Hence, any strategy of action by Negro leaders that totally alienates the white community is doomed to failure.

Yet "Black Power" advocates are probably correct in arguing that Negroes must develop an ideology that focuses upon self-determination and therefore has some "anti-white" tinges. They need an "enemy" against which to organize the Negro community. History proves that organization *against* a concrete opponent is far more effective than one *for* some abstract goal. They also need an abrasive ideology that threatens whites enough to open their eyes to the Negroes' plight and their own need to do something significant to improve it. The question is how they can accomplish these goals without going too far and thereby creating violent anti-white hostility among Negroes and equally violent anti-Negro sentiment among whites.

In the past few years, many Negro Americans—including prominent community leaders—have shifted their sights away from direct racial integration as a goal. Instead they have focused upon other goals more consistent with the "Black Power" viewpoint. They want better housing, better schools, better jobs, and better personal security within all-Negro areas—and a much stronger Negro voice in controlling all these things. These enrichment-only objectives have apparently eclipsed their desire for greater ability to enter directly into white-dominated portions of the society. This rather dramatic change in values appears to rule out much possibility of Negroes' accepting either dispersal strategy.

In my opinion, the main cause of this shift in objectives is the failure of white society to offer any real hope for large-scale integration. After years of seeking equality under the law, Negro leaders have discovered that even removal of legal barriers is not producing much progress toward a true sharing in the life of white-dominated society. Why should they keep knocking on the door if no one will answer? Why not turn instead to existing all-Negro communities and try to improve conditions there? Indeed, I believe continued white refusal to engage in meaningful, large-scale integration will make it impossible for any self-respecting Negroes to avoid espousing some version of the "Black Power" viewpoint. Understandably, they will not be able to accept the conclusion that most of the millions of Negroes whom whites force to live racially segregated lives must therefore be condemned to inferior educations, housing, culture, or anything else.

Rather, they will reason, there must be some way to make the quality of life in all-Negro portions of a racially segregated society just as good as it is in the all-white portions. And if equality in terms of the indices of desirability accepted by whites cannot be achieved, then some of these "Black Power" advocates will be willing to attain at least nominal equality by denouncing those indicators as specious. They will further claim—with some justification—that life in all-white portions of society cannot be better and may be morally worse because whites suffer from racial blindness.

The reason why this argument is and will be advanced so strongly is certainly understandable. Those who advance it would hardly be human if they were not at least tempted to do so. As long as present white attitudes and behavior persist, adopting any other view amounts to despairing of any chance at equality for most Negroes.

The "Black Power" viewpoint essentially argues that racially separate societies in America can provide equal opportunities for all their members if Negroes are able to control their own affairs. Yet there is a great deal of evidence that this argument is false.

Certainly concerning employment, equality of opportunity for Negroes cannot possibly be attained in a segregated labor market. Negroes must be provided with full freedom and equality regarding entry into and advancement within the white-dominated enterprises that are overwhelmingly preponderant in our economy. Only in this way can they have any hope of achieving an occupational equality with whites.

In education, the evidence is far more ambiguous. The recent reports of the Office of Education and the Civil Rights Commission contend that both racial and economic integration are essential to the attainment of educational equality for Negroes.[32] Yet critics of these reports point out that many types of enrichment programs were not tested in the studies conducted by the authors. Unfortunately, most alternative approaches have not yet been tried on a scale large enough to determine whether any of them will work. Yet one conclusion does seem reasonable: Any real improvement in the quality of education in low-income, all-Negro areas will cost a great deal more money than is now being spent there, and perhaps more than is being spent per pupil anywhere.

Thus, society may face a choice between three fundamental alternatives: providing Negroes with good-quality education through massive integration in schools (which would require considerably more spending per pupil than now exists), providing Negroes with good-quality education through large-scale and extremely expensive enrichment programs, or continuing to relegate many Negroes to inferior educations that severely limit their lifetime opportunities. The third alternative is what we are now choosing. Whether or not the second choice—improving schools in all-Negro areas—will really work is not yet known. The enrichment alternative is based upon the as-yet-unproven premise that it will work.

Regarding housing, the enrichment-only strategy could undoubtedly greatly improve the quantity, variety, and environment of decent housing units available to the disadvantaged population of central cities. Nevertheless, it could not in itself provide Negroes of *any* economic level with the same freedom and range of choice as whites with equal incomes have. Clearly, in this field "separate but equal" does not mean *really* equal. Undoubtedly, all-white suburban areas provide a far greater range and variety of housing and environmental settings than can possibly be found in central cities or all-Negro suburbs alone.

Moreover, there is an acute scarcity of vacant land in many of our largest central cities. Therefore, greatly expanding the supply of decent housing for low-income families in those cities at a rapid rate requires creating many new units for them in the suburbs too.

Thus, if society adopts one of the many possible versions of the enrichment-only strategy, it may face the prospect of perpetuating two separate societies—one white and one Negro—similar to those that would develop under the present-policies strategy. If the enrichment programs carried out proved highly effective, then the gap between these two societies in income, education, housing, and other qualities of life would be nowhere near so great as under the present-polities strategy. Hence, the possibility of a potentially catastrophic "confrontation" between these two societies sometime in the next twenty years would be greatly reduced.

Nevertheless, I do not believe it will really be possible to create two separate societies that are truly equal. Therefore, even if the enrichment-only strategy proved extraordinarily successful at improving the lot of disadvantaged central-city residents of all races and colors (which is by no means a certainty), it would still leave a significant gap in opportunity and achievement between the separate white and Negro societies which would continue to emerge over the next twenty years. This gap would remain a powerful source of tension that might lead to violence, for experience proves that men seeking equality are not placated by even very great absolute progress when they perceive that a significant gap remains between themselves and others in society who are no more deserving of success than they. And that would be precisely the situation twenty years from now under the enrichment-only strategy—whether linked to "Black Power" concepts or not.

Why Dispersal Should Be Seriously Considered

As pointed out earlier, either of the two dispersal strategies would require radical changes in current trends and policies concerning the location of Negro population growth. Moreover, it is likely that massive dispersal would at present be opposed by *both* suburban whites and central-city Negroes. Many of the former would object to an influx of Negroes, and many of the latter would prefer to live together in a highly urbanized environment. Why should we even consider a strategy that is not only socially disruptive, but likely to please almost nobody?

In my opinion, there are five reasons why we should give enrichment plus dispersal serious consideration. First, future job-creation is going to be primarily in suburban areas, but the unskilled population is going to be more and more concentrated in central-city ghettos unless some dispersion occurs. Such an increasing divergence between where the workers are and where the jobs are will make it ever more difficult to create anything like full employment in decent jobs for ghetto residents. In contrast, if those residents were to move into suburban areas, they would be exposed to more knowledge of job opportunities and would have to make much shorter trips to reach them. Hence they would have a far better chance of getting decent employment.

Second, the recent U.S. Office of Education and U.S. Civil Rights Commission reports on equality of achievement in education reach a *tentative* conclusion that it is necessary to end the clustering of lower-income Negro students together in segregated schools in order to improve their education significantly.[33] As I understand these reports, they imply that the most significant factor in the quality of education of any student is the atmosphere provided by his home and by his fellow students both in and out of the classroom. When this atmosphere is dominated by members of deprived families, the quality of education is inescapably reduced—at least within the ranges of class size and pupil-teacher ratios that have been tried on a large scale. Therefore, if we are to provide effective educational opportunities for the most deprived groups in our society to improve themselves significantly, we must somehow expose them to members of other social classes in their educational experience. But there are not enough members of the Negro middle class "to go around," so to speak. Hence this means some intermingling of children from the deprived groups with those from not-so-deprived white groups, at least in schools. Because of the difficulties of bussing large numbers of students from the hearts of central cities to suburban areas, it makes sense to accomplish this objective through some residential dispersal. This consideration tends to support the integrated-dispersal strategy to some extent, even though these reports have received significant criticism, as noted above.

Third, development of an adequate housing supply for low-income and middle-income families and provision of true freedom of choice in housing for Negroes of all income levels will require out-movement of large numbers of both groups from central cities to suburbs. I do not believe that such an out-movement will occur "spontaneously" merely as a result of increasing prosperity among Negroes in central cities. Even the recently passed national open-occupancy law is unlikely to generate it. Rather, a program of positive incentives and of actual construction of new housing in suburban areas will be necessary.

Fourth, continued concentration of large numbers of Negroes under relatively impoverished conditions in ghettos may lend to unacceptably high levels of crime and violence in central cities. The outbreak of riots and disorders in mostly nonwhite areas in our central cities in the past few years is unprecedented in American history. As the report of the National Advisory Commission on Civil Disorders indicates, continuing to concentrate masses of the nonwhite population in ghettos dominated by poverty and permeated with an atmosphere of deprivation and hopelessness is likely to perpetuate or intensify these disorders. This could lead to the disastrous outcome already discussed in connection with the present-policies strategy.

Fifth, a continuation of ghetto growth will, over the next three or four decades, produce a society more racially segregated than any in our history. We will have older, blighted central cities occupied by millions of Negroes, and newer, more modern suburban areas occupied almost solely by whites. Prospects for moving from that situation to a truly integrated society in which race is not a factor in key human decisions are not encouraging. In fact, by that time we will be faced with a fantastically more massive dispersal problem than the present one if we really want to achieve a society integrated in more than just words.

Thus, only the two enrichment-plus-dispersal strategies explicitly seek to create a single society rather than accepting our present perpetuation of two separate societies: one white and one Negro. Dispersal would involve specific policies and programs at least starting us toward reversal of the profoundly divisive trend now so evident in our metropolitan areas. It may seem extraordinarily difficult to begin such a reversal. But however difficult it may be now, it will be vastly more difficult in twenty years if the number of Negroes segregated in central cities is 8 million larger than it is today.

The Difficulty of Gaining Acceptance for Dispersal

I am fully aware that any strategy involving significant dispersal may now seem wholly impractical to responsible politicians and social leaders. The voluntary movement of large numbers of Negroes from ghettos to the suburbs encouraged by federal programs presupposes radical changes in existing attitudes among both suburban whites and central-city Negroes.

In spite of our social mobility, Americans are extremely sensitive to class differentiations. We have deliberately developed class-stratified suburban areas. Residents of each suburb use zoning, tax rates, lot-size requirements, and other devices to exclude persons considered farther down the ladder of social and economic prominence. As each group and each family moves upward in our mobile society, they become more concerned about creating social distance between themselves and those now below them—including those who were once equal to them.

I certainly do not deplore the historic traditions of self-improvement and protection of amenities and privileges that have been won through hard work and perseverance. These traditions should and will continue in some form, because it is proper for successful people to enjoy the fruits of their efforts.

Nevertheless, it is at least possible that the social objective of upgrading the lowest and most deprived groups in our society cannot be accomplished if we simultaneously insist upon excluding those groups from nearly all daily contact with other more fortunate people—as we do now—by maintaining extremely rigid class distinctions by geographic area. Thus, the best dispersal policy might be one that promoted day-to-day inter-class and inter-racial experiences without changing the dominant socio-economic character of the receiving suburban areas. This would allow persons moving out from the inner city to benefit from the existing character of those suburbs. Such a policy implies that the newcomers would comprise a minority in each area into which they went. This means that an integrated-dispersal strategy might ultimately provide the most desirable form of dispersal. It would enable the group that was already there to maintain nearly intact their conception of the proper standards for that community, while sharing the benefits of those standards with others.

Even this change in attitude, however, presupposes a shift in values of profound magnitude among white middle-class Americans. Furthermore, I doubt that most Negroes today want to live in white communities in which they would be relatively isolated from other Negroes. Hence they might prefer a segregated-dispersal strategy, if they were willing to accept dispersal at all. Yet, since most suburban areas are already incorporated into predominantly white communities, where and how could such a strategy be initiated?

Some Tactical Mechanisms for Encouraging Dispersal

Any attempt to achieve dispersal must involve specific answers to two basic questions:

What *mechanisms* can be designed to encourage voluntary out-movement of large numbers of Negroes into the suburbs and their peaceful acceptance and welcome by whites there?

What *incentives* can be developed leading particular interest groups in society to press politically for—or at least support—employment of those mechanisms?

Let us consider the mechanisms first. Americans have always used one basic approach to get people to overcome inertia and make voluntarily some socially desirable change. It consists of providing a significant economic or other reward for persons who behave in the desired manner. That reward might be free land (as for homesteaders and railroads in the nineteenth century), or tax reductions (as for homeowners or investors in equipment in the past few years), or direct payments (as for farmers), or services and income supplements tied to participation in specific programs (as for users of the G.I. Bill in education).

In the case of dispersion, I believe the system of rewards used should probably have the following characteristics[31]:

1. Advantages should accrue both to the Negro households moving out from central cities and to the suburban households into whose communities the newcomers move.

2. Whenever possible, these advantages should consist of rewards administered under metropolitan-area-wide organizations specifically set up for such a purpose. These organizations
could be quasi-private bodies able to cooperate directly with
existing local governments and other geographically limited
organizations. Hence they would *not* be metropolitan governments.

3. Advantages to out-moving households might include the
following:

The possibility of sending their children to top-quality
schools that receive special grants because of participation
in programs involving out-moving children.

Home-buying or renting financial aids available only to
out-moving families or at least with assigned proportions
of their total funding available only to such families.

Top-priority access to special programs concerning employment and on-the-job training in suburban industrial
and other firms. In my opinion, such programs might
be effectively built around the self-selection principle
embodied in the G.I. Bill—that is, eligible persons would
be given certificates enabling those firms who hire them
to receive special benefits to compensate for their lower
productivity or training costs. Such benefits might include tax credits or direct payments. The persons receiving these certificates would then make their own choice
of employers among firms participating in such programs.
This would preserve maximum individual choice among
program participants.

4. Advantages to households already living in the receiving
areas might include:

Special aid to schools receiving children of out-moving
Negro families. Such aid should consist of funds linked
to the students in such families. (as Title I funding under
the Elementary and Secondary Education Act is now
linked to low-income families). But the per-student
amount of aid given should greatly exceed the added
direct cost of teaching each out-moving student. Hence

the school district concerned would have a positive incentive to accept such students because of the financial "bonuses" they would bring with them. Those bonuses could be used to upgrade the entire receiving school or cut locally-borne costs therein.

"Bonus" community financing to participating suburban local governments. Again, the payments involved should significantly exceed the added costs of servicing in-coming families, so that each participating community would be able to improve other services too.

Giving higher priority in other federal programs to communities participating in out-movement programs than to those refusing to participate. These related programs could include sewer and water financing, planning aid, and selection as locations for federal installations.

5. Benefits available for out-moving families and receiving areas could be restricted by geographic area to avoid either paying people discriminately by race or wasting funds paying families who would move out anyway. A precedent for giving residents of certain neighborhoods special benefits already exists in the urban renewal and Model Cities programs. Thus, specific ghetto neighborhoods could be designated "origination" areas and largely white suburban communities designated "receiving" areas. Benefits would accrue only to persons moving from the former to the latter or to residents of the latter participating in reception programs.

6. If these programs were part of an integrated-dispersal strategy, they could be linked to quota systems concerning newcomers to each school or community involved. Thus, the special bonus aids would be available only up to a certain fraction of the total school enrollment or residential population of a given receiving community. This restriction would be aimed at retaining in the schools or communities concerned the dominance of the groups originally residing there. It is to be hoped that the result would be suburban integration, rather than a shift of massive neighborhood transition from central cities to suburbs.

The above suggestions are highly tentative and exploratory. Yet

I hope they at least indicate that practical mechanisms can be created that might achieve a substantial amount of peaceful Negro out-movement—*if* they were adopted in a general atmosphere of social encouragement to dispersal.

Some aspects of the basic approach described above may seem terribly unjust. In particular, this approach rewards the advantaged (those already living in suburbs) as well as the disadvantaged (those moving out of deprived areas into suburbs) in order to get the former to accept the latter. Yet that is a key mechanism, one which free-enterprise systems have always employed when they seek to attain high-priority ends through voluntary action. Our society abounds with arrangements that provide special economic advantages to those who are already privileged, presumably in order to evoke socially desired behavior from them. Examples are oil depletion allowances, stock option plans for top executives, profitable contracts for defense firms, lower tax rates on capital gains, and subsidy payments to wealthy farmers. I am defending neither the equity nor the effectiveness of these particular examples. Yet they illustrate that we often adopt public policies that pay the rich to undertake behavior which presumably benefits society as a whole.

A second aspect of the approach to dispersal I have described which might seem harsh is that no benefits apparently accrue to disadvantaged persons who fail to move out to the suburbs. As stated earlier, however, I believe dispersal programs should only be undertaken simultaneously with large-scale ghetto enrichment programs. The latter would provide comparable, or even greater, benefits for those "left behind" in central cities—who will undoubtedly comprise the vast majority of Negroes in our metropolitan areas for many years to come.

Developing Political Support for Dispersal

The concept of dispersal will remain nothing but an empty theory unless a significant number of Americans decide their best interests lie in politically supporting specific dispersal mechanisms. It is conceivable that such support might result from a massive "change of heart" among white suburbanites. They might view dispersal as a way to "purge themselves" of the kind of "white racism" which the National Advisory Commission on Civil Disorders described. I do not think this will occur. In fact, I believe recent urban violence has tended to make white suburbanites more hostile than ever to the idea of having Negroes live next door to them.

Yet, on the other hand, several specific groups in society are beginning to realize that dispersal might benefit them immensely. The motivation of persons in these groups varies widely, from pure moral guilt to sheer self-interest. But almost all significant social change in the United States has occurred because a wide variety of different types of people with diverse motives have formed a coalition to accomplish something. In my opinion, only through that kind of process will any of the basic strategies I have described (except the present-policies strategy) ever be achieved.

I believe the groups favorable to dispersal now include, or soon will include, the following:

> Suburban industrialists. In many metropolitan areas, they are experiencing acute labor shortages, particularly of un-skilled workers. They will soon be willing to provide open and powerful political support for the construction of low-income and moderate-income housing for Negro workers and their families in currently all-white suburbs.

> Downtown-oriented retailers, bankers, restaurant opera-tors, hotel operators, and other businessmen in our larger cities. In cities where disorders have penetrated into cen-tral business districts (such as Milwaukee and Washing-ton), many former patrons have stopped visiting these areas altogether—especially at night. If disorders in these areas get worse, the impact upon both consumer patron-age and future capital investment in big-city downtowns could be catastrophic. Those whose enterprises are "locked in" such areas will soon realize they must vigorously support both stronger law enforcement and positive pro-grams aimed at alleviating Negro discontent. At first, these programs will consist primarily of ghetto enrich-ment, but these groups will soon begin to support dispersal too.

> Home builders. They would benefit from any large-scale programs of housing construction. But the delays and difficulties of carrying out such programs within central

cities are much greater than they are on vacant suburban land. Hence they will eventually exert at least low-level support for dispersal if it means large-scale subsidy of privately built homes.

White central-city politicians in large cities. As the populations of their cities shift toward Negro majorities, they will be more and more willing to support some dispersal policies, as well as the enrichment programs they now espouse.

Businessmen in general with plants, offices, or other facilities "locked in" large central cities. An increasing number of such persons will realize that they will emerge losers from any major "confrontation" between black-dominated central cities and white-dominated suburbs, as described earlier.

Persons of all types whose consciences influence them to accept the National Advisory Commission's conclusion that dispersal of some kind is the only way to avoid perpetuating two separate societies, with the Negro one forever denied equality.

Since these groups now constitute a small minority of Americans a great many other Americans must change their existing values considerably if large-scale dispersal is ever to occur. Yet the alternatives to such a strategy—especially the one we are now pursuing—could conceivably lead us to equally grave changes in values. For example, if there is an extremely significant increase in violence in Negro ghettos which spills over into all-white areas, the white population might react with harshly repressive measures that would significantly restrict individual freedoms, as noted above. This, too, would call for a basic shift in our values. But it is a shift which I regard with much more alarm than the one required by a dispersal strategy. In fact, in this age of rapid technological change, it is naïve to suppose that there will not in the future be significant alterations in attitudes that we presently take for granted.

The Scale of Efforts Required

The foregoing discussion emphasizes that any strategy likely to have a significant impact upon ghettos will require a very much larger effort than we are now devoting to this problem. Even a "pure" ghetto-enrichment strategy, which does not eliminate or even slow down the growth of the racial ghetto, would require a significantly greater allocation of financial and manpower resources to coping with the problems of the urban poor. A dispersal strategy that addresses itself to breaking up or at least slowing down the growth of the racial ghetto would also require even more profound changes in values and attitudes. Only the first strategy—that of continuing our present activities—requires no immediate change in effort or values. But it may eventually result in significant value changes too—and perhaps far less desirable ones than are required by the other two alternatives.

Thus, there is simply no easy way to cope with this problem. In my opinion, past federal programs and many currently suggested approaches have suffered from the desire to find a cheap solution to what is an extremely expensive problem. The problem is expensive in terms not only of money, but also of our national talents and our willingness to change our basic values. In one way or another, we must and will accommodate ourselves to this problem. We cannot evade it.

Creating the Programs and Incentives Necessary to Achieve Any Desired Ghetto Future

Each strategy contains two basic parts: a desired outcome and a set of actions designed to achieve that outcome. I have not placed equal emphasis on these two parts in discussing each of the five strategies concerning ghetto futures. For example, the present-policies strategy as I have described it is essentially a set of actions—the continuation of present policies. Hence it does not emphasize a desired outcome. In fact, I have pointed out several reasons why its outcome might be quite undesirable. Conversely, my discussion of the enrichment-only strategy has focused upon its outcome. Hence I have not made many suggestions about how that outcome might be brought about. Similar emphasis upon the outcome rather than the means of attaining it also marks the discussion of the integrated-core strategy. Even my tentative analysis of how dispersal might be carried out hardly represents a complete blueprint for action.

Any strategy is really just wishful thinking until it links the outcome it envisions with some feasible means of attaining that outcome. This is especially true regarding several of the ghetto futures I have described, since they embody such radical changes in society. They are likely to remain largely fantasies, rather than real alternatives, until specific programs for achieving them can be defined. I have made some program suggestions in connection with dispersal strategies in order to prove that dispersal is not totally unrealistic. Unfortunately, the complexity of developing similar suggestions for the other strategies involving social change prevents my attempting to do so in this article.

Nevertheless, there are five basic principles crucial to formulating such programs.

1. No proposed "solution" to ghetto problems that is not eventually supported by the majority of the white middle class can possibly succeed.[35]

2. The actions designed to bring about any desired outcome must be linked to incentives that will appeal both to the self-interest of all groups concerned and to their consciences. In fact, the most difficult part of implementing any strategy (other than the present-policies strategy) will be providing effective incentives for the relatively well-off white majority. This group must be persuaded to expand many resources, and alter its own traditional behavior, in order to produce outcomes that appear to benefit mainly a small minority of the population. As indicated in the discussion of dispersal, each segment of the white majority (such as business, labor, suburbanites, senior citizens, farmers, and so forth) must be presented with arguments and incentives which appeal specifically to its interests. An example is the argument that business suffers great losses of potential profits and output because of the failure of poor Negroes to engage in high-level consumption and the inability of poorly educated Negro workers to help meet high demands for skilled labor.

3. Any program designed to achieve a given outcome should involve significant action by the private sector. Otherwise, society may relegate ghettos to a position of dependency upon government that is inconsistent with full equality in American life. On the other hand, it is naïve to suppose that the private sector can or will bear the huge expense of

coping with ghetto problems unaided. Society as a whole must pay the extra costs of on-the-job training programs, new factories located in ghettos, union training of unskilled Negro apprentices, and other actions aimed at helping the unskilled or otherwise "left out" enter the main stream of our economy. These actions must be carried out by non-governmental organizations, but financed by the government through direct payments, tax credits, or other means.

4. No program involving ghettos can be effective unless it involves a high degree of meaningful participation by ghetto residents, and significant exercise of power and authority by them. We must realize that ghettos cannot be drawn into the main stream of American life without some redistribution of authority and power, as well as income, for equality in America means exercise of significant self-determination. Admittedly, lack of skill and experience may cause that exercise to be disorderly, inefficient, and even corrupt at first—as it was among the Irish, Italians, Jews, and others in the past. Therefore, turning over more power in ghetto areas to local residents may actually cause a short-run decline in the professional quality of government there—whether in schools, the police, or local government in general. Yet it will greatly alter the attitudes of residents toward those institutions and begin to draw them into the real functioning of our society. So it should and must come.

5. The more benefits that most ghetto residents receive through programs aimed at helping them, the more dissatisfied and vocally discontent certain small parts of the ghetto community are likely to become. This makes the problem of persuading the white majority to support large-scale aid programs doubly difficult. It also means that socio-economic programs will have to be accompanied by greatly enlarged and improved law-enforcement efforts, particularly those in which ghetto leaders themselves play significant roles. Yet emphasis on improving law enforcement alone, without massively trying to meet the other needs of ghetto residents, will probably prove disastrous. Such one-sided emphasis on "law and order" could easily provoke steadily rising violence shifting in form toward guerrilla warfare. The need to avoid

this outcome further emphasizes the importance of relying more and more on ghetto communities to develop their own internal controls of violence, with outside aid, as is consistent with the preceding principle of greater self-determination.

Merely stating these principles emphasizes how far we are from having designed practical programs to achieve most of the outcomes set forth in this article. In my opinion, one of the most important tasks facing us is the formulation and public discussion of the specific ingredients needed for such programs. But even that cannot be done until we have recognized more explicitly the various possible futures of American ghettos and weighed their relative advantages and disadvantages.

At present, most public discussion and thought about racial and ghetto problems in America suffer from a failure to define or even to consider explicit possible long-range outcomes of public policy. This is one reason why such discussion seems so confused, inchoate, and frustrating. I hope that the ideas set forth in this article can serve as a nucleus for more fruitful public discussion of this crucial topic, for the future of American ghettos will determine to a large extent the future of America itself.

REFERENCES

1. The first draft of this article was written in the early summer of 1967. Subsequently, the author became a consultant to the National Advisory Commission on Civil Disorders. In that capacity, he wrote the rough drafts of several chapters in the Commission's final report. One of these (Chapter 16) contains many of the ideas set forth in this article. Nevertheless, there are sufficient differences between the contents and presentation of Chapter 16 in the Commission's Report and this article to warrant separate publication of the latter. The contents of this article express the thoughts of its author only and do not necessarily represent the views of either the National Advisory Commission on Civil Disorders or Real Estate Research Corporation.

2. Data from the Social Security Administration.

3. *Report of the National Advisory Commission on Civil Disorders* (Washington, D. C.; March 1, 1968), p. 127. This document will hereafter be referred to as the *NACCD Report.*

4. *Ibid.,* pp. 121, 127.

5. Based upon the Census Bureau's Series D projections of future population—the ones assuming the lowest of the four levels of future fertility used by the Census Bureau. See U. S. Bureau of the Census, *Statistical Abstracts of the United States, 1967* (88th Edition; Washington, D. C., 1967), pp. 8-10.

6. *NACCD Report*, p. 121.

7. *Ibid.*

8. *Ibid.*

9. Open-occupancy legislation appears to be aimed at shifting the location of some future nonwhite growth to presently all-white areas. Experience in those states which have had open-occupancy ordinances for some time indicates, however, that they have little, if any, impact in altering the distribution of nonwhite population growth.

10. *NACCD Report*, p. 227.

11. Surveys conducted annually by Real Estate Research Corporation, results unpublished.

12. *NACCD Report*, p. 216.

13. See Raymond J. Murphy and James M. Watson, *The Structure of Discontent*, Mimeographed, Los Angeles: University of California at Los Angeles, June 1, 1967.

14. *NACCD Report*, pp. 123-31.

15. Specific recommendations concerning these subjects are set forth in the *NACCD Report*, Chapter 17.

16. See John F. Kain, "The Distribution and Movement of Jobs and Industry," in *The Metropolitan Enigma*, ed. James Q. Wilson (Washington, D. C., 1967).

17. These include legislative proposals made by Senator Javits, the late Senator Robert Kennedy, and Senator Percy.

18. William Baumol and William Bowen, *The Performing Arts: The Economic Dilemma* (New York: 20th Century Fund).

19. *NACCD Report*, p. 217.

20. Insofar as I know, this principle was first formulated by my father, James C. Downs, Jr.

21. Two well-known urban specialists with such views are Jane Jacobs and Victor Gruen. See Jane Jacobs, *The Life and Death of Great American Cities* (New York, 1961), and Victor Gruen, *The Heart of Our Cities* (New York, 1964).

22. This phenomenon explains why it is so difficult to halt "massive transition" from white to nonwhite occupancy once it begins. It tends to continue

even when whites originally living in the area concerned do not "panic" at all. As long as normal turnover continues to produce vacancies, and only nonwhites fill them, such transition is inescapable. The key persons whose behavior must be affected to stop transition are not the whites living in the area at the outset, but those living scattered elsewhere in the metropolitan area or even other parts of the nation. They are the persons who must move into the areas as vacancies appear in order to maintain racial balance therein. Thus, attempts to organize existing white residents so as to prevent them from fleeing almost always fail to halt transition. Organizers can rarely identify "the whites who aren't there yet," so they cannot influence the decisions of these potential future occupants, and transition continues relentlessly.

23. The U. S. Supreme Court will soon have to face up to the consequences of this "Law." In order to attack *de facto* segregation effectively, it must recognize racial discrimination in the form of school quotas as Constitutional. At present, our society cannot achieve integration or end segregation without deliberate and explicit racial discrimination by public authorities. This is true in relation to other public facilities besides schools, including hospitals and housing.

24. This term and usage were coined by Charles E. Lindblom. See Lindblom and David Braybrooke, *The Strategy of Decision* (New York, 1963).

25. See the *NACCD Report*, Chapter 17.

26. See their statements as quoted in the Chicago *Daily News*, August 25, 1967.

27. *NACCD Report*, p. 227.

28. *Ibid.*, p. 121.

29. These figures are based upon the Census Bureau's Series D population projections. If higher fertility projections are used, the suburbs would contain slightly higher proportions of total population in 1985. See the reference cited in footnote 5.

30. *NACCD Report*, pp. 216-17.

31. This section of the article was written after Chapter 16 of the *NACCD Report* had been completed and closely parallels the contents of certain parts of that chapter.

32. See James Coleman *et al.*, *Equality of Educational Opportunity* (Washington, D. C., 1966), and the U. S. Civil Rights Commission, *Racial Isolation in the Public Schools* (Washington, D. C., 1967).

33. *Ibid.*

34. Many of the programs described in this section have been recommended by the National Advisory Commission on Civil Disorders. See the *NACCD Report*, Chapter 17.

35. This fact is recognized by most Negro leaders not committed to zealously militant separatism. For example, see Kenneth Clark, *Dark Ghetto* (New York, 1965), p. 222.

CITIZEN PARTICIPATION AND POVERTY

Martin Rein and S. M. Miller

Martin Rein and S. M. Miller, "Citizen Participation and Poverty," *Connecticut Law Review,* December 1968, pp. 221-262.

CITIZEN PARTICIPATION AND POVERTY

Martin Rein and S. M. Miller

THIS paper examines the changing character of maximum feasible participation of the poor as it has evolved over the past several years, both prior to and since the inception of the Economic Opportunity Act of 1964. Though participation of the poor can be justified on a variety of grounds, none is more compelling than the assumption that such participation contributes to the reduction of poverty. Indeed, much of the justification for the strategy of involvement grew out of a set of implicit assumptions about how poverty and participation are linked to one another. As these assumptions, both about the meaning of poverty and the contribution of participation to its reduction change, then the forms of participation change accordingly. This observation should not be taken to imply a causal argument that theory leads to action. It is perhaps more accurate to suggest that in the current history of citizen participation accident, discovery, error, and other forces contributed to the various forms of participation which have evolved.

Social policy tends not to develop in a tidy fashion. The forms of citizen participation evolve from a whole set of contradictory, conflicting, and accidental forces. There is no legislative history as to the meaning and intent of Congress in providing for maximum feasible involvement of the poor in the Economic Opportunity Act's definition of community action.[1] There is, however, an administrative history, i.e., a history based on experience.

The different forms of citizen participation embody conflicting values. No effort has been made to resolve these different perspectives. In characteristic fashion, we pursue contradictory programs, *choosing ambiguity as a way of maintaining political viability*. (Note the same reluctance to make key decisions in other OEO programs such as the Job Corps; it was never quite decided whether the program was designed primarily for those who are most deprived, those with the best potential, those who could not read, those who lacked motivation, or for those who are fully motivated but need vocational training.)

Citizen participation is largely a slogan. It has various meanings and

* Professor of Social Work and Social Research, Bryn Mawr College.
** Professor of Education and Sociology, New York University.
1. Economic Opportunity Act of 1964, 46 U.S.C. §§ 113(a)(6) (1964).

forms which co-exist and yet partially succeed each other. Its major forms are still being forged, for no resolution satisfied the diverse interest groups or the expectations invested in it. As the problems of one approach become evident, another model emerges to prominence.

In this paper then, we examine the various interpretations of citizen participation as socio-therapy, as social action, as employment, as rights, as involvement in policy making, as the redistribution of political power, and try to show how these are believed to be linked to the reduction of poverty.

POVERTY AS POWERLESSNESS AND APATHY

Poverty may be seen as caused by the spiritual emptiness of ghetto life and by the apathy of the poor who, alienated from the norms of society, retreat into a protective subculture characterized by social disengagement and indifference. This subculture is often referred to as the culture of poverty. Kenneth Clark has described the stagnation of the poor as their most striking characteristic. The poor have a pervasive sense of futility, which, according to Clark, is not even positive enough to be called cynical. It follows that it is hard to disillusion the poor, for they start with few illusions. Equally, it is hard to engage the poor, for they start with few hopes. It is this theme which explains why Haryou, the predecessor to the community action agency in Harlem, assigned crucial importance to the idea of culture building. The destruction of culture can be understood, as the sub-title of their planning report suggests, as "the consequence of powerlessness." The lack of power derives from the dependency of the Negro to control the events which shape his life. In a discussion of the Negro's crippling dependency on the white community for the solution of the problems of inadequate education of the children of the ghetto, the Haryou report redefines the traditional view of the problem:

> . . . and then the black man goes back home again and says, "I can't solve my problem unless I have a white person at my side; but I can't fight and make a change in this system unless I have a white person at my side; I can't be a man and not ask but take what is mine unless I have a white person at my side." And so he sees that he is in fact, less than a man. To reduce the demoralizing consequences of this form of welfare colonialism, the vitality, anger and energy of youth must be harnessed. Haryou must not attempt

to teach the young person . . . but Haryou must be taught by the young person in Harlem.[2]

The confidence and self-respect of the Negro was to be achieved by his own involvement and participation in shaping and creating his own life; it was the young who would provide the source of leadership. Poverty is caused by powerlessness, and the means to overcome poverty is self-help and participation. The more the Negro himself operated the strategic institutions in ghetto life, the more he would be able to reject welfare colonialism and substitute a vitality of independence and self-respect; the more would poverty defined as powerlessness decline.

This point of view stresses that poverty is not so much a lack of material advantage, in the sense of insufficient economic resources, as it is a lack of power. It assumes that there was something wrong with the poor which left them unprepared to exploit the resources and opportunities available to them. Hence, what was needed was a program to prepare the poor so that they could more effectively use available community institutions and resources. To achieve this aim, the war on poverty created remediation, employability and citizen participation programs. All of these programs share a common rationale—the reduction of the dependency and the apathy of the poor, which would, in turn, give the poor opportunity to participate in the mainstream of American society. The hallmark of OEO programs is training —training for work habits, training for skill development, training for citizenship, training for participation.

But there is a mischievous quality about the term "opportunity." The theory of opening opportunity not only implies the chance to get ahead, but it also implies a strategy of promoting conformity without coercion. Even the opportunity to overcome powerlessness is seen within these terms of reference. The link between power and conformity is contained in the program ideal of trying to promote a competent community. Residents of a community should be able to solve their own problems and control their own destinies by being able to influence the institutions which service them. When resident groups lose the capacity to solve their own problems or the capacity to modify institutional performance in accordance with their needs, one frequent

---

2. Harlem Youth Opportunities Unlimited, Youth in the Ghetto (1964) (report prepared for Presidents' Committee on Delinquency and Youth Crime).

result is a breakdown in the institution of authority. This weakness in turn leads to a breakdown in the mechanisms of social control. The grim product of the incompetent community is the collapse of its control system which leads to the expansion of crime, delinquency, and social deviancy.

This line of argument holds that poverty and delinquency are created by apathy, and by the incompetence of the residents to manage their own affairs and to encourage institutions to develop appropriate solutions to solve emergency problems. Thus, personal incompetence reinforces institutional incompetence. The apathy of the poor prevents them from demanding that the institutions which service them accommodate to their needs. The plight worsened and their capacity for effective action further weakened, a vicious cycle of poverty reinforces a vicious cycle of bureaucratic dysfunctions. To break the cycle, the vigor of local democracy must be restored, and this could best be accomplished by expanding the freedom and the competence of local residents to respond to their local problems. Citizen involvement in local decision-making, through competent local leaders, who understood how best to command the events and institutions which shape their lives, was a major ingredient of the strategy of building a competent community.

This interpretation of the dynamics which link personal and institutional incompetence was accepted by the federal panel which reviewed and passed on local projects requesting funds under the Juvenile Delinquency and Youth Offences Control Act of 1961. There was latent disagreement on the panel between the views of Lloyd Ohlin who focused on the use of established power to change institutions and Leonard S. Cottrell, Jr., who felt that whenever you could restore the competence of a community of people to act in concert on a community problem "you would lower the rate of delinquency."[8] Community organization as a strategy to reduce delinquency and crime had a long history in sociological thought. The Chicago School stressed it, and many projects in the 1930's were inspired by this theory.

NEIGHBORHOOD ORGANIZATION FOR SOCIAL THERAPY

While neighborhood groups can be organized as a means for reducing apathy and promoting conformity among the poor, they can also be organized to promote institutional change. The differences between social action for institutional change and neighborhood or-

---

3. P. MARRIS & M. REIN, DILEMMAS OF SOCIAL REFORM 170 (1967)

ganization as a form of socio-therapy need to be clarified. To use the form of one to achieve the goal of another can pose a very awkward dilemma. The experience of Mobilization of Youth in New York highlights this problem. Mobilization's prospectus makes the following point:

> Most efforts to organize lower class people attract individuals on their way up the social ladder: persons who are relatively responsible about participation, articulate and successful at managing organizational "forms" are identified as a lower class status rather than those who actually reflect the values of lower-class groups.[4]

The Mobilization proposal was clearly critical of this state of affairs and tried to attract the truly indigenous leadership in the community. But this argument can have curious implications, as Daniel P. Moynihan caustically charged in an address at a conference on poverty in Berkeley.

> Note what is to be remedied: instead of getting hold of local people who are relatively responsible about participation, articulate and successful at managing organizational "forms," Mobilization for Youth is getting hold of a lower level, true and genuine leader who is what—inarticulate, irresponsible and relatively unsuccessful? . . . I am sorry but I am suspect of that proposition.[5]

But if the major task is to reduce poverty by reducing alienation, deviancy, and the personal sense of powerlessness which is caused chiefly by isolation and apathy, then the paradox disappears. For the argument then is that people change as they try to change their world. If institutions change so as to be more relevant to the poor, and if, in the process of altering the performance of institutions, the poor change through the process of social engagement and social confrontation, then much could be accomplished in reducing both the vicious cycle of poverty and bureaucracy. In this perspective, neighborhood organization is essentially a form of therapy and only secondarily a means of changing institutions. Moynihan's argument thus becomes irrelevant to this view; for who else should be involved in therapy other than the inarticulate, the irresponsible, and the unsuccessful?

It is crucial to separate out the two agendas of reform, that of changing people and that of changing institutions. Whether each approach

---

4. *Id.* at 167.
5. P. MARRIS & M. REIN, *supra* note 3, at 185-187 reviews this debate.

supports the other remains a question to be determined empirically. Philosophically, the distinction is crucial.

In a thoughtful paper on mental health programs in model cities, Dumont reaffirms Mobilization's position on the appropriate population to be involved.

> From a preventive aspect, the community organization efforts will be directed toward the development of neighborhood and community groups among the as yet unaffiliated and disorganized people in the area; welfare recipients, public housing residents, tenement dwellers, the hard core poor who have the most severe and the most extensive psychological and social pathology.[6]

The socio-therapeutic ideals which lie behind this assertion are clear. Dumont goes on to explain that community organization "is itself a major mental health service, an end in itself."[7]

More recently the effort to link participation and conformity has been loosely extended to apply not only to individual and collective deviancy (delinquency, crime, and gang fighting) but to urban racial riots as well. The competent and conforming community according to this formulation does not call for organizing the poor, as do Cottrell, Mobilization for Youth, and Dumont, but for the restoration of power and authority to the middle classes.

Nathan Glazer recently commented that one of the glaring omissions in the analysis of the Kerner Commission Report is its failure to adequately take account of the middle class Negro and the secure working class Negro in their interpretation of the causes of urban unrest. "This is the missing man in the present crisis. And yet he must be a key factor both in the analysis of the problem . . . and in the solution of the problem."[8]

Norton Long's paper on "Politics and Ghetto Perpetuation,"[9] provides an interpretation of the role of the missing man in today's urban social unrest and the policy implications which derive from the analysis. Long's paper is an attempt to formulate a theory about ghetto instability. Long's position can be briefly summarized as follows: In American society other ethnic enclaves have created a government and

---

6. M. Dumont, A Model Community Mental Health Program for a Model Cities Area, August, 1967 (mimeo, Center for Community Planners, H.E.W., Washington).

7. *Id.* at 3.

8. Glazer, *The Problem with American Cities*, NEW SOCIETY (1968).

9. Long, *Politics and Ghetto Perpetuation*, to appear in POLITICS AND THE GHETTO (R. Warren ed., forthcoming).

economy of their own and from this political and economic base a social structure has emerged which assures social stability. However, the pattern in the Negro community is significantly different. Here a truncated occupational structure has developed which is dominated by lower class Negroes, certainly a noticeable absence of commercial interests and with control largely residing in the white community.

> The Negro middle class until recently has been escapist (and) . . . where it cannot physically flee it has sought physical coexistence and spiritual isolation. . . . The outstanding fact is that middle class Negroes do not govern the Ghetto. They are afraid of it. We thus confront a community with a unique lower class culture made possible by a missing middle class and control by an alien race. The result of the failure of self-government has been a distrust of leaders and the emergence of the lower class as the only authentic and indigenous culture. The combination of these ingredients have produced political instability and an economy of the hustle, "cashing-in" and the welfare dole and a social incapacity to mobilize resources. The costs of a purely lower class culture of immediate consumption have been a failure to make use of the economic avenues of upward mobility.[10]

This, then, is an interpretation of the causes of social unrest. The solution lies in creating a black middle class. A transition of leadership is needed, not dissimilar to the colonial transition, when blacks were taught self-government by departing white rulers. "The key question is whether there exists or can rapidly be produced sufficient middle class cadres to govern the black governed city . . . the greatest fear is clearly that the middle class Negroes . . . cannot dominate the lower class culture of Ghetto life."[11] Presumably then the Negro middle class leadership can more effectively police its own lower class ·culture if it had both the authority and the capability of exercising that leadership.

In summary, the socio-therapeutic rationale for citizen participation, with its emphasis on both personal and collective controls, can lead to efforts to organize the poor or to organize the non-poor. The rhetoric of powerlessness and apathy apply to both approaches. These views share in common, however, the commitment to produce conformity through participation.

---

10. POLITICS AND THE GHETTO (R. Warren ed., forthcoming).
11. Long, *Politics and Ghetto Perpetuation, supra* note **9**.

The major emphasis of the socio-therapeutic approach places the burden of responsibility for change upon the individual, rather than upon socio-economic institutions. But the formulation is incomplete. While competent men make competent institutions, the converse is equally compelling, for the quality and capability of the institutions affect the competence of those serviced by them. Within these terms of reference, citizen participation as social action and protest against the incompetence of institutions emerged.

Social Action and Protest for Institutional Change

How can institutions in a democratic society change? The President's Committee on Juvenile Delinquency and Youth Crime had hoped that a coalition of power (established institutions) and knowledge (research) would serve to change institutions so that they would provide increased opportunity for the poor. This was essentially an elitest approach. Like C. Wright Mills' criticism of the power elite, it argued that the wrong elite were in power, rather than that elitism was an inappropriate source of power.

This approach was a form of sophisticated naiveté; it assumed that a marginal increase in funds and the involvement of some established power groups would be sufficient to provoke change in long-established institutions. The idea of participation was crucial in this formulation, for it assumed that the institutions must be involved in their own reform. In order to prod the institutions into becoming involved in a process of self-examination, new funds were made available.

But this interpretation of how institutions change was incomplete. First, it assumed that bureaucratic rigidity, not the insufficiency of resources, was the root cause of institutional incompetence. Accordingly, the major agenda of reform sought to increase the flexibility of institutions so that they could more appropriately and creatively service the needs of the poor through small scale demonstration projects. More resources were needed to convert the demonstrations into a regular program, but these were not forthcoming. The difficulties of transforming Headstart from a summer to a year round program is a case in point for it raised problems of teacher availability and the cost of full year salaries and facilities when school buildings were in use.

Secondly, even when resources were at hand it proved difficult to get professionals to become client oriented. The hallmark of professionalism is responsiveness to the standards of colleagues, rather than to the preferences of clients. A quack, as Everett Hughes observed, is someone who is respected by his clients but not his colleagues. To change professional performance required shifting the reward system and criteria by which professionals judge quality. This demanded not so much changing the attitude of individual teachers, it required, instead, changing the view of those who teach teachers and the criteria by which a given educational system allocated rewards—wages, promotion, recognition. Institutions resisted change. Experience in trying to change institutions affirm that we know more about the forces which inhibit change than those which help to bring it about.

As limitations of the elite approach (with its emphasis on experimentation and self-study by institutions) became evident, the strategies of pressure and protest developed. It was out of the frustration of trying to change institutions that the possibility of using consumer groups emerged. Social action to promote change came to rely increasingly on organizing the poor for conflict, confrontation, and protest. The tactics of public shame, made possible by widespread newspaper coverage, were used as a source of power to promote change. Rent strikes, picketing of the schools and other forms of militant social action were encouraged by many federally financed community action programs as a way of reducing poverty by changing service institutions. But the strategy of social action as social protest was vulnerable. The experience in San Francisco helps to illuminate its underlying dilemmas.

The San Francisco Community Action Agency put its faith in organizing power. It hoped to apply massive pressure to produce massive change in institutions. The city-wide agency delegated much of its power to neighborhood boards. "Resident boards in the poverty areas gained unprecedented power over program, personnel, and budgets."[12] The director of the citywide C.A.A. explained that this strategy sought "to mobilize resident power to be able to reshape the big money institutions like the schools, employment services, and welfare to be more responsive to the poor."[13] The Western Addition Neighborhood, an area of 300 blocks with 88,000 residents of whom 50% were white and 40% were poor, devoted all its energies to this approach. The area was sub-divided into 32 sub-areas, each sub-area had its own community council, block captains and representatives to be sent to an area board. All of this involvement was to be accom-

---

12. J. Cunningham, The Struggle of the American Urbidente for Freedom and Power, a report prepared for the Ford Foundation (1967).
13. Id.

plished by fifty full time and seventy part time organizations. All the organizers were black.

But the strategy collapsed. The institutions did not respond to pressure by offering massive services or fundamental changes in policy. Moreover, massive pressure could not be generated. The efforts to organize the 32 areas proved to be very difficult as internal tension between established ghetto power and black militants was created. The focus on acquiring power through community organizations yielded no tangible and visible services.[14]

The strategy failed because it could not mobilize the poor and deliver concrete services; in other communities, the strategy failed precisely because it did deliver services and it could concert the will of the poor. When protest secures a concrete service, the very success of the project sometimes leads to the reduction in discontent and membership interest which threatens the stability of the group. Often the victory is illusory because it represents only a gesture, a token response by institutions to win peace rather than to provide lasting reform. But where social action is effective and militancy produces institutional discomfort, then a power struggle ensues. Accommodation and bargaining by established power groups is superseded by direct assault. When established power was threatened, it often fought back by striking where the protest was most vulnerable—at the source of funds which paid for organizing the poor.[15]

As the tensions in the social action strategy developed, some of the other available interpretations about the meaning of citizen participation seemed more appealing. Although protest continued, other strategies became important. Employment of nonprofessionals represented an example of attempting to deliver service and work for ghetto residents. New sources of power were sought and the power of the law was employed as a base to promote institutional change and to protect consumer rights.

INDIGENOUS WORKERS

Another of the ways that citizen participation became widely interpreted was in terms of the employment of the poor. The indigenous worker nonprofessional idea was a marvelous invention. It beautifully exploited the ambiguities in the philosophical choices

14. *Id.* at 57-69.

15. The experience in Syracuse illustrates these tensions. *See also* S. Lipsky, The Politics of Protest (1967, Institute of Research on Poverty, University of Wisconsin, mimeo).

concerning the causes of poverty. Why were indigenous personnel needed? One ready common sense answer was that the poor needed jobs. Training alone often led to blind alleys where there were insufficient job opportunities for the number of graduates of these programs.

From the time of the initial proposal for an Economic Opportunity Act, Secretary of Labor Wirtz consistently opposed the community action idea of helping young people develop their capabilities via a variety of new and immediate training, remediation, and participation programs. He saw poverty as a lack of money; money depended, in the end, primarily upon jobs. Community action, preoccupied with training, created no large numbers of new jobs. Jobs provided the opportunity for reducing poverty by providing the poor an independent source of income.

What was needed was a program of job expansion. Employment of indigenous personnel offered such an opportunity. But in order to avoid the charge of creating a large public works program, the same strategy of employing indigenous personnel could be used to satisfy the other goals of changing institutions and changing the poor. Some hoped that by introducing indigenous personnel into organizations, it would deossify rigid and irrelevant organizations. Moreover, agency workers drawn from the neighborhood were in an especially strategic position to encourage the poor to make use of existing institutions; and in the process of changing others, indigenous workers would change as well.

The program of indigenous personnel thus offered an excellent opportunity to draw together several different meanings of citizen participation. It stood simultaneously for jobs, for institutional change, and for personal therapy. This helps to account for the popularity of this form of citizen participation and its likely desirability as a form of involvement. A recent OEO report indicates that as of September 1966, approximately 132,000 nonprofessional positions have been authorized, including 25,000 positions which remained unfilled.[16]

The use of nonprofessionals, however, has raised a number of issues. There has been a great deal of creaming because many of the nonprofessional roles are being filled by people who are middle class, like housewives who have college degrees, rather than by poor people. There is a tendency to recruit those among the poor who are better off, rather than to try to recruit those who are the most disadvantaged of

16. New Careers Newsletter (August 1967).

the disadvantaged. We always have levels of disadvantage; most of our social policies skim cream off the top and neglect the bottom, with the result that the conditions of those left behind further deteriorate.

Some professionals have observed that nonprofessionals often render low quality service, and that training is essential to improve the quality. On the other hand, upgrading is limited; i.e., nonprofessionals lack opportunities to move either into the higher levels below the professional level, or to have a new route into professional life. While nonprofessional activities could become a new kind of credentialing activity, it is more often just a dead-end stage.

The nonprofessional role is frequently treated as the bottom of the status hierarchy within the social services rather than as a part of the fellowship of social service workers. Black people at the occupational bottom are labeled nonprofessionals and are looked upon as the peons of social services with a limited role and with little power within the agency. There is no active, urgent concern to change their situation, although the new organization of nonprofessionals may change this situation. Professional egality does not extend to·the new kind of nonprofessional worker. Rather than the colleague principal, the principal of hierarchy is still insisted on in most agencies.

It is not unreasonable to suggest that much more hierarchy is exhibited in the organization of services and in social agencies than in most other organizations. A consequence is that the social service nonprofessional is usually confronted with a difficult task in winning respect and compensation for his achievements. In some agencies nonprofessionals are trying to reverse this pattern, but this is not the national practice.

A possible danger in the nonprofessional role today is that there may be developing a low paid black civil and nonprofit service supervised by white professionals receiving high pay and status. This race-occupational division may become more acute rather than less with time.

PARTICIPATION AS LEGAL PROTECTION

Legal protection against administrative discretion merges with ideals of participatory democracy. Both are preoccupied with issues of the rights of marginal groups against dominant established interests. Appeal to law can serve as an instrument of reform and protest, challenging established procedures. Although militant social protest was vulnerable to challenges on the basis that its activities were inappropriate to its mission (federal funds should not be used to promote confrontation, boycotts, and protest), the law was neutral in relation to auspices, for "the law lends itself impartially to manipulation by militant radicals or repressive conservatives."[17]

When Mobilization for Youth came to recognize the limits of a cooperative strategy, it used these limits to justify a more aggressive approach of protest and confrontation. But it soon came to realize the limits of protest as well, when after the death of President Kennedy it lost its political support. The counter-attack by the schools, the police, and other institutions sorely threatened its survival. Cloward and Piven's experiences at Mobilization undoubtedly influenced their decision to turn to law as a source of support in redressing the grievances of the poor and promoting changes in institutional policy. Mobilization's neighborhood legal service came to specialize in welfare problems focusing on those administrative practices which rejected individuals who applied for welfare. They sought out test cases which could challenge the established principles by which exclusion was made possible. And so law was used as an instrument of reform.

Cloward developed another idea about how to combine law and protest. In an influential paper[18] he demonstrated that there was a high rate of under-utilization of welfare in New York, i.e., many individuals entitled to benefits were not receiving them. He argued that if non-users became users, the welfare system might collapse under the weight of the added costs. The Welfare Rights Movement was an attempt to organize the eligible non-recipients of welfare. Soon after it began, its strategy shifted from recruiting clients to getting benefits for those who were already clients. The vigorous and militant program of the Welfare Rights Movement in New York City was directed at the special grant allowance program, but supported the legal right to benefits. The protests were successful in raising the cost of the special grants for items such as household furniture, clothing, etc., from $3 million per month in 1967 to $13 million per month in 1968. These efforts did produce a change in policy from discretionary allowance, where some got more, to a flat rate where all families got $100 per year, an amount less than the average size of the special grant allowances. Organizing for entitlement did not collapse the welfare system, but it did pressure it to change. A policy change in support of flat grants was the product, but the victory was soon seen as defeat. While it reduced administrative

---

17. P. MARRIS & M. REIN, *supra* note 3, at 174.
18. Cloward & Piven, *A Strategy To End Poverty*, THE NATION 510 (May 2, 1966).

discretion and promoted more equality of benefits, it also reduced the size of the benefits for those who had learned to make the system respond to their needs.

The pressure for legal protection against administrative discretion and the effort to use law as an instrument of reform found expression in other areas as well. Interest in grievance, access, and information about rights and services developed from the consumer's point of view. The need for forms of accountability became evident. Public discussion was opened about the need for new services for the aggrieved (*ombudsmen*), for the alienated (neighborhood service centers which facilitated access) and for the uninformed (information and referral schemes, which might provide not only information on what and where services were available, but the more radical program of assessing the quality of services such as private medical care, nursing homes, and public schools).

PARTICIPATION AS POLICY DEVELOPMENT

The idea that the poor should be involved in shaping policy was entirely consistent with the ideals of the revitalization of local democracy and the increase in the competence of local leaders in managing their own affairs. This view of participation represented a form of radical democracy in which both institutional representatives of established power and the consumers of the service (not in their role as clients, but as citizens) would shape policy. The involvement of the citizen in creating policy presented no conflict with the ideals of a competent program, for the poor were to be involved in making allocative decisions. Such decisions, by their nature, involved matters of judgment and preference; they involved such questions as the relative emphasis to be assigned to programs for young children, youths, and adults, and the relative weight to be given to health, recreation, legal, and training services.

But local and national priorities are not always smoothly aligned and mutually reinforcing. Indeed, more typically they are in conflict, as in the case where a community is eager to spend its funds on recreation, while OEO rejects this type of program on the ground that recreation contributes little to the reduction of poverty. OEO, on the other hand, may be interested in promoting legal services for the poor as part of a national decision to spend funds in this area, but legal services might have a low priority on a local agenda. Thus, there might be a conflict between national and local priority systems, and assignments may conflict. To the extent that the national agenda intrudes into local decision-making, it undermines the ideal of developing the competent community. The more intrusive, insistent, and effective is the federal government, the more likely is this new form of cooperative federalism to increase the sense of local impotence.

This issue has not recieved the attention it deserves. Instead, the emphasis on involving the poor in policy-making has centered on the procedure for selecting the poor, rather than on the kinds of decisions which they are to make. Elections become the crucial battlegrounds of public policy with great debates about the most appropriate form for electing and selecting the poor on policy-making boards.

How to elect the representatives of the poor was indeed a troublesome issue. A variety of procedures were followed, including appointment by the mayor and elections. The low turn-out rate in many of the elections has been used as an argument to reaffirm the notion that the poor are apathetic and that stagnation is intense. Voting is regarded as inherently good; for many it was regarded as a form of socio-therapy on the assumption that voting strengthens the bonds of social cohesiveness.

Consistent with this assumption was the treatment of elections as only a symbolic gesture of engagement, rather than as a political act. The analysis of the low turn-out rates was strikingly apolitical, emphasizing psychological withdrawal. Had elections been accepted as political acts, the low turn out might have been interpreted quite differently. For example, it could have been pointed out that most elections were without constituencies, without issues, without rewards, and without trust since they were often held under OEO auspices, which in many communities represents the establishment.

As the debate continued, the meaningfulness of participation in formal city-wide Community Action Agencies came increasingly under question. A resilient system proved very creative in devising new administrative arrangements which devitalized the organizational structure in which the poor were advised to participate. Those who were strong advocates of participation were concerned that the procedure led to creaming off the most militant leadership in the ghetto, i.e., the leadership became co-opted, or to put it more harshly, they "sold out." Others cogently argued that they were not selling out, but simply buying into the system.

The same issues have remained alive in the implementation of the meaning of citizenship participation in model cities programs. The shift in rhetoric from "maximum feasible participation" under OEO to "widespread participation" in model cities may be interpreted as a desire to abate the intensity of engagement. But once the ideals of citizen involvement were unleashed, they were hard to contain, even in a program which set out to do so. Administrative interpretation of guidelines depended on the political climate; and as demands in Negro communities became more radical, the concern for involvement in policy shifted to control of policy.

The demand for the transfer of power took two forms, aside from the more political approach of running candidates in an attempt to win political control over the city. One form is economic development through devices such as community corporations; the other is control of the social service system by the decentralization of authority and power.

The Transfer of Power

The theme of involvement in the policies of community action agencies soon spread to involvement in other programs as well. Requirements for citizen involvement can now be found in the amendments to the Social Security Act, in recent legislation concerning the treatment of delinquents, in local legislation, and in the voluntary sector (e.g., students demand a role in policy making in the university and clients want to influence the policies of social service agencies).

The transition from involvement in policy to control of policy was perhaps less awkward than was the early struggle to win a role for local residents in the decision machinery of social service bureaucracies. The concern with law and participation had focused on the failure to give due regard to the rights of individuals, to fully implement entitlement, and to assist the aggrieved individual who was hurt by the administrative service system. Thus the concern with law and participation was primarily directed at seeing that the rules were enforced or at changing the rules by court action. By contrast, the concern with the transfer of power was directed at the issue of who should set the rules, and especially the role of consumers as rule setters.

The emphasis on the transfer of power cannot altogether be understood without recognizing the difference between issues of race and class. While policies directed only at issues of class (poverty and low income) can assign priorities to programs which emphasized service (e.g., jobs or income), policies concerned with race must today give attention to the questions of integration and separatism. The separatists black power advocates have been most preoccupied with the case for a transfer of power. The separatist hope is outlined by the following comment:

> [to achieve for their followers] group and even private political power, self-esteem and dignity, and a modicum of territory or turf over which proprietary control can be exercised . . . . This position says that if you get jobs and income without getting power, the political and economic power of the whites will be used to take the income away from you in taxes, rents, high prices . . . .[19]

The call for a transfer of power has taken two forms: community corporation and decentralization. We briefly review each.

COMMUNITY CORPORATION

"A corporation is a means which permits the blending together into one self-contained entity multi-source capital in various forms with management obtained from nonowner sources."[20] The sources of capital and management can be blended together in various combinations from public, private, and corporate areas. These types of nonprofit organizations can be identified: those organized for a private purpose (social, paternal, civic, patriotic, etc.), those created for quasi-public purposes (but outside the usual governmental machinery in order to exploit the flexibility and managerial techniques of private enterprise and also "to make possible greater citizen participation"), and finally the government corporation or public benefit corporation (e.g., T.V.A. or the proposal to change the federal postal system into a public corporation).

In a thoughtful analysis of the quasi-public, nonprofit corporation, Leshner notes that since 1932, new social legislation brought government into the position where "it not only invested the capital but took over the management in toto."[21] During this period in fields such as public assistance and child welfare, progressive reforms called for a transfer in administration from the voluntary to the public sector. The mood of the 1960's seems to have reversed the trend because "problems have developed . . . in the area of administration. The increased size of

---

19. J. Dyckman, The Organization of Metropolitan Social Planning 9 (September 1968, mimeo, National League of Cities and H.E.W., Chicago).

20. Leshner, The Non-profit Corporation—A Neglected Step Child Comes of Age, 22 Bus. Lawyer 951, 957 (1967).

21. *Id.* at 966.

government makes more difficult citizen participation and citizen communication."[22]

Without accepting the thesis that administrative problems are chiefly problems of size, it is evident that in the past several years, a great deal of interest and some experimentation with the idea of a community corporation has emerged. In 1964, OEO granted $185,000 to the East Central Citizens Organization (ECCO) in Columbus, Ohio, to cover the organizational and administrative expenses in developing a community corporation. The corporation is controlled by the residents of the community and it is organized to provide services to the community, such as job training, day care, recreation, and housing rehabilitation.

Senator Robert F. Kennedy developed the Renewal and Rehabilitation Corporation in the Bedford-Stuyvesant section of Brooklyn, New York. But the original corporation, dominated by established social welfare agencies and civic groups, did not permit control by grass roots organizations. As a result of pressure, a new corporation was created. But according to one review it remains "doubtful that it will give a significant measure of control to the poor in the community."[23]

These local experiments, reinforced by pressure from black separatists, have contributed to the newly proposed Community Self-Determination Act of 1968. The Act is supported by a curious coalition of black militant leaders at CORE, intellectuals at the Kennedy Institute of Politics at Harvard University, and by lawyers and businessmen. The legislation is inspired by the ideals of corporate capitalism and the Israeli kibbutz. "Both—through loans, technical assistance and profit making . . . [hope to] achieve self-sustaining growth."[24] Yet even a cursory examination of the legislation suggests how strongly the conservative creed for urban America influences the basic principles on which the legislation rests.

The legislation calls for the development of Community Development Corporation (C.D.C.) to manage and to own business enterprises. A network of Community Development Banks would provide the necessary investment funds. Federal tax incentives would encourage private business to enter into turnkey agreements with the C.D.C. to

22. Id.

23. Antipoverty, Community Corporations 3 COLUM. JOURNAL OF LAW AND SOCIAL PROBLEMS 94, 98 (1967).

24. Tobier, Cooperative Communities North and South: A Response to Poverty, 114 CONG. REC. S. 971 (daily ed. July 24, 1968).

turn over the business to the C.D.C. as a subsidiary. This complex structure of national boards, banks, and local corporations would hopefully generate profits to be used to finance community social services wanted at the local level.

A review of the supporting rationale set out in Section 2 of the Community Self-Determination Act[25] helps to make understandable why what might appear as a radical argument for black capital has so much appeal to conservative thought. Following are some selected quotes to illustrate this thesis:

> Programs and policies which tax some to support others offer no hope and no opportunity to those who have the capacity to become productive. . . .
> Such a program should be designed to permit the people of a community to utilize a share of the profits of community-sponsored enterprises to provide needed social services, thereby reducing the burden of taxation upon the rest of society . . .
> . . . order, stability, and progress can be achieved only when the people of a community actively participate in and are responsible for their own affairs in such areas as education . . . economic development. . . .
> As that goal is approached, government incentives should be correspondingly phased out and government investment repaid, leaving the once dependent people to make their way as independent, unsubsidized participants in our national life.[26]

The aims which inspire a conservative coalition in support of black power and black capital are clear. Conservatism views taxation to pay for the benefits to the poor as a burden, hence the poor should pay for their own services out of the profits of community corporations. Federal financing of these corporations is a temporary expedient; the ideal is self-liquidation as success fosters pragmatic extinction. Finally, the goal is to promote order, stability, and progress. The assumption is that these goals reinforce each other. Yet a compelling case could be made that token programs promote frustration and thus create the instability they are designed to overcome. Note as well the impressive lists of economic limitations imposed on Community Development Boards. They "would not be authorized to issue or deal in securities, engage in acceptable

---

25. *See* S. 3875, S. 3876, H.R. 18709, H.R. 18715, H.R. 18976, H.R. 19201, H.R. 19205, 90th Cong., 2d Sess (1968); 114 CONG. REC. S. 9274 (daily ed. July 24, 1968).
26. 114 CONG. REC. S. 9274 (daily ed. July 24, 1968).

financing, sell insurance, offer credit cards or make credit guarantees."[27] It would appear that the effect of these limitations seems to be directed at keeping the corporations away from the high profit sectors of business.

DECENTRALIZATION

The use of profits of community corporations to purchase social services and thereby transfer decision power from the public supplier bureaucracy to the user-bureaucracy appears to be limited to the class of services which the English call personal social services. In reviewing the functions of the Community Development Corporation, the Community Self-Determination bill lists the following services: "basic education, child welfare, day care, pre-school training, health, consumer education, home ownership counseling, college placement assistance, job finding, recreation, legal aid, etc."[28] The common theme which binds together what might appear as a random classification of services is the emphasis on activities which facilitate access to, or better prepare individuals to make use of, other institutional services. Although health is listed as a service, it is likely that what was intended was only medical diagnostic and referral services, rather than high-cost hospital, surgical or other direct physician services. The services then are directed at the low-cost sections of social welfare. The profits of local economic development could not, after all, realistically cover the expenses of such high cost services as education, medical care, and income maintenance.

In the high cost section of social services it is the decentralization of authority rather than the ownership of services that is being sought. To avoid a highly regressive pattern of taxation in financing these services it is necessary to regionalize or federalize the sources of funds, while localizing decisions. Education and medical care are examples.

In the area of medical care for the aged and for the medically indigent, American social policy is based on a voucher system in which the patient selects the service of his choice and the vendor is paid directly by government for the service so purchased. Alan Gartner, the associate director of the New Careers Development Center of New York University, proposed that this policy could be used to win "Community Control of the Human Resources."[29] If the users would elect to purchase their care from selected vendors, and if a group of doctors would agree to limit their practices to this clientele, then a type of

27. S. 3875, 90th Cong., 2d Sess., Title II (1968).
28. S. 3875, 90th Cong., 2d Sess., Title I (1968).
29. Social Policy Notes 2 (July 1968, New York University, mimeo.)

closed corporation could be formed. That doctors would agree in the present high demand, low supply market to an arrangement whereby a guaranteed patient load is exchanged for medical accountability to consumers, seems unlikely. However, in many communities where a limited number of physicians are already providing medical care for a large indigent population of medical care recipients concentrated in a limited geographic area, these clients could be organized to seek more control over the practice which is already dependent upon the purchase of the services. Where the public agencies already render the services directly, as they do in community health services, then the poor can serve on the boards of these agencies. But here we have only another example of participation in policy-making.

It is in the field of education, however, that a shift from participation in power to the transfer of power is being attempted. The outcome of the experiment is uncertain as illustrated by the clash in New York City between teachers seeking to protect their working conditions and neighborhood boards eager to have the freedom to select teachers of their own choosing.

In summary then, the argument for a transfer of power, whether by purchasing services from the profits of local corporations or by decentralizing authority, rests on the belief that the present principles of bureaucratic and professional accountability no longer are able to safeguard individual rights.

> . . . [I]n principle an administrator is responsible to government, and government to the people. The aggrieved citizen can protest through his representative against any intrusion on his rights. But a citizen grievance against bureaucracy cannot be simply and quickly dealt with . . . the bureaucracy . . . becomes increasingly autonomous. It is the judge of its own integrity; it controls the information by which its competence could be challenged; and it outlasts the politicians who depend upon it to execute their policies. It begins to seem an insidious threat to the whole concept of a democratic society.[30]

A professional's behavior, even in principle, is accountable not to clients but to professional colleagues who license and review the practice of other professionals. But while we cannot hope to dismantle bureaucracy or alter the essence of professional discretions, new mechanisms of accountability are being sought. Decentralization and the

---

30. P. Marris, A Report on the Scandinavian Ombudsman and the British Citizen. Advice Bureau 2 (1966, mimeo, Ford Foundation).

transfer of power to consumers represents an example of this trend. The issues of accountability have converged with the charge of welfare colonialism in the social services, and with the rise of black separatism.

CONCLUSIONS

The principle of citizen participation in public policy is not new in American political democracy. What is new, however, is the interpretation which says that citizens should be involved in the process. We are now preoccupied with finding ways of including the excluded citizens, especially the poor and the blacks. This trend must be reckoned as a significant move toward democracy in decision making, responsiveness of bureaucracies to consumer preferences, expansion of the concepts of rights and entitlement of public largess, and experimentation with new forms of protection against professional and administrative discretion. But at the same time this important step forward has generated much conflict, and it has substituted, at least in the short run, a struggle for power for the rendering of quality service. Moreover, it has in practice reduced democracy, as in the case where small cliques take over policy making without representing the interest of the majority of the residents in low income areas. Finally it has inhibited the use of professional wisdom and experience as citizens learn afresh the errors of past histories.

This brief history of citizen participation in the 1960's has reviewed the many different and simultaneously held interpretations about the form which such participation should take. Even in this short period, public policy has shifted its emphasis from one interpretation to another without abandoning or repudiating any view. Fadism has emerged as the conflicts and dilemmas of each approach have become evident, when vague ideals wrestle with practical implementation.

Our recital of difficulties and tensions in the unfolding of citizenship participation in the sixties could lead to the conclusion that it should be abandoned. That would be a grievous error. The idea of participation will be tremendously important in humanizing and democratizing institutions. It already reverberates in many fields—both students and welfare recipients assert that they have rights; legislation in many fields stipulates the involvement of the poor or the service recipient; the service bureaucracy is now viewed from the position of the user rather than the professional. Thus, the spillover effects have spread much beyond the community action programs which have been the focus of this article.

The theme of participation has fed the black revolution and, in turn, has been shaped by it..The course of race change is still uncertain; issues are still unsettled; ambiguity about goals and low faith in available means lead to stormy confrontations; the legitimacy of old and new Negro representatives and spokesmen is under challenge. These circumstances lead to the untidy situation of shifting focuses in citizenship participation. Since participation is not only a response to the issues of the past, but is constantly being assailed by the rapid cacophony of the unsettled struggle that is race relations today, it cannot be settled form.

While we see the shifting and refocusing as inevitable and recognize that experimentation is desirable, we fear that the end result is that no approach gets sufficient funding and support to have penetrating impact. Constantly changing gears may give the illusion of motion. In the next several years participation should shake down into a limited number of major models if it is to be powerful.

The other general concern we have about participation is the stress of many on its socio-therapeutic significance, which appears in many guises. It is our conclusion that the stress on socio-therapy leads to control rather than change, to spending small funds rather than large, and to presumed opportunity rather than to real opportunity.

Sometimes, groups seeking widely sweeping changes combine with more conservatively-minded groups emphasizing socio-therapy. This seems to be the case of the proposed community corporations legislation. Although strange bedfellows are sometimes the parents of effective new policies, often the end product may not be what one of the partners imagined. The partner with the broader agenda may hope to subtly influence the group with the narrow socio-therapeutic intent or to use it while yielding little of its own agenda. Our feeling is that more conservative public agendas win more than they lose to the more radical, and that if a socio-therapeutic orientation is not guarded against, it insidiously gains ascendancy. The black struggle of today may change this picture and reduce the likelihood of socio-therapy suppressing the drive for social change. But there is no assurance that protean socio-therapy will not dominate.

While the road is not easy or smooth, public policy cannot retreat from the course of expanding participation. "Maximum feasible participation" has ushered in a new era—stormy and hopeful—in the life of bureaucracy, professionalism and democracy.

THE NEGRO AMERICAN AND HIS CITY: PERSON IN PLACE IN CULTURE

Max Lerner

Max Lerner, "The Negro American and His City: Person in Place in Culture," *Daedalus,* Fall 1968, Vol. 97, pp. 1390-1408.

THE NEGRO AMERICAN AND HIS CITY: PERSON IN PLACE IN CULTURE

Max Lerner

I

THE AMERICAN city, in the late 1960's, is caught in three great testings: First: Can racial groups live together not in an uneasy coexistence punctuated by erratic flare-ups of burnings and killings, but in a going community of give-and-take, live-and-let-live? Second: Can a tolerable open society, clinging to the frame and political style of a traditional democracy, absorb and resolve the tensions of social division that are at once racial, class, and generational in character? Third: Is the modern American city viable as a social organism—that is to say, can it meet the minimum needs of the growing-up years so as to achieve a reasonably healthy personality structure with some roots in the city environment?

All three questions are obviously entangled, but I shall concentrate on the third. I should guess that whatever clues we shall find to the first two will largely depend on what clues we find to the third. My assumption in this essay is the rather obvious one—that nothing short of a total coalition of all relevant resources and talents will enable the city and the society to survive these testings. I propose not so much to argue this as to examine some of its implications.

What targets should the coalition energies focus on, by what strategies, with what guiding theories, in what spirit? The usual plea has been to make all programs "action-oriented," a plea voiced by whites and Negroes alike, by people of every political persuasion. The purpose is to avoid bureaucratic obstructions and paper constructs and to be pragmatic rather than theoretical. But action in itself can be a mindless value and in fact retrogressive. To do something about cleaning up the streets and the littered yards, getting new housing and new jobs, keeping kids in school, training and re-training young men and older men—that is obviously necessary. But it will not be adequate unless some questions are asked and answered about the action itself. Who will work at it with whom, and who will make the decisions? By what incentives will the work be sustained?

And for what good—*cui bono*? Take the job-creating task. In a technology in which speed-tape mechanisms are replacing earlier skilled and semiskilled work, the question of what kinds of jobs and for whom is of some consequence. If Peter Drucker is right in his essay in this volume, it would follow that schooling, training, and apprenticeship programs will have different impacts depending on whether the trainees are to be located in the old or the new industries. The building of new schoolhouses becomes less important than the question of what is taught, by whom, and under whose controls. As for housing, it is a truism that urban renewal programs have tended to tear down the dwellings where the poor have lived and to set up middle-income units in their place, thus leaving homeless the very people whose living conditions set the projects in motion in the first place. And if the aim is to break open the ghetto trap, I agree with Melvin Webber that coalition operations might better be focused on making low-income dwelling units available in the larger metropolitan area, especially since the location of industries is bypassing the central city.

In the broadest terms the coalition concept means the deployment of every resource upon whatever target. In a more precise sense it means a working coordination of a number of agencies in attacking the problem of the inner city—more concretely, government units at every level, independent government corporations, private corporate enterprise, banks, insurance companies, trade unions, voluntary organizations, churches, universities, school boards, foundations, media representatives, and *ad hoc* "people's groups" in the neighborhood. America is pluralistic, and every new problem must therefore be attacked by a cluster of organizations working toward a common end. But beyond the cluster itself, a coalition implies a strategy of operation for its members, articulating their roles and their relations to one another and to the program.

In every coalition, however widespread and intricate the net of membership, there are three prime partners who must carry the main burden of the support and strategy. They are government, business, and the neighborhood group. They are *primi inter pares* because among them they have the sinews of action, the first two with the money and the power, the third with the necessary good will and knowledge of life conditions and a hunger for choices. The coalition may prove to be a way of breaking the old impasse about whether government or business should take responsibility and wield power over whatever needs doing. By widening the field of discourse, increasing the partners, linking government and business with the people whose lives in the city are being affected, and by placing the stress on the how rather than the whether, on the strategy of coordination rather than on the conventional legitimacy of the cooperative action itself, the coalition method breaks away from the barren disputes of the past and opens new ground. It also tries to achieve something of that "civic religion" that Tocqueville noted in the participatory democracy of the America he visited.

In a rough typology of strategies, one can isolate five. There is the action by a single corporation (for example, Fairchild-Hiller, Aerojet General, U.S. Gypsum) or by a group of them (a consortium of life insurance companies) for a specific project in the slum area, whether for creating new jobs or building houses or whatever. Often such a project is not calculated to make a profit; although it may not be economic, it is responsive to a larger self-interest that sees corporate health as part of community health. There is the effort to attack the business-incentive problem by grants, subsidies, and especially government guarantees to cover possible losses. (The Javits, Percy, and Kennedy plans belong here, as do many others.) There is the "triggering" government corporation (Governor Rockefeller's innovative plan for New York State is the best example) whereby a government body, funded by a vast bond issue, rides herd on local obstructions and makes initial expenditures and commitments in the hope of triggering further commitments by business itself which may exceed the total governmental fund by a multiple of five or more. There is the *ad hoc* loose business alignment (for example, the National Alliance of Businessmen, under Henry Ford's chairmanship) that serves as liaison between business and governmental groups, mainly for work-training programs. There is the city or neighborhood program (Newark is an example) where a local corporation or coalition, composed of representatives of the dwellers themselves, undertakes a housing construction program on its own, with government and allied funds, instead of having the programs planned and carried out *for* it. In Philadelphia a coalition of white business-men has pledged an industrial fund, to be administered by a "Black Coalition," aimed at helping the black community to self-help measures.

Cutting across these, on a deeper level, there are several different viewpoints about the target area to which these strategies are directed. The first may see it in economic terms, as a consumption and purchasing power area whose potentials have not yet been tapped, and whose health or unhealth can affect the rest of the nation. Another sees it politically, as an explosive area where further explosions could endanger the fabric of the nation itself, and which must therefore be contained and enriched. A third sees it as an undeveloped region (like the Italian South) or even as an undeveloped country, to which a total development strategy needs to be applied (this comes close to the thinking of Hubert Humphrey), encompassing a set of feasibility studies, the use of loans and investment guarantees for job-creating programs, the dispatch of technical expertise to the city to work under local direction and with a local plan. There are doubtless other viewpoints as well. The only one about which little is said is to view the city quite simply as *a city*, a fusion of earth and ethnos and ethos, of place and personality and life style.

II

What kind of crisis does the American city face? In sheer physical terms the crisis is easy enough to describe: There is the pollution of air and water, the eyesore ugliness of billboards, the littered ugliness of vacant lots and auto graveyards, the chaos of badly planned transport, the strangling of the city by traffic, the violent explosions of the city in riots. No one can question that this chaotic ugliness and this ugly chaos are true of the American city. The city is being choked, clogged, strangled, and burned to death. Nor can anyone doubt that nothing short of a radical redesigning of the physical, social, cultural, and human environment will save the city from the body and spirit of this death.

But that begs the question: *What kind* of a radical redesigning? Conceivably one could finish the choking-strangling-burning job, level the cities of the plain, and start all over again, in different places or the same ones. But one would have to start with the same society, the same historic memories. Leveling the cities is no shortcut to a solution. To reinvent them in a better way one would have to grapple with the question of how they have come to their present situation.

This question must, in turn, be broken down into two related, and yet separable, parts. One is how the existing inequalities developed between the racial groups in the cities—inequalities in income, employment, living standards, and treatment at the hands of the society. The other is why the large-scale violence came when it did and where it did.

The answer to the first has been spelled out in a series of inquiries and reports, both governmental and academic, from President Truman's pathbreaking commission on discriminatory practices in the nation's capital to the post-Watts report in California to the Kerner Commission report. It will be found also as the background social reasoning that bolsters the judicial reasoning in a number of key Supreme Court decisions, notably under the Warren Court. It runs primarily in terms of the social and psychological heritage of slavery and Reconstruction, as well as in terms of the impact both of history and of the badge of color upon racist discriminatory practices by the whites and upon the self-image of the blacks. There can be no question that the only way to make good these injustices flowing from inequalities is through a massive institutionalizing of justice and equality. It must inform every phase of the relations between the "two societies" so as to make them one larger pluralistic society—the work and income phase, food and diet, schooling, housing, the physical setting of neighborhood and city, and above all else the phase of political power without which other gains will seem phantasmagoric.

The whole thing has the simplicity of a geometrical proposition. The only trouble with it is whatever is, at the core, the trouble with the over-rationalist, over-determinist, simplistic thinking of traditional liberalism. The determinist fallacy: Since the present situation has been determined by economic-social conditions, then change the conditions, and all will be well. The rationalist fallacy: Only do away with prejudice, repair people's ignorance, get them to understand one another, and all will be well. The liberal-ethical fallacy: Only deal with objective injustices and replace them with objective justice, and all will be well. Add two others to these: the law-and-order fallacy and the ethnic ghetto fallacy. If the others are determinist and rationalist-liberal, these two are normative. The law-and-order (crackdown) fallacy: Only apply the norms of law and order to those who are breaking both and crack down on the malefactors, and all will be well. The ethnic ghetto fallacy: There have been other ethnic minorities who have lived in ghettos, but they worked hard and educated themselves, and were able to get out; why not the blacks?

Thus the thicket of fallacies surrounding the question of the white-black relationship in the inner city. In every instance what is at fault is reductionism and abstraction—the reduction of a complex problem to one aspect of it, the abstraction of that phase from the whole.

One hears it said often that the American city is being broken apart by the forces of race, or by the forces of class conflict, or by the forces of the power struggle. It is nearer the truth to say that no single force is tearing the city apart, but that these three and several other divisive strains as well are in operation. Since the city is the loose envelope that contains, within its bounds of place, all the going strains and thrusts of American civilization, it follows that the crisis of the city is a crisis of class, race, and power divisions, and that it is also a crisis of the generational conflict and the value rebellion.

If this is true, then there is no easy gimmick that can resolve the crisis of the city. The reason why the coalition attack on it makes sense is that only a total effort could possibly hope to bring to bear a range of measures that would affect the income and daily life of the inner-city dweller as a member of a class, deal with his self-image as the member of a racial group, give him a chance to replace his powerlessness with some power, narrow the gap of generational bitterness and separation, and place within his reach the real life-options out of which a choice of values becomes possible. The existing inequalities have developed not because one particular facet has gone awry in the situation and treatment of the blacks, but in a sense because the whole alignment of the civilization-pattern has gone awry for them. Crucially, an economic, legal, political, and moral task is involved in setting it right.

The second question that I mentioned above—why the violence in the cities should have come when and where it did—is much harder to answer. Correspondingly it is more difficult to resolve in the arena of social action. Although the inequalities have been institutionalized, the discontents have been internalized. An institutional change will affect the inequalities, but not necessarily resolve the discontents.

With startling prescience, Tocqueville saw that the real problem of black-and-white relations would come after the abolition of slavery, and that it would come because the blacks, dissatisfied with formal freedom, would not stop short of anything except complete equality. "The Negroes," he wrote, "might remain slaves for a long time without complaining; but as soon as they join the ranks of free men, they will be indignant at being deprived of almost all the rights of citizens; and being unable to become the equals of the Whites, they will not be slow to show themselves their enemies." Tocqueville understood the dynamics of passionate movements, which we generally call "revolutions." Studying the French Revolution, he saw that it had not come at the point when the condition of the people was at its worst, but when important concessions had been made and conditions were on an upward arc. Every intense social movement, he saw, "grows by what it feeds on." Bukharin saw the same phenomenon much later: "In revolutions, appetite grows with the eating."

Seen thusly, it becomes clear why the great civil rights victories of the 1950's and 1960's, starting with Brown v. Board of Education, were accompanied not by social peace, but by mounting violence. Revolutions come in periods not of stagnation, but of accelerated social change. They come in periods not of apathy and hopelessness, but of rising hope—hope that is not fulfilled rapidly enough and therefore turns to frustration and bitterness. When Myrdal wrote his *American Dilemma*, it was largely an appeal to the conscience of the whites, and he wondered whether the dynamic of American idealism—both from religious and political sources—could operate effectively enough against the resistances of racism. His focus was upon the mind and personality of the whites. The Kerner report, with the same emphasis and the same focus, may be seen as the closing phase of the Myrdal approach, not as the beginning of a chapter in the story of black-white relations, but as the ending of one.

III

The next phase must focus on the psychodynamics of the Negro personality and the voyage of the mind of the blacks. The question is not only of the objective reality of whatever access the blacks get to economic and social life-chances, but also of their subjective perception of it. A good deal of the destiny of the cities will depend on the internal struggle between alienation and trust, especially in the mind of the young Negro as he grows into adolescence and beyond, whether in the ghetto streets and schoolrooms or—in the rarer cases—in middle-class homes and on university campuses.

Even a too summary glance at the development of the Negro personality will show how counterproductive it is to abstract any phase of the problem of the cities from its rich living context—a context that must always be sought at the convergence of person, place, and culture which we call the Negro ghetto. The young Negro, in his growing-up years, is subjected to a barrage of forces that zero in on his career-line. Roughly they can be put under four heads: the family, largely unstructured, mainly matrifocal; the media, at once stimulating and disillusioning, especially TV; the school, in the form of the angry classroom, lunchroom, play-yard; the street, with its cacophony of sounds and sights, its "welter of pathologies" (in Kenneth Clark's phrase), its sexual vividness, and its criminal marginalism in the form of prostitute, dope-pusher, numbers-runner. In later years, one might add to these socializing agencies the church (especially in the tightly cohesive southern communities), more than occasionally the police precinct-house or jail, and of course the Army, and for some the university.

While I have called these socializing agencies, in the sense that they bring the young Negro into the adult community in one way or another, they are not acculturating in the sense of fitting him into the larger culture, although they may in fact fit him into the ghetto subculture. One danger we run in observing the Negro family is to measure it against that of two other ethnic minorities, the Jews and the Irish or Italian Catholics, in another ghetto in the earlier history of the American city.

It is a danger because these two classic instances of access and acculturation present a false norm for the very different Negro family, with its very different historic experience, social and economic location, and life style. The Jews and the Irish, to take the best-studied ethnic minorities, started with what may be called the *dream of access,* which they never gave up. There was a good deal of family stability among the Jews, less of it with the Irish, but in both cases it was directed at "making good." They developed the rooted ties of owning (retail store, skill-shop) and running (precinct, ward); they had a tradition of the life of the mind, whether in intellectual skills or the church; they valued the winning of prestige in their subculture and larger culture. Crucially they could leave the ghetto once they got the means to leave. Although they were kept out of the social Establishment of the owning and governing caste, they did not have color as a residual badge of past subjection to keep them trapped where they were.

The dream of access has proved an eroded dream for the Negro. This is not true of the upwardly mobile middle-class Negro family, but in the other instances equal access to equal life-chances has been a cup offered, but dashed from the lips. The capacity to make use of it is less, precisely because the condition of the poor Negro family in the city—the illegitimacy, the absent father, the working mother, the cruel pressures of the relief rolls—has not been conducive to the exploration of access. There is a temptation for the Negro youth to use the obstacles in the path of access as a rationalization for inaction, a way of opting out of the competitive struggle. The result is often the drifter or operator who lives on his wits—sometimes on the margin of the criminal world, preferring the unpredictable windfalls of such a life to the burdens of an arduous job.

The media role has been disputed among a number of observers of life in the inner city. My own strong feeling is that TV played an important historic role in breaking the Negro household out of its isolation and giving it a new window on the larger world. TV and the auto have been the two ways out of the ghetto, making ghetto life tolerable for those who must stay in it, yet want to escape from it. But as often happens when the walls of isolation are broken down and when traditional culture-elements are rapidly modernized, the result may be an uprooting and confusion of the personality. That has happened a number of times in the new African states, when emigrants have left their village and tribal ties to come to the city, and when the change has left them detribalized, without any new roots and ties to take the place of the old ones. In a sense, the Negro American, torn from the roots of his church-oriented southern community with its larger joint family, a migrant to the big northern city, has used television as a way of enlarging his vistas and has ended in the same confusion of self-image as his African contemporary.

TV lighted up the little Negro flat or tenement with a view from the great world outside. It showed off the seductiveness of that world, its Babylonian surfaces and splendors, its sleek cars, its high living, its expensive fabrics, its consumers' goods, and above all its cash nexus and vendibilities as expressed in TV commercials. The urban Negro, for whom the TV screen had become a necessity no matter how low his income, was at once seduced and repelled by this view. The prizes it held out were attractive, but eluded the grasp of those who reached for them. If anything, TV may have deepened their mistrust of a society so capable of withholding what it seemed to offer, and may have widened their estrangement from it. The homes you saw were not open to you, the consumers' goods were priced beyond your range, the delicious fripperies of kitchen and boudoir could be galling if you were jobless and on the poverty level that the relief check afforded. Perhaps deeper than anything else, the white sexuality displayed was meant for whites, not blacks, and in some states it could mean death if you reached to respond to it. Thus the light that showered into the Negro flat from the TV screen, for all its brilliance, turned out for many to be a light that failed.

The trouble with the school was its inability to make what it taught, and the teachers as well, at all relevant. It was geared to a different way of life, different ordeals and ideals, a different career-line and personality-structure. But it offered a good arena for combat, a good stage on which to disport yourself. As for the vocational skills they were ready to teach you, what was the use of learning them if they fitted you for jobs that were not there or that paid worse for blacks than whites, with unions that often made the admission of blacks intolerably difficult? The Army was another matter: The black soldier or Marine got a chance to show the stuff he was made of, alongside the white, in a democracy of danger and death. Besides, the skills the services taught were skills that equipped you for work in the new electronic age, and the prestige of Army service carried over into civilian life and gave you a good chance at a job. The returned veteran was likely to find himself less estranged from the white society, more in command of himself in the black society, than any other Negro, including the upwardly mobile civilian blacks. But what an irony that the back door by which a black could enter into some kind of social normality should be a door that carried the danger of death.

Thus the career-line: family, street, media, school, Army. The inner fantasy-life that it has carried with it is one that lay ready for the spark of violence to ignite and explode. If one were to say that this fantasy-life counts for the black personality, that the disheartening gap between fantasies and the reality-principle is the clue to the discontents and therefore also to the confrontations with white authority, many "action-oriented" students of the problem might scoff. Yet I venture that there is an arena of action inside the mind and imagination that may be less dramatic than the actions outside, but without it the tearing down and building of structures, clearing and remodeling of decayed areas, the new investment, the revamping of welfare will have little focus and relevance. It forms the *cui bono* for the whole coalition approach.

Obviously I have myself been guilty of a kind of abstraction and reduction in talking as if there were a single universal personality type among the young Negroes growing up in the ghetto. One could suggest a more complex typology: the ambitious, upwardly mobile skill-oriented Negro, including not only the teachers and other professionals, but also the young men returning now from the armed services; the rooted, code-bound, church-oriented Negro, either lower-middle class or proletarian; the alienated Negro, disillusioned about white society, but still willing to move toward integration and ready to believe in the ultimate promise of an open society; the militant Negro personality, not only alienated but separatist, who has given up hope for anything but coexistence with the whites and believes that the best way to get that coexistence is to claim it, not flinching from the gun as a weapon and from fire as a symbolic leveler; the alienated Negro (again) who is not an activist, but a drifter and *Luftmensch*, making his living in the interstices of a loosely organized society, ready to make consumers' goods his own on the right occasion of violence, but uninterested in activism or revolution; and finally the Negro who has not been able to tolerate the gap between his fantasy-life and reality without becoming a drug addict and getting involved in petty crime.

I should add that in the last two types the undue postponement of the work life of the adolescent, which operates in the case of the whites to provide him with skills for a post-industrial (or knowledge-applied-to-industry) era, operates in the case of the Negro adolescent only to cast him adrift exactly when he should be putting down the roots of job, place, home, and defining his sense of selfhood.

I fear that the whites have not begun to understand the inner world of the Negro, or his fantasy-life, or the meaning that modes of personality and behavior have in the life of the Negro which would seem abnormal in the life of the whites. The norms and modalities are different, and the failure to see this has led to a failure of white psychologists and psychoanalysts to make much sense of the Negro personality in their studies of it "in depth." Where the liberal white reformer has seen the Negro on an overly rationalistic plane, the psychiatric studies have tended to see him as a set of case histories in irrationalism and psychosis, partly at least because they have not taken into account the different emotional constitution of the Negro family, the different meanings attached to male sexuality, and the different contexts in which identity is or is not achieved. If one were to take as accurate the picture of the Negro personality emerging from the psychiatric profiles-in-depth, the task of ever getting communication—not to speak of social peace—between the races would be hopeless.

I do not mean to gloss over the difficulties both of communication and social peace. They loom particularly large when you look at the whole sweeping cycle of the Negro role, from his African homeland until today, and see the progression from warrior to slave to proletarian to sullen and smoldering resister of white society and white authority. The Negro American has not passed through the stages of merchant and intellectual that the Jew has passed through, nor of lawyer and politician as in the case of the Irish. We cannot expect to cramp him into the mold of the other ethnic minorities. But it should be clear that one of the problems of the inner city is the exclusion of the Negro from the fruitful roles that have eased the acculturation of the other groups—or at least his failure to assume and fulfill those roles.

No minority can emerge from the caste status until it has been able to move into the significant elites of the society. The upwardly mobile Negro has moved into the elite of the entertainment world and of sports, but not yet into the three elites that characterize the whites: the corporate managerial elite (largely Protestant), the political elite (largely Catholic), and the intellectual and artistic elite (largely Jewish). That is why the recruiting of young Negroes for the small colleges and the great universities makes sense from an overview of the total problem. The Jews did not achieve a fully normalized life until they had shown, in the recent Israeli wars, their capacity as warriors. The Negroes, already rather formidable warriors, may not achieve a fully normalized life until they show their capacity to own, manage, and run, if not the whole city, at least those parts to which they are organic.

It is to this aspect of the Negro and the city that I turn in the final section of this essay. But not until I have asked what is meant by the violence of the Negro encounter in the inner city with the symbols of white ownership, affluence, and authority. Is it fun and games? Is it (as many of the terrified whites fear) racist hatred and death? Obviously it is a little of each. But it is also the expression of a claim on America and its Babylonian splendor. And it is a cry of anguish on the part of those who have not found their true selfhood and have not resolved the tensions between feeling and living as Negroes and feeling and living as members of the larger city and national community. It is all these and perhaps one thing more: a cry of despair at not having found suitable roles—in skills, knowledge, power—that will enable the Negro to lead an expressive life, cherishing the city he is part of, rather than threatening to level it with a flaming sword.

IV

There have been many definitions of the ghetto, some stressing its self-imposed aspect, some its other-imposed aspect. But basically a ghetto is a trap. It is a trap that may have started, as in the case of the Negroes in northern cities, when migrants moved into it to huddle together for warmth, and then continued because no other place was open to them. In some cases, they may want to continue to live there, out of a sense of the familiar and a distaste for the strange new scene. But if exit is not open to them, whether they want to avail themselves of it or not, then the trap aspect makes it a ghetto. It may also be a slum, in terms of congestion, dilapidation, or decay, but that is another matter. Psychologically, it is the ghetto aspect that counts.

Having said this, I should add that mass emigration from the city's ghettos is not necessarily the solution to the inner city's turbulence or its poverty. The whole problem has been brilliantly discussed in Anthony Downs' essay in terms of choices between possible alternative social strategies. I note only the danger we all run of falling into the fallacy that the Negro will be "happier" living elsewhere than where he is. He may or may not be. It depends on whether he can find elsewhere—in the suburbs or in parts of the central city where he is in a minority rather than a majority—the kind of social warmth and the sense of place and belonging that he finds where he is now. But what is crucial is that the Negro should be able to leave the ghettos if he chooses, able in the legal sense of open-housing laws and in the *de facto* sense of having work to do and an income that sustains him there. As for guesses about how many would leave if they had the chance, I find Kenneth Clark's estimate a credible one: that in the first generation perhaps only 10 per cent would leave, in the next 30 to 35 per cent, with enough leaving in the third generation to make it a racially balanced area, rather than a racially segregated one.

It is ironic that many who have written about the city, with the concept of place being necessarily part of it, have never themselves had an empathy for the sense of place. This is especially true of the liberal thinkers who have lived in the city, but have never been attached to a particular city. Like Jefferson, they dislike and fear the mass-city for its mass-culture aspects. Jefferson had a wonderful feeling for the farm and village and small town, and for the interaction of person, place, and culture. But a number of his followers today, although adhering to his radical views of democracy, lack his sense of the organic role of place.

A man defines himself in part by the web of his relations with others, in part by his relation to the place where he lives and works, in part by his relation to his subculture and culture. But, more precisely, what constitutes a ense of place in the city? One might say that a man has a good functional sense of place if his children are growing up there, if he has work, friends, a feeling of familiarity, and a sense of participation and some control over his destiny there. Take the classic case of the New England township in its heyday, and you will find it fulfilling each of these criteria. Take the much maligned suburb of today, with all its conformist pressures, and you will still find it measuring up tolerably. Can the same be said of the situation of the Negro in the inner city?

Only in part. His children are growing up there, but not well—largely without parental or other controls, with a series of too precocious exposures to adult experiences and too few culture-binding exposures to aspects of the larger culture. If he has work, which is a chancy if, it is likely to be elsewhere. He does have friends there and a sense of being at home in a familiar environment. He has little power or control over his destiny there, which is one of the reasons for the desolating sense that nobody cares, which we call "alienation" and which is growing rather than lessening among Negroes.

It has become a truism to say that everything will fall into place if only the Negro poor have a decent income, and there is enough truth in this to make the battle for something like a guaranteed family income a valid one. Yet income alone, or even a job alone, is not enough. It must be *work* rather than a *job*, putting back into the work concept some of the pride and sense of vocation that the Protestant ethic gave it and that, perhaps, the Negro has moved furthest from. When Ralph Abernathy organized a "poor people's march" on Washington, he defined the objective thus: "To plague the Pharaohs of this nation with plague after plague until they agree to give us meaningful jobs and a guaranteed annual income." When Lewis Mumford says that we must stop building vast high-rise urban renewal projects and pushing highway programs, stop looking for technological breakthroughs into the problem of the cities, he tells us to "listen to the poor people in every city—the unemployed, the exploited, the neglected racial minorities who are tired of being treated as subjects for computerized urban research or bureaucratic runaround." In both instances there is the hint of some special mystique of the condition of being poor that I reject.

When Abernathy talks of "meaningful jobs," however, he is talking of work in the sense I have used above. And when Mumford says that we must start not with money or technology but with men, and that we can do nothing "without restoring their self-respect, their self-confidence, and their capacity for self-government," he reaches very close to the heart of the issue, and includes work and place, power and culture.

Work—meaningful, prideful work—can do more than anything else to achieve this restoration. The Negro, migrating from the southern plantations to the cities of the North, hoped to find work and freedom in them. He found jobs in the mass-production plants for a brief spell, and in Detroit and Chicago and Watts he found freedom, but not the sense of community he had left in the more tightly knit Negro communities of the South. But the mass-production jobs needed skills and the kind of steadfast patience that many of the newcomers lacked. After the Detroit riot in the summer of 1967, the auto plants agreed to take on a number of unemployed unskilled Negroes, to open jobs for them and train them, but a dismaying percentage of them dropped out of the training course. Clearly the chances for future jobs lie less with the mass-production industries than with the new ones geared to the new technology. A massive coalition-directed program of training a large number of promising young Negroes intensively for work as technicians in these service and knowledge industries might just possibly succeed in coping with the imperative of prideful work that man needs if he is to be a person in a place. Sometimes in history the same innovating technology that dislocates a going situation and sets up a problem may help resolve it. Without going through an elaborate college education, many young Negroes can be trained by the newest technology to take their places in that same technology.

Along with work nothing can be more effective in restoring self-respect and self-confidence than the sense of having a hand in the destiny of one's neighborhood and city. This might be called participatory power. It goes beyond the voting principle, in choosing those who govern. It operates through a direct self-government on the immediate level: by decentralized school systems in which the neighborhood parents and administrators have a large share in teaching the children; by decentralized state and federal community programs in which the beneficiaries must learn to cope administratively with their own needs; by a direct share in coalition programs for developing small business ventures and for home ownership; increasingly by training more teachers, police, doctors, and politicians from the neighborhood itself so that those who live there feel that they are treated, served, represented, and governed by people with whom they feel at peace because they are their own. The way to stop the burning is to have the propertyless own their own homes, whether privately or cooperatively. The way to stop the looting is to have them own shops and small enterprises. The way to give schooling some standing is to have the schools run by those whom the people of the neighborhood know and trust. The way to anneal the sense of alienation from government and society is to see your own people become councilmen, police inspectors, mayors, governors, senators.

I am not arguing here for "Black Power" in the hostile and exclusive sense of that term, when it becomes an inverse *apartheid* and spreads the kind of *grande peur* that feeds the most extreme forces of reaction. Black Supremacy is no better than White Supremacy, and it is bound to drive whites out of any area in which the blacks seem likely to become strong. But the day is over when the ghetto was a fair preserve for proconsuls and satraps, when the whites had a prescriptive monopoly of the crucial governing posts. Today there are Negro mayors in Washington, Cleveland, and Gary; tomorrow there will be others like them in a half-dozen other great cities whose Negro component is close to a majority, if not actually one. The day after tomorrow there will be black governors, and the day after that the composition of a Presidential ticket will not easily exclude the idea of a Negro for one of the two top posts.

This is the genius of American politics, this capacity for channeling new freshets and even tumultuous currents into the main stream, whether it be in business, politics, education, or innovations in the mores and the arts. Those who speak for the necessity of a separatist Black Power movement in order to achieve a sense of pride and identity tend to forget that true self-confidence does not come when you have locked your opponent out and have your little arena to yourself; it comes when you have shown your capacity to meet your opponent on his own ground in the larger arena or to join in a coalition with him against other opponents. The relation of participant power to the sense of identity is a crucial one, and out of it can come a pride in place and a greater ease and coolness in living in it.

The other aspect of power that bears on the situation of the city is its relation to trust. The powerless cannot trust anyone: They fear the shadows as well as the realities of enmity. But some equality of bargaining power begets trust, which is needed for any coalition activity. One of the difficulties with making coalition action persuasive hitherto has been the scepticism of the Negroes not only about the good will of the whites who form the coalition but—even assuming good will—their capacity to do something about it. Before white good will can be translated into social action, there must be, so to speak, another gear—the conviction of the whites that they have personal and group interests that will be served by the action. One form of such self-interest is the idea, gaining ground steadily, that the rest of the city (or society) cannot prosper if one crucial part of it languishes. Another form, as many black militants assert, is the fear of the burning and looting that will occur unless the action is taken. Still another form is the feeling that a Negro power base—economic and political—must be wooed by actions rather than words and good will. Some whites may have as their "other gear" simply the stirring of their imagination or a more personal sense of self-interest—their image with their own children and their desire to have the approval of the young, who in many cases have identified with the cause of Negro access and power.

The growing number of young Negroes who are being admitted

into the colleges and universities raises questions of the impact the newly emerging Negro intellectual elite will have on the city. The trend among them is not only toward militancy, but a black separatism in residence and classroom and in activism outside the classroom. This is bound to affect the emotional climate of the inner city, to which most of them—as separatists—are likely to return. At the universities they have been learning invaluable lessons in political tactics and in the nature of power and the emotional frame of opinion. They need a chance to apply what they have learned to the participatory politics of city and neighborhood. There is the chance, of course, that their newly found militant separatism may lead to a break in legality and to revolutionary politics in the fragmentizing and sectarian sense. But it is a risk that has to be taken, since only the infusion of new energy and imagination into the inner city can give it the sense of ferment without which place is only location, not living.

It must be living if it is to have any meaning. One of the worst things that the white society has done to the Negro in many of the cities has been to shut him out of community, in its deepest sense of common interests and actions and the sharing of common experience and values. The Negroes had to find some common experience and values of their own. They had done so in the South, in cities like Atlanta and New Orleans. They managed to do it to some extent outside the South, in Harlem, St. Louis, San Francisco. They achieved it almost not at all in Watts, Detroit, and Newark where the Negroes came as uprooted migrants and where they found no subculture of their own to give them definition and warmth. Harlem, for example, developed its own literature, its own arts, its own dance and jazz, its own life style. The Negro in Harlem found himself to be a person not only in a place, but in a culture of his own.

Is it too wild a surmise to say that there may be some relation between this and the incidence of the riots? I have put the question earlier as to why the riots came *when* they did. But there is the added question: Why did they come *where* they did—in Newark rather than Harlem, in Detroit and Watts rather than in San Francisco? The question of the living conditions of the people is not decisive. If it were, how could one account for the trouble in Detroit, where the city administration was relatively liberal, and where the white and Negro community leaders had worked in action programs for years?

The answer about the where is complex, yet one strand of it may run through the existence rather than the absence of a conscious subculture, through some measure of the organic relations of person, place, and culture rather than the uprootedness and alienation that were true of Watts and Detroit, and supremely true of Newark.[1]

REFERENCE

1. I owe a great debt in this essay to the help of Michael Lerner at the Yale Graduate School and to his manuscript "Personality Development in the Black Urban Ghetto."

THE FORM AND CONTENT OF RECENT RIOTS

Hans W. Mattick

Hans W. Mattick, "The Form and Content of Recent Riots," *Midway,* Summer 1968, pp. 3-32.

THE FORM AND CONTENT
OF RECENT RIOTS

Hans W. Mattick

In his Introduction to the Bantam Books edition of *The Report of the National Advisory Commission on Civil Disorders*, Tom Wicker repeatedly reminds his readers that this report "derives its most devastating validity from the fact that it was drawn by representatives of the moderate and 'responsible' establishment — not by black radicals, militant youth or even academic leftists . . . these recommendations come from the moderate establishment . . . not liberals, radicals or intellectual bleeding hearts."[1] No doubt he is right but, despite their laudable desire to "tell it like it is," the commission was not insensitive to political realities. In the analytic parts of the *Report* the role of the war in Vietnam, as a contributory factor to unrest in the nation and as a diversion of national resources, was all but ignored. Similarly, in their recommendations for social change, the money and resources question remained implicit.[2]

The author was employed by the National Advisory Commission on Civil Disorders to do research on the sociological aspects of riots under OEO Contract B89-4353 during the period January 22 to March 1, 1968.

[1] (New York, 1968), pp. v–xi passim.

[2] The most comprehensive study of riots (as distinguished from studies of revolutions) in the pre-1960 period states: "The five most bitter race riots in this century have been those of East St. Louis, Washington, Chicago, Tulsa, and Detroit. Each of these riots has occurred either immediately before, during, or immediately after a major war involving the United States. The hypothesis might legitimately be raised that these disturbances have been reflections of a generalized climate of violence which results from wartime conditions" (Allen P. Grimshaw, "A Study in Social Violence: Urban Race Riots in the United States [Ph.D. diss., University of Pennsylvania, 1959], p. 180). The commission resisted the temptation to contribute toward a further test of this "legitimate hypothesis," but this will no more deter

Just as the commission displayed a tacit circumspection about the hard realities of war and money in relation to the President and the Congress, the upper staff levels displayed a cautionary sense for the presumed tolerance limits of the ideological spectrum comprising the commission. The upper staff levels, all bright, knowledgeable and ambitious young men, organized the working drafts from materials supplied by the lower staff levels and more than two hundred "consultants, contractors, and advisors." It was the upper staff levels who decided what materials would be allowed to survive in the final drafts submitted to the commission for review, acceptance, or rejection. Whether the upper staff levels were any more accurate in their perceptions about the commission than the latter were about the President and the Congress is a question that is unanswerable, but this entire process of anticipations and the exercise of restrained sensibilities underlines the conservative nature of the *Report*.

In practical terms all of this means that very little got into the analytic parts of the *Report* that could not be documented by defined data, explicit methodology, sworn testimony, affidavits, or very reliable sources. Chapter 2, on "Patterns of Disorder," with its 249 explicit footnotes, is only the most overt example of this passion for "sticking to the facts" as closely as possible while pointing to the data, its methodology and its sources. This is unexceptionable, and it resulted in the publication of a great deal of material that may be useful to future scholarship, but it was a process of exclusion as well as inclusion. The manifest aspects of civil disorders were set forth in great detail while their latent aspects were relatively neglected. The tendency to generalize, to attempt to interpret "the facts," was, by and large, resisted as too speculative an enterprise for a governmental com-

future students of riots from considering all relevant facts than it has scholars in the past. The association between wartime conditions and the outbreak of civil disorders is a historical fact frequently commented upon by sociological historians. See Lyford P. Edwards, *The Natural History of Revolution* (Chicago, 1927) or Crane Brinton, *The Anatomy of Revolution* (New York, 1938). The decision to issue the report in March rather than in July as originally planned, despite the fact that it seriously compromised the quality of much of the commission's work, which had been predicated on the longer timetable, no doubt reflects a political decision of a different order. The six months between the foreshortened publication date and the national political conventions in August may have been viewed as a sufficient "cooling off" period to help moderate the effects of the report on the political conventions or the public, or both. Neither subsequent historical events nor the political activities of "outsider" groups, however, may be as readily controllable as the publication date of the report.

mission. As a consequence, several interesting attempts to formulate a riot typology, based on the data available to the commission, simply did not survive the division of labor and editorial decision processes that resulted in the published *Report*.[3] In what follows, the tendency to generalize will be given a limited scope, an interpretation of some of the facts will be made, and a typology of both the form and the content of the riot process will be presented.

CIVIL DISORDERS SINCE WORLD WAR II

As the nation reflects on recent years of convulsive events it is only natural that some attempt be made to bring order out of chaos by an effort to understand what is happening and, insofar as possible, why it is happening. It would be a great convenience if historical and social developments unfolded themselves in rational and predictable sequences, but that is seldom the nature of the human condition. While social life and human affairs, in general, are characterized by a sufficient amount of rationality to enable men to make reasonable estimates of the probable shape of the future, the central fact about civil disorders is that they are an interruption of continuity in the orderly processes of human life. In almost every dimension in which civil disorders have been experienced and observed, they have been unusual, irregular, and, in the present state of our knowledge, unpredictable. This is not to assert that civil disorders are beyond the grasp of human understanding or that they are beyond the norms of human behavior given the necessary and sufficient conditions that tend to bring them to pass; but rather that those conditions are both numerous and complex, and our attempts to understand the products of those conditions must address them in the interrelated manner in which they confront us.

Perhaps the three safest generalizations that may be drawn from the civil disorders since World War II are all negative. 1. There is really

---

[3] Two other such attempts came to the author's attention. One was prepared by Robert Shellow, Assistant Deputy Director of Research for the commission, in an excellent paper entitled "The Harvest of American Racism," which was prominently stamped with the cautionary message: "This document has been neither submitted to, nor approved by, the members of the Commission." The other was prepared by John P. Spiegel, Director, Lemberg Center for the Study of Violence, Brandeis University, who is listed among the "consultants, contractors and advisors" to the commission. Hopefully, both of these papers will be published in order to contribute to the public understanding of recent civil disorders.

no such entity or process as a typical civil disorder. Any attempt to construct ideal types of the form or content of riots must abstract and combine predominant tendencies through analysis and synthesis. 2. Although the civil disorders since World War II were racial in character, they were not *interracial*. In general contrast to the interracial conflicts that have erupted from time to time in the past, from the colonial period through World War II, in which groups of one race came into direct conflict with groups of another, recent civil disorders, including those of 1967, have been directed against the local symbols of white American society: authority and property. 3. Despite the extremist rhetoric of some unimportant fringe groups, there has been no serious attempt, either actual or ideological, to systematically subvert the democratic and pluralistic social order based on the Constitution of the United States. In effect, what those who are now attacking white authority and property are saying (and have been saying for the past hundred years) is, "We want fuller participation in the goods, services, and amenities enjoyed by the vast majority of American citizens." In this sense, the conflict between the majority and the minorities represents a *conservative movement*. At this juncture in history the remaining minorities still want "in," not out; they want to play a role in the American dream; not create a nightmare of the extreme right or left.

ELEMENTS TO BE COMBINED IN A TYPOLOGY

While all of the commission's findings may be drawn upon to contribute toward a typology of riots, some aspects of their analysis are more useful than others. For the first nine months of 1967 the commission compiled a list of 164 civil disorders occurring in 128 cities. These were classified by the criteria of levels of damage and violence into "major," "serious," and "minor" civil disorders, and then subclassified by month, region, and population size of cities in which they occurred.[4] In addition, the commission made a detailed study of 24 civil disorders in 23 cities;[5] conducted more than 1,200 interviews in

[4] *Report of the National Advisory Commission on Civil Disorders* (Government Printing Office [Catalog No. Pr 36.8: C 49/R29; price $2.00], Washington, D.C., March 1, 1968), pp. 65–66. (Hereinafter this official document will be cited as *NACCD Report*.)

[5] Ibid., p. 67. The 20 cities and three university settings were: Atlanta, Bridgeton, Cambridge, Cincinnati (June disorder), Dayton (June and September dis-

20 cities to study the content, frequency, and intensity of grievances in Negro communities;[6] and made a special study of riot participants based on all the foregoing, supplemented by arrest records and two probability samples, from Detroit and Newark.[7] These parts of the commission's *Report* are singled out because they are important baselines and constitute the source materials for what follows. Although the commission's conclusions are clear, a detailed examination of the analysis will reveal that questions related to the causes, motives, and objectives of the riots are left implicit. Similarly, the only distinctions made between riots are those based on low-level intensity scales of quantifiable categories. The commission's grievance study, the detailed study of 24 disorders and the studies of the riot participant will enable us to be more explicit and to make some qualitative distinctions. At the same time, the commission's classifications of 164 civil disorders will tend to limit any generalizations incident to the construction of a riot typology.

In proportion to the degree to which one is familiar with the complexity and interrelated details of civil disorders, one is prevented from drawing easy generalizations from such involved social processes. One must, therefore, resort to a series of methodological strategies designed to contribute to an understanding of the nature of the civil disorders of 1967 and to enable one to make some positive generalizations. We are thus aware that we are engaged in an enterprise of vast oversimplification in which we will lay stress on the central tendencies of manifest and latent social phenomena. We can only do what the nature of the data reasonably permits and enter a disclaimer to the effect that the riot processes we will try to describe have multiple facets, contradictory movements, elements that have been ill-defined, misjudged, and unknown, and the task before us can only result in a product based on limited, though informed, judgment.

The twenty-four disorders in twenty-three cities studied in detail by the commission revealed only the most general and elementary uniformities directly deducible from time and place, challenge and

---

orders), Detroit, Elizabeth, Englewood, Grand Rapids, Jersey City, Milwaukee, Newark, New Brunswick, New Haven, Paterson, Phoenix, Plainfield, Rockford, Tampa, and Tucson; Houston, Tex. (Texas-Southern University), Jackson, Miss. (Jackson State College), and Nashville, Tenn. (Fisk University and Tennessee A. & T. State College).

[6] Ibid., pp. 80–83.
[7] Ibid., pp. 73–77.

response, ambiguous beginnings and indeterminate ends. Each was a process of social interaction developing over a period of time out of a state of increasing grievance and tension on the part of the Negro community, and a correlative degree of apprehension on the part of the white community, particularly as reflected in a series of police incidents.[8] As tensions increased, a variety of attempts were made to achieve new, or maintain old, levels of racial accommodation. As these attempts broke down, the potential for violence increased, resulting in a variety of explosions related to the particular cluster of circumstances and social forces that characterized that particular locale and its problems.

In the majority of cases a particular confrontation can be labeled the "precipitating incident" that apparently preceded the eruption of violence; but in almost all cases there had also been a series of prior incidents that, in their cumulative impact, merged into the last of the series. Whether these earlier incidents happened a few days, or a month, or a year or more before, they all contributed directly to the increasing grievance and tension in the Negro community and helped precipitate violence. Once violence was abroad, it varied widely in intensity and duration from city to city and in quality over time within the various cities.[9]

THE GRIEVANCE BANK: CAUSES AND MOTIVES

One cannot understand riots without a historical perspective. Nowhere do they simply "break out" in a "spontaneous" fashion from a preexisting state of calm. If they were merely the irrational expression of a perverse human nature we would have to ask ourselves: Why Watts rather than Beverly Hills in Los Angeles? Why the Central Ward rather than some outlying ward in Newark? And why Twelfth Street in Detroit rather than Grosse Pointe? We do not propose to go over the history of race relations in the United States once more. This was more than adequately done by Gunnar Myrdal in his *An American Dilemma*, more than twenty-five years ago. The historical perspective that we seek lies in the personal or vicarious experience and memory of living men in a peculiarly intimate way. These are the events and relations that enter the mind early and deeply; they

[8] Ibid., pp. 68–71 and 81–83.
[9] Cf. the "Charts on Levels of Violence and Negotiations," ibid., pp. 360–407.

are pervasive, long-lasting, and tend to structure one's future perception of the world. If a disproportionate amount of that experience and memory is filled with pain, disappointment, and anger, the result is a person who conceives of himself as being aggrieved.

If a number of men have similar experiences with similar reactions, and if they share their experience and memories with others, the basis has been laid for a community of interest whose common denominator is a set of shared grievances. This is the situation of the Negro community in the United States and, to a greater or less degree, the situation of other disadvantaged minorities. Since, however, the overwhelming majority of civil disorders in 1967, including all of the twenty-four under consideration here, involved mainly Negro participants, we will confine our remarks to Negro grievances. It is worth noting, however, that everyone, including the white majority, has some grievances. The latter may be less demonstrable in an objective fashion, may be less widely or intensely shared, and are therefore less likely to form the basis for a community of interest, but they are present; and, insofar as they have a racial focus, they can play an important part in contributing to violence.

Reference has been made to the commission's study of the content, frequency, and intensity of grievances in the Negro community. Here we are mainly concerned with the qualitative nature of these grievances, the relationships between them and how they interact with other social processes to form what we will call the *grievance bank*. The grievance bank may be conceived of as a combined metaphor, including elements of a memory bank, a data bank, and an exchange bank, with inputs and outputs that accumulate, draw variable interest, and convert into each other through actual or symbolic forms of exchange.

The content of this grievance bank, whether that of the Negro minority or the white majority, consists of an intricately related set of factors that we will separate conceptually in order to simplify the description. By and large those contents may be classified under three headings: (1) objective factors, (2) mixed objective and subjective factors, that is, subjective perceptions and values placed on the objective factors, and (3) purely subjective factors. The main difference between the Negro and white grievance banks, as will soon be apparent, is that *on the average*, the values that can be assigned to the more objective factors are higher or positive for whites and lower or negative for Negroes, while the values that can be assigned to the more ʳ subjective factors are similar in their intensity or central tendency.

1. The Objective Factors in the Grievance Bank

The objective factors, as the term implies, are those on which there is a high level of agreement. They have a high degree of validity and reliability, and separate investigations into their essential nature would result in similar findings. They can be classified, counted, defined, and described with a high degree of precision. They have an existential base and constitute the basic categories for an analysis of social life. If they have been accurately assessed, they can only be reflected upon; they cannot be changed, for they are history. More concretely, they include: the population distribution and characteristics of a defined area, income levels, employment rates, housing conditions, educational achievement, physical and mental health, recreational facilities, political representation, the administration of justice, welfare services, municipal services, and commercial practices. It will be noted that attitudes, and future promises or threats, enter only indirectly, if at all, into the objective factors of the grievance bank.

2. The Mixed Factors in the Grievance Bank

The mixed factors are products of individual or group judgment based on past experience. Something exists or happens, and its meaning or value is perceived from a point of view that is structured by the perceiver's position or function in society. The perception and its interpretation may be accurate or distorted, but whatever their nature, the final product has been largely predetermined. This is the area in which white and black attitudes diverge most sharply, and since we are constructing a grievance bank from the Negro point of view the meanings and values we assign to these factors will be largely negative. In so doing we do not mean to imply that either Negroes or whites are more or less reality-oriented, but rather that this is one of those methodological strategies that will enable us to make a point about central tendencies in Negro grievances. More concretely, these mixed factors include: demeaning or "brutal" police incidents; low wages, unemployment, underemployment, and job discrimination; poor housing in bad areas; substandard schools without quality education; ill health and mental stress; disorganized family life; inadequate recreational facilities, underrepresentation and political exploitation; a double standard in the administration of justice; inadequate and demeaning welfare services; lack of municipal services resulting in dirt and rats; unfair credit and commercial exploitation; and prejudicial white attitudes.

3. The Purely Subjective Factors in the Grievance Bank

The purely subjective factors are myths, rationalizations, and paranoid projections based on the other two sets of factors in the grievance bank. This is the sphere of rumor, propaganda, conspiratorial "plans," and political agitation; the realm of political opportunism, charismatic rhetoric, threats and promises addressed to the future, and the folklore of the streets. It is that proportion of ideology that is designed to appeal to the emotions rather than reason, and while it may move men, it moves them in unpredictable ways. By and large, in comparison with the objective and mixed factors, these purely subjective factors are sound and fury signifying relatively little.

These are the contents of the grievance bank that pervade the Negro community. They constitute social forces that move some Negroes to take social action and to challenge the level of social accommodation in contemporary society, and even to engage in acts of violence. Similar social forces contribute to the motivations of the white majority and move some whites to resist any challenge to the level of social accommodation that exists.

Since our pluralistic and democratic society is constitutionally grounded on a division of powers between the three major branches of government, in a system of checks and balances, it can, for the purpose of constructing an ideal type, be defined as approximating an unstable equilibrium model of social organization. Such a society tends to exercise minimal controls over social forces. Competitive processes in the economic sphere are, for the most part, regulated by market conditions; in the political sphere they are determined by numbers, power, influence, and negotiation; and in the social sphere they are controlled through voluntary association and informal channels of communication. The competition and interaction of such social forces tends to result in a relatively stable level of accommodation between majority and minority interest groups. The same competition and interaction also results in social change, tending to upset that level of social accommodation. But when the more peaceful mechanisms of social control break down or are not responsive to the needs and demands of competitive interests, the stage is set for potential violence.

Ordinarily, there is then resort first to the civil law and then to the criminal law, in a final attempt to contain the potential violence. If however, the law as it impinges on the personal lives of people, in its ultimate role as the arbiter of justice, is itself perceived as being unresponsive or contaminated with prejudice, then the potential for violence is increased. In the construction of the grievance bank and much more thoroughly, in the commission's study of grievances, the importance and salience of Negro grievances about police incidents is manifest. This is the sensitive area that more frequently than any other was the occasion for the eruption of violence in the civil disorders of 1967.

Thus, our inferred "causal chain" begins with a postulate of grievance based on objective factors, leading to an increase in social tension; attempts at challenging the existing level of social accommodation; the achievement of a new and more satisfactory level or, failing that, the maintenance of the old level or perhaps even a less satisfactory one; and renewed cycles of challenge and response, until a viable equilibrium with satisfactory adjustment and continuity is achieved. Like most causal analyses of social phenomena, this is not definitive; but it is not an unreasonable inference in the light of the civil disorders that disturbed the nation in 1967.

The objective factors in the grievance bank may thus be conceived of as a classification of causes, and the mixed factors as a classification of motives. This is not to assert that unitary causes lead to simple motives that move men to precipitate riots, nor is it to deny that the purely subjective factors in the grievance bank do not make a significant contribution to the eruption of violence. On the contrary, it is necessary to emphasize that many causes and motives combine in diverse ways, under various conditions, in differing settings; and yet whether violence erupts or not still remains problematic. More frequently than not, the question turns on the nature of the response from the side of authority. Indeed, in some cases violence is precipitated by the anticipatory behavior on the part of an overapprehensive authority.

More generally, however, a community of interest whose common denominator is a set of shared grievances contains enough free-floating

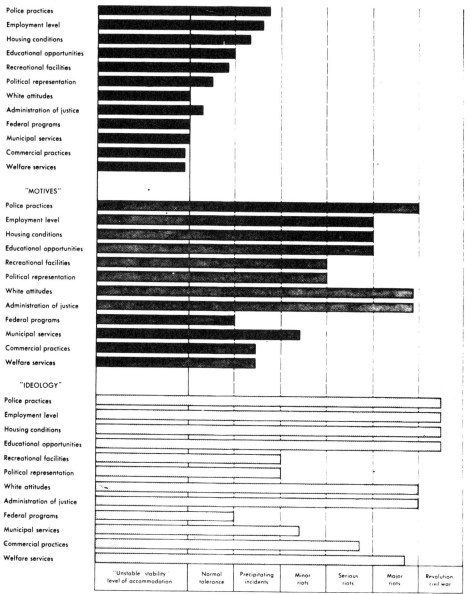

"CAUSES"
Police practices
Employment level
Housing conditions
Educational opportunities
Recreational facilities
Political representation
White attitudes
Administration of justice
Federal programs
Municipal services
Commercial practices
Welfare services

"MOTIVES"
Police practices
Employment level
Housing conditions
Educational opportunities
Recreational facilities
Political representation
White attitudes
Administration of justice
Federal programs
Municipal services
Commercial practices
Welfare services

"IDEOLOGY"
Police practices
Employment level
Housing conditions
Educational opportunities
Recreational facilities
Political representation
White attitudes
Administration of justice
Federal programs
Municipal services
Commercial practices
Welfare services

"Unstable stability" level of accommodation — Normal tolerance — Precipitating incidents — Minor riots — Serious riots — Major riots — Revolution, civil war

Grievances and potential behavior in an unstable equilibrium model of social organization. In this model the social forces interacting in the "grievance bank," and tending toward increasing levels of social instability, are classified in terms of intensity and seriousness. The more "objective factors," which are measurable, valid, reliable, and existential, are defined as "causes." The "mixed objective and subjective factors," which are structured perceptions of objective factors that are value-judged subjectively, are defined as "motives." The more "subjective factors," which are myths, rationalizations, opportunistic rhetoric, and street folklore, are defined as "ideology," that is, largely irrational. The dimension from left to right indicates increasing intensity and the dimension from top to bottom indicates decreasing seriousness. The darkness of shading suggests the relative potential seriousness of the three groups of factors.

hostility in search of a target or a scapegoat that the potential for violence is always present. Given an indeterminate amount of such free-floating hostility, combined with an apprehensive authority that tends to identify with the aggrieved portion of the white majority (which is also seeking an outlet for its hostilities), under the conditions of a precipitating incident and the rehearsal of past grievances, the outcome is civil disorder. All of the foregoing must enter, to a greater or lesser extent, into the typology of the form and content of the riot we propose to construct.

SOME LIMITATIONS ON GENERALIZATIONS

The commission reported that due to widely varying definitions, "between 51 and 217 disorders were recorded by various agencies as having occurred during the first nine months of 1967. From these

COMPARISONS OF TWO SAMPLES OF CIVIL DISORDERS
(All values percentages)

Categories and Subcategories	Sample of 164	Sample of 24	Differences
Violence and Damage			
"Major"	5	25	+20
"Serious"	20	42	+22
"Minor"	75	33	−42
Month of Occurrence			
January	0.5	0.0	−0.5
February	0.0	0.0	——
March	0.5	0.0	−0.5
April	2.0	4.0	+2.0
May	7.0	8.0	+1.0
June	10.0	17.0	+7.0
July	63.0	63.0	——
August	10.0	4.0	−6.0
September	7.0	4.0	−3.0
Region of Occurrence			
East	35	38	+3
Midwest	36	29	−7
South and Border	16	25	+9
West	13	8	−5
City Population (thousands)			
0–50	25	17	− 8
50–100	18	4	−14
100–250	19	33	+14
250–500	18	25	+ 7
500–1,000	9	17	+ 8
Over 1000	11	4	− 7

sources we have developed a list of 164 disorders which occurred during that period." [10] It was this sample of 164 "civil disorders" occurring in 128 cities which were classified in readily quantifiable ways. Similarly, when the commission made its careful inquiry into the riot process, concluding that "the differences between various disorders were more pronounced than the similarities," [11] they "examined 24 disorders which occurred during 1967 in 20 cities and three university settings." [12] Since we intend to draw upon the data and descriptions of the latter in the development of our typology, it is necessary to compare the sample of 164 with the sample of 24, by the commission's own classifications, in order to note any important differences. (See table.) We do not quarrel with the commission who admit that "We found a common social process operating in all 24 disorders in certain critical respects . . . [but] the differences between various disorders were more pronounced than the similarities"; [13] we are simply saying that there is a difference between history and sociology. Sociology seeks to generalize from history and contemporary social life, and so long as assumptions, hypotheses, and methods are made reasonably explicit, rational discussion can go forward about the adequacy of the generalizations that are derived from human experience.

The most important differences between the larger and smaller samples of disorders are that the smaller sample that we will draw on is heavily weighted in the direction of greater seriousness and larger cities. Such a skewing has both advantages and disadvantages. The main disadvantage is that any generalizations derived from such a biased sample are apt to mislead the reader about the character of civil disorders in general and contribute to a greater degree of public apprehension than the facts warrant. The advantages of such a bias are all informational. The six major and ten serious riots, in contrast to the eight minor ones, [14] occurred, for the most part, in large urban locations with many agencies and observers to record information and supply testimony. This will tend to lend our analysis and generaliza-

---

10 Ibid., p. 65.

11 Ibid., p. 67.

12 Ibid., p. 67; see n. 5, above.

13 Ibid., p. 67.

14 "Major": Cincinnati, Detroit, Milwaukee, Newark, Plainfield, and Tampa. "Serious": Atlanta, Cambridge, Dayton (June), Grand Rapids, Houston, Jackson, Nashville, New Haven, Paterson, and Phoenix. "Minor": Bridgeton, Dayton (September), Elizabeth, Englewood, Jersey City, New Brunswick, Rockford, and Tucson.

tions a decidedly serious and urban cast, but it is not intended to imply a necessary correlation.

Despite these reemphasized cautions, we will utilize the major riot as a methodological strategy to generalize about riot processes. A major riot is an enormously complex social phenomenon with mixed causes, motives, and objectives. Therefore, we must resort to a process of abstraction, which makes conceptual separations from a combined reality possible. In so doing we are imposing logic; we are not re-creating reality. In our typology we will present the predominant character of some riots and combine elements or strains from several riots in order to exemplify the central tendencies of different kinds of riots.

Our method will be to present first the form and then the content of the riot. The form of the riot will describe the most general social processes that take place, quite apart from any particular time, place, or person. It will appear to be the chronological sequence of a major riot that runs its course. Only the most general and neutral labels of identification for the participants and contributors will be used, and events will be set forth in an impersonal fashion. In using a major riot as a methodological strategy we do not mean to imply that serious or minor civil disturbances are interrupted or aborted major riots. A civil disturbance is an emergent situation, and what its ultimate character or course might have been, in the absence or presence of events that did not happen, must remain unknown.

THE FORM OF THE MAJOR RIOT: SOCIAL PROCESSES

The form of the riot is symmetrical, like a mirror image. It consists of challenges and responses between the official and the private partici-pants to the riot, with the challenge and the response originating, potentially, from either side. Within this predominant pattern there are contributors and participants who are only indirectly involved, but who, from time to time, help determine the general course of events. Included in the definition of official participants are: local, state, and national officials, elected and appointed, especially the police and the military. Private participants include local citizens, members and leaders of local community organizations, morbidly curious outsiders, and petty criminals. The indirect contributors are the mass media, electronic and printed, counter-rioters, irrational opportunists, and discussants and negotiators, who may be somewhat removed in space and social distance but are trying to affect the course of events. There is, obviously, some overlap and interchange among all these categories of persons, many of whom play both formal and informal and active and passive roles in the entire process.

An Ideal-Typical Riot Process

1. *The Final Incident* occurs: There is acute interaction between some official and private persons in the presence of an initial audience.
2. *The First Violence* erupts: The official and private persons conflict, with some degree of audience participation; the initial audience grows tense, but the official and private participants diverge, usually leaving each other's presence.
3. *The Interstimulation and Early Definition Process:*
   a) The private group *intra*-acts and increases in number through communication and movement.
   b) The official group *intra*-acts and increases in number through communication and movement.
   c) Both groups seek to "define" the ambiguous, emergent, social process.
4. *The Mass Media*, first electronic and then printed, report the event, including the early definitions gained from official sources.
5. *The Conflict Preparation Process:*
   a) The private group congregates at the original scene or migrates to the location of the official group. *Intra*-stimulation, communication, feedback, and movement increase tension.
   b) The official group returns to the original scene or meets the private group at the migration location. *Intra*-stimulation, communications, feedback, and movement increase tension.
   c) Conflicting definitions of the situation are voiced. Complaints, demands, threats, and insults are exchanged in the presence of an audience.
6. *The Second Incident* occurs: Uncontrolled elements in the official and private groups interact intensely and acutely in the presence of a larger audience.
7. *The Second Violence* erupts: The official and private groups conflict and diverge; the entire audience, official and private, is highly stimulated and seeking an outlet for the increasing tensions.
8. *The Mass Media* continue to report these events with the selection of dramatic elements in headlines and pictures. News sources are both official and private, and the early definitions of the situation are qualified.
9. Both the official and private participants, and many members of the larger audience, *activate their full communications spheres*, formal and informal and receive feedback that contributes to further stimulation and tension.
10. *Unofficial counter-rioters and irrational opportunists intervene* and attempt to decrease or increase the level of violence and tension by redefining the situation.
11. *In the background*, near the scene of action or removed from it, putative representatives and leaders of both *the private and official participants meet to discuss, define, and control* the riot. Formal statements of demand and response are made, threats and promises are voiced, some negotiations begin, and tactical, nonviolent plans are formulated.

12. *Preparations for the Final Resolution or Exhaustion:*
    a) The official group rallies nonlocal forces to the scene of greatest potential danger or violence in order to deal with it.
    b) The private group is congregated at, or gravitating toward, the scene of final confrontation.
        (1) The official group has increased in number, changed its basic identity and behavior, and becomes both more threatening and more impersonal (nonlocal, usually state police, National Guard, or federal military forces).
        (2) The private group has increased in numbers, changed some elements of its identity and behavior, and responds more impersonally to the new authority (more older persons, more crimes of opportunity, officially recognized counter-rioters).
13. *The Final Confrontation:*
    a) The official group disperses or contains the riot participants or withdraws from the scene of interaction.
    b) The private group interacts and *intra*-acts intensely in response to the actions of the official group.
    c) There is violence and destruction on both sides, unless the official group has withdrawn, in which case there is destruction and looting within the riot area.
14. *The Mass Media report more objectively* about events, including violence, counter-violence, background meetings, and negotiations. Some "in depth" reports are included with the "news."
15. *The Terminal Process:*
    a) The private group begins to resume normal routines, with diminishing frequency of contact with authorities. Basic human needs for food. shelter, and safety assert themselves.
    b) The official group begins a withdrawal pattern and transfer of responsibility and identity to local authority.
    c) Peaceful emergency measures are taken, on both sides, to deal with the immediate consequences.
16. *Plans for the future* are formulated by representatives of the official and private groups together, and by some members of the official and private groups separately.
    a) Cooperative plans are formulated with full participation and democratic process.
    b) A facade of planning is enacted with many reservations on both sides.
        (1) *"We will all do our best for a peaceful future together."*
        (2) *"Next time we'll really get the dirty bastards."*

THE CONTENT OF THE MAJOR RIOT: ECONOMIC, POLITICAL, AND IRRATIONAL PROCESSES

The content of the riot is reciprocal, like a broken bargain. It cor. sts of claims and denials made in the substance and conceptions of life, liberty, and the pursuit of happiness. The parties to the bargain are the Negro community and the white majority, living under the rule of law, at some level of social accommodation. In process of time the predominant social forces come to shape the law in accordance with the differential distribution of power between the white majority and the black minority. Such consolidations of power are reinforced with irrational myths about black inferiority and white supremacy, and supported by discriminatory behavior patterns and prejudicial attitudes. As a result the Negro community experiences unfair treatment at the hands of the white majority and grievances accumulate. When claims of grievance are made, they are denied, minimized, and rationalized away. When legal attacks are made on discriminatory patterns, the formal law is changed in a grudging, rearguard action and represented as progress. Meanwhile informal procedures are devised to subvert the formal changes in the law. Grievances continue to accumulate and soon the grievance bank of the Negro community is full: almost every aspect of social life that has a significant effect on the life chances of Negroes seems blocked. The progress of the law has been too little and too late. At this juncture of history, after a series of prior incidents of similar character, the final incident takes place and violence erupts.

Any attempt to understand the nature of a riot based on final incidents is, more frequently than not, to deal with symptoms rather than causes. Indeed, final incidents are routine and even trivial. They are distinguished in retrospect because they happen to have been the occasion for the eruption of violence; otherwise they resemble ordinary events. To get at causes, motives, and factors that contribute to the momentum of a riot, we must return to the grievance bank of the Negro community. And, while there is no simple or direct line of progression from cause to motive to action, groups of related grievances can be converted into clusters of causes that motivate men to actions that result in riots. Out of this moving image of social process and content, a phenomenon of infinite complexity, we now propose to construct a number of ideal types. The methodological strategy that we shall adopt is to name a heuristic type, describe its qualitative content, and point to examples among the twenty-four civil disorders of 1967 especially studied by the commission.·

IDEAL-TYPICAL RIOTS CLASSIFIED BY CONTENT

1. The "Rational" Riot of a "Rising" Negro Class

The "rational" riot is rational in the sense that, out of a confused, emergent situation, collective purposes of a "realistic" nature become clear in process of time, and means are relatable to ends. The rioters and their sympathizers, to a greater or lesser degree, attempt to achieve these ends. Such riots tend to take place within nonsouthern, metropolitan centers. When the setting is southern, a university location or large-scale student participation tends to offset the regional character of the setting. Such riots tend to have longer periods of duration, in which their objectives become increasingly clarified. They tend to be preceded, or accompanied, by new or intensified competition among leadership elements within the Negro community, in addition to leadership struggles between elements of the black and white communities. These competitive strivings follow the major leadership dimensions: young and old, radical and conservative, and black-dominated and white-dominated ideological values. During the course of the riot the leadership structure and ideology within the Negro community tends to shift in the direction of the young, radical, black ideology. In response the white leadership tends to make some public concessions to the traditional Negro leadership in an attempt to subvert the new, rising, black leadership and its more radical demands. Participation in the riot involves large numbers and generates widespread sympathy in the Negro community. Both the rioters and their sympathizers become increasingly more task-oriented over time, relating basic causes and motives to short- and long-term objectives. The participants in the rational riot tend to change in identity and character over time. In the early stages of the riot they are younger, less firmly related to the local and wider social structure, and more likely to run great risks and engage in actual and symbolic acts of aggression and defiance. In the later stages of the riot the participants tend to be older, more firmly rooted in the local and wider social structure, in terms, for example, of family relations, employment, and prior legitimate behavior, and they are less likely to engage in irresponsible actions. The participants in a rational riot and their sympathizers are better educated, more politically aware, and slightly better off financially than a true underclass. They are also more self-aware and identify with the mystique of black power and cultural negritude. In descending order of preference, they refer to themselves as black rather than Negro, and Negro rather than colored. The causes that emerge over time are related to the objective factors in the grievance bank — employment, housing, education, political representation, administration of justice, etc. The motives that members of the Negro community exhibit and verbalize tend to stress the more objective factors in the grievance bank — police brutality, low income, unemployment and job discrimination, poor housing and untoward effects of urban renewal, substandard schools with low-quality education, etc. The purely subjective factors in the grievance bank — propaganda, agitation, conspiracy, etc. — add fuel to the riot but contribute nothing new. Both violence and rationality assert themselves in a complementary fashion. Immediately before the riot and in its early stages, the Negro community sees the white majority, and particularly its local representatives, as unresponsive to claims, with channels of communication blocked. During the riot, some elements of both the Negro and the white communities seek opportunities for meetings where more rational discussion and some negotiation of salient grievances can be undertaken. Such meetings tend to alternate with periods of violence, almost as if violence, or the threat of violence, were the medium of exchange in a bargaining session. The new leadership structure that tends to come to the fore in the rational riot participates to a greater degree in such meetings and negotiations, that is, there is more youthful, radical, and black-ideological representation in these attempts to communicate. On the streets, however, in the violent interaction, there is a greater tendency on the part of local authority to engage in retaliatory violence, but this is soon brought under control by the importation of outside military forces. As the rational riot wanes and begins to pass into the aftermath, a fairly clear set of economic, political, and legal proposals for change will have been put forward by the Negro community, and there is at least an initial disposition on the part of the white power structure to address them seriously, within the limits of political survival.[15]

2. The "Expressive" Riot of a Negro "Underclass"

The expressive riot is a "sentimental" riot in the sense that it is a catharsis of accumulated feelings and attitudes. Such riots certainly

[15] With due regard to the necessary qualifications imposed by the internal complexities of all riots, nevertheless, the following classification of riots into our typology is hazarded here and in the next three footnotes. The major riots in Cincinnati, Detroit, and Newark are the best examples of "rational" riots among the twenty-four civil disorders under consideration. The major riot in Plainfield, the serious riot in New Haven, and the minor riots in Englewood and New Brunswick also exhibited strong "rational" themes. The three serious riots at university settings, Houston, Jackson, and Nashville, while including some "rational" themes, are classified as "expressive" riots (see n. 16) because the riot participants lacked a sufficiently firm community base to be taken seriously by the local white power structure.

have latent causes and motives, but these causes and motives do not emerge clearly. Thus the predominant character of the riot remains an expression of sentiments. As a consequence, the objectives of the riot are not formulated in sufficiently general terms to achieve sufficient consensus for more rational action; or the apparent objective is a specific, concrete, local facet of a more general problem that is not focused upon. The latter may be a direct reaction to the final incident, that is, to a symptom; or it may be a high degree of preoccupation with, for example, the failure to serve Negroes in a particular restaurant, rather than the more general problem of equal access to public accommodations. With such unclear or highly specific objectives, resistance to change, in the short run, is usually successful. As a result, the level of tension and frustration either has no clear target or the identified target represents an aggravating defiance. The feelings of frustration are first dammed up and then they overflow into action that becomes violent. Such riots tend to take place in southern, less urban, locations; especially southern university towns with largely nonlocal student populations. The "underclassness" of the Negro groups involved in such a riot may be underclassness in an absolute sense, but it does not have to be. It may be a socially mobile group that views its situation through the lens of relative deprivation in comparison with white peer groups. Black consciousness characterizes the relative deprivation group but is absent or denied in the true underclass. The former identify themselves as *black*, the latter as *colored*. Expressive riots are also preceded, or accompanied, by competition among leadership elements in the Negro community, but there is a relative absence of leadership competition between blacks and whites. The leadership struggles are intergenerational and largely ideological. The older Negro leadership is relatively resigned to the level of social accommodation that obtains between the races; the younger black leadership is challenging these traditional leaders. However, whether the participants in an expressive riot are a true underclass or whether they perceive themselves as such in terms of relative deprivation, neither group has sufficiently firm roots in the local social structure to generate the minimum of power required to elicit a serious response from the representatives of the white power structure — the true underclass because they ordinarily are disorganized and apathetic, the relative deprivation group because they are young and nonresidential. Participation in the riot involves small numbers, generates great hostility in the white community, and receives relatively little sympathy from the wider Negro community. The duration of the expressive riot is relatively shorter than the rational riot and after the incident of first violence is kept alive by large infusions of purely subjective factors in the grievance bank: rumors, propaganda, political agitation, and the folklore of the streets. These are retailed by temporary charismatic rhetoricians in the streets or by student speakers and nationally prominent black militants invited to participate in local protest. The identity and character of the rioters does not change over time, or from prior incidents to the current incident. Such causes as emerge in the course of the riot are closely related to the motives for action in that they flow from the more subjective of the mixed factors in the grievance bank, such as discriminatory behavior and prejudicial attitudes on the part of whites. Attempts to communicate and negotiate with the highest leaders in the white power structure seldom succeed; instead, the meetings and negotiations that take place are mediated through middle-range representatives (both black and white) of the white majority, school superintendents, police captains, aldermen, or a top executive's assistant. The relationship between such meetings and the violence in the streets is remote, however, for the white leadership sees the violence as a problem to be dealt with by major reliance on repressive measures. The violence plays itself out in a relatively short period of time, in any case. As the expressive riot wanes, very little that is substantive has been accomplished by the rioters, but the riot itself has been a form of communication. The white majority becomes more aware that local Negro grievances are more serious than they were thought to be, but the more significant reaction is a generalized sense of disturbance and an increase in polarization. The Negro rioters, on the other hand, feel they have made their point and adopt a wait-and-see attitude. In the final result, threats and promises are made on both sides, and a few token, or symbolic, changes are made in the short run; but the basic causes, motives, and objectives are a potential legacy for future outbursts.[16]

[16] The major riots at Milwaukee and Tampa, the three serious riots at university settings, and the serious riots at Cambridge and Dayton (June) are the best examples of "expressive" riots. The major riot at Milwaukee actually began as a "reified" riot (see n. 17) that turned into an "expressive" riot. The serious riot at Atlanta and the minor riot at Dayton (September) also included strong "expressive" themes.

3. The "Reified" Riot of Social "Contagion"

The reified riot is a "stimulated" riot in the sense that it is the answer to a self-fulfilling prophecy. Such riots may be subsclassified according to the predominant source of the prophecy into (1) media-created riots, (2) authority-created riots, and (3) conformity-created riots on the part of some elements in the Negro community. The reified riot is, essentially, an abstraction made real through the repetition of news about other riots, proximate in space or time, resulting in anticipatory or conforming behavior. The other riots are real enough, but *locally* reports of their nature are filtered through the subjective factors in the grievance banks of both the white and the Negro communities: rumors, propaganda, political agitation and opportunism, charismatic rhetoric, paranoid projections, and the folklore of the streets. Thus major riots in other cities create satellite riots by a process of communication and social contagion. Reified riots can develop into "rational" or "expressive" riots — indeed, develop in almost any direction — or they may remain indeterminate. At the time of the final incident and the eruption of first violence, they have no "real" character of their own, although they develop out of a social environment that is 'ready" for them, that is, enough grievances have accumulated in process of time, and through prior incidents, that the grievance bank on both sides is nearly full.

Media-created riots are an unintended consequence of a competitive and narrow functionalism, and a generalized stimulus to the authority- and conformity-created riots. The media conceive of themselves as doing their normal jobs; they are simply "reporting the news" about a riot that is underway in some nearby location. In the early stages of that civil disorder, however, they are reporting on an emergent situation, and in so doing they help shape its definition. At the same time they are helping to shape the definition of an incipient local civil disorder that might have remained a routine police action or a mere protest activity. Indeed, the working press and still and television photographers sometimes directly provoke unstable elements among the public and the authorities in order to "manufacture" news. Editorial policies in the selection of headlines, stories, and pictures in an emergent situation overshadow the later background articles and studies "in depth." Thus they contribute to the purely subjective factors in the grievance banks of both the white and Negro communities and are put into the service of rumor and the folklore of the streets.

On the side of authority, reified riots can be said to be "planned for" in the sense that the police and city administrations adopt such a posture of readiness that they grow top-heavy and topple over, creating a riot by their anticipatory statements and behavior. The authorities activate their full communication spheres and are *intra*-stimulated through repetition, preoccupation, and feedback. They are usually in direct contact with some elements of the removed authority structure that is dealing with the proximate riot that is the source of news and rumor. Their intention is to be rational and to remain task-oriented, but their focus is too narrow, and they increasingly lose their capacity for making an objective appraisal of all the social forces at play in the local situation. As a result, they are the midwives at the premature birth of a riot.

The conformity-created riot is a direct outgrowth of the two foregoing types, the authority- and media-created. With the background stimulation of a nearby riot, and with the perception of the state of readiness and apprehension on the part of the authorities, youthful and unstable elements in the Negro community in effect say to themselves, "They're expecting it; they're asking for it; let's give it to them." As tension increases with a typical final incident, the reaction seems out of proportion to a routine or trivial event, and the ensuing eruption of violence has the appearance of a "spontaneous" riot. It is, however, the product of the complex interaction between the media, the authorities, and the least stable elements of the public.

Reified riots tend to be short or intermittent and, when intermittent, tend to last about as long as the nearby major riot of which they are a satellite. There are many halo effects from the reports of the proximate riot, as reflected in the perceptions of the local authorities and members of the white and black communities. The intermittent, "stop-and-go" pattern of alternating violence and relative calm is a confused and delayed response to the news as it is received through the media and through the formal and informal communication spheres that are activated by the authorities and the public. The objectives of the reified riot are short-term and reactive, growing directly out of social interactions in the streets. Such riots can occur anywhere but tend to occur most frequently in middle-sized cities or towns surrounding the central city of a metropolitan region. Participation in these riots involves small numbers if they are contained on the first day. If the reified riot is over-reacted to by the authorities or constantly fueled by "atrocity stories" from the proximate major riot, its duration is increased, and it may change its form and content into that of a rational or expressive riot. As the reified riot wanes, the entire community is pervaded by a generalized sense of disturbance and an increase in polarization, the public coming to realize that "it can happen here." Very little has been accomplished, however, and there is not even the feeling that significant communication has occurred. There is an air of unreality about the whole experience, and, although threats and promises have been uttered in the course of tactical maneuvers, the basic situation remains essentially the same. No basic causes, motives, or objectives particularly related to the *local* community have emerged with clarity, the future outlook remains vague, and the white community assumes that the old accommodation patterns will continue to obtain.[17]

4. The "Irrational" Riot of an "Irresponsible" Group

The "irrational" riot is a "counterfeit" riot in a double sense of the term. It is irrational because it has no real, or no legitimate, objectives. It is not based on any of the more objective factors in the grievance bank, except in a very attenuated sense and, therefore, has no real causes, but it does have false motives. It is also irrational in the sense that it is a stereotypical interpretation of the character of other types

[17] The major riots at Cincinnati, Detroit, and Newark served as the riots of reference in space and time for a whole series of "reified" riots in the metropolitan regions surrounding these cities. While such satellite riots may also be subsumed under other headings, their "reified" character is the predominant element in either the final incident preceding the eruption of violence or in their duration, or in both. The major riot at Milwaukee exhibited strong elements of a "reified" riot that developed into an "expressive" riot, with Detroit as the riot of reference. The serious riot at Grand Rapids was also a "reification" of the Detroit riot. The "New Jersey string" of riots — Bridgeton, Elizabeth, Englewood, Jersey City, and New Brunswick (all minor), the major riot at Plainfield, and the serious riot at Paterson — all reflected "reification" effects from Newark as the riot of reference. The minor riot at Rockford was a "secondary reification" from Milwaukee which was, itself, a "reified" riot. Four incipient civil disorder incidents from nearby Chicago also cast their "halo effects" over Rockford. Three other "reified" riots whose later predominant character was "expressive" were the serious riots at Cambridge, Dayton (June), and Phoenix. The minor riot at Tucson was a "reified" riot that seemed to remain largely "irrational" (see n. 18).

of riots, but the stereotype takes the part for the whole and, most frequently, the less important part. Nevertheless, there are irrational components in most riots, and in a few cases it may be said that irrationality is their predominant character. Irrational riots may be divided into a subclass which can be analyzed and explained and a residual category that can be described but not explained because it is irrational. The former is the "irrational" riot with no legitimate objectives and false motives, and the latter is the pure type of the irrational.

The "counterfeit irrational" riot is a diversionary maneuver by a group of criminal, conspiratorial, or simply disorderly persons who are "raising hell." The criminal and conspiratorial groups "stage" some elements of civil disorder in order to achieve some organized and illegitimate purpose, whereas in the case of the disorderly group, the civil disorder is an unintended consequence of exaggerated recreational behavior, like drinking or horseplay. The criminal and conspiratorial activities of such groups represent an opportunistic expression of long-term "life styles"; their behavior is the product of some degree of planning and organization among persons who are "professional" criminals or agitators. They and their activities must be sharply distinguished from persons who commit situational crimes in the course of a riot or who engage in short-term tactics in the fluid situation of a riot. The more professional criminals loot not only for personal aggrandizement, but for resale and profit. The situational criminal loots mainly for personal aggrandizement, but also out of need created by the disruptions of a riot. Similarly, the more professional conspirator wants to control the course of the riot in order to implement some ideological plan of the extreme left or right, but more frequently than not, he is the captive of the riot rather than the reverse. The short-term tactician, who must be distinguished from the professional conspirator, is at best a would-be negotiator in the more rational discussions that go on in the background of riots or at worst merely provocative or reactive in relation to the authorities in the streets. By and large, insofar as such "irrational" elements succeed in precipitating a civil disorder, the participants are few in number and their activities are quickly brought under control. Otherwise, they are a minor element in a different kind of a riot and their motives and activities are confused with more basic social causes, motives, and objectives.

The pure irrational riot is an unintended consequence of the purely irrational activities of individuals or very small groups. It may be an anticipatory or reactive paranoia, striking out blindly at a presumed "enemy" or a random "settling of old scores" (as between blacks and whites) or a reaction of unstable personalities to some natural disaster (fire, flood, breakdown of public utilities), which erupts in violence. Such persons are essentially unpredictable and such events unpreventable; they are the by-products of a complex social organization that takes its toll at its weakest points.[18]

5. The Interracial Riot

The interracial riot is the riot that did *not* happen in 1967, nor, indeed, has there been such a riot in the past twenty-five years. It is the specter that has haunted Americans whose historical frame of reference is the nineteenth-century rural economy. The nature of race and class relations has undergone a radical shift in character since World War I, and the old-style interracial riots that have taken place since then may well be a historical survival from this earlier period. Interracial violence, as one form of social violence, has been well defined by Grimshaw: "Social violence . . . refers to assault upon individuals, or their property, solely or primarily because of their membership in social categories." [19] This definition encompasses much more than interracial violence and our earlier ideal types of the "rational" and "expressive" riots reveal some indications of the shift from racial to class competition. In recent riots the violence of Negroes was directed against the symbols of the white community: authority and property, rather than the white community as a whole. The violence of whites, while much less discriminating, was still not directed against the Negro community as a whole. The "expressive" riot was accompanied by leadership struggles *within* the Negro community and the "rational" riot was accompanied by leadership struggles both *within* the Negro community and *between* the Negro and white communities. At the same time, over the past fifty years there has been a

---

[18] The minor riot at Tucson had the nearest resemblance to an "irrational" riot of the pure-irrational type. At one stage of the serious riot at Grand Rapids, underworld vice elements almost succeeded in exploiting a "reified" riot by trying to turn it into an "irrational" riot of the illegitimate-irrational type. Cf. *NACCD Report*, p. 379.

[19] Grimshaw, "A Study in Social Violence," p. 10.

gradual increase in the proportion of Negroes who have achieved middle-class status. From the standpoint of a shift from race to class competition, these historical developments indicate that "expressive" riots may be a transitional type to the "rational" riot, and that it is the latter that are more likely to recur in the future, unless alternative means to achieve their ends intervene to prevent them. Moreover, regardless of local and transient appearances, this historical development in the United States is essentially a *conservative movement.* The "rising" Negro class does not want to change the American system. What they are saying (and have been saying for the past hundred years) is, "We want fuller participation in the goods, services, and amenities enjoyed by the vast majority of American citizens."

A POSTSCRIPT ON COMMUNICATION: "IMAGES OF ORGANIZATION" AND "PHANTOM SNIPERS"

All civil disorders, anticipated and actual, increase the frequency and intensity of communication among and between the individuals and groups who are most concerned, directly and indirectly. The authorities in particular, with their immediate and constant access to a large variety of communication methods, their more intimate contacts with the mass media and with authorities in other locations, are able to activate an intense and resonating network of communication, which we have referred to as their communication sphere. Similarly, the public caught up in anticipatory or actual civil disorders, as well as those who comprise the wider public audience, also increase the frequence and intensity of their communications.

The mass media, with their constant and repetitious reporting of the news of civil disorders, feed directly into both the official and the public communication spheres. In addition, the authorities, mass-media workers, and members of the public have not only formal but also informal capacities and relations with one another. During the course of a major riot these interrelated communication spheres link everyone, from the President down to the lowliest street gang member, in a resonating network of communication and feedback. All of these communications, rational and irrational, contribute to the creation of a "riot climate."

We have seen how, in the case of reified riots, the activation of these official and public communication spheres, together with the unintended effects of the mass media reporting the news, contributed directly to the "creation" of some civil disorders. There is, however, a secondary effect of the relation between the official communication sphere and the mass media that may help to account for the puzzling contradiction between the theory that riots are the products of organization and the absence of evidence of such organization in subsequent investigations. It may also help account for the great disproportion between the large number of reported snipers and the relatively few that are identified or arrested and charged.

We have characterized civil disorders, in their initial stages, as being emergent situations without clear definition. Both local authorities and other observers, confronted with what was perceived as an ambiguously dangerous social situation, tended to define such emergent situations in operational terms, for the sake of dealing with an unknown, future, potential situation. Similarly, the mass media, reporting such emergent situations, tended to select the most newsworthy and dramatic elements from developing events. Both the authorities and the mass media were simply doing their jobs; had they not done it, they would have been subject to severe criticism. Nevertheless, the functional rationality [20] of a narrow or specialized task orientation had many unintended consequences, one of which was the creation of the image of organization and the multiplication of phantom snipers.

The authorities in their communications and in their deployment of manpower and resources attract the attention of interested members of the public. If, for example, five squad cars from three local beats converge on some location, together with two squadrols sent out from the police station, they will attract an audience even though they may be responding to a false "officer needs help" signal. Similarly, reporters coming on the scene somewhat later are apt to pick up the folklore of the streets rather than descriptions of a real event. Several such false alarms, or small skirmishes, taking place in the atmosphere

[20] Karl Mannheim, *Man and Society* (New York: Harcourt Brace, 1940) distinguishes between "functional" and "substantial" rationality. "The common soldier, for example, carries out an entire series of functionally rational actions accurately without having any idea as to the ultimate end of his actions or the functional role of each individual act within the framework of the whole." On the other hand, "We understand as substantially rational an act of thought which reveals intelligent insight into the inter-relations of events in a given situation" (pp. 56 and 53). It is worth noting that Mannheim associated an increase in "functional rationality" with a tendency toward totalitarianism.

of a "riot climate," soon begin to take on substance. One of the earliest and simplest explanations of "what is going on" is a theory of conspiracy and organization by a group that was previously perceived as being capable of inciting or agitating a "riot."

Somewhat similar processes are at work when the authorities are deployed in several locations simultaneously under a fragmented command or on their own. Any firing of heavy weapons like Stoner rifles and Magnum pistols, whose muzzle velocity sends their missiles through flesh, wood, brick, and metal, creates a dangerously ambiguous situation for the authorities, rioters, and innocent bystanders near

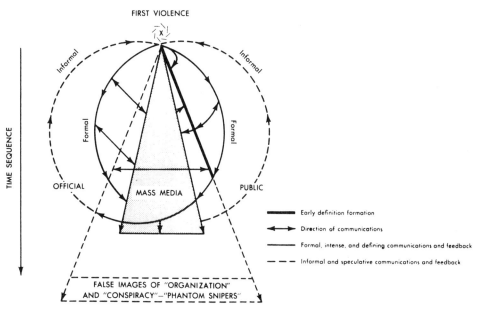

The activation of official and public communication spheres, the mass media, and mutual feedback following upon the outbreak of first violence. In this figure the "operational necessity" of defining the nature of civil disorders in their early, ambiguous, and emergent stages, so that they can be dealt with and reported to the public, results in an interpretation of what first violence means. The simplest and earliest theory is that the developing violence is organized, represents a conspiracy, and is being implemented by snipers. Once the theory is asserted, it is repeatedly fed back to the interest groups engaged in the defining process through the selective perception of "verifying instances" present in a highly complex event, and the definition begins to crystallize. In process of time, and upon more intensive investigation, however, these "images" grow dim for lack of supporting evidence. The "organization" cannot be described, the participants in the "conspiracy" cannot be identified, and the gunfire seems to emanate from "phantom snipers." For true believers the very lack of objective evidence is simply further "evidence" of the depth, deviousness, and elusiveness of "organized conspirators and snipers."

and far. The scene is also set for the inferential creation and multiplication of nonexistent snipers.

Thus the conspiratorial theory and the phantom sniper are fed into the communication spheres of the authorities and the mass media at an early stage, and they keep coming back from what appear to be other, and independent, sources through feedback channels. As a result the images of organization and the phantom sniper are created, projected, and reflected, and they continue to resonate in the atmosphere until more thorough and dispassionate investigation seeks the evidence for them. Insofar as the twenty-four disorders studied by the commission are concerned, no evidence of conspiracy or organization, whether from the left or the right, or black or white, was uncovered.[21] Similarly, reports of sniping were found to be highly exaggerated.[22]

[21] *NACCD Report*, p. 89.
[22] Ibid., p. 180.

PART II
RACE AND
EQUAL EDUCATIONAL OPPORTUNITY

RACE AND EQUALITY OF EDUCATIONAL OPPORTUNITY: DEFINING THE PROBLEM

Charles H. Thompson

Charles H. Thompson, "Race and Equality of Educational Opportunity: Defining the Problem," *Journal of Negro Education,* Summer 1968, Vol. 37, pp. 191-203.

RACE AND EQUALITY OF EDUCATIONAL OPPORTUNITY: DEFINING THE PROBLEM

Charles H. Thompson

The general purpose of this paper is to define the complex problem involved in the attainment of educational opportunity by the Negro racial minority in the United States as compared with the white majority. More specifically, it is the purpose to indicate the present status of the problem, to note in some detail a few of the significant factors which presently define it, and to suggest what seem to be some of the most important next steps in its solution.

Present Status of the General Problem

It should be noted from the outset that the task of obtaining equality of educational opportunity by Negroes, or any other minority group for that matter, obviously is not an isolated problem. It is only one aspect of the larger task of assuring all citizens the opportunity of participating equally in the pursuit of the "American dream." The attempt, therefore, to secure equality of *educational* opportunity by Negroes can not be divorced from their efforts to obtain equal opportunity for employment, equal access to decent housing of their choice and financial ability to purchase, equal opportunity to enjoy public accommodations without conditions based upon race, equal opportunity to participate in the body politic

through the free exercise of the franchise, equal opportunity to obtain impartial administration of justice; in short, equal opportunity to enjoy on the same basis all rights and privileges available to all other citizens, unconditioned by race, color, sex, class, religion, national origin, or any other similar limiting factor.

The extent of the Negro's achievement or lack of achievement of equality in these various areas is generally well known. For example, the late President John F. Kennedy very frankly and aptly noted in his message to Congress in 1963[1] an observation which is equally true to-day. He observed that a Negro child born in America in 1963, regardless of the section in which he was born, had about half as much chance of completing high school as a white child, one-third as much chance of completing college, one-third as much chance of becoming a professional man,[2] one-seventh as much chance of earning $10,000 a year, a life expectancy which was seven years shorter, and prospects of earning only half as much during his lifetime. He might have added that that same Negro child was two and one-half times as likely to have come from a broken home in a slum-ridden ghetto; four times as likely to have been a member of a family eking out an existence on welfare; three

---

* This discussion "is limited to Negroes," as suggested by the Editor, because they are "the largest and most visible minority," and have "been the specific concern of this magazine since its founding."

1 February 20, 1963.
2 The chances of getting into certain professions are even more remote. See *Infra* footnote 35.

and one-half times as likely of running afoul of the law; and so on, *ad infinitum.*

It is not the purpose here to discuss in any detail the history of the Negro's struggle for equality of opportunity in general in this country. However, it will be instructive to recall a few selected highlights for perspective. For much of the Negro's present plight stems from his unhappy past.

Few Americans — Negro or white — know much about, much less understand or appreciate, the nature and history of the abnormal relationship which the Negro has borne to the American social order during the past three and a half centuries, and their influence upon his present status. In fact, as pointed out in the *Report of the National Advisory Commission on Civil Disorders:*

> Few appreciate how central the problem of the Negro has been to our social policy. Fewer still understand that today's problem can be solved only if white Americans comprehend the rigid social, economic and educational barriers that have prevented Negroes from participating in the main stream of American life.[3]

The Commission shocked some of the Nation with its main conclusion: "Our Nation is moving toward two societies, one black and the other white."[4] Why the Commission used the phrase "moving toward" is not clear, except to emphasize that the situation is much worse than we think. Otherwise one would be led to wonder what the Commission thought the American social order had been during the three and a half centuries since 1619.

Whatever the Commission meant by this ambiguous phrasing of their conclusion is not so important here as the fact that they recognized and reported that

> Discrimination and segregation have long permeated much of American life . . . Race prejudice has shaped our history decisively . . . [and] White racism is essentially responsible for the present explosive mixture which has been accumulating in our cities since the end of World War II.[5]

It should be emphasized that "white racism" is not only "essentially responsible" for the present situation but has been at the root of most of the Negroes' troubles ever since they landed on these shores. Beginning shortly after they arrived in 1619, Negroes were separated by law and custom from the remainder of the population. Deprived of their African traditions and dispersed among Southern plantations, they quickly lost tribal and family ties. Moreover, Negroes have been forced to remain more or less apart ever since and by and large are still looked upon as members of an inferior caste.

As slaves, and even as free Negroes during slavery and afterward as freedmen, Negroes have been held in a subordinate position in the American social order, at first by brute force; and later by more sophisticated but equally effective methods. As suggested by Grimes,[6] slavery and the general subordination of the Negro were rationalized on the basis of the legitimizing myth of a master race — reminiscent of Hitler's pronouncement of a master race in the late 1930s. This myth eventuated in the explicit doctrine

---

[3] See: *New York Times* edition of the Report, pp. 206-7.
[4] *Ibid.,* p. 1

[5] *Ibid.,* p. 10.
[6] Alan P. Grimes, *Equality in America* (New York: Oxford University Press, 1964), p. 49.

of white supremacy which survives to this day in less blatant but more subtle and latent form. In support of this doctrine an extensive body of literature and folklore was developed. It purported to prove that Negroes were inherently inferior, that they belonged to an inferior order of humanity, and hence were predestined to be "hewers of wood and drawers of water" for the master race. Often the Bible was quoted and distorted at length to support the contention.

This sort of rationalization has been used to justify slavery, the overthrow of Reconstruction, the disfranchisement of Negroes by law in many of the former slave states, peonage, and other inequities perpetuated against Negroes up until World War II. Moreover, similar rationalizations are being used to justify discrimination in employment, education, housing, and in other rights and privileges enjoyed generally by the white majority.

The point of this discussion is that the problem of attaining equality of *educational* opportunity on the part of Negroes is crucially defined by the difficulties in the attainment of equality of opportunity in general. Two of these difficulties are immediately apparent.

The first difficulty is the fact that the Negro has been and is not only a victim of his high visibility but even more of his checkered past. Much of white America has been conditioned by its own mythology which has been used to rationalize its inequitable treatment of Negroes. Consequently, they have developed what Kenneth Clark calls, "residual psychological prejudices"[7] which come to the surface

whenever a specific problem involving race arises. For example, the automatic assumption underlying the question, Why don't Negroes get out of poverty as the European immigrant did? is that Negroes are inferior, lazy, or both. Thus, there is displayed not only an amazing lack of knowledge of history but a typical automatic assumption concerning Negroes. And many white Americans still cling to this assumption despite the very perceptive explanation in the Report of the Commission on Civil Disorders.

The second and crucial difficulty is that "white racism" — which Tom Wicker so aptly defined as "white refusal to accept Negroes as human beings, social and economic equals . . ."[8] — is the root cause of the denial of full equality of opportunity to Negroes in general. There has been considerable progress made in the past 10 or 15 years in the recognition of the legal right to equality of Negroes in the form of Civil Rights legislation and court decisions. However, there has been considerable "foot-dragging" in implementation. And the stumbling block has been that not enough white Americans have made up their minds to accept Negroes as fellow Americans with equal rights and privileges.

As suggested, the dynamics of this "foot-dragging" is "White racism," although, as noted, in much more subtle form. The fact of the matter is, and may be it is a hopeful sign, that much of "white racism" is going or has gone underground; certainly it is becoming

---

[7] See: Kenneth B. Clark, "Alternative Public School Systems," *Harvard Educational Review*, XXXVIII (Winter, 1968), 102.

[8] See: Introduction to the *Report of the National Advisory Commission on Civil Disorders*, p. vi.

more latent. It tends to rise to the surface, however, whenever some specific issue of personal interest is raised, such as open housing, integration of education, interracial marriage, and the like. The crucial dimension of the definition of the problem of equality of opportunity in general, and of *educational* opportunity for Negroes specifically, is a fundamental change in "the racial attitude and behavior of white Americans toward black Americans . . .";[9] in short, the elimination of "white racism" from American life.

Some Significant Factors Defining the Problem

The task of securing equality of educational opportunity for Negroes is an educational as well as a political problem. Not only does it involve the development of a reasonable consensus in support of the idea, but poses a number of pressing questions relative to implementation. Despite the fact that practically every advance made in the attainment of equality of opportunity for Negroes in general, as well as specifically in equality of educational opportunity, has come through legal coercion, the problem is at the stage now where an almost equally difficult task is that of educational implementation. For even if every racial barrier were entirely removed immediately and everyone agreed that Negroes should have full equality of educational opportunity, such a consensus would constitute only a partial solution of the problem.

The Concept of Equality of Educational Opportunity

What are some of the difficulties to be

resolved relative to educational implementation? The answer to this question is obviously predicated first upon one's definition of the concept of equality of educational opportunity. There is a fairly widespread consensus that public education in the United States should provide equality of educational opportunity. But there is considerable lack of agreement, even disagreement, as to what "equal" educational opportunity means or should mean.[10]

What does equality of educational opportunity mean? Does it mean the *same* opportunity to get an education? Or does it mean an opportunity to get the *same* education? Or opportunity to be educated up to the level of one's capabilities and future occupational prospects? Or opportunity to learn whatever one needs to develop one's own peculiar potentialities? In the case of the "culturally-deprived," whose "background . . . has built-in resistance to learning," does equal educational opportunity mean compensatory education? Is only racially integrated education equal, irrespective of whether lack of integration is intentional or accidental? Is equality of educational opportunity a moral as well as a mathematical concept? And so on.

9 *Report of the National Advisory Commission on Civil Disorders,* p. 10.

10 See: B. P. Komisar and Herrold R. Coombs, "The Concept of Equality in Education," *Studies in Philosophy and Education,* III (Fall 1964), 223-244; Herbert A. Thelen, *Education and the Human Quest* (New York: Harper & Brothers, 1960), pp. 11-12; Myron Lieberman, "Equality of Educational Opportunity," *Harvard Educational Review,* XXIX (Summer 1959), 133 ff. John Gardner, Excellence (New York: Harper and Row, 1961), p. 12; Alan P. Grimes. *op. cit.,* pp. 41-88; A. F. Kleinberger "Reflections on Equality of Education," *Studies in Philosophy and Education,* V (Summer 1967), 293-340; James Coleman "The Concept of Equality of Educational Opportunity," *Harvard Educational Review,* XXXVIII (Winter 1968), 7-22.

It is not the purpose here to engage in an extended discussion of the various definitions of this concept. Rather, it is to suggest that a very important aspect of the problem of race and equality of educational opportunity is the question of the meaning of the concept of equality. It will be illuminating, as well as illustrative, to note briefly the definitions of equality, or rather inequality, as employed in the Coleman survey.[11]

In planning the survey, Coleman observed that "it was obvious that no single concept of equality of educational opportunity existed and that the survey must give information relative to a variety of concepts."[12] The *first* type of equality was defined in terms of the community's "input" to the school, such as per capita expenditure and equality of school plant, library, teachers, and other similar items. A *second* was defined in terms of racial composition, in view of the Court's pronouncement that separate schools were inherently unequal. A *third* type included various intangibles such as "teacher morale, teacher expectations of students, level of interest of the student body in learning or others."

All of these three definitions involved "input" of resources to the school; a second set involved the "effects of schooling." Thus a *fourth* type of equality was defined in terms of the *effects* of the school on "individuals with equal backgrounds and abilities." Here, Coleman explained that equality comprised equal results, "given the same individual input." A *fifth*

type was defined in terms of the effects of the school on "individuals of unequal backgrounds and abilities." In this instance, equality consisted of equal results "given different individual inputs."

In stressing the difference between inputs and effects, the Coleman survey made explicit the basis upon which concepts of equality of educational opportunity have been predicated in general, namely, "*effective* equality of opportunity; that is, equality in those elements that are effective for learning." Thus, instead of employing *inputs* as measures of quality by definition,[13] *effects* of inputs have replaced them as a basis for assessing school quality and hence equality of opportunity.

As suggested by Coleman, this is the latest stage in the evolution of the concept of equality of educational opportunity, namely, that equality of output is determined not so much by the equality of inputs as by the power of these in bringing about achievement. The reason this principle has been half-hidden, obscured by definitions that involve inputs, Coleman explained, is that research has until recently been unprepared to demonstrate what elements are actually effective.[14]

Moreover, as noted by Dyer,[15] the result of the Coleman study, despite flaws, has been to enable us to get a truer national assessment of educational opportunity than we have ever been able to get before. He explained that this definition means that student-teacher ratios,

---

11 James S. Coleman, *et al.*, *Equality of Educational Opportunity* (Washington, D.C.: U.S. Government Printing Office, 1966), pp. 735.

12 Coleman, "The Concept of Educational Opportunity," *loc. cit.*, pp. 18-19.

13 For example, assuming that "small classes are better than large, higher paid teachers are better than lower paid ones, by definition."

14 *Ibid.*, p. 18.

15 Henry S. Dyer, "School Factors and Educational Opportunity," *Harvard Educational Review*, XXXVIII (Winter, 1968), 39.

teachers' salaries, classroom footage per pupil, and similar characteristics can legitimately enter into the assessment of educational opportunity only to the extent that they can be shown to be related to the intellectual, emotional and social development of pupils. "In the absence of information about such relationships, any attempts to equalize education [or even to determine whether it is equal] will of necessity be blind."[16]

This revised concept of equality of educational opportunity has special significance in the definition of the problem of the Negro and the attainment of equality of educational opportunity. If the responsibility to create achievement lies with the school and not the child, as Coleman argues, as a logical implication of this concept, then he is correct in suggesting that the difference in achievement between the average white and average Negro at grade 12 is in effect the degree of inequality of opportunity. Moreover, he correctly insists under the circumstances that "the degree of inequality of opportunity, and the reduction of that inequality is a responsibility of the school."[17] As will be noted later, the implications of this concept have considerable relevance for compensatory education which has special significance in the education of minority groups.

Recent Studies and the Further Definition of the Problem

The definition of the problem of attaining equality of educational opportunities by Negroes has been considerably sharpened by recent studies and critical

discussions.[18] The most ambitious and comprehensive of these studies, popularly referred to as the "Coleman Report," was a response to a Congressional mandate in the 1964 Civil Rights legislation. Section 402 required that a survey be made to ascertain the extent of inequality of educational opportunity "for individuals by reason of race, color, religion or national origin in public institutions of all levels in the United States." The other studies are either replications or reanalyses of parts of the Coleman survey, or critical evaluations of it and its implications.

It is not the purpose here to make an extended critique of this research. The aim is rather to note a few of the important findings which raise in some detail certain basic questions underlying the problem of the attainment of equal educational opportunity by Negroes.

Undoubtedly, one of the most important findings of these studies, if not the most important from the point of view of race, is that Negroes in predominantly (more than half) white schools achieve at a higher level than those in all-Negro or predominantly (fewer than half white) Negro schools. The Report noted "that as the proportion white in a school increases, the achievement of students in each racial group [Puerto Ricans, Orien-

16 Ibid.
17 Coleman, "The Concept of Equality of Educational Opportunity," loc. cit., p.22.

18 See: James S. Coleman, et. al., Equality of Educational Opportunity loc. cit.; U.S. Commission on Civil Rights, Racial Isolation in the Public Schools (2 volumes). (Washington, D.C.: U.S. Government Printing Office, 1967); "Equal Educational Opportunity" (A Special Issue), Harvard Educational Review XXXVII (Winter 1968), 3-175; Samuel Bowles and Henry M. Levin, "The Determinants of Scholastic Achievement — An Appraisal of Some Recent Evidence," The Journal of Human Resources III (Winter 1968) 3-24.

tals, Mexican-Americans, Negroes, and American Indians] increases."[19] The Report explained that the general pattern was an increase in average test performance as the proportion of the whites increased. However, it was noted that in many cases the average for Negro students in totally segregated classes was higher than the average for those in classes where half or fewer of the students were white.[20] Moreover, analysis of the Coleman survey data by the Commission on Civil Rights, revealed "that the achievement of white students in classes which are roughly or more than half white is no different from that of similarly situated students in all white classes."[21]

Coleman explained his main finding by noting that it was a result of the social-class composition of the groups. "This means," he explained, "that the apparent beneficial effect of a student body with a high proportion of white students comes not from racial composition per se but from the better educational background and higher educational aspirations that are, on the average, found among white students."[22]

Other studies corroborate the general finding that the scholastic achievement of students of various racial and ethnic groups is enhanced as the proportion of white students is increaesed and that the reason is the fact of the addition of a larger proportion of middle- and upper-class students. For example, a later study found that "Given similar social-class compositions the racial balance of a school

has slight bearing on academic performance of students."[23]

It should be noted, however, as pointed out in the Report of the Commission on Civil Rights, that "there has been disagreement on whether the differences are due entirely to factors associated with the social class level of schools or whether racial composition is an important additional factor."[24] Despite an elaborate attempt on the part of the Commission's staff to demonstrate that differences in achievement are due to race as well as class -- or as Pettigrew put it, that "there is a *critical* racial composition correlate" — the methodological defects of their analyses cast serious doubt upon the validity of their findings. The point is well made by Moynihan after his review of the data: ". . . it is important that we begin to see that the underlying reality is not race but social class. And this has not got to do with whether you are white but whether you are a very low paid and intermittently employed worker or whether you're a school teacher or whatever."[25]

What does such a finding, as noted above, mean as far as the Negro and the attainment of equality of educational opportunity are concerned? First, it obviously means that since pupils irrespective of their backgrounds — racial or otherwise — achieve more scholastically in schools with a predominantly middle-class student body, there must be considerable social-class integration, in order to provide a

19 *Coleman Report*, p. 307.
20 *Ibid.*, p. 331.
21 *Racial Isolation in the Public Schools*, I, p. 160.
22 *Coleman Report*, p. 309.

23 Alan B. Wilson, "Educational Consequences of Segregation in a California Community" in *Racial Isolation in the Public Schools*, II, p. 202.
24 *Racial Isolation in the Public Schools*, I, p. 90.
25 Southern Education Reporting Service, "Moynihan Believes Class is the Issue," *Southern Education Report*, May 1967, p. 7.

more effective learning situation (or equality of educational opportunity) for lower-class pupils in general. Second, since not more than 25 or 30 per cent of the Negro population can realistically be designated as "middle class," any appreciable attempt to provide Negro pupils with an effective social class climate would necessitate racial integration on an unprecedented scale.

In what way does this finding further sharpen the definition of the problem? It should suffice for the purpose at hand to indicate briefly a few of the unanswered questions that come to mind immediately.

1. In view of the hunch in some quarters, "that racial composition is an important additional factor"[26] and the acknowledgment that "Research has not given clear answers to this question,"[27] there should be an intensive testing of this hypothesis under much less questionable conditions. In fact, many of the Coleman findings, as well as the results of the re-analyses of the data made by, or under the direction of, the Civil Rights Commission (as suggestive as these have proved to be as fruitful hypotheses) should be repeated under much more rigidly controlled conditions. Not only has this recommendation been made by practically all of the persons who have reviewed the studies but it has been voiced by most of the investigators themselves. Moreover, this step is most significant, in view of the fact that important policy decisions may be based upon these findings.

2. How would or could this finding

26 Racial Isolation in the Public Schools, I, p. 90.
27 Ibid., p. 89.

be applied to pupils in schools in large urban centers who are largely Negro, or lower class, or both, with few or no middle-class whites, or even middle-class Negroes, with whom to integrate them? In such a situation, how does one get an effective social class mix? In view of the recent court rulings that real racial integration must be realized, what are the most effective means to effect it? Do the data in the Civil Rights Commission's study on "Racial attitudes" support the conclusion that there is advantage in integrating lower-class Negro pupils with lower-class white pupils?

3. The above finding was obtained from data collected on common school pupils. Logically, if the finding is valid for lower schools, one would expect it to obtain for students in higher institutions, collegiate and professional. However, the hypothesis should be tested under more carefully controlled conditions. If it is found, as one has reason to anticipate a priori, that this finding holds for higher institutions also, how would or should this fact affect the status of the predominantly Negro college or university?

SOME PRACTICAL ASPECTS OF
THE PROBLEM

The basic premise upon which this discussion is predicated is that the provision of real equality of educational opportunity must of necessity require racially integrated schools. Research has found that an effective learning situation is the product of a predominantly middle-class student mix, whether white or Negro. In view of the small proportion of middle-class Negroes it will be absolutely necessary to integrate Negroes practically wholesale with whites. Moreover, the courts[28] have recently ruled in effect that "token" desegregation and other evasive and delaying tactics will not be tolerated longer; and the compliance criteria authorized in the 1964 Civil Rights Act are being tightened accordingly.

Some questions posed by this situation — which are equally as much political as educational, if not more so — are illustrated by the following:

1. How does one get to integrated predominantly white schools from the present all but wholly segregated Negro ghetto schools which are almost invariably considered low prestige institutions, manned by teachers who, according to Clark, "tend to resist assignments in Negro and other underprivileged schools and generally function less adequately in these schools . . . [whose] morale is generally lower [and] who tend to see their students as less capable of learning."[29]

2. In view of the fact that residential segregation has made the "neighborhood" school an inevitable instrument of continued school segregation, what can be done to replace it, especially in view of the great respect in which it is held as one of America's great traditions?

3. How does one solve the problem of unequal distribution of teachers in the schools where the best teachers by their own preference as well as community pressure are placed in the middle-class white schools and positions in Negro ghetto schools go begging or are filled to a much greater extent by teachers of lesser ability and experience?

4. How does one solve the sticky public relations problem created by middle-class white parents — and even many middle-class Negro parents — who oppose the integration of their children with slum Negro children because they are afraid that the "cultural deprivation" and educational backwardness of such pupils will restrict the learning of their children if taught in the same classes; in spite of the fact that if the ghetto children are taught in separate classes in the integrated school, segregation of the worst sort obtains again?

Current efforts to answer such questions fall into two general categories: compensatory education in predominantly Negro schools and school desegregation. At the present time there is considerable difference of opinion as to the efficacy of the two approaches. Some of the points of difference of opinion are illustrated in the following observations.

Compensatory programs have been indicted primarily because there is little hard evidence indicating that current programs "have raised significantly the [academic] achievement of participating pupils . . ."[30] thus casting considerable doubt upon their efficacy. The answer to this criticism, say proponents, is that compensatory education has not been given the financial support it should have in order to make a difference. In fact, as noted by Day,[31] such support as has been given is largely understandable as a political response "aimed at containing Negro aspirations and challenge within the bound-

---

[28] See: Particularly Hobson et al. v. Carl J. Hansen et al., Congressional Record H7656-7697, J. Skelly Wright, U.S. Circuit Judge.
[29] Kenneth B. Clark, op. cit., p. 101.

[30] See Racial Isolation in the Public Schools, I, p. 138.
[31] Noel E. Day, "Implementing Equal Educational Opportunity," Harvard Educational Review, XXXVIII (Winter 1968), 139.

aries set by the white majority's demand that their comfort and convenience not be unduly imposed upon."

This observation raises the question as to what an effective compensatory program would cost and the possibility of securing the funds to support it. Some indication of the cost of an effective compensatory program is estimated by Cohen[32] who found that if the "More Effective Schools Program" in New York City were made national policy and if it were accomplished over a five-year period it would cost as a minimum between five and six billion dollars annually. However, if the MES Program standard were raised so as to assure a more effective program — namely, maintain a student-teacher ratio half that of MES — it would require an increase in annual expenditure for instruction alone of poor children of some $1.7 billion to around $8.6 billion, or from 8 per cent to 43 per cent of present total annual public school expenditures for *all* children.

This estimate indicates that an effective compensatory program is not only a pressing educational problem but an even more difficult if not impossible political one. It is seriously doubted that middle- and upper-class whites who control the purse strings and have the political power can be convinced that this sort of expenditure is worthwhile to be made upon slum Negroes and poor whites at the expense, as they see it, of their own children's education.

Despite the apparent ineffectiveness of current compensatory efforts and the all but prohibitive cost of an effective program from the political viewpoint, compensatory education as a transitional program seems inevitable. As noted by the Commission on Civil Disorders:

We support integration as a priority educational strategy, it is essential to the future of American society. . . . We recognize that the growing dominance of pupils from disadvantaged minorities in city school populations will not be soon reversed. No matter how great the effort toward desegregation, many children of the ghetto will not, within their school careers, attend integrated schools.[33]

Moreover, the Commission concluded: "If existing disadvantages are not to be perpetuated, we must improve the quality of ghetto education."[34] The important question is, how can this be done in such a manner as to make the effort the first stage in real desegregation rather than the means of furthering the segregated school?

An even more striking example of the inevitability of a temporary and transitional stage of compensatory education is seen in the predominantly Negro higher institution. The current justification of the predominantly Negro higher institution is that it performs a necessary compensatory function in the higher education of Negroes which most predominantly white higher institutions are not willing to undertake. Many Negroes with average and above native capacity find themselves victims of their past inferior educational preparation. Unless some special machinery is available by which they can be helped to overcome their handicaps, they will not be admitted to the predominantly white higher institu-

[32] See: David K. Cohen, "Policy for Public Schools: Compensation and Integration," *Harvard Educational Review*, XXXVIII (Winter 1968), 122-123.

[33] *Op. cit.*, p. 25.
[34] *Ibid.*

tion, or, if admitted, are most likely to fail.

At the present time, Negroes constitute a highly disproportionate group in higher educational institutions. Only 15 per cent of the Negroes of college age are in college as compared with 45 per cent of the white college age group. Moreover, at least half of the Negroes in college are in predominantly Negro higher institutions.

In the professional fields the disparity is even greater. For example, there are six times as many white medical doctors as Negro in proportion to their respective populations; almost seven (6.7) times as many white dentists; forty times as many white engineers; forty-five times as many white pharmacists; fifty-seven times as many white architects; and ninety-seven times as many white lawyers, as their Negro counterparts. What is even more striking is the fact that the majority of Negroes who are currently being educated in these fields are enrolled in some predominantly Negro higher institution.[35]

Earl McGrath made a comprehensive survey of predominantly Negro higher education three years ago. He reported his findings under the suggestive title of "The Predominantly Negro Colleges and Universities in Transition." He

strongly recommended that "None of the predominantly Negro colleges should be allowed to die until their present and prospective students can be fully assured of better educational opportunities elsewhere."[36] The difficulty with this obviously sound advice is: how can it be implemented without further entrenching segregation?

Whatever research or critical discussion may have to say about the relative merits of compensation in the predominantly Negro school versus desegregation is not likely to be decisive in determining whether we shall have one or the other or both. For, as it has been noted, the courts have recently indicated that they expect increased and continuous efforts toward segregation, and the Civil Rights compliance division is tightening up its machinery of implementation as a consequence.

Most educators have concluded that the main if not the only way to effect desegregation in the public schools on a reasonably comprehensive scale is to restructure the educational set-up. The idea is to organize larger units that cut across present local lines, enlarging attendance areas, and eliminating one of the main barriers to desegregation – the neighborhood school.

There are a number of plans which have been proposed, and many are being tried, to effect desegregation on a wider scale. But progress in desegregation has not been extensive, according to the Commission on Civil Rights.[37] In a number of smaller communities efforts have been successful. A variety of techniques has

---

35. At the present time, for example, there are approximately 300 Negroes enrolled in all of the dental schools in the country. All except a tenth of them are enrolled in Howard University and Meharry Medical College — both accredited predominantly Negro medical and dental schools. A similar situation obtains in medicine. A little over 800 Negroes are estimated to be enrolled in all medical schools. All except a fourth of them are enrolled at Howard and Meharry. This situation is typical of all of the professions.

36 See: p. 160.
37 See: *Racial Isolation in Public Schools*, I, p. 154.

245

been used, but the one common element in all of the efforts involved the enlargement of school attendance areas to overcome residential segregation.

In large urban centers comparatively little progress in desegregation has been made. "Larger areas of racial concentration and rapid racial turnover in peripheral areas have made it difficult for big city school systems to reduce racial imbalance."[38] In some cities the Negro elementary school enrollment comprises a majority of the public school enrollment. Moreover, the situation is getting worse because of the growing concentration of Negroes and other minorities in the inner city and the continued flight of middle-class whites to the suburbs. In such cities, says the Civil Rights Commission, desegregation not involving suburban participation is no longer possible.[39] And it is obvious that the chances of such participation is politically highly unfeasible.

Some educators see little hope of achieving effective school desegregation as a feasible short-term (the next 15 or 20 years) goal for varied reasons. First, as noted earlier, there is fear on the part of upper- and middle-class whites who possess the political power and hold the purse strings that mixing their children with ghetto Negro pupils, practically all of whom are lower-class, will be detrimental for the education of the white pupils academically and otherwise. Data from the Coleman survey indicated that white pupils did not suffer academically when mixed with Negroes in predominantly white schools. While *a priori* such a situation should bring better race rela-

tions, no study has given a convincing factual demonstration of the advantage of such a mix for white pupils. Thus, this is one of the pressing questions that needs an answer if desegregation is to be achieved as a feasible short-term goal.

A second reason for skepticism has been noted immediately above in the description of the unpromising demographic situation characterizing many of our large urban centers. In such cities, it was the conclusion of the Civil Rights Commission that without suburban cooperation desegregation was no longer possible. One need only recall the difficulty in getting cooperation from such units in less sticky matters to realize how politically unpromising such a proposal is.

A third reason grows out of the fact that what seems to be the most promising proposal to effect desegregation on a wider scale — The Education Park[40] — has an unprecedented price tag attached to it. The term unprecedented is used because so much more than normal construction is involved, as well as funds for busing students, and providing special services for a larger number of children. Cohen,[41] who estimated the cost of an effective program of compensatory education vis-a-vis school desegregation, concluded that the latter would cost 20 per cent more than the former which was calculated to be between $100 and $160 billion over a ten-year period. Obviously, the present climate — and even that in the foreseeable future — does not appear at all favorable for such an additional expense.

Other educators see little hope in

---

38 *Ibid.*
39 *Ibid.*

40 See chapter in this issue on "School Parks and Equal Opportunities."
41 Cohen, *op. cit.*

any efforts to reform the present public school system because it is an entrenched monopoly, as Clark[42] calls it. And as a monopoly it need not be concerned about real reform, he says, as long as it can get financial support "without the accountability which inevitably comes from aggressive competition." Thus, he recommends what he calls "Alternative forms of public education [as] realistic, aggressive and viable competitors" of the present public system. This same idea has been suggested in different forms by others. Such suggestions indicate that something is radically wrong with our present school system. One wonders, however, whether the suggested remedies are feasible.

---

42 Clark, *op. cit.*, pp. 108-111.

EQUALITY OF EDUCATIONAL OPPORTUNITY

James S. Coleman

James S. Coleman, "Equality of Educational Opportunity," *Integrated Education,* September-October 1968, No. 35, pp. 19-28.

EQUALITY OF
EDUCATIONAL OPPORTUNITY

James S. Coleman

The writer is Professor, Department of Social Relations, The Johns-Hopkins University, and was co-director of the U. S. Office of Education Equal Educational Opportunity Study of 1966. His article is based on an address to an in-service training program attended by teachers in School District 65, Evanston, Illinois, July 8, 1968.

> *When Mexican-American children are taught about the Alamo in their classrooms, it should be standard procedure to mention that the Alamo was followed by over 100 years of rigid segregation and severe exploitation of Chicanos [i.e., Mexican-Americans] in Texas. In absolutely no sense of the word, therefore, does the word "Alamo" symbolize freedom for Mexican-Americans.*
>
> —Octavio I. Roman-V,
> *El Grito,* Spring, 1968

Evanston is one of the few cities to attain an objective important to attain throughout the United States—consciously integrated schools.

One of the problems that arises in such a step is the ability of a school to cope with a much wider range of family background than it does in homogeneous areas. As a consequence, I would like to examine the importance of children's background for activities in school through discussing some of the results of the survey, *Equality of Educational Opportunity,* that I directed for the Office of Education.

251

It was designed to assess the amount and sources of inequality of educational opportunity by race in the schools of America. Thus, it was not concerned with the effect of a child's background upon his performance in school, upon his chances in school and life. Yet, as it turned out, in order to successfully answer the primary question about differential opportunity in schools, it became necessary to investigate in some detail the question of the effect of the child's home.

The first way in which the home intruded itself into the examination of schools came in our search for those aspects of schools which made the most difference in a child's achievement. As we examined the performance of children in different kinds of schools, we found a fact which occasioned some surprise on our part and some reassessment. The variation in performance in different children within the same school is far larger than, in fact several times as great as, the variation in performance between schools. This held true in the North, in the South, in rural and urban settings and for each of the six racial groups examined in the survey. (This means, along with Negroes and whites, four other groups, Mexican Americans, Oriental Americans, American Indians, and Puerto Ricans. For each of the groups separately, the school factors having most influence on achievement, that is, achievement on standardized tests, were examined, as a preliminary step to examining how these factors which affected achievement were distributed differently among the different groups.) The importance of the result, the much greater variation in performance within schools than between, lies in what it begins to tell about the relative influence of the school and home on achievement. It shows that children subject to the same school influences but coming from different homes are more different in achievement than the average child in different schools. Thus, the effect of different schools could not be as powerful as we had anticipated in the survey, when most of the difference in achievement lay within the very school itself.

INTERACTION IN SCHOOL

I should point out, however, what every good teacher knows, that the variation in achievement of different children within a school is not a result wholly of what the children bring to the school. There is often a subtle interaction, and sometimes not so subtle, between the child's characteristics and the opportunities he finds in school. If he is eager but well-disciplined, neither too passive nor too unruly, the teacher often establishes a different kind of interaction with the child, stimulating, building him up, often unconsciously using such a child as a model for the other children in the class. But quite apart from this the first result of the study of inequality of educational opportunity among schools was that the effective opportunity provided by different schools was far overshadowed by other sources of variation in opportunity, which had nothing to do with the school. These are not achievement differences between Negroes and whites in the same school, but between different Negroes in schools attended by Negroes and between different whites in schools attended by whites.

In a situation like that which has just been created in Evanston, where the racial and socio-economic variatiins between student bodies in different schools have been consciously and purposefully reduced, the achievement differences w i t h i n schools are even greater. In one respect, the results I've just described provide some reassurance for teachers faced with a new and greater heterogeneity in their classrooms. Know it or not, they've already been confronting wider ranges of performance within their classroom than exist on the average between different schools. Those teachers have learned various techniques, some good and some bad, of dealing with diversity in the classroom. But the increased diversity that now exists should lead to some reassessment of just what those techniques are and how they may have been reinforcing the initial diverstiy of skill with which children enter the classroom.

This first result of the survey, the diversity within the schools, pointed directly to the relatively great importance of the child's home for his level of achievement than of the school itself. The result obviously presents a challenge to schools and it is one which has not gone unrebutted by some persons who feel, as I also feel, that schools should play a far more important role in providing equality of opportunity than these results suggest.

James Skelly Wright, Washington, D. C.

A federal judge in the Nation's capital has struck a judicial blow against school segregation with a decision that orders sweeping reforms in the District of Columbia Public School System. If it is upheld by the Supreme Court, the decision could be as important in the North as the 1954 desegregation opinion was in the South. In his opinion, U. S. Circuit Court of Appeals Judge James Skelly Wright, sitting, as a District Court judge, set major precedents in the heretofore gray area of de facto segregation — segregation reflecting housing patterns rather than that established by law. His opinion found: "racially and socially homogeneous schools damage the minds and spirit of all children who attend them — the Negro, the white, the poor, and the affluent — and block the attainment of the broader goals of democratic education whether the segregation occurs by law or by fact. . . ." The decision tells school officials, in effect, that they cannot absolve themselves of responsibility for overcoming segregated schooling simply because it reflects discriminatory housing patterns. Judge Wright therefore ordered Washington to integrate all its faculties, pointing out that the racial composition of school staffs there has generally tended to coincide with the racial composition of the schools. His decree orders the school system to bus Negro pupils from overcrowded slum schools to undercapacity white schools in affluent sections of the city. Judge Skelly Wright was born and educated in New Orleans.

—Editors, *Who's Who in America,* 1968 edition, text of award for field
of Law, Citation for Significant Contribution to Society

We firmly believe in the positive value of intercultural and interracial educational experiences for all children. Integrated schools expand the knowledge and understanding of the child, increase his awareness of others, and provide lessons of tolerance and fairness that are important assets to the individual and to society.
—Republican Coordinating Committee, *Urban Education: Problems and Priorities*, March 18, 1968

(The Republican Coordinating Committee includes the following persons, among others: Dwight D. Eisenhower, Barry Goldwater, Richard M. Nixon, Thomas E. Dewey, Alf M. Landon, Senators Everett M. Dirksen, Thomas H. Kuchel, Bourke B. Hickenlooper, Margaret Chase Smith, George Murphy, Milton R. Young, and Hugh Scott; and Reps. Gerald R. Ford, Leslie C. Arends, Melvin R. Laird, William C. Cramer, Robert Taft, Jr. and Albert H. Quie.)

WHAT CAN SCHOOLS DO?

This first result then led to a modification of the initial design of the survey, to examine in somewhat more detail the effects of family background differences on achievement levels. For if the major variations in educational opportunity are due to processes lying outside the school, then it becomes important for the school itself to know more about them if the schools will significantly affect the inequalities of opportunity they have now largely perpetuated. In this examination the survey found that not only did family background differences show large relation to achievement differences in the same school, they counted for a considerable part for the differences in achievement between schools. Even the differences between achievement levels in different schools which one might first put down to the effect of the different schools themselves, can be partly explained by differences in the average family background of students within them. And these variations in achievement by different family background were not something which showed up only in the early years of school, to be diminished by the impact of school over the twelve years. The survey covered five grade levels, grades 1, 3, 6, 9, and 12. And it found that the relation between family background and achievement both within schools and between schools with students with different family background was approximately constant over the twelve school years. Again, this is true among Negroes and it is true among whites. This provides still another indication of the importance that a child's family background has for his achievement of those skills which a school attempts to impart, and it provides another evidence of the challenge to the schools, the challenge to have some effect in reversing the inequality with which children begin school. It is not, I suggest, that schools cannot have a powerful effect in reducing inequality. It is rather that they have not yet learned how to do so. Schools are still learning how to teach children who traditionally, fifty years ago, left school at an early age, children for whom the school must be both preparatory and motivational, the latter a task which the schools have traditionally left to family.

Beyond the primary fact that the home has an important effect on achievement, several points stand out in the survey. First, it was clear that of three separate aspects of family background, each played an important part in the child's achievement. These aspects were the economic level of the home, the educational

> I get the feeling that this drive by business [to employ hard core unemployed ghetto residents] is orchestrated for a symphony but is being played on tin horns. If the country raises a lot of false hopes and then doesn't follow through in a lasting fashion, the ghetto letdown could be very bad.
>
> —Richard Clark, June 29, 1968

> Why Run in Mexico and Crawl at Home?
> —Sign appealing to Negro American athletes to boycott the 1968 Olympic Games in Mexico City

background and educational influence in the home (such things as the amount of reading matter that was there, together with educational level of the mother and father), and finally the interest taken by the parents in the child's performance in school and any further education As one might expect, these three factors, the economic background, the educational background, and the parents' interest, are interrelated. Many children have very high levels of all three and many have low levels of all three. However, some children have one, but not the others, and it is thus possible to note the separate importance of each. Although the survey does not go into the details of how each has its effect, I commend to your attention a study in Britain which shows these mechanisms by Brian Jackson and Dennis Marsden, entitled Education and the Working Class. In this study, Jackson and Marsden took 88 working class children who had passed the several hurdles infrequently overcome by working class children in Britain: first, they passed the 11-plus examination and had gone to grammar school, that is, instead of secondary modern school, which provides no academic credentials for further education. Secondly, they stayed until the sixth form of grammar school, a step which is a prerequisite for university entrance, which even most grammar school students do not do; and finally, they passed A-level examinations, that is, entrance examinations to the University. Jackson and Marsden were interested in just what it was about these working class families that led their children to take these unusually difficult paths. They found several things.

First of all, a large number of the families had been in the working class for only one generation. The family history, tradition and interests were toward higher education and economic level than they currently held. The higher economic and educational background was most often on the mother's side of the family, a level that she had lost by the marriage she made. Secondly, the study showed the enormous efforts made by the family in overcoming both economic and social difficulties to bring their child over the educational hurdles. Often the physical arrangements of the home made studying difficult, and the families already cramped for space set aside a room for several hours of the evening in which the child could study.

In numerous ways, the families deprived themselves, often including deprivations for the other children, to make possible physical conditions which would lead the child to continue. The family also exerted special effort in another way, to protect the child from the influences of the neighborhood, from the children of the neighborhood, all of whose activities led in a direction away from those they had planned for their child.

HARLEM AND BRITAIN

A circumstance similar to this was described to me some years ago when I lived on the edge of Harlem in New York. I had a friend who taught the fifth grade in a school in Harlem. She described one set of children in her class, a minority of children, who were subject to what appeared a peculiar and harsh restriction. These children were under strict rules to be in the house 15 minutes after the close of school and were not allowed to leave the house until school time the next morning, except with the parent. My friend described the parents of these children as absolutely determined that their child would not be pulled down by the neighborhood, that they be subject only to the influences of the home and school. They were absolutely determined that the child go up and out of the neighborhood to further education and a good job.

These parents were aspiring to economic and educational levels very different from those of the neighborhood, and in order to do so had to institute controls that many middle-class parents would regard as unduly restrictive. Both of these examples, one from Britain and the other from Harlem, show one major point. That for families at lower economic levels in a neighborhood where influences outside the home, pull away from education, it requires much more effort, much stronger discipline, much stricter constraint and a much higher level of motivation on the part of parents to provide the *same* level of conditions for educational achievement as in a middle class family in a middle class neighborhood.

In the usual simple way we see these things we see them separately: the same level of interest and motivation on the part of parents, we assume, will produce children with equal levels of motivation and interest. But they are not separate. In the middle class family a lower level of motivation and effort on the part of the parents can be compensated by the external neighborhood influences which support educational achievement. And there is the greater ease of providing appropriate conditions for achievement in the home itself. In effect, the rest of the child's environment more often reinforces educational goals in a middle class setting, while in a lower class setting parents interested in their child's education must fight the environment to achieve their goals.

This interaction between the family and the other aspects of the child's environment is important information for the school and the teacher. It means, if the teacher is to work through the home in any way, she must provide *more* aid to the lower class family to have the same effect, and the lower class family must work *harder* to have the same effect. A laissez faire orientation of parents, which produces average achievement for children subject to middle class economic and social environment, will produce disastrous results when these other environmental influences push in a direction away from school. This knowledge should also lead the teacher in the school to recognize the more difficult task that the lower class parent has, and to recognize that many parents will not be up to this task, just as many middle class parents, facing the same difficulty, would not be up to the task.

SCHOOL IS IMPORTANT

I turn now to another result from the study of *Equality of Educational Opportunity*, a result which may appear contradictory to the experience of teachers. This is that children from poor family background are more affected by the differential quality of schools than are those from family backgrounds that contain more educational resources within them. And children from poor family backgrounds are more affected by the aspirations and achievements of the other students in their class than are those from family backgrounds in which they had more educational resources. This does not mean that children from poor backgrounds get more out of school. It means instead that a good school or

a good teacher, and particularly the latter, makes more difference for a child who has few educational resources in the home than for one who has many. The child with many educational resources in the home gets a lot out of school, whether or not the teacher is good, whether or not his classmates are also achieving highly. A child without these resources in the home is one for

> There is in America today a generation of white youth that is truly worthy of a black man's respect, and this is a rare event in the foul annals of American history. . . . The sins of the fathers are visited upon the heads of the children—but only if the children continue in the evil deeds of the fathers.
>
> —Eldridge Cleaver, *Soul on Ice* (1968)

whom the extra efforts of the teacher and for whom the climate provided by the other students in the classroom make most difference in his achievement.

This result may be viewed in another way. There are three major places in which a child can find educational resources necessary to his achievement, the home, the environment provided by his peers in school and neighborhood, and the resources provided by the school itself. If the resources are provided by the first, the additional importance of the second and third is less. If the resources are provided by the first or the second, the additional resources provided by the third, that is the school, are less important to his ultimate level of achievement. Indeed, there are studies of middle class children who for one reason or another have been prevented from attending secondary school, and these studies show that they achieve about as high as their counterparts who have attended school.

This leads to another result of the study, which is particularly relevant to the policy of school integration as implemented in Evanston. This is the fact that children's achievement is very much related to the social composition of their classroom. The survey showed that Negro students, for example, performed at a higher level according to standardized tests, even though their school grades were lower, when they were with children who were from higher socio-economic levels, most often white students, than when they were in schools with children of lower socio-economic levels.

CLASSROOM INTEGRATION

A further examination of the data by James McPartland showed that this effect was principally the result of integration of the classroom rather than merely integration of the school. He showed also that there is a beneficial effect due to the socio-economic level of students in the classroom, and a beneficial effect due to the proportion of white students in the classroom. Both these sources provided for children who had few educational resources at home, an alternative set of resources that had an impact on achievement. The most important way in which this occurs is not so evident but there are several ways in which it can occur.

One is the interaction of the child with other children having larger vocabularies. An English-speaking child, for example, will learn French much more quickly in a classroom of French children than from the best French teacher. Or an adolescent girl in interaction with other adolescent girls must learn certain things about popular culture whether she wants to or not if she's to be part of the crowd. She must learn the top tunes, the latest fashions, and so on. In much the same way, children come to learn the things which are necessary to get along with their peers, and if these things are part of school learning it reinforces what they learn at the hand of the teacher. A second way this cause and effect occurs is by the level of teaching, the level of demands by the teacher herself.

Every teacher must adjust to the level of teaching that she can carry out in the particular classroom. And in some classrooms, as graphically portrayed by recent essays, such as Jonathan Kozol's, the adjustment involves very low levels of challenge indeed. Major attention is given to discipline rather than learning. Thus, the effect is important because of its effect on the teacher, and what

> What the hell is a white teacher going to do when students say: "Tomorrow we want to start learning some black history"? He wouldn't know what to do. He might come in and do something about Black Sambo or something like that. Or, talk about Booker T. Washington or George Washington Carver.
> —Bill Cosby, May, 1968

the teacher does. At one extreme is maintaining discipline, and at the other extreme is challenging and demanding high levels of achievement.

This is not to suggest that the integration of students with low level past performance in the classroom with much higher levels is not a psychological trauma. Anyone who has learned a foreign language by being alone in a foreign country has experienced that same sort of trauma. And the eagerness with which one, in such a situation, seeks out English-speaking persons indicates the efforts which new and different environments entail. But the evidence indicates that such psychological discomforts are not lasting, even though the child may be receiving lower grades than in a more comfortable environment in the past. In fact, another result from the survey indicates that Negro children in an integrated school come to gain a greater sense of their efficacy to control their destiny. It is very likely due to the fact they see that they can do some things better than whites and can perform in school better than some whites, a knowledge which they never had so long as they were isolated in an all-black school.

By the very fact of bringing the classroom environment toward equality through racial integration, Evanston has taken an important step in the direction of equality of educational opportunity. But the challenges lie in the use of integration to increase the educational resources available to lower class children of whatever race. In part, this involves things other than direct teaching It implies achieving a high level of social integration in out-of-class activities, an achievement which is greatly affected by collective projects, extra-curricular activities, and other things which make for high morale in the school and bring the student body closer together. In part, it implies modifying classroom activities to create more interaction among students and less reliance upon direct communication from teacher to student. One way this can be achieved is academic games, a mode of teaching that I and others at Johns Hopkins have been working on for several years. But most of all it is recognizing that social integration creates an opportunity to use special and conscious means to bring about equality of opportunity.

STRATEGY OF EQUALITY

Having examined some of the direct and indirect ways a child's family background and the backgrounds of other children in his class affects his achievement, I turn to the question of which strategy teachers in schools might use to bring about equality of educational opportunity in view of these effects.

Two opposite strategies naturally occur. First, to modify the home environment, bring the parent in as an aid and resource toward learning. Second is its opposite, attempting to wean the child as much as possible away from harmful family and neighborhood influence. The extreme of the first strategy is to incorporate community into the school, modifying the community in those ways that make its effect educationally beneficial. The extreme of the second would be integrated public boarding schools in which the total environment of the child is shaped by the school. Both strategies are based on the recognition that the school at preesnt modifies only a small portion of the child's environment and that strong educational impact can only occur when a much larger portion of his social environment than is now provided by the school points in the direction of learning. But these two strategies differ greatly. Neither extreme, of course, is available to the classroom teacher. Nevertheless, the alternative strategies in a less extreme form do confront the teacher; to work through gaining the help of the parent, or to provide the support that insulates the child from negative influences of home and background.

No simple answer can be given to the question of which strategy is most effective. If the support of the home can be obtained, it will be a powerful support, as evidenced by the general importance of the home for learning as shown by numerous studies such as I have described above. But the research has shown also that it takes a remarkable amount of determination, a remarkable amount of strength for a mother in a lower class environment to provide those educational resources to support the school. And the consequence, the effort a teacher or school expends in this direction, that is working with the parent, may be far greater than the benefit gained, except with a few parents. For the greatest number of children, the opposite strategy may prove more valuable.

In the very process of education, the fact that achieving in school means gaining a better occupation has always to some degree alienated lower class children from their parents. This has been shown in the British study I mentioned, and in various studies of immigrant groups in America. Such an alienation occurs through education, as every parent knows who has seen his children come to move in different circles and enjoy different activities from his own. No attempt to bring the parent into the school can ever fully avoid it, nor does the aspiring parent even wish that. What the school can do is provide a more intense social environment for the child that leads him to invest a larger portion of himself in the school and in school activities. Most important, I think, as part of the strategy in substituting for the home is to make the child aware that he himself is in the end responsible for his own

---

The principal beneficiaries of Black Power have been the black middle-class. Jobs have opened up to professional blacks. . . . Those who have benefited least from Black Power . . . are those whose needs are the most acute — the black poor. They have gained pride and self respect, but unlike the black intelligentsia, there has been no opportunity for them to parlay this new pride and self-respect into something more concrete.

—Julius Lester, May 25, 1968

. . . The white middle class has "turned" the public colleges into bastions of racial reaction. Blacks and Puerto Ricans must realize this and push for a lowering of the artificial standards which deny them entrance to these schools. Public colleges must go back to being truly public and must go back to serving those that cannot afford a private education.

—Fred Beauford, Black Allied Student Association at New York University, May 24, 1968

development. For the child to become consciously aware that he has options in shaping his activities, and that it is his choice among options that largely determine his future, is an important step in his education.

USE OF GAMES

It is in developing such awareness that I suggest the use of academic games that I mentioned before. In general, the use of such games opens and stimulates discussion around areas that are of great importance to children, but areas that we seldom discuss seriously and non-threateningly in school. For example, in a life-career game that has been developed for high school students, a player takes the profile of a child aged 14 or 15, in a given family background and a given level in school. In a sequence of steps he plans the hypothetical person's life, first making decisions about courses to take next year in school, then how long to continue in education, perhaps in the face of poor grades, and how much time to devote to it, together with various decisions along the way about the use of one's free time, what kind of an education to pursue, and choices that may range all the way from leaving high school for a trade school to continuing high school and then a four-year college. The details of this game situation are not important. What is important is the fact that it confronts the

It was almost impossible up until very recently to get research support for work on any aspect of racial integration. With the passage of the Civil Rights Act of 1964, federal agencies suddenly awoke to responsibilities which they did not feel previously.
—Peter H. Rossi, June 2, 1967

child, sometimes for the first time, with the fact that the decisions he makes today affect the possibilities open to him tomorrow. He learns that he does have a choice, that these are decisions whether he realizes he makes them consciously or merely accepts the obvious and easiest activities.

In another game, a parent-child game, the children in a higher elementary grade gain a recognition that the child in choosing the action that affects him operates within the context of his interaction with parents. In using this game with children of poorer background, we found a remarkable product in the form of free, open discussions and the analysis of the relations between parents and children, including the various strategies their parents use to cope with them and their strategies for coping with their parents. The value of the game appears to lie as much in freeing children to discuss openly the relationships between parents and children as in any other effect.

More generally, I suggest that one valuable strategy in coping with diverse family background with which children come to school is to bring it into the open—not through direct and threatening discussion of the child's own family, but through other means such as games, discussions of stories involving children from diverse backgrounds, and other devices that a teacher can evolve. Once in the open, the relation of home environmnet to the various activities of the child becomes something he can begin to cope with, something that he himself can recognize some responsibility for and and above all, something over which he himself can exercise some control.

These, then, are the matters to which I direct your attention. First, the fact that a child's home environment, as well as the environment of other children in which he finds himself, is a very crucial influence on his performance in school. Secondly, the kind of influence the family has and the ways in which it has such influence have been described. Finally, I have made some suggestions about possible strategies for teachers and for schools to bring about equality of educational opportunity for children of whatever family background.

DESEGREGATION OF PUBLIC SCHOOLS: AN AFFIRMATIVE DUTY TO ELIMINATE RACIAL SEGREGATION ROOT AND BRANCH

G. David Vann Epps

G. David Van Epps, "Desegregation of Public Schools: An Affirmative Duty to Eliminate Racial Segregation Root and Branch," *Syracuse Law Review,* Fall 1968, pp. 53-65.

DESEGREGATION OF PUBLIC SCHOOLS: AN AFFIRMATIVE DUTY TO ELIMINATE RACIAL SEGREGATION ROOT AND BRANCH

G. David Vann Epps

In the first *Brown v. Board of Education of Topeka* decision, the Supreme Court of the United States was asked to decide whether the educational opportunity offered by racially segregated schools is equal to that offered by non-segregated schools; if not, whether it can be made equal; and whether assignment to racially segregated schools deprives students of the equal protection of the law. In its opinion, the Court specifically called attention to the finding that the schools involved had been or were being equalized in terms of the quality of their buildings and curricula, the qualifications and salaries of their teachers, and other "tangible" factors.[2] Thus, its decision did not turn on a comparison of the presence and quality of such material factors in the "Negro" and "white" schools, but looked "instead to the *effect of segregation itself on public education.*"[3] The Court unanimously held that opportunity to obtain an education is "a right which must be made available to all on equal terms."[4] Indeed, "in the field of public education the doctrine of 'separate but equal' has no place. Separate educational facilities are inherently unequal."[5] The plaintiffs were held to have been deprived of the equal protection of the law guaranteed by the fourteenth amendment, as a result of their assignment to racially segregated schools.[6] In the second *Brown* decision, the Court unanimously held that "all provisions of federal, state or local law requiring or permitting such discrimination must yield to this principle."[7]

It is well documented that separation of the races (whether by segregation or as a result of other influences) in public schools, inferior educational opportunities offered by schools serving nonwhite students, and overwhelming attendance of nonwhite students in predominantly or wholly "nonwhite" schools have been persistent and frustrating facts.[8] Despite the seemingly clear

---

1. Brown v. Board of Educ. of Topeka, 347 U.S. 483, 488 (1954) [hereinafter cited as *Brown I*].

2. *Id.* at 492.

3. *Id.* (emphasis added).

4. *Id.* at 493.

5. *Id.* at 495.

6. *Id.*

7. Brown v. Board of Educ. of Topeka, 349 U.S. 294, 298 (1955).

8. The matter has been portrayed thoroughly by the multitude of law review articles concerned with the problems of school desegregation. The situation in the District of Columbia, which bears

statements of *Brown I*, argument has raged as to whether there is any duty upon school officials beyond the duty of the state to refrain from *de jure* racial segregation[9] of public school pupils. Three broad theories have been advanced. First, it has been suggested that school officials have no affirmative duty to deal with racial imbalance[10] in public schools' if there has been no segregation imposed by the state. Second, courts have taken the position that there is an affirmative obligation upon school authorities to eliminate racial imbalance in public schools where it is the product of a history of *de jure* segregation and such imbalances are maintained by *de facto* racial segregation.[11] A third position has been advanced to the effect that there is a duty to eliminate any unjustified racial imbalance in the public schools. The Supreme Court in three recent cases[12] has addressed itself in a modest way to the problem of securing equal educational opportunity for all.

THE ARGUMENTS

A.   The Constitution commands only mere restraint from de jure racial segregation of public school pupils. It was first proposed in cases of *de jure* segregation of public schools that, while the Constitution prohibits *de jure* racial

---

many fruitful analogies to the other large ghettos of the United States, is described in prodigious detail in Hobsen v. Hensen, 269 F. Supp. 401, 408-514 (D.D.C. 1967). *See generally* the materials cited by Judge Wright. *Id.* 498, 504 n.186-89.

9. The general concept, *segregation*, is here used to denote geographic separation and separate use of facilities which is forced by a group upon subordinate categories and groups of persons by law or custom. BAIN, SEGREGATION, A DICTIONARY OF THE SOCIAL SCIENCES 628, ¶ 2 (1964). *De jure segregation* here denotes the imposition of racial segregation by one group upon another through law. Note that the term segregation is used by courts, often in a journalistic fashion, without explicit recognition of the essence of the concept, *imposition* of racial separation and separate use of facilities.

10. *Racial imbalance* is used colloquially by the courts to denote the proportion of nonwhite students in a given school compared with the proportion of nonwhite students in the school district generally. Since the concept appears most often in a context of near total separation of the races, a more precise notion has been slow to develop.

11. *De facto segregation* denotes racial segregation of public schools by school authorities through the manipulation of school district rules, transfer of students, drafting of district boundaries, construction of facilities, selection of students into tracks or other groups purportedly consolidated on the basis of learning ability, and in other ways, non segregative on their face, but administered at least partly to maintain segregation of the races. As with *de jure* segregation, it is imposition by one group upon another which distinguishes this form of segregation from mere "racial separation".

Racial separation denotes the results of ecological processes by which people settle or locate in those areas of a community occupied by people of similar social characteristics or activities. BAIN, *supra* note 9, ¶ 1. While it is arguable that this process is still another form of segregation, it is here distinguished from segregation by the directness of the process. Racial separation is indirect, a product of the cultural, social, and material resources at the command of the groups involved.

12. Green v. County School Bd. of New Kent County, 391 U.S. 430 (1968); Raney v. Board of Educ. of Gould School Dist., 391 U.S. 443 (1968); Monroe v. Board of Comm'rs of City of Jackson, 391 U.S. 450 (1968).

segregation, it does not command racial integration of these schools.[13] This argument was carried over in various forms to apply to situations of *de facto* racial segregation of public schools. Racial imbalances in public schools resulting from residential segregation were held not to be violative of any constitutional right.[14] School officials were held not to have an obligation to mitigate racial imbalances in public schools which resulted from strict adherence to the neighborhood system of school location, where the selection of the neighborhood plan was not motivated by the purpose of maintaining segregation.[15] Courts have held that there is no duty to reduce racial imbalances resulting from demographic shifts where the school attendance zones were innocently derived.[16] The location of schools in areas heavily populated by nonwhites was held to be within the permissible discretion of school officials if based upon considerations of population density, distance, accessibility, ease of transportation, safety, and other "relevant and reasonable" tangible factors, even though students are generally required by school regulations to attend their neighborhood schools.[17] Students have been held not to have a constitutional right to attend a public school outside the attendance area in which they live.[18] Similarly, where "tangible" factors are equal, students have been held to have no constitutional right to attend a school in which the student body is of a different race.[19] School officials have been held not to have a constitutional duty to bus children out of their neighborhoods to alleviate racial imbalances resulting from racial separation.[20] Public school authorities were permitted to delay for a year involuntary transfers of students to alleviate racial imbalance, where the students were accorded an unfettered right of free transfer from their assigned school to any other school.[21] Such plans of free transfer and freedom of

---

13. Stell v. Savannah-Chatham County Bd. of Educ., 333 F.2d 55 (5th Cir.), *cert. denied*, 379 U.S. 933 (1964); Downs v. Board of Educ. of Kansas City, 336 F.2d 988 (10th Cir.), *cert. denied*, 380 U.S. 914 (1964); Bradley v. School Bd. of City of Richmond, 345 F.2d 310 (4th Cir.), *vacated on other grounds*, 382 U.S. 103 (1965).

14. Webb v. Board of Educ. of City of Chicago, 223 F. Supp. 466, 468 (N.D. Ill. 1963). The court declared that the Constitution forbids "actively pursuing a course of enforced segregation." Absent such, "irreparable harm is, by itself, insufficient . . ." to raise a constitutional question. *Id.*

15. Bell v. School City of Gary, 324 F.2d 209, 213 (7th Cir. 1963), *cert. denied*, 377 U.S. 924 (1964).

16. *Id.*; Downs v. Board of Educ., *supra* note 13, at 998.

17. Henry v. Godsell, 165 F. Supp. 87, 90 (E.D. Mich. 1958).

18. *Id.* at 91.

19. Lynch v. Kenston School Dist. Bd. of Educ., 229 F. Supp. 740, 744 (N.D. O. 1964). Note the court's reverse application of *Brown I.* "Plaintiffs have a constitutional right not to be objects of racial discrimination . . . , but they do not have a constitutional right to attend or to refrain from attending a particular school on the basis of racial considerations when there has been no actual [*de jure*] discrimination against them." *Id.*

20. Deal v. Cincinnati Bd. of Educ., 369 F.2d 55, 61 (6th Cir. 1966).

21. Swann v. Charlotte-Mecklenburg Bd. of Educ., 369 F.2d 29, 32 (4th Cir. 1966). The court noted that "there is no constitutional requirement that [the School Board] act with the conscious

choice have been held not to be constitutionally objectionable even though large segments of white and nonwhite students chose to continue attending their assigned schools.[22] One court, asked to rule that intermixing of races in public schools is constitutionally required, flatly rejected the notion.[23] The court ruled instead that freedom of choice, when used to describe "a system in which each pupil, or his parents, must annually exercise an uninhibited choice, and the choices govern the assignments",[24] raises no constitutional objection.[25] In another recent case, the court ruled that "the Fourteenth Amendment did not command compulsory integration of all of the schools regardless of an honestly composed unitary neighborhood system and a freedom of choice plan."[26] In still another decision, the court declared that it was "firmly committed" to the principle that freedom of choice plans are not unconstitutional *per se*.[27] Summarizing this current of judicial opinion, the United States Court of Appeals, Second Circuit, said that "[a]lthough there may be some dissent, . . . , courts generally agree that communities have no constitutional duty to undo bona fide *de facto* segregation."[28] However strange these concepts may seem in the light of the *Brown I* holding that segregation itself renders educational opportunities inherently unequal and thus constitutionally offensive,[29] they continue to govern substantial numbers of decisions.

B. The Constitution commands affirmative action to disestablish de jure racial segregation of public school pupils. In *Branche v. Board of Education of Town of Hempstead, School District Number 1*,[30] a second theory involving a general notion of affirmative duty can be seen beginning to take shape. The court held that racially segregated education is inadequate and when the segregation is attributable to state action, it is a deprivation of constitutional

---

purpose of achieving the maximum mixture of races in the school population. . . . So long as the boundaries are not drawn for the purpose of maintaining racial segregation, the School Board is under no constitutional requirement that it effectively and completely counteract all of the effects of segregated housing patterns." *Id.*

22. Clark v. Board of Educ., 369 F.2d 661, 666 (8th Cir. 1966). "In short, the Constitution does not require a school system to favor mixing of the races in school. . . ." *Id.*

23. Bowman v. County School Bd. of Charles City Co. 382 F.2d 326, 327 (4th Cir. 1967).

24. *Id.*

25. *Id.* Extrinsic circumstances would be viewed, the court said, to determine if the choice was in fact free.

26. Monroe v. Board of Comm'rs of City of Jackson, 380 F.2d 955, 957 (6th Cir. 1967), *vacated*, 391 U.S. 450 (1968).

27. Jackson v. Marvell School Dist. No. 22, 389 F.2d 740, 744 (8th Cir. 1968). The court's resolve to require the School Board to act "responsibly and adopt a procedure which will assure full attainment of constitutional rights . . ." involved, is belied by its analysis of the facts. *Id.* 744-47. *See* Spriggs v. Altheimer Arkansas School Dist. No. 22, 385 F.2d 254 (8th Cir. 1967).

28. Offerman v. Nitkowski, 378 F.2d 22, 24 (2d Cir. 1967). *De facto* segregation is used by the court in the same sense as racial separation is used herein. *Supra* note 11.

29. *Brown I, supra* note 1, at 492-95.

30. 204 F. Supp. 150 (E.D.N.Y. 1962).

rights.[31] The defendant School Board asked for summary judgment on the ground that it had not by design, pattern of conduct, or contrivance created or maintained segregated education in the schools of the district.[32] The distribution of students in the schools, it said, was due solely to the residential pattern of the district.[33] The court appraised the facts and stated that they could be interpreted as indicating an absence of the Board's direct responsibility for the existing separation of the races in the schools, but denied the motion as the facts fell short of a demonstration that there had been no segregation.[34] The defendant claimed that it had no affirmative duty to integrate the educational system. The court held that failure to deal with a known condition of racial imbalance in public schools amounts to inflicting segregation, as much as any gross imposition of *de jure* segregation.[36]

The situation in *Blocker v. Board of Education of Manhasset*[37] was one in which demographic shifts within the school attendance zones had resulted in a change in the racial composition of the school population from seven per cent Negro during the 1920's to approximately ninety per cent Negro by 1950.[38] The school in question was stipulated by the parties to be equal to the all-white schools in facilities, programs, teaching materials, and teaching and administrative staff.[39] The court found the school system racially imbalanced and this, combined with the "Negro" status of the school in question, rendered inferior the educational opportunity offered by that school.[40] The Constitution requires more than mere passivity.[41] The school officials' prolonged awareness of the racial imbalance, coupled with the rigid no-transfer system, constituted segregation attributable to the state, a violation of plaintiffs' constitutional rights.[42]

The court found an absence of deliberate intent by public school authorities to racially segregate students in *Barksdale v. Springfield School Committee*.[43] Such racial separation as did exist was the result of adherence by the school

31. *Id.* at 153. The court notes that "[t]he central constitutional fact is the inadequacy of segregated education. That it is not coerced by direct action of an arm of the state cannot, alone, be decisive of the issue. . . ."

32. *Id.* at 151.

33. *Id.*

34. *Id.* at 153.

35. *Id.* at 151.

36. *Id.* at 153. The court declares that "[t]he educational system that is thus compulsory and publicly afforded must deal with the inadequacy arising from adventitious segregation: it cannot accept and indurate segregation on the ground that it is not coerced or planned but accepted." *Id.*

37. 226 F. Supp. 208 (E.D.N.Y. 1964).

38. *Id.* at 211.

39. *Id.* at 219.

40. *Id.* at 228-29.

41. *Id.* at 223.

42. *Id.* at 226-27.

43. 237 F. Supp. 543, 544 (D. Mass.), *vacated on other grounds*, 348 F.2d 261 (1st Cir. 1965).

officials to a neighborhood system of school location.[44] The court held that educational opportunities for Negroes in racially imbalanced schools are inadequate because of the separation of the races.[45] School officials have an affirmative obligation under the fourteenth amendment to eliminate racial imbalances within their schools to the fullest extent possible within the framework of effective administration.[46] Neighborhood plans are not unconstitutional, but the court required that the plans be modified or abandoned where they lead to racial imbalance tantamount to segregation.[47]

In *United States v. Jefferson County Board of Education*,[48] the United States Court of Appeals for the Fifth Circuit declared that "the law imposes an absolute duty to desegregate, that is, disestablish segregation. And an absolute duty to integrate, in the sense that a disproportionate concentration of Negroes in certain schools cannot be ignored; rather, a mixing of students is a high priority educational goal."[49] The court cautioned that "[t]he only school desegregation plan that meets constitutional standards is the one that works."[50] School officials are obligated by an affirmative duty to take corrective action to insure attainment of the goal of one, integrated school system.[51] The court pointed out that in the Fifth Circuit the problem is *de jure* segregation. This Circuit has not had to deal with racial imbalances arising fortuitously in single school systems.[52] The court pointedly rejected the notion that transfer systems are a means for the disestablishment of *de jure* segregation of Negroes in public schools. In formerly *de jure* segregated public school systems, the courts must require school boards to desegregate the schools from which transferees come, as well as the ones to which they go:[53] *i.e.*, they must require the "conversion of the dual zones into single system[s]".[54] The court unequivocally stated that "the only adequate redress for a previously overt system-wide policy of segregation directed against Negroes as a collective entity is a system-wide policy of integration."[55]

---

44. *Id.*

45. *Id.* at 546.

46. *Id.* at 547.

47. *Id.* at 546.

48. 372 F.2d 836 (5th Cir. 1966).

49. *Id.* at 846-47 n.5.

50. *Id.* at 847.

51. *Id.* at 845-46. The court said, "[w]e use the terms 'integration' and 'desegregation' of formerly segregated public schools to mean the conversion of a de jure segregated dual system to a unitary, nonracial (nondiscriminatory) system . . . ." *Id.* at 846 n.5.

52. *Id.* at 852, 876.

53. *Id.* at 867-68.

54. *Id.* at 868. *See generally* Broussard v. Houston Independent School Dist., 395 F.2d 817, 818 (5th Cir. 1968), for a case in which the Fifth Circuit dealt with an instance of racial imbalance found in a racially desegregated school system. In such a case, the court held that racial imbalance in public schools, where it is the result of the exercise of freedom of choice, is not evidence of the deprivation of constitutional rights. *Id.* at 820.

55. *Id.* at 869.

C. The Constitution commands affirmative action to disestablish de jure segregation of public school pupils and, further, to eliminate any unjustified racial imbalance resulting from other causes. A third view is expressed in *Hobsen v. Hansen.*[56] The court's argument flows from the initial premise that segregation[57] *per se* renders public education inferior.[58] Relying upon an elaborate and thorough array of empirical evidence,[59] the court concludes that "[r]acially and socially homogeneous schools damage the minds and spirit of all children who attend them—the Negro, the white, the poor and the affluent and block the attainment of broader goals of democratic education, whether the segregation occurs by law or fact."[60] Such schools (at least on the facts of the instant case) offer objectively inferior opportunities to the children assigned to them.[61] They preclude the democratic social encounter[62] the court believed to be so important in "learning to live interracially."[63] And, they exact personal harm to the children assigned to "Negro" schools by maintaining in the minds of these children a stigma of their alleged inferiority.[64] The court emphasized its evaluation of the basic importance of public schools in unequivocal terms. "For the disadvantaged child, handicapped as he is by home and community circumstances, the school remains as the last hope for overcoming academic deficiencies."[65] Segregation was defined somewhat broadly as denoting "the state of racial separateness in the schools, regardless of cause."[66] *De jure* segregation is used to denote "segregation specifically mandated by law or by public policy pursued under color of law."[67] The court had no doubt that if a valid educational purpose is in fact joined with an "outright segregatory purpose" that *de jure* segregation was established.[68] Indeed, "deliberately discriminatory" action is not required by this definition. It is sufficient to raise the issue of *de jure* segregation if the "government action [is] without justification [and] imposes unequal burdens or awards unequal benefits. . . ."[69] School officials may not stand by and watch objective factors conjoin to deprive students of their educational opportunities.[70] Such *de jure* segregation, the court

---

56. *Supra* note 8.
57. Segregation is defined by the court as "the state of racial separateness in the schools, regardless of cause." *Id.* at 411 n.9.
58. *Id.* at 406, 419-21, 480-83, 504.
59. *Id.* at 408-514.
60. *Id.* at 406.
61. *Id.* at 504.
62. *Id.* at 504-5.
63. *Id.* at 419.
64. *Id.* at 506.
65. *Id.* at 483.
66. *Id.* at 411 n.9.
67. *Id.* at 493.
68. *Id.* at 418.
69. *Id.* at 497.
70. *Id.* at 441-42.

clearly regarded as proscribed by the *Brown* decisions.[71] The court did not find that the facts of the case were sufficent to warrant a holding of *de jure* segregation[72] and chose instead to dispose of the issue with what it termed a "new approach".[73] Had it found *de jure* segregation, the court was of the opinion that it had the power to insist upon actual integration. This is so, it argued, since a court has a right to real assurance that the school district has abandoned its unconstitutional policy and, secondly, to wash away the stigma attached to racially segregated schools.[74] In cases of *de facto* segregation,[75] the court did not believe that it could reach so far as to demand the absolute integration of the schools.[76] In such situations, a reinterpreted *Plessy* doctrine[77] was held to be applicable.[78] In this view, the courts must demand that disadvantaged minorities receive equal treatment where the "crucial right to public education is concerned."[79] Indeed, "the minimum the constitution will require and guarantee is that for their objectively measurable aspects, these schools be run on the basis of real equality, at least unless any inequalities are adequately justified."[80] The court holds that the mere fact that there is *de facto* segregation and that it redounds to the detriment of Negro students and seriously undermines the democratization of racial attitudes is insufficient to conclusively determine that action by school officials is unconstitutional. There remains with every such situation the question of justification.[81] Note that it is probably safe to predict that this court will not easily be persuaded as to the existence of justification for practices resulting in *de facto* segregation. The court points out that while theoretically any purely irrational inequalities between two schools would raise a constitutional question, such inefficiencies can be tolerated in the white suburbs.[82] They can not be tolerated where these inadequacies touch the Negro poor. "[T]he law is too deeply committed to the real, not merely theoretical . . . equality of the Negro's educational experience to compromise its diligence . . . ."[83] The court declares that to justify the denial

---

71. *Id.* at 493.

72. *Id.* at 419, 494.

73. *Id.* at 496.

74. *Id.* at 494-95.

75. The court defines *de facto* segregation as segregation which "results from action of pupil assignment policies not based on race but upon social or other conditions for which the government cannot be held responsible." *Id.* at 493. This corresponds to the notion of racial separation as used herein. *Supra* note 11.

76. *Id.* at 496.

77. Plessy v. Ferguson, 163 U.S. 543 (1896). This case enunciated the "separate but equal" doctrine.

78. Hobsen v. Hensen, *supra* note 8.

79. *Id.* at 496-97.

80. *Id.* at 496.

81. *Id.* at 506.

82. *Id.* at 497.

83. *Id.*

of qualitatively equal, if not integrated, educational opportunities to nonwhite students, the school authorities must show that they cannot further their legitimate objectives by narrower or less offensive measures. They must also show that their objectives are of such importance as to override in the court's opinion, the "evil of inequality" which the measures engender.[84] The court said that because the subject is a vital personal right, involving a voiceless, invisible, minority that courts must subject such practices to closer scrutiny than would otherwise be necessary.[85]

GREEN, MONROE, RAINEY: THE RESPONSE OF THE SUPREME COURT

In *Green v. County School Board of New Kent County*, the Supreme Court undertook to consider the constitutionality of a "freedom of choice" plan of school desegregation.[86] The facts of the case blatantly indicated a history of segregation. The population of New Kent County was approximately one half Negro and there was no residential segregation. The school system, however, was first directly segregated by law and then indirectly segregated by the application of a pupil placement law.[87] In order to remain eligible for federal aid, the school authorities adopted a freedom of choice plan of school desegregation. Under the terms of this plan, each pupil could annually choose between the "white" New Kent school and the "Negro" Watkins school. Pupils not making a choice were to be assigned to the school they previously attended, except for pupils of the first and eighth grades who were required to affirmatively choose one or the other school.[88] Mr. Justice Brennan writing for a unanimous Court noted that the racial identification and segregation of the schools involved was complete and was attributable to the state acting through local school authorities.[89] The Court held that "freedom of choice" was insufficient as a means to desegregate the schools.[90] The Court required the School Board to formulate a new plan which would "fashion steps which promise realistically to convert [the dual school system] promptly to a system without a 'white' school and a 'Negro' school, but just schools."[91] The Court viewed the *Brown* decisions as establishing that "[t]he transition to a unitary, nonracial system of public education was and is the ultimate end to be brought about . . . ."[92] Indeed, "*Brown II* was a call for the dismantling of well-entrenched dual systems tempered by an awareness that complex and

---

84. *Id.* at 507.
85. *Id.* at 507-08.
86. 391 U.S. 430, 431-32 (1968).
87. *Id.* at 432-33.
88. *Id.* at 433-34.
89. *Id.* at 435.
90. *Id.* at 441.
91. *Id.* at 442.
92. *Id.* at 435.

multifaceted problems would arise which would require time and flexibility for a successful resolution."[93] Even though problems were anticipated, the *Brown* decisions "clearly charged [school officials] with the affirmative duty to take whatever steps might be necessary to convert to a unitary system in which racial discrimination would be eliminated root and branch."[94] The time for mere "deliberate speed" has run.[95] Today, there is a burden on school authorities to come forward with desegregation plans which promise realistically to work, and promise "realistically to work *now*."[96] "[A] plan that at this late date fails to provide meaningful assurance of prompt and effective disestablishment of a dual system is intolerable."[97] Freedom of choice plans are not *per se* unconstitutional. Rather, district courts must assess such plans and others in the light of the circumstances and options available to school officials in each instance. Where the court finds the school board to be acting in "good faith" and the proposed plan has "real prospects for dismantling the state-imposed dual system 'at the earliest practicable date,' " the plan raises no constitutional objection. The existence, however, of other more promising alternatives places a "heavy burden" on school officials to explain their preference for methods less effective in breaking down the established, segregated educational system. Whatever plan is adopted, it is to be evaluated in practice.[98] The factual context of the decision and the constant referral to disestablishment support the second theory that there is an affirmative duty going beyond mere restraint from *de jure* segregation to the actual disestablishment of *de jure* segregation. The responsibility of school officials for *de facto* segregation and their obligations regarding racial imbalance resulting from racial separation remain undecided.

In *Monroe v. Board of Commissioners of the City of Jackson*, the school district coincided with the city limits of Jackson, Tennessee.[99] Unlike *Green* and *Raney*, the district's Negro residents lived predominantly in the confines of the central city.[100] The school authorities, in response to the order of the district court, filed a desegregation plan establishing attendance zones based upon geographic division of the district along natural boundaries and the capacities of the schools within the zones. In addition, the plan called for the "free transfer" of any child to the school of his choice after he registered in his assigned school. The choice, however, was limited by the proviso that there be space available for him in the school selected. Zone residents were to be given priority in their own zones. Transferring students were required to provide their

---

93. *Id*. at 437.
94. *Id*. at 437-38.
95. *Id*. at 438.
96. *Id*. at 439.
97. *Id*. at 438.
98. *Id*. at 439-41.
99. 391 U.S. 450, 452 (1968).
100. *Id*.

own transportation, as the district did not operate buses.[101] The Supreme Court held unanimously that the adequacy of "free transfer" plans of school desegregation are to be tested by the principles announced in *Green*. The Court noted that the plan had been operated in a discriminatory fashion and that it had resulted in segregating students.[102] "Plainly the plan does not meet respondent's 'affirmative duty to take whatever steps might be necessary to convert a unitary system in which racial discrimination would be eliminated root and branch.' "[103] The Court required the School Board, as in *Green*, to formulate a plan which would promise realistically to convert the dual system of racially segregated schools into one system. It said that no transfer plan of which racial segregation is the "inevitable consequence" may stand under the fourteenth amendment. Free transfer plans were not made *per se* unconstitutional, but give rise to the burden of proving their adequacy as tools for the disestablishment of racially segregated school systems.[104]

In *Raney v. Board of Education of Gould School District*, petitioners had sought injunctive relief from the District Court.[105] They had asked, *inter alia*, for relief from being required to attend a "Negro" school, from the provision of inferior school facilities to Negroes, and for the enjoinment of the operation of racially segregated schools.[106] In an unreported opinion, the district court dismissed petitioners' complaint and denied all relief. The Court of Appeals for the Eighth Circuit affirmed the dismissal.[107] The Supreme Court held this improper. "Dismissal will ordinarily be inconsistent with the responsibility imposed on the district courts by *Brown II*."[108] Instead, district courts should retain jurisdiction to insure that a constitutionally acceptable plan is adopted and to insure that it is operated "so that the goal of a desegregated, non-racially operated school system is rapidly and finally achieved."[109]

REFLECTIONS

Within the flury and tempest of the school desegregation controversy, three related and much confused elements are present: racial segregation of public school pupils, the quality of objective educational facilities, and the subjective characterization of segregated schools in the minds of students and the public. The courts in struggling with desegregation have often treated segregation as the cause of the objective inferiority of educational facilities accorded Negroes and

---

101. *Id.* at 453-54.
102. *Id.* at 456-57.
103. *Id.* at 458.
104. *Id.* at 459-60.
105. 391 U.S. 443, 445 (1968).
106. *Id.* at 446.
107. Raney v. Board of Educ. of Gould School Dist., 381 F.2d 252 (8th Cir. 1967).
108. *Id.* at 449.
109. *Id.*

as the cause of the subjective stigma attached to "Negro" schools. These factors are, however, discrete phenomena and, though they may have been previously found together, there is no logical nor empircal necessity that they conjoin. Failure to recognize these elements as independent, as ways in which a general right to educational opportunity may be lost, has tempted some courts to seek a solution to the problem of securing to all, equally a meaningful educational experience in the mechanical fixing of quotas and the mixing of races. If segregation is the evil, then integration must be the means to exorcise that evil. This disposition to frame the issue in terms of segregation-integration has been reinforced by the factual contexts of cases in which the quality of the educational experience offered to Negro children could actually be substantially improved by integrating the "white" schools of formerly dual systems. Failure to recognize that the right which must be accorded constitutional protection is not the limited right to be free from segregation (though we may wish for other reasons to secure this right constitutional protection), but the more general right to educational opportunity has had anomalous results. Three hypothetical children in three hypothetical situations could reasonably expect different treatment, though in each case the educational opportunity of the child (and with it his personal development and chances for useful life) is destroyed. Child A attends a segregated school (irrespective of the quality of the education offered). The courts have held that such segregation deprives him of a constitutional right. Child B attends a segregated school, but is transferred or bussed to a "white", middle class school in which he is expected to function in roughly the same manner as the middle class students. His educational opportunity may be destroyed by cultural shock and/or the inability of the school to meet his special needs and requirements; and yet, once his segregation has ceased, it is unlikely that a court would find his constitutional rights to have been breached. Child C attends a nonsegregated school which offers an inferior education experience due to inadequate objective facilities and a stigma of inferiority attached to the school and its students. His hope for personal and social fulfillment may well be dashed, but under present thinking he has not been denied his constitutional rights. To call such reasoning artificial is to indulge in understatement! Those courts which have sought solutions to the vexing problem of guaranteeing meaningful education to all have been led astray by the unfortunate focus upon segregation in the *Brown* and subsequent lower court decisions. Such attention has tended to a preoccupation with mechanical devices to homogenize the racial composition of schools and a failure to deal with situations lacking in segregation (in the usual sense) though individuals are nonetheless crushed by effectively preventing them from attaining their potential. There must be recognition by the courts that segregation is but one way that the right to education may be lost. There must also be recognition that when children are placed in schools competent to teach only middle class, white children, without more this is not an "equal" educational opportunity. Minority children may not have the cultural and social requisites to bring such opportunity to fruition and, if they do not possess these characteristics, to call such exposure opportunity is illusory. There must be recognition that to bring the potential of these special children to reality, special treatment is required. Equality must not become a slogan which thwarts the attainment or real equality. Instead educational opportunities must be judged in terms of their reasonably anticipated results.

There is awareness in *Brown I* of the nature of this problem and recognition there of a constitutionally protected right to education, but the cases decided under its mandate have shifted judicial focus from securing the right to preoccupation with abolishing one means by which the right may be lost. It is time, after fourteen years, for the Supreme Court to clear away the intellectual and political debris and return judicial attention to the essential problem, guaranteeing meaningful educational experience to all. As phrased by Chief Justice Warren in *Brown v. Board of Education of Topeka*:

> Today, education is perhaps the most important function of state and local governments. Compulsory school attendance laws and the great expenditures for education both demonstrate our recognition of the importance of education to our democratic society. It is required in the performance of our most basic public responsibilities, even service in the armed forces. It is the very foundation of good citizenship. Today it is a principal instrument in awakening the child to cultural values, in preparing him for later professional training, and in helping him to adjust normally to his environment. *In these days, it is doubtful that any child may reasonably be expected to succeed in life if he is denied the opportunity of an education. Such an opportunity, where the state has undertaken to provide it, is a right which must be made available to all on equal terms.*[110]

---

110. *Brown I, supra* note 1, at 493 (emphasis added).

SCHOOL DESEGREGATION: THE NEED TO GOVERN

Morton Inger and Robert T. Stout

Morton Inger and Robert T. Stout, "School Desegregation: The Need to Govern," *The Urban Review* (A Publication of the Center of Urban Education), November 1968, pp. 35-38.

SCHOOL DESEGREGATION: THE NEED TO GOVERN

Morton Inger and Robert T. Stout

School desegregation is dead — at least temporarily — at least in the opinion of some observers. And white opposition is frequently cited as the reason for its demise. The findings of research conducted by the present authors suggest that this opposition, though unmistakably present, could not have been the cause of the demise. It could not, because it was not even the main cause of the defeat or the delay of desegregation plans.[1] What is more, in the opinion of the authors, the reports of the death of integration are greatly exaggerated.

In view of what were (and are) believed to be the prevailing white attitudes toward Negroes and toward integration, the response of whites in the eight cities studied was surprising. In four of the cities, there was either no conflict or else the opposition took forms — such as legal action — which helped to legitimate the school system's integration plan. In the other four cities, there was active opposition (in varying amounts), but the school system in all four except Englewood was able to retain control of the situation. (Please note that we are talking here about the absence or presence of open conflict, not mere dissatisfaction. In all eight cities there was dissatisfaction.) In seven of the eight cities, even including Englewood, the community ultimately accepted the school system's plan. The exception is Syracuse, but the school administration's plan was withdrawn because of opposition by the city's *Negro* leaders.

During the period studied — the mid 1960s — school integration was perhaps the chief demand of the civil rights movement, and school administrators greatly feared the issue. They thought whites would be so aroused over integration that they would rebel against the school system in general and refuse to support needed bond issues, and, in the case of elected school boards, turn the incumbents out of office. Certainly, this happened in some cities. But our study indicated that this need not happen. It depends to a great extent on how the school leaders handle the issue. If the issue is presented and handled properly, we have evidence that the white community not only can accept the desegregation plan but will subsequently give positive support to the school system and its financial needs.

Boston, Chicago, Cleveland, Oakland, and Buffalo are vivid examples of cities whose school systems were believed by school administrators and others to have been hurt in general by the school desegregation issue. No realistic educator would willingly subject his school system to the strains and wrenches experienced by the school systems in those cities. A public controversy is anathema to the school administrator. Like any

---

[1] The eight cities studied were Berkeley, California; Coatesville, Pennsylvania; Englewood, New Jersey; Greenburgh School District #8 (Westchester County, New York); Rochester, New York; Syracuse, New York; Teaneck, New Jersey; and White Plains, New York. The cut-off date for the study was October 1966. Except for the case of Rochester, our remarks are confined to events occurring prior to October 1966.

administrator, he prefers to 'get on with his work.' But from 1960 through 1966, it was difficult if not impossible for a school system to avoid the issue of school desegregation. Despite the impression one may have received from newspaper accounts, some cities achieved desegregation without experiencing harmful public conflict.

What distinguished the successful school systems from the unsuccessful ones? (Success here being defined as the ability to achieve school desegregation without disrupting the school system.) To begin with, the troubled cities (those that did not achieve desegregation and experienced public disruption of the school system) had school superintendents who took the stand that desegregation was not an essential educational goal. In some of those cities, and in other cities that achieved desegregation only after great delay and cost, the school officials asked the public — through referenda and the submission of the issue to *ad hoc* citizens committees — what *they* thought about the question. This was an indication that the school officials did not believe that integration was a proper educational goal, for few school systems ask the voters to decide educational matters as they arise. In Buffalo, in 1964, when the school system went to the public with the issue of the racial composition of a new school, the result was the adoption of a proposal for a school *more* segregated than even the most ardent neighborhood-school advocates on the board had hoped to achieve.

In the four cities that achieved desegregation with little difficulty, the school officials were convinced that integration was an important goal of the public schools. In two of these four cities, the superintendent went beyond this and proclaimed integration to be a moral necessity. White Plains superintendent Dr. Carroll Johnson could see no reason for submitting the issue to the voters. "Who would ask for a show of hands on a moral issue?" he explained. In an official statement, Rochester superintendent Herman Goldberg announced that segregation was *the* problem with education in Rochester. In addition, he made many public appearances arguing the moral and educational rightness of integration. School integration in Greenburgh School District #8 (Westchester County, New York) began in 1951 as an *educational* necessity for the community. Since that time, the superintendent and school board have become committed to 'heterogeneous' education (i.e., racial and achievement mixtures in the classroom) as a goal in itself. Even in Coatesville, Pennsylvania, where the school board and superintendent exerted little leadership to achieve desegregation and seemed relatively uncommitted to the idea, the school system moved rapidly to desegregate because of the school board's conviction that desegregation was the law of the land. In a fifth city, Berkeley, which differs from the above four in that it achieved desegregation only after a long and bitter public fight, the school board tried as much as possible to leave the issue up to citizens committees. Nevertheless, the Berkeley school staff helped CORE present its statement on de facto segregation (and actually found more segregation than CORE knew about), the school superintendent said that integration was good in itself and needed no further justification, and the desegregation plan was presented to the public as an *education* plan.

Indeed, the differences among the eight cities can be seen as differences in the way the school systems presented their plans to the public. The eight cities range from Englewood (where first the school officials and later the city administration asked the community to vote on how and whether to integrate) to White Plains, where the school administration worked skillfully to keep the issue from ever going to the public. It is relatively easy to rank these eight cities ranging from (top) the ones with the greatest noise level over school integration to the cities (bottom) in which there was virtually no conflict.

If we rank the eight cities on the extent to which the school system opened the issue to the public, we see a striking similarity to the first ranking.

Extent of open conflict and difficulty in obtaining acceptance	*Extent to which the schools opened the issue to the public*
high	*high*
Englewood	Englewood
Berkeley	Berkeley
Teaneck	Syracuse
Syracuse	Teaneck
Coatesville	Coatesville
Rochester	Rochester
Greenburgh	Greenburgh
White Plains	White Plains
low	*low*

Despite many differences between these cities, the school systems that opened the issue to the public the most had the greatest difficulty in obtaining community acceptance. The ones that opened the issue the least had the least difficulty in obtaining acceptance.

To explain our ranking of the cities on their opening the issue to the public:

Englewood is at the top because of the repeated polling of the public.

Berkeley is ranked second because of the school board's constant referral of the issue to citizens committees.

Syracuse is third because, among other things, the school board's vacillation and indecision drew into the issue many public voices during the policy formation stage.

Teaneck and *Coatesville* clearly belong in the middle, with perhaps Teaneck being placed higher than Coatesville. The Coatesville school board opened up the issue by asking the PTAs to suggest plans for the integration of the schools; no specific plan was suggested by the school board or the superintendent. On the other hand, when the PTA majority urged the board to fight any attempt to integrate, the school board went ahead and integrated anyway. The Teaneck board publicly announced its intention to come up with an integration plan, asked the public for suggestions, and made frequent, heated appearances before public forums on the issue. A clash at one of these forums led one of the neighborhood-school proponents to decide to run for the school board against the 'integrationists.' Yet, unlike the Coatesville board, which never did come up with a plan of its own but adopted the plan suggested by the PTA minority, the Teaneck school board made its own decisions and plans and went against the open hostility of a large and vocal segment of the public and community leaders.

The remaining three cities clearly belong at the 'absence of public referral' end of the table:

In *Rochester*, for the period studied by the authors (that is, prior to 1967), the school board and superintendent made all decisions without referring the question to the public. (As we shall discuss more fully below Rochester's superintendent made an abrupt change in tactics in 1967, putting the issue of whether and how to the public.)

Greenburgh and *White Plains* run a close race for the position of opening up the issue the least, but we believe White Plains stands by itself because of the finesse with which community organizations were co-opted by the school officials and community acceptance was won.

We have considered and rejected the possibility that the *reason* some cities opened up the issue more than others was that they had more opposition. Such a premise is based, in part, on the assumption that the cities with the least open conflict were somehow made up of nicer, more liberal people who would not oppose integration. This notion is not totally supported by the evidence. In all eight cities large numbers of citizens expressed their dissatisfaction with the very notion of integration as well as with the specific plans under consideration.

One lesson of these eight cities is clear. The less the public is asked for its opinion during the period of policy-formation, the greater the likelihood that the public will accept the integration plan. One can pick cities from any point in the scale and find support for this argument. White Plains is especially 'satisfactory' because community acceptance was won from a rebellious community which, one year earlier had twice decided that the schools were already spending too much money.

Coatesville, too, is a good example because, even though the school board went against the opinion of the community organization from which it had solicited suggestions, the community accepted the integration plan without incident. (And this in a city with many Southern rural mores!)

Teaneck is another good example, for despite the vitriolic open conflict *while the board members were making up their minds,* the community quietly accepted the integration plan once it was put into effect. Thirty neighborhood-school advocates tried to get a boycott started, but their own friends dissuaded them.

Even Englewood is a good example. Despite the openness of the conflict, despite the militancy of the civil rights movement, once the school system adopted a plan and put it into effect, the community accepted it without incident.

Because Rochester's superintendent changed tactics in 1967, that city provides a sharp. illustration of the point we are making.[2] From 1963 through 1966, the Rochester school system made progress toward integrating its all-white and predominantly white schools. All steps taken were made by the school officials and school board members without referring the question to the public. Except for a few easily handled legal challenges, the Rochester citizenry quietly accepted all the steps taken by the school system. So successful (in their limited way) were these steps and so committed did the superintendent and the school board seem, that the United States Commission on Civil Rights chose Rochester for the location of hearings on school desegregation in the fall of 1966. Yet, in response to his own school board's unanimous directive (May 1966) to have ready by February 1967 a plan for the desegregation of all of Rochester's elementary schools, the superintendent did *not* adopt a plan. Instead, he broadcast four plans to the public without indicating any moral or educational necessity for adopting any particular plan. Thus having been asked *whether* as well as how to integrate, Rochester's

---

[2] As we have indicated, our study ended as of October 1966. Our information on Rochester since that date was obtained by Morton Inger while working in the Center for Urban Education's Rochester project, directed by Dr. Gladys E. Lang. See *Resistance and Support for School Desegregation Proposals: A Study of Parental Reactions in Rochester,* by Gladys E. Lang, Morton Inger, and Roy Mallett (Center for Urban Education, 1967). The interpretation of the Rochester events expressed herein is that of the authors of the present article and should not be ascribed to the Center or to Dr. Lang.

white citizens — some of them, anyhow — expressed their strong opposition to the idea of cross-busing. Six weeks after the superintendent threw the plans out to the public, the school board, which had ordered a plan, rejected all four desegregation plans.

Although an argument could be made that the public opposition arose because the rejected plans were more far-reaching than the earlier steps which had been accepted, we believe the earlier steps would have been rejected as well, had they been placed before the voters without the educators having argued strongly for their acceptance. The experience of the other cities indicates that it is not the size of the step taken but the way it is presented that elicits widespread, active opposition. When Berkeley's small step — to desegregate just one junior high — was opened to the public, intense opposition forced the board into a bitter recall election. When Teaneck opened up its decision, there was great trouble, but when the board closed it down — *not reducing the plan,* but taking responsibility for the decision — the trouble ended.

Contrary to the fears of schoolmen that a school system could not escape being hurt if the integration issue came up, in all eight cities the public — as of our cut-off date of October 1966 — had not only accepted the system's integration steps but had supported bond issues and re-elected the school board members who had taken these steps.[3] When school board elections occurred *before* implementation of a plan, incumbent school board members did not fare well. But when the elections occurred *after* implementation, the incumbents were re-elected. The other side of the coin can be seen in Rochester. So long as Rochester's school board was strongly urging desegregation and implementing desegregation plans without consulting with the public, the school board members were easily re-elected. But after the board *retreated* from its stand, a neighborhood school advocate was elected to the board for the first time.

The hallmark of these success stories is that the school officials presented desegregation as a proper goal of the educational system and, in some cities, as an educationally beneficial change. In the cities where

[3] Though Syracuse's integration *plan* had to be withdrawn, all the *steps* it had taken were accepted by the public.

[4] Syracuse and Englewood witnessed a battle between white and Negro groups; but in these two cities the battle was over specific integration plans, not over whether to integrate or not.

acceptance was won with the least conflict, an additional key element is that the public was not asked for its prior approval. The important consequence of this form of presentation is that the issue did not become a battle between Negroes and whites.

In Chicago, Cleveland, Boston, Buffalo, and some Southern cities, the school issue stirred up a battle between the civil rights organizations and the whites who are opposed to integration. In our eight cities, by contrast, the school system adopted integration as its own goal, thereby giving legitimation to the idea. If a battle arose in these cities, it was between an accepted governmental body and a group of dissident citizens.[4] It is important to note, in this connection, that even the relatively uncommitted Coatesville school board told the community that segregation was in violation of the law of the land and indicated its intention to desegregate *before* it even had a plan. It was only after the Coatesville board made its intentions clear that it went to the community for suggestions. Thus, the people of Coatesville were asked for suggestions in the context of governmental (the school board) approval of integration. The people of Coatesville, then, were not asked for·a show of hands on integration. This would explain why the Coatesville School Board was not deterred by the PTA vote against integration; the school board had already made its decision.

In Teaneck, the school board was uncommitted to any specific integration plan. Indeed, the Teaneck board did not agree on a plan until two nights before the meeting at which they formally adopted it. This uncertainty, which was known to the public, did have the effect, as we have noted, of opening up the issue and making it a public controversy. An election campaign for the school board was fought out over the issue; and when word leaked out that the board had agreed on a plan, three councilmen crashed an executive session of the board to protest their decision. At the public meeting the next night, 1,400 people (estimated to be 3 to 1 against the plan) crowded into the meeting room, shouting and shaking their fists. Overwhelmed by the commotion, the board members called a five minute recess to collect themselves; they then came back and adopted the plan by a vote of 7 to 2.

From that point on, any community response had to be to a governmental decision. Governmental decisions are legitimate; for many people, this is enough to settle the issue. For the committed opponents, the road of opposition is difficult. This was clearly the case in Teaneck, for the outburst at the school board meeting was the last open attack on the Teaneck school board. The opponents filed law suits (and lost) and conducted a vigorous election campaign a year later. The legitimating effect of the governmental decision can be seen by comparing that election with the school board election which was held while the board was still making up its mind. In February 1964, while the board was still uncertain, two proponents of the neighborhood school 'concept' were elected to the board, while one incumbent who was known to be favoring the superintendent's integration plans squeaked past a third pro-neighborhood school candidate by only 21 votes. To indicate the virulence of the feelings in Teaneck at that time, one of the pro-neighborhood school candidates told the superintendent during the campaign, "I know you're not a Communist, but you talk like one, you act like one, and you propose policies the Communists favor." That candidate was elected. But in the election *following* the adoption of the integration plan, all three candidates favoring the board's integration plan defeated the three neighborhood-school candidates by a 7 to 5 margin.

The importance of governmental action as a legitimating force can be seen further in the matter of attitudes toward integration. In three of our cities — Syracuse, Englewood, and Coatesville — the school board members were unanimous in their negative feelings toward civil rights demonstrations, yet they approved of integration. It is generally believed that the public as a whole *dislikes* civil rights marches and school boycotts and integration, but our study indicates that when the issue is presented in a certain way, the public *accepts* integration. Apparently, the community tends to accept the idea if it comes from a legitimate governmental body such as the school board. The significant task for government, then, would be to prevent race relations from becoming simply a conflict between 'those Negroes' and 'us whites.'

When the government opposes integration, as superintendent Benjamin Willis did in Chicago, or abstains from the issue and defers to the public, as the city government did in New Orleans from 1956 to 1961 and as the school board and superintendent did in Buffalo at one point, integration is robbed of legitimacy, and the issue becomes a matter of competing demonstrations. When the school systems in Syracuse and Englewood referred the issue to the public at critical points, the void left by the abstention of the government was filled by competing white and Negro groups. The conflict that emerges from such confrontations frightens most people away, and many whites say no to the whole disturbance, including the idea of integration which 'caused' it.

By contrast, the *actions* of the board in Rochester, White Plains, Greenburgh, and Coatesville were accepted by the public. Integration in these cities was achieved not by demonstrations and boycotts but by legitimate school officials who promoted it in the name of educational and moral values. Consequently, the actions taken by these school boards, though not exactly what the public would have demanded if they had been asked what to do, were accepted by the public.

Does this analysis speak against democracy? We think not. We are not advocating secrecy in government or deals made behind closed doors. Although we feel that public leaders should not ask the people what to do, we do believe they should say what they did and why. More specifically, asking the public what to do on issues as they arise is a particularly dangerous thing for a *school official* to do.

School administrators and — in most cities — school board members are not politicians. Hence, they can make no demands upon the parties or their leaders. Yet, being in the public sphere, they are subject to demands from all sectors of the community. The consequence is that school governing bodies are unprotected from mass grievances. Furthermore, not being politicians, school officials are not skilled at 'reading' the grievances. That is, they can not discriminate among the many voices they hear. Is the man or the group who shouts the loudest the one you should listen to? What is the significance of a petition bearing 6,000 signatures opposing desegregation? A political leader with a ward organization can answer these questions, but a school administrator or board member has only hunches — and these are the hunches of amateurs.

There *is* a way for schoolmen to go to the public: to act and later stand for re-election. Schoolmen who ask the public what decisions they should make — especially on such a hot issue as desegregation — risk the incapacitation of the school system. Furthermore, this violates the trust of the public, for these men were elected (or appointed by elected officials) to govern the schools.

Why did the eight communities we studied accept the plans and re-elect the officials responsible for them? The citizens in these cities are certainly no more liberal on race relations than the citizens in most other cities. The answer must be that the people in these cities were satisfied with the men and the desegregation policies. Democracy does not mean that all the people make all the decisions. The fundamental requirements of democracy are met if the people have ample opportunity to influence or unseat the decision makers, if those who govern can be held accountable by the people. Actual day-to-day decisions are left to representatives of the people, who expect these representatives to 'get on with it' without referring all the decisions to them. In fact, democracy is served when the representative accepts responsibility for the decisions. The people of Englewood and Syracuse wanted the same things the people in the other cities wanted: peace, progress, and prosperity. By dodging responsibility and asking the people how and whether to integrate, the officials of Syracuse and Englewood failed to give their citizens what they wanted. The officials in the other cities desegregated the schools (in varying degrees), kept the peace, and were able to get on with other fundamental educational problems.

By way of a summary, we offer the following advice to school officials. If you will treat integration as a routine educational matter and proceed to implement your integration plan without asking for a show of hands, the community will accept the steps you take. Furthermore, integration is not dead. So long as America remains a plural nation, integration shall remain a continuing *internal* need, one that is not dependent upon the demands of individuals and groups. Certain *groups* may no longer speak as though they want integration, but the *nation* needs integration as much as it ever did.

THE BUSING OF STUDENTS
FOR EQUAL OPPORTUNITIES

Thomas W. Mahan

Thomas W. Mahan, "The Busing of Students for Equal Opportunities,"
Journal of Negro Education, Summer 1968, Vol. 37, pp. 291-300.

THE BUSING OF STUDENTS FOR EQUAL OPPORTUNITIES

Thomas W. Mahan

THE PROBLEM — AND SOME EFFORTS TOWARD SOLUTION

The evolution of the concept of "busing" as a technique for increasing the probability of equal educational opportunity for black or other minority youth comes from two rather distinct sources. The first of these has lost some of its popularity in recent months and revolves about the role of the public school as a dynamic force in the acculturation process. It views the strength of the society as an outgrowth of its ability to absorb divergent, even conflicting, traditions and forge a "mainstream" which can be "owned" by all segments. With the repeated failure of the white educational establishment to demonstrate the viability of this concept (except on very paternalistic terms) and the growing sense of alienation between white and black traditions, this basic premise has been seriously questioned especially by the black community. This problem will receive more attention later.

The second source for interest in "busing" is a more empirical one. Public school research bureaus are filled with data (long zealously ignored) which underline the limited output (as measured in terms of achievement, mental ability or social adaptation) of the ghetto school. Even beyond this the cumulative, if not definitive, impact of efforts in the areas of enrichment and intensive compensatory programs has provided little basis for hope that the relatively easy solutions such as smaller classes, better teachers, new facilities, revised curricula or combinations of these will correct the problem. In other words, "busing" is an intervention which faces up to the evidence about the overwhelming burden which faces the neighborhood school in the ghetto; that is, it faces all the facts except that of numbers. Once again this issue will be delayed until later.

Yet to write about "busing" even within this context is too general. For example, does this concept include those operations which transport Negro youngsters from a highly segregated school to a less segregated school only to place them into highly segregated classes because of the principle of homogeneous grouping? For the purposes of this paper "busing" will be limited to those programs which transport ghetto youth into essentially white schools and place them in classes where they are a clear-cut minority (less than 25% of the total class). This arbitrary definition is invoked because it seems essential to clarify the issues: busing is here viewed as an intervention designed to enhance the performance of ghetto youngsters along the dimensions of traditional school success. This in no way implies an unawareness of the philosophical or value issues involved, but it does involve an immediate, pragmatic orientation: within the present system ghetto youngsters have few, if any, alternatives and the range of possibilities for subsequent movement is extremely constricted. In the long run it may be that the public school system will be dramatically changed and its relation to higher education and occupational structure much altered; in the meantime it exists and demands recognition.

At this point it may be well to set forth the rationale behind the intervention. Clearly, there is no magic in sitting next to a white child that suddenly transforms the non-white child into a better student. Rather, the assumptions have to do with styles of learning, reinforcement, level of expectations and modeling. In brief, the ghetto child enters school with a "style of learning" which does not generally facilitate school success. Because of the homogeneity of the ghetto school this style or pattern is reinforced by the general population and eventually the expectation is that this pattern will persist and dominate. In contrast, when the ghetto child is placed in a suburban school, his crystallized pattern is confronted with new situations and reactions. There is a tendency for the pattern to become less stable because of different response sets and different expectations. Theoretically, the change will be in the direction of the other models present — particularly if supportive assistance is provided in the initial explorations. In other words, it is felt that the characteristics of the majority of the pupils in a classroom are a powerful determinant of individual pupil behavior and of teacher interaction, including teacher expectation. Viewed in this light busing constitutes a frontal attack upon two highly-valued educational myths: the neighborhood school and homogeneous grouping.

The present paper is an early survey of four attempts to introduce quality education by way of busing. The choice of case studies is primarily a function of availability of· data although the major emphasis has been placed on urban-suburban plans because these most dramatically illustrate the problems and promises of this intervention. The urban communities involved are Boston, Hartford, and Rochester, New York, all of which have ghetto youth now attending schools in white suburbs and White Plains, New York, which has introduced an extensive intra-city program. Table I summarizes some of the information about these communities and their plans.

Clearly, the size of the programs is limited and each of the urban-suburban efforts has· been characterized as a "pilot" endeavor. Within this context it appears that there are some beginning signs of breakthrough. Boston's METCO program continues to expand and will reach a figure of 800 pupils in 22 towns by September, 1968; in similar fashion Hartford's Project Concern is now assured of a program of 1000 pupils in 11 communities — a figure which is approximately 13 per cent of the total nonwhite population in grades K − 6. These figures, however, take on much more meaning in the light of the difficult road to existence.

THE QUEST FOR A DREAM: A BRIEF HISTORY

The American dream of equal rights and equal opportunity has been shattered in the ghetto schools of our major cities for years and yet it has continued to persist. This dream has been part of the motivation which has led to busing, but it has had to overcome a series of impressive obstacles. In each of the com-

TABLE I

TABLE I

Descriptive Data on Four Communities

Program Title	Year Initiated	Nonwhite School Population	No. of Children	No. of Towns
Boston METCO	1966	24%	220 (1966)	7
			425 (1967)	15
Hartford Project Concern	1966	56%	266 (1966)	
			284 (1967)	5
Rochester	1965	28%	64	1
White Plains	1964	18%	750 (est.)	N.A.

munities which are mentioned above there has been active, vigorous objections to the concept of busing. The form of the objection has followed a rather consistent pattern with voiced objections taking the following lines: (a) it is the city's problem and let them solve it, (b) if "they" want to move out there, let "them" work their way up as we did, (c) busing will dilute the quality of our suburban schools, (d) the disparity of experience will be psychologically traumatic, (e) "they" will be happier in their neighborhood schools, and (f) it would be better to spend the money for improvement in the ghetto school.

Beneath these objections as they were voiced in crowded and often tumultous public hearings was an intensity of feeling which appeared to bring serious disharmony into the community. It seemed obvious in most suburban towns that a popular plebescite would result in rejection of the plan. Consequently, the cry for a referendum was frequent and loud: "let the people decide," was the plea. In each of the three states involved (Connecticut, Massachusetts, and New York) the statutes clearly placed the responsibility for such decisions in the hands of the boards of education or school committees. In Connecticut, a number of towns requested rulings from their legal officers as to the legality of an "advisory referendum" which would have no binding force but would give the board of education the benefit of the town's opinion. In four towns the legal authorities declared that such an action would not be legal; in two others the decision stated that, if no expense was involved (i.e., if the question were placed on an already scheduled ballot), it would be legal, but not binding. As a result, two such "popular votes" have been held with results given in Table II. This illustrates the fact that even in a town which has had two years of successful experience in the program and where the local school authorities have gone on record as enthusiastically supportive, there

TABLE II

Distribution of "Popular Votes" in Two Towns on the Issue of Busing

Town	Question	% Voting	% Favor	% Opposed	Final Decision
Bolton	To Join	38	40	60	Joined
Manchester	To Continue	35	49	51	Continued

remains much divergence of feeling within the town.

Yet in some ways these figures are misleading. The natural history of events seems to follow a rather determined sequence. There is the excited, turbulent period charged with emotion and attack; the predictions of dire results (and perhaps reprisals in the form of opposition to bond issues, etc.) may accompany the courageous decision of the school authorities to move ahead. Then comes a period of watchful waiting coupled with a sense of surprise when the largest problems turn out to be logistical (how to get the buses to be at the different places at the same time, for example). When the question is again formally before the board of education to decide upon continuation, it now evokes limited interest. Where in the beginning, 2,000 taxpayers may have turned out for a meeting only 25 to 50 come, and statements are simple, to the point, and without vindictiveness.

This simplified and generalized account in no way conveys the tremendous pressures which are exerted in the midst of the controversy nor the remarkable sources of support which are sometimes rallied. These will probably vary from town to town, but it seems safe to infer that at least some elements of the "power structure" must encourage participation if there is to be substance to the proposal. The alignment of the liberal "civil rights" groups or those commonly dismissed as "do-gooders" is essential, but not sufficient in itself.

Operational Design: An Overview

Each of the four places considered by this paper has a basic similarity in that nonwhite youngsters (mostly black, but including Puerto Rican) are placed in predominantly white schools where there is room. In White Plains where the program is contained within the city limits, the plan called for the closing down of a core city school and dispersion of these youngsters into the other ten elementary schools with certain guidelines as to ethnic percentages. This procedure is most directly contrasted with Hartford where there are eight elementary schools containing 12,000 youngsters that are 90 per cent or more nonwhite. Under such conditions, where the total school population is 56 per cent nonwhite, the closing of schools and redrawing district lines will not work. For Hartford, time had made that approach obsolete. Yet, in a sense, the suggested solution was the same except that it called for a redefinition of the geographic limits of the community. Perceived in this way each of the plans is similar with the following exceptions:

A. Only in White Plains has the action solved the segregation problem; in the other three communities only the possibility of a solution has been demonstrated.

B The youngsters involved differ

1. White Plains — all the pupils of one inner-city school and 20 per cent of other elementary schools have been reassigned to create reasonable uniformity in ethnic balance.

2. Boston — volunteers were solicited through various media and applicants selected by interview.

3 · Hartford — random selection from all segregated schools.

4. Rochester — selection by school authorities.

C. The grade levels involved differ in that Hartford and Rochester bus only elementary school youngsters (although in 1968-69 Hartford will include secondary school youngsters who have completed two elementary school years in the project), White Plains reassigned only elementary school youngsters since its secondary schools were already integrated and Boston buses youngsters through senior high school.

D. The research implications differ in that Hartford's Project Concern was initiated as a research study of the effectiveness, and a design involving a comparison group of controls within the inner city has been carefully implemented; in the other three plans evaluation procedures have been continually developed but a research design has been lacking.

E. Hartford has operated an experiment within an experiment in that it has provided a supportive team (teacher and paraprofessional aide) to supplement the suburban school's resources in some instances and not in others in the hope of being able to determine whether suburban placement or supportive assistance or both is the "treatment of choice."

Still, within these program differences, the operation has been similar. Black youth are "bused" to white schools and are given the encouragement and opportunity to partake in all school related activities. In other words, an effort is made to re-create the advantages of the neighborhood school (after-school activities, parent involvement, school-community programs such as scouting or religious instruction) in a school which is not within walking distance.

THE EFFECTIVENESS OF BUSING:
SOME TANTALIZING RESULTS

An effort to report on the four programs is exceedingly difficult because of the differences mentioned above. However, each program does provide at least some beginning data from which to assess its effectiveness and these data will be presented here within a framework of areas of concern. However, before setting these forth it might be well to sketch the characteristics of youngsters and families in *Project Concern* since this program will provide a larger proportion of the evidence available. Since the Hartford children were randomly selected, they provide a good base from which to make inferences for future efforts. The following figures were given by the parents to interviewers:

Living Situation

Mother & Father, 56%
Mother only, 37%
Step parent(s), 4%
Other than parent, 2%
Father only, 1%

Parental Birthplace

Connecticut, 18%
Other North, 6%
South, 65%
Puerto Rico, 17%

Number of Siblings

1-3, 23.5%
4-6, 44.5%
7 or more, 32%

Income Source

Both Parents, 23%
Father only, 36%
Mother only, 12%
Welfare, 36%

In addition to the data given above, it is relevant to note that 94 per cent of the families live in multi-family rental situations and that only two parents report themselves as above the unskilled or semi-skilled occupational scale.

What Is the Reaction of the Black Community?

A major question in the development of busing programs continues to be the conflict over the desires of the Black community. In the light of their increased sense of separation and the continuing gulf between white opportunity and black opportunity, many Negro leaders have stated a preference for separatism and local (i.e. Black) control of schools. Yet, with this cry much in the news media, the burden of the evidence suggests that most Negro parents see the white school as providing increased educational opportunity for their children. Some of the indicators of this feeling are:

(a) In an anonymous questionnaire in White Plains 66 per cent of the respondents from the predominantly Negro school indicated that they saw only positive effects from the plan, 28 per cent saw "no difference" and the remainder reported both positive and negative effects.

(b) In Rochester a visiting team of professionals from the New York State Department of Education interviewed parents of children being bused to West Irondequoit and reported that all parents interviewed wholeheartedly supported the program.

(c) In Hartford where the original selection was random it was also necessary to obtain parental permission. Ninety-six per cent of the parents of the children selected agreed to participate and presently there is an extensive waiting list.

(d) No program has reported any difficulty in obtaining youngsters to fill spaces available.

In other words, the basic response of the Negro parent has been favorable. Even among those youngsters who have been lost from the Hartford program for various reasons most of the parents would like to have them readmitted. This desire is found even in the face of feeling that the white school is prejudiced. This may be, as some claim, one more instance of the Negro's ingrained sense of inferiority and subservience — or it may be his assertion of his ability to prove himself even on white middle-class America's grounds.

The most striking data to support this latter hypothesis come from the bused children themselves. In a structured interview directed by a Negro *not* associated with the project, a random sample of 50 youth bused from Hartford expressed very directly their desire to continue to attend suburban schools. They expressed themselves in a manner which the interviewer saw as indicative of much greater self-esteem and self-confidence than was true of the inner city control child, were able to be more specific, felt strongly that they were receiving a better education (frequently referring to siblings or friends in the inner city schools as illustrative examples), and were aware of both subtle and direct prejudices against them.

What Will Happen to the Academic Standards of the White Schools?

In two of the four programs (Hartford and White Plains) this has been carefully surveyed by using each child as his own control and comparing children who have been in class with Negro youngsters with those who have not. In both studies the results underline the fact that there is *no* evidence of a drop in achievement among white youngsters when black children are placed in a previously all white class; in fact, what evidence exists suggests that the opposite may be true.

What Are the Attitudes of White Parents?

Again, Hartford and White Plains present direct evidence in this question based on an anonymous questionnaire. The rate of return was 31 per cent in White Plains

and 40 per cent in Hartford. The general design of the questionnaire was considerably different with the Hartford one requesting reaction to the program while the White Plains questionnaire directed attention to the impact of the program on that parent's child. Yet the results have interesting similarities: 50 per cent of the White Plains respondents saw the plan as positive while 54 per cent of the suburban Hartford respondents endorsed continuation without condition; 14 per cent of White Plains parents saw the program as negative while 15 per cent in the Hartford groups wanted it discontinued. Although there may be no clear mandate in these data, it appears that white parents with contact with the program tend to see it favorably.

How Will the Black Child Adjust Socially?

This is a complex question and the data reported here refers only to elementary grade children. Preliminary reports from White Plains indicate that Negro youngsters are making "satisfactory peer adjustments." In Hartford the following indices are available:

(a) Sixty-eight per cent of *Project* youngsters take part in after school activities in the suburb on a regular basis;

(b) On sociometric measures *Project* children are selected by suburban children in a proportion which is slightly greater than their numerical proportion in the room; (many of the choices were mutual choices);

(c) Suburban teachers report 70 per cent of the bused pupils as making a superior social adjustment and only 12 per cent of making a poor adjustment (on a three point scale).

What Is the Impact of Placement in a White or Racially Balanced School on the Academic Performance of Negro Youth?

Again, the differences in the characteristics of the pupils in the various programs pose real difficulty for comparisons. For example, the mean I.Q. of the Boston pupils on a group administered instrument is 102 while Hartford youth in an individually administered instrument where their reading disability would not penalize them had a mean I.Q. of 89. However, both groups are reported as considerably depressed on measures of achievement according to national norms. Still, a consistent pattern arises from the tentative results reported in these two projects (results are based upon one year of operation and must be viewed with caution until replicated in a second year). Both show project participants as reversing the trend toward greater deviation from national norms; in fact, they show growth rates in excess of normative expectations in both verbal and numerical achievement tests. In addition, Hartford youngsters show a growth of I.Q. which, though far from miraculous, is statistically significant (6.5 points).

Perhaps most important is the finding, again tentative, that the Hartford youth bused to suburbs show a growth pattern in achievement and mental ability that is clearly and significantly superior to their controls in the inner city *including those controls who are receiving intensive compensatory assistance.*

Can Busing Solve the Problem of Inequality of Educational Opportunity?

This question has geographic, economic and political aspects, but it does seem safe to state that there is no intrinsic reason for busing programs to operate at a token level. Many communities (including the three involved in this paper) are ringed by essentially, all-white suburbs where there exists a large pool of potential classrooms for participation. For example, within the present busing radius of *Project Concern* there are over 2000 classrooms (K-6) exclusive of Hartford schools.

The economics of the program are somewhat demanding. The major expenses are the per pupil tuition charge which is paid to the suburban town and the cost of transportation ($250-$270 per child). At the same time these costs are not excessive when compared with the cost of educating the child in the inner city school with the additional expense of compensatory program. Also, the Commonwealth of Massachusetts under legislation passed in 1966 (Chapter 506) and the State of Connecticut under Public Act 611 have both given some state subsidizing as well as legal sanction to cooperative programs between communities designed to provide quality education for ghetto youth.

In other words, for most cities (and this obviously does *not* include cities like Washington, D. C., or New York) the problem which inhibits large-scale busing is not lack of suburban classrooms or lack of funds, but rather it is the political obstacle. The issue is not often "can it be done"; rather it is usually "do we really want to do it!"

SUMMARY AND CONCLUSIONS

Any inferences or conclusions must be made within the limitations of the available information, but at the same time the available information demands serious study. Perhaps the most striking element is the consistently favorable response from all who have been associated with these projects: educators, pupils, Negro parents, research personnel, and, to a large extent, white parents. Opposition tends to come from sources, varied as they be (from white conservative newspaper columnists to black militant leaders), who have had little, if any, direct contact with the programs. At the least, it can be said that busing has created a climate of hope for the families and has resulted in greater self-esteem for the pupils selected. In addition, the evidence of greater motivation for educational development can be interpreted from such items as attendance records, dropout rates, and teacher ratings. Under such circumstances the following conclusions appear justified:

(a) Busing is a logistically and economically feasible intervention for many cities.

(b) There is no evidence to support claims of psychological trauma among the participants nor is there evidence that they become alienated from their own community. In fact, the evidence available is in contradiction to both of these fears.

(c) There is no evidence that the quality of academic achievement among white pupils is depressed by placing educationally disadvantaged black children in their class. Again, the existing evidence points in the opposite direction.

(d) Black pupils bused into white elementary schools are quickly assimilated socially and appear to hold their own in the area of peer group relationships. This finding holds in spite of the fact that the children are alert to signs of prejudice among some students and staff members.

(e) Teachers in white schools experience no particular problem in coping with the educational disadvantages of inner city nonwhites when these youngsters constitute less than 25 per cent of the classroom membership.

(f) Pupils transported to white schools show significant gains in achievement and mental ability scores when compared with their own prior performance (Boston and Hartford) or when compared with a comparable control group (Hartford).

(g) Again evidence is found which indicates the relatively slight impact of intensified services and programs when these are initiated in the ghetto school (Hartford); in fact, there appears to be no difference between these ghetto youngsters and those in the typical ghetto school situation.

(h) Observer ratings and film illustrate a consistent difference in the classroom climate and teacher-child interaction between inner city and suburban classrooms. It appears that this difference is not easily modified by introducing changes into the ghetto school.

(i) There are signs which suggest that the busing is a more effective intervention in the primary grades than is the case later on.

These conclusions, based as they are on interim materials, make a strong case for the effectiveness of busing as a means for moving toward equal educational opportunity. They raise serious questions about the concepts of the neighborhood school and homogeneous grouping, both of which appear to be bulwarks for the maintenance of the status quo. Yet these conclusions fail to convey the dramatic reality of the human experience which is expressed in a child's discovery that he is somebody because *he* can do things or a parent's feeling that things can be better for her child. Put very simply it seems that the white school, with all its weaknesses, is more attuned to Yeats' words when he wrote:

> But I, being poor, have only my dreams;
> I have spread them under your feet;
> Tread softly because you tread on my dreams.

Bibliography

Archibald, D. *Report on changes in academic achievement for a sample of elementary school children.* Boston (METCO), 1967. Mimeo.

Johnson, C. *White Plains racial balance plan,* White Plains, N.Y. (White Plains Public Schools,) 1967, Mimeo.

Kurland, N. *et al.* "Urban-Suburban Cooperation: A Report," *Integrated Educational Education,* 1966, 4, 65-69.

Mahan, T. *Project Concern: A Preliminary Report on an Educational Exploration.* Hartford (Hartford Public Schools), 1967.

——————, *Project Concern: Interim Report II (A working draft).* Hartford (Hartford Public Schools), 1968. Mimeo.

——————, Project Concern: A Supplementary report on non-academic factors. Hartford (Hartford Public Schools), 1968. Mimeo.

METCO, Suburban education for urban children (revised edition). Boston (METCO), 1967. Mimeo.

THE REALPOLITIK OF RACIAL SEGREGATION IN NORTHERN PUBLIC SCHOOL: SOME PRAGMATIC APPROACHES

Leroy D. Clark and W. Haywood Burns

Leroy D. Clark and W. Haywood Burns, "The Real-politick of Racial Segregation in Northern Public Schools: Some Pragmatic Approaches," *Howard Law Journal,* Summer 1968, pp. 217-240.

THE REALPOLITIK OF RACIAL SEGREGATION IN NORTHERN PUBLIC SCHOOL: SOME PRAGMATIC APPROACHES

Leroy D. Clark and W. Haywood Burns

NEIGHBORHOOD legal service programs, financed by the federal government to give legal assistance to indigents, particularly in the North, may find themselves asked to represent indigents who have legal problems in the civil rights area. Although civil rights litigation has not been the fare of most legal aid societies because illegal racial discrimination in the North has typically been handled by state agencies or private organizations, there is no technical reason why an indigent ought not to have access to a legal aid lawyer to handle a legal problem which just happens to involve racial discrimination. This article provides some practical approaches to the solution of one of the most pressing social and legal problems faced by Negro indigents — poor schooling because of Northern-style isolation.

I. DE FACTO SEGREGATION

A. *The Factual Background*

The pervasive experience for Negroes in education is separation from the majority community. Prior to the 1954 decision in *Brown* v. *Board of Education*,[1] which sought to end government-enforced racial segregation in the schools, every Negro child and teacher in 17 Southern and border states was separated from every other white child and teacher in separate schools by mandate of state law. The picture could not have been much different in the rest of the country, for a 1966 report by the Department of Health, Education and Welfare found that 80% of all white pupils in the country in grades 1 through 12 attended schools that were from 90% to 100% white.[2] In 75 cities surveyed, 9 out of every 10 Negro elementary students attended schools in which the majority of students were Negroes; 43 of these cities were in the northeast, midwest, and west.[3]

---

* The authors are staff counsel, National Association for the Advancement of Colored People Legal Defense and Educational Fund, Inc.
[1] 347 U.S. 483 (1954).
[2] HEW, Report on Equality of Educational Opportunity, Summ. 3 (1966).
[3] United States Commission on Civil Rights, Racial Isolation in Public Schools 3 (1961).

Nor are Negro students merely isolated within the public school systems of the country, but they are typically subjected to grossly inferior facilities, curriculum, and teachers. Nationwide, the number of pupils per room is lower for white elementary school children (29) than for Negro students (30 to 33).[4] This is even more aggravated in particular areas: in the metropolitan midwest, the average number of pupils per room for Negro students is 54 as compared with 33 per room for whites. Minority groups tend to have less access to physical facilities which are related to academic achievement (such as accelerated curriculum, more frequent intelligence testing, etc.). Negro students are less likely to attend secondary schools that are regionally accredited than are white students. Indices of teacher quality (such as number of advanced degrees, years of teaching experience) demonstrate that a greater percentage of the teachers in "Negro schools" fall below the median than teachers in "white schools". The result of the isolation and the inferior facilities is not surprising: Negroes show progressive deterioration in achievement scores as they proceed through the public school system.[5] The fact that many Negroes are in the low-income group might qualify this finding since lower academic achievement bears some relationship to lower socio-economic status. There are, however, other studies which show that Negro students of the same socioeconomic level of white students score lower on achievement tests when they are in racially-isolated schools.[6]

B. *Brown v. Board of Education — A Support for De Facto School Litigation?*

All discussion of *de facto* litigation has proceeded from an analysis of the Brown case where the Court held racially segregated public schools unconstitutional. The problem consistently presented to litigants in a *de facto* school segregation suit is that the opposition quickly points out that *Brown* arose in jurisdictions where the segregation of the races was total and mandated by state or local law — the pure *de jure* segregation. Many commentators, by analyzing the fact that some social science data was introduced, state that *Brown* was not decided solely on the principle of law that legislatively mandated school

---

4 HEW, Supra note 2, at summ. 3.
5 HEW, supra note 2, at summ. 9-20.
6 HEW, supra note 2, at app. C.

segregation is unconstitutional, but went further and said that it was the "harm" done to Negro children resulting from segregation which was unconstitutional and, therefore, Brown stands for the principle that equal educational opportunity is what is required by the Constitution.[7] The problem with this argument is that the social science data introduced in the *Brown* case was slight and could not be characterized as definitive.[8] The Court did not have before it a full and exhaustive study of the harm done to Negro children so that it could hold, as a matter of law, that this harm would obtain in the same degree throughout any *de jure* system. While the most recent and comprehensive appellate decision on racial segregation in schools, *United States, et al. v. The Jefferson County Board of Education*,[9] states in dicta that *Brown* points toward a duty to integrate *de facto* segregated schools. The same court also distinguished *de facto* from *de jure* segregation in a way which could increase the burden of proof for litigants in the North:

> The similarity of psuedo *de facto* segregation in the South to actual *de facto* segregation in the North is more apparent than real.
>
> [and] although psychological harm and lack of educational opportunities to Negroes may exist whether caused by *de facto* or *de jure* segregation a state policy of apartheid aggravates the harm.[10]

The key question is whether formal legislation explicitly requiring racial segregation in public schools is a necessary quantum of "state action" to have segregation in schools held unconstitutional as a matter of law. This would limit *Brown* to the Southern and border states which had legislated segregation and would require plaintiffs outside of that context to prove that the school board had actively gerrymandered school zone lines with the sole purpose of achieving racial segregation.

Since racial discrimination was by no means solely a Southern phenomenon and, in fact, has been practiced in literally every state in the country, in one form or another, the segregation

---

[7] Fiss, Racial Imbalance in the Public Schools: The Constitutional Concepts, 78 Harv. L. Rev. 564 (1965); Wright, Public School Desegregation: Legal Remedies For De Facto Segregation, 40 N.Y.U.L. Rev. (1965).

[8] Kaplan, Segregation, Litigation and the Schools — Part II: The General Northern Problem, 58 Nw. U.L. Rev. (1963).

[9] 372 F. 2d 836, 875 (5th Cir. 1967).

[10] Id. at 876.

in Northern schools is probably not, in most instances, fortuitous. Probably with adequate time and resources, one could prove that a school board (or a school board in conjunction with housing authorities or other state agencies) had at some time actively patterned their decisions about school organization so as to isolate Negroes into Negro schools. While this may be true, attorneys who instituted litigation in the North knew that the average Negro community did not have the resources to undertake a detailed investigation to show such a pattern. They also knew that attempts to prove unequal facilities and the resultant unequal achievement would have to be repeated for each future case. Therefore, they wisely emphasized the principle that Northern school boards have a constitutional obligation to relieve segregation in the school system, without proof that school districts were gerrymandered or that racial isolation worked a detriment to educational opportunities.

Unfortunately (but perhaps predictably) the early *de facto* school litigation, at the Court of Appeals level, has been unsuccessful. In *Bell* v. *the School City of Gary, Indiana*,[11] plaintiffs asserted that the school board had a constitutional obligation to relieve racial imbalance. The district court held against them. Plaintiffs lost on appeal and the Supreme Court of the United States denied certiorari.[12] The same results followed in *Downs* v. *Board of Education*,[13] *Gilliam* v. *School Board* (Hopewell)[14] and *Deal* v. *Cincinnati Board of Education*.[15] All held that the plaintiffs had the burden of excluding all alternative explanations for the existence of racial segregation in the public schools and were required to show that such segregation was solely the intentional act of the school board.

There have been three successful federal court suits against school systems not previously having *de jure* segregation.[16] They may not be particularly helpful since one court simply rejects

---

11 213 F. Supp. 819 (N.D. Ind. 1963).

12 324 F. 2d 209 (7th Cir. 1963), cert. denied, 377 U. S. 924 (1965).

13 336 F. 2d 988 (10th Cir. 1964), cert. denied, 380 U.S. 914 (1965).

14 345 F. 2d 988 (4th Cir. 1964), vacated and remanded on other grounds, 382 U.S. 103 (1965).

15 369 F. 2d 55 (6th Cir. 1966), cert. denied 389 U.S. 847 (1967).

16 Branche v. Bd. of Educ., (Hempstead), 204 F. Supp. 150 (E.D.N Y 1962); Blocker v. Bd. of Educ., (Manhasset), 226 F. Supp. 208 (E.D. N.Y. 1⁰ Barksdale v. Springfield Sch. Comm. 237 F. Supp. 543 (D. Mass. 1965), vac on other grounds, 348 F. 2d 261 (1965).

the holding in *Bell*,[17] and two make direct findings that racial imbalance denies equal educational opportunities, without extended discussion as to how the court ruled out explanations, other than discrimination, as the cause of poor achievement in Negro schools.[18]

E. *Fiss Theory: Duty of the school board to respond affirmatively to changing conditions.*

Owen Fiss, in a long and definitive article,[19] argues that the *de jure — de facto* distinction may obscure many of the lines of state responsibility which occur in the *de facto* situation. He is cognizant of the extreme proof difficulties involved in showing a denial of equal opportunity through concentrating on a comparison of the achievement levels between Negro and white students.[20]

Fiss argues along these lines: one must look to surrounding state agencies to see if the confluence of their activities and the school board's activity has caused the results of racial imbalance in schools. Here one would examine the site selection policies of public housing authorities or any prior ordinances requiring racial segregation in residence. Since these are state agencies the school board cannot escape responsibility because it maintains that it did not segregate by itself — the "state" is the sum of activities of its disparate agencies regardless of whether there was a planned intention for their separate activities to result in school segregation. The school board cannot be passive in the face of activities of other state agencies, or, indeed, in the face of privately achieved racial segregation in neighborhoods,

---

[17] Blocker v. Bd. of Educ., 226 F. Supp. 208 (E.D. N.Y. 1964).

[18] "The central constitutional fact is that of the inadequacy of segregated education." Branche v. Bd. of Educ., supra note 16, at 153; "Opportunity of Negro children in racially-concentrated schools to obtain equal educational opportunities is impaired and I so find." Barksdale v. Springfield Sch. Comm., supra note 16, at 546.

[19] Fiss, supra note 7.

[20] Id. at 595-96:

". . . in each case the court will be called upon to decide whether the racial imbalance that exists in the schools of a particular community results in systematically and substantially inferior educational opportunity for Negroes. No matter how conscientious the court that decides this question, an irreducible amount of uncertainty will remain. It is doubtful that any experiment or survey can be devised that will satisfy the vigorous standards of a scientific method and still eradicate this uncertainty . . , if such an experiment were to be devised, it would have to include an almost infinite set of variables. . . ."

but has an affirmative duty to construct its school assignment policies in response to these activities.

Fiss says that although there is a degree of "uncertainty" in the proof of unequal educational opportunities the courts have, in other contexts, made normative judgments about large scale social facts. He suggests that the court use that technique in the school segregation area.

F. "Reasonable Alternative" Theory

Other commentators have suggested that the analysis in *Bell* and like cases are wrongly conceived. As one stated:

> The courts in these cases (*Bell* and *Downs*) seem to have applied the principle that as long as there was a rational relationship between what the school board did and a legal end to be achieved the courts' inquiry was concluded. The courts rejected the suggestion that the end intended was racial segregation and held that the boards' action perpetuated segregation was reasonable under the circumstances.
>
> But, as we shall see, the rational relationship doctrine has no application to cases involving racial discrimination in public education. Even if it did, it would be highly questionable whether permitting segregation of Negroes is racially related to the education of those children who must attend them.[21]

The argument essentially is that once the plaintiffs prove substantial racial concentration in a school system, the burden then shifts to the school board to show that they have no "reasonable alternative" for relieving the segregation. This reasoning assumes that since there is such massive denial of equal educational opportunity in isolated Negro schools, that it is not a sufficient defense to assert that some minor educational ends are being served, such as avoiding the expense of bussing or drawing zone lines along "natural" boundaries.

II. PRAGMATIC APPROACH TO DE FACTO SCHOOL LITIGATION

The Fiss and "reasonable alternative" theories must be stressed in all *de facto* school litigation. A part of the failure of school litigation in the North is probably related to the court's lack of acquaintance with the concepts in litigation involving racial discrimination, particularly since most of them have been

---

21 Wright, supra note 7, at 294.

314

spun out of the general language of the fourteenth amendment. An educational job will have to be done with judges before success can be obtained at the appellate level. The theories have the attraction of being couched in terms which would be respectable in the writing of an opinion. However, they do have problems attached to them. Fiss' theory of the joint-action of state agencies would probably present a litigator with almost the same degree of proof problems that he would have in trying to show a school board has actively gerrymandered school zones. While it may be simple to present prior legislation of the state or local government which required racial segregation in housing or other areas, charting the action of a public housing authority in its total site selection activities would be a substantial job. While the "reasonable alternative" theory is a more adequate analysis of the question which a Northern court should ask in *de facto* segregation, it is in essence a reformulation of a theory advanced by Fiss and, therefore, will not essentially alter the resistance of courts in a *de facto* case.

Theories, or concept construction which have been the sole thrust of comments on *de facto* segregation, are not addressed to the real and underlying resistance of the courts in this area. It is instructive that very few courts at the District Court level and none at the appellate court level have responded to the common sense judgments which every "reasonable man" might make about how schools become segregated or about the resultant deficiency of educational opportunities in all-Negro schools. It cannot be that these courts are totally ignorant of the abundance of social science data which point heavily towards the consistently poor quality of education in Negro schools; it can only mean that they have used judicial techniques for avoiding the obvious. This article will explore the unstated reasons for opposition and advance some suggestions for long-range and short-range activities by legal aid lawyers which may aid in coping with resistance to dis-establishing inferior Negro schools.

A. *Maximum Proof on Inequality and Gerrymandering*

If expert resources were no problem, one could skirt the theoretical problems in *Bell* by showing direct denial of educational opportunities to Negro students due solely to school board action. In *Hobson* v. *Hansen*,[22] the plaintiffs took on this full

---

[22] 269 F. Supp. 401 (D. D.C. 1967). The school board as a body voted not to appeal. The superintendent (now resigned), one dissenting school

burden and showed manipulation of zone lines to achieve predominantly-white schools, and, in the Negro schools, overcrowding, unequal facilities and curriculum. In *Bell*, plaintiffs proved that Negro students had lower achievement levels, but the trial court stated that they had not proven that this was due solely to the unequal facilities provided by the defendants. Plaintiffs in *Hobson* undertook this task and linked poor achievement with lack of equivalent educational resources (e.g., there was expert testimony that Negro students could not achieve as well as white students because they had no kindergarten classes, which all the predominantly-white schools had). They also showed that some of the poor conditions in Negro schools were correctable (e.g., there were vacancies in white schools which could have relieved the overcrowding in Negro schools). The substantiality of the proof is attested to by a trial court opinion of 118 pages, most of which is a summary of the evidence. Plaintiffs used six experts and the trial took approximately twenty days. Unfortunately *Hobson* can probably be reproduced in the same form of thoroughness in only a few school systems.

B. *Prior Mandatory Segregation*

Taylor v. *Board of Education*[23] is one of the few *de facto* school segregation cases in which plaintiffs were successful, and it may provide an approach calling for fewer resources than *Hobson*. While the court found that there had been active gerrymandering until 1934 and a transfer plan until 1949 which permitted white students to leave predominantly Negro zones, in essence, it held that once there had been active gerrymandering the school board had an obligation to make affirmative efforts to relieve racial imbalance in schools even though the imbalance which had occurred since 1949 was largely due to changed residential patterns. This offers one line for reducing the proof effort; namely if plaintiffs can prove some "past gerrymandering," coupled with an acquiescence in growing racial imbalance thereafter, *Taylor* is some precedent for fastening a duty

---

board member, and white parents who sought to intervene are attempting to appeal. The motion to dismiss their appeal has not been decided.

23 191 F. Supp. 181 (S.D. N.Y. 1961), appeal dismissed as premature, 288 F. 2d 600 (2d Cir. 1961), remedy considered on rehearing, 195 F. Supp. 231 (S.D. N.Y. 1961), aff'd, 294 F.2d 36 (2d Cir. 1961), cert. denied, 368 U.S. 940 (1961), order modified by application of school board, 221 F. Supp. 275 (S.D. N.Y. 1963). For a description of this litigation, see Public Schools North and West 27-103 (1962).

on the school board to restructure. *Taylor,* however, is a district court opinion which was never reviewed on the merits by the Court of Appeals or the Supreme Court of the United States, and is substantially at variance with *Bell.*[24]

C. *Securing Data*

In order to evaluate the litigation potential in a *de facto* school situation, an attorney must first secure some minimal data about the school system and the placement of Negro students and teachers. HEW is now surveying all school districts in the North with over 3,000 students as to the assignment and employment of minority groups.[25] This is the opening in a projected effort to more adequately assure compliance with nondiscriminatory pledges in the North. The Freedom of Information Act[26] a recent Amendment to the Administrative Procedure Act, requires every federal agency to make its records available to the public with certain exemptions, such as purely intra-agency data about personnel and secret information relating to the national security. Should the federal agency refuse to make its records available upon demand, litigation is authorized to require the agency to do so.

D. *Limited Proof of Gross Irremediable Inequality*

One cause of the major resistance of the courts must be the sheer size of the problem presented to them. Essentially, they are asked to have a thorough and complete description of an entire school system (alternative zoning, transportation provided, transfer policies, etc.). The courts are now aware of the substantial political and social forces arrayed against any major system-wide reorganization. A court maintains respect for itself by taking on only those tasks with which its limited coercive powers can cope. It is a strong institution when dealing with disputes between single individuals, but it becomes a

---

24 The trial court in Bell attempted to distinguish the Taylor case by stating that there the plaintiffs had proved that the school board had deliberately drawn the lines so as to create an all-Negro school. This does not adequately distinguish the Taylor case since in Bell the school board had maintained segregated schools under state law and had only ceased that policy in response to a change in state law in 1949. The school board, in Taylor had also ceased its practice of active segregation and in exactly the same year, but the court there still used the prior practice as a part of establishing a present duty to avoid racial imbalance.
25 See Wall Street Journal, Dec. 11, 1967, at 1, col. 1.
26 5 U.S.C. §1002 (1964).

progressively weaker institution as it moves out into the area of public law and attempts to structure widespread public activity. (In arguing before the court, one frequently is asked whether school desegregation is now a "legal problem" or has not become essentially an educational administration problem which would be handled by some federal agency.) One can clearly see, for example, that the Supreme Court of the United States is taking a "hands-off" attitude toward *de facto* litigation. As recently as December, 1967, it denied certiorari in another Northern school case.[27] The Supreme Court must be aware of the almost total resistance of school boards in the South to the *Brown* decision over the last 13 years. It is probably not anxious to make another sweeping school decision which would cover all non-southern school systems and have the spectacle of open resistance and non-compliance which they have had to countenance under *Brown*. Even the *Jefferson* case implicitly recognizes the vulnerability of the court in this area — after a long and affirmative opinion which argues for complete reorganization of the dual school system, the actual implementing decree gives nothing more than individual Negro students the right to demand transfer to white schools.

The tactical response to the caution of the court is to scale down substantially the size of the problem presented. The *Hobson* case suggests one approach to achieve some desegregation on a more limited and manageable basis.

While attorneys may not be able to fully canvass an entire de facto school system as was done for *Hobson,* it is probably possible to get a quick index of courses and facilities missing from a few of the all-Negro schools but present in all the predominantly-white schools, e.g., science laboratories, honor programs, or certain academic courses. (Negro administrators or principals, if assured of confidentiality, are generally knowledgeable enough to point towards the grosser deficiencies.) Or one might limit the inquiry to a gross disparity with regards to double sessions, pupil-teacher ratios, or the lack of accreditation in Negro high schools. Here, one probably need not show the connection between poor achievement and the absence of these facilities or curriculum, for the equal protection claim is that a school board cannot always provide certain educational oppor-

---

27 Deal v. Bd. of Educ., 369 F.2d 55 (6th Cir. 1966), cert. denied, 389 U.S. 847 (1966).

tunities in predominantly white schools, and always deny them to predominantly Negro schools. At the least the burden should shift to the school board to justify the inequality. If the disparity is gross, the school board may not be able to correct the deficiencies in Negro schools.

In that event, *Jefferson* outlines one remedy:

> If for any reason it is not feasible to improve sufficiently any school formerly maintained for Negro students, where such improvement would otherwise be required by this sub-paragraph, such school shall be closed as soon as possible, and students enrolled in the school shall be reassigned on the basis of freedom of choice.[28]

If the school board claims that there are insufficient funds to correct deficiencies in Negro schools,[29] the immediate alternative may be to close them and assign the students to predominantly white schools which are not deficient.

(1) *Right to Transfer*

If the deficient Negro schools cannot be closed, any Negro student there should have the right to transfer into a predominantly white school pending the full correction of the deficiencies. In *Bell*, the court appeared to hold contra. Although plaintiffs proved that certain academic courses were not available in Negro schools, but were present in all predominantly-white schools, the court commented that the curriculum was made up in response to student demands and that if the demand for some courses in a given school was inadequate, the school board was justified in not providing those courses. (There was no comment as to whether the school board regularly canvassed students to find out, however, what courses they wanted to be added to the present curriculum). *Bell* did not take the next step, however, and place a responsibility on the school board to permit as many Negro students as possible to transfer to the predominantly-white schools which had the courses the Negro schools lacked. *Jefferson* specifically requires that a Negro student be permitted to transfer under these circumstances.

---

[28] United States v. Jefferson County Bd. of Educ., 372 F. 2d 836, 900 (5th Cir. 1967).

[29] Cf. Griffin v. Bd. of Educ., 377 U.S.218 (1964). It is no defense once a denial of equal protection is established that the school board does not have sufficient funds to correct the denial. In Griffin, the court merely added the tax authorities as parties-defendant and ordered them to raise sufficient funds to provide equal protection for Negro students.

(2) *General Transfer Policies*

While litigation might establish a "right to transfer" because of unequal curriculum or facilities, attorneys should also study transfer rules which can be employed to effect some limited integration. Typically, the transfer rules will permit some students to leave their present school. (For example, some school boards permit students to attend schools near their parents' place of employment. This exception might be used by Negro teachers who work in predominantly white schools or by Negro domestics in white residential areas). Attorneys could lecture parent-teacher·associations on the school board's transfer policies, urging them to transfer their children where this would mean assignment to an integrated school. If the school board refuses to honor these transfer applications, litigation should follow. White students who would be assigned to all-Negro schools because of their residences are usually assigned to white schools. A suit could assert that the school board was operating a racially discriminatory transfer policy.

One may query — will this at best produce piece-meal student-by-student integration? How can this remedy an entire system of poor Negro schools? Worse, won't the students who transfer be the brightest students of the more alert aggressive Negro parents? All of this cannot be refuted entirely. To some degree this pessimistic prognosis is true. The only answers are partial and speculative. School boards that do not mind short-changing Negro children can do so more easily where there are identifiable Negro schools. Therefore, individual Negro students may benefit by moving into predominantly white schools because the school board will more likely prevent a drop in educational standards in these schools (unless the white children in the schools are from poor families who are themselves prone not to protest inferior education.) Community concern is a more potent weapon than litigation. The attorney can only hope that the pressures for transfers will generate demands from the Negro community for greater change — partial inadequate solutions may create a demand for more complete solutions. Transfer of a few Negroes into white schools will feed more information into Negro communities about the gross disparity between the white school and their former Negro school. Here the lawyer can set the stage for generating community concern — "outside agitation" at its best.

One attractive device for reassuring the court that its de-cisions will meet with greater public acceptability is to link the desegregation process to financial economies. While many oppose racial desegregation per se, their opposition might be greatly lessened if it can be shown that the school budget would substantially benefit from some reorganization.

Therefore, where one seeks to integrate Negro students through school closings, it would be wise to start with small, inadequate Negro schools in a system where there is some possi-bility that the entire student body can be absorbed into predomi-nantly-white schools. Indeed, since many schools attended by poor whites are as deficient as some Negro schools, an attorney can increase the acceptability of a suit by including them in a school-closing effort. A taxpayers' action could be instituted on the ground that the continued operation of these schools is a waste of public funds since there is an alternative which is much less costly. Such an action was instituted in Florida to close a Negro law school with an average total enrollment of 12 to 13 students.[30] The courts in Alabama have also ordered the closing of small inadequate Negro schools.[31] Even the increased expense of bussing students might be less than the cost of keeping these schools open.

(2) Plans for New Schools

Taxpayer's actions can be utilized to achieve desegregation in other ways. New schools, with new equipment and facil-ities, act as a "magnet" for white students and may be a deterrent to the typical Northern pattern of the white, middle class parents placing their children in private or parochial schools. A limited amount of information may show that, in-stead of building two new schools, one in a predominantly Ne-gro community and another in a predominantly white community, one larger school, built midway between two such communities,

---

30 Due, et al. v. Florida Agricultural and Mechanical University (FAMU), et al. Civil No. 947 (N.D. Fla., filed Feb. 1961). Plaintiffs acquiesced in a dismissal of the suit when assured that these plans were to close the school. The school is now closed.

31 Carr v. Montgomery County Bd. of Educ., 253 F. Supp. 306 (1967).

would achieve substantial savings.[32] Here, no theoretical question arises of whether school boards have a duty to locate schools to achieve integration, because the thrust of the suit would be preventing a waste of public funds. This suggestion is particularly relevant for junior and senior high schools for which residential proximity is normally less important.

(3) *Consolidation of School Districts*

The trend in the United States has been towards the consolidation of small school districts into a single one.[33] Typically, this was not done to achieve school integration but rather to reduce duplication and to effect savings. For example, one school district may be building schools because its present ones are filled beyond capacity, while an adjoining district may have unused classroom space. In the rural areas of a state, where there are many small school districts, a taxpayer's suit to require a consolidation of these districts might succeed in integrating some Negro student populations into a larger, white-student population.

F. *Public Housing: Bringing the Mountain to Mohammed*

To the extent that the Negro population falls in the low-income group, many will be eligible for low-rent public housing projects. Since the "neighborhood school" policy is the primary means for assignment to public schools, an attorney might secure school integration indirectly by litigation to place new public housing in predominantly white residential areas.

The Department of Housing and Urban Development (HUD) has reversed its earlier "hands off" policy as regards racial segregation in federally supported public housing.[34] This was done largely in response to Title VI of the 1964 Civil Rights Act[35] which explicitly prohibits racial discrimination in any federally supported program. HUD has promulgated regulations which require local housing authorities to select sites

---

32 See, Racial Isolation, supra note 3 at 143-46 for survey of communities which achieved greater integration in this manner.

33 In 1932 there were 127,530 school districts; in 1955 the number was 59,270 and in 1962 it was 37,025. Advisory Commission on Intergovernmental Relations, Performance of Urban Functions: Local and Areawide 63 (1963).

34 See J. Greenberg, Race Relations and American Law 286-93 (1959), for early history of federal agency on this issue.

35 42 U.S.C. §2000d (1964).

for new housing projects outside of Negro ghettos.[36] One *who* wishes to complain that a local housing authority is about to select a site which will maintain racial segregation can file a complaint with HUD. HUD can investigate and, if the charges are well founded, it can negotiate for new sites. Ultimately its sanctions are to cut off federal funds or ask the Attorney General of the United States to sue to enjoin the construction.

Attorneys may also file a direct suit asserting that the site selection is unconstitutional because it increases racial concentration (although it is probably wise to exhaust the federal administrative remedies first). The suit might also be brought under Title VI of the Civil Rights Act on a claim that the Negro plaintiffs are the third-party beneficiaries of the non-discriminatory agreements made between the housing authority and the federal agency.[37] Tenants or applicants for public housing have been found to have standing to challenge the site-selection policies of a local housing authority.[38]

G. ABILITY GROUPING: THE NEW SEGREGATION

(1) *Track System*

A "track" system classifies and programs the instruction of students along the lines of their supposed abilities. This kind of ability grouping, though not defective in concept, often in execution works to the detriment of the poor or minority-group pupil.[39]

The tests which determine the groupings are usually culturally biased — favoring the middle-class white child to the disadvantage of the already economically-deprived or racially-discriminated against student. Pupils from this underclass are in a disproportionate number, thus locked into the lower tracks at an early stage, with little likelihood of movement between tracks. This phenomenon is often found in previously *de facto* segregated schools that have recently integrated. The resulting pattern is one of the internal desegregation of what are now at least nominally "integrated" schools.

---

[36] 24 C.F.R., §1.4 (Supp. 1967).

[37] Lemmon v. Bossier Parish Sch. Bd., 240 F. Supp. 709 (W.D. La. 1965).

[38] Gautreaux v. The Chicago Housing Authority, 265 F. Supp. 582 (N.D. Ill. 1967).

[39] See "Public School Segregation and Integration in the North," 4 J. Intergroup Rel. 71-73 (1963) [Hereinafter cited as "Public School Segregation"].

One federal court has indicated that when the track system builds in this structural bias it is amenable to legal attack. *Hobson*[40] held that where disadvantaged children, primarily Negro, are relegated to lower tracks based on intelligence tests largely standardized on white middle-class children, and there given reduced education, such disadvantaged children are denied equal protection of the laws. Recent studies have produced highly persuasive evidence of the inappropriateness of standard tests.[41] Social scientists claim that more accurate methods are needed for testing the aptitude of the disadvantaged child.[42]

In evaluating any track system in contemplation of litigation, an attorney should look to such indices as the number and proportion of underclass children in the different tracks; the nature of the tests that put them there; the possibility of movement between tracks — especially the frequency of retesting and the quality of remedial instruction given to students in lower tracks.

Attorneys in *Hobson* presented the court with detailed data on the operation of the track system in the Washington, D. C. schools. One might try, as attorneys there did, to tap the Social Research Department of a local university. However, the track system involved in the *Hobson* case was found remiss on many grounds, and there may be some more expedient ways to show the defects. Since much of the evidence was cumulative, the quantum of proof necessary to challenge a discriminatory track system successfully need not be nearly so great. It would be sufficient, for example, to show that predominantly Negro schools did not have the honors or highest track (as was the case in Washington, D. C.), and that over the years no provision had been made for taking the qualified students out of the predominantly Negro schools and placing them in schools with an honors track. This more simplified approach to this proof problem is more realistic, given the exigencies of a legal aid practice.

Social science data in this type of litigation may be of substantial value. Recent research indicates that ability grouping may be detrimental to students in the average and low

---

40 Hobson v. Hansen, 269 F. Supp. 401, 443-93 (D.D.C. 1967).
41 See, e.g., The Lorton Study, discussed in Hobson v. Hansen, Id. at 485.
42 See, F. Riessman, The Culturally Deprived Child, passim (1962); Sexton, Education and Income, passim (1961).

ability categories.[43] The students suffer from the lack of intellectual stimulation provided by brighter children while, on the other hand, the brighter children do not appear to be harmed when left with average and lower group children — at least through elementary school.[44]

Studies show that ability grouping can have a deleterious effect upon the social and emotional development of children.[45] Children are aware of a "class" system and those in the less gifted section evince feelings of worthlessness and rejection as a result.[46]

One study has pointed out, that

[S]o-called "homogeneous groups" — whether based on I.Q. or some other measure, or even on several criteria — not only reveal a substantial range of individual differences in function or functions used for the classification, but they also reveal still wider ranges of difference in other functions. The pupils may be fairly homogeneous in reading achievement, for example, but very heterogeneous in arithmetic achievement.[47]

This "Heterogeneity of 'Homogeneous Groups'" has been well documented.[48]

This is not to say that all ability grouping is harmful, or even that all harmful ability grouping is vulnerable to legal attack — only that a lawyer working on *de facto* segregation should be aware of this problem. A system of ability grouping with proper supplemental learning assistance and frequent retesting with properly designed tests, could be of advantage to all children involved. "The new problem (racial integration in the classroom) is simply the old problem — how to create a harmonious working group in which each individual is encouraged to develop to the fullest extent of his capacities."[49]

---

[43] See e.g., Elkstrom, "Experimental Studies of Homogeneous Grouping: a Critical Review," 69 Sch. Rev. 216-26 (1961).

[44] Eash, "Grouping: What have We Learned?", 18 Educ. Leadership 429-34 (1961).

[45] Byers, "Ability Grouping-Help Or Hindrance to Social and Emotional Growth?", 69 Sch. Rev. 449-56 (1961).

[46] Eash, supra note 44.

[47] "Public School Segregation," supra note 39 at 72.

[48] See, e.g., Tyler, "Intraindividual Variability" in Nat. Soc. for the Study of Educ., Individualizing Instruction, 61 Y.B. 164-74 (1961).

[49] H. Giles, The Integrated Classroom 215 (1959).

(2) *Special Schools and the "difficult" child*

There is a definite need for special educational facilities for the retarded and the emotionally disturbed child. However, the designation has sometimes been used as a convenient means of shunting off difficult discipline problems. School authorities who lack a full appreciation of some of the cultural differences involved may be causing many underclass children to end up in the "special" schools.

Attacking improper classification through legal avenues presents many problems. Generally, the placement of children in special schools is viewed by the courts as purely an internal administrative matter not subject to judicial intervention.[50] However, where the removal of the child from a regular school is of a questionable nature, certain legal arguments are available to challenge the placement.

Most state constitutions provide for public schools, which "normal" children of certain ages have a right and a duty to attend. It can easily be shown that placing a normal child in a school where the other children are genuinely retarded or emotionally disturbed is injurious to him. Whenever government acts to injure an individual, or to deprive him of his educational rights, it must comply with the guarantees of due process.[51] This line of argument, along with an expert witness or two, may permit a challenge to the procedures for faulty assignments. The difficulty with constitutional claims in this area is that a court is likely to interpret the *Brown* case as requiring an intent or motivation to harm children and as noted earlier, this in almost all cases will be difficult or nearly impossible to show.[52]

Even where the designation has been proper, there may

---

50 For a treatment of the general reluctance of courts to intervene in what they regard as internal school policy where the problem is discussed in the context of school suspensions and expulsions, see 58 A.L.R. 2d 903 (1958).

51 Dixon v. Alabama Bd. of Educ., 294 F. 2d 150 (5th Cir. 1961), cert. denied, 368 U.S. 930 (1961); Knight v. Bd. of Educ., 200 F. Supp. 174 (M.D. Tenn. 1961); Woods v. Wright, 334 F. 369 (5th Cir. 1964); In the matter of Goldwyn, 51 Misc. 2d 97, 281 N.Y.S. 2d 903 (1967); Madera v. Bd. of Educ., 267 F. Supp. 356 (S.D. N.Y. 1967).

52 This theory has recently been advanced in the case of a supposedly emotionally disturbed child who had been barred from attendance at regular public school. Kirkland v. Bd. of Educ., Civil No. 67C698 (E.D.N.Y. filed Oct. 1967). The student is being represented by the Nassau County Law Services Committee, Inc., located at 150 Old Country Road, Mineola, New York 11501.

still be a litigable issue on the question of whether the special schools are doing the job they were established to do — i.e., teach the children. Special public schools for "socially maladjusted" children often become little more than custodial institutions — thus effectively depriving the students of the education which is their right.[53] The *Hobson* case, *supra,* is a good example of the depth to which a court can go in evaluating the educational process within a school system when there are questions of constitutional dimension at stake. The district court in *Madera* v. *Board of Education of the City of New York* though for another purpose, inquired into the nature of schools for emotionally disturbed or "socially maladjusted" children.[54]

H. CHOICE OF APPROPRIATE REMEDIES: SOLVING THE COURT'S DILEMMA

Litigation to close inadequate schools, to consolidate the construction of new ones or to rearrange a track system may run into one of the substantial but unexpressed fears of the courts, namely, that they will be saddled with the task of reorganizing the school system, when they have no particular expertise in this area. Many opinions give evidence of this unstated hesitation in the deference shown to any reason the school board offers as to the basis for its decisions, or in the comments that the courts cannot "substitute their judgment" for that of the school board. One way to reduce the spectre of the unmanageability or reorganization is to demand in a complaint that experts in school administration, attached to, or funded by, the Department of Health, Education and Welfare (HEW), be called in to advise the courts and assist the school boards in designing a feasible desegregation plan. This has been expressly authorized in the *Jefferson* case, and one district court has already ordered a school board to avail itself of the desegregation resources of HEW.[55] The HEW funds for assistance in desegrega-

---

[53] See, Mackler, A Report on the "600" schools: Dilemmas, Problems, and Solutions, passim (1966) [unpublished report prepared for the N.Y. city Bd. of Educ.]

[54] Madera, supra note 51 at 367. See also, Matter of Skipwith, 14 Misc. 2d 325, 180 N.Y.S. 2d 852 (Dom. Rel. Ct. 1958), the court upheld Negro parents' defense to a proceeding for neglect following withdrawal of their children from a racially imbalanced school, saying that parents had a constitutionally guaranteed right to choose no education for their children rather than expose them to discriminatory-inferior education.

[55] Braxton et al. v. Bd. of Pub. Instr., Civil No. 4598 (D. Md. filed Aug., 1967).

tion, are not limited to southern school systems.

Assistance is also available from some private companies. To the extent that reorganization of school systems requires the manipulation and accommodation of many variables, companies dealing in computer systems analysis are entering the field.

III. THE LAWYER AS NEGOTIATOR FOR THE COMMUNITY

The legal aid attorney should not limit his role to litigator but should act more broadly as a representative of groups of poor persons whose problems may be resolved by legislation, negotiation, or securing additional private and governmental resources. This was the original conception of the role of a lawyer by those who encouraged new legal service programs.[56] An expanded definition of the attorney's role in school desegregaton is necessary because litigation may have but a limited possibility of success where courts decide that its task of making neat findings of fact is incompatible within the evaluation of complicated and extended social data. While one can say that courts make these judgments in other areas of the law, the fact is that they are unlikely to make decisions which have the permanence of constitutional findings in sensitive areas like racial integration where school boards may actively resist court orders and the Congress has provided no direction and few resources. The lawyer confronted with this fact may approach the state legislature since it, unlike the courts, can experiment and adopt solutions which utilize massive social data. Each legal service program could attach a lawyer as "house counsel" to the local parent-teacher's association in schools servicing low-income communities. The attorneys so designated could form a state-wide group which could jointly draft and endorse model legislation, to be submitted to the state legislature which would place a legal duty on school boards to work, as much as is feasible, toward reducing racial imbalance. Such state legislation has achieved some desegregation of schools.[57]

If a convention to reorganize the State Constitution were in the offing, attorneys might submit some general provisions assuring equal educational opportunities regardless of race (or

---

[56] Cahn & Cahn, "The War on Poverty: A Civilian Perspective," 73 Yale L. J. 317 (1964).

[57] Ill. Rev. Stat. ch. 122, §§ 34-18 (7) (1965); Mass. Gen. Law. ch. 71, § 370 (1965).

economic status, which might be a more tactical approach). A concerned state educational agency might do as others have done and avoid the federal constitutional problems by findng that there was a duty under the state constitution to relieve racial imbalance.[58] Or one might subsequently seek interpretation of the state constitution in litigation, where a court would not have the greater burden of interpreting the Federal Constitution.[59]

Attorneys could also function as the negotiators for parent-teacher groups, by drafting applications to private foundations to provide funds on an experimental basis to assist with local educational problems. Typically, the average Negro community (and perhaps some school boards) will not have knowledge of these resources, and an intervening attorney could lend substance to an application to a foundation. For example, a foundation might finance a program to bus Negro children into white schools where there were vacancies. An attorney might simultaneously seek a university study of a comparison of the achievement levels of students who were bussed to their equivalents who remained in Negro schools. The school board could not make the usual objection to the bussing of the Negro students, if it was to be conducted without taxing the regular school budget, and there were spaces to absorb the transferees. Further, if Negro students were shown to be performing better in their new setting, negotiation with the school board might encourage them to continue the bussing. There are funds under Title I of the *ESEA* for this kind of program.[60]

IV. Decentralization of School Board Authority and Compensatory Education

While an attorney may want to direct his efforts toward integration, if he is in a school system where the prospects for desegregation are minimal, because of residential segregation, he may be met with a demand by the Negro community that he draft and propose legislation giving them greater local control over the operation of their schools.[61]

---

[58] See, e.g. N.J. Const. art 1, § 5 (1965); Fisher v. Bd. of Educ., 8 Race Rel. Rep. 730 (N..J. Comm'r. of Educ. 1963).

[59] See, e.g. Jackson v. Pasadena City Sch. Dist., 59 Cal. 2d 876, 382 P. 2d 878 (1963).

[60] See Racial Isolation, supra note 3, at 238.

[61] See e.g. "Separate Schools for Harlem Urged by 2 Civil Rights Chiefs," N. Y. Times (Nov. 22, 1967).

This demand is, in part, an outgrowth of the "Black Power" demand that Negroes control their local institutions. There is also the desire to achieve more effective education, where school boards have failed to attend to the specialized needs of ghetto schools. Proponents of decentralization of school board authority claim that, in a large city school system, many programs are impeded by complicated bureaucratic structures, and school boards tend to get out of touch with the community. They argue that shifting greater control to smaller units will yield more immediate response to the local school needs, and those responses would be fashioned by persons closer to the problems.

The major study in this area was done in New York City, and is commonly referred to as the "Bundy Report."[62] It was made in response to the rapidly declining quality of education in the New York schools. Working upon a premise that a greater sense of community control will result in increased achievement, the report proposes legislation to achieve a major shift in authority from the present central board of education to 30 community-school districts. Each school district would have a board of directors, elected by persons living within that school district.[63] This board would have control over the selection of the district supervisor, principals, and the teaching staff (with teachers, however, continuing to be protected by the tenure provisions in state law). The board would also be able to reshape curriculum, plan construction, reassign students, and contract for special programs. The central board of education would retain the power to tax, as well as the responsibility for distributing a fair share of the total budget to the 30 community school districts. This central board would also engage in research, have authority to require the local community school board district to meet minimal state education standards, and assist in training persons for the task of sitting on the local community school board.

There are positive elements in decentralization, for example, teachers who evidence hostile and demeaning attitudes toward

[62] Report, Mayor's Advisory Panel on Decentralization of the New York City schools, Recommendation for Learning: A Community School System (1967).

[63] Persons could serve on the board regardless of whether they had children in school. The Mayor's Committee thought that persons without school children, but with the interest, time, and capacity for contribution. should be among those who could be selected to serve on the board.

the "unwashed" poor may be made more accountable if one of their parents is a school board member. But the report wisely stresses that decentralization is no panacea, and that its success will be strongly related to an increase in financial resources, particularly if many innovations are undertaken. However, even with adequate financial backing, there is still the more basic question of just how much fundamental and lasting change can be brought about through decentralization when the personnel that the local boards will use for the day to day running of the schools will be made up of the same teachers and administrators currently directing the system. Although control is shifted closer to the "consumers" of the school product, there may be certain built-in limitations on how much difference they can make.

The primary vehicle for the decentralization of a school board to improve the quality of education for disadvantaged children would be compensatory education.[64] Studies show, however, that initial gains in achievement are not sustained over a period of years, and that racial and socio-economic isolation are the primary impediments to the learning process.[65] Attorneys must be aware that emphasis on "quality" education within ghetto schools tends to divert integration efforts and to institutionalize and ossify the *de facto* segregation that characterizes these schools. There are those who dispute these findings and claim that achievement might have been greatly different had the schools themselves been different, and found that the schools themselves might have been different had there been greater community control.

CONCLUSION

School desegregation is a political problem — but as with most "political" problems, the courts, despite their disclaimers to the contrary, can give rational direction to its resolution. An attorney must assay the strengths and weaknesses of the litiga-

---

[64] Compensatory education includes programs of remedial reading, cultural enrichment, and preschool instruction which are designed to counter the lack of intellectual stimulation in the lower socio-economic environment. Title 1 of ESEA provides a major source of funds for these programs, most of which tend to be in predominantly Negro schools.

[65] Racial Isolation, supra note 3, at 115-40; Cohen, "Policy for the Public Schools: Compensation or Integration?" passim (1967) prepared for the National Conference on Equal Educational Opportunity in America's Cities, sponsored by the U.S. Commission on Civil Rights.

tion system and structure the problems in the most palatable form. Poor people not only get inferior "private" goods (like slum housing and shoddy foodstuffs); but they get inferior "public" goods, like schools, although personal wealth, theoretically, should not determine the right to equal benefits in the public sector. The legal aid attorney can increase the power of his clients to "purchase" quality schools through litigation with limited, circumscribed goals.

THE EFFECT OF FAMILY INCOME ON CHILDREN'S EDUCATION: SOME FINDINGS ON INEQUALITY OF OPPORTUNITY

Stanley H. Masters

Stanley H. Masters, "The Effect of Family Income on Children's Education: Some Findings on Inequality of Opportunity," *Journal of Human Resources*, Spring 1969, pp. 158-175.

THE EFFECT OF FAMILY INCOME ON CHILDREN'S EDUCATION: SOME FINDINGS ON INEQUALITY OF OPPORTUNITY *

Stanley H. Masters

In this paper an attempt is made to estimate the degree of inequality of educational opportunity at the secondary school level. Data from the 1/1,000 sample of the 1960 Census are used to estimate the probabilities of falling behind in school or dropping out for children from different family backgrounds. For children whose parents have little education or income, the probabilities are more than 20 times greater than for children from well-to-do families where both parents have graduated from high school. The determinants of the dropout and retardation rates are also investigated, with the discussion focusing on the possible effects of new transfer programs, such as the negative income tax. While the short-run effects are likely to be quite small, the long-run effects may be important, especially for the Negro retardation rate.

This paper investigates the extent to which children's education is related to family income and the education of the parents.[1] By studying this

---

The author is Assistant Professor of Economics at Rutgers—The State University of New Jersey

* This study was begun at the Brookings Institution where helpful comments were made by Jesse Burkhead, Henry Levin, Alex Maurizi, Stephan Michelson, and Michael Taussig. At Rutgers, Monroe Berkowitz, C. Harry Kahn, Collette Moser, Jeffrey Schaefer, Joseph Seneca, Richard Burkhauser, and other participants in two research seminars contributed many useful suggestions. Glen Cain provided valuable suggestions during the initial stages of the study and again at the final draft. While at Brookings the work was financed by the Department of Health, Education, and Welfare. A grant from the Rutgers Research Council helped with later expenses. The computer programming was done first by the Assist Corporation and then under the supervision of Kate Tallmadge at Rutgers. Without this very competent assistance, the study never would have been completed.

1 David *et al.* [5] and Nam *et al.* [8] have done closely related studies based on data from special surveys. The David study emphasizes the relation between children's education and the education of their parents, while the Nam study

question, we may be able to learn more about inequality of opportunity and, in addition, we may gain better insight about some of the effects of possible new transfer programs, such as the negative income tax.

The War on Poverty has emphasized equality of opportunity as one of its major goals, and the importance of this objective may help to explain why education programs have been favored over transfer payments. But increased transfer payments may lead to better education as well as higher incomes for the poor. Therefore, if equality of opportunity is an important goal, it is important to know whether changes in transfer payments are likely to have any significant effect on educational opportunities.

I. ESTIMATING INEQUALITY OF EDUCATIONAL OPPORTUNITY

In this paper equal opportunity is defined as a situation in which each individual's chances of achieving his goals depend only on his own inherited ability and are unaffected by his parents' income and education. The empirical work is an attempt to measure inequality of educational opportunity, using data from the 1/1,000 sample of the 1960 Census. Children's education is measured by (1) whether the youth has dropped out before graduating from high school, and (2), for those who are in school, whether the youth is behind the average grade for his age.[2] The observations consist

---

relates children's education to the occupation of the family head and several other variables. The Coleman Report [4] includes an investigation of the effect of family background on children's education, but its data on families are limited to information supplied by the children. For a general critique of this report, see [1].

2   This measure could be affected by different promotion policies in different schools, but the Coleman Report ([4], pp. 113–14) indicates that (stated) school policies are reasonably similar regardless of region, metropolitan status, and racial composition. Policies on dropouts could also vary, although dropout prevention appears to be a very widely held goal.

Another very interesting measure of educational attainment is scores on standardized tests. Data by race ([2], p. 49) show that in the twelfth grade, the average Negro has an achievement level of 9.2 years compared with 12.7 for the average white. By comparison, the Census data show a retardation rate of 29 percent for Negroes versus 13 percent for whites, and a dropout rate of 22 percent versus 11 percent. While it is difficult to make a precise comparison here, the differences by race may be most important for the test score results. If this is true and if an analogous result holds for differences in socioeconomic status, then our measures will underestimate the total inequality in educational opportunity.

Note: In this paper the term "dropout" includes those few youths who have never attended school.

of single youths who are living with their families. For the dropout rate, 16–17-year-olds are investigated; for the retardation measure, 14–15-year-olds.[3]

In this section only family income[4] and parents' education are included as independent variables. Although these variables are essential in considering inequality of opportunity, some measures of the children's "natural" ability and motivation should also be included. Since no measures of ability or goals are available from the data, the results will include the effect of differences in these factors as well as the effect of unequal opportunities.[5]

In the regression analysis, family income and parents' education are each represented as a series of dummy variables.[6] The regression equations, estimated by ordinary least squares,[7] are as follows:

---

3   Many youths over age 17 have married and/or left home. For these youths there are no data on parents' education or the income of their original families. Below age 16, school attendance is often compulsory and dropout rates are low. Therefore, 16 and 17 look like the best ages for studying dropouts. For the retardation rate, age 15 was picked as the upper limit since the figures for older youths would be heavily biased by a high dropout rate among those who have fallen behind. The lower limit of 14 was chosen mainly so that the sample size would be about the same as the one for the dropout rate analysis.

    See Appendix A for a discussion of the biases introduced by excluding those youths who have married and/or left home.

4   Family income is defined here as the family's total money income minus the youth's earnings.

5   Although the question of differences in inherited ability is beyond the scope of this paper, more can be said about the question of goals or motivation. Can it be assumed that all youths want (1) to keep up with their age group while in school, and (2) to stay in school until they receive a diploma? While most youths probably want to be promoted each year with their class, the dropout question is more complicated. It is not known what percentage of youths (1) drop out because they are hopelessly behind in school, (2) wish later on in life that they had not dropped out, or (3) have the ability· to complete high school but drop out and never regret it because they feel that school has little to offer. To the extent that case (3) is important and does not result from inferior schools, then the results· from the dropout rate may overestimate the inequality of opportunity. Despite this ambiguity, reducing the dropout rate is a widely held social goal. Therefore, the results for the dropout rate are given as much emphasis as those for the retardation rate.

6   Although continuous variables might seem more appropriate, especially for family income, preliminary results from a large number of dummies indicated that a few dummies would provide an acceptable fit.

7   Given a number of assumptions, ordinary least squares is generally considered the most appropriate estimating technique. Since the dependent variables are dummies, however, the homoscedasticity assumption is violated. Therefore, although the ordinary-least-squares estimates are unbiased, they are not efficient, and the standard errors cannot be interpreted in the usual manner. While some

For the retardation rate (ages 14–15)—

$$N = 5142 \qquad \overline{R}^2 = .102 \qquad F = 65.9$$

$$\begin{aligned}
(1) \quad RR = .122 &+ \underset{(.014)}{.095Y_1} + \underset{(.013)}{.056Y_2} - \underset{(.015)}{.006Y_3} + \underset{(.020)}{.175HE_1} \\
&+ \underset{(.015)}{0.55HE_2} - \underset{(.012)}{.043HE_3} + \underset{(.016)}{.080ME_1} - \underset{(.011)}{.055ME_2}
\end{aligned}$$

For the dropout rate (ages 16–17)—

$$N = 5287 \qquad \overline{R}^2 = .067 \qquad F = 43.0$$

$$\begin{aligned}
(2) \quad DR = .114 &+ \underset{(.012)}{.062Y_1} + \underset{(.012)}{.019Y_2} - \underset{(.013)}{.007Y_3} + \underset{(.017)}{.145HE_1} \\
&+ \underset{(.014)}{.067HE_2} - \underset{(.011)}{.042HE_3} + \underset{(.014)}{.012ME_1} - \underset{(.011)}{.054ME_2}
\end{aligned}$$

where

$RR = 1$ if the youth is 14 and has completed less than seven grades or if he is 15 and has completed less than eight.

$DR = 1$ if the youth has left school but has not graduated from high school.

$Y_1 = 1$ if the family income is less than $3,000 in 1959.

$Y_2 = 1$ if the family income is less than $5,000 but not less than $3,000.

$Y_3 = 1$ if the family income is greater than $10,000.

$HE_1 = 1$ if the family head has completed less than five grades of school.

$HE_2 = 1$ if the family head has completed at least five grades but less than eight.

$HE_3 = 1$ if the family head has graduated from high school.

$ME_1 = 1$ if both parents are present and the mother has completed less than eight grades of school

$ME_2 = 1$ if both parents are present and the mother has completed high school

The mean values of all the variables presented in this paper are presented in Appendix C.

---

more advanced techniques have been proposed for dealing with this problem (see [6], pp. 248–51), it would have been rather costly to make them operational on the computer. Therefore, the analysis is limited to ordinary least squares.

Another statistical problem in this analysis is multicollinearity. Although parents' education and family income are fairly highly correlated, there are enough observations to provide reasonably accurate estimates for the effect of each variable.

The regression equations can be interpreted in terms of conditional probabilities. For any youth, there is an associated set of values for the independent variables. Given these values, the corresponding estimate for the dependent variable is an estimate of the probability that this youth will be retarded at school or a dropout. If two youths have similar abilities and goals, then the difference in their estimated probabilities is a measure of the differences in their educational opportunities. For example, consider a youth whose family has less than $3,000 annual income, whose father has completed less than five grades of school, and whose mother has completed less than eight. If this youth is in school at age 14 or 15, he has a 0.47 chance of his progress in school being retarded. If he is 16 or 17, then he has a 0.33 chance of being a dropout. In contrast, the chances of an average youth[8] are 0.12 and 0.11, respectively, and, for a youth whose family has an income of over $10,000 and whose parents have both graduated from high school, the probabilities are 0.02 and 0.01. If one is willing to accept the necessary assumptions about motivation and inherited ability, the differences in these odds represent a rather striking degree of inequality of opportunity.

It is also possible to estimate how the retardation and dropout rates would change if the chances of the disadvantaged youths were improved. If all children from a family with less than $5,000 annual income or with a parent who has completed less than eight grades of school had as good a chance of "making it" as those from average families, then the retardation rate would fall by 40 percent and the dropout rate by 34 percent.[9]

II. DETERMINANTS OF CHILDREN'S EDUCATION

While limiting the independent variables to family income and parents' education makes sense for analyzing inequality of opportunity, a more comprehensive analysis will provide better insight into what determines the dropout and retardation rates. In addition to family income and parents' education, data are also available on housing, family size, occupation of

---

8 In this context, an average youth is one whose family has an annual income of $5,000 to $10,000 and whose parent(s) have completed 9 to 11 years of school. For such a youth, all the independent variables have a value of zero.

9 The assumptions about family income and parents' education would be fulfilled if Y_1, Y_2, HE_1, HE_2, and ME_1 became zero for all youths. To calculate the corresponding decline in RR or DR that could be expected, the coefficients of these variables are multiplied by their mean values (which are given in Appendix C) and the products are summed. To get the expected percentage changes, the sum is divided by the mean value of RR or DR.

family head, presence of the parents, geographic location, mobility, age, sex, and race.

Why might we expect the retardation and dropout rates to be affected by these variables? Family income seems likely to have its most direct effect on the dropout rate since a poor youth may be under strong pressure to leave school and get a full-time job. However, family income may also have a more general effect on children's education since more income should lead to better food and medical care and thus to brighter, more attentive students. Increased income should also lead to better housing.

Better, less crowded housing may improve a child's health. At the least, it should give him more opportunity to study and to get a good night's sleep before coming to school. The housing variable may also be important for another, more indirect reason. The income data are for current annual income; yet past (or permanent) income is likely to be at least equally important in explaining children's education. Quite possibly, the housing variables will serve as proxies for permanent income.[10]

If family income is held constant, differences in family size will affect a family's economic position. Consequently, large family size and low family income should have many of the same effects on children's education. Children from large families may have an additional disadvantage if their parents cannot give each child as much attention as do parents with small families.[11]

Better educated parents may provide more encouragement to their children to do well at school. Moreover, children learn at home as well as at school. Consequently, a child will have an advantage in school if his parents speak "good" English and are well informed. The regression coefficients for parents' education may also have an upward bias since (1)

---

10   The concept of permanent income includes past and expected future income as well as present income. As another possible test of the hypothesis that permanent income is important and that housing is a reasonable proxy for it, dummy variables were used for high and low values of (1) the rent-to-income ratio, and (2) the value-of-owner-occupied home-to-income ratio. For the dropout rate, the coefficients were positive for the low values and negative for the high values, as had been expected. For the retardation rate, however, the equivalent results were obtained only for the renters. For homeowners, the signs of the coefficients were reversed. None of the coefficients were twice as large as their standard errors.

   Note that the housing variables may also be proxies for the type of neighborhood and perhaps for the type of school.

11   Another related factor is the labor force status of the mother. A dummy variable for youths whose mothers were home and not in the labor force had a negative coefficient for the retardation rate but a positive coefficient for the dropout rate. Neither coefficient was statistically significant.

parents' education may be another proxy for permanent income, and (2) part of the relation between parents' education and children's education probably results from inherited differences in ability. This second factor is also likely to affect the results for family income.

Parents' occupation may be important since parents with white-collar occupations may put more emphasis on children's education.

If one, or both, parents are absent, the child may be deprived of emotional support and encouragement in his school career. In addition, the absence of the parent (especially the father) is likely to make the family much poorer economically. The family's current income may underestimate their average income in the past,[12] but the child may also be under heavy pressure to help maintain the family's income. Consequently, the child may drop out of school and seek a full-time job.

Geographical location is likely to be important for a number of reasons. Rates of return to education may vary from one area to another, and so may community attitudes towards education. Although school policies on promotions and dropouts do not appear to vary very much from one area to another (see footnote 2), there may still be some differences. Moreover, because of differences in the cost of living and in the relative importance of imputed income, a given level of money income will usually leave a farmer better off than an urban resident.

The frequency with which a family moves may be even more important than its present location. Changing schools means adjusting to new friends and teachers, and possibly also to a new curriculum. At any age curriculum differences are likely to force the child to repeat a grade. If the youth is old enough to consider leaving school, all the adjustment problems may encourage him to drop out.

Other things being equal, the older the youth, the more likely that he has dropped out or fallen behind the normal grade for his age. Boys may be more rebellious than girls in school and thus more likely to have to repeat a grade or two. With regard to dropouts, most boys probably leave school to get a full-time job and start asserting their independence, while many girls leave school to get married. Since data limitations restrict the regression analysis to single youths living with their families, the regression results may show that boys are more likely to drop out, even if the over-all rate is fairly similar for boys and girls.[13]

---

12 When we use a dummy for families with one or both parents absent, this factor could lead to a negative coefficient. The other hypotheses predict a positive coefficient.

13 The dropout rate equations are estimated separately for boys and girls in Appendix A. A general discussion of the biases resulting from this data limitation is also included.

Many Negroes, American Indians, and Mexican-Americans attend schools that are of relatively low quality. These schools may have different policies towards promotions and potential dropouts. Moreover, if the children from these minority groups attend integrated schools, they may still be subject to discrimination within the schools.

In addition to considerations directly related to our present schools, there are other reasons why racial variables may be important. Race is also related to the quality of the parents' schooling, which may affect parental attitudes toward education. Second, a given level of education or income may be associated with greater ability and ambition for members of the minority groups because of discrimination.[14]

When all these variables are included in the regression analysis, equations (3) and (4) are obtained. Except for low family income, the only variables included are those having a regression coefficient larger than its standard error.

For the retardation rate—

$$N = 5142 \qquad \overline{R}^2 = .142 \qquad F = 36.4$$

$$
\begin{aligned}
(3) \quad RR = .118 &+ \underset{(.015)}{.057Y_1} + \underset{(.013)}{.042Y_2} + \underset{(.020)}{.127HQ_1} + \underset{(.013)}{.031HQ_2} \\
&+ \underset{(.019)}{.085HC_1} + \underset{(.014)}{.025HC_2} + \underset{(.012)}{.017FS} + \underset{(.020)}{.122HE_1} \\
&+ \underset{(.015)}{.035HE_2} - \underset{(.012)}{.035HE_3} + \underset{(.016)}{.054ME_1} - \underset{(.012)}{.037ME_2} \\
&- \underset{(.011)}{.014HO} + \underset{(.014)}{.014PP} + \underset{(.011)}{.022S} - \underset{(.016)}{.022RF} \\
&- \underset{(.017)}{.048CC} + \underset{(.013)}{.075M_1} + \underset{(.011)}{.038M_2} + \underset{(.009)}{.024Ag} \\
&+ \underset{(.009)}{.066Ma} + \underset{(.031)}{.039MA} + \underset{(.072)}{.198AI}
\end{aligned}
$$

For the dropout rate—

$$N = 5287 \qquad \overline{R}^2 = .120 \qquad F = 33.7$$

---

14 On the other hand, if the rate of return on the investment in education is an important factor, then *ceteris paribus*, the dropout rate might be higher for Negroes than for whites since Negroes appear to have a much lower rate of return on their educational investment (see [7]). In recent years, however, the expected rate of return for Negroes may have increased considerably.

$$(4) \quad DR = .055 + .016Y_1 + .002Y_2 + .148HQ_1 + .038HQ_2$$
$$ (.013) \quad\quad (.012) \quad\quad (.019) \quad\quad (.013)$$
$$+ .094HC_1 + .032HC_2 + .028FS + .103HE_1$$
$$ (.019) \quad\quad (.014) \quad\quad (.012) \quad\quad (.018)$$
$$+ .055HE_2 - .032HE_3 + .016ME_1 - .014ME_2$$
$$ (.013) \quad\quad (.011) \quad\quad (.015) \quad\quad (.011)$$
$$- .032HO + .078PP - .023RF + .052CC$$
$$ (.011) \quad\quad (.014) \quad\quad (.014) \quad\quad (.016)$$
$$+ .092M_1 + .031M_2 + .039Ag + .046Ma$$
$$ (.012) \quad\quad (.010) \quad\quad (.008) \quad\quad (.008)$$
$$- .044Ne$$
$$ (.015)$$

where

$HQ_1 = 1$ if the housing is dilapidated.
$HQ_2 = 1$ if the housing is deteriorating.
$HC_1 = 1$ if there are over 1.5 persons per room.
$HC_2 = 1$ if there are 1.01 to 1.5 persons per room.
$FS = 1$ if there are more than five current members in the family.
$HO = 1$ if the family head has a white-collar occupation—professional, manager, clerk, or salesman.
$PP = 1$ if the youth does not live with both his parents.
$S = 1$ for a Southerner.
$RF = 1$ for a rural youth living on a farm.
$CC = 1$ for a youth living in a central city of more than one million people.
$M_1 = 1$ if the family has moved in the last 15 months.
$M_2 = 1$ if the family has moved in the last five years but not in the last 15 months.
$Ag = 1$ for 15-year-olds in the retardation rate equation and for 17-year-olds in the dropout rate equation.
$Ma = 1$ for a male.
$MA = 1$ for a Mexican-American.
$AI = 1$ for an American Indian.
$Ne = 1$ for a Negro.

The results contain few surprises.[15] With the other independent variables added, the dummies for family income and parents' education have

---

15   One surprising finding is the lower values for the coefficients of Y_1 and Y_2 in equation (4) compared with equation (3). Since poor youths might need to drop out to help support their families, these coefficients were expected to be larger in equation (4).

smaller coefficients in equations (3) and (4) than in equations (1) and (2).[16]

Let us assume that equations (3) and (4) represent causal relations. Then, if all families had at least $5,000 annual income, the retardation rate would fall by 12 percent and the dropout rate by 3 percent. These changes are relatively small, but they represent estimates for the effect of low annual family income,[17] while inequality of opportunity is probably more closely related to differences in families' permanent income, a concept that includes past and expected future income. Although annual income is one proxy for permanent income (especially for families at the same stage of the life cycle), the housing variables are alternative proxies. If it is assumed that low-quality housing results only from low permanent income and not at all from discrimination or differences in tastes, then the estimates for the effect of low (permanent) family income increase dramatically. The retardation rate would fall by 30 percent and the dropout rate by 27 percent.[18] Some, but not all, of the effect of poor housing probably derives from low permanent income. Therefore, the results with and without

---

The negative sign for the Negro coefficient in the dropout rate equation is also a little surprising. The most plausible explanation seems to be that, as a result of discrimination, a given level of education and income is associated with greater ability and ambition for Negroes than for whites. After accounting for other variables, David et al. [5] and Nam et al. [8] still find that Negroes have less education. In the Nam study, the net effect of race is quite small, however.

An additive model has been used. Interaction effects have not been examined. The Nam study finds interaction effects among race, religion, region, urbanization, and household head's occupation to be relatively unimportant in explaining dropout rates.

16   There appears to be considerable multicollinearity among the variables for low income, poor housing, and few years of parents' education. This multicollinearity could help account for the relatively large values for the standard errors of the coefficients for these variables. On the other hand, the standard errors do have a downward bias (see footnote 7).

Although the $\bar{R}^2$ values are low, we are trying to predict the behavior of individuals, and such predictions are much more difficult than predicting average rates for large groups of people.

Note that the regression equations can no longer be interpreted as conditioned probabilities since the predicted values of the dependent variable will sometimes be negative.

17   These results could be underestimates since changes in income are likely to lead to changes in housing. On the other hand, they could easily be overestimates if changes in family income are not accompanied by corresponding changes in the children's inherited ability or the families' attitudes towards the schools.

18   These results are based on the assumption that all youths move out of the Y_1, Y_2, HQ_1, HQ_2, HC_1, and HC_2 categories. Then the estimates are derived by calculations similar to those discussed in footnote 9.

changes in housing could represent upper and lower bounds to the effect of low family income.[19]

Given these results, what can one conclude about the likely effect of an increase in transfer payments to the poor? The short-term effects are likely to be rather slight. Not only are the coefficients for the annual income variables quite small (especially in the dropout equation), but factors such as the ability and ambition of the parents are likely to affect both family income and the child's educational attainment.

The size of the long-term effect would depend on (1) the extent to which increases in transfer income and increases in earned income will have similar effects, (2) the validity of estimating the effects of changes in income from cross-section data, and (3) the extent to which the statistical importance of the housing variables results from their being proxies for a family's permanent income.

III. DETERMINANTS OF NEGROES' EDUCATION

Much of the recent concern about poverty and inequality of opportunity has focused on the problems facing Negroes. Consequently, it is interesting to see how the results differ for Negroes.

For the Negro retardation date—

$$N = 548 \qquad \bar{R}^2 = .132 \qquad F = 4.8$$

$$
\begin{aligned}
(5) \quad RR = .227 &+ \underset{(.053)}{.117Y_1} + \underset{(.055)}{.059Y_2} + \underset{(.051)}{.096HQ_1} + \underset{(.045)}{.047HQ_2} \\
&+ \underset{(.056)}{.109HC_1} - \underset{(.055)}{.017HC_2} + \underset{(.049)}{.014FS} + \underset{(.052)}{054HE_1} \\
&+ \underset{(.051)}{.077HE_2} - \underset{(.067)}{.033HE_3} + \underset{(.055)}{.007ME_1} - \underset{(.074)}{.013ME_2} \\
&- \underset{(.074)}{.056HO} + \underset{(.052)}{.004PP} - \underset{(.054)}{.056S} + \underset{(.059)}{.119RF} \\
&+ \underset{(.068)}{.137CC} + \underset{(.050)}{.120M_1} + \underset{(.045)}{.082M_2} + \underset{(.037)}{.098Ag} \\
&+ \underset{(.037)}{.162Ma}
\end{aligned}
$$

---

19 Low permanent income is also likely to be related to other variables, such as those for parents' education, the presence of both parents, and mobility. Therefore, it is not strictly accurate to refer to the results in the text as upper bounds for the effect of low family income. On the other hand, the lower bound argument must be qualified by the discussion in footnote 17.

For the Negro dropout rate—

$$N = 603 \quad \bar{R}^2 = .069 \quad F = 3.0$$

$$
\begin{aligned}
(6) \quad DR = .101 &- .087Y_1 - .044Y_2 + .156HQ_1 + .056HQ_2 \\
&(.047) \quad\;\; (.048) \quad\;\;\; (.047) \qquad\;\; (.041) \\
&+ .059HC_1 + .011HC_2 - .020FS + .115HE_1 \\
&(.052) \quad\;\;\; (.050) \qquad (.044) \quad\;\; (.047) \\
&+ .128HE_2 - .022HE_3 - .009ME_1 - .049ME_2 \\
&(.045) \qquad (.063) \qquad (.051) \qquad (.066) \\
&- .027HO + .061PP - .016S - .098RF \\
&(.074) \qquad (.046) \quad\;\; (.047) \quad\;\; (.056) \\
&+ .093CC + .111M_1 + .041M_2 + .103Ag \\
&(.058) \qquad (.046) \quad\; (.039) \quad\;\; (.033) \\
&+ .085Ma \\
&(.033)
\end{aligned}
$$

The most surprising results are those for annual family income. Although there is a strong positive relation between low family income and the retardation rate, there is a negative relation between low family income and the dropout rate. Perhaps this negative relation results from the exclusion of those dropouts who have left home (see Appendix A) or from the omission of many young Negroes from the entire Census. Or perhaps the answer lies with welfare eligibility criteria and the fear of reporting dropouts to interviewers.[20]

Since both the dropout and retardation rates are inversely related to housing quality, the long-run effects of an increase in transfer payments are likely to be more favorable than the short-run effects. If equations (5)

If the housing variables are added to equations (1) and (2) and low-quality housing is considered a sign of low permanent income, then the three sets of probabilities would change to 0.60, 0.47; 0.10, 0.09; and 0.02, 0.01; where the first set applied to youths who satisfy HQ_1 and HC_1 as well as Y_1, HE_1, and ME_1.

Based on the same equations, if all children with a parent who has completed less than eight grades of school or from a family with less than $5,000 annual income or from a family with crowded or low quality housing have as good a chance as those from average families, then the retardation rate would fall by 52 percent and the dropout rate by 49 percent.

20   Reporting errors on family income or parents' education create no serious problems unless they would affect ordinal measures of income or education. If the rankings are not disturbed, the only changes necessary would be in the values of the cutoff points for some of the variables. If the rankings are disturbed, however, then the effects could be especially important because of the multicollinearity problem. Note that the coefficients for family head's education are much larger in equation (6) than in equation (5).

and (6) do represent causal relations, then we can look at what would happen if all Negro families had at least $5,000 annual income and all Negro children lived in good housing. Under these assumptions, the Negro retardation rate would decline by 53 percent and the dropout rate by 9 percent. Under analogous assumptions for the entire population, the retardation rate falls 30 percent and the dropout rate 27 percent. In absolute terms, the retardation rate declines 16 percentage points for Negroes and five for whites, while the dropout rate declines two percentage points for Negroes compared with three for whites. These results suggest that, if the housing variables are good proxies for permanent income, then the long-run effects of increased transfer payments on children's education are likely to be greatest for the Negro retardation rate.

APPENDIX A: THE EFFECTS OF EXCLUDING YOUTHS WHO HAVE LEFT HOME

For those who have left home, the 1/1,000 Census tape contains no data on parents' income or education. Consequently, these youths had to be excluded from the study. Since the excluded youths represent less than 2 percent of all 14- and 15-year-olds enrolled in school, their absence is not likely to have any serious effects on the results for the retardation rate. For the dropout rate, however, the results may be affected. Almost 9 percent of all 16- and 17-year-olds are excluded from the regression analysis. Even more important, the exclusions are heavily concentrated among dropouts, where they represent about 30 percent of the total.[21]

To evaluate the effect of these exclusions, we need to know some of the characteristics of these youths. In particular, we need to know whether the excluded dropouts are likely to be from poor families. If they are more likely to be from poor families than the included dropouts, then we will have a downward bias in our coefficients for the low income variables.[22] Otherwise we will have an upward bias.

More than two-thirds of the excluded dropouts are married girls. It seems likely that many of these girls would come from relatively poor families. The rest of the excluded dropouts are almost all boys. Some of their characteristics are presented in Table 1.

---

21 For the 14- and 15-year-olds enrolled in school, less than 5 percent of the retarded had to be excluded.

22 The 16- and 17-year-olds who are excluded but who remain in school constitute only about 6 percent of all those who are in school. Since they probably include a large number of youths from well-to-do families who are attending boarding schools, their exclusion may create a slight downward bias in the coefficients for Y_8 (the variable for family income over $10,000).

TABLE 1

CHARACTERISTICS OF EXCLUDED DROPOUTS

	Boys	Girls
Married	26	187
Unmarried	62	7
Military	30	
Delinquent or criminal	13	
Mental disease or handicap	7	
Roomer or lodger	7	
Household head	4	
Other	1	

TABLE 2

PERCENTAGE OF CHILDREN IN POOR FAMILIES, BY SEX

	Boys	Girls
Y_1	19.7	18.4
Y_2	18.5	17.6
HE_1	9.4	8.7
HE_2	15.1	15.0
ME_1	14.0	14.3

Among the boys, the largest group is in military service. Here youths from poor families may be under-represented since they are less likely to meet the physical and mental standards. On the other hand, youths from poor families may be very heavily represented among delinquents and criminals. For the other categories, including married men, and for the group of excluded male dropouts as a whole, it is not at all clear whether poor boys are likely to be over- or under-represented.

On balance, the exclusions seem more likely to affect the results for girls than for boys. To test this hypothesis, we can look at the percentage of girls and boys living in poor families. If birth and death rates are the same for each sex, then our hypothesis predicts that there will be relatively fewer girls living in poor families. The results in Table 2 are generally consistent with the hypotheses, although they are not as dramatic as expected.[23]

Since the bias may be greater for girls than for boys, regression (2) has been run separately by sex.[24] The results are as follows:

---

23 For a listing of the figures for all the variables, see Appendix C. For poor housing, the results are less consistent.

24 When regression (4) is run separately for boys and girls, analogous results are obtained.

TABLE 3

CHARACTERISTICS OF EXCLUDED NEGRO DROPOUTS

	Boys	Girls
Married	4	35
Unmarried	10	1
Military	3	
Delinquent or criminal	5	
Lodger	1	
Household head	1	

For boys, $N = 2671$ $\bar{R}^2 = .089$ $F = 30.0$

$$(7)\quad DR = .136 + .088Y_1 + .030Y_2 + .002Y_3 + .168HE_1$$
$$(.018)\quad(.018)\quad\;(.020)\quad\;(.026)$$
$$+ .058HE_2 - .063HE_3 + .026ME_1 - .061ME_2$$
$$(.020)\quad\;(.016)\quad\;(.021)\quad\;(.016)$$

For girls, $N = 2616$ $\bar{R}^2 = .043$ $F = 14.1$

$$(8)\quad DR = .095 + .031Y_1 + .007Y_2 - .013Y_3 + .115HE_1$$
$$(.016)\quad(.017)\quad\;(.017)\quad\;(.023)$$
$$+ .077HE_2 - .023HE_3 + .001ME_1 - .046ME_2$$
$$(.018)\quad\;(.014)\quad\;(.017)\quad\;(.014)$$

Almost all the variables are more closely related to the male dropout rate. Since a higher proportion of female dropouts are excluded and since the excluded females may have come more frequently from poor families, the results for males are probably more accurate. Therefore, the exclusions probably create a downward bias in the coefficients for the low income variables in equations (2) and (4).

For Negroes, the exclusions also represent a little under 10 percent of all 16- and 17-year-olds and about 30 percent of the dropouts. Moreover, married girls again account for just over two-thirds of the exclusions. For the excluded Negro males, the findings are a little different, however (see Table 3). For Negroes, the delinquent or criminal category accounts for a larger proportion of the excluded boys than does the military. Consequently, there may be more downward bias in the results for Negro boys than for all boys.[25]

---

25   When equation (6) is rerun separately for boys and girls, the coefficients of Y_1 and Y_2 are still negative for both groups.

APPENDIX B: THE EDUCATIONAL ATTAINMENT OF DROPOUTS

In addition to looking at the relation between the dropout rate and variables such as family income and parents' education, it is also interesting to investigate the relation between these variables and the grades of school completed by the dropouts. For this analysis, the dependent variable is defined in Table 4. Since the exclusion problem appears to be more serious for girls than for boys, the regressions are run separately by sex.

For boys, $N = 381$ $\bar{R}^2 = .149$ $F = 3.7$

$$
\begin{aligned}
(9) \quad GC = 2.52 &- \underset{(.13)}{.14Y_1} - \underset{(.13)}{.05Y_2} + \underset{(.21)}{.06Y_3} + \underset{(.14)}{.02HQ_1} \\
&- \underset{(.12)}{.05HQ_2} - \underset{(.15)}{.15HC_1} - \underset{(.14)}{.10HC_2} - \underset{(.12)}{.09FS} \\
&- \underset{(.14)}{.34HE_1} - \underset{(.12)}{.04HE_2} + \underset{(.17)}{.07HE_3} - \underset{(.14)}{.16ME_1} \\
&+ \underset{(.16)}{.06ME_2} + \underset{(.17)}{.07HO} - \underset{(.13)}{.10PP} - \underset{(.11)}{.30S} \\
&- \underset{(.14)}{.16RF} + \underset{(.17)}{.22CC} - \underset{(.11)}{.01M_1} - \underset{(.11)}{.02M_2} \\
&+ \underset{(.09)}{.13Ag} + \underset{(.23)}{.27MA} - \underset{(.13)}{.11Ne} + \underset{(.64)}{1.15AI}
\end{aligned}
$$

For girls, $N = 225$ $\bar{R}^2 = .300$ $F = 5.4$

$$
\begin{aligned}
(10) \quad GC = 2.94 &- \underset{(.14)}{.14Y_1} - \underset{(.14)}{.05Y_2} + \underset{(.20)}{.18Y_3} + \underset{(.15)}{.16HQ_1} \\
&- \underset{(.13)}{.08HQ_2} - \underset{(.17)}{.65HC_1} - \underset{(.14)}{.33HC_2} + \underset{(.13)}{.07FS} \\
&- \underset{(.15)}{.68ME_1} - \underset{(.13)}{.19HE_2} - \underset{(.17)}{.53HE_3} - \underset{(.14)}{.15ME_1} \\
&+ \underset{(.17)}{.18ME_2} + \underset{(.17)}{.39HO} - \underset{(.14)}{.13PP} - \underset{(.11)}{.21S} \\
&- \underset{(.17)}{.12RF} - \underset{(.16)}{.10CC} - \underset{(.13)}{.08M_1} + \underset{(.11)}{.06M_2} \\
&+ \underset{(.10)}{.01Ag} + \underset{(.24)}{.12MA} + \underset{(.13)}{.25Ne} - \underset{(.80)}{2.68AI}
\end{aligned}
$$

Although few of the coefficients are much larger than their standard errors, low family income and low parents' education do tend to be associated with few grades completed. If this conclusion is valid, it would add another dimension to the inequality of educational opportunity.

TABLE 4

DEFINITION OF DEPENDENT VARIABLE, GC

Highest Grade Completed	Value of GC
0–4	0
5–7	1
8	2
9–11	3

APPENDIX C: MEAN VALUES FOR THE VARIABLES IN EACH REGRESSION

In considering the importance of the various dummy variables, it is often useful to know their mean values as well as their regression coefficients. For example, the mean values are essential in calculating the possible effects of increases in family income and parents' education. In Table 5, these mean values are given for each regression.

REFERENCES

1. S. Bowles and H. M. Levin. "The Determinants of Scholastic Achievement—An Appraisal of Some Recent Evidence," *Journal of Human Resources*, 3 (Winter 1968), pp. 3–24.
2. Bureau of Labor Statistics–Bureau of the Census. *Social and Economic Conditions of Negroes in the United States.* Washington: 1967.
3. Bureau of the Census. *U.S. Census of Population and Housing: 1960 1/1,000 and 1/10,000. Two National Samples of the Population of the United States* (processed).
4. J. S. Coleman *et al. Equality of Educational Opportunity.* Washington: U.S. Office of Education, 1966.
5. M. David, H. Brazer, J. Morgan, and W. Cohen. *Educational Achievement—Its Causes and Effects.* Ann Arbor: 1961.
6. A. Goldberger. *Econometric Theory.* New York: John Wiley & Sons, Inc., 1964.
7. G. Hanoch. "An Economic Analysis of Earnings and Schooling," *Journal of Human Resources*, 2 (Summer 1967), pp. 310–29.
8. C. B. Nam, A. L. Rhodes, and R. E. Herriott. "School Retention by Race, Religion, and Socioeconomic Status," *Journal of Human Resources*, 3 (Spring 1968), pp. 171–90.

TABLE 5

MEAN VALUES FOR THE VARIABLES IN EACH REGRESSION

Variable	Regression Number							
	1,3	2,4	5	6	7	8	9	10
RR	.15	—	.29	—	—	—	—	—
DR	—	.12	—	.22	.14	.10	—	—
GC	—	—	—	—	—	—	2.13	2.35
Y_1	.18	.19	.53	.48	.20	.18	.37	.31
Y_2	.18	.18	.23	.24	.18	.18	.22	.21
Y_3	.14	.14	.02	.01	.14	.15	.06	.07
HE_1	.08	.09	.30	.30	.09	.09	.24	.20
HE_2	.15	.15	.25	.27	.15	.15	.24	.27
HE_3	.38	.35	.12	.12	.36	.34	.12	.15
ME_1	.14	.14	.30	.29	.14	.14	.27	.25
ME_2	.39	.35	.10	.12	.36	.35	.12	.13
HQ_1	.07	.06	.25	.22	.06	.07	.19	.19
HQ_2	.16	.15	.30	.29	.16	.14	.27	.22
HC_1	.11	.09	.41	.35	.09	.10	.25	.23
HC_2	.17	.17	.23	.25	.17	.16	.24	.24
FS	.36	.33	.61	.59	.32	.35	.49	.52
HO	.31	.28	.08	.06	.28	.29	.10	.13
PP	.15	.17	.36	.36	.17	.16	.30	.29
S	.33	.32	.69	.66	.33	.32	.46	.39
RF	.10	.11	.13	.12	.11	.11	.13	.09
CC	.08	.08	.14	.15	.08	.09	.10	.12
M_1	.18	.15	.20	.17	.16	.15	.31	.22
M_2	.26	.25	.26	.26	.24	.26	.24	.32
Ag	.49	.48	.49	.47	.49	.47	.56	.54
Ma	.52	.51	.51	.50	1.00	.00	1.00	.00
MA	.02	.02	.00	.00	.03	.02	.05	.05
AI	.004	.003	.00	.00	.003	.002	.005	.004
Ne	.11	.11	1.00	1.00	.11	.12	.20	.21

COMPENSATORY EDUCATION IN THE EQUALIZATION OF EDUCATIONAL OPPORTUNITY I

Edmund W. Gordon and Adelaide Jablonsky

Edmund W. Gordon and Adelaide Jablonsky, "Compensatory Education in the Equalization of Educational Opportunity, I," *Journal of Negro Education,* Summer 1968, Vol. 37, pp. 268-279.

COMPENSATORY EDUCATION IN THE EQUALIZATION OF EDUCATIONAL OPPORTUNITY I

Edmund W. Gordon and Adelaide Jablonsky

Compensatory education is a term which has come into use since 1960 to refer to those pedagogical efforts directed at overcoming or circumventing assumed deficiencies in the background, functioning, and current experiences of children from economically deprived, culturally isolated, and/or ethnically segregated families. A wide variety of elements have been introduced under this banner. They include: (1) modifications in training, recruitment, and utilization of staff; (2) remedial reading and language development; (3) enrichment and modification of curriculum; (4) expanded guidance services; (5) enrichment of extracurricular activities; (6) increased parental and peer involvement; (7) extended reciprocal involvement of school and community; and (8) extensions and appendages to the school day and school year. Particular emphasis has been given to the prevention and salvaging of school dropouts and to the preparation for school through preschool programs. Although most of these programs have concentrated on improved or increased cognitive input, some have

sought to introduce affective experiences or affect laden materials designed to improve self-concept and motivation. Compensatory education models have been widely and enthusiastically accepted. However, when one looks at their impact on academic performance in the target population, it is obvious that compensatory education as presently practiced is either insufficient or irrelevant to the needs of disadvantaged young people. There are some aspects of compensatory education which seem to have some promise with some children. There are other aspects projected — but not yet tried — which would logically seem to have good potential for success. Some of these more promising elements are in the direction of what we might expect excellent programs of education to be. Others are in the direction of what we might expect of a good and humane social order. Both of these utopian but obtainable goals are costly in terms of material resources and humanitarian concern; however, they may be prohibitive in cost in competition with distorted national values.

In this paper we review a number of primary and secondary sources for data and information concerning the nature, effectiveness and cost of compensatory ed-

---

* This chapter is based on a paper prepared under contract with the U. S. Commission on Civil Rights. It was undertaken independently from the Commission and is the responsibility of the authors alone.

ucation. From identifiable programs and practices and from implicit needs and theoretical projections, we have outlined what might be an adequate program (continued in the next chapter). From too limited information and even more limited experience, we have estimated the cost of such a program based upon the cost of present efforts.

EVALUATION OF CURRENT PROGRAMS

The several programs of special education for the disadvantaged have been described as compensatory because they are usually attempts to compensate, to make up for or to overcome, the effects of hostile, insufficient, different and/or indifferent conditions of prior experience and stimulation. The aim of these programs is to bring children from these backgrounds up to a level where they can be reached or served by existing educational practices. To the degree that these young people improve in academic achievement and approach the mean age-grade achievement levels established for the general population, compensatory education would be said to be effective or successful. It has been this standard which has guided practically all of our efforts at evaluating compensatory education.

For all of these programs the question is asked, "What changes can be observed in the academic achievement or intelligence test scores of the children served?" Although many aspects of these programs have been directed at other categories of function, and despite the growing skepticism that cognitive function is the optimal system through which immediate gains are reflected, the prime criterion of success or failure of these programs is academic achievement. Whether one likes this circumstance or not, it is at least understandable since the central thrust has been focused on bringing these children up to levels of performance comparable to those of the children with whom the school feels it succeeds.

Project Head Start

The largest compensatory education program undertaken to date is Project Head Start. This nationwide program has served almost one million children since its inception. It was designed to take children immediately preceding school entry, and through a broad-based program of educational, medical, and social services to better prepare them for primary school. Despite the broad-based program, the many efforts at evaluating Head Start have emphasized changes in children's intelligence scores. These evaluation efforts have resulted in varied findings.

In general, the test scores of children served by the program have been higher at the end of the program than they were when the children entered. When compared to expected growth patterns, the Head Start children tended to be performing better than would have been expected without the program. When compared to children not served by Head Start, the children in the program tended to show better progress. Although the dominant trend was in the direction of improved performance, there were many instances in which Head Start children showed no significant differences in scores from children not served by Head Start.

In several attempts to determine the persistence of these gains, equivocal findings are reported. In some of these studies children served by Head Start continued to show higher achievement levels throughout the first grade (the longest period reported so far). At the other extreme there are studies which indicate no persistent difference in achievement levels after two, four or six months in kindergarten or first grade. In the latter studies, which are often cited when "fade out" is discussed, it should be noted that it is the difference between the two groups that fades and not the prior gains. Equalization of performance seems to be a function of the non-Head Start children having caught up, rather than of Head Start children having lost some of their developmental gains.

After reviewing almost 100 major and minor studies of Head Start as an approach to compensatory education, it is clear that the introduction of broad-based but highly diversified services at the three to four year old level is associated with some gains in intellectual function for the population served. These gains are reflected in higher performance levels by these children than by children not served. The persistence of these gains is not consistent. Subjectively assessed changes in social-emotional maturation and in general readiness to benefit from the formal learning experiences of the primary school are more universally reported and are perceived by teachers as being more persistent. However, the long term impact of Head Start as an antidote to the destructive influence of poverty and inferior status on educational and social development is yet to be established.

Title I and Title III Projects

A second category of program is that which has been developed with support from Titles I and III of the Elementary and Secondary Education Act. With even more diversity with respect to program elements and quality than is true of Project Head Start, the Title I program in particular has been directed at improving the capabilities of the schools, in areas where disadvantaged children are concentrated. The legislation and regulations give the states and school systems wide degrees of freedom to develop programs and resources directed at the needs of poor children. Most of the eligible school systems have eagerly accepted this challenge. Some have mounted elaborate programs. Practically all of the 50 states have done something under one or both of these titles.

Reports on these efforts are available for 1965 and 1966. The review of these data is not encouraging. The reports indicate that: (1) In most instances money was made available in such haste that the quality of planning and development of programs was severely limited. (2) Many programs have been operative for too brief a period to be effectively evaluated. (3) Many programs were funded at levels insufficient to meet the requirements necessary to do an adequate job. (4) Most programs could not find adequate and appropriate specialized personnel to mount major efforts. (5) Most programs were unable to report appreciable improvement in academic achievement for the target populations. (6) Most programs tended to increase the quantity of services available without any substantive change in content and quality.

Among programs reporting positive findings, the tendency was toward improved morale, higher teacher expectation, improved staff-perceived climates for learning, improved attendance, and reduced school dropout rates. These gains are not to be demeaned. But the development of compensatory education under

357

support from Titles I and III has not yet resulted in a major change in the schools' success patterns with children from disadvantaged backgrounds.

Upward Bound

Upward Bound is a national program designed to assist and increase the number of disadvantaged youth who enroll in some sort of post-secondary education. The program's primary focus is on developing interest in higher education among tenth and eleventh grade pupils from poor families.

In the summer of 1965, pilot programs were conducted on eighteen college campuses. In 1966 the program was expanded to include two hundred twenty colleges, universities, and residential secondary schools, and the number of students increased from 2,000 to 20,000. Elements common to these programs are (a) a six to eight week residential summer phase designed to remedy poor academic preparation and increase the pupils' possibilities for acceptance and success in college and (b) a follow-up phase conducted during the regular academic year which is designed to sustain the gains made during the summer months. In general, both phases include academic content that does not make an attempt to parallel the regular secondary school work. Both phases also include cultural enrichment experiences designed to increase total effectiveness.

Data from six of the original programs indicate that 80 per cent of students enrolled continued their education; 78 per cent of the students entered college in contrast to the 8 per cent who would normally have gone on to college. Data on college retention rates show that the dropout rate for Upward Bound youth in college is the same rate as for all other college youth. In 1965 the freshman year dropout was 12 per cent, the sophomore year dropout was 21 per cent, and the retention rate was 67 per cent. The project staff feels that the impact of Upward Bound should be judged not only on its short term effect on students but also on long term influences, e. g., sensitizing the secondary education system, bringing the most effective teachers into Upward Bound related secondary schools, and making the schools responsible for "brokering" their students into appropriate employment or higher education. It is, of course, too early to evaluate such structural impact.

School Dropout Programs

In the early 1960s considerable national attention was directed at the problems of the school dropout. In the summer of 1963 President Kennedy set into motion a large scale national campaign focused on 63 of the larger cities in this country. Almost 60,000 young people were contacted in that initial effort. Other school dropout projects have expanded on that crash program. They have generally been organized by high schools, community groups and by private industry. These projects have included intensive guidance services, remedial education, specific job training in and out of formal school settings and large scale "Stay in School — Return to School" publicity campaigns.

Data on the initial effort in 1963 indicate that 52 per cent of the youth contacted actually returned to formal school affiliations. National figures on the total effort subsequent to that time are not available. The need for large scale programs which combine intensive guidance services with remedial education, specific job training and remunerated work is clear. A review of the nation's attempt at doing this indicates that money and resources, when applied, are seldom sufficiently concentrated to achieve the obvious goal.

Project 100,000, *United States Department of Defense*

Project 100,000 was designed as an attempt by the armed services to become involved with and to help alleviate social and educational problems of the poor. In October 1966, 40,000 young men were taken into the armed services under lowered entrance standards. These men fell between the tenth and thirteenth percentile on Defense Department qualifying tests.

The 40,000 soldiers were tested in July on the Metropolitan Word Recognition, Reading and Arithmetic Fundamentals sections. The average was grade 6.5 on word recognition and arithmetic fundamentals, and grade six on reading. Seventeen per cent of this group were reading below the fourth grade level.

The first program which is basic training takes eight weeks for the majority of soldiers. In the total army population 98 per cent of these are expected to pass the performance and academic tests given at the end of the program. Of the 2 per cent that fail, one-half fail because of medical reasons.

In the special program, 95 per cent are expected to succeed in passing the performance and academic tests. However, about 8 per cent of this group require re-cycling, which means doing a week or several weeks' work over again,

before they can be passed; 4 per cent are discharged for physical and academic reasons.

After basic training some soldiers are sent directly into a combat area; most go through advanced training. For many of these advanced training courses, the language used by the instructors and in printed materials has had to be simplified in order to accommodate the program to the low reading level of these soldiers. In addition to the change in language, there are programmed texts in basic arithmetic skills, video tape and simulators with which it is hoped that soldiers will be trained to do a specific job in the service. For the individuals in this project, however, instructors in the practical courses such as automobile mechanics take the slow learners for after-hours tutoring. This tutoring may include either mechanical or basic academic assistance. In a recent speech, former Secretary of Defense, Robert McNamara, indicated that the earlier estimates of anticipated success were, in general, consistent with the performances of these men.

Banneker Project of St. Louis, *Missouri*

"Operation Motivation" was initiated in the Banneker School District of St. Louis, Missouri, in 1957, under the direction of Dr. Samuel Shepard. The program is an attempt to raise the academic achievement of children in kindergarten through eighth grade by concentrating on attitude change on the part of pupils, teachers, and parents rather than through specific curriculum modification.

The Banneker Project attempted to appeal directly to the sense of pride and competitive spirit of the pupils. Techniques employed were pep rallies, honor assemblies, competition contests, a radio program giving children suggestions on "how to succeed in school," and ungraded classes with heavy emphasis on reading. Teachers were encouraged to give pupils a sense of the direct relation between present day school work and future employment, to "quit teaching by I.Q. . . . quit their attitudes of condescension . . . assign homework . . . and visit the homes of the parents." Meetings were held with parents at which they were persuaded to look forward to a better future for their children and to inspire their children to regard school as the best means of self-fulfillment 'and upward mobility.

In the evaluation of the Banneker Project, student performance was compared with national norms and with norms found in other nearly all-Negro and all-white schools. When compared with other all-Negro schools, the Banneker school's academic standing showed no advance during the Project years. In 1965-66 the position of the Banneker schools relative to nearly all-white schools remained inferior. In looking at more than academic achievement test scores, Dr. Shepard has reported that the children have been more interested in school, have been better behaved, and have had better attendance, that teachers have been working harder, and that there has been excellent cooperation from parents.

More Effective Schools Program of New York, New York

The More Effective Schools program was initiated in 1964 in ten New York City elementary schools and expanded in September 1965 to include eleven additional city schools. The Program was intended to create basic changes in curriculum, personnel, school plant and organization and school-community relations. Specific program elements were to include provision of teacher specialists, team teaching, reduced class size, heterogeneous grouping, and intensive work with parents and community.

Attention has recently been turned to the evaluation of the More Effective Schools program. Perhaps the most important finding of one such study was that despite certain administrative and organizational changes "little has happened in the way of innovation or restructuring in the basic teaching process." There was general agreement among both observers and • school staff that "teachers have not revised techniques of instruction to obtain the presumed instructional advantages" of reduced class size and the availability of specialized services.

In reviewing the data on cognitive and attitudinal changes in MES classes, one must note both the provision of reduced pupil/teacher ratios and specialized psychological, social, and health services and the absence of any radical revision in instructional practices. On the basis of standardized tests and classroom observations, children in some ME schools made significant achievement gains over children in designated control schools and in other special service schools. In general, reading retardation was reduced in ME schools more so than in control schools. Comparisons of achievement in reading grade show some MES classes scoring from 2 to 5 months above control and comparison classes. It should be noted, however, that these findings are derived from a longitudinal analysis of MES pupil data.

On an earlier cross-sectional analysis the gains of MES pupils were less obvious.

In addition to measured cognitive gains, a clear sense of "enthusiasm, interest, and hope" has been reported among administrative staff and teaching faculty as well as parents and the community in general. As indicated in one evaluation, "The creation of such positive feelings and climates in a school system which in recent years has evidenced considerable internal stress and school-community conflict is an important accomplishment" and, we might add, a rather ironic one.

Higher Horizons Program of New York, New York

The Higher Horizons Program was conceived in large measure as an extension of the "successful" Demonstration Guidance Project. The Demonstration Guidance Project involved approximately 700 junior and senior high school students in Harlem. Counseling and remedial education staffs were significantly increased in the schools involved to provide a high concentration of supplementary help. The results were quite dramatic. Approximately 60 per cent of the students who had joined the Project in seventh grade gained an average of 4.3 years in reading achievement after 2.6 years in the Project; the dropout rate from high school for these children decreased from 40 to 20 per cent, and a significant portion were motivated to continue their education beyond high school.

The Higher Horizons Program was an attempt to replicate the Demonstration Guidance Project on a much wider scale and at minimum extra cost. Higher Horizons was begun in 1959 to serve 12,000 children from 31 elementary schools and 13 junior high schools, and was expanded in 1962 to include 64,000 children. The major purpose of Higher Horizons was to "develop techniques for the identification, motivation, enrichment, and education of the culturally disadvantaged children and to perfect means for stimulating them and their families to pursue higher educational and vocational goals." The foci of the program were intensive individual and group counseling, cultural and occupational experiences, remedial services and parent education. Several hundred specialized personnel were added to the staffs of the project schools. The extra teachers were used as curriculum assistants, teacher training specialists, or subject matter (particularly reading) specialists; each teacher was expected to spend a good part of his time on parent and community education, cultural activities, and inservice training, as well as on curriculum improvement and remedial work.

Any evaluation of the Higher Horizons Program must take into account that at least as far as budgeting was concerned, the Program was not supported financially to the extent originally planned. For example, in 1959 one additional teacher or counselor was provided for every 108 children, but by 1962 there was only one teacher or counselor provided for every 143 children. On a per capita basis, more than three times as much money was spent on the Demonstration Guidance Project as on Higher Horizons. In 1964 an evaluation was completed for the New York City Board of Education. The study concentrated on students in eight Higher Horizons schools matched on a one-to-one basis (on I.Q., reading comprehension, ethnic composition, geographic location, and size of school) with non-Higher Horizons students. For the period of the study (1959-62), the Higher Horizons schools had a somewhat smaller average class size, lower rates of pupil and teacher transiency, and larger percentages of regular teachers. The evaluation reported that there were no significant differences between Higher Horizons and control group children on reading and arithmetic achievement, ratings of school attitudes, self-image, and educational-vocational aspirations. The only significant differences noted were gains made by Higher Horizons elementary school children in arithmetic. Despite these disappointing results, the professional staff in the program were observed to be favorably disposed to the Program. They felt that it was most successful in providing cultural opportunities and extra remedial guidance services and that its least effect was on students' behavior, study habits, and educational goals.

Project Case II: MODEL

The Institute for Behavioral Research began its project Case II: MODEL (Contingencies Applicable to Special Education-Motivationally Oriented Designs for an Ecology of Learning) in February 1966 under the direction of Harold Cohen. Twenty-eight young men in the National Training School for Boys were involved. The basic goals of the project were to improve the academic behavior of all twenty-eight and to prepare as many as possible within a one-year time schedule for their return to school. The age range of the group was fourteen to eighteen, their average I.Q. was 93.8; 85 per cent were dropouts from school, and only three had never been sentenced and institutionalized before.

Case II was based on the idea that each learning experience should have built into it a series of reinforcing steps to maintain the students' interest. This meant direct tangible reinforcement as well as an individual sense of success and group approval. Cohen used money as an extrinsic immediate reinforcement — ". . . our student-inmates want to know, 'Man, what's the payoff now?' For them, as well as for the bulk of Americans, they work for money." Students became Educational Researcher's and went to work on 140 programmed educational courses in 18 programmed classes. When they performed on tests at 90 per cent or better, they were paid off. A point system was utilized, each point representing one penny. With his money earned, the student provided for his room, food, clothing, gifts and an entrance fee and tuition for special classes. "A student who does not have sufficient funds goes on relief — sleeps on an open bunk and eats food on a metal tray. No student has ever been on relief more than two weeks."

A specially designed 24-hour contingency-oriented educational laboratory was designed to provide, in effect, 24 hours of educational therapy. "Where and when a student sleeps, eats, makes contact with another student, with a machine, with a group, a program or a teacher is part of the educational ecology. . . . Every student in this program is being counseled by those people he selects during the day. He talks to his friends, to the librarian, the teacher, the cook, the secretary, the research staff and visitors. He can select a particular counselor on request, e. g., his minister, psychologist, or caseworker, for which he pays a small professional service fee."

The vital aspect of the structured environment is that it programs the individual for success. This is attained basically by (1) structuring each curriculum unit at a level where the individual can perform successfully step by step and (2) providing direct pay-off for achievement. This work is primarily directed at developing new and more appropriate behaviors under a schedule of reinforcement while eliminating inappropriate antisocial behaviors by a schedule which is non-reinforcing.

Cohen's intermediate findings are quite impressive. Increases of the I.Q.'s of the students have averaged 12.09 points. For every 90 hours of academic work, there was an average increase of 1.89 grade levels on the Stanford Achievement Test and 2.7 grade levels on the Gates Reading Survey.

General Criteria and Promising Models

The rather modest success of these and many other efforts at compensatory education, when combined with the Coleman findings indicating that school factors account for a small amount of the variation in school achievement, could lead to the conclusion that improvements in the equality of education are hardly worth our effort. But just as the Coleman finding is based upon an examination of several factors which are probably not crucial in the determination of the quality of education, much that we see in the several approaches to compensatory education consists of educational features which may be necessary to the educational process, but evidently are not sufficient to make the difference in terms of greatly improved academic achievement in socially disadvantaged children.

Most of these programs have either attempted to modify basic cognitive processes, to change levels of content mastery, or to change the motivation of the young people served. However, most of these programs represent vast increases in the *quantity* of effort directed at improving function with very little improvement in the *quality* of program offered. The efforts directed at changed cognitive function are very traditional and have brought little that is new or changed in pedagogy. One does not see in these programs any reflection of current thinking relative to learning theory and behavioral organization. With but one exception, there is no representation in the programs reviewed of the application of behavioral analysis and contingency management to the learning experiences of these youngsters. Yet, as we have indicated, this is one of the few approaches to compensatory education which seems to be bearing fruit. In approaching improved content mastery, the programs seem to have concentrated on either an enriched or watered-down presentation of material to pupils. Again, drastic reorganization in the presentation of material, the quality of material and the conditions under which materials are presented are not present in these programs. At the level of increased motivation and attitude change, we have somewhat more promising signs in the effort of many of these programs. Several programs have sought more active involvement of parents and representatives of the communities from which these children come in the planning and conduct of educational programs. This emphasis, however, is by no means a widely accepted and dominant one. At least at the level of meaningful participation there continues to be strong resistance on the part of the education establishment. This has been particularly exhibited in recent struggles between school personnel and community groups. Despite the tradition of community control of the public school, when that control is likely to pass into the hands of poor and minority group persons the school resists strongly. If compensatory education is to compensate for the learning problems of young people who are thought to come to school without the necessary background of experience to optimally benefit from school, of youngsters who come to school poorly motivated toward the goals of the school, of youngsters who come to school lacking certain cognitive habits and skills, and of young people who come to the school attitudinally unprepared to participate or to sustain participation in academic learning tasks, there are then several criteria which might guide the development of compensatory education.

1. Effective instructional programs and practices must be a part of such an effort. If this is to be achieved, we will need to give greater attention to the dynamics of group interaction in their relationship to the teaching-learning process. Professionals concerned with such fields as psychotherapy and decision processes have developed elaborate systems of theory and practice based upon concepts of group dynamics. This sophistication has not yet been appropriately applied to education. Effective instruction will also require that we explore different ways of organizing learning experiences to meet individual differences in readiness and style. Readiness and style may vary with respect to the functional capacity to discriminate between things seen, heard, tasted, or felt. They may vary with respect to habit patterns that have been established around these sensory functions. They may vary based upon the dominance of one aspect of sensory function over another. It may well be that children whose life experiences vary drastically may also have significant variations in the hierarchical organization of sensory function and response modalities. Furthermore, if individuals, independently of experience or station in life, differ with respect to the degree to which they are inclined to respond with one or another of the senses, it may be that one of the significant variables in learning ability and disability is the quality of support provided when the learning task presented does not complement the sensory organization of the learner.

Another emphasis deserving of attention in our efforts at more effective instruction involves the utilization of behavioral analysis and contingency management in the design of learning experiences. In another context, one of the authors, (Edmund W. Gordon) has stressed the importance of qualitative as opposed to quantitative analysis of intellectual and other behavioral functions as a prerequisite for the development of prescriptions for learning. In behavioral analysis one is concerned with the detailed analysis and description of behavioral function, so that strength, weakness, style, preference, etc., are identified and a course of action for directed learning may be established. In contingency management, one is concerned with limiting the contingencies surrounding behavior so that the possible outcomes can be controlled, enabling the anticipation of consequences of the behavior. Such understanding and manipulation permit us to tie consequences of behavior to the antecedents of behavior and to use these consequences as reinforcers of desired behaviors.

2. If effective instructional programs can be achieved, compensatory education will need to reach children earlier, serve them over longer periods of the day, week, and year, and possibly follow them later into life. This latter need may increase as the need for continued learning and instruction as lifetime processes becomes more accepted in our society. The program then must provide for intensive and extensive care from the cradle until at least productive work or college. In many instances, it will need to provide, through the school, child care and instructional services ten to twelve hours a day, six or seven days a week, and twelve months of the year. If we are concerned with insulating the child from many of the destructive elements in disorganized communities and families, there is little choice but to drastically expand the periods for which the school is responsible for the child.

3. The enriched school experience will have little effect unless it can come to be valued and respected by the children and families served. Unless involvement in the school and respect for its values can become positive norms in the lives of the children, the productiveness of the school will be impaired. There is mounting evidence suggestive of the relationship between goal determination and task involvement. It would appear that participation in the determination of the policies of schools which these children attend by their parents and community members with whom they identify would be positively reflected in increased commitment to the objectives and programs of the school. A corollary of this involvement

is another attitudinal asset. The increasingly recognized sense of environmental control would seem also to be a potential product of this increased involvement in decision-making in school affairs. Participation in decision-making is by no means the only road to personal involvement. Of equal importance is the need that the school, the curriculum, and the materials it uses provide points of identification for the learner. In this connection materials which are widely representative of the variety of cultural, economic, and ethnic groups in this country are essential. Staff members who also represent this variety of backgrounds are necessary.

4. If the school is to meet the special needs of youngsters who are handicapped by lower economic status, special attention and provision will need to be made to protect and insure good health, adequate nutritional status, and the material resources necessary for effective school learning. In some instances this will mean elaborate programs of health care. In other situations food supplements will be required. In many situations, stipends may be necessary to enable the youngster to provide the necessary supplemental school materials and pocket money for minimal social interaction. For these children, the school must alleviate or circumvent economic, cultural, social, experiential, and educational deficiencies in their environment. Many of these are functions the school was not originally designed to perform.

5. The influence of the school is by no means limited to the period during which the youngster is responsible to the school. What the youngster perceives as opportunity to utilize the school's products and

to participate in the mainstream of the society may be as important to his adjustment and progress within the school as it is to his development in the post-school period. Again, in reference to the all-important sense of environmental control, it may be that in the absence of perceived opportunity to do something with his life, all of our innovations and educational improvements will be for naught.

6. Since so much of the school's influence is mediated through verbal interaction, its program for these children will have to reflect respect for the languages with which these children come to school. In some instances, basic education may have to be provided in the vernacular of the child until development has progressed to a point where a transition to standard language forms may be achieved.

7. Since high degrees of mobility and transiency are characteristic of many families in the target populations, special provisions to accommodate transiency must be made. This may require comparability of basic goals and programs at each level of instruction and sufficient intimacy in teacher-pupil relationships to provide for emotional and physical security particularly at points of transition. This goal can be partially achieved through the provision of sufficiently small organizational units so that each child is enabled to achieve a sense of identity and involvement in the essential aspects of the educational process. In this setting the child will need to experience a real sense that what he does and what he decides can influence his progress, achievement, and future.

8. The implementation of programs which approach these criteria will to a large extent depend upon the availability of excellent school staffs. In the achievement of this goal special attention will need to be given to the preparation, supervision, and circumstances of work of the school's personnel. The dimensions of the necessary training programs have not yet been specified. Wide variations are possible in the backgrounds and training of persons utilized if emphasis is placed upon supervision and accountability. Nonprofessionals and paraprofessionals indigenous to the backgrounds from which the children come should be utilized, and these persons like all other staff members should be actively represented along with non-school employed members of the target community in decision-making in all aspects of the school's functioning.

9. The school must be adequately provided for in terms of material support. For the target population, facilities and resources do make a difference. Quality of teachers is important. There must be available the monetary and status rewards necessary to attract and hold able teachers in classroom instruction.

10. Cultural, economic, and ethnic integration in education is often viewed as alternative to compensatory education. Increasingly, it must be viewed as integral parts of compensatory or quality education. Probably more efficient than all the above stated factors excellently provided would be the mixing of children from more limited backgrounds in schools where the majority of pupils come from more privileged circumstances of life. Instead of a choice between integration and compensatory education, we advocate integration as an essential feature in compensatory education.

COMPENSATORY EDUCATION IN THE EQUALIZATION OF EDUCATIONAL OPPORTUNITY II

Edmund W. Gordon and Adelaide Jablonsky

Edmund W. Gordon and Adelaide Jablonsky, "Compensatory Education in the Equalization of Educational Opportunity, II," *Journal of Negro Education,* Summer 1968, Vol. 37, pp. 280-290.

COMPENSATORY EDUCATION IN THE EQUALIZATION OF EDUCATIONAL OPPORTUNITY II

Edmund W. Gordon and Adelaide Jablonsky

Within the framework of the several criteria discussed in the preceding chapter, a comprehensive model for compensatory or quality education can be projected to meet the needs of socially disadvantaged children. The model which follows provides programs at the early years particularly for the disadvantaged. As we move into the elementary school, the plan is particularly designed for children from disadvantaged backgrounds, but optimally it should include children of all backgrounds. At the level of secondary school, our plan requires inclusion of the total population in that age group. It is clear that the authors of this paper feel that when education is appropriate to the characteristics of the learners and adequate to the achievement of certain basic criteria of academic and social function, compensatory education and integration become less the issue and education of high quality available to children in relation to their needs the primary concern.

Early Child Care: Birth through Two Years of Age

For families where economic, social and /or psychological factors make it difficult or impossible to afford the infant and young child care which insures optimal development, provisions should be made for optional services. In addition to physical, nutritional, and medical care,

there must be provided warm personal relationships and opportunities for the kinds of experiences which help to develop facility in the use of language, perceptual discrimination skills, integrated perceptual-motor functioning, conceptual problem solving skills, and attitudes of appreciation for and challenge by learning.

Where the parents so elect, the child should be placed for the first two months in an extended nursery facility. The facilities should provide for an option of daytime care or around-the-clock care. They should provide an opportunity for mothers and/or fathers to visit with and remain with their children for as long and as often as they are able. The nursery should care for children until they are able to walk and understand simple directions at which time they should be transferred to a new unit. For children from this stage until three years of age, several organizational units should be designed to accommodate progressive phases of maturation.

These programs should be implemented by a Bureau of Child Welfare within the criteria previously established. They should provide the children of this age opportunities to develop, experience, and learn to the point where within the third year of life the following achievements have been met: (1) The child has the physical coordination and skill required for walking comfortably, feeding

---

* This chapter is a continuation of Chapter IX.

himself and is capable of normal control of toilet functions for this age level. (2) The child has the verbal ability and vocabulary to make his wants understood, understands simple directions from adults, and has basic language facility for this age level. (3) The child has begun to show a balance between dependence and independence in his behavior, reflecting a view of the environment as phenomena to be explored, manipulated, utilized, and mastered. (4) The child is judged sufficiently mature by the faculty of the school to make the transition to the primary school. Transfer to the primary school could take place on previously established dates six times during the year so that the receiving school would begin orientation programs for newly admitted children in groups sufficiently large to permit group orientation to the structure and program of that school.

The Primary School: Three through Five Years of Age

This school should be patterned on the present Head Start program with several alterations. Each school should be directed by a head teacher and should accommodate about 150 children, in five groups of thirty. Each group of thirty should have a head teacher, one assistant teacher, two student teachers or paraprofessionals, and two community nonprofessionals. Each school should have two social workers, a nurse, and a parttime psychologist.

A coordinating council should be established for each six to eight schools in a neighborhood to be headed by an administrator who is not necessarily an educator but is responsible for all the business affairs of the cluster of schools. Working with him should be a coordinator

of food services and the full-time educational psychologist serving the center. A science specialist and a recreation specialist should not be based at the central headquarters but should be assigned on a rotating basis to each of the schools to work with the children in enhancing those aspects of the program.

This school would function six days a week from before breakfast until after dinner. It would be segmented into two levels, one primarily for the three to four year olds, and the other level for children ready to make the transition at the five year old level. At both levels there should be explorations beyond the school facility itself into the community in order to learn its various elements. However, these experiences should be much more frequent and enriched at the five-year old level.

In addition to the usual rest periods, specific blocks of time of several hours should be established for purely recreational purposes using neighborhood parks, or, if necessary, providing transportation to parks for these activities when weather permits. The parks could also provide the environment for nature studies.

Transition from the lower to the upper level of this school should take place when the child is judged by the faculty to have developed maturity, attitudes toward learning which are demonstrated by normal curiosity and desire to explore, normal problem solving skill and evidence of the concept that what the child does influences his present and his future.

At the upper level, the transition should be begun to a cognitive emphasis with a strong drive toward pre-reading and reading skills, introduction to writing and drawing, introduction to basic arithmetic and listening skills.

Transfer out of the primary school should take place four times a year. The later fives and early sixes would be transferred when they were judged by the faculty of their school to have developed sufficiently in perception, cognition, motor, emotional and social skills to adjust to the program of the elementary school.

Each executive committee of a cluster should be held accountable to a central city or school district board for the achievement and development of the children in its care. As previously established in the basic criteria, this executive committee would consist of administrators, teachers, parents, and community representatives.

The Elementary School: Six through Eleven Years of Age

While it would probably be more desirable to provide new educational structures for all children in these schools, reality forces us to design the schools around the presently existing facilities. The utilization of these facilities, however, will require the changes indicated below. Due to the lack of sufficient facilities to provide these accommodations for all disadvantaged children, it will probably be necessary to secure other available space in apartment houses, community structures, stores, business facilities, or temporary structures until the building program can provide sufficient and appropriate space for this level.

Starting with the smallest unit, a class will consist of approximately 54 children under a master teacher, further subdivided into two groups of approximately 27 children each, each with a fully licensed teacher. Each teacher is to have working with her one student teacher or paraprofessional and one nonprofessional parent or community person. Each unit (of 54) is to have complete use of three standard contiguous classrooms. Two of the classrooms remain as presently structured for group instruction of 25 to 30 children at a time. The third classroom would have partitions constructed to provide cubicles varying in size from individual study carrels to small group instruction rooms for three to nine children at a time.

Each unit of children and their teachers would remain together for approximately two years with children being admitted at each level (6-7, 8-9, 10-11) four times a year as children are judged by the faculty as being ready for the next level. Each school would consist of six or nine units depending on population needs. The school would be headed by a head teacher or principal whose major responsibilities would be educational leadership for the school, quality control and accountability. He would have two major assistants, one in charge of administrative affairs including maintenance, the supervision of nonprofessionals, and feeding. The second assistant would concern himself with educational matters. His assignment would be within the classrooms rather than in an office. He would fill in for master teachers when they are absent, take part in daily instruction and remediation and coordinate in-service education of the teachers, paraprofessionals, and subprofessionals.

Each elementary school would have a library for books and all other educational resources including film strips, films, records, etc. It should be staffed by two librarians, one whose major function would be to work with the teachers, supplying them with materials and the understanding of the use of new and useful materials, and a second who would work directly with the children providing their needs for materials in individual projects or in group or class projects. They are to be assisted by a nonprofessional, preferably a man, who would take care of audiovisual equipment and make it available to teachers on request and assist in physical care of the library.

Each school would have a science teacher whose responsibilities would be to codinate all science activities in the school, having all equipment and supplies necessary for a rich program. He would have a separate facility for housing materials and displays which would be difficult to move from class to class, but would also give lessons weekly in each of the classes and supply the teachers with necessary materials and background to carry on the science lessons he initiates with their co-planning.

A physical education consultant would have a staff of three paraprofessionals and six to nine selected high school students. This staff would be responsible for the recreational activities.

At each school, there should be an Independent Study Center (ISC) available to all children in the school. Pupils would use the ISC as a resource where they could obtain advanced work and direction if they were moving ahead of the class to which they were assigned or special remedial help or modified curriculum materials if they were lagging behind. The center staff would help with the study skills, would provide brief, intensive refresher or compensatory units of courses, assistance with special projects or indi-vidualized instruction as requested by pupils. The staff would also serve as a consultant resource to teachers.

A medical doctor on call, a full-time nurse, a full-time psychologist or psychiatrist, two social workers, one guidance person, and a community coordinator would complete the cluster staff. The present day strictures on curriculum would be lifted, and master teachers, teachers, and central staff would have the responsibility for evolving an appropriate curriculum for each school which would result in the following outcomes:

1. Each child would have developed self-concept characterized by awareness of his worth as an individual and an awareness that his own behavior influences his present and his future.

2. Each child would have the social development which would make him comfortable in relating with peers and adults.

3. Each child would have the communication skills which would make it possible for him to express himself adequately at his age level in face-to-face conversation and in informal and formal reports to larger groups. He would also have the ability to listen attentively and to demonstrate a follow-up on what he has heard.

4. Each child would have the literacy competence expected of his age level. He should be able to read and enjoy reading, to comprehend increasingly more difficult materials. He should have the ability to write standard English.

5. Each child should be able to think in mathematical concepts and to do appropriate arithmetic computations for his level.

6. Each child should have an ever growing awareness of his relationship and

man's relationship to his family, his neigh borhood, his society, his school, his country, and the world. The social studies curriculum would focus on the present, with the past being introduced where appropriate for reinforcement but with the major purpose of preparing the child to function in tomorrow's world.

7. Each child should understand and be able to function in the use of scientific method and have an adequate content background in science for his level.

8. Each child should have experiences which provide a growing awareness of expressive and receptive art forms. Where talent can be developed, these experiences should also lead to the development of competence and skill in the art medium of his choice.

The Secondary School(s): Twelve through Seventeen Years of Age

The schools for the 12-17 year olds present certain problems at this time and in the near future because of the need to provide two approaches to education for disadvantaged youth. One program would provide for those students who had proceeded through the quality education program outlined above and were functioning at or beyond the expected level of performance. The second, however, would need to be heavily remedial in order to overcome the problems in learning which had been established through the experiences in today's schools and to overcome the serious deficiencies in basic skills and in content which are demonstrated by current measures of academic performance by a large percentage of the disadvantaged secondary school population.

All of the basic elements indicated at the elementary level would be continued into the secondary schools with several additions and organizational changes. We take no strong position in the present controversy concerning the relationship between junior and senior high schools, although we have some preference for keeping the seventh to twelfth grade classes within one building. This will again place accountability on the shoulders of one professional group for this six year span of education and will eliminate the projection of blame for failure onto a prior school organization.

Realizing the many advantages which can be derived from enlarged educational complexes at the secondary level, we are proposing the establishment of facilities to serve a large geographic area. This will provide for representation of broader social, ethnic, and economic groups. Centralized facilities such as gymnasiums, theaters, swimming facilities, and highly specialized academic centers could be provided to enrich the school experiences of these children. However, since anonymity is a serious problem in large installations of this kind, we propose that units or clusters be established for each group of 600 students consisting of two units of 100 students at each of the following age levels, 12-13, 14-15, and 16-17. While current educational statistics indicate a drop off in attendance at the upper age levels, we are assuming that quality education will lead toward student retention through the 18th birthday. Each school could service any multiple of 600 and still give each student in the smaller units real and meaningful participation in decision-making in relation to his own activities and the welfare of the group.

Each 100 children would have four teachers, an English-speech instructor, a social studies teacher covering all the disciplines, a science teacher capable of teaching general science, earth science, astronomy, chemistry, and physics at this level, and a math teacher. This would constitute the basic responsible unit of staff. They would be responsible for four classes among themselves, preferably for the entire six year span. For each two units, that is for each eight classes totaling 200 children, the teaching staff would be augmented by a foreign language instructor, an art teacher, a music teacher, a physical education teacher, vocational and academic counselors, and a battery of shops including carpentry, automobile, electronic, commercial, plumbing, electrical, etc. As at the elementary level, provision would be made for additional space for small group and individual study, the availability of rich library resources of materials and personnel, and an Independent Study Center would be available to each cluster.

The administration of a school of 1,200 students would be similar to the central administration at the elementary level, with the addition of a coordinator for work experiences and whatever staff would be needed to implement a work-study program.

Each child should be expected to participate in a work-study program in which he would be exposed to a graduated series of work experiences from his admission at 12 years of age to the secondary school until his completion of the program at the age of 18. The early phases of this program should provide several hours of work a week at appropriate levels of remuneration. These should be exploratory in nature, affording each child several opportunities to learn from appropriate models in different institutions or or-

ganizations. The program should heavily involve the concept of apprenticeship, using skilled community resources wherever appropriate. The program should provide assistance for younger children and leadership roles for the 16 and 17 year olds in preparation for their transition to out-of-school employment or for higher education.

The school would be opened from breakfast through ten p.m., providing periods for instruction, recreation, study and the work periods, with flexible grouping and student selection of some units of learning. Units of study should be organized for short-term completion (six to eight weeks), providing frequent and periodic appraisal and review. Programs as agreed to by the central executive committee for the school would extend for six days a week and twelve months a year, including a period of camping.

Camping

Of the several possible approaches to extension of the influence and service of formal instruction, the use of camping offers unique opportunities. The change in pace, the change in setting, the esthetic values of nature, the intimacy of small group leadership, and other advantages of camp life make this an untapped resource which can be developed for compensatory education. It is proposed that beginning with all ten year olds a two month per year camp experience be provided through the summer of the year of completion of high school.

The camp experience would be used to serve several purposes. The program would include a strong component of cultural enrichment with intensive exposure to arts, crafts, nature, trips, etc. Equal attention, however, would be given to personal relationships, the identification and fostering of values and to contemplation and recreation. A third component of the camp program would be an extension of the Independent Study Center services. Aspects of the ISC would be available in camp with the study resources utilized in relation to pupil need and interest. Some pupil-campers would be doing supplementary and advanced studies. Some would be doing remedial work. Some would concentrate on refresher units. Others would be doing special projects designed to extend specific competencies or to compensate for specific deficits in knowledge or skill.

The camp season which could run from late spring through early autumn, April to October in the Northeast, should run concurrently with the extended school year. Grouping patterns should provide for age group mixing and certainly accommodate ability group mixing. Camper to counselor ratio should not exceed seven to one, yet opportunities for larger and smaller group activities must be available. Camp facilities need not be elaborate but should be adequate to protect health and safety.

Health and food services should permit special or remedial treatment for children with chronic diseases or nutritional problems. Hosteling and other combinations of camping and travel should be provided. For some, apprenticeships in nature-related industries should be developed. For youngsters of advanced high school age, work as counselor aides and other working camping experiences should be provided. For the recent high school graduate, the camp season might be used for

an introduction to post high school study or work.

ESTIMATED COST

The accurate estimation of the cost of establishing a nationwide system of compensatory or quality education for all disadvantaged children is a task which will require more time, money, and resources than the nation is likely to allocate at this time. Based upon the experiences of several school districts and projections by groups which have struggled with this problem, it is possible to arrive at crude estimates which suggest the magnitude of this undertaking.

If we define the disadvantaged primarily and realistically in terms of family income, we may be talking about 30,000,000 to 35,000,000 individuals of all ages. The Office of Economic Opportunity has taken both family size and urban and rural factors into consideration in establishing annual cash income thresholds to poverty. Some selective figures from their present criteria are given in Table I.

TABLE I

PRESENT O.E.O. CRITERIA FOR POVERTY CLASSIFICATION

Family Size Persons	Non-farm	Farm
2	$1,990	$1,390
5	$3,685	$2,580
7	$4,635	$3,245
10	$6,135	$4,295

Using these criteria, O.E.O. provides the information given in Table II for children and youth:

TABLE II
POVERTY GROUPS AS CLASSIFIED BY O.E.O. CRITERIA

Persons in Poverty

Age	Millions	% of Poor who are nonwhite	% of all poor and nonpoor in this age group
Under 6	5.8	40	24
6-15	8.1	38	21
16-21	3.0	30	17

The total of almost 17 million children and youth then forms the hard core of the poverty group. It is patent, however, that the group of disadvantaged children and youth to whom the educational establishment is relating extends far beyond this number. Since these income figures are minimal, factors such as one-parent families, father absences, inadequate housing, physical malfunctions, malnutrition, and others are not taken into consideration. One-fourth to one-fifth of all young people are in the poverty group. Many others must be considered disadvantaged when we include educational criteria.

Minimum educational standards should be established for 14-18 year old youth with moderate intelligence and limited background that our education system can bring them to the level of demonstrating basic skills in reading and arithmetic equivalent to the expectation at the eighth grade level, with commensurate content acquisition for that level. We then present a base upon which each young man and woman can be ready for at least apprenticeship or vocational education to equip the graduate with the knowledge and skills required for full employment as an adult. Thereafter, every child at younger age levels should be considered disadvantaged if his academic development is not progressing at a rate which will assure the accomplishment of eighth grade academic achievement by ages 14-18. Each of these criteria is measurable.

We have purposely eliminated from our statistical estimates criteria such as educational background of parents, housing conditions, and behavioral disorders because of difficulty in securing appropriate measures. Included in these projections is the small proportion of youngsters from backgrounds of poverty who nevertheless are making acceptable progress in school. Our proposed organization for instruction must both compensate for deficiencies which exist and complement the assets of these pupils. We have not segmented the statistics by farm and nonfarm populations or by white and nonwhite populations, because we assume that compensatory education in the United States must serve all children who require it.

Taking 50 per cent of the population at each age level as operating at/or below grade level and reducing that by 10 per cent representing the mentally retarded and seriously physically handicapped or other children needing intensive professional attention, we can establish a 40 per cent overall figure. The figure of 10 per cent is used by the armed services in screening out men for their special

Project 100,000. The 10 per cent, therefore, will not be reflected in our budget; however, the Federal Government will need to make provision for these children. The budget for these purposes would probably exceed the per capita figures indicated in this report.

It would perhaps be justified if we were to include in the target population most nonwhite children in the United States since their education is routinely retarded by factors of discrimination beyond the problems faced by the poor. Another group requiring special attention (but not included as a special category) are children above the poverty level with language difficulties and/or cultural or social deficiencies resulting from geographic isolation or from limited resources of home and community. If we were to include these children and youth we would need to add another 5 per cent to each category of persons.

The following total population, then, requires compensatory education. We have rounded figures to represent the annual average for the period 1967-1970.

Birth to 2 years of age	5,000,000
3-5 years of age	5,000,000
6-7 years of age	3,200,000
8-9 years of age	3,200,000
10-11 years of age	3,000,000
12-13 years of age	3,000,000
14-15 years of age	2,500,000
16-17 years of age	2,500,000
18-19 years of age	3,000,000
	30,400,000

In the review of compensatory education programs by Gordon and Wilkerson, per pupil cost for isolated and at times limited special programs ranged from $25 per pupil to more than $1,000 above basic educational costs. The average for the more active and better-rated ancillary programs would be approximately $500 per child. These programs were modest in design and in effect, yet to apply them to the entire target population would cost $15 billion per year over current costs for 30 million children. This does not provide for additional basic costs for children under six years of age not presently served by the education system. None of these programs approximates the intensity, comprehensiveness, and quality of the programs we have proposed. From evaluation reports of many of these programs we could not anticipate the desired results from this limited additional financial investment.

Another way of establishing this budget is to take the average per pupil expenditure in our more advanced school systems and to add to it the amount needed for quality education. Exclusive of capital investment and of federally funded programs, the average per pupil cost in five of these systems ranges from $700 to $1,200. The round figure of $1,000 per child represents a nine to ten month school year, five days a week, from 9 a.m. to 3 p.m. Considering: (1) the lengthening of the school day from 8 a.m. to 6 p.m. or 10 p.m. at the different age levels, (2) the inclusion of a sixth school day each week, (3) the need to further improve teachers' salaries and working conditions, with upgrading for the master classroom teacher, (4) the need to enhance the technical preparation and employment circumstances of the paraprofessional and the nonprofessional, (5) the funds required for inservice refreshment and enhancement of teacher competence, (6) the reduced adult-pupil ratios, (7) the addition of nutritional, health, medical, and social services, (8) the urgency of continuing intensive research and evaluation, and (9) the desirability of multiple and varied programs and activities for involving parents and community representatives in the education of these children, the lowest defensible estimate for the ten month program is $2,500 per child or youth each year exclusive of capital investment or about $75 billion. The summer program providing care for the young children for the two months of the summer and camping for two months for the older children and youth would cost about $600 per individual for a total of $18 billion.

The monetary supplements for the work program at the secondary level should provide $15 to $30 a week per youth from 12-17 years of age. We assume that the income for the 18-19 year olds would come from industrial or other sources. These supplements for 8 million youths would total approximately $8 billion.

To summarize the budget, therefore, we must take: (1) the expensive capital investment needed to provide adequate facilities, (2) cost of school program — $75 billion, (3) cost of summer program — $18 billion, and (4) monetary supplements for work program — $8 billion, (a total of $101 billion). Since this budget relates only to the 30.4 million disadvantaged children, and since all children in our country are entitled to this high quality level of education, it is clear that this figure must be extended to educate 77 to 80 million children and

youth under 20 years of age. In addition, higher education of equal quality should be provided for all those who qualify for advanced study.

Is Compensatory Education the Answer?

It can be argued that no price is too high to pay for good and effective education for all of our children. In a cost-conscious society, however, social programs are judged in relation to economy of operation. Given our concern with improving or even optimizing educational achievement for poor and minority group children and in considering the economics of compensatory education, we might ask the question: "Is the most effective approach one which involves major and extensive innovations in curriculum content and school organization?" The data presently available to us indicate that most of the things we know how to do and have been willing to apply to improve education are of modest help to the target population. These efforts do not represent substantive changes in quality nor have they resulted in greatly improved academic performance. On the other hand, a much less complex innovation, economic and racial integration in the schools, seems to be associated with more substantial gains in quality of functioning in the target groups. If, based on our present level of knowledge and practice, we are forced to make a choice between compensatory education as currently practiced and school integration, it appears that school integration is the treatment of preference.

To dichotomize this issue, however, may be an error. One should not be forced to choose the treatment which will provide the greatest gain but rather the treatments necessary to achieve the goal. There is increasing conviction that just as compensatory education alone may be insufficient, ethnic integration alone in the school may also be insufficient. In many instances where movement toward integration has been achieved, further separation by race or economic group has nonetheless occurred as pupils have been grouped on the basis of their present achievement. Clearly, where youngsters come to a learning situation with different backgrounds and different degrees of readiness, we have no choice but to institute educational programs which build upon and compensate for their functional characteristics. At the same time, since we know that a large measure of pupil functioning seems to be influenced by noncognitive factors related to the social-psychological circumstances under which they study, the school also has responsibility for the manipulation of those circumstances to serve the learning needs of pupils. In this instance, the provision of learning experiences in the context of culturally, economically, and ethnically integrated pupil groupings is indicated.

Even if compensatory education could do the job, several leaders have cautioned against dropping the demand for integration. They feel it is only the threat of racial integration which will lead the white majority to provide the resources we need to do an acceptable job of compensatory education. We recall that it was the threat of racial mixing that pushed the Southern schools of the 1940s and 1950s to equalize at least the educational facilities available to Negroes. We wish that the estimate of the nation's values in this area were wrong. But given the immorality of our destructive "defense" of autocracy and corruption masquerading as "democracy" in Vietnam, the inhumanity of our pursuit of that military victory, and the financial drain and waste involved in that military effort, the disadvantaged of our nation would be wise to expect little gratuitous assistance. Equalizing educational opportunity is not yet a priority goal in our country.

PART III
URBAN SCHOOL ORGANIZATION
AND CHANGE

COMMUNITY CONTROL
AND THE PUBLIC SCHOOLS —
PRACTICAL APPROACH FOR ACHIEVING
EQUAL EDUCATIONAL OPPORTUNITY:
A SOCIO-LEGAL PERSPECTIVE

Michael Flynn

Michael Flynn, "Community Control of the Public School-Practical Approach for Achieving Equal Educational Opportunity: A Socio-Legal Perspective," Suffolk University Law Review, Spring 1969, pp. 308-342.

COMMUNITY CONTROL AND THE PUBLIC SCHOOLS— PRACTICAL APPROACH FOR ACHIEVING EQUAL EDUCATIONAL OPPORTUNITY: A SOCIO-LEGAL PERSPECTIVE

Michael Flynn

> In these days, it is doubtful that any child may reasonably be expected to succeed in life if he is denied the opportunity of an education. Such an opportunity, where the state has undertaken to provide it, is a right which must be made available to all on equal terms.[1]

INTRODUCTION

Until recently, the struggle to achieve equal educational opportunity for Negro school children in the ghetto areas of our major cities, has been primarily concerned with the elimination of racial imbalance. Prior to the decision in *Brown v. Board of Education*,[2] the 1896 Supreme Court ruling in *Plessy v. Ferguson*[3] judicially sanctioned the existence of "separate but equal" public schools on the basis of "substantial equality."[4] *Brown* gave birth to a prolific amount of litigation which essentially focused on removing the effects of "separate but equal" by alleviating causes of racial imbalance through the busing of children, redrawing of residential zones, and selection of school sites.[5] Nearly all of the cases were indigenous to what was then considered the fundamental *Brown* objective—desegrega-

---

[1] Brown v. Bd. of Educ., 347 U.S. 483, 493 (1954). In essence, *Brown* held that segregation of Negro pupils solely on the basis of race was a denial of equal protection of the laws guaranteed by the fourteenth amendment. The Court stipulated that "the history of the Fourteenth Amendment is inclusive as to its intended effect on public education," and that "the question presented in these cases must be determined, not on the basis of conditions existing when the Fourteenth Amendment was adopted, but in the light of the full development of public education and its present place in American life throughout the Nation." *Id.* at 483.

[2] 347 U.S. 483.

[3] 163 U.S. 537 (1896).

[4] McLaurin v. Oklahoma State Regents, 339 U.S. 637 (1950); Sweat v. Painter, 339 U.S. 629 (1950); Missouri *ex rel.* Gains v. Canada, 305 U.S. 337 (1938); Pitts v. Bd. of Trustees, 84 F. Supp. 975 (E.D. Ark. 1949); Carter v. School Bd., 182 F.2d 531 (4th Cir. 1950).

[5] Northcross v. Bd. of Educ., 333 F.2d 661 (6th Cir. 1964); Bd. of Pub. Instruction v. Braxton, 326 F.2d 616 (5th Cir.), *cert. denied*, 377 U.S. 924 (1964); Clemons v. Bd. of Educ., 228 F.2d 853 (6th Cir.), *cert. denied*, 350 U.S. 1006 (1956); Jackson v. Pasadena City School Dist., 59 Cal. 2d 876, 382 P.2d 878, 31 Cal. Rptr. 606 (1963). *See also* Rousselot, *Achieving Equal Educational Opportunity for Negroes in the Public Schools of the North and West: The Emerging Role for Private Constitutional Litigation,* 35 GEO. WASH. L. REV. 898 (1967). *See also* MASS. GEN. LAWS ch. 71, § 37c (1965).

tion. In the past few years, new developments in the law have altered the original judicial perspective. Constitutional impermissibility of segregation continues to be the direct legal progeny of *Brown*, but new emphasis is on "the law of equal opportunities."[6]

Recent interpretations of the 1954 ruling have found an affirmative duty to integrate on the premise that equal protection under the Fourteenth Amendment requires equal educational opportunity.[7] The underlying theme of these cases is the constitutional obligation of the states to provide positive remedies for the resolution of educational inequality in ghetto public schools.[8] In this context, community control of inner city schools by Black parents has emerged with a dual function and possessed of a bilateral nature: (1) as an interim, self-rectifying educational remedy to accelerate integration; (2) as a right or privilege vested with constitutional powers. Thus far, however, the revolutionary nature of this concept has limited its application, reduced its effectiveness, and drained it of substance. As a social remedy, local control has received partial legislative sanction and judicial recognition; as a constitutional right, it has been overtly ignored.

This Note will explore the self executing applicability of equal protection to the inequalities that are causatively traceable to a centralized urban school system. As a standard of review, it will employ the principle of equal educational opportunity and analyze the evolutionary transformation of this doctrine in the desegregation cases. Specific application of the 1967 "tracking" and *de facto* segregation rulings in *Hobson v. Hansen*[9] will be made to the recent decentralization decision of a New York Federal District Court.[10] The Note will also discuss the exclusive control exercised by state legislatures over the public schools, and examine the possibility of federal judicial intervention. Finally, it will assess the remedial effect of local control and consider the broader implications of this concept on the educational and judicial process.

---

[6] United States v. Jefferson County Bd. of Educ., 372 F.2d 836 (5th Cir. 1966) interpreted *Brown* as making "equal educational opportunity" the constitutional equivalent of equal protection. It was expounded upon and applied as the standard of review in Hobson v. Hansen, 269 F. Supp. 401 (D.D.C. 1967). Currently, it is the view of a limited minority.

[7] *Id. See also* Barksdale v. Springfield School Comm., 237 F. Supp. 543 (D. Mass.), *vacated and remanded with direction to dismiss without prejudice*, 348 F.2d 261 (1st Cir. 1965).

[8] For support of the premise that *Brown* requires affirmative measures to provide equal educational opportunity, *see* Fiss, *Racial Imbalance in the Public Schools: The Constitutional Concepts*, 78 HARV. L. REV. 564, 570 (1965) and Wright, *Public School Desegregation: Legal Remedies For DeFacto Segregation*, 40 N.Y.U. L. REV. 285 (1965).

[9] 269 F. Supp. 401 (D.D.C. 1967).

[10] Oliver v. Donovan, No. 68-C-1034 (E.D.N.Y., Nov. 26, 1968).

Negro communities in many cities are demanding control, or at least a greater degree of participation, in the operation of neighborhood schools.[11] Parents of ghetto school pupils want the right to superintend teacher selection, qualification, tenure, methods and curriculum. More importantly, they seek a decentralization of authority and a voice in the allocation of state controlled funds. Their quest has brought them into conflict with the United Federation of Teachers,[12] central boards of education and state legislatures and constitutions.[13]

Three recent state and federal court decisions as well as the enactment of a "decentralization" statute, are the result of a two year campaign by Negro parents in New York to provide a community oriented approach to education problems in the city generally, and the ghetto specifically.[14]

The first test of local control occurred in 1966 when a group of East Harlem parents simply demanded removal of a white principal, and the institution of Black history and literature courses. This attempted usurpation of a power legislatively vested in the City's Central Board of Education assumed official respectability when the Ford Foundation, under McGeorge Bundy, declared that it would finance planning for three decentralized "demonstration districts."[15] In this climate, the Board of Education became committed to a policy of decentralization which resulted in the immediate enactment of Chapter 484 of the Laws of 1967,[16] and the

---

[11] In New York's Ocean Hill-Brownsville District, parents set up an experimental local control project. In Boston's Roxbury ghetto at least two schools are being run by local control groups. Parents in Washington's Adams Morgan area selected their own fifteen member Community School Council. See Roberts, *The Battle for Urban Schools*, SATURDAY REVIEW, Nov. 16, 1968, at 97; NEWSWEEK, Oct. 28, 1968, at 84.

[12] *See* N.Y. Times, Sept. 9, 1968, at 1, col. 8.

[13] *See* N.Y. Times, Nov. 8, 1967, at 1, col. 1; *Id.*, Nov. 12, 1967, at 1, col. 2; *Id.*, Jan. 5, 1968, at 1, col. 1; *Id.*, April 11, 1968, at 1, col. 6. *See also* Boston Globe, Sept. 4, 1968, at 1, cols. 5 & 6.

[14] Although the concept of community control has currently emerged in many cities due to pressures from the ghetto, which have caused the above stated controversies, the decision to decentralize in New York has a legislative history traceable to other factors, including fiscal considerations. *See, e.g.*, MAYOR'S ADVISORY PANEL ON DECENTRALIZATION OF THE NEW YORK CITY SCHOOLS, RECONNECTION FOR LEARNING: A COMMUNITY SCHOOL SYSTEM FOR NEW YORK CITY at 1 (1967) (hereinafter cited as the BUNDY REPORT). In addition, as early as 1962, ch. 615, § 4 of the New York Session Laws, required the city board of education to submit a plan "for securing the most effective possible participation of the people of the city of New York in the affairs of the city school system, through the development of local school boards."

[15] Roberts, *supra* note 11, at 98.

[16] This statute, ch. 484, (1967) N.Y. Acts 495 provides in part:
Section 1. Legislative findings. Increased community awareness in the educational process is essential to the furtherance of educational innovation and excellence in the public school system within the city of New York. The legislature hereby finds and declares that the creation of educational policy units within the city school district

eventual enactment of Chapter 568 of the Laws of 1968.[17] The former directed the Mayor of New York to prepare a program for decentralization and the latter put a revised plan into limited effect.

Partial legislative submission to the community demands for local self-determination had as its stimulant the awakening realization that ghetto schools are constitutionally deficient in providing equal educational opportunity.[18] Low student performance among disadvantaged minorities, specifically the Negro, could be traced to a number of factors, ranging from high pupil and teacher absenteeism, to the physically overcrowded, run-down and understaffed conditions of the ghetto school. In this context, denial of equal opportunity became readily apparent when compared to the white suburban, and white city schools.

B. *The Social Background*

Urban education in the United States, specifically in the ghetto, stands in stark contrast to that in smaller, more prosperous, locally governed communities. In essence, America has developed a dual system of public education; one half consists of the suburban, middle class white, while the other includes mostly urban, lower class Negroes.[19] The allocation of resources illustrates this discrepancy:

> The contrast in money available to the schools in a wealthy suburb and to the schools in a large city jolts one's notions of the meaning of equality of opportunity. The pedagogic tasks which confront the teachers in the slum schools are far more difficult than those which their colleagues in the wealthy suburbs face. Yet the expenditure per pupil in the wealthy suburban school is as high as $1000 per year. The expenditure in the big city school is less than half that amount.[20]

---

of the city of New York for the formulation of educational policy for the public schools within such district will afford members of the community an opportunity to take a more active and meaningful role in the development of educational policy closely related to the diverse needs and aspirations of the community.

Section 2. The mayor of the city of New York shall prepare a comprehensive study and report and formulate a plan for the creation and development of educational policy and administrative units, within the city school district of the city of New York with *adequate authority* to foster greater community initiative and participation in the development of educational policy for the public schools within such district and to achieve greater flexibility in the administration of such schools. . . . (Emphasis supplied.)

[17] Ch. 568, (1968) N.Y. Acts 1163, *as amended*, N.Y. EDUC. LAW § 2564 (McKinney 1968). A partial text of § 2564 is given at p. 321 of this Note.

[18] This is the contention of local control proponents in Ocean Hill-Brownsville. Ch. 568, (1968) N.Y. Acts 499 provides: . . .

[t]he need for adjusting the school structure in the city of New York to a more effective response to the *present urban educational challenge* requires the development of systems to insure a community oriented approach to this challenge. . . . It is appropriate therefore that a detailed program for decentralization be formulated by the Board of Education of the City of New York against the *background of urban educational problems in the city of New York.* (Emphasis supplied.)

[19] *See* SCHRAG, VILLAGE SCHOOL DOWNTOWN 154 (1967).

[20] J. CONANT, SLUMS AND SUBURBS 2-3 (1961). SCHRAG, *supra* note 19, at 182, corre-

The Willis Harrington Report[21] to the Massachusetts legislature in 1965 makes an accurate analysis tracing the economic development of this condition. Traditionally, the education bill for a local district was paid for by local property taxes. Higher land values and decreased costs for social disorders enabled the affluent, suburban communities to give educational expenditures higher priority in the town budget. Recognizing the need for educational excellence, they invested greater sums of money because they could afford to spend it. Large cities struggled along on "the verge of poverty with very high and costly levels of social calamity."[22] They did not possess enough money for the maintenance of proper educational facilities, and generally, the Black community was the first to be deprived. The resulting discrepancy in the two systems increased as sons of the rich enjoyed the fruits of educational opportunity and children of the poor forsook education to pursue the struggle for existence.[23]

Overriding the economic problems, and contributing to them, is the question of centralization. It is not difficult to uncover books, articles and reports denouncing the labyrinthian bureaucracy which characterizes the large urban school systems. "As most big city schools now operate, the employees are not directly responsible to the people. . . . There are many layers of authority, but it is impossible to pin down just where the responsibility lies."[24] At the center are boards of education which generally are too removed from the neighborhoods to cope with local problems, and too musclebound with numerous administrative employees to act with efficiency.[25] "Decisions made in the central office are remote from the

---

lates improper allocation of funds with the bureaucratic system and lack of parental involvement:

> Not enough money has been allocated, and what has been allocated often went to the wrong people through the wrong channels. While superintendents and politicians (who are collecting all the money) warn of federal control, the real danger is that the money will make no difference at all, that it will merely reinforce the existing hierarchies and the machines that are creating the problems in the first place. *The schools do not require aid nearly as much as do children and education, and until far greater influence is exercised by the parents and those most beholden to public education, most of the money will make no impact at all.* (Emphasis supplied.)

[21] REPORT OF THE SPECIAL COMMISSION ESTABLISHED TO MAKE AN INVESTIGATION AND STUDY RELATIVE TO IMPROVING AND EXTENDING EDUCATIONAL FACILITIES IN THE COMMONWEALTH (1965) (hereinafter cited as THE WILLIS HARRINGTON REPORT).

[22] *Id.* at 57.

[23] *Id.* at 55-56:

> These towns, then could invest heavily in education, and they did because their citizens knew from their own experience how rich were the returns of good education. The educational climate in such communities, the educational expectations of their residents as parents, the educational investments by their taxpayers and educators, all combined to produce, quite systematically, children who continued their own educations, prospered, and moved into communities like those they had come from. . . . *The operation of this locally controlled and inspired circle of education, society and economics was responsible in large part for the Commonwealth's eminence.* (Emphasis supplied.)

[24] Roberts, *supra* note 11, at 101.

[25] New York has 3,000 officials in its administration alone. It has a 1.4 billion

many diverse neighborhoods that constitute the city and may or may not make sense in a particular school. . . . [T]his procedure tends to isolate the community from what goes on in the school."[26]

The size and impersonality of the urban system tends to decrease parental involvement in school affairs.[27] This is especially true in the ghetto areas where participation by parents in school affairs is so negligble that there is virtually no pressure on the child to learn. In effect, it is here that the school system of the city differs from that in the suburb. School boards in suburban communities are more responsive to the people and, consequently, greater reciprocity of action exists between them. Total community involvement is lacking in the ghetto due to non-access and a failure of communication between school committee and parents. The Report of the National Advisory Commission on Civil Disorders states that "[e]xpansion of opportunities for community and parental participation in the school system is essential to the successful functioning of the inner city schools."[28]

Politics, however, is a critical factor preventing dispersal of authority and decentralization of urban schools. As one commentator states, "Boston is probably no more or less typical of the situation of urban education than any other metropolis. . . . In Boston, for better or worse, all school issues are political issues. . . . [E]verything is political."[29] Decentralization involves disruption of the political status quo and transfer of authority from those who now possess it. The educational establishment, like most institutions, has become captive to vested interests. The detrimental effects of a centralized political bureaucracy on the ghetto are stressed throughout the United States Riot Commission Report. It states:

---

dollar school budget, 1,100,000 students, 57,000 teachers and 3,700 principals and other administrators, all controlled by the central board of education, which "has become synonomous with frustration." NEWSWEEK, *supra* note 11, at 84. For statistics, *see* Roberts, *supra* note 11, at 97.

[26] CONANT, *supra* note 20, at 69.

[27] Boston, for example, has no parents organization, other than the Home and School Association which, under its constitution is forbidden to attack the schools and therefore is virtually ineffective. *See* SCHRAG, *supra* note 19, at 139.

[28] REPORT OF THE NATIONAL ADVISORY COMMISSION ON CIVIL DISORDERS 440 (1968) (hereinafter cited as U.S. RIOT COMMISSION REPORT). The report states:

Teachers of the poor rarely live in the community where they work and sometimes have little sympathy for the life styles of their students. Moreover, the growth and complexity of the administration of large urban school systems has compromised the accountability of the local schools to the communities which they serve, and reduced the ability of parents to influence decisions affecting the education of their children. Ghetto schools often appear to be unresponsive to the community, communication has broken down, and parents are distrustful of officials responsible for formulating educational policy.

The consequences for the education of students attending these schools are serious. Parental hostility to the schools is reflected in the attitudes of their children. Since the needs and concerns of the ghetto community are rarely reflected in educational policy formulated on a city-wide basis, the schools are often seen by ghetto youth as being irrelevant. *Id.* at 436.

[29] SCHRAG, *supra* note 19, at 3.

First, there is a widening gulf in communications between local government and the residents of the erupting ghettos of the city. As a result, ghetto residents develop a profound sense of isolation and alienation from the processes and programs of government. This lack of communication exists for all residents in our larger cities; it is, however, far more difficult to overcome for low income, less educated citizens who are disproportionately supported by and dependent upon programs administered by agencies of local government. Consequently, they are more often subject to real or imagined official misconduct ranging from abrasive contacts with public officials to arbitrary administrative actions.[30]

All the foregoing political, social, and economic considerations retard urban education. Moreover, ghetto environment and its interaction with the schools reinforces the causative relationship between the type of schools found in the ghetto and the type of pupil it produces. The Coleman Report[31] and the U.S. Civil Rights Commission Report[32] emphasize the depressant effect of socio-economic conditions in the inner city and support the conclusion that "improvement in school quality will make the most difference in achievement."[33] Reconstruction of a child's social and intellectual environment necessarily involves his parents and his teachers. In this regard, parental control over the institutions that shape the lives of their children should provide an additional incentive in the development of essential literary skills by both parent and child, as well as yield a productive educational conduit between the home and the school.

C. *The Community Control Solution*

Certainly, there is no panacea which can overcome all the factors contributing to the poor quality of education in ghetto schools. Often it is difficult to ascertain specific causes of particular problems. In the past, integration has been considered the ultimate solution in achieving equality between the races. "Community control" represents a departure from this view, at least in so far as it offers more immediate and concrete solutions to local problems. Creation of decentralized school boards, operated by parents, may have a greater chance of success than those methods used in the past, if given the benefits of certain aid programs, such as compensatory education. A few studies have formulated proposals through which a locally controlled system could be implemented.

The plan for the reorganization of the New York City School System—

---

[30] U.S. Riot Commission Report, *supra* note 28, at 284; *see also Id.* at 144, 279-99. *See also infra* notes 79, 80, 82.

[31] U.S. Office Of Education, Equality Of Educational Opportunity (1966) (hereinafter cited as the Coleman Report).

[32] 1 U.S. Commission On Civil Rights, Racial Isolation Of The Public Schools (1967).

[33] Coleman Report, *supra* note 31, at 22.

The Bundy Report[34]—is perhaps the most comprehensive plan to date. The fact that it proposed extensive and sweeping changes in the educational hierarchy in New York City led to its rejection by the legislature, but it did have the beneficial effect of initiating a temporary and limited decentralization plan. Essentially, the Bundy Report proposed legislation designed to shift the authority from the present Central Board of Education to thirty community school districts, each headed by an eleven member school board. The parents of children in the schools would name six of the members and the mayor would assign five others. The powers of the local board would include: selection of district supervisors, principals and other teaching staff, determination of curricula, allocation of funds and formulation of budgets. The Central Board would retain the power to tax, the responsibility for distributing a portion of the budget, and the responsibility to uphold minimum state education standards. The primary objective of the plan was to create in New York a school system "that in imagination, flexibility and innovation could match or surpass the most dynamic suburban or small-city school district in the country."[35]

The Willis Harrington Report proposed many changes in the Massachusetts school system after intensive study revealed that communities with a great deal of local control were eminently superior to those without it. Recognizing the vast discrepancy in educational standards in different parts of the Commonwealth, the report states:

> Elementary and secondary schooling in Massachusetts is *municipally rather than educationally diversified. This condition results in thoroughgoing lack of equality of educational opportunity* for the one million individuals of compulsory school age in the Commonwealth today. The sum total of this disparity presents, in a period of unsurpassed affluence, an unnecessary modern-day disaster and a direct challenge to the state and every one of her people. This is not to say that there are not many examples of excellent teaching, good schools, and fine students within our educational system. On occasion *local independence has been used to produce a richness of educational opportunity without a conformity to mediocrity.* (Emphasis supplied).[36]

---

34 BUNDY REPORT, *supra* note 14. For an explanation of this report, *see* Hechinger, *Decentralization: The Whys*, N.Y. Times, Nov. 12, 1967, § 4, at 9, col. 4:

Decentralization, as proposed by the Bundy Panel, is an effort at both racial change and pacification of a strife-torn city and school system. It aims essentially at the following: (1) To recreate within the huge city some of the devices of the small town or suburb—quasi-independent local school boards . . . (2) To create a sense of competition, both for personnel and for effective instruction . . . (3) To give the local districts the chance to pick their own educational leadership—still within the confines of professional certification or, if persons from outside the education fields are chosen, with approval by the education authorities . . . (4) To defuse the present guerilla warfare by giving elected parents—and only parents, not outside agitators—the kind of powers and responsibilities normally enjoyed by suburban school board members. At least part of the idea is to deprive the local community of the alibi that 'they' are not educating 'our children.'

35 Quote by Mayor Lindsay, N.Y. Times, Nov. 8, 1967, at 94, col. 1.

36 THE WILLIS HARRINGTON REPORT, *supra* note 21, at 59.

The report found enormous variations in student IQ as well as curriculum materials, course offerings, textbooks, libraries, audio-visual aids, and general educational services.[37] To counteract this trend, it made many and varied recommendations: that the "Department of Public School Education should be reorganized into a vital and useful adjunct to local schools;"[38] that special consideration be given large cities like Boston, in the distribution of state funds;[39] that districts "develop programs which are especially planned to meet the specific needs of children enrolled in schools in disadvantaged areas."[40] In essence, the impact of the entire study reinforces the need to transfer greater control to smaller units and to place in their hands compensatory programs designed to meet local problems.[41]

The Willis Harrington Report did not propose the sweeping local administrative changes suggested by the Bundy Report, but the pervasive similarity of their basic concepts was prodigious. The dominant theme of both was the effectiveness of community involvement in the expansion of educational opportunity. To date, recognition of its remedial effect, and the authority needed for its implementation have not corresponded. The fundamental assumption that educational policy-making resides in the legislature may be an inherent obstacle to significant local control legislation. Transfer of public school control to ghetto parents appears to be repugnant to an educational structure politically dominated by a majority controlled legislature.

D. *The Legal Framework of the Public School*

The body of law governing education in the United States consists essentially of state statutes regulating the rights and duties of both parents and state. Although the Federal Constitution contains no direct provisions or specific references concerning education, the "welfare clause" of Article I, § 8[42] may be construed as implicitly authorizing the government to participate in educational affairs. However, it is the Tenth[43] and Four-

---

37 *Id.* at 61-89.

38 *Id.* at 203.

39 *Id.* at 584.

40 *Id.* at 570.

41 *Id.* at 545: "Local districts should be encouraged to study their present patterns and the possible alternatives and to decide what is best for themselves." For a thorough treatment of the concept of community involvement in politics, economics and education, *see* U.S. RIOT COMMISSION REPORT, *supra* note 28.

42 "The Congress shall have power to lay and collect taxes, duties, imposts and excises to pay the debts for the common defense and general welfare of the United States." U.S. CONST. art. I, § 8.

43 "Powers not delegated to the United States by the Constitution, nor prohibited by it to the state, are reserved to the states respectively, or to the people." U.S. CONST. amend. X.

teenth Amendments[44] which have the greatest constitutional impact. The former delegates to the state the authority to establish school systems, and the latter insures equal educational opportunity to all children in whatever state they reside, regardless of race or color.[45]

State constitutions and legislatures are the primary sources of authority in the establishment, support and control of the public school. The legislatures possess plenary authority over all educational matters within state and Federal Constitutional limits.[46] Although they are the ultimate decision makers, a good portion of the responsibility of policy-making, curriculum control and apportionment of funds is delegated to state boards of education.[47] The following excerpt from Madeline Remmlein's treatise on school law succinctly states the relationship between the legislature and the board of education:

> In any phase of school management wherein the state board of education has been given powers of operation, the rules and regulations of the state board have the force and effect of law. However, being a creature of the legislature in most states, the state board has only the powers delegated to it or implied in the delegated powers. In the states where the state board is created by constitutional provision, its constitutional powers are very general, and in specific instances it depends upon the legislature for its authority to act. In either case, if the state board acts outside its delegated or implied power, the rule or regulation is void. There is, however, a presumption of authority, and until challenged in court, all rules and regulations of the state board are presumed to be valid and have effectiveness as enforceable as a statute enacted by the legislature.[48]

Since state legislatures and boards of education cannot effectively operate an entire public school system, local school districts and school boards possess a measure of administrative autonomy. A school district differs from a school board in that the former "is a territorial subdivision of the state in which the state function of education is performed; whereas, 'the school board' is an agency, composed of citizens, representing the territorial subdivision of the state in performing essentially the same state

---

44 "No state shall make or enforce any law which shall abridge the privileges or immunities of citizens of the United States; nor shall any state deprive any person of life, liberty or property without due process of law, nor deny to any person within its jurisdiction the equal protection of the laws." U.S. CONST. amend XIV.

45 347 U.S. 483.

46 Bd. of Educ. v. State Bd. of Educ., 116 Ohio App. 515, 189 N.E.2d 81 (1962). "When the General Assembly speaks on matters concerning education it is exercising *plenary* power and its action is subject only to the limitations contained in the Constitution." *Id*. at 518, 189 N.E.2d at 83-84.

47 *See, e.g.*, MASS. GEN. LAWS ch. 15, § 16 (1965), outlining the functions of a state board of education.

48 BOLMEIR, THE SCHOOL IN THE LEGAL STRUCTURE 92 (1968), citing from REMMLEIN, SCHOOL LAW 3 (1950).

function."[49] Neither of these entities possess any common law powers because they are solely the creation of the legislature.[50] School boards are generally considered "quasi corporations" or agencies of the state and suits against them are suits against the state and its property.[51] Their members, as individuals, have no more authority than any other citizen, and to be legally effective they must be assembled and act as a board.[52] Although there has been a great deal of litigation over the authority of school boards, it must be kept in mind that this authority is always subject to legislative will. Generally, the courts have held that school boards have the power to select school sites,[53] control property,[54] manage school funds,[55] prescribe standards for teacher qualification,[56] determine curricula,[57] and exercise a reasonable degree of discretionary authority over pupils.[58]

These areas basically represent the type and degree of control sought by Negro communities in the inner city. However, an effective transition of such control within the existing legal framework is confronted with two basic obstacles: (1) municipal rather than educational diversification of school districts;[59] (2) legislative centralization of school authority. City boards of education are expected to administer to multiple segments of the population as efficiently as small, suburban boards administer to

---

[49] BOLMEIR, *supra* note 48, at 117.

[50] Languis v. DeBoer, 181 Neb. 32, 146 N.W.2d 750 (1966). "[T]he state is supreme in the creation and control of school districts and may, if it thinks proper, modify or withdraw any of their powers or destroy such school districts without the consent of the legal voters or even over their protests." *Id.* at 32, 146 N.W.2d at 751.

[51] State *ex rel.* Rogers v. Bd. of Educ., 125 W. Va. 579, 25 S.E.2d 537 (1943).

[52] State v. Consolidated School District No. 3, 281 S.W.2d 511 (Mo. 1955); Wayman v. Bd. of Educ., 5 Ohio St. 2d 248, 215 N.E.2d 394 (1966).

[53] Smith v. City Bd. of Educ., 272 Ala. 227, 130 So.2d 29 (1961).

[54] Demers v. Collins, 98 R.I. 312, 201 A.2d 477 (1964).

[55] Bd. of Educ. v. Town of Ellington, 151 Conn. 1, 193 A.2d 466 (1963). *See generally* BOLMIER, *supra* note 48, at 148-52.

[56] Tripp v. Bd. of Examiners of City of New York, 44 Misc. 2d 1026, 255 N.Y.S.2d 526 (1964). But, where statutes vest sole authority in the state board to determine the qualifications of teachers, the local school board is without power to prescribe qualifications for teachers. Coleman v. School Bd., Dist. of Rochester, 87 N.H. 465, 183 A. 586 (1936).

[57] *See* BOLMIER, *supra* note 48, at 227.
Most of the statutes pertaining to curricula and its administration are rather general—as they should be—with delegated authority to local boards or professional personnel to determine the specifics. The high degree of local autonomy in this respect should not be construed as a surrender of state authority over the curricula or other school matters. . . .

[58] Discretionary authority of a school board over pupils has, of course, been the subject of much litigation. The area *per se* is beyond the scope of this Note and shall be discussed only as it relates to the community control objective of giving ghetto parents the same degree of authority and participation in their local schools, as have many middle and upper class suburban communities.

[59] *See* THE WILLIS HARRINGTON REPORT, *supra* note 21, at 49.

lesser numbers. In addition, the citizens of middle and upper class suburbs generally have mutual interests and seek similar goals, whereas the varying ethnic segments of a city's populace may, and usually do, have conflicting political, social and economic interests. If sufficient control of a city's central board is vested in any one group, the legal structure of the entire system may be used as a device to protect their interests. Community control may provide an effective remedy to this condition through an adequate dispersal of authority. As has been observed, legislative sanction for this proposition is a fundamental necessity. The following two "community control" decisions illustrate this fact.

1. *Council of Super. Ass'n of Pub. Sch. v. Board of Ed.*[60]

The Board of Education of New York City pursuant to section 2554, subdivision 2 of the Education Law[61] appointed a community representative to the newly created position of "administrator"[62] of the Ocean Hill-Brownsville Decentralization Project. It also originated the position of "Demonstration Elementary School Principal"[63] and assigned three persons, nominated by an elected governing board of the project area, to three separate schools in this new capacity. The Board of Education made the appointments without qualifying the nominees as principals according to the experience and professional requirements of the City of New York,[64] and without regard to an eligibility list prepared by the Board of Examiners pursuant to the civil service provisions of the New York

---

[60] 56 Misc. 2d 32, 288 N.Y.S.2d 135 (1968). As far as known to this writer, this is the first case directly involving a community control issue.

[61] N.Y. EDUC. LAW § 2554(2) (McKinney 1962), vests the board of education with the power to:

> create . . . such positions . . . as, in its judgment, may be necessary for the proper and efficient administration of its work; to appoint . . . employees and other persons or experts in educational, social or recreational work in the business management or direction of its affairs as said board shall determine necessary for the efficient management of the schools and other educational, social, recreational and business activities. . . .

[62] The administrator of Ocean Hill-Brownsville, is the much publicized Rhody McCoy, who acts as a liaison between the local board of the project area and the board of education.

[63] Allegedly, a "demonstration school principal" was a novel position not directly related to the ordinary office of "school principal." On this basis, the board of education made the appointments pursuant to N.Y. EDUC. LAW § 2554(2) (McKinney 1962).

[64] The experience requirements for a principal of an elementary school in the city of New York are five years of teaching, supplemented by three years of supervising experience, all under appointment; three years of experience must have been in elementary schools or junior high schools. In addition to the experience requirements there are professional requirements such as possession of a baccalaureate, thirty semester hours of graduate work and professional courses. . . . Council of Super. Ass'n of Public Schools v. Bd. of Educ., 56 Misc. 2d at 38, 288 N.Y.S.2d at 142. None of the appointees so qualified, but they were given an examination designed to test their attitudes toward children in disadvantaged areas.

Constitution,[65] and section 2573 of the Education Law.[66] The licensed personnel eligible for appointments as principals sought to restrain the Board of Education from making the appointments. In an opinion, prefaced with a summary of the decentralization and community control campaign taking place in New York City at the time, the New York Supreme Court held: (1) that the position of "administrator" was a "novel creation" that "in no way impugns the dignity of any law intended to maintain the strength of the merit system . . . nor . . . [does the position] do violence to any law enacted for the protection of the educational system. . . .";[67] and (2) that since the position of the "demonstration school principal" was in no way different from that of the ordinary elementary school principal, these appointments were made in violation of the New York Constitution and Education Law regarding eligibility and civil service promotions.

The diverse results on the two basic issues in this case made it both a success and a setback for advocates of local control. Judicial recognition of a new and official position, "administrator," gave the parents a spokesman where he could effectively convey the educational needs and aspirations of the community to the Board of Education; but the court's revocation of the "demonstration school principal" appointments defeated their basic demand for an authoritative voice in the selection of teachers.

Primarily, the community desired "unlimited domination over school personnel with the right of transfer, dismissal, appointment and assignment without regard to examinations, merit system or eligibility lists."[68] Their argument was premised on the fact that effective local control could only operate apart from the bureaucratic laws which served to perpetuate the present, nonfunctional system; the purpose of the decentralization project was to experiment in adaptation and modification of the existing educational hierarchy. The court rebuked this contention stating:

> The stress by the Board of Education that the schools are in an experimental stage does not alter in any manner the fact that the appointments were illegal. I cannot see why there cannot be experimentation with those on the eligible list who have already demonstrated their training, experience and devotion to educational principles.[69]

---

[65] N.Y. CONST. art. V, § 6 provides:

"Appointments and promotions in the civil service of the state and all of the civil divisions, thereof, . . . shall be made according to merit and fitness to be ascertained, as far as practicable, by examinations which, so far as practicable, shall be competitive.

[66] N.Y. EDUC. LAW § 2573 (McKinney 1953) provides that recommendations for appointment shall be from the first three persons on an appropriate eligible list prepared by the Board of Examiners. The appointees were not on it.

[67] Council of Super. Ass'n of Public Schools v. Bd. of Educ., 56 Misc. 2d at 37, 288 N.Y.S.2d at 141 (1968).

[68] Id. at 34, 288 N.Y.S.2d at 138.

[69] Id. at 40, 288 N.Y.S.2d at 143.

Despite this denial, community control proponents can find some redemption by way of judicial concession to the necessity of parental involvement in local schools. The court concluded as a matter of fact, *"that in certain communities, specifically disadvantaged areas, the performance of pupils in those schools was far below the level of pupils in other communities and that there was a definite correlation between the schools' performance and parents' involvement in the subject schools."*[70] (Emphasis supplied).

With this fact finding, the court placed itself in a rather contradictory but traditional position. It recognized the need and educational effectiveness of local control, but denied the power and authority to employ it, even though a rational alternative on which to find such power did exist. Stress on the "experimental" character of the decentralization project might have led to a liberal construction of section 2554, subdivision 2 of the Education Law, thus bringing the "demonstration school principals" within its provisions. The exercise of judicial restraint reflects the traditional perspective of the courts to leave the formulation and interpretation of educational policies entirely in the hands of the legislature. In this case there was a rational basis on which to intervene. The court in the following case did not possess a similar alternative.

2. *Ocean Hill-Brownsville Gov. Bd. v. Board of Ed.*[71]

The aforementioned decentralization statute, section 2564 of the Education Law,[72] essentially gave the Board of Education the power to create local school districts; delegate its powers, functions and obligations to the local districts; and retain the power "to remove at its pleasure" a local school board in any such district. The law became effective when the powers of the local boards were advisory only, and after the local "administrator" (referred to the case above) had removed a number of teachers in the district from their teaching assignments.[73] The Board of

---

[70] *Id.* at 34, 288 N.Y.S.2d at 138.

[71] — Misc. 2d —, 294 N.Y.S.2d 134 (1968).

[72] N.Y. Educ. Law § 2564 (McKinney 1968) provides in part:

1. The board of education . . . shall divide the city school district into such number of local school board districts as such board in its discretion may determine. The board of education may from time to time alter the boundaries of such districts, consolidate two or more districts as it shall consider necessary. . . .

2. Such board of education, upon the establishment of such local school board districts, shall have the power to appoint, or provide for the election of, and remove at its pleasure, a local school board for each local school board district, which shall consist of such number of members as the board shall determine from time to time.

3. The board of education, with the approval of the regents, shall have the power to delegate to such local school boards, any or all of its functions, powers, obligations and duties in connection with the operation of the schools and programs under its jurisdiction, and may modify or rescind any function, power, obligation and duty so delegated.

[73] The chronology of events is as follows:

April 19, 1967—Board of Education became committed to a policy of decentralization.

Education ordered the reinstatement of these teachers, the local district refused, and the Board suspended the local governing board for thirty days. The members petitioned the court for (a) immediate termination of the suspension and (b) to restrain the Board of Education from interfering with local decision making. The Supreme Court, Appellate Division, held that the Board of Education possessed the statutory authority "to remove at its pleasure" a local school board whether elected or appointed, and without notice, charges, nor opportunity to be heard.[74]

Petitioners contended that the statute should not be construed to give the Board of Education the power "to remove at its pleasure" an "elected body." Rejecting this contention, the court said that their status as an elected body was "subject to serious doubt,"[75] and that the statute made no exception for an "elected" local board as distinguished from an appointed one. It reasoned that since the legislative intent was framed in language sufficiently plain and clear, the court could not "hold that the legislature had an intention other than that which the language of the statute imports."[76]

In contrast to the previous case, the explicit language of section 2564 left no latitude for judicial construction. The statute clearly intended that the delegation of certain powers to the local board, and the exercise thereof, be "subject to the control, supervision, and directives of the Board of Education. . . ."[77] As the court stated, "the Board of Education and its Superintendent are, and were intended to be, paramount and superior. No local school board, or its administrator, is, or was intended to be, autonomous."[78]

The phrase "remove at its pleasure" concisely points out the legislative compromise made to proponents of local control and the existing educational establishment. Section 2564 fulfilled the community's objective of decentralization, but in form only. The apparent transfer of control from the Board of Education to local districts was illusory in fact. Important

---

April 24, 1967—Chapter 484 of the Laws of 1967 was enacted directing formulation of a decentralization plan.

August 3, 1967—Local election financed by the Ford Foundation selects local board.

August 21, 1967—Local project developed by the board of education.

May 9, 1968—The "Administrator" removed a number of teachers from the Ocean Hill-Brownsville District.

June 5, 1968—Section 2564 of the Education Law enacted.

October 6, 1968—Local Board suspended for second time.

October 17, 1968—Board of Regents approve Section 2564.

October 24, 1968—This decision.

[74] Ocean Hill v. Bd. of Educ., — Misc. 2d at —, 294 N.Y.S.2d at 138 (1968).

[75] Of the eighteen members of the local board, only seven were "elected," and they were not elected pursuant to any statute. — Misc. 2d at —, 294 N.Y.S.2d at 138.

[76] Id.

[77] Id. at —, 294 N.Y.S.2d at 139.

[78] Id.

powers and functions such as teacher selection, allocation of funds and curriculum determination remained where they always existed—in the central educational bureaucracy. The Negro community's attempt at self-determination met the resistance it always met, and was confronted with the same result. The impact of this decision was similar to that of *Super. Ass'n v. Board of Ed.*; community control continued to be a recognized remedy for the cure of various educational ills, but lack of access to the medicine cabinet prevented its effectiveness.

Statutory interpretation by each of the above courts demonstrates the necessity of obtaining legislative approval for achieving effective decentralization. However, the local educational needs of disadvantaged minorities are generally subject to a majority oriented legislature representative of majority interests.[79] Legislative centralization of school authority in a central board operates as a stimulant to those with a strong political and economic base but as a depressant to those without one.[80] Political alienation of the Negro is exacerbrated by his economic isolation. Decentralization proposes a dispersal of political-educational authority and a corresponding distribution of the attendant benefits.[81]

The U.S. Riot Commission Report compares the Negro political experience in this country with that of other immigrant minorities. It traces the lack of adequate Black representation to the "centralized political machines" that dominated the ghetto areas during their development. In contrast, the "political machines" were decentralized when the earlier immigrants settled, "which gave them economic advantages in exchange for political support."[82] As government became more complex,

---

[79] U.S. RIOT COMMISSION REPORT, *supra* note 28, at 145 states:

The political structure was a source of grievance in almost all of the cities and was one of the most serious complaints in several. *There were significant grievances concerning the lack of adequate representation of Negroes in the political structure*, the failure of local political structures to respond to legitimate complaints and the absence or obscurity of official grievance channels. . . . (Emphasis supplied).

[80] *Id.* at 205:

Finally, many Negroes have come to believe that they are being exploited politically and economically by the white "power structure." Negroes, like people in poverty everywhere, in fact lack the channels of communication, influence and appeal that traditionally have been available to ethnic minorities within the city. . . . (those unburdened by color).

[81] For a compendious and specific illustration of this fact *see* Epstein, *The Battle of Ocean Hill*, XI NEW YORK REVIEW, Nov. 21, 1968, No. 9. He states at 4:

To dispense with this nonsense is what decentralization is about. So much of the uproar against it arises from the bureaucrat who will be dispensed with as well. But decentralization also means community control, and community control means that blacks and Puerto Ricans will control millions of dollars with which to hire not only teachers but the contractors and the architects, the plumbers and electricians, to say nothing of the custodians and the teamsters, who have, up to now, been able to make their favored arrangements with the central bureaucracy. This is what has brought the city's Central Labor Council into the struggle and this is why the UFT has chosen to close the city's schools to their million students in order to crush an experimental district which, for its own part, shows every sign of succeeding.

[82] U.S. RIOT COMMISSION REPORT, *supra* note 28, at 279. It further states:

bureaucratic and impersonal, the gulf between ghetto residents and·public officials widened, and local educational needs suffered as a result.

The role of the judiciary in responding to educational problems in the ghetto is a difficult one. Traditional control of public schools by the legislature and the traditional "one man-one vote" concept of representation present a united front to constitutional intervention. In an effort to increase Black political power, challenges have been made to at-large voting systems that pursue statutory schemes which undermine the strength of the Black vote.[83] Discriminatory voting systems, however, need not be the *cause celebre* in an attempt to invoke constitutional protection.

The evolutionary interpretation of the Fourteenth Amendment as a self-executing[84] mandate for equal educational opportunity raises a permissible inference that centralization of educational authority which either causes or preserves inequality in ghetto schools may be a denial of equal protection. Re-analysis of the *Brown* decision in light of the "law of equal opportunities" suggests the possibility that federal courts will initiate community control as an interim remedy in. the pursuit of equal and integrated schools. Moreover, the United States Supreme Court has enunciated the right of parents to educate their children free from undue state control. Juxtaposition of the right to equal educational opportunity and the parental right to educate theoretically provides a substantial constitutional base for according community control the status of a right or privilege.[85]

[W]ard-level grievance machinery, as well as personal representation, enable the immigrant to make his voice heard and his power felt. Since the local political organizations exercised considerable influence over public building in the cities, they provided employment in construction jobs for their immigrant voters. Ethnic groups often dominated one or more of the municipal services . . . even public education. . . . By the time the Negroes arrived, the situation had altered dramatically.

[83] "Voting Power" cases ordering abolition of at large systems are: Simms v. Baggett, 247 F. Supp. 96 (M.D. Ala. 1965); Smith v. Paris, 257 F. Supp. 901 (M.D. Ala. 1966). Supreme Court decisions turning down challenges to at-large systems are: Fortson v. Dorsey, 379 U.S. 433 (1965); Burns v. Richardson, 384 U.S. 73 (1966). But the following dictum from *Fortson* limited validation of an at-large voting system:

Our opinion is not to be understood to say that in all circumstances such a system as Georgia has will comport with the dictates of the Equal Protection Clause. It might well be that, *designedly or otherwise*, a multi-member constituency apportionment scheme, under the circumstances of a particular case, would operate *to minimize or cancel out the voting strength of racial or political elements of the voting population*. When this is demonstrated it will be time enough to consider whether the system still passes constitutional muster. (Emphasis supplied.) 379 U.S. at 439.

[84] Self-execution of the fourteenth amendment implies application of equal protection in certain limited areas such as *de facto* segregation, to review state action that causes unequal treatment or produces unequal results, and which is not traceable to a specific discriminatory law.

[85] Practical distinction between a right and a privilege is difficult for exact defini-

The following discussion explores the concept of local control of public schools both as a remedy, and as a right within the confines of equal protection and the class action doctrine.

II. Constitutional Questions Examined

A. The Individual Right of the Parent to Educate

The individual right of a parent to control the education of a child has long been the subject of human controversy.[86] In the United States, the respective rights and duties of parent and state developed with the organization and growth of the public school system. The state's source of authority premised itself on the necessary assumption that protection of the general welfare of its citizens included supervision of education.[87] The right of parents to educate according to their own desires is protected by the Fourteenth Amendment's guarantee that no person be deprived of "liberty . . . without due process of law."[88] The countervailing interests of both are balanced by "a rule of reasonable conduct on the part of each."[89]

The Supreme Court has decided a group of cases, which place greater stress on the paramount *right of the parent* as opposed to that of the state; but the protection afforded by these decisions only prohibits arbitrary state laws, which are not rationally related to a valid state purpose.[90]

---

tion. In·certain areas of the law, mutually exclusive interpretations as to the intended effects of each category have been made, and different results have been reached; in other areas, they have been used interchangeably by the courts. For purposes of this Note, only a vague and imprecise distinction could be made and, therefore, will be avoided. For analytical discussion of the two concepts in the public sector, *see* Van Alstyne, *The Demise of the Right—Privilege Distinction in Constitutional Law*, 81 Harv. L. Rev. 1439 (1968).

[86] *See generally* Note, *Constitutional Law: Parents' Right to Educate the Child*, 13 Okla. L. Rev. 432 (1960).

[87] Near v. Minnesota, 283 U.S. 697 (1931); People v. Levison, 404 Ill. 574, 90 N.E. 213 (1950).

[88] Meyer v. Nebraska, 262 U.S. 390 (1923). The Court said:

While this Court has not attempted to define with exactness the liberty thus guaranteed, the term has received much consideration. . . . Without doubt, it denotes . . . the right of the individual to . . . marry, establish a home and bring up children, to worship God according to the dictates of his own conscience. . . .

Id. at 399.

[89] In State v. Hoyt, 84 N.H. 38, 41, 146 A. 170, 171 (1929), the court said:

In the adjustment of the parent's right to choose the manner of his children's education, and the impinging right of the state to insist that certain education be furnished and supervised, the rule of reasonable conduct upon the part of each toward the other is to be applied.

In Parr v. State, 117 Ohio St. 23, 157 N.E. 555 (1927), the right to educate is restricted by certain societal standards.

[90] *See generally* Note, *The Right Not To Be Modern Men: The Amish and Compulsory Education*, 53 Va. L. Rev. 925 (1967), where it is noted that the right to have a compulsory system of education is balanced by a "countervailing though largely undefined policy of pluralism and deference to minority ethnic groups. . . ." *Id.* at 931.

Meyer v. Nebraska[91] is the first United States Supreme Court decision affecting the curriculum of a state school system. The Court struck down a state statute, which forbade the teaching of German to any child under twelve. It gave birth to the *Meyer Doctrine*, which recognized the constitutional right of parents to educate free from state legislation that "unreasonably interferes with the liberty of parents and guardians to direct the upbringing and education of children under their control."[92]

In *Pierce v. Society of Sisters*,[93] decided two years after *Meyer*, litigation resulted from the enactment of an Oregon statute requiring children between the ages of eight and sixteen, to attend public schools. Invalidating the statute, the Court said:

> *The fundamental theory of liberty upon which all governments in this Union repose excludes any general power of the state to standardize its children.* . . . The child is not the mere creature of the state; those who nurture him and direct his destiny have the right, coupled with the high duty, to recognize and prepare him for additional obligations.[94] (Emphasis supplied).

Since *Meyer* and *Pierce*, other cases have upheld the constitutionally mandated duty of the state not to "unreasonably interfere" with the *parents' right* to control the education of their children.[95] One fundamental characteristic common to all such cases is their recognition of an inherent constitutional privilege possessed by every parent; but which privilege has never been properly defined.[96] Lack of adequate identification essentially results from the negative approach employed by the courts in a circumspect attempt to deal with due process in the area of education, which in itself is not considered a constitutional right. In addition, all the aforementioned cases have arisen due to infringement by a state law bearing no rational relation to a valid state interest. The invalidity of these statutes has produced a vague and nebulous area into which the states are not allowed to intrude, but the boundaries of which have never assumed concrete form.

In contrast, community control presents itself as a positive factor attempting to establish a firm constitutional footing on which to increase parental control. The concept of local control bears no specific relation to

---

[91] 262 U.S. 390 (1923).

[92] Pierce v. Society of Sisters, 268 U.S. 510, 534-35 (1925).

[93] *Id.*

[94] *Id.* at 535.

[95] *See, e.g.,* West Virginia State Bd. of Educ. v. Barnett, 319 U.S. 624 (1943). The Supreme Court invalidated a statute requiring salute of the flag in all public schools. It concluded that, "The Fourteenth Amendment, as now applied to the states, protects the citizens against the State itself and all of its creatures—*Boards of Education not excepted.* . . . That they are educating the young for citizenship is reason for scrupulous protection of constitutional freedoms of the individual. . . ." (Emphasis supplied). *Id.* at 637.

[96] 262 U.S. at 399.

a particular statute, which may be considered constitutionally suspect. Therefore, these cases, by themselves, do not necessarily afford a viable constitutional basis for implementing a community controlled educational system in the ghetto. Nor does substantive due process, as applied in them, provide an entirely satisfactory standard for reviewing the possible constitutional deficiencies of a centralized school system.

However, their relevance and applicability to community control issues is twofold. Primarily, they recognize a parental right to exercise some degree of educational control over the public schools. Secondarily, they offer a precedent for federal intrusion into the legislatively controlled school system. Both these factors assume substantial importance in view of the expanded role of equal protection, and the class action doctrine as delineated in the segregation cases.

B. As a Group Right—The Class Action Doctrine

The Court in *Meyer v. Nebraska* failed to delineate the exact extent of the individual right of the parent to the educational control of children, but it did proceed on the assumption that it is a personal one. Thus, Negro parents are confronted with the question of whether they, as a distinct class in the community, possess this right.[97] Federal courts have repeatedly held that the personal nature of the right to equal protection does not preclude the use of class actions under Rule 23 (a) of the Federal Rules of Civil Procedure. In *Williams v. Kansas City*,[98] the Court of Appeals for the Eighth Circuit stated:

Violations of the Fourteenth Amendment are of course violations of individual or personal rights, but where they are committed on a class basis or as a group policy, such as a discrimination generally because of race, they are no less entitled to be made the subject of class actions and class adjudications under Rule 23. . . .[99]

Local control of public schools by the Black community has particular appeal as a class action. Their claim to equal educational opportunity, causatively denied by a centralized educational structure is "typical of the claims . . . of the class" that they represent, and there are "questions of law or fact common to the class."[100] Extension of the parental right to

---

[97] A "class right" has been defined as the "multiplicity of individual, personal rights resulting from the fact that all individuals have the same characteristics (*i.e.*, racial characteristics) typical for the group." *See* KING & QUICK, LEGAL ASPECTS OF THE CIVIL RIGHTS MOVEMENT 42 (1965).

[98] Kansas City v. Williams, 205 F.2d 47 (8th Cir. 1953), *cert. denied,* 346 U.S. 826 (1953).

[99] *Id.* at 52.

[100] These are two of the prerequisites under Rule 23(a). The last two require that the group be "so numerous that joinder of all members is impracticable . . . ;" and that the representative parties must "fairly and adequately protect the interests of the class." FED. R. CIV. P. 23(a).

educate to all class members, presupposes two assumptions: (1) that centralization of school authority does produce inequality in education, even if it is not intrinsically discriminatory; (2) that equal educational opportunity is a "critical right" sufficiently broad to correct the inequalities. In view of their revolutionary nature, a successful suit by the local community necessarily would involve a measurable degree of abstraction on each of these issues. However, modern social scientific data and the historical evolution of equal protection in the segregation decisions support such an action.

C. Equal Protection Evolved

1. Before BROWN

Prior to the Desegregation Case, the Equal Protection Clause was not considered an acceptable standard for reviewing the then prevailing racial segregation in public schools.[101] On principle, *Plessy v. Ferguson* confirmed previous holdings that permitted "separate but equal" facilities in public education, if maintained under the guise of "substantial equality."[102] Essentially, *Plessy* embraced a dual tendency of the judiciary at that time toward pervasive nonactivism in the interrelated areas of education and social relationships. Exercise of judicial power in both fields was negatived by the view that, "if one race be inferior to the other socially, the Constitution of the United States cannot put them upon the same plane."[103] Thus, school segregation was held to be constitutional on the premise that "equal school facilities and accommodations . . . are required to be furnished, and not equal social opportunity."[104]

2. BROWN and Its Progeny

Plessy's rejection by the Supreme Court in *Brown v. Board of Education* heralded an era of virtually unprecedented activism in nurturing social and educational equality. Its revolutionary nature, however, demanded gradual application to the multiple areas of society which were vitally affected by its far-reaching implications. Education, more than anything else, was indelibly stamped with the *Brown* constitutional

---

101 For an excellent discussion of *Brown, Plessy* and the fourteenth amendment, concluding that *Brown* was correctly decided, *see* Forkosch, *The Desegregation Opinion Revisited: Legal or Sociological?*, 21 VAND. L. REV. 47 (1967). For a criticism of the doctrine of equal educational opportunity, *see* Kurland, *Equal Educational Opportunity: The Limits of Constitutional Jurisprudence Undefined*, 35 U. CHI. L. REV. 583 (1968).

102 163 U.S. at 540. Essentially, *Plessy* upheld the constitutionality of a Louisiana statute requiring "equal but separate accomodations for the white, and colored races. . . ." Plessy was prosecuted for violating this law by taking possession of a seat in the white section of a railroad coach.

103 *Id.* at 552.

104 People v. School Bd., 161 N.Y. 598, 600, 56 N.E. 81 (1900).

mandate. For this reason, attempts to correct the inequalities existing in the public schools provided the greatest source of litigation, and ignited the most amount of resistance.[105]

The social consequences implicit in the *Brown* ruling led to rejection, qualification and diverse interpretation as to its intended effects. Aware of its potential explosiveness, the Court adopted a "go slow" policy of implementation,[106] which was designed to pacify discontented state and federal courts, particularly in the South. On this basis, the often cited case of *Briggs v. Elliot* assessed *Brown* in the following manner:

> [I]t is important that we point out exactly what the Supreme Court has decided and what it has not decided in this case. . . . It has not decided that the states must mix persons of different races in the schools or must require them to attend schools or must deprive them of the right of choosing the schools they attend. What it has decided, and all that it has decided, is that a state may not deny to any person on account of race the right to attend a school that it maintains. . . . The Constitution, in other words, does not require integration. It merely forbids discrimination. It does not forbid such segregation as occurs as the result of voluntary acts. It merely forbids the use of governmental power to enforce segregation.[107]

The analysis offered by this court laid the foundation for what proved to become the prevailing interpretation of *Brown* and its directives under the Fourteenth Amendment.[108] It made the illegality of segregation dependent on racially motivated state action arising either pursuant to a statute, or through the office of a public official. If discriminatory state policies could not be uncovered, there remained no constitutional basis on which to promote equality of opportunity in education. In effect, the majority of the segregation decisions neutralized *Brown* to the point of ineffectiveness. However, acceptance of the illegality of *de jure* segregation may have let the proverbial horse out of the barn.

The sociological limitations that necessitated a "go slow" policy in 1954 have undergone substantial transformation. The awakening of society

---

105 *See, e.g.,* Avins, *Towards Freedom of Choice in Education,* 45 J. URBAN LAW 23 (1967), citing from Davis v. East Baton Rouge Parish School Bd., 214 F. Supp. 624 (E.D. La. 1963). The Judge declared at 625:

> I could not, in good conscience, pass upon this matter today without first making it clear, for the record, that I personally regard the 1954 holding of the United States Supreme Court in the now famous Brown case as one of the truly regrettable decisions of all times. Its substitution of so-called 'sociological principles' for sound legal reasoning was almost unbelievable. As far as I can determine, its only real accomplishment to date has been to bring discontent and chaos to many previously peaceful communities, without bringing any real attendant benefits to anyone.

106 Brown v. Bd. of Educ., 349 U.S. 294 (1955).

107 Briggs v. Elliot, 132 F. Supp. 776, 777 (E.D.S.C., 1955).

108 *See, e.g.,* Monroe v. City of Jackson, 221 F. Supp. 968 (W.D. Tenn. 1963); School Bd. v. Allen, 240 F.2d 59, 62 (4th Cir. 1956); Avery v. Wichita Falls Indep. School Dist., 241 F.2d 230 (5th Cir. 1957).

to the basic reality that "no child may reasonably be expected to succeed in life if he is denied the opportunity of an education"[109] has induced several federal courts to take somewhat affirmative steps toward achieving equal educational opportunity.

Although, the majority of the courts have reached few conclusive results, most of them have qualified the original desegregation cases to some degree. In the absence of discriminatory intent, they have shifted the focus from the causes of *de jure,* to the effects of *de facto* segregation.[110] New emphasis has been placed on the harm done to Negro children whether caused by racially motivated state action or not. In this perspective, the real meaning of *Brown* comes to light. Denial of equal protection does not necessarily depend on the presence of specific instances of discriminatory practice, but on whether the state public school system serves to promote equal educational opportunity. When *Brown* overruled *Plessy,* it rejected the thesis that "equal school facilities and accommodations . . . are required to be furnished and not equal social opportunity."[111]

In this context, nearly all of the *de facto* segregation cases have produced a somewhat ambivalent result. As the standard of review, the courts have employed the availability of rational alternatives to determine whether existence of *de facto* racial residential patterns and school attendance zones violates the Fourteenth Amendment.[112] In such cases, they have generally found that if *de facto* "classifications" bear a clearly based and "rational relationship" to a valid governmental objective, there is no violation.[113] Hence, equal has come to mean "equal unless a fairly tenable reason exists for inequality."[114] The ambivalence and/or contradiction

---

[109] 347 U.S. at 493. *See supra* note 1.

[110] For cases holding that *de facto* segregation is not unconstitutional, *see* Deal v. Cincinnati Bd. of Educ., 369 F.2d 55 (6th Cir. 1966); Gilliam v. School Bd., 345 F.2d 325 (4th Cir.), *vacated,* Bradley v. School Bd., 382 U.S. 103 (1965); Downs v. Bd. of Educ., 336 F.2d 988 (10th Cir. 1964), *cert. denied,* 380 U.S. 914 (1965). For cases holding that *de facto* segregation is unconstitutional with a duty to integrate, *see* Barksdale v. Springfield School Comm., 237 F. Supp. 543 (D. Mass.), *vacated and remanded with direction to dismiss without prejudice,* 348 F.2d 261 (1st Cir. 1965); Blocker v. Bd. of Educ., 226 F. Supp 208, *enforced,* 229 F. Supp. 709 (E.D.N.Y. 1964); Branche v. Bd. of Educ., 204 F. Supp. 150 (E.D.N.Y. 1962).

[111] People v. School Bd., 161 N.Y. 598, 600, 56 N.E. 81 (1900).

[112] The Supreme Court has not yet ruled on the constitutionality of *de facto* segregation. For a thorough discussion of the "rational relationship and alternatives" standard for reviewing *de facto* segregation cases, *see* Horowitz, *Unseparate but Unequal—The Emerging Fourteenth Amendment Issue in Public School Education,* 13 U.C.L.A. L. Rev. 1147 (1966). *See also* 11 A.L.R.3d 780 (1967).

[113] *See, e.g.,* Norvell v. Illinois, 373 U.S. 420 (1963); Ferguson v. Skrupa, 372 U.S. 726 (1963); McGowan v. Maryland, 366 U.S. 420 (1961). Generally, equal protection cases conclude that a classification will not be held invalid if it has a rational basis and it will not be held arbitrary unless there is no reasonably conceivable state of facts which would justify it, or it is not related to a governmental objective.

[114] Black, *The Lawfulness of the Segregation Decisions,* 69 YALE L. J. 421, 422 (1960).

in this approach is manifest. If the courts concede that *de facto* segregation causes inequality of educational opportunity, then the Fourteenth Amendment, as interpreted by *Brown*, should require a finding that *de facto* segregation is inherently unconstitutional. The availability of rational alternatives, other than as a practical solution to the problem, should not determine the constitutionality of something that denies equal protection by simply existing.

Of course, this proposition rests on the fundamental assumption that *Brown* intended to make equality of opportunity in education the constitutional equivalent of equal protection. On this basis, the standard of review in *all* segregation cases should not depend on whether segregation is given *de jure* or *de facto* denomination. Affirmative response to the problems of disadvantaged minorities becomes a constitutional requirement. A few cases have enunciated this standard and validated the "law of equal opportunities" on principle.

3. The Law of Equal Opportunities

The aforementioned *Briggs v. Elliot*[115] decision created an interpretive principle that still lingers in the minds of the majority of judges and legislators. The courts' dichotomization of *Brown* on a negative desegregation—positive integration basis, reflected the traditional tendency of non-intrusion into state educational policy through negative exercise of judicial power. Rejection of the *Briggs* standard first occurred in 1965,[116] and later received elaborate exposition by a federal court of appeals in *United States v. Jefferson County Board of Education*. The court declared in dictum:

> The mystique that has developed over the supposed difference between "desegregation" and "integration" originated in Briggs v. Elliot. . . . This dictum is a product of the narrow view that Fourteenth Amendment rights are only individual rights; . . . as we see it, the law imposes an . . . absolute duty to integrate, in the sense that a disproportionate concentration of Negroes in certain schools cannot be ignored; racial mixing of students is a high priority educational goal. . . . We emphasize, therefore, the governmental objective and the specifics of the conversion process, rather than the imagery evoked by the pejorative "integration." Decision making in this important area of the law cannot be made to turn upon a quibble devised over ten years ago by a court that misread Brown, misapplied the class action doctrine in the school desegregation cases, and did not foresee the development of *the law of equal opportunities*.[117] (Emphasis supplied).

Although only hortatory, the court's denunciation of the *Briggs* doctrine has validity. Stressing the detrimental effects of *de facto* segregation,

---

[115] 132 F. Supp. 776.

[116] Kemp v. Beasly, 352 F.2d 14 (8th Cir. 1965).

[117] United States v. Jefferson County Bd. of Educ., 372 F.2d 836, 846-47 n.5 (5th Cir. 1966).

the court shifts from a negative to a positive judicial stance. It transcends previous analysis of *Brown* by enlarging the reviewing power of equal educational opportunity beyond the context of coerced segregation, to a level where the inadequacies of segregated education are deemed violative constitutional facts. On this issue, the affirmative "duty" to integrate as expounded by the *Jefferson* court represents a departure from prevailing constitutional interpretation; but in one essential, it continued to be restrictive. The "racial classification" approach to equal protection remained as the "touchstone" in reviewing public school education. *Hobson v. Hansen*[118] appears to have further expanded the doctrine of equal educational opportunity to encompass educational policies that are not necessarily "racial classifications."[119]

Hobson v. Hansen[120]—The *Hobson* court formalized the scope of "equal educational opportunity;" developed a test to review educational policies in general; and rigorously applied this test to the factual issues confronting it. It decreed that the District of Columbia Public School System abolish the "track system,"[121] diminish *de facto* segregation, and initiate compensatory programs. To accomplish these ends, the court embraced a latitudinous standard of review which it justified within the confines of equal protection.

In examining the multifaceted causes of educational inequality, *Hobson* did not require a finding of discriminatory intent. It simply took notice of the fact that "the power structure . . . may incline to pay little heed to even the deserving interests of a politically voiceless and invisible minority."[122] To balance the possible detrimental effects of educational policies so employed, even when non-discriminatory, the court weighed the benefits to be derived from them. If the "adverse effects" overrode the beneficial, then a finding of unconstitutionality was justified.

The "balancing test" had as its foundation, the precept that opportunity for education is a "critical right." Proceeding on this assumption, the

---

[118] 269 F. Supp. 401 (D.D.C. 1967). For analytical treatment of this case, *see* Note, *Hobson v. Hansen: Judicial Supervision of the Color-Blind School Board*, 81 Harv. L. Rev. 1511 (1968).

[119] A classification, as used in the desegregation cases, includes a number of considerations. Generally, it denotes separation of certain groups by race, nationality or economic class. Such a separation may or may not connote discrimination. For example, students may be assigned to neighborhood schools through a school zoning plan solely related to geographic criteria; or a geographic arrangement may be formulated (gerrymandering) which is designed to restrict students to certain schools on the basis of race. The latter implies discrimination. To invoke equal protection under *Brown*, generally, some type of classification must be alleged. This Note applies *Hobson* to support the thesis that any state action that denies equal educational opportunity, is unconstitutional even if a distinct racial classification cannot be uncovered.

[120] 269 F. Supp. 401 (D.D.C. 1967).

[121] Tracking is a form of ability grouping which tests the aptitudes of children and places them in specific "tracks" with others achieving within the same range.

[122] 269 F. Supp. at 507-08.

court drew the "conclusion that the *doctrine of equal educational opportunity—the equal protection clause in its application to public school education—is in its full sweep a component of due process . . . ."*[123] (Emphasis supplied). In doing so, it relied on certain "critical right" cases[124] which justify judicial intervention when the rights of a "disadvantaged minority" are threatened.

Application of the test resulted in expansive solutions to the facts presented in issue. The court easily adjudged *de facto* segregation, and "tracking" as having little or no redeeming value when scrutinized as to their "adverse effects." It correlated the disadvantages of *de facto* segregation to associational deprivation from white students; and it found that the deleterious consequences of "tracking" directly corresponded with the socio-economic class of those tested. The court decided that these fact findings necessitated abolition of both, and institution of affirmative programs and policies designed to correct them.

The cogency of the *Hobson* appeal to the problems of disadvantaged minorities requires neither social, moral nor legal vindication. Although the law of equal opportunities may be criticized as too broadly conceived, limitless in its implications, and unrealistic in its application, the potential societal advantages are enormous. The dimensions of the court's inquiry envelop political, economic, social, psychological and legal considerations that remarkably comprehend the evolutionary pattern of modern day problems in light of modern day solutions.[125] In this context, the court succinctly analyzed the role of equal protection in responding to basic social and educational needs when it declared:

> Orthodox equal protection doctrine can be encapsulated in a single rule: *government action which without justification imposes unequal burdens or awards unequal benefits is unconstitutional.* The complaint that analytically no violation of equal protection vests unless the inequalities stem from a deliberately discriminatory plan is simply false. Whatever the law was once, it is a testament to our maturing concept of equality that, with the help of Supreme Court decisions in the last decade, we now firmly recognize that the arbitrary quality of thoughtlessness can be as disastrous and unfair to private rights and the public interest as the perversity of a willful scheme.[126] (Emphasis supplied).

D. Application of the Hobson Standard to Community Control

At the risk of undue excrescency, the *Hobson* interpretation of equal protection has special and circumstantial application to the factual issues

---

123 *Id.* at 493.

124 Carrington v. Rash, 380 U.S. 89 (1965); Reynolds v. Sims, 377 U.S. 533 (1964); Harper v. Virginia Bd. of Educ., 383 U.S. 663 (1966). These cases attacked statutory voting schemes. *See supra* note 83 for other voting rights cases.

125 In the Federal Supplement the findings of facts cover 85 pages.

126 269 F. Supp. at 497.

at hand. Administrative mismanagement, lack of experienced teachers, unequal allocation of resources, and bureaucratic indifference to ghetto needs, are all traceable to "government action which without justification imposes unequal burdens or awards unequal benefits."[127] This "government action" consists of legislative centralization of school authority in central boards of education, which in turn, propogate the entire spectrum of causative factors that undermine equal opportunity for education. Inability of the Black community to obtain redress through proper political and economic institutions necessitates invocation of equal protection; especially in a period when arbitrary governmental action is demonstratively instrumental in shaping the institutions that control the lives of those in the ghetto. The doctrine of equal educational opportunity requires substantive application to those areas where state regulation is predominant. Centralized school authority readily falls into this category.

It would be senseless and unnecessary to ascertain the exact intent of the framers when the Fourteenth Amendment was adopted in 1866, and thereby discern the constitutional propriety of employing it to review public school control in the teeming ghetto areas that have come to be a societal reality in 1969. Although it is safe to conclude that the mutatious potential of equal protection did not quite comprehend its use as an affirmative standard for achieving equal educational opportunity after the Civil War, the early cases adumbrated its role in resolving the educational woes confronting disadvantaged minorities, specifically the Negro. Equal protection prior to 1954, at least required "substantial equality" on principle, even though the schools were "inherently unequal"[128] in fact. The tides of history and social progress have expanded constitutional interpretation to insure "inherent" equality in the face of a political, economic and social structure unsympathetic to Black self-determination and self-realization.

Application of the *Hobson* standard to review the adverse effects of centralization, in contrast to the beneficial consequences of local control, is constitutionally sound, at least within the abstract concept of "equal educational opportunity." However, practical assessment of detrimental educational policies, directly traceable to centralization, under the more reductive "balancing test," may present problems of exact specification. All of the segregation cases, *Hobson* not excepted, are concerned with state classifications, that tend to categorize certain disadvantaged minorities. These classifications have included flagrant gerrymandering, optional residential zoning and most recently "tracking."[129]

---

[127] *Id.*

[128] 347 U.S. at 495.

[129] *Supra* note 118.

The *Hobson* departure from the traditional classification cases has a dual aspect. It removed the necessity of finding "race" as the basis of state classification, and introduced judicial review of an educational policy not implicitly associated with race. "Tracking" may be correlated to the socio-economic backgrounds of racial minorities, but it essentially comprises an "educational policy" rather than a "racial classification."[130] Thus, it appears that the *Hobson* court has in fact looked beyond state classifications to review educational policies in general.[131] Judge Skelly Wright has declared, "the touchstone in determining equal protection of the law in public education is equal educational opportunity, not race."[132] In this context, judicial review of a centralized school system presents at least two problems: (1) traditional focus on "race," in terms of state classification, rather than examination of educational policies in general under the doctrine of "equal educational opportunity;" (2) presentation of specific evidence caused by centralization. Both are essentially inter-related and each was raised in the following case.

---

[130] The issue here may be one of law or simply one of definition depending on the standard employed by the court. If race is used as the basis of reviewing centralization, then it would be virtually impossible to find overt discrimination, or even characterize a centralized school system as a "classification," but if equal educational opportunity is the standard, then centralization may be reviewed as an educational policy that adversely affects a disadvantaged minority, whether adjudged a "classification" or not, and whether or not racial discrimination is present.

[131] Although the court does focus on *de jure*, and *de facto* segregation, and tracking, as three "classifications" which are made in relation to the "race" of those classified, it makes a number of statements implying that the reviewing power of "equal educational opportunity" does encompass educational practices in general, when they harshly affect a disadvantaged minority. "To fathom and apply the content of the principle of equal educational opportunity is the Court's next project." 269 F. Supp. at 493. After defining *de jure* and *de facto* segregation, the court stated:

> A third equal protection approach to the problems presented by this case questions whether the principle of equal educational opportunity does not require that schools must be materially equal *whenever, for whatever reasons*, these schools are substantially segregated racially or economically. (Emphasis supplied).

Id. at 494. After analyzing equal protection (*see* quote p. 333 of this Note), the court observes at 497: "Theoretically, therefore, purely irrational inequalities even between two schools in a culturally homogenous, uniformly white suburb would raise a real constitutional question."

[132] Wright, *supra* note 8, at 301. Judge Wright goes on to say that: "If classification by race is used to achieve the invidious discrimination, the constitutional insult is exacerbated. *But the focus must remain on the result achieved*. If the untoward result derives from racial classification, such classification is per se unconstitutional. When the result is segregation, and therefore unequal educational opportunity, the classification used, whatever it is, is constitutionally suspect and a heavy burden is placed on the school board and the state to show, not only innocent intent, but also lack of a suitable alternative." (Emphasis Supplied).

Rev. C. Herbert Oliver v. Bernard E. Donovan[133]

The local governing board of Ocean Hill-Brownsville brought this suit in a New York Federal District Court to enjoin the defendants from interfering with the right to run and control public schools through representatives of the community. As a constitutional basis, they asserted that the Fourteenth Amendment imposes "a duty not to interfere with the development of quality education for Black and Spanish-speaking children of New York and equality of education with white children."[134] The court granted the defendants' motion to dismiss for want of jurisdiction on the ground that none of the facts alleged or proven came within the purview of the Fourteenth Amendment. It held that the plaintiffs did not establish any "overt act" denying them a "right or immunity created by the Constitution."[135]

Dismissal of the suit for lack of jurisdiction resulted from a failure to allege "overt acts" violative of anyone's constitutional rights to equal protection. The plaintiffs claimed that proof of specific violations was unnecessary on the basis that equal protection imposed an affirmative duty on the defendants not to interfere with their right to equal educational opportunity, as decided in *Brown v. Board of Education*. This position was premised on the assertion that "the adoption of an educational system based upon decentralization and the involvement of the local community is an attempt to correct the denial of rights under the . . . Fourteenth Amendment. . . ."[136] In effect, the plaintiffs contended that the enactment of the decentralization statute was the result of a legislative finding that a centralized system was one of the causes in the failure to provide equal educational opportunity. Therefore, local control became a constitutionally mandated obligation.

Rejecting this contention, the court refused to be drawn into an analysis of those cases which have discussed the "law of equal opportunities" and have found an affirmative duty to take positive steps in the equalization process.[137] Its holding was predicated on the conclusion that education is not a right guaranteed by the Constitution, and that the existence of

---

[133] No. 68-C-1034 (E.D.N.Y. 1968). This case involves the statutory and factual developments of Ocean Hill-Brownsville Gov. Bd. v. Bd. of Educ., — Misc. 2d —, 294 N.Y.S. 2d 134 (1968), and has, of course, the same parties, the same factual background, and concerns the decentralization statute, § 2564 of the Education Law. *See supra* notes 72 and 73.

[134] No. 68-C-1034 at 7.

[135] *Id.* at 25. Petitioners also invoked the thirteenth amendment on the grounds that control of ghetto public schools by the white community was a "badge or indicia" of slavery. This contention is not discussed in this Note.

[136] *Id.* at 32. *See* ch. 484 (1967) N.Y. Acts 495.

[137] The plaintiff cited *Brown*, United States v. Jefferson County Bd. of Educ., and *Hobson*, but the court stated: "This Court fails to see the similarity in any of these cases with the case at bar," and did not discuss them. No. 68-C-1034 at 27.

educational inequalities, "without more, does not make out a case of constitutional violation."[138]

In its final analysis, the court revealed the foremost reason for denying jurisdiction: "The injunctive relief sought would require this court to order the Board of Education of the City of New York to take action which would be illegal under the Education Law of the State of New York. . . . For this reason . . . relief could not be granted."[139] The implications of this statement are vast. If the court demanded performance of an act which was illegal under state law, it would have had to declare the state law unconstitutional. A ruling of this kind, in turn, would have necessitated a finding that local control of public schools is constitutionally required. Creation of such a precedent would have entailed consideration of a number of revolutionary principles and resulted in unprecedented innovations. First, the court might have invoked the *Meyer* doctrine and ascertained whether centralization of educational authority in the ghetto, when balanced against the degree of control exercised by other communities, was a sufficiently valid state purpose, as to permit certain infringements on parental liberty which deny equal educational opportunity. In this manner, community control of education might have assumed the character of a constitutional right or privilege, even though education, *per se,* does not possess this distinction. As an alternative, the court might have pursued a less revolutionary approach and achieved the same result. Application of the doctrine of equal educational opportunity, by itself, might have required implementation of community control as an interim remedy to accelerate educational equality. This would have unconstitutionalized centralization, in some of its present forms, without recognizing local control as a right, though employing it as a remedy. Essentially, however, the court was confronted with only two real alternatives—to decide for or against community control. One was revolutionary in scope; the other was traditional in conformity. It chose the latter.

In making its choice, the court considered a number of factors. Primary among them, was the comparison of decentralization to desegregation, both as an educational remedy and as a constitutional right. The plaintiffs contended that segregation in the schools caused a denial of equal educational opportunity and resulted in a constitutional mandate to desegregate. Although reluctantly conceding that centralization, unlike segregation, "as it has existed is not inherently unconstitutional . . . ,"[140] they asserted that its effects are the same. Therefore both are unconstitutional when they tend to dilute equality of opportunity in education.

Rejecting this proposition, the court noted a number of dissimilarities. It observed as a practical matter, that "segregation obviously connotes

---

138 *Id.* at 24.
139 *Id.* at 25-26.
140 *Id.* at 22.

inferiority. But no finding or general feeling is present stating that centralized school systems are *inherently* inferior."[141] The court further stated that, "in the well known segregation cases, the alternative was desegregation. We cannot assume that decentralization is the only constitutional alternative if we say centralization is unconstitutional."[142] Although it conceded that "the concept of community involvement is one that appears to have great possibilities,"[143] the court disposed of this argument with the following reasoning:

> The Ocean Hill experiment is just that, an experiment. It is an attempt to see how the effectiveness of the educational structure may be improved. But the State should not be put into a Constitutional straight jacket, forbidding it from attempting other experiments. The alternative to segregation was some form of integration—that was the clear alternative. There is no such obvious solution to the educational problems of the large cities. The State should not be prevented from ending one experiment and trying others, if the action is taken in good faith, without discriminatory intent or result.[144]

After making the aforesaid statement, the court concluded that it did not possess jurisdiction over the cause of action. These views and much of the court's reasoning do not have appeal. Its rejection of local control on the premise that it is "only an experiment;" that its legalization would put the state into a "Constitutional straight jacket;" and that, unlike integration, it does not provide a "clear alternative" to the problem of centralization, appears to be ambiguous and unrealistic. Characterization as an "experiment" does not, in itself, warrant non-consideration of community control either as a constitutional right or as an educational remedy. Such a position fails to apprehend the evolutionary nature of the law in the field of race relations. The many and varied interpretations of *Brown* reflect the developing and still "experimental" condition of integration. Yet, decentralization does not necessarily afford any more of a "Constitutional straight jacket" for the solution of educational problems at this stage, than did desegregation in 1954.

In its analysis that integration offers the only alternative "in the well known segregation cases," the court adopts the restrictiveness it seeks to avoid. This proposition assumes that "race" is the basis for interpreting *Brown*. By making this assumption, the court introduces itself into the company of the segregation cases that adhere to the *Briggs* standard, and it falls into the same trap. According to such a view only racial classifications that are inherently arbitrary must be struck down, without regard to

---

141 *Id.* at 28.

142 *Id.* at 22.

143 *Id.* at 32.

144 *Id.* at 33.

the inequalities that they produce.[145] Experience has proven that this type of reasoning has a tendency to create constitutional cubbyholes without resolving the inequalities themselves.

The constitutional straight jacket sought to be avoided tightens itself in the vein of logic that the court pursues. If "racial classifications" are made the determinant of equal protection and integration is the corresponding mandate, "with no alternative," then freedom of choice and social advancement become synonomous with compulsory, constitutionalized integration. Forced association of White and Black is a two-sided coin. It is discriminatory to force one to mix with the other, as it is vice-versa. This is legally illogical and socially impractical. As a philosophical dictum and as an inherent right, man cannot be forced to co-mingle for social progress, as he cannot be forced to succeed; he can only be given the appropriate opportunity.

An acceptable solution, is to vest equal educational opportunity with self-executing constitutional powers as a critical right. So construed, centralization, segregation, or any lesser category can be reviewed under this broader and extensively more flexible standard. Under *Hobson*, "objectively measurable aspects" of the schools must be equal. This allows scrutinization of any school board policy, practice, method or classification, according to a balanced assessment of their detrimental and beneficial effects. By focusing on the inequalities that are "objectively measurable," necessity for finding overt discriminatory acts, which *Oliver v. Donovan* required,[146] is avoided. It would be sufficient to present evidence, proving that equal educational opportunity is denied when a particular policy is pursued, regardless of racial motivation.

Equal educational opportunity is the ideal approach to social equalization and certain disadvantages must necessarily be encountered. Educational advancement is made to depend on the institutional competence of the courts to implement educational policies, which in their judgment, achieve the desired goals. If local control proves to be beneficial, then factual determinations must be reached as to what degree of parental con-

---

145 Since the *Brown* decision, there has been little progress in desegregating the schools. Focus on racial classification rather than the equal educational opportunity principle has not resolved the inequalities in ghetto schools. Practical application of *Brown* requires full development of this principle. *See* Fiss, *supra* note 8, at 588-98.

146 Judge Travia did not apply the doctrine of equal educational opportunity and required a finding of discriminatory intent. No. 68-C-1034. He stated:

I am permitting them an opportunity to at least give the Court some background in preparation for, I hope, will be a move on the plaintiff's part here to show some violative acts. . . . I think they should be entitled to bring in a little bit of background . . . and then try to join it with any overt acts which they claim then are violative of the 13th and 14th Amendments. . . . We have to have something more specific. . . . *Id.* at 29.

There has been no allegation that less qualified teachers were forced, in a discriminatory manner, upon Negro schools, nor of any arbitrary, discriminatory, or capricious action that could be deemed to violate the right of the inhabitants of the experimental district to equality of education. *Id.* at 24.

trol and/or participation is required. Specific decrees must be rendered delegating various powers and capacities to local groups or leaving them with the educational structure. Remitting such decisions to the educational institution appears to be more realistic, but its apparent failure to respond to ghetto urgencies necessitates active judicial intervention.

The doctrine of equal educational opportunity provides a more flexible constitutional base on which to intervene. Even if integration is pursued as the "governmental objective," it does not preclude employment of interim remedies.[147] If the Black community is given control of the political, economic and educational structure that vitally affects the operation of its local schools, they may become their own architects for social progress.[148] Given this opportunity, personal growth through self-esteem in the creation of its own institutions would tend to produce a more natural and evolutionary economic, political and finally, social integration.[149] As the excellence of ghetto schools improves through increased community concern, paralleled with local control, the white community may seek to benefit from this progress as it has done in other areas.[150]

---

[147] If equal protection under *Brown* does require integration, practical steps must be taken to achieve it. The courts have pursued various plans and intruded into other areas of state regulation to attain the desired goal. For example, in Griffin v. School Bd., 377 U.S. 218 (1964), the Supreme Court made local officials levy school taxes and reopen public schools. In Bush v. Orleans Parish School Bd., 191 F. Supp. 871 (E.D. La. 1961) a federal court blocked the state legislature from removing a school board and school board attorney. In Lee v. Macon County Bd. of Ed., 267 F. Supp. 458 (E.D. Ala.), *aff'd,* Wallace v. United States, 389 U.S. 215 (1967), the Court allowed positive measures to be taken by Negro petitioners, which have a "community control" character. They were entitled to set up an interim choice of a school plan where the state board of education so controlled the public school system, including construction of schools, teacher assignments, use of funds, transportation, consolidation of schools, and assignment of students.

[148] As parental involvement increases, so too will student ambition and achievement. If Negro parents are allowed to directly participate in the education of their children, the atmosphere of rebellion and powerlessness now prevalent in the ghetto may be dissipated. Community control of education may serve as the catalyst in stimulating Negro equality. For an illustration of the beneficial effects of community control, *see* 65 LIFE, Nov. 8, 1968, No. 19, at 67-68.

[149] U.S. RIOT COMMISSION REPORT, *supra* note 28, finds no conflict between integration and community control. It supports the latter and concludes that both are reciprocally beneficial. It states at 439:

No matter how great the effort toward desegregation, many children of the ghetto will not, within their school careers, attend integrated schools.

If existing disadvantages are not to be perpetuated, we must drastically improve the quality of ghetto education. Equality of results with all-white schools must be the goal.

We see no conflict between the integration and quality education strategies we espouse. Commitment to the goal of integrated education can neither diminish the reality of today's segregated and unequal ghetto schools nor sanction the tragic waste of human recources which they entail.

Far from being in conflict, the strategies are complementary. The aim of quality education is to compensate for and overcome the environmental handicaps of disadvantaged children. The evidence indicates that integration, in itself, does not wholly achieve this purpose.

[150] Athletics and entertainment are two prime examples.

E. A Social Necessity

Lack of opportunity, in this era of revolutionary technological advancement, yet extreme social unrest, can only be made the predicate of one thing—education. Former President Johnson has stated, " 'One great truth' . . . is that 'the answer for all our national problems, the answer for all the problems of the world comes down, when you really analyze it, to one simple word—education'. . . . The dependency of democracy on popular education has been a continuing theme in our history."[151] The relationship of education to the continuation of the democratic process has been obvious. An informed and knowledgeable electorate is the backbone of freedom. Political and economic alienation of the Black community from the mainstream of an affluent society has served to enslave as effectively in 1969, as was accomplished by physical and legal coercion prior to 1864.

A long history of oppression has profoundly affected Negro self-esteem. Unlike immigrant minorities who freely emigrated to this country, the Negro was brought and sold as chattel with no property or personal rights. Since his release from bondage, an entire century of fears, suspicions and feelings of inadequacy have generated a sense of impotency and powerlessness over his fate.[152] Today, however, there is a surge of new-found pride in his race. Prominent Negro leaders, entertainers and athletes are joining in a common plea for equality. Society has the responsibility and the duty of aiding this cause, by breathing new meaning into the self-evident truths, "that all men are created equal, that they are endowed by their Creator with certain unalienable Rights, that among these are life, liberty, and the pursuit of happiness."[153]

The Black community has historical privilege, social justification, and the constitutional precedent to propogate self-determination through control of education. The Administrator of the Ocean Hill-Brownsville decentralization district in New York compendiously recapitulated one hundred years of "token" emancipation: "everyone else has failed. We want the *right* to fail for ourselves."[154] (Emphasis supplied).

SUMMARY

Transfer of neighborhood school control from central boards of education to local parental groups involves some degree of social upheaval. Implicit in most social change is the desire of the participants to find sufficient authority within the law to effectuate meaningful reform. The desire of the federal courts to provide equal educational opportunity for Negroes has already led to radical and affirmative measures which are anomolous to the traditional characterization of education as a state function. Judicial intrusion into state public school systems, mostly on

---

151 T. PARSONS & K. CLARK, THE NEGRO AMERICAN 491 (1966).
152 *Id.*
153 THE DECLARATION OF INDEPENDENCE.
154 Roberts, *supra* note 11, at 117.

integration issues, has become the rule rather than the exception, and may presage a period of closer scrutiny and stricter supervision of local schools.

The evolutionary trend of the segregation cases, as well as the personal right cases before 1954, suggest the possibility that federal courts might intervene on behalf of community control in the ghetto if sufficient evidence is presented to substantiate two facts: (1) the educational advantages to be derived; (2) the denial of equal educational opportunity as a component of equal protection, through centralization of educational authority. If proven as a sociological fact that, in the words of *Hobson*—a "power structure"—has so controlled ghetto education as to deny equal educational opportunity, or even failed to promote it, federal courts may be prone to granting a transfer of some degree of control, or at least allowing greater participation in local decision making.

Conclusion

Whether community control of the public school is theoretically characterized an an educational remedy or dynamically vested with constitutional powers is, in reality, irrelevant to the poor and alienated segments of our society that suffer the disadvantages of educational inequality. As a legal concept, it has meaning only in the minds of its outspoken advocates and forceful opponents. If the judiciary hopes to enhance the status of the underprivileged and promote the cause of social justice, it must reassess traditional constitutional premises in the reality of modern day conditions. Mr. Justice Brennan has concisely proclaimed this irrefragable truth:

> The day is past when the law erected the Constitution into a barrier against social and economic reform, and at the same time watered down the guarantees of human rights and liberty into mere admonitions against government. Today, Constitutional interpretation leaves the people wide latitude to experiment with social and economic reforms which further social justice, and, in the area of the guarantees of human rights and liberties, courts are giving Constitutional restraints on government full sweep to prevent oppression of the human spirit and erosion of human dignity."[155]

Michael Flynn

[155] Brennan, *Education and the Bill of Rights*, 113 U. Pa. L. Rev. 219, 223 (1964).

PRIVATE SCHOOLS FOR BLACK CHILDREN

Christopher Jencks

Christopher Jencks, "Private Schools for Black Children," *The New York Times Magazine,* November 3, 1968.

PRIVATE SCHOOLS FOR BLACK CHILDREN

Christopher Jencks

T HE public school system of New York City is on the brink of collapse. No compromise between the teachers' union and the school board is likely to resolve the fundamental conflicts between the school staff and the advocates of black community control. Until the basic political framework of public education in New York City is altered, strikes and boycotts—or both—are likely to recur on an annual basis.

Nor is New York unique. It is simply first. All the forces which have brought New York City to its present condition are at work elsewhere, and the New York story will certainly be repeated in dozens of other major cities around the country during the next decade.

The origin of the crisis is simple. The public schools have not been able to teach most black children to read and write or to add and subtract competently. This is not the children's fault. They are the victims of social pathology far beyond their control. Nor is it the schools' fault, for schools as now organized cannot possibly offset the malignant effects of growing up in the ghetto. Nonetheless, the fact that the schools cannot teach black children basic skills has made the rest of the curriculum unworkable and it has left the children with nothing useful and creative to do for six hours a day. Ghetto schools have therefore become little more than custodial institutions for keeping the children off the street. Nobody, black or white, really knows what to do about the situation.

The traditional argument of both black and white liberals was that the problem could be solved by integrating black children into predominantly white schools, but experience has shown that many whites are reluctant to allow this, and that many blacks are not willing to move into white neighborhoods

423

or bus their children across town even if the opportunity is available. Furthermore, studies such as the one done in New York City by David Fox have shown that most black children's academic performance improves only a little or not at all in integrated schools. Most people have therefore abandoned integration as a solution, at least in big cities.

Most educators are now concentrating on "compensatory" and "remedial" programs to bring academic competence in all-black schools up to the level of all-white schools. Unfortunately, none of these programs has proved consistently successful over any significant period. A few gifted principals seem to have created an atmosphere which enables black children to learn as much as whites in other schools, but they have done this by force of personality rather than by devising formulas which others could follow. Programs like More Effective Schools in New York City may eventually prove moderately effective, but evaluations to date have not provided grounds for great optimism.

The widespread failure of both integration and compensation has convinced some black nationalists that the answer is to replace white principals and teachers with black ones. But experience with this remedy is also discouraging. The schools in Washington, D.C., for example, have predominantly black staffs, and yet their black pupils learn no more than in other cities. So, many black militants are now arguing that the essential step is not to hire black staffs but to establish black control over the schools. There is little evidence one way or the other on this score, but the schools in America's few predominantly black towns are not especially distinguished.

THE available evidence suggests that only a really extraordinary school can have much influence on a child's academic competence, be he black or white. Within the range of variation found in American public schools—and by traditional criteria this range is quite broad —the difference between a "good" school and "bad" school does not seem to matter very much. James S. Coleman's massive Equality of Educational Opportunity survey, conducted for the U.S. Office of Education, demonstrated this point in 1965. Coleman's work was much criticized on methodological grounds, but most subsequent analyses have confirmed his conclusions. Indeed, recent work at Harvard suggests that Coleman probably overstated the effect of school quality on student achievement. This means that the gap between black and white children's academic achievement is largely if not entirely attributable to factors over which school boards have no control.

There are, of course, both educators and scholars who disagree with this conclusion, and who argue that the schools play a substantial role in perpetuating inequality between the races. Such skeptics must, however, explain two facts documented by the Coleman survey and never seriously disputed since.

FIRST, Coleman's work confirmed previous studies showing that even before they enter school black children perform far less well on standard tests than white children. The typical black 6-year-old in the urban North, for example, scores below five-sixths of all white 6-year-olds on tests of both verbal and nonverbal ability. These tests obviously measure performance on tasks which seem important to educators and psychologists, not tasks which seem important to the children being tested or most of their parents. But for precisely this reason they provide a fairly accurate indication of how well any particular cultural group is likely to do at such "white - middle - class"

games as reading and long division. In the case of poor black children, the tests predict disaster.

The prediction, moreover, is all too accurate. Twelve years later, after the schools have done their best and their worst, the typical black 18-year-old in the urban North is still scoring at about the 15th percentile on most standard tests. The schools in short, have not changed his position one way or the other. This obviously means that his *absolute* handicap has grown, for he is 12 years older and both he and his classmates know far more than before, so there is more room for differentiation. Thus a first-grader who scores at the 15th percentile on a verbal test is less than a year behind his classmates; a 12th-grader who scores at the 15th percentile is more than three years behind.

The second fact which must be reckoned with is that while black children go to many different sorts of schools, good and bad, integrated and segregated, rigidly authoritarian and relatively permissive, their mean achievement level is remarkably similar from school to school. By the sixth grade, for example, the typical lower - class Northern black child is achieving a little above the fourth-grade level. There is a great deal of *individual* variation around this average, both because black lower-class families vary considerably in the amount of support they give a school child and because individual children differ in native ability. But there is very little variation from one school to another in such children's *average* level of achievement. The black lower-class average is within one grade level of the over-all black lower-class average in 9 schools out of 10. This uniformly depressing picture cannot be attributed to uniformly depressing conditions in the schools Coleman surveyed. Many of these schools were predominantly white, and some had excellent facilities, highly trained and experienced teachers, relatively small classes and high over-all levels of expenditure. These differences show no consistent relationship to the mean achievement of black elementary school pupils.

The last word has certainly not been written on this subject. Indeed, a group at Harvard is planning another whole book on it. But at the moment I think the evidence strongly indicates that differences in school achievement are largely caused by differences between cultures, between communities, between socio-economic circumstances and between families—not by differences between schools.

None of this provides any adequate excuse for the outrageous and appalling things which are often done in ghetto schools. But it does suggest that even if black schools had the same resources and the same degree of responsibility to parents that the better suburban schools now have, ghetto children would still end up much less academically competent than suburban children.

It follows that the pedagogic failure of the ghetto schools must not be blamed primarily on the stupidity or malice of school boards or school administrators. It must be blamed on the whole complex of social arrangements whose cumulative viciousness creates a Harlem or a Watts. This means that, barring a general improvement in the social and economic positions of black America, black children's school achievement is unlikely to improve much in the foreseeable future, no matter who runs the schools or how they are run.

Some will challenge this depressing conclusion on the ground that black children's achievement scores could be substantially improved if really radical changes were made in the character and organization of black schools. This may well be true, but such changes are unlikely. Nor is it clear that they would be worth the cost. Despite a great deal of popular mythology, there is little real evidence that improving black children's academic skills would help any appreciable number of them to escape poverty and powerlessness.

On the contrary, studies by Otis Dudley Duncan at the University of Michigan suggest that academic competence probably explains only 10 per cent or 15 per cent of the variations in men's earnings. Research by Stephan Michelson at the Brookings Institution likewise indicates that staying in school is not likely to be much help to a Negro who wants to break out of poverty unless he stays through college.

IN these circumstances, it seems to me that we should view the present urban school crisis primarily as a political problem, and only secondarily as a pedagogic one. So long as militant blacks believe they are the victims of a conspiracy to keep their children stupid—and therefore subservient—the political problem will remain insoluble. But if we encourage and assist black parents with such suspicions to set up their own schools, we may be able to avert disaster.

These schools would not, I predict, be either more or less successful than existing public schools in teaching the three R's. But that is not the point. The point is to find a political *modus vivendi* which is tolerable to all sides. (After that, the struggle to eliminate the ghetto should probably concentrate on other institutions, especially corporate employers.) How, then, might independent, black-controlled schools help create such a *modus vivendi?*

The essential issue in the politics of American education has always been whether laymen or professionals would control the schools. Conflict between these two groups has **taken a hundred forms. Professionals always want more money for the schools, while laymen almost always want to trim the budget. Professionals almost always want personnel hired and promoted on the basis of "fair" and "objective" criteria like degrees, examination results and seniority. Laymen are inclined to favor less impersonal criteria, such as whether the individual has roots, whether they personally know and trust him, whether he gets on well with his colleagues, and so forth. Professionals almost** never want anyone fired for any reason whatever, while laymen are inclined to fire all sorts of people, for both good and bad reasons. Professionals want a curriculum which reflects their own ideas about the world, and this often means a curriculum that embodies "liberal" ideas and values they picked up at some big university. Laymen frequently oppose this demand, insisting that the curriculum should reflect conservative local mores.

The development of big-city public schools over the past century has been marked by a steady decline of lay control and an increase in the power of the professional staff. Until relatively recently, this has meant that control was exercised by administrators. Now the teaching staff, represented by increasingly militant unions and professional associations, has begun to insist on its rights. This is, however, an intraprofessional dispute. It has done nothing to arrest the staff's continuing and largely successful resistance to nonprofessional "intervention" by parents, school-board members and other laymen. About the only thing such laymen can still decide in most big cities is the over-all level of expenditures.

The extent to which the professional staff gets its way seems to be related to the size of the administrative unit in which it works. Laymen usually have more power in small school districts, while the staff usually has more power in big districts. Until relatively recently, most liberals saw this as an argument for bigger districts, since they thought that the trouble with American education was its excessive deference to local inter-

66Given racial and economic segregation in housing, localism in education means de *facto* segregation in schooling.99

ests and its lack of professionalism. In the past few years, however, liberals and radicals have suddenly joined conservatives in attacking bigness, bureaucracy and the claims of enterprise. Most people on the left are now calling for more participation, more responsiveness, more decentralization, and less "alienization."

LIBERAL thinking on this question is in large part a response to black nationalism. More and more Negroes believe there is a cause-effect relationship between the hegemony of what they call "white middle - class" (read professional-bureaucratic) values in their schools and the fact that their children learn so little in those schools. So they think the best way to improve their children's performance would be to break the power of the professional staff. This, they rightly infer, requires Balkanizing big - city systems · into much smaller units, which will be more responsive to parental and neighborhood pressure. (There are, of course, also strictly administrative arguments for breaking up systems as large as New York City's into units the size of, say, Rochester. But that would not do much for parental control.) So black militants want to strip the central board of education and central administrative staff of authority, elect local boards, have these boards appoint local officials, and then let these locally appointed officials operate local schools in precisely the same way that any small-town or suburban school system does.

This scheme has been at-tacked on two grounds. First, given racial and economic segregation in housing, localism in education means *de facto* segregation in schooling. In New York City, for example, almost everyone agrees the so-called "Bundy Plan" would foreclose any serious effort to reduce racial and economic segregation in the schools. Furthermore, if big-city school systems are broken up, the more affluent neighborhoods will presumably pursue the logic of Balkanization a step further by asking for fiscal as well as administrative autonomy. This demand would be politically difficult to resist. Yet if it were met, the expenditure gap between Harlem and Queens would almost certainly become wider than it now is.

The second common objection to the Balkanization of big-city school systems is that it would produce more parental "interference." (The distinction between "participation" and "interference" is largely a matter of where you think parents' rights end and staff prerogatives begin.) Parental interference would, it is plausibly argued, make it even harder to recruit staff members whose values are significantly at odds with the community's. This would make schools even more homogenized and parochial than they now are. Indeed, a local district which does not give its staff substantial autonomy is likely to have some difficulty recruiting even teachers who have grown up in the neighborhood and share the parents' values, simply because most teachers do not want parents constantly second-guessing them. Once the first flush of idealistic enthusiasm had passed, locally controlled schools in poor areas would probably have a harder time getting staffs than they do now. Like small rural districts confronted with the same problem, small impoverished urban districts would probably have to depend mainly on local people who could not get better jobs elsewhere.

These two arguments against local control of big-city schools naturally carry little weight with black militants. They have little patience with the liberal claim that the way to make black children learn more is to give them more white classmates and more middle-class teachers from Ivy League colleges. When liberals oppose decentralization on the grounds that it would legitimize segregation, the black militants answer: "So what? Integration is a myth. Who needs it?" When professional educators add that decentralization would create working conditions unacceptable to highly trained (and therefore potentially mobile) teachers, the black militants again answer: "So what? Teachers like that don't understand black children. Who wants them?"

DIFFERENCES of opinion like this probably cannot be resolved by "experimentation"—though more reliable information about the consequences of various school policies would certainly help. For reasons already indicated, the solution must be political.

In seeking such a solution, however, we should bear in mind that a similar crisis arose a century ago when Catholic immigrants confronted a public school system run by and for Protestants. This crisis was successfully resolved by creating two school systems, one public and one private.

It seems to me that the same approach might be equally appropriate again today. Since such an idea is likely to shock most liberals, it may be useful to recall certain neglected features of the parochial - school experiment.

The motives of the Catholic immigrants who created the parochial-school system were different in many important respects from the motives of the black nationalists who now want their own schools. Nonetheless, there were also important similarities. Just as today's black nationalist does not want his children infected by alien, white "middle-class" values, so many devout Catholic immigrants did not want their children to imbibe the alien values of white Protestant "first families." Just as today's black nationalist deplores the public schools' failure to develop pride and self-respect in black children, so, too, many Irish immigrants felt they needed their own schools to make their children feel that Catholicism and Irishness were respectable rather than shameful. And just as many black parents now want to get their children out of public schools because they feel these schools do not maintain proper discipline, so, too, many Catholics still say that their prime reason for sending their children to parochial schools is that the nuns maintain order and teach children "to behave."

Why, then, did not devout Catholics press for Balkanization of big-city school systems? Why did they not turn their neighborhood schools into bastions of the faith rather than creating their own separate system?

The answer is that there were very few neighborhoods in which literally all the residents were Catholic. Even where everyone was Catholic,

not all Catholics wanted their children educated in self-consciously Catholic schools. Some Catholics, especially those of Irish ancestry, were extremely suspicious of the Anglo-Protestant majority, were strongly attached to the church, and eager to enroll their children in church schools. But others, of whom Italian immigrants were fairly typical, felt as suspicious of the Irish who dominated the church here as of the Anglo-Saxons who dominated the rest of America. Such Catholics were often anticlerical, and they wanted to send their children to schools which would stick to the three R's and skip ideology.

Thus, even in the most Catholic neighborhoods, there was a large minority which thought priests, nuns and theology had no place in the local schools. This minority allied itself with the Protestant majority in other parts of the same state. These state-wide majorities then kept strict limits on local control, so as to prevent devout Catholics from imposing their view of education on local Protestant (or lax Catholic) minorities. In particular, most state constitutions contain some kind of prohibition against the introduction of church personnel and teaching into the local public

431

schools. **When they do not, it is only because the Federal First Amendment was thought sufficient to prevent the possibility.**

THIS points to a difficulty with neighborhood control which black militants have yet to face. Blacks are not a majority in many of the areas where they live, at least if these areas are defined as large enough to support a full school system. Nor are black Americans of one mind about Balkanization and its likely consequences. Some black parents still believe in integration. They think the only way to get the social and material advantages they want is to stop being what they have always been, however difficult and painful that may be, and become culturally indistinguishable from the white majority. They therefore want their children to attend integrated schools, to study the same curriculum as white children, and to have teachers from good colleges (most of whom will be white for the foreseeable future). What these families want is thus very similar to what the present professional staffs of big-city school systems want.

Other black parents feel that they can never become indistinguishable from whites, that attempts to acquire white culture only make black children feel miserable and incompetent, and that if such children are to succeed they will have to develop their own style. Such parents want their children to attend schools which try to develop distinctive black virtues and black pride, and which maintain the discipline which is so sorely lacking in the public schools. This cannot, I fear, be reconciled with what the present professional staff wants (or knows how to do).

FOR convenience, I will label these two sorts of black parents "integrationists" and "nationalists"—though the flavor of the distinction is perhaps better captured in the militants' rhetorical distinction between "Negroes" and "blacks."

Balkanizing big-city school systems would clearly be a victory for the nationalists at the expense of the integrationists. Schools in predominantly black neighborhoods would almost certainly end up with fewer white students and teachers. Local control would also make it easier for white neighborhoods to resist open enrollment, busing and other devices for helping black integrationists send their children to predominantly white schools. The curriculum might or might not be substantially revised once black neighborhood boards held power, but whatever revisions were made would certainly please the nationalists more than the integrationists.

Yet for this very reason state legislatures are unlikely to let black separatists exercise complete control over "their" schools. Just as legislatures earlier protected the rights of Protestant and anticlerical Catholic minorities in devout Catholic communities, so they will almost certainly protect the rights of white and black - integrationist minorities in predominantly black neighborhoods.

If, for example, the local Ocean Hill - Brownsville board wins control over the schools in that part of New York City, the New York State Legislature will almost surely go along with union demands for tight limits on the local board's right to discriminate against whites in hiring teachers and principals. (No such discrimination appears to have taken place in Ocean Hill-Brownsville's hiring of teachers, but the local board does seem to have had a strong and entirely understandable prejudice in favor of black principals.) State certification requirements are also likely to be strictly enforced, so as to restrict black local boards to hiring teachers who have enough respect for white culture and white standards of competence to have got through four or five years of college. New restrictions are also likely to be put on the curriculum, perhaps in the form of a law against teaching "racial hatred," so as to keep LeRoi Jones, etc., out of black schools. Such action would be defended on the same grounds as the rules barring religious teaching in public schools.

Restrictions of this kind are both reasonable and necessary in public institutions which must serve every child in a community, regardless of his race or his parents' outlook on life. They are, however, likely to mean that black nationalists end up feeling that, even though they have a majority on the local board, they do not really control their schools. Once again, whitey will have cheated them of their rightful pride. Local control is, therefore, likely to enrage the professional educators, work against the hopes and ambitions of the integration-minded black and white parents, and yet end up leaving black nationalists as angry as ever. An alternative strategy is badly needed.

THE best alternative I can

see is to follow the Catholic precedent and allow nationalists to create their own private schools, outside the regular public system, and to encourage this by making such schools eligible for substantial tax support.

The big-city school systems could then remain largely in the hands of their professional staffs. (A major change in the distribution of power between teachers and administrators would still be required, and some decentralization of big cities would also be advisable on bureaucratic grounds, but these are negotiable issues.) The public system would continue to serve white and black integrationists. Separatists who found this system unacceptable would have the option of sending their children to other schools at relatively low cost.

The beginnings of such a parallel system can already be seen in some big cities. Black middle-class parents are already far more likely than their white counterparts to enroll their children in private schools. A number of private "community schools" have also sprung up in the ghettos during the past few years. The Muslims run several schools. These schools have found many black parents are willing to make considerable financial sacrifices in order to send their children to a school they think superior to the public one. What these ventures lack, however, is substantial political and financial support. Without this they are likely to remain isolated and relatively unusual.

Some will ask why an independent black school system should need or deserve white support when the parochial schools get no such support. The most relevant answer is that, without the unity and legitimacy conferred by religion, the black community cannot go it alone. It is, perhaps, an unfortunate historical accident that black America lacks its own church, but it does—and even the Muslims have not been able to remedy the situation. Yet black America still needs its own schools, free to serve exigencies of black nationalism. Given the inevitable hostility of both professional educators and laymen who believe in integration, black nationalists are unlikely to be able to create such schools within the public sector.

Is there any justification for funding black private schools without funding other private schools on the same basis? My answer is "No."

Indeed, it seems to me that the only way a black private-school system could hope to get tax subsidies would be to ally itself with a parochial school system in demanding Federal and state support for all private schools. Many traditional liberals feel this would violate the constitutional separation of church and state. The Supreme Court has never ruled on this question, however; until it does, it seems reasonable to assume that there is no constitutional objection to Federal or state subsidies for private schools —so long as these subsidies are earmarked to achieve specific public purposes, and so long as the schools are accountable for achieving these purposes.

An analogy may clarify this point. Back in the 19th century, the Supreme Court ruled that the Government could legally contract with Catholic hospitals to care for public charity patients, and today only the most strict separatist would argue that the Federal Government cannot contract with a Catholic university or a Catholic hospital to carry out scientific research. Why, then, should it not contract with a Catholic school to teach physics to 16-year-olds or reading to impoverished 6-year-olds?

Private schools should, of course, be required to show that they had actually done what they promised to do, rather than devoting public funds to the construction of chapels or the production of antiwhite propaganda. But accountability of this kind is essential with all tax subsidies, whether to private schools, private corporations or local government.

EVEN if a coalition between the church and the black community were put together, is it realistic to suppose that white Protestant America would actually support black schools? My guess is that it would, so long as the financial burden remains within reason. Remember, I am *not* proposing that white legislators should help create a private system for blacks which would be more expensive than the one now attended by whites. I am only proposing that black children who attend private schools should be eligible for at least part of the tax subsidy which is now available if they choose to seek an education in the public system. Far from increasing the overall tax bill, then, a scheme of this kind would actually lower it. In particular, it would help slow the rise in local property taxes, by providing black parents with state and Federal incentives to withdraw their children from locally supported schools, thus cutting local costs. Many local white taxpayers would probably greet such a development with considerable enthusiasm. It would also reduce some white parents' anxiety about the public system's being "overrun" by black children. (It would not actually diminish integration - minded blacks' interest in desegregation, but if it reduced over-all black enrollment it might make desegregation seem a little less threatening and more practical.) In addition, the creation of an independent black school system might strike many whites as a relatively easy and painless way to buy political peace and sweep the whole racial problem under the rug. I doubt if it would succeed in doing this, but it might at least help shift the focus of racial conflict away from the schools and into other more critical arenas.

At this point, somebody always says, "Well, what about private schools established by white supremacists to escape integration?" The answer to that question is already clear. The Supreme Court has held subsidies for such schools unconstitutional, and neither legislatures nor Congress should provide them. Indeed, I would go further and argue that the state should not subsidize any school which is not open to every child who wants to enroll — regardless of race, religion or ability. Not many non-Catholics want to attend parochial schools, but some already do and others will. Their admission should certainly be a precondition for public subsidies. Similarly black schools should be required to admit white applicants in order to get tax support. No rush of applicants need be anticipated.

ONE final objection to the establishment of independent black schools should be mentioned. Many whites fear that such a system would preach black nationalism and racial hatred, and that this would make racial reconciliation even more difficult than it now seems.

This is a reasonable fear. The same objections were raised against the Catholic schools for more than a hundred years. Yet despite all sorts of horror stories about anti-Semitism and other forms of prejudice in Catholic schools, a 1964 survey by Andrew Greeley and Peter Rossi of the University of Chicago demonstrated fairly conclusively that Catholics who attended parochial schools were no more intolerant, narrow-minded or socially irresponsible than Catholics who attended public schools. Indeed, the survey suggested that, all other things being equal, parochial schools had a more liberalizing effect on Catholics than did public schools.

And similarly, the Greeley-Rossi survey suggests that the black schools would not have to be especially affluent to do an acceptable job. While the parochial schools spent far less per pupil than the public schools, used less extensively trained teachers, had much larger classes, were housed in older buildings, had smaller libraries and relied on a curriculum even more medieval than did the public schools, their alumni did at least as well in worldly terms as public-school Catholics.

All other things being equal, parochial-school Catholics ended up with slightly more education and slightly better jobs than public-school Catholics. The only really significant difference Greeley and Rossi found between the two groups was that parochial school products were more meticulous and better informed about their religious obligations. This suggests that fears for the future of black children in black-controlled schools may also be somewhat exaggerated.

THE development of an independent black school system would not solve the problems of black children. I doubt, for example, that many black private schools could teach their children to read appreciably better than white-controlled public schools now do. But such schools would be an important instrument in the hands of black leaders who want to develop a sense of community solidarity and pride in the ghetto, just as the parochial schools have worked for similarly placed Catholics.

Equally important, perhaps, the existence of independent black schools would diffuse the present attack on professional control over the public system. This seems the only politically realistic course in a society where professional control, employe rights and bureaucratic procedures are as entrenched as they are in America. The black community is not strong enough to destroy the public-school bureaucracy and staff. Even if it did, it now has nothing to put in its place. What the black community could do, however, would be to develop an alternative — and demand tax support for it.

Some radicals who expect black insurgency to destroy the whole professional hierarchy in America and create a new style of participatory democracy will regard this kind of solution as a cop-out. Some conservatives whose primary concern is that the lower orders not get out of hand will regard it as an undesirable concession to anarchy. But for those who value a pluralistic society, the fact that such a solution would, for the first time, give large numbers of non - Catholics a choice about where they send their children to school, ought, I think, to outweigh all other objections. ■

SCHOOL PARKS FOR EQUAL OPPORTUNITIES

John H. Fischer

John H. Fischer, "School Parks for Equal Opportunities," *Journal of Negro Education,* Summer 1968, Vol. 37, pp. 301-309.

SCHOOL PARKS FOR EQUAL OPPORTUNITIES

John H. Fischer

Of all the plans that have been put forward for integrating urban schools the boldest is the school park. This is a scheme under which several thousand ghetto children and a larger number from middle-class white neighborhoods would be assembled in a group of schools sharing a single campus. Placing two or more schools on one site is not a new idea, but two other aspects of the school park are novel. It would be the largest educational institution ever established below the collegiate level and the first planned explicitly to cultivate racial integration as an element of good education.

A small community might house its entire school system in one such complex. A large city with one or more large ghettos would require several. In the most imaginative and difficult form of the proposal a central city and its neighboring suburban districts would jointly sponsor a ring of metropolitan school parks on the periphery of the city.[1]

The characteristic features of the school park — comprehensive coverage and unprecedented size — are its main advantages and at the same time the chief targets of its critics. Is the park a defensible modern version of the common school, perhaps the only form in which that traditionally American institution can be maintained in an urban society? Or is it a monstrous device that can lead only to the mass mistreatment of children? Whatever else it is or may in time turn out to be, it is neither a modest proposal nor a panacea.

Since even one such project would require a substantial commitment of policy and money, it is obvious that the validity of the concept should be closely examined and the costs and potential benefits associated with it carefully appraised.

The purpose of this paper is to assist that process by considering the relevance of the school park to present problems in urban education and by analyzing, although in a necessarily limited way, its potentially.

THE PROBLEM

Twelve years of effort, some ingeniously pro forma and some laboriously genuine, have proved that desegregating schools — to say nothing of integrating them — is much more difficult than it first appeared. Attendance area boundaries have been redrawn; new schools have been built in border areas; parents have been permitted, even encouraged, to choose more desirable schools for their children; pupils from crowded slum schools have been bused to outlying schools; Negro and white schools have been paired and their

*This chapter is excerpted from a paper entitled "The School Park" prepared by Dr. Fischer under contract with the U. S. Commission on Civil Rights. It was undertaken independently from the Commission and is the responsibility of the author alone.

[1] Thomas B. Pettigrew, "School Desegregation in Urban America," unpublished paper prepared for NAACP Legal Conference on School Desegregation, October 1966, pp. 25-33.

student bodies merged; but in few cases have the results been wholly satisfactory. Despite some initial success and a few stable solutions, the consequences, for the most part, have proved disappointing. Steady increases in urban Negro population, continuing shifts in the racial character of neighborhoods, actual or supposed decline in student achievement, unhappiness over cultural differences and unpleasant personal relations have combined to produce new problems faster than old ones could be solved.[2]

Underlying the whole situation are basic facts that have too seldom been given the attention they merit. Some of these facts bear on the behavior of individuals. Few parents of either race, for example, are willing to accept inconvenience or to make new adjustments in family routines if the only discernible result is to improve the opportunities of other people's children. A still smaller minority will actually forego advantages to which their children have become accustomed merely to benefit other children. Most parents, liberal or conservative, hesitate to accept any substantial change in school procedures unless they are convinced that their own children will have a better than even chance of profiting from them. While prejudice and bigotry are not to be minimized as obstacles to racial integration, resistance attributed to them is often due rather to the reluctance of parents to risk a reduction in their own children's opportunities.

. . . .

The controversy over what constitutes viable racial balance in schools or neighborhoods remains unsettled, for the data are far from complete. There is abundant evidence, however, that few middle-class families, Negro or white, will choose schools enrolling a majority of Negro children if any alternative is available. Additional complications arise from social class and cultural relationships. Although borderline sites or school pairing on the periphery of a ghetto may produce temporary racial desegregation, these devices rarely bring together children of different social classes. As a consequence, the predictable antagonisms between lower class white and Negro groups increase the school's burden of adjustment problems and diminish the benefits of cultural interchange.

. . . .

The moral and legal grounds for desegregating schools are clear and well-established. The factual evidence that integration can improve the effectiveness of education is steadily accumulating.[3] For the purposes of this paper there is no need to review either. But it will be useful to examine what is now known about the conditions that must be met if schools are to be well integrated and effective.

The first requirement is that the proportion of each race in the school be acceptable and educationally beneficial to both groups.[4] This means that the proportion of white students must be high enough to keep them and, more importantly, their parents from feeling overwhelmed and to assure the Negro student

2 Jeanette Hopkins, "Self Portrait of School Desegregation in Northern Cities," unpublished paper prepared for NAACP Legal Conference, October 1966, pp. 1-3.

3 James S. Coleman, Equality of Educational Opportunity (Washington, D. C.: U. S. Department of Health, Education, and Welfare, 1966), p. 332.

4 Pettigrew, op. cit., p. 17.

the advantage of a genuinely integrated environment. On the other hand, the number of Negro students must be large enough to prevent their becoming an odd and isolated minority in a nominally desegregated school. Their percentage should enable them to appear as a matter of course in all phases of school life. No Negro student should have to "represent his race" in any different sense than his white classmates represent theirs.

Many efforts have been made to define a racially balanced school, but no "balance," however logical it may be statistically, is likely to remain stable and workable if it results in either a majority of Negroes, or so few that they are individually conspicuous. This suggests in practice a Negro component ranging from a minimum of 15 to 20 per cent to a maximum of 40 to 45 per cent.

School districts with small Negro minorities, even though they may be concentrated in ghettos, can ordinarily devise plans to . meet these conditions without large scale changes in the character of their school systems. Central cities with sizeable ghettos and smaller cities with larger proportions of Negroes will usually be required to make substantial changes in order to attain integrated schools.

But even when such acceptable racial proportions have been established, an effectively integrated school can be maintained only if a second condition is met: The school must respond to the educational needs of all its students better than the schools they might otherwise attend. The school must possess the capacity, the physical facilities, the staff strength, the leadership, and the flexibility required not only to offer a wide range of programs and services, but also adapt them to the special circumstances of individual students.

THE PARK AS A POSSIBLE SOLUTION

In school districts where redistricting, pairing, open enrollment, and busing offer little hope of producing lasting integration and high quality school programs, the school park may well offer a satisfactory solution. School parks (called also educational parks, plazas, or centers) have been proposed in a number of communities and are being planned in several. The schemes so far advanced fall into several categories. The simplest, which is appropriate for a small or medium-sized town, assembles on a single campus all the schools and all the students of an entire community. As a result the racial character of a particular neighborhood no longer determines the character of any one school. All the children of the community come to the central campus where they can be assigned to schools and classes according to whatever criteria will produce the greatest educational benefits. The School Board of East Orange, N. J., has recently announced a 15-year construction program to consolidate its school system of some 10,000 pupils in such an educational plaza.[5]

Another variant of the park is a similarly comprehensive organization serving one section of a large city as the single park might serve an entire smaller town. Where this plan is adopted the capacity of the park must be so calculated that its attendance area will be sufficiently large and diversified to yield a racially balanced student body for the foreseeable future. Merely to assemble two or three

[5] "Desegregation. Ten Blueprints for Action," *School Management*, X (October 1966), 103-105.

elementary units, a junior high school and a senior high school would in many cities produce no more integration than constructing the same buildings on the customary separate sites.

Less comprehensive schemes can also be called school parks. One, applicable to smaller communities, would center all school facilities for a single level of education — e.g., all elementary schools, or middle schools, or high schools, on a single site. Single-level complexes serving less than a whole community are also possible in large cities. . . .

A fourth, and the most comprehensive, type of park would require a number of changes in school planning and administration. This is the metropolitan school park designed to meet the increasingly serious problems posed by the growing Negro population of the central cities and the almost wholly white suburbs that surround them. The proposal, briefly stated, is to ring the city with school parks that would enroll the full range of pupils from the kindergarten to the high school and possibly including a community college. Each park would be placed in a "neutral" area near the periphery of the city. Each attendance area would approximate a segment of the metropolitan circle with its apex at the center of the city and its base in the suburbs. Since many students would arrive by school bus or public carrier, each site would be adjacent to a main transport route.[6]

The potentialities of school parks in general can be explored by projecting what might be done in such a metropolitan center. We can begin with certain assumptions about size and character. In order to encompass an attendance area large enough to assure for the long term an enrollment more than 50 per cent white and still include a significant number of Negro students from the inner-city ghetto, the typical park, in most metropolitan areas, would require a total student body (kindergarten to Grade 12) of not less than 15,000. It would thus provide all the school facilities for a part of the metropolitan area with a total population of 80,000 to 120,000. The exact optimum size of a particular park might be as high as 30,000, depending upon the density of urban and suburban population, the prevalence of nonpublic schools, the pattern of industrial, business, and residential zoning, the character of the housing, and the availability of transport.

The site, ideally, would consist of 50 to 100 acres but a workable park could be designed on a much smaller area or, under suitable circumstances, deep within the central city by using high-rise structures.[7] Within these buildings individual school units of varying sizes would be dispersed horizontally and vertically. On a more generous plot each unit could be housed separately, with suitable provision for communication through tunnels or covered passages.

The sheer size of the establishment would present obvious opportunities to economize through centralized functions and facilities, but the hazards of overcentralization are formidable. To proceed too quickly or too far down that path would be to sacrifice many of the park's

---

6 Pettigrew, op. cit., pp. 25-33.

7 Harold B. Gores, "Education Park; Physical and Fiscal Aspects," in Milton Jacobsen (ed.), An Exploration of the Educational Park Concept (New York: New York Board of Education, 1964), pp. 2-7.

most valuable opportunities for better education.

Because of its size the park would make possible degrees of specialization, concentration, and flexibility that are obtainable only at exorbitant cost in smaller schools. A center enrolling 16,000 students in a kindergarten-4-4-4 organization, with 1,000-1,300 pupils at each grade level, could efficiently support and staff not only a wide variety of programs for children at every ordinary level or ability, but also highly specialized offerings for those with unusual talents or handicaps.

Such an institution could operate its own closed circuit television system more effectively, and with lower cable costs than a community-wide system, and with greater attention to the individual teacher's requirements. A central bank of films and tapes could be available for transmission to any classroom, and the whole system controlled by a dialing mechanism that would enable every teacher to "order" at any time whatever item he wished his class to see.

The pupil population would be large enough to justify full-time staffs of specialists and the necessary physical facilities to furnish medical, psychological, and counseling services at a level of quality that is now rarely possible. Food service could be provided through central kitchens, short distance delivery, and decentralized dining rooms for the separate schools.

The most important educational consequences of the park's unprecedented size would be the real opportunities it would offer for organizing teachers, auxiliary staff, and students. In the hypothetical K-4-4-4 park of 16,000, for example, there would

be about 5,000 pupils each in the primary and middle school age groups, or enough at each level for 10 separate schools of 500 pupils.

Each primary or middle school of that size could be housed in its own building, or its own section of a larger structure with its own faculty of perhaps 25. Such a unit, directed by its own principal, with its own complement of master teachers, "regular" teachers, interns, assistants, and volunteers, would be the school "home" of each of its pupils for the 3, 4, or 5 years he would spend in it before moving on to the next level of the park. A permanent organization of children and adults of that size employing flexible grouping procedures would make possible working relationships far superior to those now found in most schools. Moreover, since a child whose family moved from one home to another within the large area served by the park would not be required to change schools, one of the principal present handicaps to effective learning in the city schools would be largely eliminated.

While not every school within the park could offer every specialized curriculum or service, such facilities would be provided in as many units as necessary and children assigned to them temporarily or permanently. Each child and each teacher would "belong" to his own unit, but access to others would be readily possible at any time.

The presence on a campus of all school levels and a wide range of administrative and auxiliary services would present the professional staff with opportunities for personal development and advancement which no single school now affords. The ease of communication, for example, among the guidance specialists or mathematics teachers would exceed anything now possible. It would become feasible to organize for each subject or professional specialty a department in which teachers in all parts of the park could hold memberships, in much the way that a university department includes professors from a number of colleges.

For the first time, a field unit could justify its own research and development branch, a thing not only unheard of but almost unimaginable in most schools today. With such help "in residence" the faculty of the park could participate in studies of teaching problems and conduct experiments that now are wholly impracticable for even the most competent teachers.

Much would depend, of course, on the imagination with which the park was organized and administered and how its policies were formed. Since the metropolitan park, by definition, would serve both a central city and one or more suburban districts, its very establishment would be impossible without new forms of intergovernmental cooperation. At least two local school boards would have to share authority, staffs, and funds. The State educational authority and perhaps the legislature would be required to sanction the scheme and might have to authorize it in advance. Public opinion and political interests would be deeply involved as would the industrial and real estate establishments of the sponsoring communities.

The planning of a metropolitan park would have to be viewed as a concern not merely of school people, parents, and legislative or executive officials. It would have to be approached from the outset as a fundamental problem in metropolitan planning. Its dependence on quantitative projections of population and housing data is obvious, but equally important is its relation to the character of the housing, occupancy policies, and ethnic concentrations. To build a park only to have it engulfed in a few years by an enlarged ghetto would be a sorry waste of both money and opportunity. No good purpose, educational or social, would be served by creating what might become a huge segregated school enclave. A school park can be undertaken responsibly only as part of a comprehensive metropolitan development plan. Where such planning is not feasible, the establishment of a metropolitan school park would be a questionable venture.

It may be reasonable in some circumstances to project a park within the limits of a single school district. Where the analysis of population trends and projected development justify a single district park, the intergovernmental problems disappear, but agreements within the municipal structure will still be important and may be quite difficult to negotiate. The need for comprehensive community planning to assure the future viability of the park is certainly no less necessary within the city than in the metropolitan area.

Once the park is authorized, the question of operating responsibility must be addressed. In a sense that no individual school or geographic subdivision possibly can, the school park permits decentralized policy development and administration. Because of the natural coherence of the park's components and their relative separation from the rest of the district — or districts — to which it is related, the park might very well be organized as a largely self-contained system. The argument for placing the park under a board with considerable autonomy is strong whether it is a metropolitan institution or a one-city enterprise. For the first time it could thus become possible for the citizens in a section of a large community to have a direct, effective voice in the affairs of a school serving their area. . . .

Citizen participation would have to occur at points other than the board, however. If the park is to be strongly related to its communities, and integrated in fact as well as in principle, parents and other citizens would have to be involved, formally and informally, in many of its activities. These might range from parent-teacher conferences to service on major curriculum advisory groups. They could include routine volunteer chores and service as special consultants or part-time teachers. The specific possibilities are unlimited but the tone of the relationships will critically affect the park's success.

. . . .

Obtaining the necessary cooperation to build a metropolitan park will not be easy but the financial problems will be equally severe. A park accommodating 16,000 pupils can be expected to cost in the neighborhood of $50 million. The financial pressures on cities and suburban districts make it clear that Federal support on a very large scale will be required if school parks are to be built. But it is precisely the possibility of Federal funds that could provide the incentive to bring the suburbs and the central city together.

While categorical support through Federal funds will continue to be needed,

effective leverage on the massive problems of urban education, including, particularly, integration, can be obtained only through broadly focused programs of general aid, with special attention given to new construction. Little can be done toward equalizing opportunities without a sizeable program of school building expansion and replacement. Such aid, moreover, must be available for both the neglected child and the relatively advantaged.

If much of this new assistance were expressly channeled into creating metropolitan parks, on a formula of 90 per cent Federal and 10 per cent State and local funding, it would envision equalized, integrated schools of high quality in most cities within a period of 10 to 15 years.

Would such a program mean abandoning usable existing school buildings? Not at all, since most districts desperately need more space for their present and predictable enrollment, to say nothing of the other uses that school systems and other government agencies could readily find for buildings that might be relinquished. The impending expansion of nursery school programs and adult education are only two of the more obvious alternate uses for in-city structures.

Is the school park an all-or-nothing question? Is it necessary to abandon all existing programs before the benefits of the park can be tested? Short of full commitment, there are steps that can be taken in the direction of establishing parks and to achieve some of their values. The "educational complex" put forward in the Allen Report for New York City is one such step. As described in that report, the complex is a group of two to five primary schools and one or two middle schools near enough to each other to form a cooperating cluster and serving sufficiently diversified neighborhoods to promote good biracial contact.

An educational complex should be administered by a *senior administrator*, who should be given authority and autonomy to develop a program which meets appropriate citywide standards but is also directly relevant to the needs of the locality. Primary schools within the complex should share among themselves facilities, faculties, and special staff, and should be coordinated to encourage frequent association among students and parents from the several units. Within the education complex teachers will be better able to help children from diverse ethnic backgrounds to become acquainted with one another. Parent-teacher and parent-school relations should be built on the bases of both the individual school and the complex. The children — and their parents — will thus gain the dual benefits of a school close to home and of membership in a larger, more diverse educational and social community. The concept of the educational complex arises in part from the view that the means of education and much of their control should be centered locally.

Although it may not be possible to desegregate all primary schools, ultimately most of them should be integrated educationally. This will aid the better preparation of students for life and study in the middle school; it will more nearly equalize resources; and it will give the staff in the primary schools new opportunities for innovation and originality in their work.[8]

Experimental projects on a limited scale

might also be set up between city and suburban districts to deal with common problems. The Hartford and Irondequoit projects transporting Negro students to suburban schools are examples of what can be done.

Additional efforts could include exchanging staff members; involving students, particularly at the secondary level, in joint curricular or extracurricular activities; setting up "miniature school parks" during the summer in schools on the city-suburban border; conducting work sessions in which board and staff members from metropolitan school systems examine population changes, common curriculum problems, and opportunities for joint action.

Establishing school parks would mean a substantial shift in educational policy. In addition, as has been pointed out, the metropolitan park would require concerted action among governmental units. New forms of State and Federal financial support and sharply increased appropriations would be essential. . . . Parents and other citizens, school leaders, public officials and legislators will be justified in asking for persuasive factual and logical support for such radical proposals.

The response must be that critically important educational, social, and economic needs of a large part of urban America are not being met by our present policies and practices and that there is no reason to think that they will be met by minor adjustments of the present arrangements. The evidence is irresistible

8 State Education Commission's Advisory Committee on Human Relations and Community Tensions, *Desegregating the Public Schools of New York City* (New York: New York State Department of Education, 1964), p. 18.

that the consequences of racial segregation are so costly and so damaging to all our people that they should no longer be tolerated. Through bitter experience we are learning that the isolation of any race is demeaning when it is deliberate and that it is counterproductive in human and economic terms, no matter how it is caused or explained. The elimination of this debilitating and degrading aspect of American life must now be ranked among the most important and urgent goals of our society. The task cannot be done without concerted action among many forces and agencies. Participation by private agencies and by government at every level will be needed. But central to every other effort will be the influence and the power of the public schools. Those schools, which have served the nation so well in achieving other high purposes, can serve equally well in performing their part of this new undertaking — if the magnitude of the task is fully appreciated and action undertaken on a scale appropriate to a major national purpose.

The steps that have heretofore been taken to cope with segregation have been of no more than tactical dimensions. Most of them have been relatively minor adaptations and accommodations requiring minimal changes in the status quo. It should by now be clear that we cannot integrate our schools or assure all our children access to the best education unless we accept these twin goals as prime strategic objectives.

. . . .

Establishing rings of school parks about each of our segregated central cities would, to be sure, require decisions to invest large sums of money in these projects. The prior and more important commitment, however, must be to the purpose to which the money will be dedicated: effective equality of educational opportunity at a new high level for millions of our young people.

The school park is no panacea. In itself it will guarantee no more than a setting for new accomplishment. But the setting is essential. If we fail to provide it or to invent an equally promising alternative, we shall continue to deny a high proportion of our citizens the indispensible means to a decent and productive life.

THE REAL MEANING OF THE NEW YORK CITY TEACHERS' STRIKE

Albert Shanker

Albert Shanker, "The Real Meaning of the New York City Teacher's Strike,"
Phi Delta Kappan, April 1969, pp. 434-441.

THE REAL MEANING OF
THE NEW YORK CITY TEACHERS'
STRIKE

Albert Shanker

Educators and parents in cities throughout the country have observed the New York school crisis with intense interest and apprehension. Their interest grows out of their need to find a solution to educational problems remarkably similar to those faced by New Yorkers—segregated schooling, inadequate resources, overworked and undertrained teachers, unwieldy central bureaucracies, and most significantly, the massive educational retardation of the poor. And they are apprehensive because they wish to avoid the kind of tragic racial and ethnic conflicts and political polarizations that were caused by the controversy over decentralization and due process for teachers.

I think they can avoid these difficulties—indeed, they must—which is also to say that the New York conflict was not inevitable; that, in fact, it was the result of

---

MR. SHANKER is a former junior high math teacher who at one time studied for a doctor's degree in philosophy at Columbia. He has headed the United Federation of Teachers since 1964 and is a vice-president of the AFL-CIO-affiliated American Federation of Teachers.

certain political errors that need not be repeated and intellectual confusions that can be corrected by a critical analysis of the problems involved. I am, therefore, somewhat discouraged by the decision of the PHI DELTA KAPPAN to run a series of articles in its January, 1969, issue—particularly "The UFT Strike: Will It Destroy the AFT?" by Stephen Zeluck; "Local Control and the Cultural Deprivation Fallacy," by S. Alan Cohen; and "Strategies for Improving Inner-City Schools," by Robert G. Owens and Carl R. Steinhoff—which justify past errors, reinforce present confusions, and do little to shed light on a situation that has been obfuscated by slogans and clichés.

Mr. Zeluck's article is a rehearsal of half-truths and simplifications which are often used today to "prove" that the United Federation of Teachers has become anti-Negro and conservative. His argument is based on the false assumption that the UFT has abandoned the civil rights movement and liberalism when, in fact, it is certain segments of the liberal and black communities that have abandoned the principles of integration, nonviolence, and democracy which are the essence of the civil rights movement

453

and which remain the fundamental beliefs of the UFT This is a complicated question involving a crisis in American liberalism and race relations which I shall consider at a later point. For the moment I shall deal with Mr. Zeluck's specific allegations which, sadly, serve best the interests of those who desire to see the UFT divided from minority communities.

Mr. Zeluck claims that the UFT did not support the school boycotts of 1964, yet our staff was involved in the organization of those boycotts, and we defended any teacher who participated in them. He also interprets the contract demand for special facilities for "disruptive children" as "punitive" and anti-black, a position popularized by the mayor and the Board of Education to mobilize community support against the 1967 strike. Mr. Zeluck fails to note that a far stronger "disruptive child" proposal was adopted in 1965 by the Detroit Federation of Teachers. The proposal was drafted by Ed Simpkins, a black vice-president of DFT, a responsible educator, and Zeluck's leader in the opposition caucus within the American Federation of Teachers. The point is that the "disruptive child" proposal was not racist but a meaningful educational demand. One emotionally disturbed child *can* disrupt a class of 36 children, and that child *should* receive special attention. Mr. Zeluck's treatment of this material is significant not in terms of its validity, but as an indication of his consistent attempt to impose a racially divisive interpretation on educational issues.

This is equally true of his discussion of the controversy over due process for teachers which led up to the 1968 teacher strikes. The history of these events is long and complicated,* but this is no excuse for Mr. Zeluck's errors and oversimplifications. His central point is that the UFT used the due process issue as "a smoke screen for its hostility to community control."** This is a highly subjective judgment based upon preconceptions and hearsay, and there is absolutely no evidence to support it.

There is evidence, however, to show that the UFT cooperated with the Ocean Hill-Brownsville experiment in school decentralization in the hope that it would stimulate greater parent involvement in the schools and provide more effective education for the children. As early as 1966, the UFT was involved in joint parent-teacher efforts to secure improvements at Junior High School 178 and its feeder schools. It was largely as a result of these efforts, in fact, that Ocean Hill was chosen as an experimental district.

---

*The most thorough accounts of these events are Martin Mayer's "The Full and Sometimes Very Surprising Story of Ocean Hill, the Teachers' Union and the Teacher Strikes of 1968," *The New York Times Magazine*, February, 2, 1969, an expanded version of which has just been published in book form by Harper & Row; and Maurice Goldbloom's "The New York School Crisis," *Commentary*, January, 1969. These pieces were published subsequent to Mr. Zeluck's article, so he did not have the benefit of reading them.

**The "smoke screen" accusation was made by the New York Civil Liberties Union. Point-by-point refutation has been made by Maurice Goldbloom in "A Critique of the New York Civil Liberties Union Report on the Ocean Hill-Brownsville School Controversy" and by Sandra Feldman in "The Burden of Blame: An Answer to a Statement by the New York Civil Liberties Union." The former is available from the Ad Hoc Committee To Defend the Right To Teach, Room 1105, 112 East 19th St., New York 10003 and the latter from the UFT, 260 Park Ave. South, New York 10010.

Our hope was that the experiment would bring parents and teachers closer together in search of solutions to educational problems, and that their task would be facilitated by the infusion of more resources into the district. Yet during the summer of 1967, the first signs began to appear that neither of these objectives was to be realized and that the interests of some influential participants in the planning of the project were hardly educational at all. The proposal submitted by the Ocean Hill Planning Council to the Board of Education to establish the project abandoned a previous request for additional resources and supplementary educational services. More significantly, there emerged the first tendencies toward extremism and confrontationism which were later to bring so much harm to all parties involved. The Planning Council began to receive its political direction from Father John Powis of the Church of Our Lady of the Presentation, ·whose chief concern was not raising the reading level of children but forcing "a confrontation with a sick society;" and Herman Ferguson, an anti-white black separatist who at the time was under indictment (he was later convicted and his case is now being appealed) for conspiracy to murder moderate civil rights leaders, who was extremely hostile to the UFT. (Ferguson was later chosen by the governing board to be principal of the new I.S. 55.) These were hardly conditions conducive to parent-teacher cooperation. A statement made by the teachers in the district in September, 1967, noted that the atmosphere at the meetings "became so hostile that teachers hesitated even to ask a question or express an opinion. Any attempt at teacher comment was met with insults and charges of obstruction."

The atmosphere of hostility persisted throughout the fall to the point where many teachers wanted to leave the district, but UFT representatives met with them regularly, urging them to stay with the experiment until high feelings cooled and cooperation might be possible. As a result of the union's entreaties, very few teachers left—fewer, in fact, than the 10 percent quota which had been permitted by a special transfer policy. Moreover, a district teacher committee was formed which met monthly with Rhody McCoy, the unit administrator, to discuss problems and help formulate educational programs, and UFT representatives

> "... the UFT has [not] abandoned the civil rights movement and liberalism ... in fact, it is certain segments of the liberal and black communities that have abandoned the principles of integration, nonviolence, and democracy...."

also held regular meetings with McCoy to offer him any technical assistance he might need. Not only did McCoy never act upon any of the ideas brought forth by the teachers, he never once informed the Ocean Hill governing board of his meetings either with the teacher committee or with the UFT. He thus helped maintain the atmosphere of hostility that divided the governing board and other parents from the teachers.

In March, 1968, the day following the Rinaldi decision invalidating the appointment of elementary school principals by the Ocean Hill governing board, Frederick Nauman, the UFT chapter chairman at J.H.S. 271, sent a letter to the president of the Board of Education urging him to appeal the decision in the hope that the principals might be retained. Nauman feared that if the principals were removed the experiment in decentralization would be destroyed. The letter was signed by almost the entire staff of J.H.S. 271.

It is against a background of these efforts of the Ocean Hill staff to cooperate with the project that we must try to understand why the governing board made the infamous decision to dismiss summarily 13 teachers and six administrators. The decision had nothing to do with the educational competence of the dismissed personnel. Indeed, the governing board can hardly be assumed to have been aware of their performance in school when they were not even certain of some of the *names* of the dismissed teachers. Nor were the teachers dismissed because of political differences with the project, although that was the reason given, and the charge has been made—by Zeluck, among others—that they were trying to "sabotage" the experiment. One of the "saboteurs" was Nauman, who had supported the experiment from its inception. Moreover, McCoy and the governing board at first refused to bring charges against the teachers—they had no charges to bring—and those which they finally did compile were found to be invalid by the Negro trial examiner, Judge Francis E. Rivers. One teacher was accused of having no control over his class because his children had been observed throwing chairs around the classroom, but on closer examination it was found that the chairs in the room were of the stationary type, fastened to the floor. Another teacher was accused of being hostile to the project because he remarked at a Christmas party that certain conditions in the schools were unwholesome and should be improved. Judge Rivers found that not only was this teacher protected by the First Amendment, he was "actually attempting to give constructive criticism of the project."

The teachers were dismissed because certain individuals on the governing board and extremist elements from both within Ocean Hill and around the city, who claimed to represent "the community," desired a confrontation. They wanted one in order to test whether they had total control, and also because they felt that by creating a *racial* confrontation (the only Negro teacher among the 13 dismissed was immediately reinstated) they could mobilize community support behind them. For they did not have this support, however much they invoked and claimed to embody that mythical entity, "the will of the community." A Harris poll taken that spring found that the community was generally dissatisfied with the performance of McCoy (44 percent evaluated him negatively and only 29 percent positively) and the governing board (47 percent were negative and 38 percent positive) and only 29 percent supported the decision to oust the teachers. And during the summer a local Committee for Democratic Education circulated a petition throughout Ocean Hill demanding new elections for the governing board. Although over 2,000 signatures were gathered—twice as many people as had originally voted the previous summer—the Board of Education refused to act. This inaction was one more factor obstructing a settlement of the dispute.

It was because of the desire for a confrontation that McCoy did not go through established procedures for dismissal or transfer of teachers. And it was for this same reason that he and Oliver[*] refused to submit the dispute to binding arbitration or to mediation by Theodore Kheel, to whose recommendations the UFT agreed in June. For McCoy and Oliver to have accepted such arbitration would have meant the loss of their confrontation.

It is within this context that the three fall strikes must be understood. The issue had nothing to do with decentralization, but rather with the right of teachers who are threatened with dismissal to have charges brought against them, to

be able to defend themselves at hearings before a neutral third party, and to have the right of appeal. These are rights which must be guaranteed every American worker—particularly black workers, who have so often been fired without due process as a result of racial and political prejudices. To threaten some workers with the loss of these basic rights is to threaten all workers—black and white. And, I might add, Mr. Zeluck, as a union leader, should deal very carefully with these issues.

It was the guarantee that the dismissed teachers would have the right to return to their classes which ended the first strike on September 10. And it was the violation of this settlement on the following day which brought on the second strike. For when the UFT teachers returned to Ocean Hill on September 11, they were told to report to the auditorium of I.S. 55 for a special "orientation" session. There they were terrorized and told that they would be killed if they did not leave the district. This terrorism, prearranged by McCoy and others and participated in by a minority of extremists, was referred to as an uprising of the "community." I should add in this context that the real community in Ocean Hill never turned up at any of the rallies called by these militants. On those rare occasions when they were able to muster as many as 300 people at a demonstration, the vast majority always consisted of anti-UFT teachers and traveling extremists; there were at best a very small handful of parents.

The second strike was ended when John Doar, president of the

[*]The Reverend C. Herbert Oliver, chairman of the Ocean Hill project governing board, a former Southern Christian Leadership Conference worker from Alabama.—*The Editor*

Board of Education, assured the union that he would set up an enforcement procedure in Ocean Hill similar to the one he had established in 1962 to secure the admittance of James Meredith to the University of Mississippi. This procedure, however, broke down almost immediately. Union teachers were not given classes, and they had to face daily abuse and insult. There was still hope, though, that passions would cool—until October 9, when there was another eruption of violence and threats at J.H.S. 271. Extremists were allowed into the school and they, together with teachers hostile to the union, incited the children and threatened union teachers and the acting principal with violence. (The latter, a Negro lady, was so shaken by the events of October 9 that she refused to return to the school.) At all of the schools, principals refused to give union teachers class assignments. Superintendent of Schools Bernard Donovan reacted to this by suspending the principals and closing J.H.S. 271 for the following two days. But then when he decided to reopen it *without taking any action to insure that the horrors of October 9 would not be repeated* and to reinstate the principals without any assurances that they would comply with the agreement, the union was forced to embark on its third, tragic, but ultimately necessary, strike. The strike lasted for five weeks, until a settlement could be worked out that put Ocean Hill under a state trusteeship. I should add as a final, ironic commentary on the situation that many of those young, enthusiastic teachers in Ocean Hill who opposed our strike but who also have been unable to control their classes can today find themselves on new lists of unwanted teachers.

In this brief chronology of the events in Ocean Hill, I have omitted any substantial discussion of decentralization itself because this was not an issue in the dispute—at least as far as the UFT was concerned. But certainly it *was* an issue to the extent that many people believed it to be, and in that the events took place within the context of a controversy over the kind of decentralization that would best contribute to the improvement of New York schools. For, indeed, there have been many *kinds* of decentralization proposed, and more obscurantism than intellectual clarity has emerged from the debate over which might be the best kind. In the space remaining, therefore, I shall try to answer two questions which seem to me fundamental: What is the educational relevance of decentralization and why has it become such a powerful issue at this particular point in history?

The UFT has stated repeatedly that it is in favor of decentralization. I think it has great constructive potential, particularly those aspects of it which should enhance both parent concern for the learning of the children and creative community participation in matters of educational policy. Parents have a legitimate grievance against the rigidities and the remoteness of the central bureaucracy. To the extent these difficulties have increased the alienation and apathy of parents, to that extent they must be remedied by bringing the decision-making power closer to where its effects are felt. I favor this because if parents have no

> "The teachers were dismissed because certain individuals on the governing board and extremist elements from both within Ocean Hill and around the city, who claimed to represent 'the community,' desired a confrontation."

interest or influence in their children's education, then the kind of militant parent-teacher alliance that the UFT has always advocated as a means to improve the schools will be impossible to achieve. And, more fundamentally, I favor increased parent and community participation because I know from my experience in the trade union movement that individuals cannot have human dignity until they participate in decisions affecting their lives.

The UFT, therefore, has supported (and lobbied for) a decentralization plan that would give locally elected boards, among other things, the power to hire and fire their district superintendents and guaranteed funds, over and above centrally mandated costs, for use as they see fit in developing innovative programs. We have also sup-

ported the establishment of a civilian review board to which parents could bring complaints against teachers and which, in turn, would guarantee those teachers a fair hearing. And our union has fought for the enlargement of the role played by paraprofessionals whose contribution represents the most creative form of community participation to date in our schools. They have freed the teacher to teach by performing many important non-professional tasks, and in the process they are receiving the training that will enable them in the future to assume more professional responsibilities. Even more significantly, their employment (there are 20,000 of them working in New York City schools) is a pioneering effort in the area of "new careers for the poor" which has tremendous social implications at a time when automation is eliminating jobs for the unskilled.

We have also argued for the retention of a central focus, which would involve the determination, by the central board, of city-wide educational standards and a minimum curriculum required of each district, as well as the evaluation by that board of the performance of each district. We have also felt that the hiring and licensing of teachers should be done by a central agency. The reasoning here is that if districts compete for staff (as was suggested, for example, by the Bundy plan) those areas of greatest educational need will have the most difficult time recruiting adequate personnel while middle-class districts would have a surplus of teachers. Even McCoy, whose district was a *cause celebré*, could not find enough teachers this past summer to staff his schools and was, therefore, forced to turn to the Board of Education. (Dismissal of incompetent personnel would be initiated, of course, at the local level, by the supervisor closest to the staff and by the district superintendent, who can be fired by the local board if he does not weed out incompetents.) And finally, we have urged that local districts be large enough to provide a basis for integration and to prevent the institutionalization of segregation.

But the union's program for improving the schools does not—and must not—end with decentralization, for the basic educational problems that confront parents and educators today cannot be solved with only administrative changes. James Coleman, for example, in his massive study *Equality of Educational Opportunity,* found that the two most important variables affecting the achievement of a child are his socioeconomic class and the skill of his teacher. In relation to the first variable, S. Alan Cohen (KAPPAN, January, 1969) hardly clarifies matters by postulating "the cultural deprivation fallacy," and then noting that "enriched verbal home environments . . . make children in Scarsdale less dependent upon the school to learn to read and write than children from Bedford-Stuyvesant." He can not have it both ways; nor can our society, which must begin to spend the billions of dollars that are needed to attack the problem of economic deprivation. And we must also be willing to spend money on programs that will help the teacher to teach more effectively, for even if

poverty persists I am convinced that we can make our teachers and our schools good enough to enable children to overcome its constricting and debilitating effect. We must improve our teacher recruitment and training programs and, most importantly, we must expand the More Effective Schools program which, despite the Owens and Steinhoff report (KAPPAN, January, 1969), has proved highly effective in New York City schools. The basis of their study was an evaluation of the program made in 1967 by the Center for Urban Education.° But a study conducted *a year later* by the Board of Education showed that children in ME schools had made dramatic advances in reading over children in comparable control groups—as much as three-tenths of a school year at the third- and fifth-grade levels. Owens and Steinhoff call for "greater trust" and "social warmth," and I too would like to see these qualities predominate in our schools. But in order to achieve this we must have smaller classes and better trained teachers, both of which require massive social expenditures. Owens and Steinhoff forget that individuals do not act autonomously, that they are affected by the conditions under which they must work and live.

The inadequacies of the Fox evaluation are analyzed in Sidney Schwager's "An Analysis of the Evaluation of the MES Program Conducted by the Center for Urban Education," *The Urban Review,* May, 1968, p. 18, which shows that the poor results reported for MES were due to Fox's failure to control for pupil mobility. Achievement scores were lowered by testing pupils who transferred into MES schools and had not had the advantages of this program. When the results of students who had the benefit of MES were isolated, they showed the program was successful.

(George Orwell once wrote that "a 'change of heart' "—which is essentially what Owens and Steinhoff are asking for—"is in fact *the* alibi of people who do not wish to endanger the status quo.") I think it is asking too much of a teacher to be warm, open, and relaxed when every day he must confront a class of 36 children most of whom are brutalized by poverty and are more concerned with survival than learning to read and write. In this regard, pointing to the success of Herbert Kohl under present conditions hardly confronts the fundamental difficulty of enabling hundreds of thousands of teachers—of average, not exceptional, ability who, unlike Kohl, make teaching a career—to perform systematically at a higher level. And I must add that local control is marginal to this central issue. It is an administrative reform that can bring parents and teachers closer together; but to think that it can provide the fundamental changes that are required for educational excellence is to substitute social myth for public policy.

Which brings me to the final question of why local control has become such a myth, to the point where its educational significance has been distorted out of all proportion to the contribution it can make. For I believe that the difficulties with demands for local control arise not from these demands per se (which, as I have suggested, have constructive possibilities), but from their potential effect on educational and social policy that derives from the political context in which decentralization is proposed. This political context has been shaped by the failure to achieve either racial integration or the massive resources necessary for quality education. Within this context decentralization, while not in inherent contradiction to massive funding or integration, is put forth as an alternative to both of them. And once it has been so proposed, it is justified on the grounds that both of the previous policies have proved educationally invalid, an empirical judgment based on the false assumption that massive funding and integration "didn't work," when in fact they had never even been tried. Mr. Cohen, therefore, can write that "half a decade of federal funds" has failed to make substantial changes in our schools. He does not understand that the funds provided urban schools under Title I of the 1965 Elementary and Secondary Education Act are infinitesimal compared to what is needed. And in the same sense we can see how Kenneth Clark, a strong and influential proponent of decentralization, can make the following statements rejecting greater public investment in education:

One of the best things that could happen to public education in the United States in the next two or three years is that it not get any extra money from the federal or state governments and that it be required to raise the quality of performance within its present budget. (*The Center Magazine*, November, 1968)

If the sentiments of Cohen and Clark are widely shared, I am afraid that it will be far more than two or three years before our schools get any extra money, because the political pressure for

461

such funds will have been channeled into demands for decentralization.

The same political context has produced a situation in which many former integrationists have not only become resigned to segregation but have become active enthusiasts of racial separatism. The reasons for this are highly complicated and deserve close analysis. On one level there has been the attempt on the part of city officials and foundation executives to accommodate to the most militant and separatist elements in the black community in order to de-fuse what they consider to be an explosive situation. They have operated on the basis of a "riot psychology" which has prevented them from taking any action opposing the militants for fear there might be a violent reaction. This was most evident during the events in Ocean Hill when militants like Sonny Carson had the ear of city officials and therefore became in effect community spokesmen. More moderate community leaders were not listened to, for they were not to be feared, and a confrontation became inevitable.

This de-fusing has taken the form of community control, I think, for two reasons. First, community control provides separatism with a cloak of respectability that can make it acceptable to the American public. The concept of hiring and firing people on the basis of race is both morally offensive and politically impractical, but when transformed into the demand that each community have the right to control its schools, it can be accepted as part of our progressive democratic tradition. And, second, community control provides a vehicle for shifting the burden of responsibility for educating black children from the whole society to the black communities themselves. The former is thus "let off the hook" (even though it is the whole society that is responsible for the brutalities blacks have suffered), while the latter are left with only themselves to blame for their children's failure. The art of political de-fusing is to induce the protester to protest against himself.

The dilemma which remains to be explained is why blacks and liberals who support their cause should .permit, and even desire, such a reactionary situation to develop. The answer lies, I feel, in the crisis in American liberalism and race relations that I have already noted and which has manifested itself as a process of the mystification of racial separatism. It has occurred in segments of the black community largely as a consequence of the failure by our society to meet Negro demands for full equality. For those blacks who have despaired of progress, there has been a withdrawal into nationalism, a turning away from social institutions that have proved difficult to change, and a concentration on psychological problems which are more immediate and seem to be more manageable. And there has been the inevitable rationalization that this is a progressive shift of emphasis—that one can obviate the need for more and better jobs, homes, and schools simply by thinking that "black is beautiful."

A similar process of mystification and withdrawal has taken place in the white community as well. Many liberals who have grown weary of the struggle for social justice are using the rhetoric of black nationalists as a means of justifying their fatigue. They have now convinced themselves that the black poor need "identity" and "pride" rather than economic and political equality, and that the primary task of white people is to purge themselves of their racism. I am in agreement with these liberals only to the extent that I *do* find an undercurrent of racism in their attitudes. Having assumed that the Negro is in need of psychological rehabilitation, they act towards him in a manner that is both condescending and insulting. They romanticize his poverty, pardon all of his misdeeds, and project him into the role of revolutionary come to save the white middle class from their boredom and their sins. Like conventional bigots who say "No" to every black demand, they now mindlessly say "Yes," thus refusing to treat the Negro as an equal—and fallible—human being. And by choosing as the "real" black man those who are most extreme in their behavior—regarding the others as "Toms"—they unwittingly sanction the racist myth that the Negro represents a dangerous element and a social liability.

Those attitudes might be ludicrous did they not contribute to an atmosphere in which racial separatism has become acceptable public policy. For example, Thomas Pettigrew, one of the principal authors of one report of the United States Commission on Civil Rights, *Racial Isolation in the Public Schools*, has pointed out (*The Urban Review*, January, 1969) that decentralization of the kind proposed in the Bundy Plan will produce a separatist situation in which there will be "60 ghettos, sealed in structurally, where local people have a vested interest in keeping the structure that way, even if the education is inferior." Moreover, the redistricting proposed by Mayor Lindsay's "liberal" Board of Education in its decentralization plan of December 15, 1968, was a deliberate attempt to impose racial apartheid on the city of New York.

> "When the UFT teachers returned to Ocean Hill on September 11, they were told to report to the auditorium of I.S. 55 for a special 'orientation' session. There they were terrorized and told that they would be killed if they did not leave the district."

What is even more threatening is that as a result of the separatist and nationalist framework within which decentralization has developed, a mood of intellectual oppression and moral absolutism has set in which has made it impossible to discuss social problems with any degree of rationality. The separatists have posed the issue as that of a people struggling to overthrow an oppressor. They have imported concepts of imperialism and colonialism which provide the ideological justification for calling people to arms on the basis of ethnic loyalties. Their cry is, "We destroy you or we perish."

The logical outcome of defining the issue in terms of racial oppression is that demands become absolistic and non-negotiable. And because it is impossible to meet these demands within the context of competing centers of influence, a climate of violence and racial hostility must inevitably develop. I think that we must understand the problem of anti-Semitism as a subsection of this larger difficulty. The Jews are a convenient and proximate object of hatred, and so they have been singled out, but ultimately they are but one of the many so-called "oppressors." The fundamental problem remains the environment of hostility that has been created by those who use primitive oversimplifications, racial myths, and irresponsible revolutionary rhetoric to interpret complex social issues.

These attitudes have also helped divide the Negro from the American trade union movement. Thus John Doar can write that

> Union concepts of security and seniority were formulated in the period of struggle between company and union. Now the struggle is between the Negro and the unions. . . . It is our position that a basic conflict exists between labor-union concepts and civil

rights concepts. Something has to give. (*Fortune*, January, 1969)

And S. Alan Cohen, a "reading specialist" with varied interests, can offer us an analysis of "the real issues" involved in decentralization: "the union chief's play for power," "unionism," and "white racism." What Doar and Cohen do not seem to understand is that they cannot help Negroes by destroying the rights of unionists—2,000,000 of whom *are* Negroes. What they will succeed in doing is reinforcing the political and racial polarizations upon which George Wallace will thrive, and they shall find themselves in an alliance with the most reactionary elements in the country who are both anti-labor *and* anti-Negro. For the Negro ultimately has common —not conflicting—interests with lower-middle class whites. Each group will benefit from more jobs, better housing, and superior schools and they must struggle together to achieve those ends. Anyone who encourages them to fight against each other *over scarce resources* rather than with each other *for more resources* is, however noble his intentions, the worst enemy of both.

The mystification which I identified in relation to racial separatism has, like a contagious psychological disease, infected other areas of social thought as well. A mystique has been built up around decentralization and participation that has distorted the genuinely democratic character of these concepts. Some decentralists, I feel, would prefer to dismember rather than democratize social institutions which they despise for being impersonal, technological, and centralized. Their protest is in the form of a cult of localism and antisocial individualism which is most evident today among educated and alienated members of the middle class. This movement is inevitably separatist in its effect, since it glorifies and reinforces those characteristics —racial, ethnic, class, or otherwise— which differentiate social groups. And it is also reactionary in that it is fundamentally opposed to political and economic equalization, as well as to those centralized institutions—such as the federal government, the labor movement, and the public school system— which have been most responsible for the social advancement of the poor.

Which is all a complicated way of saying that we must be very careful to disassociate the regressive features of decentralization from the progressive ones. I am not certain, for example, that decentralization will necessarily promote innovation, since small districts have been traditionally conservative and highly dependent on conventionalized commercial products. In fact, the most innovative school systems today are those which are consolidating the resources of localities, thereby broadening the scope and range of their activities. Nor does it follow that decentralization will eliminate bureaucracy, inefficiency, and unnecessary costs. On the contrary, it might very well establish inefficient and expensive local bureaucracies which would perform the same dull administrative chores that are presently centralized—only with greater duplication.

And although I have stated that decentralization can enhance democracy, it can also inhibit it by creating power vacuums that extremists can move in to fill. For once they have moved in, they will not only deny academic freedom and due process to teachers, they will intimidate the less aggressive members of the community who disagree with their views. More fundamentally, decentralization can be antidemocratic insofar as it caters to local differences and prejudices. Liberal teachers will be unwanted in conservative neighborhoods, and ethnic and racial affinities with the local population may become the prime criteria for selecting staff. In a pluralist society such practices are discriminatory and intolerable.

I have offered these criticisms of decentralization because I fear that many people with progressive intentions are rushing blindly into actions which may have seriously reactionary consequences. We must not forget that Louise Day Hicks, the Boston segregationist, ran for the School Committee in that city on a neighborhood school/segregation platform which is not substantially different from what many decentralists propose. We must therefore proceed cautiously with decentralization without abandoning the principles of integration and full economic and social equality to false hopes and illusions. For these principles are not only morally just, they are also the basic values which must be preserved if our pluralist society is to endure as a stable and unified democracy.

OCEAN HILL: EDUCATION, COMMUNITY POWER, AND, THE MEDIA

Agee Ward

Agee Ward, "Ocean Hill: Education, Community, Power and the Media," *Center Forum* (A Publication of the Center for Urban Education), November 13, 1968, pp. 1-10.

OCEAN HILL: EDUCATION, COMMUNITY POWER, AND, THE MEDIA

Agee Ward

WHEN social conflicts become public controversies, much depends upon the quality of information available to the citizenry at large. In situations where the general public is not immediately involved, most people have no direct experience of the conflict and no perception of their own as to what the issues are. The mass media and other channels of public information automatically become the chief sources of knowledge for most people who are interested in the controversy. The immense power of these communications media thus becomes a highly significant factor in the conflict itself. Even when, operating from certain limited points of view, the purveyors of mass information generally represent only one side in the clash and present only one view of the issues, they usually convey the impression that their projections are impartial and objective. When biased reporting and analysis of this kind become the general rule, there is little hope that the public will favor a resolution of the conflict that is either realistic or just. There are a number of issues in recent American affairs around which just such a pattern has emerged. One of the most serious instances of this pattern is now emerging in the area of public education and its relationship to community life among urban minority groups.

The entire New York school crisis, and the Ocean Hill-Brownsville conflict in particular, are being presented to the American public in extremely misleading terms. These matters have been widely discussed on the basis of inaccurate and incomplete information. This in turn leads to widespread acceptance of quite unreasonable interpretations and conclusions. My own comments are offered from three perspectives fortuitously com-

bined by circumstances over the past several months. In addition to being a resident of the community most directly affected by the school crisis, I have been a continuous direct observer of the struggle from a community viewpoint, and I am a professional social scientist. From these perspectives the following report includes four kinds of information, each presented in the hope of correcting the general ignorance and misinformation about the case of Ocean Hill-Brownsville. First, most of the article simply describes the behavior, the experience, and the sentiments of community residents which I have observed and recorded. Second, the reader will find some descriptions of significant otusiders as I have directly observed them and their actions within the community. In the third place, some references are made to relevant portions of the public record available in the press and other media. Finally, a few passages will readily be perceived by attentive readers as analysis, judgment, or prediction which I present as my own in my capacity as a professional researcher.

Much misunderstanding arises from a failure to give due emphasis to the background and context of current conflicts. Even the best of the discussions tend to gloss over the fact that these conflicts are expressions of extremely long-standing grievances all across the country. The articles therefore fail to make it fully clear that the case of Ocean Hill-Brownsville and the crisis of New York City are deep-lying and explosive national issues. Likewise, they fail to communicate effectively how the demand for community control over schools derives its credibility and relevance from the experience of life in the urban areas in America populated by the poor and racial minority groups.*

The aggrieved parents of these deprived communities have been pressing their case in the area of education for many years now. They have been through the whole range of educational challenges and responses from desegregation to compensatory schooling, in all their many forms. Yet neither the achievement levels of their youngsters nor the opportunities open to their school graduates have improved significantly. The conclusion has been drawn in these areas that the ruling central bureaucracies are not really interested in improving the lot of the minority poor. A sizable number of residents perceive that in spite of all the centralized "solutions," many youth are still pushed into the status of dropouts. Parents are aware that those who graduate generally are not regarded as qualified to live the kind of life to which they aspire. Youth and adults increasingly believe that the few who become successes are frequently committed to a system which oppresses their own home communities. Out of this perspective—and the long and frustrating experience behind it—has come the demand for community control over the schools. The central goal of this movement is to make local institutions *accountable* to the people whom they are supposed to serve.

There has long been a widespread feeling that many members of neighborhood school staffs care little about children

* Three recent documents present much useful and enlightening background for the present account. (1) New York Civil Liberties Union, *The Burden of Blame: A Report on the Ocean Hill-Brownsville School Controversy*, mimeographed, October 1968. (2) Richard Karp, "School Decentralization in New York: a Case Study," *Interplay*, August-September 1968. (3) Niemeyer Commeyer Commission, *An Evaluative Study of the Process of School Decentralization in New York City*, July 1968.

from racial minority groups and have little faith in their ability to learn. Exceptional individual teachers and principals are known and recognized for their positive contributions. By far the most common perception in the community, however, is that school faculties generally underestimate black and Puerto Rican students, "teach down" to them, judge them unfairly, and show little empathy either with children or with parents. (Community opinion, incidentally, does not ignore other popular explanations for low scholastic achievement. Poor motivation and irresponsibility on the part of both pupils and parents are among the additional factors most commonly cited in black and Puerto Rican neighborhoods. For many community people, however, these factors do not lessen the responsibility of school personnel for what is seen as a lack of commitment, dedication, sympathy, or understanding on the part of professional educators.)

A pervasive effect of all this experience has been a sense of being powerless to influence local educational institutions. For many this frustration has led to apathy and resignation on the educational front, reactions which are reinforced by the fact that most poor families are confronted daily with problems of more immediate urgency. Yet in spite of all this there are also many black people and Puerto Ricans who respond to their situation by struggling through the years to find some way to obtain quality education for their children. This struggle is motivated by attitudes and values that are common and familiar throughout American society. Citizens of deprived communities want their children to receive effective schooling because they believe this will enable them either to remake their communities or to leave the world of menial jobs, welfare dependency, and slum living behind them. But active strivers and uninvolved spectators alike are faced year after year with the fact that the struggle brings individual success to very few and little if anything in the way of effective institutional improvement for the community as a whole.

The view of the matter frequently stated by community people directly associated with the experiences described in this article is that very few of the analysts, commentators, or reporters who interpret the school issue to the public have been through the general experience described above. Further, few of them have been close to those whose experience this is, and few have made a conscientious effort to expose themselves directly to this background. In short, most individuals and institutions responsible for projecting the struggle over community control to the public are simply not qualified to report it accurately or understand it well. Moreover, these purveyors of information are deeply conditioned by their own life experience, a conditioning which typically leads to more or less automatic respect for the conventional institutions which people in the deprived urban areas increasingly feel have failed them. These institutions include governmental and educational bureaucracies, teaching and allied professions, police forces, news media, and others, all of which respond primarily to centralized power centers extremely remote from the world of ghetto citizens.

This is what spokesmen for oppressed minorities and the poor mean, in part at least, when they refer to the insensitivity of White America. This is the reason why many of these spokesmen despair of ever being treated fairly by existing dominant institutions. Quite apart from the other institutions involved, this challenge for responsible fair play has received no adequate response on the part of information media, including the news industry, the publishing business, and the academic world. My contention is not that no efforts have been made in the several areas of national life concerned with information and communication. The point is rather that with very few exceptions current attempts to develop new directions in informing the public about the national crisis in intergroup relations are so inadequate in scale and quality that they can only be described as a failure. We have a national situation in which even those members of the public who might be receptive to a less one-sided presentation of issues involving life among oppressed Americans are literaly denied the relevant information.

The present crisis in public education, as I have noted, is a case in point. To begin with, public attention is continually diverted from the central issue that most concerns advocates of community control and most conditions their conduct in the conflict. *This issue is the quality and relevance to local needs of local institutions.* Yet the major sources of public knowledge generally focus on the power struggle surounding this issue, pronouncements by well-known individual figures, institutional actions such as strikes, group actions like demonstrations and street confrontations, and numerous more or less manufactured false issues. Little is said about what has gone on or is going on in the everyday business of the classroom, the principal's office, teachers meetings, or gatherings of parent associations. Outsiders are told almost nothing about the many and frequent expressions of interest in the process of education itself by involved community residents or the day-to-day labors of leaders, professionals, and volunteers in and around the schools.

Indeed, the nature of the crisis itself—of which both the school situation and information discrepancy are parts—is such that many of these very people have been more or less diverted from direct dealings with educational processes as such and forced to channel their energies into the power struggle because they see no other way to act for what they want in the present situation. They find themselves engaged in defending their movement and its achievements against numerous false and irrelevant attacks. Similarly, this very essay must deal at length with many side issues in an attempt to set the record straight. So pervasive is the mental set created and perpetuated by conventional sources of information that all parties to the conflict, as well as anyone who wishes either to learn or to inform about the dispute, is forced to deal with considerations that are irrelevant both to the central issues and to the essential interests of the contending forces.

One of the fundamental failures of most published accounts is quite independent of the whole question of the absolute validity of contending positions. Most discussions do not even begin to convey to the wider public the coherence that the community control position achieves in the words of community leaders or the credibility that this position holds for community members in terms of their experience. Without this indispensable quality of reportage, advocates of community control are easily made to seem simply unreasonable and extremist. This impression may well be given even by writers who profess sympathy for the communities involved.

A factor that contributes to this effect is that most writers and commentators seem to take the public presentation of positions by the educational and political establishment more literally and seriously than do many residents of Ocean Hill-Brownsville. For example, they generally assume that the central government of New York City is resolutely opposing the entrenched interests of the teaching and allied professions by working actively to shift power in the educational system to constituent communities throughout the city. This is difficult to believe from the perspective of the concerned and involved parent or educator in Ocean Hill-Brownsville.

Factually speaking, the metropolitan establishment has proposed a plan for "decentralization" which actually would retain all crucial options of educational policymaking in the hands of the central bureaucracy. This centralized decentralization is accomplished by vesting in the superintendent of all city schools and the central board of education a decisive veto on matters of budget, personnel, and contractual relations with such bodies as professional associations and unions. This veto power is an essential provision of the official proposal put forward by the city school board, a majority of whose members were recently appointed by Mayor Lindsay. Moreover, it is this same body that has repeatedly settled or averted teachers strikes by agreeing to all major union demands without acceding to any of the principal points made by proponents of community control. A considerable spectrum of community leaders are well aware of these political realities. Many ordinary blacks and Puerto Ricans also understand these things, and the city government is losing its credibility in the ghettos. Yet by and large the news media and journals of opinion continue to purvey the official myths of "decentralization" as if there were no question about their literal verity.

Similarly, even the repeated claim by the teachers federation that they favor decentralization is parroted by the media without reporting the facts which contradict this claim. Nevertheless, many black and Puerto Rican people are aware of the fact that the educators professional association played a major role in defeating legislation designed to make the schools accountable to local areas within the city. This knowledge comes from the fact that ghetto leaders and citizens were present during the last session of the state legislature when the United Federation of Teachers carried out its successful lobbying effort to defeat legislation proposed to serve local community interests. Moreover, many black and Puerto Rican people were also present during public hearings held late this past summer on the "decentralization" plan proposed by the central city board of education. There they heard the teachers spokesmen oppose the central plan as "going too far too fast," while their own ghetto community leadership denounced the same plan as failing to provide genuine accountability to local communities.

More than anything else, however, it is the series of teachers strikes during the past year that has persuaded black and Puerto Rican community people to see the position of the teachers professional establishment quite differently from the way it is generally presented to the public at large. The first of these strikes took place in September 1967, in a context that was locally significant but little known in the outside world. Somewhat prior to the strike, the newly constituted Ocean Hill-Brownsville governing board had been confronted, just as its experimental local district was being set up, with the resignation, by voluntary transfer to other districts, of incumbent principals in five of the district's eight schools. The local board met this situation by appointing replacement principals of its own choice who had certified qualifications but who did not come from the "approved waiting list" through which the teachers union and principals association customarily exercise influence over such appointments. This early exercise of local authority provoked protests from teacher representatives on the local board. A few days later the teachers federation struck the citywide school system.

The U.F.T. declared that its main strike goals were higher salaries and smaller classes, both of which, it suggested, would improve education in minority communities as well as elsewhere. The Ocean Hill-Brownsville governing board and its supporters, on the other hand, perceived the strike as being at least partly an attempt, provoked by the dispute over the five principals, to exert pressure against local authority. The local board refused a request that it support this strike, whereupon the teacher representatives resigned from the board. These union representatives have never resumed their membership in the local board.

At this stage, particularly in areas neighboring but outside Ocean Hill, many parents accepted the U.F.T. declaration of aims at face value and supported the strike. From this time forward, however, the people of Ocean Hill-Brownsville have seen the attack by the teachers organization against their elected representatives and their schools mount through several stages of escalation. It has been repeatedly reported (through word of mouth, at public meetings, and in written form by the governing board) and is widely accepted in the community that union teachers in the Ocean Hill schools carried out a sustained campaign throughout the last school year to discredit and undermine the entire program of the local administration. Specifically it is believed that opposition teachers often spoke against the local program to students, advised Puerto Rican pupils that they would be discriminated against by black power advocates in the local system, encouraged or allowed extremes of rowdy and destructive behavior by school children, and generally neglected their teaching duties. It is also understood in the community that the governing board repeatedly asked for aid in this situation from the central board of education but received no action. Further, it is a matter of public record that large numbers of teachers left the district at their own request to the central authorities, sometimes in such large numbers that substantial teacher shortages resulted. The wider public does not know, as do many in the local community, that there were mothers who begged some of these teachers to stay and instruct their children. Many in the community have heard these mothers report that in some cases they were told bluntly by the teachers that they would not work under black administrators. Nothing in community experience makes these reports difficult to believe, for its residents. It is also a matter of record that during these months the teachers federation and other sources mounted a rising campaign to persuade the public that Ocean Hill-Brownsville is ruled by black racists, extremist mobs, and violent revolutionaries. Community people know full well that militant as well as moderate forces support community control. Yet, for those who see their elected representatives and their community-employed educators in operation, these sweeping accusations have the hollow rings of manufactured hysteria.

In view of this background it is not

surprising that there was no visible community opposition when in May the local board notified some 20 teachers that they were to be transferred out of the district because they were considered unsuitable for the local program. The reaction of outside groups initially produced confusion within the community but ultimately solidified support for the governing board. Comparable teacher transfers have long been customarily arranged between district superintendents, the central authorities, and even the union. In this case, however, the city superintendents of schools and the central board of education refused to approve the transfers requested by the district board—a refusal which stands to this day. The reaction by union teachers represented to the community a more directly perceivable punitive show of power designed to defeat local authority over the schools. Some 350 of these teachers walked off their jobs, remaining on strike for the remaining six weeks of the school year —in support of their colleagues' alleged right to refuse transfer to another district.

The people of Ocean Hill-Brownsville saw that this move crippled their already limping schools. Parents found their children without instructors or supervisors, and it soon became clear that the school year could not be completed without a new kind of community effort. People became involved in the situation in a new way, through a volunteer effort by parents and others that managed to keep the schools from closing and to carry on through graduation.

With no assurance that the locally striking teachers would ever return, or function constructively from a community viewpoint if they did return, the local board and principals worked through the summer to recruit replacements. The community soon found that it had a new kind of loyal teaching corps. This predominantly white group includes idealistic young Ivy League graduates attracted to the special challenge of Ocean Hill-Brownsville, black educators committed to a concept of self-determination for the community, and Spanish-speaking teachers devoted to an innovative bilingual program specially designed for Puerto Rican children. Other innovations dictated by local perceptions of community needs were planned. Hope rose that in spite of everything, community control in service of local interests was becoming a reality in Ocean Hill-Brownsville.

Then came the series of events this autumn which are perceived by proponents of local authority as concerted attacks from the major centers of metropolitan power, designed to destroy the Ocean Hill-Brownsville project and to prevent community control from being realized in other areas as well. Three teachers strikes, supported by principals and custodians, have prevented most of the city's schools from functioning during all but a few days of the first several weeks in the new term. The union's initial demand was that the unwanted teachers be forced back into the Ocean Hill schools by any means necessary to overcome the community's resistance. By the time the middle of October had passed, however, the teachers federation and its allies were openly demanding that Ocean Hill-Brownsville be reabsorbed into the centralized system and that decentralization be officially declared a failure (see the New York *Post*, October 14 and 15; the *Amsterdam News*, October 19; the New York *Times*, October 22). In response the central authorities, as seen from the local community, have temporized and compromised in word while favoring anti-community forces in deed. The unwelcome teachers have been repeatedly forced into the schools by the police. All local personnel from governing board members to loyal teachers have operated for weeks under varying degrees of actual or threatened official suspension from their positions.

The most visible response to these events within the community has been an enthusiastic rallying to the support of the governing board against its perceived external enemies. A concrete indication of this growing force of community opinion is the recent behavior of the one previously visible source of opposition within the community. A single local politician had earlier conducted a semi-public campaign opposing the local authorities. By mid-September he declared publicly that he supports the governing board "one thousand percent." (The events in this situation were: the man in question was repeatedly denounced in public meetings for his earlier stand. He was decisively rebuffed in governing board meetings. His wife was defeated in a P.A. meeing on the same issue. Finally, his home was picketed by community control advocates. Then he publicly stated his new position at a mass rally.) Other examples are the impromptu rallies in support of community control which regularly have attracted many hundreds of enthusiastic participants. Sizable street demonstrations against the impositions of central authorities have periodically occurred for several days running. Local groups ranging from anti-poverty agencies to churches to organized militants are active and committed in varying degrees. As public expressions of support and tangible help begin to come in from many organizations and personages in other minority communities, as well as a small number of groups with primarily white constituencies, Ocean Hill is becoming conscious of having meaningful allies and of being a focus for attention rather widely in the nation. *Even though historically the locality has not been a social or political unit, the force of events and the response of local residents are beginning to forge a sense of community identity in and around Ocean Hill.*

On the other hand, it would be quite inaccurate to visualize Ocean Hill as a unanimously aroused and totally mobilized community. The people actively involved in the events just mentioned are actually a rather small part of the local citizenry. In this sense they are like the minority activists who initiate most movements for radical social change.

Nonetheless, there is no indication that the initiative for change in Ocean Hill-Brownsville is either actively or passively opposed by a majority or even a substantial minority of local people. There are certain individuals who disagree with the community-control movement on various grounds of principle or of strategy. One may hear individual expressions of most of the various public arguments presented by parties to the dispute. But dissent from community control has not crystallized into any visibly active opposition to the local governing board. The chief impression one receives from the masses of neighborhood people is that they remain uninvolved in the overt, observable aspects of the current struggle.

The behavior of this inactive majority seems to reflect varying combinations of incomplete knowledge or conflicting information, reluctance to participate in public conflict, and overriding concern with personal or family affairs and other aspects of existence not immediately related to community education. That is non-participation does not seem to be a passive or indirect expression of any widespread position on the issues. (Attendance at Ocean Hill schools has sometimes been below normal during the crisis, but this has not been accompanied by any exodus of pupils to other districts or alternative sources of schooling.) Some of the commonest sentiments of non-participants appear to reflect individual concerns. When children are out of school (less a problem in Ocean Hill than elsewhere in the city this fall), mothers complain that this complicates home life, job holding, and other family affairs. One often hears people wish that somehow the situation could settle down and cease to be a source of upset and concern.

The principal leadership of the local movement consists of educators, clergymen, and neighborhood mothers. These men and women are certainly authentic leaders who are much respected in the community. Yet creating and managing a mass movement is not their prime expertise. Nor is this a job for which they have very much time or energy. They are primarily preoccupied with running the school district and coping directly with what they see as destructive and self-serving power plays by the external opposition. Means for mobilizing and organizing large numbers of people within the community are not extensively developed or readily available on a continuing basis. It is therefore not surprising that purposeful and continuous mass public action has largely been absent in Ocean Hill-Brownsville. Five or six hundred people at an evening rally may express unanimous enthusiasm for the idea that everyone must be in the streets ready for action in the morning. Yet the next day very few people may appear. Demonstrations that march through the neighborhood streets inviting bystanders and passersby to join do not produce massive numbers of recruits. When large numbers of people do act publicly, there may be no unified leadership or generally understood plan of action. Always in the background one is conscious of the seemingly inert majority.

Among community people participating actively in the conflict there is considerable speculation about this seemingly uninvolved mass. Some view the non-participants as a reservoir for new recruits to the movement for community control, while one occasionally hears fears that they may be a potential source for the kind of significant local opposition that has not yet materialized. There seems to be little disagreement that the present role of this segment of the populace is a force for continuing inertia within the community. Active citizens are aware that the changes of individual or organizational position that have been visible over the past few months have been from detachment to involvement and from neutrality or opposition to commitment for community control as symbolized by the governing board. It is commonly predicted that this trend will continue and perhaps accelerate as long as the conflict is further escalated by forces outside the community. While such

forecasts are no doubt conditioned by partisan feelings, there certainly is also objective evidence to support them. Over the past several months, new moves against the local district authorities and citizenry have repeatedly aroused new and stronger popular resentment.

One form of escalated intervention, much on the minds of Ocean Hill people this autumn, evokes spirited predictions of the uttermost resistance from the more militant residents, while more moderate citizens tend to shake their heads and fall back on the hope that the crisis does not reach such proportions. This anxiety is expressed over the possibility that central authorities may act decisively to impose total physical control or paramilitary subjugation on Ocean Hill. Within the community some such eventuality has indeed seemed imminent from time to time. Thousands of policemen have swarmed through the streets with a great array of motorized constabulary equipment, established impressive field headquarters complete with elaborate communications and supply units, and displayed many high ranking officers in command of this armed establishment. For weeks these forces have been stationed throughout the district and neighboring areas, inside and outside schools, in playgrounds and parks, on rooftops, and in low-flying helicopters.

In spite of all this, a wide array of community forces have continued to express their defiance of the combined attempt by the entire city government, all of organized labor, and their various allies to force the return of unwanted teachers. Only one among many forms this defiance has taken is a series of mass rallies, demonstrations, and marches carried out directly in the face of armed intimidation and despite repeated and severe physical punishment systematically administered by the police arm of the official authorities. The demonstrators knew that as they marched and rallied in the streets, school children in classrooms were telling the rejected teachers why they are not wanted, community clergymen were issuing defiant manifestoes from their vestries, secular community groups were doing their best to mount organizational and informatioanl support efforts, and the governing board was standing firm.

As this situation continued over weeks stretching into months, it gradually became apparent to everyone involved that the teachers federation, the educational bureaucracy, and the city government were all failing in significant respects to impose their will on the people and institutions of Ocean Hill-Brownsville. This prompted many thinking people in the community to ask themselves and discuss with one another what the central authorities and other outside forces could try next. From such questions was born the not uncommon observation that state troopers and the national guard are about the only remaining untried instrumentalities short of the U.S. Army. Along with the head shaking and wishful thinking already referred to, these considerations also provoked a revival of earlier discussions as to how well the community may be prepared in terms of arms, organization, and determination to resist and defend itself against fullscale paramilitary or military intervention.

In the midst of all this, came the well-publicized threat by the teachers federation to send tens of thousands of white members marching into Ocean Hill to occupy physically the community's schools. While many people may regard this as a scare tactic empty of any real possibility as to action, others have heard or seen evidence of similar threats from picketing teachers not only in Brownsville but also as far away as Canarsie. In any case, these expressions of intent to initiate massive invasions of the community have provoked great anger in Ocean Hill-Brownsville. In response to these various threats of intervention there have been both individual and organizational commitments to resistance by whatever means seem necessary and possible. The wider public should know that today it is not a rarity for Ocean Hill citizens of both sexes and many ages to declare either publicly or privately and with utmost seriousness, that they will die if necessary to defend community control of education as it now exists in their district.

These human realities may not provide a secure basis for confident or detailed predictions as to future developments. Nevertheless, these circumstances do call upon us to give real attention to the opinion of some serious people in and around Ocean Hill, that the interventionist threats noted earlier could produce a community insurrection which might attain locally disastrous proportions. The predicted target of such a rebellion is whatever group might be perceived as conducting a finally unbearable invasion, whether teachers, policemen, or soldiers. There should be no doubt in anyone's mind that a great many people in Ocean Hill already feel sorely oppressed by outsiders or that large numbers are in a mood of rebellion against those whom they perceive as their oppressors. If such local rebelliousness should reach the level of sustained mass physical resistance and retaliation, it could, of course, be easily suppressed by powers unmindful of the cost to the insurrectionary community. That is, military suppression could be swift and rapidly effective, provided the explosion remains local. From the perspective of Ocean Hill, and with recent experience in other minority areas around the country, however, your author wonders how clear a picture the central authorities have of the potentialities for explosive conflict beyond local boundaries.

The growth of involvement and commitment within the community does not come about only through perception of the public events cited earlier or through the dramatic lessons of the Ocean Hill streets to be noted below. It also occurs at numerous different levels of experience and through many little happenings that are unknown in the wider world. For example, a small number of ordinary citizens, including this writer and his wife, as well as recognized community leaders, have now had the experience of meeting face to face in private negotiations with the chief public figures of the central establishment. One such occasion afforded the enlightening spectacle of recent appointees to the city's board of education, including those with the greatest recognized power, stating that Ocean Hill-Brownsville is right both legally and morally and then "begging" the community to give in on all major outstanding issues for the sake of ending the teachers strike and opening the rest of the city's schools. Citizens and observers have also heard private commitments to specific action in favor of the community from the lips of the highest responsible officials, only to see these promises completely violated within a matter of days.

Related experiences are occurring—with the same consequences—at a different level in neighboring black and Puerto Rican communities where, until recently, there has been considerable disposition to stay clear of Ocean Hill's struggle as not one's own. One group of parents with children in an elementary school not very far from Ocean Hill supported the teachers strike of last year and remained aloof from the subsequent crises involving the nearby governing board. Yet this fall they have worked with a small group of community-oriented teachers to keep their school open during this year's strikes. During the third strike of the present term they organized a line of picketing mothers to counter the intimidating daily picket line of striking teachers at their school. This led to a mild confrontation where the author and other community observers watched the police obviously and roughly discriminate against the mothers in favor of the striking teachers.

The mothers then called a parent-teachers association meeting to which the observers and the strikers were invited. Teachers and supervisors stated their position that the strike was neces-sary to end the present regime in Ocean Hill-Brownsville but insisted that this was not inconsistent with their support for "decentralization" or their declared dedication to the welfare of pupils and parents of the school they were picketing. Mothers replied that they supported the Ocean Hill governing board, but since they were more immediately concerned with their own school, they requested that the strikers support their union in some way that would allow them to teach, while the Ocean Hill issue was settled, to stop picketing the local school, or at least to cease blocking the main entrance. All these requests were refused by the striking teachers. Parents came away angry that even their most modest request—to stop blocking the door—had been summarily rejected, they questioned both the logic and the sincerity of the teachers, and they determined to continue counterpressure against the strike.

These are the merest samples of proliferating citizen experience which leads them to perceive their situation as one opposing powerful groups that act to prevent accountability to local needs and sentiments, all the while justifying their actions with the rhetoric of decentralization and proclaiming devotion to local interests. Partly in response to this obfuscation, advocates of local accountability have made great efforts to distinguish between "decentralization" as officially proposed or as embraced by the teachers federation and "community control" in the sense of representative local authority over educational policy and the resources to implement policy. Although the two labels, "decentralization" and "community control," have come to appear widely enough, the net result is confusion, because the press and the broadcast media have generally failed to make the distinction clear in terms of meaning. For example, the media generally have not even picked up the simple analogy that is most widely current in local discussions: proponents of community control feel they are demanding no more than what is taken for granted by any suburb or small town that has its own school board which is elected, otherwise representative, or at least open to citizen pressure. Instead of clarifying this point, the major sources of public information have largely allowed the obfuscation to stand. This again creates public confusion over who stands where in the whole controversy. It also fosters the impression that advocates of community control are either being extremely unreasonable or really aiming for something other than their stated demands.

Again and again, one must return to the inaccuracies in the reportage that has examined the conflict in Ocean Hill-Brownsville. Many writers maintain that the teachers strike occurred because the Ocean Hill-Brownsville local governing board "fired" 19 teachers. The fact is that the governing board requested the city's superintendent of schools to transfer out of Ocean Hill-Brownsville this small group of teachers who were locally judged incompatible with the district program. This action was taken by the unit administrator and the local governing board on the basis of parents' complaints and information from relevant principals and observers. The local board has subsequently maintained the position that if this request is not granted and implemented, then the local community has no meaningful control over its schools. It is well known, though not often mentioned by newsmen or analysts, that the superintendent of the schools not only has the power to grant the request but, in fact, routinely transfers large numbers of teachers from school to school and district to district as a matter of course.

Thus, some months ago, when the Ocean Hill-Brownsville staff still included many teachers and supervisors who were hostile to the community-selected administration, all 14 assistant principals in the district were transferred elsewhere in one day at their own request. This autumn 16 teachers from one Ocean Hill school were allowed to transfer out voluntarily just as the system was about to reopen following the summer. Indeed there seems to be no record of any Ocean Hill teacher or supervisor being denied his or her own wish for transfer by the central bureaucracy. Yet from last year into the present month of October, the same authorities who granted these transfers continue to refuse the request for 19 transfers made by the governing board which is supposed to administer the district. The local board and its supporters have understandably concluded that the central powers regularly side with the teachers federation and remain determined not to grant meaningful powers to local community bodies.

Even as I write this, the news media mindlessly intone the latest threat of action by the central school establishment. This is a threat which must surely be the ultimate absurdity in the already ridiculous game of "due process" and "legal authority." The superintendent of schools is solemnly decribed as considering using his powers to transfer summarily out of Ocean Hill-Brownsville a group of teachers whom he considers unsuited for their present duties because they are opposed to the return of the original teacher group whose removal the local board has sought for many months. Thus the exercise of central power comes full circle with a threatened action which is the closest possible parallel to the attempted action for which the local board has been so roundly condemned. The real function of "law" and "principal" as invoked by the establishment stands revealed—to the community and in fact—as a mere facade for maneuvers and manipulations to preserve the status quo of power relations between localities and the metropolitan authorities.

The basic position of the Ocean Hill-Brownsville governing board on the disputed teachers was first enunciated in May 1968, and has remained consistent since then. This position is that the board, acting under existing regulations, initiated legitimate, lawful action to transfer several teachers out of the Ocean Hill district schools, supporting this action by documenting grossly unsatisfactory performance on the part of the teachers in question. Ever since May the governing board has been waiting for the superintendent of schools to accept and sanction this action, just as he regularly approves and implements comparable initiatives from other district administrations. This is normally and legally done without charges or hearings. In the absence of positive action by either the superintendent or the city board of education, large numbers of concerned Ocean Hill citizens have refused, ever since last spring, to accept the return of the 19 teachers whose transfer had been set in motion. As an elected representative body, the local board has felt that it must abide by this popular initiative of its constituency—the community. The following account of the subsequent dispute, with special reference to the due process issue, presents the conflict as it has been experienced by both leaders and followers of the movement for local control in Ocean Hill, together with their supporters from elsewhere. Many ordinary local citizens are well acquainted with the outline of these developments as presented here, though, of course, not everyone has followed all the details. Quite apart from purely local knowledge and sentiment, and in addition to the events reported by the author as an observer, the factual statements made below can all be documented from the public record: the press, other media, and material published by the various parties to the controversy.

The effective positions maintained by the actual conduct of contending parties in this situation will never be exposed to public understanding as long as most writers and information agencies persist in a basic distortion of one of the central issues. Most sources continue to treat the initial and continuing cry by the teachers union for "due process" on the original locally sanctioned transfers as if this were a genuine assertion of legal and ethical principle. In fact, it is a manufactured pseudo-issue. The union demands, in effect, that the unwanted teachers be guaranteed the unprecedented privilege of defying and ignoring the judgment of the local administration and its citizen constituency on teacher fitness for its particular program. The teachers organization demands this even for substitute teachers without tenure who are legally subject to unchallengeable dismissal by school principals. Yet anyone really well acquainted with the dispute knows that the problem of the contested transfers could be resolved in at least three ways that are closer to presently established procedures or to ideal due process than the solution demanded by the teachers federation.

The first solution is one of long-established practice, both legal and customary. This is the solution that the local board originally and repeatedly requested, hoping that the central school authorities would show that they really meant their proclaimed support of decentralization and the Ocean Hill experiment. The board simply asked the superintendent of all the city schools to approve the inter-district transfers on the request of the district administrator, just as he so often does when requested by other district administrations. There is nothing either illegal or unusual about this request; it does not infringe upon any contract with the union or any regulation of the school system. This gave the superintendent a perfect opportunity to use his traditional powers to facilitate rather than to thwart local initiative, responsibility, and accountability. Instead the superintendent not only refused the request but has steadfastly declined to give any reason for this refusal that makes sense to the aggrieved community. This same official has reaffirmed to the local board in recent weeks, speaking before community residents and observers, that he has exercised and frequently continues to do so the power to transfer any teachers within and between districts. Asked by parents as well as by local board members why he does not use this power to honor the legal and legitimate Ocean Hill request, he replied, "I prefer not to." In short, the traditional form of due process in such cases has been denied not to the teachers but to the local administration and its community.

The second available procedure would invoke another form of due process normally employed to resolve disputes that have reached an impasse. That is, a solution could be arrived at if the principal parties would agree to binding arbitration. Then if either side felt that the other had violated the settlement imposed by the arbitrator, the proper recourse would be to the courts. This procedure has been recommended several times during the present dispute by the Mayor and others. This recommendation has been accepted by the Ocean Hill-Brownsville governing board but rejected by the federation of teachers. With respect to this potential solution, then, it is not the community but the teachers organization that has refused to submit to due process.

The third available resolution is one that would appear ideal because it explicitly provides for due process guaranteed by the courts while at the same time actually serves to establish the decentralization which all sides claim to favor. Here the solution would be to grant full authority over the administration of staff and personnel to the governing board and local administrator in accordance with existing proposals for community control, as put forward by Ocean Hill and other districts. These provide that state-established criteria of teacher qualifications will be followed, that teacher tenure rights will be respected, and that duly established contracts will be honored. Obviously any unlawful deviation from these provisions could be dealt with in the courts. These proposals have been put forward again and again by Ocean Hill and the entire

citywide movement for community control. The other parties have all responded negatively to these proposals—even as they continue to proclaim their devotion to decentralization. The local control plans have been ignored by the Mayor, rejected in favor of central control by the city board of education together with the superintendent, and denounced by the teachers federation as well as the principals and supervisors association.

In short, Ocean Hill-Brownsville and its supporters are on record as favoring legal resolutions through any one of three alternative arrangements for legitimate due process. Each of these routes to a settlement is blocked by the educational establishment: the educators professional associations with their total rejection, the centralized school bureaucracy which insists on retaining central control and using it to thwart local initiatives, and the educationist institutions and publications which participate, actively or passively, in perpetuating the fiction that teachers are being denied due process in Ocean Hill-Brownsville. This creation of bureaucratic, professional, and specialist imaginations has been further promoted by the mass media, so that it is now a well established public myth, apparently taken for granted by most people outside minority communities who are interested in the controversy. This ubiquitous misinformation also makes it clear what results can be expected from proposals made by opponents of community control, such as the convening of a special session of the state legislature or a citywide public referendum. The reader may judge how likely it is that this conflict can be settled either fairly or realistically while this myth is allowed to hole sway over the minds of the general public.

Faced with this situation and immense public pressure generated by it, the local governing board has been forced several times against its will to compromise on the issues of principal by agreeing to take the unwanted teachers back into its schools. The conditions for these returnees were not to the liking of the teachers federation. The community continued to object to these returnees after they were repeatedly forced into the schools by police power. On occasion this opposition

Eleanor Maġid

was expressed by angry and verbally threatening crowds. Teachers who had been loyally serving the local administration since early September or since last year also objected to the returnees and told them so, sometimes loudly and bluntly. Pupils often expressed similar views. In two classes which this writer observed, students refuted the union position point by point in debates with returned instructors. In other classes pupils walked out and refused to attend lessons offered by the unwanted teachers. Some of these teachers were also assigned to duties other than classroom teaching.

Despite extended and intensive observation and lengthy discussion with numerous participants in these events, I am unable to report any evidence of physical harm, other than allegations by returning teachers, publicized by the union and the news media. My own evidence is entirely negative and, of course, does not prove a total lack of physical threats. It does make

me skeptical of the widespread reports that the returning teachers were subjected to a horrifying reign of terror. (On the other hand, I have witnessed many aggressive exercises in intimidation and harassment by striking teachers, including physical assaults on school buildings open in spite of the strike; I have been present when dire threats were uttered by picketing teachers; I know many people publicly opposed to the strike who tell me they receive frequent threatening telephone calls; and incidents of physical attacks against 'non-striking teachers, students, and parents have been related to me by numerous independent witnesses, including some of the victims.)

By the end of October, the situation had reached the stage at which the Ocean Hill board offered an unconditional return to the remaining teachers who wished it. The teachers federation immediately rejected this offer, charging that the local board was not sincere. The union followed this up by reasserting its earlier demands that the entire Ocean Hill district administration be removed and all the local schools be reabsorbed into the centralized system. No one in the local-control movement was surprised. They have long believed that the real purpose of the teachers federation and its allies is to destroy decentralization and prevent community control.

From the local community viewpoint, there is no question of firing the disputed teachers from the city school system. They would presumably be welcome in one of the other 30-odd school districts that make up the city. Of course, some advocates of the community control add, if no district wants these teachers then presumably they should be fired, but that is a central bureaucratic responsibility. If someday there should be effective decentralization, just this kind of facilitation of inter-district relations would appear to be a remaining legitimate role of the central authorities. A major tenet of the local-control movement, however, is that under the existing system, medocrity and incompetence are protected through cooperation between the central bureaucracy and the associations of professional educators. It is a fact that it has long been extremely rare for a licensed educator to be discharged from the city school system. This is seen as reason enough for many teachers and supervisors to fight for preservation of the status quo. This fight can hardly be convincingly justified, however, in terms of moral or constitutional principles.

A number of writers properly have credited the Ocean Hill-Brownsville community forces with recruiting a loyal multiracial teaching corps, building a strong and innovative educational program especially well suited to community needs, and keeping this program running normally in spite of the teachers strikes which crippled or closed most other city schools. Yet these same writers fail to make clear that all this constructive community effort was made in the face of repeated mutually reinforcing blockages and attacks from the United Federation of Teachers, the central board of education, and the city government. At least one author (Jason Epstein, "The Brooklyn Dodgers," *The New York Review of Books,* September 20, 1968) goes so far as to project the fantasy of an "alignment" between the "upper middle class" and "the racial minorities," supposedly presided over by Mayor Lindsay. Against this fine fairytale we must recognize a series of hard actualities. Only one editorialist of the entire conventional press has belatedly presented the community position (Murray Kempton in a number of New York *Post* columns during September and October). Likewise only a handful of academies or other professionals have publicly supported community control in terms that are meaningful to those whose daily struggle is in deprived urban communities. Meanwhile the entire establishment of organized labor has issued thinly veiled threats of a general strike to bring Ocean Hill-Brownsville to its knees. Most politicians have either remained silent or denounced the local board; until mid-September the chief representative

of the political establishment within the community had attempted to pressure the local board into accepting the union's terms. The Ford Foundation has delayed funds previously committed to support the local board and its program. The machinery of the central school bureaucracy has become unaccountably paralyzed with respect to the ordinarily routine matters of confirming staff appointments made at the local level. The Mayor has declared that the disputed teachers will be reimposed upon the community even if it takes "the full resources" of his administration. The New York Police Department has become the chief instrument for enforcing this decree.

Again, a number of publicists deserve credit for setting part of the record straight on the false issue of how representative the Ocean Hill-Brownsville school board may be in view of the fact that it was elected by some 25 per cent of those eligible to vote. Yet these writers generally fail to mention the really relevant comparisons on this question of representativeness. The politician who headed the only publicly organized opposition to the local board within the community was himself elected to a state office by a much smaller proportion of the electorate than participated in choosing the governing board. Likewise it is seldom noted that when the leadership of the United Federation of Teachers has called for strike votes, the total number of ballots cast has been approximately 10 per cent of the membership. No realistic observer would suggest that *all* the people of Ocean Hill-Brownsville are enthusiastic, involved, or even visibly interested in support of community control. Nevertheless, it does seem clear that the local board is substantially more representative than some of its principal opponents. Moreover, this body consults regularly, almost daily, in many informal ways with its constituency. Its meetings are generally open to the interested public, and local citizens who are not members do attend and voice their opinions. Further, the context of this issue of representativeness is additionally obscured by the general failure to report that the original exercise of democracy which created the local governing board was achieved only by overcoming the obstruction of the central school administration. The central bureaucracy was somehow unable to supply any names and addresses of pupils' parents when the nascent Ocean Hill-Brownsville organization sought to hold its first election. The election then had to be arranged by door-to-door canvassing and registration. The nominations and voting were later declared legitimate and valid by a commission appointed by the central board of education itself.

All in all, what journalist has sought out the source or given the lie to the belief in white communities that the Ocean Hill-Brownsville administration seeks to get rid of all of its white teachers and replace them with blacks? Who has exposed the insidious campaign to persuade the Puerto Rican minority that community control is a black plot against them? Who has placed this calumny against the act that Ocean Hill-Brownsville has appointed the only Puerto Rican principal and established the only bilingual school for Spanish-speakers in all of New York? The union propaganda that the local district is run by anti-semitic, black supremist union busters backed up by mob rule has not been faced squarely or compared with relevant factual observations. It must be made clear that as the teachers federation and its allies agitate to promote intergroup tensions, they are also carrying out a series of illegal strikes with the more or less open backing of the police and the passive connivance of the central authorities. While all this has gone on in the wider community, the institutions more or less controlled by the local community have been running smoothly with an impressive degree of interracial and interfaith harmony, backed by pro-community militancy against the impositions of established central power.

Journals concerned with the conflict in Ocean Hill-Brownsville should be calling upon the enemies of community control to explain how their accusations of black racism are related to the following undisputed facts. The Ocean Hill-Brownsville governing board is made up of men and women from many walks of life who are blacks, Puerto Ricans, and non-Latin whites. Moreover, as I have suggested, this is no mere paper organization; board members in each of these categories actually work together every day. Further, the principals who were either hired or retained by this board to head the eight schools in this little district are four black men, two non-Spanish-speaking whites, at least one of whom is Jewish, one Puerto Rican, and one Chinese. Finally, the district faculty chosen by the board is 70 per cent white and 50 per cent Jewish. The pupil population served by this staff, on the other hand, is about 65 per cent black and 30 per cent Latin.

It cannot be denied that some partisans of community control, including some who are active in Ocean Hill-Brownsville, believe that many black teachers are uniquely qualified by life experience, as most whites can hardly be, to communicate with black students and respond with empathy to their needs. This position need not be racist in conception; to brand it as such without further evidence is quite unreasonable. More important perhaps, the people of Ocean Hill are being exposed, through the staff their representatives have hired, to a lesson in interracial communication. Contrary to much quite real past experience and despite all the tensions of the present situation, it is being demonstrated now that a multiethnic but largely white teaching corps can function effectively in Ocean Hill, with loyalty to a largely nonwhite authority and in service to a program especially designed for black and Puerto Rican students. It would be hard to find in the United States today a more striking expression of the antithesis of racism in actual operation. The lesson is not lost on the local citizenry. They publicly applaud and otherwise warmly express their appreciation of the nonblack educators serving their community.

A related lesson seems available to anyone who has witnessed and compared the mass rallies with citywide participation organized by the teachers federation and those organized by community control forces. The teachers rallies, with all their hundreds of signs denouncing racism, are virtually all white to the last individual participant. The demonstrations for local control, carrying banners asserting the rights of self-determination for minorities, are multiracial and thoroughly integrated. Once again it is clear that the accusations of black racism played up by the press neither square with the actual behavior of the accused nor reflect a genuine non-racialism on the part of the accusers.

With respect to the exercise of police powers in Ocean Hill-Brownsville, the press has presented a picture to the outside world which cannot be reconciled with the reality in the streets. Here it should be understood that I am writing as a daily eye-witness. Jason Epstein (in the article already noted) writes that unwanted teachers were physically prevented from entering a school by *demonstrating parents*. (The context makes it clear that he is referring to an incident that occurred at JHS 271 on September 11th.) He suggests that this event occurred as he described it (evidently from press reports) because it would be, in his words, "obviously unthinkable" for Mayor Lindsay to allow *the police* to drag the parents away from the schoolhouse door. Yet if he had been there he in fact could have seen the police aggressively push their way into a group that had agreed with the commanding officer on the scene to take no physical action as long as the police took none. He could have watched as the men in blue carried out precisely the action which he describes as unthinkable, inflicting a number of painful injuries in the process. He could then have observed—as I did—that the disputed teachers, surrounded by a flying wedge of constabulary, were rushed through the open doors into the school.

It was from that time forward that Ocean Hill-Brownsville was occupied continuously over several weeks by an army of up to several thousand police. On each of the few school days when the teachers federation has not been on strike, the unwanted teachers have been brought into the schools surrounded by massive armed force, with uniformed officers often stationed inside the school buildings, sometimes even in classrooms. For nearly a month no member of the community has stood in the way of any teacher. Yet I have now witnessed Mr. Epstein's unthinkable scene on several occasions at four different schools. The only qualitative difference between the events described above and subsequent confrontations is that in the October incidents the parents were trying to get *into* the schools of their *own* community. There have been numerous clubbings and beatings by the police. Many of the victims—in my direct observation—have been mothers and grandmothers. Others who have been attacked are teachers—male and female, black and white—who are loyal to the local governing board. In more than one confrontation, the Mayor's highest personal representatives were on the scene, with no observable effect on the behavior of the constabulary.

During this time, it has been publicly charged by organizations within the community that one man was beaten to death by the police. Further information has proved impossible to obtain on this case; apparently no official notice has been granted to these charges. In the case of a young woman publicly assaulted by police and struck unconscious to the ground, there was good reason to fear that she had lost her unborn child. Only after this woman was released by the police were the community leaders able to learn through a private physician that her hemorrhages, mercifully enough, were not in fact a miscarriage. Again officialdom remained mute while rage and fear grew in the community.

Only on one occasion have the major

485

newspapers of New York printed any-thing approaching a fully circumstantial description of the aggressive and provocative police tactics. Significantly enough, perhaps, this was an event in which a couple of reporters were roughed up or had their notes taken from them by officers, this being but a small part of what almost amounted to a police riot. During these days I myself—acting in my role as observer—have twice experienced the physical pain and personal humiliation produced by extremely forceful and totally unprovoked police aggression. I have also taken a seriously injured victim to receive urgently needed medical attention—which was refused to him by the police department. My perspective is therefore perhaps a little different from that of most writers, readers, or viewers of the news media. Indeed, these experiences have convinced me—just as many community citizens are convinced—that there is no hope for reconciliation between communities like Ocean Hill-Brownsville and comfortable White America until some part of the information media begins to communicate the experience of the oppressed within our own society.

Probably the failure of the media in this respect cannot be appreciated without further direct comparison between observed events and newspaper accounts. Except where otherwise stated, the following abbreviated description is based upon observations at the scene made by my wife and myself.

During a recent demonstration, a common pattern developed in which a crowd verbally taunted and harangued the lines of police blocking access to a local school. The demonstrators were deliberately slow to obey commands that they move back or clear a given area of the street outside the police lines. There was, however, no direct physical resistance, much less any active forcible aggression, against the police. Presently a young man announced defiantly that he would move no further. In an instant he was pushed violently by over a half dozen policemen who then chased him for half a block or so and beat him to the ground with flailing nightsticks. We could hear uniformed officers at their posts on nearby rooftops shouting, "Hit him, hit him!" Another man, caught in the same constabulary rush, was clubbed to the pavement and then beaten until his face and/or head bled profusely, while policemen ringed the immediate scene to prevent photographers from recording it.

Yet another assault in this same outbreak involved the pregnant woman mentioned above. We did not observe this case ourselves but were given identical independent accounts of it by numerous witnesses who have proved reliable in the past. According to these reports, the young woman was pushed in the chest by a policeman. She began a movement which might have been an attempt either to defend herself or to retaliate, but she never completed it, for the officer struck her to the ground with a blow of his baton on her head. She was knocked unconscious and carried or dragged limp to a police vehicle. Before the whole outburst was over, we saw a number of other individuals being less violently seized and taken away. We did not observe or hear about any injuries to police officers.

The entire direct description of these events in the principal evening newspaper reads "a demonstration outside [the school] that injured two policemen and resulted in the arrest of seven persons" (New York *Post*, Oct. 10). Several general statements in the same story describe the police in Ocean Hill-Brownsville as guarding against violence and seeking to avert violence. Toward the end of the story a two-sentence statement about the female victim is attributed to a "community relations officer for Ocean Hill-Brownsville" without further comment or evaluation. The most respected morning newspaper (New York *Times*, Oct. 10) printed a photo of one man being clubbed on the ground and carried a fairly circumstantial report of police action against other men in the same incident. This material again appeared at the end of the story. This newspaper made no reference whatever to a woman being struck or to the charges later made on her behalf. Readers thoroughly accustomed to assuming that the police department employs physical force only when it is necessary to prevent violations of the law or apprehend serious violators would not have their assumptions disturbed by these press accounts;

A few days later an instructive study in contrasts was made available to some of the same people, including the writer, who experienced the events just described. A group of Brownsville citizens journeyed to a high school in a nearby largely white district. They made their little trip to show support for students and teachers who were attempting, against heavy opposition, to keep the high school open and functioning during the strike. Their special interest in this situation derived from the fact that black and Pureto Rican students attend this school because Brownsville and Ocean Hill have no high school of their own. Brownsville youngsters have attended this school ever since it opened a few years ago, in spite of such welcoming signs posted around the institution as, "Nigger Go Home" (according to reports from both youngsters and adults). Moreover, a minority of the pupils involved in trying to keep the school going despite the strike were sons of black parents living in Brownsville.

When the racially mixed delegation from Brownsville arrived, they found a group of at least 100 vocal and high-spirited all-white pickets, including both teachers and local parents as well as teenagers who presumably were students, massed on the sidewalk in front of the school. These demonstrators appeared to be confined behind lines established by the same police force (one or two black officers were present, a matter of constant attention to people in the area) that has been upholding law and order in Ocean Hill. It was early morning, school-opening time. A few white pupils and even fewer black students walked in past the yelling pickets while the Brownsville people watched quietly.

Then a substantial number of white demonstrators walked past unmoving police officers and ran inside the school. Once a sizable number were safely inside, policemen made quite a show of denying entry to the remaining crowd of strikers and supporters. But intense observation failed to detect a club raised, a blow delivered, or even an energetic push carried out on the part of the police. For reasons that were difficult to determine from where the Brownsville people stood behind unguarded wooden barricades on the sidewalk, the police proved unable to apprehend any of the strikers in the school or remove them from the building. Presently it was announced that the school had been closed by the district superintendent because of "disruptions" inside the building. Then some of the strikers came over to the Brownsville people to argue their dedication to equal rights for everyone, while others announced that they would march on to Ocean Hill. As we walked away, one prominent black leader from Ocean Hill was heard to say that this was indeed a lesson in comparison between one community and another. Before the day was out, the lesson had been widely communicated in Brownsville and Ocean Hill.

The account of these events printed in the New York *Times* (October 19, page 26) was the following: "Picketing teachers at Canarsie High School in Brooklyn walked through police barricades to enter the building. However, the school was later closed by the district superintendent." While this brief passage says a lot to those who were there about the role of the press, it must surely be impossible for other readers to gain from this report any accurate impression of the major events that actually occurred.

By the time the crisis had extended through nearly two months of the fall school term, increasing alarms had been expressed by public figures and editorialists that the dispute is taking on "racial overtones" or arousing intergroup tensions. One may hear similar descriptions of the problem from residents of Ocean Hill and neighboring areas. It is much more common, however, for people of communities to conceive the problem in a significantly different way. It is commonly stated that the sudden attention to the racial factor in the conflict is only a belated recognition of something that has always been there. Many add that it is the opponents of community control who have made this controversy into a racial conflict. This is not a contradiction, for the assignment of responsibility is not intended to refer only to contemporary actions. It refers to the organization of our entire society by racial groupings, as well as the historical development of American race relations, as many black and Puerto Rican citizens conceive these larger entities and processes.

Thus the present fight for community control is very widely seen as a current phase of the long struggle against a racially discriminatory system. Only a few black residents of poverty-districts literally blame all their troubles exclusively on the white man. Self-criticism and negative evaluations of qualities attributed to the minority community itself are not at all uncommon. At the same time, however, there is a very general disposition to attribute difficulties with intergroup dimensions to past iniquities by outsiders and to general attitudes or practices of white-dominated society. Inhabitants of minority districts often take it for granted that the conflict is inherently an intergroup clash imposed upon them by the nature of the world. They commonly see this world as one in which the primary actors are outsiders: residents of distant communities, enjoyers of advantages that are rare or unknown in poverty areas, whites.

Present-day experience seems, in Ocean Hill-Brownsville, perfectly consistent with these long-standing views of the world. Though not every community member shares all these perceptions, what is happening today in Ocean Hill is easily perceptible as White society, penalizing the minority poor for asserting and defending its own interests. Many inhabitants of Ocean Hill and Brownsville feel that White power holders are attempting to teach them a lesson: a stark demonstration that they can not control their own collective destiny. They feel they are being shown that what happens in their non-white community is determined by an essentially White government structure and its non-official White allies. They see wealthy White liberal leadership which does not respond to local community needs or protect Black and Brown collective interests when the chips are down. They interpret recent events as revealing political leadership and its bureaucracy in collusion with White professional associations of teachers, administrators, and others who make their comfortable livings by staffing local neighborhoods overrun and occupied by armed White legions, apparently to make sure that this racial status quo is not upset. Watching these constabulary hordes at work, a sober and respected local black leader muttered, "The rape of Ocean Hill-Brownsville."

For those who have been close enough to the inner workings of the educational system as it operates in Ocean Hill, the racial lessons seem obvious: White teachers and supervisors come and go at their own request, but a Black administrator and a multiracial governing board headed by a Black man are not allowed to transfer a few unwanted White employees. Those parents who remember being told pointblank by voluntarily departing or striking White teachers that they would not work under a Black administrator have understood the message quite literally. Some people who have been through a variety of recent experiences like those described here now find that some of their beliefs and attitudes are changing. One now finds a certain sense of having been deceived by seemingly positive changes in the social policies of White America during recent years. Having a sprinkling of Black and Puerto Rican people in political and government posts seems to have done Ocean Hill little good, and so people begin to wonder whether such men can be more than figureheads or underlings. While a small company of non-white educators and other professionals has provided indispensable service to Ocean Hill, their numbers compared with the need, plus the knowledge that many of their brethren have escaped into the outer White world where they do not serve the local community—all this has given new meaning in the community to the already existing concept of token integration. The Black policeman occasions the most comment of all, for many people cannot help seeing him, stationed in Ocean Hill during these weeks of mass conflict, as betraying his own people by serving non-community interests.

These experiences and the human responses to them create a consciousness which outsiders with their own world view rooted in their own experience do not begin to appreciate. In Ocean Hill-Brownsville this is a consciousness—by no means universal but noticieably widespread in the community—that is dynamic, in flux, and open to new ideas which seem to speak to the condition of the community as its people perceive it. Thus commonly given to ideas and proposals which most comfortable White Americans would unhesitatingly label as irrational, extremist, or worse. Not far beyond the currently conspicuous movement to make educators accountable to the local community, there is in the making an organized demand for local community control over the police. Support for this proposal is by no means confined to a few intellectuals, alienated individuals, or any other lunatic fringe which might be imagined.

Much more daring ideas than this are current in far wider circles than the little groups of theorists or underground groups which outsiders might imagine. Anyone in the community may hear articulate, intelligent, and well informed men seriously develop conceptions of self-determination, autonomy, and even nationhood for American ethnic minorities. Audiences ranging from several hundred in local gatherings to several thousand when many Ocean Hills come together in city-wide meetings listen very attentively and applaud most enthusiastically as speakers present a host of ideas related to those just cited. An impressive sense of unity and determination is evident on these occasions. It should not be understood that the orientations described here are sweeping suddenly over the entire population of the minority poor. Nevertheless, these ways of viewing the world are a significant part of the context in which the movement for community control of education exists. Moreover, this is not only a local or metropolitan context. There is strong evidence of quite comparable trends among oppressed minorities—Mexicans Americans and American Indians as well as black people and Puerto Ricans—in many areas across the country.

Conventional sources of information trumpet the accusation or exude the implication that advocates of community control willfully insist, for reasons of their own, upon defining the issues in racial terms. The fact remains that black and Puerto Rican communities are simply faced with a racial reality for which most of their members feel White America is primarily responsible. A common analysis is that the definition of issues is dictated by white racism. As a matter of fact, quite a number of thoughtful black people are actively engaged in a search for modes of discourse and thought which will free them from the influence of ideologies closely identified with white interests or traditions. This effort quite explicitly includes a search for alternatives to racism and racist thought which will be meaningful in terms of minority experience. Moreover, participation in the multiracial scene of Ocean Hill has convinced me that black and Puerto Rican people—often to a degree that is hard to match among their white counterparts—welcome mutual participation with non-blacks and non-Latins whenever the latter demonstrate rather than merely proclaim that they are committed to the interests of the minority community as these interests are locally understood. This context lends credibility to the claim of partisans for community control that when they speak of racial issues in relation to their movement they are merely recognizing a long-standing actuality imposed upon them. A watchful eye has not enabled me to detect any evidence that these partisans are adding extraneous racial considerations beyond their view of the structure of American society which has grown directly from their experience as minority people.

Perhaps the question of racialism within or outside the community can be further clarified by considering some of what this observer has seen inside the Ocean Hill schools under community control. Then the reader may compare this with the earlier descriptions of activities by outside forces ranging from striking teachers to policemen. During this fall term, the Ocean Hill schools have been in full operation regardless of the citywide teacher strikes and, except when they were forced in, without the unwanted teachers being present. Under these circumstances, repeated visits showed teachers and supervisors—white and black, Jewish and gentile, Latin and Oriental—enthusiastically working together with an obvious spirit of comradeship. Also present and ready to help when called upon by the district administration were parent volunteers, community leaders, and interested citizens — mostly Negroes, West Indians, and Puerto Ricans but also including some whites. The focus of attention for all these people was the children and the educational process to which they all felt they were contributing. Along with this went a conspicuous pride in Ocean Hill's achievements, enthusiastic loyalty to the governing board and its district administration, and a quiet determination that all this must not be destroyed by outside forces.

Inside the classrooms, orderly and attentive groups of children participate in lessons such as basic typing skills, English literature (British and American classics), the chemical elements (complete with simple experiments), a social studies discussion of issues in the teachers strike, bilingual exercises in language arts, studies of Puerto Rican culture, and a lecture on Afro-American history illustrated with slides and recordings. Jewish teachers, who say they have encountered no anti-Semitism, relate happily that for the first time they are being allowed to use non-traditional teaching approaches and speak enthusiastically about the positive results in pupil achievement. One teacher in African garb asserts that he personally is an adherent of black nationalist philosophy, and he adds without rancor that most of his colleagues of all races disagree with him. This man shares responsibility for Afro-American studies at a junior high school with a young white teacher who is completing his doctorate from a Midwestern university after studying in Africa. Without sharing all of one another's personal views, these men agree that Afro-American studies are important for black children to help them develop their own sense of dignity as worthwhile human beings. Turning from classroom activities and teacher discussions, the observer roaming corridors, visiting lunchrooms, and watching playgrounds sees plenty of youthful energy displayed but fails to find any destructive rowdyism.

When the unwelcome teachers are brought into the classrooms, additional observations are made. In two different classes returning strikers are paired under team-teaching arrangements with instructors who have been in school since early September. In one case the paired teachers are black and white respectively; in the other case both are white. In both classes each teacher states his or her view of the strike, community control, and related issues. This is followed by questions and comments from pupils. It is obvious that student sentiment opposes the strike and favors community control. Elsewhere a returning teacher, who is notorious among community people for his leading role in the conflict, emerges from his classroom to complain heatedly that the children are uncontrollable. This instructor is persuaded to return to his class accompanied by a group of adult observers, including the author. The small class bombards the teacher with rapid-fire queries and challenges, only a few of which does he manage to answer, none to the satisfaction of the students. Why does he do such a poor job as a teacher? Why did he leave the school when they needed him? How can he expect them to want him back now? Is he really interested in anything but money for himself and power for the teachers union? The children are obviously aroused emotionally, but they do not shout or scream. They are sitting at their desks as they rattle off their questions. They are not physically threatening. Their language is blunt and colloquial, but they utter no racial epithet. As a matter of fact, there is no mention of race during the entire session. Afterwards a community leader among the observers comments privately that this teacher has lost all respect from the students and will never be able to teach successfully here.

These observations on the racial dimensions of the crisis as they appear from within the community have been presented at some length because the general public has little access to such information either through its own experience or from the news media. With Ocean Hill-Brownsville in the news every day for weeks and weeks, active community participants have had many opportunities to observe reporters and cameramen in action, as well as numerous occasions to compare their own daily experience with the version of the same events which appears in print or over the airwaves. Humble citizens and community leaders alike often express the conclusion that the media not only show the blindness of White America to non-white experience but continually perpetuate and reinforce his same extreme insensitivity. There is much comment by citizens on one-sided reporting, distorted presentations, and suppression of information favorable to community causes.

The many people who know what is going on in their schools because of the high degree of citizen participation in Ocean Hill's educational process, are first puzzled and then outraged by the continual projection in the media of anti-community propaganda unaccompanied by any factual correctness. Examples include the constant reiteration of such charges as "mob rule in the schools" or "teaching race hatred to children," contained in union leaders' statements, reports on teachers meetings, stories about strikers rallies and demonstrations, photos of picket signs, excerpts from teacher federation leaflets, full-page ads giving the union positions, pro-strike columns, and anti-community editorials. People ask where one can read or see the other side, and with few exceptions there is no answer. The inhabitants of Ocean Hill know well enough that community control exercised by an elected board of clergymen, educators, and parents cannot be equated with mob rule, that attempts to communicate the dignity of black and Puerto Rican heritage or the reality of intergroup relations are not race hatred.

Experience with media personnel in Ocean Hill-Brownsville has many other facets. Many hundreds, if not thousands, of citizens have watched daily contingents of dozens of newsmen lounging for hours behind police lines instead of interviewing demonstrators, observing the schoolrooms in operation, or going into the community to talk to ordinary people. Hundreds have watched while, on three separate occasions, television crews refused to record a demonstration of black-Puerto Rican unity. Importance is attached to this because people are proud of this intergroup solidarity, and they feel that this achievement has never been reported to the outside world. Smaller numbers of ordinary residents have been through the experience of reporters refusing or terminating interviews when they discovered that the citizens they were talking to had no publicly recognized position or title. Parents and others who are present when their own community leaders are interviewed frequently comment that the questions are hostile and the reports that emerge are full of distortions. People say they have long since given up looking for accurate press reports of the brutality practiced by police. The catalogue of reasons given for distrusting the media cannot be exhausted in available space. The resulting loss of credibility is such that newsmen are now sometimes excluded from meetings and other events where they once would have been welcome and more recently tolerated.

The mass media have yet another effect on the crisis in Ocean Hill, one which greatly concerns activists in the movement for community control. The outpourings from the major public information sources have a considerable persuasive effect on many members of the black and brown communities, especially those who are least in touch with relevant community events but also on the populace as a whole. Many observations and conversations indicate that mass communications do often counteract the direct experience of the people, distorting and reinterpreting the evidence of their daily lives. There seem to be at least two main reasons why these powerful effects are possible. First, many or perhaps most members of these communities are no less deeply conditioned to accept the persuasions of the mass media, no less schooled in the conventional assumptions and values through which popular appeals are made, than most other Americans. Second, the continual dinning barrage from mass communications cannot be matched, either in sheer volume or in technical skill, by the information networks of small and struggling community organizations. This seems to be true even for many people who have derived direct and immediate lessons from experience in the streets and schoolhouses of Ocean Hill-Brownsville. People go home to rest in their tenements and housing projects, open up their tabloids and turn on their television sets. With their defenses down, whatever ingrained loyalty they have to the conventional order is aroused, and all their hopes for a comfortable niche in the existing system are mobilized. Before long the lessons of more direct experience begin to blur, perceptions from the street to dim. The hurts of the day may be assuaged, lulling recently aroused fears of oppression, and the remaining anger may even be turned against some of the very men who strive to protect the local community.

On the other hand, intellectual toughness, emotional resilience, and shared commitment to a cause that is meaningful in terms of strong needs can enable people to resist such pressures. There is ample evidence that these human qualities are sufficiently common among the minority poor so that they support their leaders in showdowns like the conflict over the Ocean Hill-Brownsville schools. It may be that these same strengths enable so many people in Ocean Hill to maintain a clear vision of the central issues as they and their leaders have defined them, in spite of powerfully tempting distractions.

My knowledge of this sizable body of individuals convinces me that if they could speak directly to you, the reader, rather than through this author, this is what they would tell you. The power struggle, the racial conflict, the battle in the streets, and the dispute with the media may all be important, necessary, or inevitable—but none of these is the central problem. The crucial issue as seen within the movement for community control is the quality of public institutions and their relevance to local needs. The goals are quality education, effective social services, responsible police forces, livable housing, dignified employment, adequate income, a pleasant community environment, and a modicum of respect from people outside the community. Surely these aims must sound very familiar to most Americans.

Minority communities have long struggled for—and long been promised—these things under numerous concepts ranging from emancipation to integration. Contemporary existence among the minority poor daily brings it home that these approaches have failed. More and more people of these communities are becoming convinced that these failures came about primarily because of resistance by comfortable whites to the pleas and demands made by the poor and the nonwhite. From this consciousness has been born the drive for local self-determination and community control. The people who make up this movement see it as another means to well established and long familiar but endlessly deferred goals. In terms of their experience, this is a rational and relevant means to humane ends. If this basic message cannot be communicated to the wider American public, there can be little hope for reconciliation between the contending forces.

Agee Ward

Mr. Ward is a social scientist on leave from a university teaching post. He is currently conducting research in New York designed to achieve the special understanding of poverty areas to be derived from living with their people and participating in their life for an extended period.